# BEST PLACES®
## SAN FRANCISCO

Edited by
**MATTHEW RICHARD POOLE**

**EDITION** 2

**SASQUATCH BOOKS**
SEATTLE

Printed in the United States of America
Published by Sasquatch Books
Distributed by Publishers Group West

Second edition
09 08 07 06 05 04 03 02          5 4 3 2 1

ISBN: 1-57061-313-3
ISSN: 1526-9663

Series editor: Kate Rogers
Cover and interior design: Nancy Gellos
Cover illustration/photograph: Gary Moon
Maps: GreenEye Design
Composition: Patrick David Barber and Holly McGuire

**SPECIAL SALES**

Best Places guidebooks are available at special discounts on bulk purchases for corporate, club, or organization sales promotions, premiums, and gifts. Special editions, including personalized covers, excerpts of existing guides, and corporate imprints, can be created in large quantities for specific needs. For more information, contact your local bookseller or Special Sales, Best Places Guidebooks, 615 Second Avenue, Suite 260, Seattle, Washington 98104, 800/775-0817.

**SASQUATCH BOOKS**
615 Second Avenue
Seattle, Washington 98104
206/467-4300
books@SasquatchBooks.com
www.SasquatchBooks.com

# CONTENTS

# Acknowledgments

If you knew how much time and effort went into creating this second edition of *Best Places San Francisco,* you would steer well clear of a career as a travel guide writer. Which is why I can't give enough gratitude, kudos, and accolades to everyone who helped create what I firmly believe is the finest and most comprehensive guidebook to San Francisco.

For fear of reprisal I must first thank my sister, Rebecca Poole Forée, for the countless hours she spent writing and editing much of the first edition of *Best Places San Francisco.* Next in line are my editors at Sasquatch Books, Kate Rogers and Laura Gronewold, whose combined patience and professionalism can make even hack writers like me look good. To my smooth talking friend Regi Robles, who spent weeks on the phone fact checking thousands of details, you da man. For her help with updating the Shopping chapter, a huge dose of gratitude to fellow writer/ photographer Heather M. Reidy. Mark Magiera, thanks for your help with the Restaurants chapter and good luck with your new post as general manager at Five Points restaurant in NYC. And a final thank you to Delynn Parker for her help with the Exploring and Performing Arts chapters. To all of you I say with sincerity that I couldn't have done it without you.

—MRP

# Contributors

**MARK MAGIERA** has enjoyed and long and varied career in the food and wine industry. After working his way through graduate school as a waiter in San Francisco (earning a degree in poetry), he went on to spend the next seven years as a waiter and cafe manager of the world-famous Chez Panisse restaurant in Berkeley. In 1995 he moved to Singapore where over the next four years he worked as a food book editor, freelance writer, and voice-over announcer. Subsequent pursuits included the creation of a successful wine importing business, and a brief foray into the dot-com craze as a writer and editor for various wine- and food-related start-ups. Mark is currently the General Manager for Five Points restaurant in lower Manhattan.

**DELYNN PARKER,** a graduate of UC at Santa Barbara, has worked as a teacher, wrangler, cafe owner, and massage therapist, but her favorite occupation is giving in to her strong wanderlust and traveling off the beaten path in her trusty old Toyota 4-Runner. Born and raised in the Bay

Area, there is little left of San Francisco that she has not experienced or photographed. She hopes her future will take her to many more exciting places, but will always return her home to enjoy the mountains, the sea, and the exciting San Francisco scene.

Born in Manila in 1964, **REGI ROBLES** migrated from the Philippines to the Bay Area with his family in 1979, where he eventually majored in political science at UC Berkeley. Since then he's traveled the world extensively and held various jobs ranging from mobile disc jockey to music promoter, bartender, marketing and sales manager, and nonprofit administrator. He is currently a music promoter for Red Melon Records, and his turn-ons include spinning and dancing to house music, making travel plans, eating Thai food, and drinking Starbucks' Venti Caramel Macchiato.

A cosmopolitan artist who finds life in the world we live in through writing and photography, **HEATHER REIDY** is a motivated, passionate, and versatile writer and photographer. She developed a passion for writing and photography because she wanted to capture and express the beauty of the natural world that surrounds us. Heather's work has allowed her to travel extensively throughout the United States, Mexico, Europe, and Australia to capture the magnificence of these amazing places. Originally from the Chicagoland area, she now resides in San Francisco.

A native Californian, **MATTHEW R. POOLE** has authored and contributed to more than two dozen travel guides to California and abroad, including guides to Hawaii and Las Vegas. A graduate of UC Santa Barbara, Matthew has managed to combine three of his stronger passions—writing, photography, and traveling—to his advantage. Before becoming a full-time travel writer/photographer, he was an English tutor in Prague, a ski instructor in the Swiss Alps, and a scuba instructor in Maui. He currently resides in Marin County, but spends most of his time on the road doing research and avoiding commitments.

# About Best Places® Guidebooks

People trust us. Best Places guidebooks, which have been published continuously since 1975, represent one of the most respected regional travel series in the country. Each guide is written completely independently: no advertisers, no sponsors, no favors. Our reviewers know their territory, work incognito, and seek out the very best a city or region has to offer. Because we accept no free meals, accommodations, or other complimentary services, we are able to provide tough, candid reports about places that have rested too long on their laurels, and to delight in new places that deserve recognition. We describe the true strengths, foibles, and unique characteristics of each establishment listed.

*Best Places San Francisco* is written by and for locals, and is therefore coveted by travelers. It's written for people who live here and who enjoy exploring the city's bounty and its out-of-the-way places of high character and individualism. These are the very characteristics that make *Best Places San Francisco* ideal for tourists, too. The best places in and around the city are the ones that denizens favor: independently owned establishments of good value, touched with local history, run by lively individuals, and graced with natural beauty. With this second edition of *Best Places San Francisco*, travelers will find the information they need: where to go and when, what to order, which rooms to request (and which to avoid), where the best music, art, nightlife, shopping, and other attractions are, and how to find the city's hidden secrets.

We're so sure you'll be satisfied with our guide, we guarantee it.

**NOTE:** *The reviews in this edition are based on information available at press time and are subject to change. Readers are advised that places listed in previous editions may have closed or changed management, or may no longer be recommended by this series. The editors welcome information conveyed by users of this book. A report form is provided at the end of the book, and feedback is also welcome via email: books@SasquatchBooks.com.*

# How to Use This Book

This book is divided into eleven chapters covering a wide range of establishments, destinations, and activities in and around San Francisco. All evaluations are based on numerous reports from local and traveling inspectors. Best Places reporters do not identify themselves when they review an establishment, and they accept no free meals, accommodations, or any other services. Final judgments are made by the editors. **EVERY PLACE FEATURED IN THIS BOOK IS RECOMMENDED.**

**STAR RATINGS** *(for Top 200 Restaurants and Lodgings only)* Restaurants and lodgings are rated on a scale of one to four stars (with half stars in between), based on uniqueness, loyalty of local clientele, performance measured against the establishment's goals, excellence of cooking, cleanliness, value, and professionalism of service. Reviews are listed alphabetically, and every place is recommended.

| | |
|---|---|
| ★★★★ | The very best in the city |
| ★★★ | Distinguished; many outstanding features |
| ★★ | Excellent; some wonderful qualities |
| ★ | A good place |
| **NO STARS** | New or undergoing major changes |

(For more on how we rate places, see the Best Places Star Ratings box below.)

**PRICE RANGE** *(for Top 200 Restaurants and Lodgings only)* Prices for restaurants are based primarily on dinner for two, including dessert, tax, and tip (no alcohol). Prices for lodgings are based on peak season rates for one night's lodging for two people (i.e., double occupancy). Peak season is typically Memorial Day to Labor Day; off-season rates vary but can sometimes be significantly less. Call ahead to verify, as all prices are subject to change.

| | |
|---|---|
| $$$$ | Very expensive (more than $125 for dinner for two; more than $250 for one night's lodging for two) |
| $$$ | Expensive (between $85 and $125 for dinner for two; between $150 and $250 for one night's lodging for two) |
| $$ | Moderate (between $35 and $85 for dinner for two; between $85 and $150 for one night's lodging for two) |
| $ | Inexpensive (less than $35 for dinner for two; less than $85 for one night's lodging for two) |

**RESERVATIONS** *(for Top 200 Restaurants only)* We used one of the following terms for our reservations policy: reservations required, reservations recommended, no reservations. "No reservations" means either reservations are not necessary or are not accepted.

**ADDRESSES AND PHONE NUMBERS** Every attempt has been made to provide accurate information on an establishment's location and phone number, but it's always a good idea to call ahead and confirm. For establishments with two or more locations, we try to provide information on the original or most recommended branches.

**CHECKS AND CREDIT CARDS** Many establishments that accept checks also require a major credit card for identification. Note that some places accept only local checks. Credit cards are abbreviated in this book as follows: American Express (AE); Carte Blanche (CB); Diners Club (DC); Discover (DIS); Japanese credit card (JCB); MasterCard (MC); Visa (V).

**EMAIL AND WEB SITE ADDRESSES** Email and web site addresses for establishments have been included where available. Please note that the web is a fluid and evolving medium, and that web pages are often "under construction" or, as with all time-sensitive information, may no longer be valid.

**MAP INDICATORS** The letter-and-number codes appearing at the end of most listings refer to coordinates on the fold-out map included in the front of the book. Single letters (for example, F7) refer to the San Francisco map; double letters (FF7) refer to the Greater Bay Area map on the flip side. If an establishment does not have a map code listed, its location falls beyond the boundaries of these maps.

**HELPFUL ICONS** Watch for these quick-reference symbols throughout the book:

 **FAMILY FUN** Family-oriented places that are great for kids—fun, easy, not too expensive, and accustomed to dealing with young ones.

 **GOOD VALUE** While not necessarily cheap, these places offer you the best value for your dollars—a good deal within the context of the city.

 **ROMANTIC** These spots offer candlelight, atmosphere, intimacy, or other romantic qualities—kisses and proposals are encouraged!

 **UNIQUELY SAN FRANCISCO** These are places that are unique and special to the city, such as a restaurant owned by a beloved local chef or a tourist attraction recognized around the globe. (Hint: If you want to hit several of these special spots at once, turn to the Top 25 Attractions in the Exploring chapter. They're all uniquely San Francisco!)

 Appears after listings for establishments that have wheelchair-accessible facilities.

**INDEXES** In addition to a general index at the back of the book, there are five specialized indexes: restaurants are indexed by star-rating, features, and location at the beginning of the Restaurants chapter, and nightspots are indexed by features and location at the beginning of the Nightlife chapter.

**MONEY-BACK GUARANTEE** Please see "We Stand by Our Reviews" at the end of the book.

## BEST PLACES® STAR RATINGS

Any travel guide that rates establishments is inherently subjective—and Best Places is no exception. We rely on our professional experience, yes, but also on a gut feeling. And, occasionally, we even give in to a soft spot for a favorite neighborhood hangout. Our star-rating system is not simply a checklist; it's judgmental, critical, sometimes fickle, and highly personal. And unlike most other travel guides, we pay our own way and accept no freebies: no free meals or accommodations, no advertisers, no sponsors, no favors.

For each new edition, we send local food and travel experts out to review restaurants and lodgings anonymously, and then to rate them on a scale of one to four, based on uniqueness, loyalty of local clientele, performance measured against the establishment's goals, excellence of cooking, cleanliness, value, and professionalism of service. That doesn't mean a one-star establishment isn't worth dining or sleeping at—far from it. When we say that all the places listed in our books are recommended, we mean it. That one-star pizza joint may be just the ticket for the end of a whirlwind day of shopping with the kids. But if you're planning something more special, the star ratings can help you choose an eatery or hotel that will wow your new clients or be a stunning, romantic place to celebrate an anniversary or impress a first date.

We award four-star ratings sparingly, reserving them for what we consider truly the best. And once an establishment has earned our highest rating, everyone's expectations seem to rise. Readers often write us letters specifically to point out the faults in four-star establishments. With changes in chefs, management, styles, and trends, it's always easier to get knocked off the pedestal than to ascend it. Three-star establishments, on the other hand, seem to generate healthy praise. They exhibit outstanding qualities, and we get lots of love letters about them. The difference between two and three stars can sometimes be a very fine line. Two-star establishments are doing a good, solid job and gaining attention, while one-star places are often dependable spots that have been around forever.

The restaurants and lodgings described in *Best Places San Francisco* have earned their stars from hard work and good service (and good food). They're proud to be included in this book—look for our Best Places sticker in their windows. And we're proud to honor them in this, the second edition of *Best Places San Francisco*.

**READER REPORTS** At the end of the book is a report form. We receive hundreds of reports from readers suggesting new places or agreeing or disagreeing with our assessments. They greatly help in our evaluations, and we encourage you to respond.

# PLANNING A TRIP

# PLANNING A TRIP

## How to Get Here

### BY PLANE

Two international airports serve San Francisco: the perpetually delayed San Francisco International (SFO) and the smaller, more user friendly Oakland International (OAK).

#### SAN FRANCISCO INTERNATIONAL AIRPORT

**SFO** (650/876-2377; www.flysfo.com; map:KK5-LL5) lies 14 miles south of San Francisco directly off the Bayshore Freeway (Hwy 101). The fifth-busiest airport in the United States and the seventh busiest in the world, SFO is the stopping-off point for more than 1,000 flights a day via four dozen airlines. Although the snazzy new international terminal has improved the look and flow of SFO, until an additional runway is built you can expect up to hour-long delays in even mildly bad weather, especially fog. All major domestic airlines and many international ones fly into SFO, and each of the three main terminals is linked by adjoining walkways. Most gates are no more than a 10-minute walk from the check-in counters.

For travel information on how to get from SFO to the city and back, go to the **INFORMATION DESK** on the terminal's lower level near baggage claim. You can also call the airport's toll-free hotline (800/736-2008) from 7am to 5pm weekdays for information (via a real live person!) on how to find your way into the city.

SFO's **PARKING COMPLEX**, which currently holds 7,000 cars, is undergoing a massive expansion, and the construction has further complicated what was already barely controlled chaos. Scarce space and high prices can make parking a chore, and passengers are advised to call ahead (650/877-0227) for availability. There is also a **CONSTRUCTION HOTLINE** (650/821-6400) for information on which parking lots have been temporarily closed (this can change at short notice). Short-term parking costs $1 for each 15 minutes, with a maximum of $28 for the first 24 hours and $35 per day thereafter. Long-term parking, limited to 30 days, costs $15 per day for the first week and $12 per day thereafter. Valet parking is also available for $38 per day with a minimum of one day's stay and $45 per day thereafter. MasterCard, Visa, American Express, and Discover cards are accepted. For those who have a disability, parking is offered on the first four levels of the short-term parking area at a reduced rate of $12 per day. Passengers with a disability are required to show their special ID card, placard, and dashboard driver's license when they exit.

If the airport parking lots are full, a number of more affordable nearby **COMMERCIAL LOTS** offer free shuttle service to the airport (a 5- to 7-minute drive). Sky Park (650/875-6655), Park & Fly (650/877-0303), Parking Company of America (650/877-0250), and SMA Parking

(650/871-7275) are open 24 hours a day and do not require reservations, though at peak travel times it's wise to call ahead about availability. Rates range from $9 to $16 per day.

### AIRPORT TRANSPORTATION

While public transportation via **BAY AREA RAPID TRANSIT** (a.k.a. BART; www.bart.org) will not extend to the airport until 2002 (or so they say), there are several ways to get to and from SFO without driving. Airport shuttles are the most convenient door-to-door transit service and the Bay Area's favorite way to travel. Of the variety of reasonably priced shuttle companies, most charge around $10 to $16 (one way) and will take you anywhere in the city. Reduced rates apply for pickups of two or more people, and rides are shared with other passengers, so expect multiple stops en route. Shuttles leave every 15 to 20 minutes from the upper level of each airport terminal; look for the red signs posted on the curb.

**SUPERSHUTTLE** (415/558-8500; www.supershuttle.com), whose ubiquitous blue-and-yellow vans can be found at all major California airports, serves SFO from San Francisco and the Peninsula and charges $12.50 per person to a hotel, $17.50 to a residence or business, and $8 for each extra person in your party. Equally reliable services (often with shorter waiting lines) are the **BAYPORTER EXPRESS** (415/467-1800; www.bayporter.com), which runs to the East and South Bay from SFO for $19 per person; **LORRIES AIRPORT SERVICE** (415/334-9000), a 20-year-old business that whisks travelers into the city for $14 per person; and **QUAKE CITY SHUTTLE** (415/255-4899), which runs from 5am to 11pm and charges $13 per person (reservations are required only for the SFO-bound).

No reservations are needed for shuttle rides from SFO, but you should definitely make them traveling to the airport from your hotel or home; you can call anytime, day or night. All shuttles demand that you be packed and ready two hours before your domestic flight and three hours during holidays and for international flights. For service from the airport, most passengers just get in line after they've landed and hop on the next available shuttle; the wait is usually no longer than half an hour. While most shuttles operate until midnight, they're few and far between in the wee hours; service picks up again around 5am.

The **SFO AIRPORTER** (650/624-0500; www.groundnet.com/sfo-airporter/hotels.html) buses serve the downtown area and run every 15 to 30 minutes, departing from outside the lower-level baggage-claim area and stopping at most of the major hotels in the Union Square and Financial District areas. The service operates from 5am to midnight and costs $10 one way; children under 2 ride free. No reservations are required.

The cheapest (and least convenient) hitch to the city is by bus. **SAMTRANS** (800/660-4287) buses 7F and 7B run every half hour from the airport's upper departure level to the Transbay Terminal at Mission and

First Streets. The 7F costs $3 and takes 35 minutes; passengers are restricted to one carry-on bag. The 7B costs $2.20 and takes about 55 minutes, with no luggage restrictions. Another cheap (but more complicated) bus route: Take either the 3X to Colma BART station or the 3B to Daly City BART station (for $1), then catch BART (510/464-6000) into San Francisco. The ride takes roughly 40 minutes and costs only $2.25 to downtown, but it might be a strain on travelers with heavy luggage.

An equally inexpensive option is to take the free **CALTRAIN** (800/660-4287; www.caltrain.com and www.samtrans.com) shuttle from the airport's North and South Terminals to Millbrae Station. The trains run frequently during the day, and from there it's only a 25-minute ride ($2) to the CalTrain Depot at Fourth and Townsend Streets in San Francisco (map:O4). This is not recommended at night; although the neighborhood is rapidly improving, it's pretty isolated after dark.

**TAXIS** are a reliable but expensive option, costing approximately $28 to $33 plus tip. You'll find them outside the lower level of the terminal. Taxi sharing isn't prohibited but is rarely an option.

### OAKLAND INTERNATIONAL AIRPORT

Another often overlooked way to fly into San Francisco is through Oakland International Airport (1 Airport Dr, off Heggenberger Rd; 510/577-4000; www.flyoakland.com; map:JJ2-KK2), or **OAK** for short, located off Interstate 880 in the East Bay. The midsize airport serves more than 9 million passengers a year, and a $600 million expansion project will enable it to handle another anticipated 5 million. More kudos: Parking is cheaper and far more convenient, the airport staff is friendlier, and the new elevated freeway connecting the east end of the Bay Bridge to I-880 makes driving to and from OAK a veritable pleasure cruise.

OAK, far less hectic and much easier to navigate than SFO, has only a fraction of the maddening delays that SFO incurs daily due to high winds and foggy weather. Its two terminals serve 10 domestic airlines (including **UNITED** and **ALASKA AIRLINES**), along with international flights to Europe and the Pacific. **SOUTHWEST AIRLINES** (800/I-FLY-SWA) offers more than 80 flights in and out of Oakland each day, much of it commuter service to Los Angeles. Terminal 1 houses most of the kiosks and restaurants. A walk to Terminal 2 from the check-in counters takes no longer than 10 minutes.

For ground information, visitors to OAK can call the **VISITOR SERVICES VOLUNTEERS** (510/577-4015 from 8am to 8pm, or 510/577-4000 after hours). Transportation into San Francisco and the surrounding Bay Area is straightforward. Hotel shuttles, taxis, rental cars, and shuttles into Oakland are all available outside the baggage-claim area; signs are clearly marked. The cheapest way to downtown San Francisco from the Oakland airport is to take the **AIR-BART** shuttle bus to the BART terminal and hop on a city-bound train—about a 45- to 55-minute ordeal.

The Air-BART Shuttle (510/577-4294) runs about every 15 minutes Monday to Saturday from 6am to 11:30pm and Sunday from 8:30am to 11:30pm, stopping in front of Terminals 1 and 2 near the ground transportation signs. Tickets cost $2 and must be bought inside the airport from machines marked Air-BART. Once you arrive at the BART station, you then need to buy a $2.45 ticket for the 20-minute train ride to San Francisco (yes, it's a bit of a hassle, particularly if you have a lot of luggage). For more information visit BART's website at www.bart.org.

Private shuttle services such as **BAYPORTER EXPRESS** (415/467-1800; www.bayporter.com) will take you into San Francisco and drop you off at your home or hotel for $25 to $35, not including driver's tip; the journey takes half an hour to 45 minutes, depending on traffic, but it's very convenient. Advance reservations aren't necessary but are recommended, particularly for late-night shuttles. A taxi to or from downtown San Francisco costs around $45, so unless money's not a concern, it's advisable to take a shuttle instead.

Short-term **PARKING** (510/633-2571) costs $1 every 20 minutes or $25 per day; long-term parking costs $1 every 20 minutes up to five hours or $18 per day; economy parking (located across from Terminal 1) costs $1 every 20 minutes up to five hours or $15 per day—a big savings compared to the lots at SFO. That makes the Oakland airport quite popular with those who fly down to L.A. for a few days. All lots are directly across from the airport, and shuttle service is provided. Parking lots fill up quickly, so you may want to get there early to make sure you secure a spot.

## BY TRAIN

Two train services go to and from San Francisco. **CALTRAIN** (800/660-4BUS or 415/546-4461) offers regular service from the city depot (700 4th St, at Townsend St) along the Peninsula down to San Jose and stops at smaller cities along the way, including Palo Alto (Stanford University) and Mountain View. The trip to San Jose costs $5.25 one way and takes an hour and a half. Other, slower trains make several stops and take longer. Bikes are allowed on all trains.

**AMTRAK** (800/USA-RAIL; www.amtrak.com) trains from major cities, including Chicago, San Diego, Seattle, and Sacramento, stop at four East Bay stations: Richmond (16th St and MacDonald Ave), Berkeley (3rd St and University Ave), Oakland (245 2nd St at Jack London Square), and Emeryville (5885 Landregan St). A free connecting Amtrak shuttle bus from the Emeryville station drops passengers off at the San Francisco Ferry Building, located at the intersection of Market Street and the Embarcadero. If requested, the shuttle also makes stops at the CalTrain station, Pier 39, and the Union Square area (be sure to tell the driver in advance). Fares vary accordingly. The average round-trip train ticket from Los Angeles to the Bay Area (a 12-hour trip one way) ranges anywhere from $88 to $148, but a one way from Sacramento is only about $14.

## THE GOLDEN GATE BRIDGE

San Francisco's most famous landmark took 13 years to plan and build and is a masterpiece of engineering and design. More than a mile long, the bridge was conceived by engineer Joseph Strauss to withstand winds of more than 100 miles an hour and is supported by cables that measure more than 3 feet in diameter. Standing 220 feet above the channel, the bridge has endured the wind, fog, more than 1,000 suicides, and the misconception that it was ever truly golden. Each year it's painted with 5,000 gallons of International Orange, a weather-resistant paint chosen by consulting architect Irving F. Morrow because he thought it would accentuate the area's natural beauty (that, and it's visible through fog). In contrast to the gray hue of most bridges, orange is a great change of pace, and it glows like gold in the setting sun.

You can get one of the best views of the bridge by walking across it, which allows you to admire the metal gussets that allow it to sway more than 27 feet at its center. The bridge's engineering was put to the test in 1987 when, during the structure's 50th birthday commemoration, nearly one-third of San Francisco's population showed up to celebrate by strolling across it. The mass of people literally flattened the span, making bridge officials noticeably nervous. Fortunately, Big Red held firm.

## BY BUS

GREYHOUND (800/231-2222) operates out of the Transbay Terminal (425 Mission St at 1st St; 415/495-1569; map:N2) in San Francisco, traveling to cities around the Bay Area and throughout the United States. For popular destinations such as Lake Tahoe, it's an efficient way to travel, but local out-of-town destinations are better served by SamTrans buses (San Mateo County Transit District; 800/660-4287). You'll find Greyhound on the third floor of the Transbay Terminal—but since this isn't the best part of town, you should plan your trip so you get there during the day.

## BY CAR

San Francisco can be accessed by several major highways. US Interstate 80 is the major artery from the east and the turnoff for those heading south via INTERSTATE 5. Expect a $2 toll (and major traffic during morning rush hour) as you approach the Bay Bridge from the eastern side. More scenic yet often equally congested is US HIGHWAY 101, which snakes north-south from Marin County across the Golden Gate Bridge (a $3 southbound toll), through San Francisco, and on down to San Jose. Known as the Pacific Coast Highway, HIGHWAY 1 is a narrow, winding coastal road that passes along the majestic Pacific both north and south of the city, merging with 101 on the Golden Gate Bridge and, up north, eventually heading back toward the coast at the Stinson Beach exit in

Marin County. Yes, it's a gorgeous drive, but it's recommended only for those who have plenty of time and don't get carsick.

Driving up from Los Angeles there are two main routes. The longer coastal route along Highway 101 (437 miles and an 11-hour drive) is a beautiful scenic ride until you reach San Jose, at which point traffic, even under good conditions, slows to a crawl. From there it will take an hour and a half to reach the city. The inland route, Interstate 5 (389 miles and 8 hours), is a long, flat, boring stretch, but it will get you there in good time. From Sacramento it's 88 miles to San Francisco (1½–2 hours); from Yosemite it's 210 miles (4–5 hours).

# When to Visit

## WEATHER

If you've decided to come to San Francisco in the summer because you expect it to be warm and sunny, think again. Epitomized in Mark Twain's infamous (mis)quote, "The coldest winter of my life was the summer I spent in San Francisco," the city's weather should be factored into the timing of your visit—although you never really know what to expect. In recent years, flash flooding and El Niño's storms ravaged the area during the winter, followed by an unusually (for San Francisco) hot summer. But the city normally enjoys mild weather year-round, with temperatures seldom rising above 70°F (21°C) or falling below 40°F (5°C). Be forewarned, however, about the morning and evening fog, which makes the temperature dip precipitously when it rolls in. Locals tend to dress in layers of clothing, and lightweight clothes often aren't enough, especially during the foggy summer months.

Typically, San Francisco enjoys its best weather in September and October. January is when the rain hits hardest, although it rains often throughout the winter, and it's windy year-round. The Bay Area is home to several "microclimates," which means that while one part of the city may be hot (typically the Mission District and Potrero Hill), another part (e.g., the Sunset and Richmond Districts) will be blanketed in icy fog. The National Weather Service Forecast (831/656-1725), therefore, may not suffice; bring an extra sweater instead.

### Average temperature and precipitation by month

| Month | Daily Maximum Temp. degrees F | Daily Minimum Temp. degrees F | Monthly Precipitation in inches |
|---|---|---|---|
| JANUARY | 56.1 | 46.2 | 4.48 |
| FEBRUARY | 59.4 | 48.4 | 2.83 |
| MARCH | 60.0 | 48.6 | 2.58 |

| APRIL | 61.1 | 49.2 | 1.48 |
|---|---|---|---|
| MAY | 62.5 | 50.7 | 0.35 |
| JUNE | 64.3 | 52.5 | 0.15 |
| JULY | 64.0 | 53.1 | 0.04 |
| AUGUST | 65.0 | 54.2 | 0.08 |
| SEPTEMBER | 68.9 | 55.8 | 0.24 |
| OCTOBER | 68.3 | 54.8 | 1.09 |
| NOVEMBER | 62.9 | 51.5 | 2.49 |
| DECEMBER | 56.9 | 47.2 | 3.52 |
| ANNUAL AVERAGE | 62.5 | 51.0 | 19.33 |

*Source: San Francisco Convention and Visitors Bureau*

## TIME

San Francisco is on Pacific Standard Time (PST), which is three hours behind New York, two hours behind Chicago, one hour behind Denver, and two hours ahead of Honolulu.

## WHAT TO BRING

Be ready for anything by wearing layers, layers, layers. In the winter dress for rain and carry an umbrella, but in Indian-summer autumn you may want to have a T-shirt on hand. In the summer months wear shorts only if you're brave or visiting the Mission District. Always bring a lightweight jacket or sweater with you just in case. If you're sitting on crowded public transportation you can take it off; if you're walking along the windy streets to do a bit of shopping you can put it back on.

As for clothing style, in San Francisco anything goes. This being home to Levi Strauss and Esprit, the fashion is casual, clean chic. Suits and ties are worn solely in the Financial District; most people dress as if they've just dashed out of the house for a cup of coffee. This is not to say San Franciscans dress down: In a town where Banana Republic rules, expensive T-shirts and khakis are considered good taste. Areas like Haight-Ashbury ("the Haight") still attract leather-clad punks and tie-dyed hippies, while secondhand-clothing stores are popular everywhere, and retro fashion still makes a splash. In short, be yourself—nobody's going to notice anyway.

# General Costs

Until just recently California's economy was booming, thanks mostly to the continued success of the computer industry in Silicon Valley, the proliferation of Internet start-ups, and flourishing national companies such as the Gap, which originated and have their headquarters here. Even with the fizzle of the dot-com industry, San Francisco still draws an incredible amount of money—and people—to this small, windswept peninsula.

The high-tech industry is big business in San Francisco. Hewlett-Packard, Intel, Sun Microsystems, Apple Computer, and Adobe Systems all reside in nearby Silicon Valley. There are more than 2,000 computer companies in the area, and new software, multimedia, communications, and networking companies launch literally every day. Then, of course, there's the big banking industry: Wells Fargo and Charles Schwab & Co., for example, are all longtime city residents.

The high cost of living (San Francisco's is one of the highest in the country) coupled with the housing crunch stands as a glaring contradiction to the city's 14,000 homeless people. Nonetheless, San Francisco has always drawn—and continues to draw—a diverse, well-educated, and creative workforce. Thousands move to the city every month to start a business or a lucrative career. Many are lured by the city's history of open-minded thinking and an entrepreneurial spirit that has prevailed here since the Gold Rush.

It is worth mentioning that the record-low tenant vacancy rate (which, due to all the dot-com bombs, is increasing slowly) and climbing (indeed, astronomical) rent in nearly all neighborhoods has changed the housing market in recent years. Those who opt to stay are compromising their budgets to live here, while old-timers who bought their homes decades ago for $40,000 are guaranteed a comfortable retirement. The introduction of live/work spaces to formerly industrial neighborhoods is also changing the housing game. In short, affordable housing has all but disappeared even as the economy has flattened out.

## Average costs for lodging and food

Double room:

| | |
|---|---|
| **CHEAP** | $99 |
| **MODERATE** | $120–$150 |
| **EXPENSIVE** | $220 |

Lunch for one:

| | |
|---|---|
| **CHEAP** | $5–$8 |
| **MODERATE** | $10–$15 |
| **EXPENSIVE** | $15–$25 |

Beverage in a restaurant:

| | |
|---|---|
| **GLASS OF WINE** | $3.50–$9 |
| **PINT OF BEER** | $3.50–$5 |
| **COKE** | $1.50 |
| **DOUBLE LATTE** | $2.75 |

Other common items:

| | |
|---|---|
| **MOVIE TICKET** | $8.75 |
| **ROLL OF FILM** | $6 |
| **CABLE CAR** | $2 |
| **TAXI PER MILE** | $1.80 in town; $2.30 out of town |
| **SOUVENIR T-SHIRT** | $10 |

# Tips for Special Travelers

## FAMILIES WITH CHILDREN

In an emergency call 911, 24 hours a day. For questions about your child's health call Pediatric Health Services at UCSF (415/476-2507). You will have to pay for any emergency service, so you may want to contact your medical insurance carrier before seeking treatment. Emergency rooms are at San Francisco General Hospital (415/206-8111), UCSF Medical Center (415/476-1000), Davies Medical Center (415/565-6060), Saint Francis Memorial Hospital (415/353-6000), and California Pacific Medical Center (415/600-0600). In addition, downtown Medical/Travel Medicine (415/362-7177) offers same-day appointments for travel-related medical conditions and is open from 8am to 6pm.

Watch for this icon throughout the book; it indicates places and activities that are great for families.

## SENIORS

Seniors are well looked after in the city and receive discounts at museums and tourist attractions and on public transportation. The Senior Citizen Information line (415/626-1033) offers info on city services, and the Friendship Line for the Elderly (415/752-3778) is a support service that also offers crisis intervention.

## PEOPLE WITH DISABILITIES

California is one of the leading states when it comes to providing social services for people with disabilities. Transportation organizations have created an ID card that gives people with disabilities discounts on travel throughout the Bay Area. For information, contact San Francisco Muni's Elderly and Handicapped Discount ID Office (415/923-6070). For information on disability-related needs/rights and referrals to state and national resources, call Americans with Disabilities Act (800/514-0301). A crisis line for the disabled offers advice on everything from public transportation to stress and operates 24 hours a day (800/426-4263). Locally, the American Foundation for the Blind (415/392-4845) offers catalogs to help people access resources. Lighthouse for the Blind and Visually Disabled (415/431-1481) has devices such as walking canes to help people get around the city.

Most of San Francisco's major tourist attractions are wheelchair accessible, and many hotels offer services for visitors with wheelchairs or other special needs. The San Francisco Visitor Information Center (900 Market St, lower level Hallidie Plaza; 415/391-2000; map:N3) has the most up-to-date information.

## WOMEN

San Francisco is a safe place for female travelers, but as in any major city, it's advisable to take more precautions at night. Many women's services are tied to lesbian resources, and the most comprehensive center for both is at the Women's Building (3543 18th St btwn Valencia and Guerrero Sts; 415/431-1180; map:L6). The building houses nine women's organizations and offers everything from classes in yoga and aerobics to social services. Another important health resource is Planned Parenthood (815 Eddy St btwn Van Ness Ave and Franklin St; 800/967-7526; map:L3), which offers contraception and the morning-after pill at sliding rates. The Bay Area Women's and Children's Center (318 Leavenworth St; 415/474-2400; map:M4) also offers specialized services to women. The Rape Crisis Hotline (415/647-7273) is open 24 hours a day.

## PET OWNERS

San Franciscans love their dogs, some to the point of militancy. Organized groups like to express their views to the city council, and the focus tends to be on one thing: letting canines roam freely through city parks. The San Francisco Dog Owners Group maintains a web site, www.sfdog.org, and a lively email network through which like-minded owners can come together and wag their tongues.

San Francisco's off-leash areas are well delineated in *The Bay Area Dog Lover's Companion* (Foghorn Press), available at most local bookstores. Dogsbythebay.com is another good resource, providing info on hotels and restaurants that will welcome your pooch. Off-leash areas within San Francisco include:

**FORT FUNSTON,** along Skyline Boulevard next to Lake Merced.
**CRISSY FIELD,** on the north edge of the Presidio, at Marina Boulevard.
**MISSION DOLORES PARK,** on Dolores Street between 18th and 20th Streets.
**ALTA PLAZA PARK,** at Steiner and Clay Streets.

## GAYS AND LESBIANS

San Francisco is renowned as a gay-friendly city and a mecca for gay and lesbian travelers. Its large gay community—gays and lesbians form one-fourth to one-third of the population of San Francisco—is centered in the Castro neighborhood (at Castro and 18th Sts), where festive rainbow flags fly and the streets are lined with upscale shops and gay bars. The neighborhood is extremely close-knit and supportive, and its vitality owes much to its denizens' long struggle for equality and civil rights. The city's lesbian population tends to concentrate around 16th and Valencia Streets in the Mission District, but you can find clubs and bars catering to the gay community in all parts of San Francisco. Non-queers are usually welcome to join the scene as long as tolerance is exercised; stare, point, harass, and/or sneer in a homophobic fashion and you'll probably be asked to leave (and trust us, those gay guys are in far better shape than you are).

## SAN FRANCISCO'S LITERARY LEGENDS

Like any artistic enclave, San Francisco has drawn its share of literary talent. Great authors such as Mark Twain, Dashiell Hammett, Robert Louis Stevenson, Oakland-born Jack London, Jack Kerouac, and Allen Ginsberg have all written about the city, lending their genius to the backdrop of its rolling hills. San Franciscans in general are well read, which explains the hundreds of bookstores here: The city has more than 200—new and used, intimate and colossal, nonprofit and corporate—for every political bent, sexual leaning, and cultural interest. Many well-known authors live and work in the area, and new writers are always making their presence known.

**Nonfiction**

*California: An Interpretive History* by Walton Bean (McGraw Hill, 1993). An account of California's (sometimes shady) past.

*California Coastal Access Guide* by the University of California (Seven Hills, 1997). True to its title, a guide to the coastal regions.

*Literary San Francisco* by Lawrence Ferlinghetti and Nancy Peters (Harper & Row, 1980). An account of the writerly circles that have helped shape the city's history. (Out of print but available through Amazon.com.)

*The Mayor of Castro Street* by Randy Shilts (St. Martin's Press, 1988). A landmark work on the political career of Harvey Milk and the development of gay politics.

*San Francisco Confidential* by Ray Mungo (Birch Lane Press, 1995). A look at what goes on behind the city's closed doors.

*San Francisco Stories: Great Writers on the City* by John Miller (Chronicle Books, 1990). Includes contributions by locals Herb Caen, Anne Lamott, Amy Tan, and many others.

*San Francisco: The Ultimate Guide* by Randolph Delehanty (Chronicle Books, 1995).

There are literally too many resources for gays and lesbians to list here. Several local publications and online resources cover news, culture, and events, including **DAMRON LESBIAN AND GAY TRAVEL GUIDES**, which provide information for lesbians and gays looking for travel and accommodations; **GAY-MART** (www.gaymart.com), a gay and lesbian travel and resource guide that lists accommodations, bars and clubs, tea rooms, and cafes; **GAYCITY SAN FRANCISCO** (www.citycentral.net/gaycity), with links to nightlife coverage, community news, live chat, classifieds, and discussion boards; **QSF GUIDE** (www.qsanfrancisco.com); and **WWW.SANFRANCISCOLEATHER.COM**. The *Bay Area Reporter*, the gay community paper that's distributed free on Thursdays, has comprehensive listings of goings-on around town for gays and lesbians, including a weekly calendar of events. It can be found stacked in bars, bookshops, and various stores around town, as well as at the corner of 18th and Castro Streets and at Ninth and Harrison Streets.

A meticulously researched compendium of 13 walking tours through the city. (Unfortunately, it's out of print also, but copies can be ordered through Amazon.com.)

*16th Street: Faces in the Mission* by Bert Katz (Gulliver Books, 1997). A photo collection of Mission residents. Local coffee shops on 16th and Valencia Streets tend to have a copy lying around.

**Fiction**

*As Francesca* by Martha Baer (Bantam Doubleday Dell, 1998). An exploration of the allure of cybersex.

*Beyond Definition: New Writing from Gay and Lesbian San Francisco* by Marci Blackman and Trebor Healey, editors (Manic D Press, 1994). Poetry and fiction from a cross section of queer San Francisco.

*The First $20 Million Is Always the Hardest* by Po Bronson (Avon, 1998). A high-tech novel from the Silicon Valley chronicler and writer for *Wired* magazine.

*The Grapes of Wrath* by John Steinbeck (Turtleback, 1976). The classic epic of California during the Depression, by one of America's best observers.

*The Joy Luck Club* by Amy Tan (Ivy Books, 1994). The lives of several generations of Chinese and Chinese-American women are explored in this sensitive novel.

*The Maltese Falcon* by Dashiell Hammett (Vintage Crime/Black Lizard, 1992). A great detective novel set in a dark and dangerous San Francisco.

*On the Road* by Jack Kerouac (Penguin, 1991). Sex, drugs, and rock 'n' roll in San Francisco and across the world, from the notorious Beat.

*Tales of the City* (six volumes) by Armistead Maupin (HarperPerennial Library, 1994). A soap opera following the lives and loves of a group of friends in the sexually liberated 1970s right on into the post-AIDS '80s.

For those eager to chat it up in person, Cafe Flore (2298 Market St; 415/621-8579; map:K6) is a great spot. The restaurant, a favorite gathering place, has a good coffee selection, and you're bound to bump into a local enjoying their latte who can shoot the breeze or offer good advice. For guidebooks and other publications, check out the community bookstore A Different Light (489 Castro St; 415/431-0891; www.adlbooks. com; map:K6), which has a wide array of gay-oriented literature and a helpful staff.

For information on AIDS, contact the San Francisco AIDS Foundation (415/487-3000) or the AIDS Nightline (800/273-AIDS; 415/434-AIDS).

## FOREIGN VISITORS

The city has a number of services for travelers from abroad, including money exchange and translation services. Thomas Cook Currency Services (75 Geary Blvd; 415/362-3452; www.us.thomascook. com; map:N3) offers currency exchange, wire transfers, and sale and cashing of traveler's checks. Worldwide Foreign Exchange (150 Cyril Magnin St at 5th and Market Sts; 415/392-7283; map:M3) will exchange foreign currency and traveler's checks for U.S. dollars and vice versa. International Effectiveness Center (690 Market St, Ste 700; 415/788-4149; map:N3), one of San Francisco's oldest translation services, provides simultaneous interpretation and guided tours with interpreters.

For a complete list of consulates, consult the Yellow Pages.

| | | |
|---|---|---|
| **AUSTRALIA** | I Bush St, 7th floor | 415/362-6160 |
| **AUSTRIA** | 41 Sutter St, Ste 207 | 415/951-8911 |
| **CANADA** | 555 Montgomery St, Ste 1288 | 415/834-3180 |
| **FRANCE** | 540 Bush St | 415/397-4330 |
| **GERMANY** | 1960 Jackson St | 415/775-1061 |
| **GREAT BRITAIN** | I Sansome St, Ste 850 | 415/617-1300 |
| **IRELAND** | 44 Montgomery St, Ste 3830 | 415/392-4214 |
| **ITALY** | 2590 Webster St | 415/931-4925 |
| **MEXICO** | 870 Market St, Ste 528 | 415/392-5554 |
| **NETHERLANDS** | 275 Battery St | 415/981-6454 |
| **NEW ZEALAND** | I Maritime Plaza, Ste 700 | 415/399-1255 |
| **NORWAY** | 20 California St, 6th floor | 415/986-0766 |
| **RUSSIA** | 2790 Green St | 415/928-6878 |
| **SPAIN** | 1405 Sutter St | 415/922-2995/96 |
| **SWEDEN** | 120 Montgomery St, Ste 2175 | 415/788-2631 |
| **VENEZUELA** | 311 California St, Ste 620 | 415/955-1982 |

## WEB INFORMATION

If you're hooked up to the Internet, just about any info involving San Francisco is easily accessible online—from local news and traffic reports to hotel and restaurant reservations. The top four San Francisco sites are www.sfgate.com, http://bayarea.citysearch.com, www.bestofthebay.com, and www.bayinsider.com. All offer an incredible amount of info about the Bay Area's restaurants, hotels, attractions, nightlife, and current performances.

Along with the big four above, the following websites are also a good place to start when planning your visit:

**WWW.SFVISITOR.ORG** for the San Francisco Convention and Visitors Bureau

**HTTP://SFBAY.YAHOO.COM** for general city information

**WWW.HOTELDISCOUNT.COM** for a complete list of hotels and rates

**WWW.HOTELRES.COM** for reserving San Francisco hotel accommodations online

**WWW.QSANFRANCISCO.COM** and **WWW.GAYGLOBALSF.COM** for gay and lesbian information, attractions, and events

**WWW.SFNORTHBEACH.COM** for information on San Francisco's North Beach neighborhood

**WWW.SFTRAVEL.COM** for travel advice on San Francisco restaurants, hotels, performances, and attractions

**WWW.OPENTABLE.COM** for online restaurant reservations

# LAY OF THE CITY

# LAY OF THE CITY

## Orientation

Situated at the tip of a peninsula, San Francisco is surrounded by large expanses of water on three sides: the roiling Pacific Ocean to the west, the treacherous Golden Gate to the north, and the calm San Francisco Bay to the east. The northern border is graced by the world's most famous bridge, the **GOLDEN GATE BRIDGE**. On the eastern side, the San Francisco Bay is dotted by the natural wonders of Alcatraz Island, Angel Island, and Yerba Buena Island as well as the human-made **SAN FRANCISCO–OAKLAND BAY BRIDGE** and Treasure Island. The city itself packs a bounty of beauty into its compact 47 square miles. From rolling hills and eucalyptus groves to towering skyscrapers and a colorful urban fabric, it strikes a harmonious balance between natural and human-made attractions.

Incorporated in 1850, San Francisco was a Gold Rush town, built on the wishes and whims of citizens who came here from around the world seeking their share of the new wealth. Much of that pioneering freewheeling spirit still thrives in the city's many diverse neighborhoods, each with a flavor and texture uniquely its own. The grid of the city's streets originated at Chinatown's Portsmouth Square and emanated from there; **MARKET STREET** diagonally intersects the grid from the waterfront to Twin Peaks and beyond. **SOUTH OF MARKET**, or **SOMA**, as it's known today, has long cultivated a sort of "other city" identity. Flatter than much of this notoriously hilly city, and with wider streets, today's SoMa is home to large, low-slung warehouses, industrial and high-tech businesses, artists' lofts, funky and hip restaurants, lively nightspots (many along 11th and Folsom Sts), and the **PACBELL BALLPARK** (2nd and Townsend Sts; map:O4). Still being developed in leaps and bounds, SoMa has also become a high-culture focal point with the building of the **SAN FRANCISCO MUSEUM OF MODERN ART** and **YERBA BUENA CENTER FOR THE ARTS** (3rd and Mission Sts; map:N3), where a verdant park provides a tranquil spot to admire the city's fascinating skyline.

Just north of Market Street are two areas that form the city's commercial core. The **FINANCIAL DISTRICT** (Kearny St to the Embarcadero) is marked by such mercantile monuments as the **TRANSAMERICA PYRAMID** (Montgomery and Washington Sts; map:N2), the **BANK OF AMERICA** building (Kearny and California Sts; map:N2), and the four shopping and high-rise office complexes of **EMBARCADERO CENTER** (bounded by Battery St and the Embarcadero and Sacramento and Clay Sts; map:N2). To the west are the department stores and luxury hotels of **UNION SQUARE** (an area bounded by O'Farrell and Sutter Sts and Powell St and Grant Ave; map:N3). The square itself is a terraced green expanse surrounding the granite Dewey Monument, which commemorates

Admiral Dewey's 1898 victory over the Spanish Navy at Manila Bay in the Spanish-American War.

Northeast of Union Square are the endlessly fascinating alleys and streets of **CHINATOWN**. Enter through the arching, dragon-adorned Chinatown Gate (Bush St at Grant Ave; map:N3) to explore this city-within-a-city, where the herb shops, Taoist temples, and strains of numerous Chinese dialects combine for an intoxicating effect. Along Stockton Street this exotic enclave flows seamlessly into the Italian neighborhood of **NORTH BEACH**, where excellent restaurants and espresso cafes vie for your attention on Columbus Avenue. North Beach is also home to the remnants of the Beat Generation, best exemplified by City Lights Bookstore (Columbus Ave and Broadway; map:N2), where poet-proprietor Lawrence Ferlinghetti still keeps shop.

Head farther north to the waterfront and you come to San Francisco's most popular tourist attraction, **FISHERMAN'S WHARF** (Jefferson St btwn Mason and Hyde Sts; map:M1). Once the true domain of fishermen and their nets, the neighborhood is now a collection of knick-knack shops, restaurants, souvenir stands, and walk-away crab cocktail vendors. Rising above it all is affluent, mostly residential **RUSSIAN HILL**, named for the immigrant Russian population that settled here a century ago, now boasting a fine array of restaurants, coffee shops, bars, and book and antique stores along Polk Street. To the south is posh **NOB HILL**, whose pinnacle atop California Street is home to the city's grande dame hotels—the Fairmont, the Mark Hopkins, the Huntington, and the Stanford Court—and the soaring, neo-Gothic Grace Cathedral, modeled after Notre Dame in Paris.

On the south side of town the outlying neighborhoods have an entirely different feel. The **HAIGHT-ASHBURY** district (Divisadero St to Stanyan St and Oak St to Frederick St; map:J5) hasn't lost touch with its '60s flower-power roots; in today's undeniably seedy yet gentrified Haight, an eclectic mix of shops, restaurants, and vintage clothing stores, attracts an equally eclectic mix of locals and tourists. South of here is the famous **CASTRO** district, nerve center of the city's large, politically active gay and lesbian population. You can experience a good cross section of this interesting, vibrant neighborhood on Castro Street between Market and 17th Streets, anchored by the fabulous Castro Theatre, one of San Francisco's best repertory film houses.

To the west, the city's residential areas have plenty to offer the eager sightseer. **PACIFIC HEIGHTS** (anchored by Fillmore St btwn Jackson and Post Sts; map:K2) is a tony enclave replete with chic shopping boutiques, small but popular restaurants, and a mix of beautiful old Victorians and sleek modern homes. Visit Alta Plaza Park (Jackson and Steiner Sts; map:K2) for incredible views in every direction. Stroll down the hill along

FILLMORE STREET and you'll go through the youngish, postcollegiate neighborhood of COW HOLLOW, so named because dairy farms once flourished here. The main drag is UNION STREET, turf of savvy boutique shoppers by day, single bar-hoppers by night. Farther down Fillmore is the MARINA DISTRICT, as famous for its great views and warm microclimate as for its instability in earthquakes (it's built almost entirely on landfill and sustained major damage in the Loma Prieta quake of 1989). The Marina nowadays is generally a calm, sun-washed sea of Mediterranean-style homes along meandering streets. On weekends, though, the main artery of CHESTNUT STREET is a riot of folks in college alma-mater sweatshirts jockeying for a free table in one of the many trendy juice joints and cafes. The Marina is also home to the Palace of Fine Arts, the Exploratorium, and the Golden Gate Promenade.

Farther westward still, GOLDEN GATE PARK stretches from the Haight-Ashbury area at Stanyan Street to the Great Highway and the Pacific Ocean. This immense swath of green (between Fulton St on the north and Lincoln Ave on the south) is home to the California Academy of Sciences and a slew of other botanical and cultural sites. South of the park, the SUNSET DISTRICT, a quiet residential bastion of postwar middle-class homes, is currently in the throes of becoming trendy. North of the park, the RICHMOND DISTRICT, another up-and-coming working-class neighborhood, boasts a mind-boggling assortment of ethnic restaurants, from Russian to Thai to kosher delis; just venture down Clement Street or Geary Boulevard and take your pick. The Richmond, also known informally as Chinatown West, has an Asian population bigger than Chinatown's. Its northern neighbor is the PRESIDIO, a former military base converted a few years ago into a national park, with walking and biking trails and historic sites galore. At the Presidio's northernmost tip is Fort Point, a Civil War fortress that still houses the San Martín Cannon, cast in Peru in 1684. And directly above the fort looms the city's crown jewel: the GOLDEN GATE BRIDGE.

# Visitor Information

With tourism as the city's number-one source of revenue, it's not unusual to see people trying to get their bearings on street corners as they battle with huge maps flailing about in the wind. But locals are known for their willingness to help—and there are ample resources to turn to. Foremost is the SAN FRANCISCO VISITOR INFORMATION CENTER (900 Market St at Powell St; 415/391-2000; map:N3), in the lower level of Hallidie Plaza, next to the cable car turnaround near Union Square. Open Monday through Friday 9am to 5pm, weekends 9am to 3pm, and closed on major holidays, the center presents a cornucopia of helpful expertise (in German,

Japanese, French, Italian, Spanish, and English), from city maps and tour books to hotel and restaurant advice. There's a hotline—also in six languages—with schedules for citywide entertainment and events. For non-English events information call 415/391-2003 (French); 415/391-2122 (Spanish); 415/391-2101 (Japanese); or 415/391-2004 (German). The center is operated by the **SAN FRANCISCO CONVENTION AND VISITORS BUREAU** (201 3rd St, Ste 900; 415/391-2000; map:N3), another valuable tourist resource; an easy way to access its font of information is on the Internet at www.sfvisitor.org. Other visitor information kiosks are sprinkled throughout town, including one near the front entrance to the San Francisco Shopping Centre (5th and Market Sts; map:N3) and at the San Francisco International Airport (800/736-2008; map:KK5–LL5).

# Getting Around

## BY BUS

With the possible exception of New York, no other U.S. city has more locals who pride themselves on living a sans-auto lifestyle. By foot, bike, or bus, it is relatively easy to get around in San Francisco without a car—especially if you're willing (and able) to hike up the many hills. In fact, given the scarcity of parking spots, walking is often preferred. The **MUNICIPAL RAILWAY SYSTEM** (415/673-6864; www.sfmuni.com), or **MUNI**, as it is known around here, is San Francisco's public transportation network. Efforts always seem to be under way to improve the system's punctuality, but if you need to be somewhere at a specific time, play it safe and hail a taxi (see the By Taxi section, below). Muni operates an extensive system of diesel- and electric-powered buses, as well as a handsome line of historic streetcars that amble up and down Market Street from First Street to the Castro district. The streetcars, collected from cities around the world and restored to their original beauty, include a wood-sided car from 1920s Italy and a convertible car that locals call "the Boat."

The Muni system also operates light-rail trains as well as the famous cable cars, the nation's only moving national landmarks. Cable car fares are $2 one way. Bus and streetcar fares are $1 for adults (ages 18–64); 35 cents for seniors (age 65 and up), youth (ages 5–17), and disabled persons; and free for children under 5. Exact change is required except on cable cars, where conductors can make change for $20. Adults can save on fares by buying Muni tokens at 80 cents each in rolls of 10, 20, and 40. (Cable car conductors accept a token plus $1.)

An even better deal for frequent riders is the Muni Passport. Available for one day ($6), three consecutive days ($10), or seven consecutive days ($15), Passports allow you to ride buses, streetcars, and cable cars as many times a day as you wish. Passports will also get you a reduced transit fare to ballgames at 3Com Park or PacBell Ballpark and other special events; the three- and seven-day passes are good for discounts at various local attractions, including the San Francisco Zoo, museums in Golden Gate Park, and some sights near Fisherman's Wharf. You can buy one-day Muni Passports from conductors on cable cars; in addition, Passports and cable car tickets are sold at several locations throughout town, including the information booths in the baggage claim areas at San Francisco International Airport; the downtown Visitor Information Center; the cable car ticket booth at the turnaround at Powell and Market Streets; and TIX Bay Area (251 Stockton St on Union Square; 415/433-7827; map:N3). For a complete list of locations call 415/923-6050 or 415/923-6051, or visit the Muni Revenue Department (949 Presidio Ave at Geary Blvd; 415/673-6864; map:J3).

For detailed route information either phone Muni (415/673-6864), consult the bus maps located at most bus stops and in the front of the Yellow Pages, or go to the Muni website. If you're planning on using public transportation often, you might as well purchase a $2 route map, sold at the San Francisco Visitor Information Center (see above) and in many downtown retail outlets.

## BY BART

Bay Area Rapid Transit (insider tip: Don't call it "the" BART, it's just BART) is an excellent way to travel longer distances. The clean, safe underground rail network links San Francisco to East Bay destinations including Berkeley, Oakland, Fremont, and Pleasanton, as well as cities as far south as Daly City and Colma. BART fares range from $1.10 to about $5, depending on how far you're going. Call 650/992-2278 for schedules and more information; better yet, go to the BART website at www.bart.org.

## BY TAXI

It's an ongoing debate: City officials say there aren't enough taxis in San Francisco, while cabbies say there are too many. Caught in the middle are everyday San Franciscans, standing on street corners with outstretched arms trying to flag down a cab. While you can usually hail a taxi from a downtown sidewalk without too much trouble, it can be a terribly frustrating endeavor during rush hour and on weekend evenings. Your best bet during these times is to call ahead from your hotel room, restaurant, or wherever you happen to be. Rates for most taxi companies are about $2.50 upon entering the cab, then either 30 cents for each sixth of a mile or 40 cents for each minute. Trips to and from the airport usually cost between $30 and $40; some drivers will offer a flat rate before the trip starts. A few of the bigger companies, all radio dispatched, are DeSoto Cab (415/970-1300), Yellow Cab (415/626-2345), Veteran's Cab (415/552-1300), Luxor Cabs (415/282-4141), and City Wide (415/920-0700).

# LOW-PRICED PARKING

It borders on the absurd what some garages charge for parking in the city. In the Financial District, for example, rates go as high as $5 per 20 minutes, and a day's parking at the Pier 39 Garage will set you back a whopping $30. Heck, that's a decent lunch for two.

Ergo, you'll want to keep this page earmarked if you're touring the city by car, because the best parking deals are the city-owned garages, which charge a fraction of what the private parking sharks demand for a tiny patch of oily cement. We've put together the following list of city-owned garages to save you both time and lunch money.

Note: After you park, take your ticket with you, because you'll have to present it and pay up before you return to your car (and be sure to remember where you parked, because some of the garages are huge). The parking rates below may have increased since this book went to press, but they're likely still the cheapest in the city.

In Chinatown, park at the Portsmouth Square Garage, with an entrance on Kearny Street between Washington and Clay Streets (504 spaces; $1.50 for one hour, $8 for four hours, $5 flat after 5pm), or the Golden Gateway Garage, with an entrance on both Washington and Clay Streets between Battery and Davis Streets, (1,095 spaces; $4 per hour for the first four hours, $5 flat after 5pm).

In the Nob Hill/Union Square area, park at St. Mary's Square Garage, with entrances on Pine, Kearny, and California Streets, bordered by Grant Avenue (828 spaces; $1 per hour after 6pm, $2 per hour on weekends, $4 per hour for the first four hours on week-days), or the Sutter-Stockton Garage, with entrances on Stockton and Bush Streets, bordered by Grant and Sutter Streets (1,865 spaces; $2 per hour, $6 for four hours, $1 per hour after 6pm and on Sundays). Right in Union Square is the Union Square Garage, with an entrance on Geary Street, bordered by Powell, Post, and Stockton Streets (1,030 spaces; $2 per hour, $10 for four hours), or the Ellis-O'Farrell Garage, with entrances on O'Farrell and Ellis Streets, bordered by Powell and Stockton Streets (925 spaces; $6 for four hours, $1 per hour after 6pm).

If you're headed to SoMa or near the San Francisco Museum of Modern Art (SFMOMA), your best bet is the Fifth & Mission Garage, with entrances on Mission and Minna Streets, bordering 4th and 5th Streets (2,622 spaces; $2 for one hour, $7 for four hours), and the Moscone Center Garage, with an entrance on 3rd Street, between Howard and Folsom Streets (732 spaces; $2 per hour, $7 for four hours).

At the Civic Center and Hayes Valley, try the Civic Center Garage, with an entrance on McAllister Street between Polk and Larkin Streets (840 spaces; $6 for four hours, $1.50 per hour after 7pm), and the Performing Arts Garage, with an entrance on Grove Street between Gough and Franklin Streets (612 spaces; $1 per hour for the first four hours).

## BY CAR

About five years ago city officials estimated there were 450 registered automobiles in San Francisco for every mile of paved roadway. It doesn't take a civil engineer to figure out that that's too many cars. In spite of the city's reputation for good public transportation, cars still abound. The by-product, of course, is traffic—tons of it. And parking? Fuhgeddaboudit. Everyone here jokes about being tempted to stop and park if they see a good spot, even when they don't need one. Still, driving in San Francisco can be a convenient—if sometimes adventurous—way to get around. And a car definitely comes in handy for trips outside of town. The San Francisco International Airport has outlets for most **RENTAL CAR COMPANIES**; most have downtown and other San Francisco locations as well, including Avis (800/331-1212), Budget (800/527-0700), and Hertz (800/654-3131). The California State Automobile Association (CSAA), a division of AAA (800/272-2155), has a traveler's service providing information on rental cars, trips, and road and weather conditions, as well as tour books and maps. For CSAA emergency roadside assistance, call 800/222-4357.

Your best bet for **PARKING** downtown is in one of the many centrally located lots. Metered parking is available but hard to come by, and once you find a spot, you can't stay long; most downtown meters allow 30 to 60 minutes of parking or are located in loading or rush-hour tow-away zones. The garages on average charge $1.50 per hour, $7 for four hours, or about $15 to $25 for the day. There are a few relatively low priced garages in the Union Square area; see the "Low-Priced Parking" sidebar in this chapter for details.

In outlying neighborhoods, street parking is usually easier to find. Most areas have two-hour metered parking along the commercial strips at 25 cents (quarters only) for each half- or quarter-hour; noncommercial streets typically have two-hour parking limits enforced by ever-vigilant patrolling officers of the Department of Parking and Traffic (415/554-7275), who time your visit by marking your tires with chalk. Parking tickets range from $25 or $30 for a minor violation to $250 and more for parking illegally in a space reserved for the disabled. If your car is towed, call the **AUTO IMPOUND** (415/553-1235) and expect to pay at least $100 to retrieve it. If you think your car may have been stolen, call the California Highway Patrol (415/557-1094), but always check first to see whether it has been towed.

## BY BICYCLE

One look at the steep hills that rise and fall all over San Francisco, and you might think only an Olympic athlete or a fool would use a bicycle to get around. But bikes are actually one of the best ways to see the city. And there are plenty of places to ride that don't overtax your legs or lungs.

Great **BIKE TRAILS** trace the Embarcadero along the waterfront, from the northern piers around to the Ferry Building and toward the South Beach Marina; the more rustic Golden Gate Promenade, along the northern edge of the city, takes you by the foot of the Golden Gate Bridge. Both offer flat terrain and spectacular views of the city and the bay. Bicycling is also an excellent way to see the Presidio. While this military-base-turned-national-park has its inclines, the Presidio trails—some of which are unpaved—offer a wooded, tranquil respite from the urban hubbub just a stone's throw away. Golden Gate Park is another great choice for leisurely biking, with a web of trails meandering throughout its length, many leading all the way out to the ocean. On Sundays the park is closed to auto traffic, so all you have to look out for are daredevil inline skaters (and other bikes). Riding the hilly streets in the heart of the city is more of a pastime for bike messengers than for pleasure bikers, but bikes are hugely popular just beyond the city limits.

**MOUNTAIN BIKING** was invented in Marin County, and that is where you'll find an army of enthusiasts keeping the tradition alive on any given day. You can ride across the Golden Gate Bridge to access the myriad trails in the Marin Headlands and Tennessee Valley, which begin just north of the bridge. Call the Golden Gate National Recreation Area (415/556-0560) for details and map information.

Another outstanding choice for trail riding is Angel Island State Park (415/435-1915), an oasis of tranquility in the center of the bay. Ferries will take you and your bike to and from the island (see the By Ferry section, below). Several places in San Francisco have good-quality **BIKES FOR RENT** at reasonable day and weekend rates. On Stanyan Street near the eastern entrance to Golden Gate Park, several bike shops coexist in neighborly harmony as a sort of "bicycle row"; among these are American Cyclery (858 Stanyan St at Frederick St; 415/876-4545) and Avenue Cyclery (756 Stanyan St at Beulah St; 415/387-3155). Other good bets near the wharf and North Beach area are Adventure Bike Rentals (968 Columbus Ave; 415/771-8735) and Blazing Saddles Bike Rentals (Pier 41, at Fisherman's Wharf, and 1095 Columbus Ave at Francisco St; 415/202-8888).

## BY FERRY

As you might imagine in a city bounded by water, passenger ferries populate the bay. In fact, before the bridges were built, ferries were the only way to reach the city from the east and the north without an overland detour of several hours. Now less widely used, they're still a scenic and fun way to get across the water. Commuters, tourists, and weekend bike warriors share the decks (alas, no automobiles are permitted). Ferries go to the Marin County towns of Sausalito, Larkspur, and Tiburon as well as to Alcatraz and Angel Island; East Bay destinations include Alameda,

## SAN FRANCISCO'S FERRY FLEET

One of the most fun and motivating ways to explore the Bay Area is by ferry. In addition to the popular ride over to Alcatraz, there are a number of options for cruising the bay. The Blue & Gold Fleet (415/705-5555; www.blueandgoldfleet.com) offers ferry service to Alcatraz, Angel Island, Sausalito, and Tiburon, as well as bay cruises throughout the week. All tours depart from Pier 39 or Pier 41 at Fisherman's Wharf; call for the latest schedules and rates. Also located on Fisherman's Wharf is the Red & White Fleet (415/447-0597 or 877/855-5506; www.redandwhite.com). It offers a one-hour Golden Gate Bridge Cruise that takes in all the city's waterfront sights and also cruises under the Golden Gate Bridge, along the Marin Headlands, and past Sausalito, Angel Island State Park, and Alcatraz Island. Also offered is a 45-minute "Round the Rock Cruise" that circles Alcatraz. It's based at Pier 43 on Fisherman's Wharf; call for schedules and rates.

Oakland, Berkeley, and Vallejo farther to the north (you can even get as far as Davis and Sacramento via connecting buses). Boats for the various **FERRY SERVICES** depart from the Ferry Building at the foot of Market Street and from Piers 39, 41, and 43½. Services include Blue & Gold Fleet (415/705-5555), Red & White Fleet (877/855-5506), Golden Gate Ferries (415/923-2000), the Angel Island–Tiburon Ferry (415/435-2131), the Harbor Bay Ferry (510/769-5500), the Oakland/Alameda Ferry (510/522-3300), and Baylink Ferries (877/643-3779). Call ahead for fare, bicycle, and schedule information.

# Essentials

## AREA CODES

The area code for all of San Francisco and Marin County to the north is 415. Oakland, Berkeley, and much of the East Bay is 510, and for the peninsula to the south, generally 650. The Wine Country, including Napa and Sonoma, is 707.

## MAJOR BANKS

The easterly hub of San Francisco's downtown area is called the Financial District, and it's easy to find a banking institution here to meet your needs. All major banks can exchange currency. The self-proclaimed "Bank of the West" is Wells Fargo, founded right here in the City by the Bay in the mid-1800s to handle the "new" money that folks were pulling down from the hills in the form of gold nuggets. Wells Fargo has many branches throughout the Bay Area, along with several in downtown San

Francisco, including its beautiful banking hall at the corner of Market and Montgomery Streets (800/411-4932). Until not very long ago the world headquarters for Bank of America was in San Francisco, in the massive granite-clad skyscraper that still bears the bank's name (Pine and Montgomery Sts; map:N2). While the actual headquarters have moved east, the "BofA" building and the bank itself still exert a strong presence in San Francisco. Downtown you'll find branches of the bank at the corner of Market and New Montgomery Streets, in the One Market Plaza building (1 Market St; map:O2), and near Union Square (420 Powell St; map:M3). Call the 24-hour customer service number (800/227-5458) for a complete list of local branches and other recorded information.

## BUSINESS AND COPY SERVICES

HQ Global Work Places (425 Market St at Fremont St; 415/781-5000; 2 Embarcadero Center, Ste 200, at Sacramento and Front Sts; 415/835-1300; and 1 Sansome St at Sutter St; map:N3, N2) has everything the traveling business executive could possibly need, from part- or full-time corporate office suites and videoconferencing facilities to secretarial, computer, and graphic services and high-speed Internet access. Ascribe Business Services (1245 Folsom St between 8th and 9th Sts; 415/551-0555) is a respected outfit specializing in legal documents, oversize printing, presentation blowups and mounting, and digital color print-outs. Copy Central is a popular service center, with four locations downtown (705 Market St at 3rd St; 415/882-7377; 603 Battery St at Jackson St; 415/433-5792; 110 Sutter St at Montgomery St; 415/392-6470; and 4 Embarcadero Center, lobby level, Drumm and Clay Sts; 415/576-0430; map:N3-O2). The city is rife with Kinko's outlets as well, all open 24 hours a day, including locations downtown (201 Sacramento St at Davis St; 415/834-0240; map:N2), in Pacific Heights (3225 Fillmore St at Lombard St; 415/441-2995; map:K1), and in the Upper Market area (1967 Market St at Duboce St; 415/252-0864; map:L5).

## COMPUTER REPAIRS AND RENTALS

The people at PC Repair Center (415/452-0955) will pick up your ailing laptop and give you a loaner while they fix it. They promise a four-hour response time, with no charge for traveling to your location. For exclusive, factory-authorized Macintosh service, a good choice is Computer-Ware (Cupertino office, 800/434-9622; ask the operator for a location near you), where the friendly, knowledgeable staff can often fix your problem within a day. Rent-A-Computer (6082 Steuart Ave, Fremont; 510/687-1200; ask the operator for a location near you) offers reasonable rental rates on a full line of products by Apple, Compaq, IBM, and Sun Microsystems.

## DRY CLEANERS AND LAUNDROMATS

Most hotels offer dry cleaning and laundry service for their guests. In addition, a good service in the Financial District is Embarcadero Cleaners (2 Embarcadero Center at Clay and Front Sts; 415/986-7627; map:N2), a full-service operation with express cleaning available. Ray's French Cleaners (1205 Union St at Hyde St; 415/885-4171; map:M2), on Russian Hill, offers same-day service for shirts as well as complete laundry service; it's open every day except Sunday.

You can find full-service and self-service laundries in almost every neighborhood in town, but you can clean your clothes *and* enjoy a social night out at Brainwash (1122 Folsom St at Langton St, between 7th and 8th Sts; 415/861-3663; map:M4), a laundromat and cafe in the hip South of Market area. In addition to several self-serve laundry machines, the place has a full-fledged singles scene, complete with live music.

## GROCERY STORES

If you can't find what you're looking for at one of the farmers markets held during the week in the city, several good grocery stores dot the downtown periphery. Whole Foods Market (1765 California St at Franklin St; 415/674-0500; map:L3) has a cultish following among locals, who flock to the bright, warehouselike store for its gourmet products, health-conscious inventory, and fresh-prepared foods to go. In Pacific Heights, Mollie Stone's Market and Deli (2435 California St btwn Steiner and Fillmore Sts; 415/567-4902; map:K3) is also popular for its fresh-made foods and its outstanding fish and meat department. Open daily till 10pm, this is a great place to stop for a huge deli sandwich and a good bottle of wine for a picnic in Golden Gate Park. The Safeway chain has several locations in San Francisco, including one in the North-point Centre (350 Bay St btwn Powell and Mason Sts; 415/781-4374; map:M1), open daily until midnight, and a 24-hour store in the Marina District (15 Marina Blvd; 415/563-4946; map:J1).

## HOSPITALS AND MEDICAL/DENTAL SERVICES

San Francisco, one of the nation's leading health-care and research centers, is home to myriad top-quality hospitals and medical centers. The California Pacific Medical Center (2333 Buchanan St btwn Clay and Sacramento Sts; 415/563-4321; map:K3) is based in the Pacific Heights area and offers a physician referral service (800/225-5637). The University of California at San Francisco (UCSF) (505 Parnassus Ave btwn 2nd and 3rd Aves; 415/476-1000; map:I6), one of the nation's leading cancer research facilities, has a medical center on its campus. And the San Francisco City Health Center (800/533-7344) is a network of community health facilities offering a complete range of medical services. Call to locate a participating branch near you.

## EARTHQUAKE ADVICE

If you're lucky enough to be in San Francisco during a big one (it's truly a thrill), it helps to know a few tips on how to avoid getting hurt. First off, don't panic—chances are you're only feeling a baby quake (we get these all the time). If it's a super shaker and you're inside a building, seek cover. Don't run outside or you might get creamed by falling debris such as those 100-pound windows. Stand under a doorway or against a wall, and stay away from windows. When you exit a building after a substantial quake, use the stairwells, not elevators. If you're outside, stay outside and away from power lines, trees, and large buildings. If you're around tall buildings (such as in the Financial District), run to the nearest doorway to avoid falling debris. If you're in your car, pull over to the side of the road and stop, but first make sure you're well away from over-passes, bridges, telephone poles, power lines, and anything else that might crush your car (by the way, experiencing an earthquake while driving feels like having a wobbly flat tire). Stay in your car until the tremor stops. And don't forget about the aftershocks.

The Dental Referral Service (800/422-8338) can put you in touch with a dentist who accepts your insurance or can treat you in an emergency. The San Francisco Dental Society Referral Service (415/421-1435) also offers information on low-cost clinics and emergency care.

### LEGAL SERVICES

The Lawyer Referral Service (a branch of the Bar Association of San Francisco) offers attorney referrals (415/989-1616). The San Francisco Trial Lawyers Association provides free legal advice and referrals (415/956-6401). The AIDS Legal Referral Panel (205 13th St, Ste 2170, at Natoma St; 415/291-5454; map:N3), composed of volunteer attorneys, helps individuals with AIDS/HIV handle everything from wills to power of attorney to discrimination. Fees are based on a sliding scale; Spanish- and Farsi-speaking attorneys are available. Centro Legal de la Raza (474 Valencia St, Ste 295, at 16th St; 415/575-3500; map:L5) gives legal services to Spanish-speaking people and has 12 attorneys and dozens of volunteers on staff.

### MESSENGER SERVICES

More than just a delivery method, messengering in San Francisco is almost cultlike. The bicycle couriers that zip in and out of traffic, slipping at full speed through the tiniest openings between cars and trucks, have reached near-legendary status. Two of the most reliable, and fastest, radio-dispatched services are Ultraex (1177 Howard St at 8th St; 415/243-8600) and Citisprint (1900 3rd St at Mariposa St; 415/495-8333).

## PETS AND STRAY ANIMALS

If you see a stray or any animal in need of help, or if you've lost your furry or feathered travel companion, call San Francisco Animal Care and Control (1200 15th St at Harrison St; 415/554-6364; map:M5), which also has a lost pet service (415/LOST-PET). If the little critter gets sick or injured, Pets Unlimited (2343 Fillmore St between Clay and Washington Sts; 415/563-6700; map:K3) is one of the top animal health-care facilities in the city, offering everything from 24-hour emergency service to grooming to flea control.

## PHARMACIES

Walgreens drugstores, where in addition to a full-service pharmacy, you'll find a large assortment of sundries, are in abundance in San Francisco. Some stores are open 24 hours and have 24-hour prescription services. There are several locations downtown, including 825 Market Street at 4th Street (415/543-9534) and 141 Kearny Street at Post Street (415/834-0231). For a complete list of store locations, call 800/925-4733. Other good locally owned full-service pharmacies include the One Market Plaza Pharmacy (1 Market St Plaza btwn Spear and Steuart Sts; 415/777-0404; map:N2), downtown in the Financial District; the Four-Fifty Sutter Pharmacy (450 Sutter St, 4th fl, btwn Stockton and Powell Sts; 415/392-4137; map:N3), which will deliver your prescription anywhere in the city; and the Fairmont Hotel Pharmacy (801 Powell St at California St; 415/362-3000; map:N3), in the lobby of the landmark Nob Hill hotel.

## PHOTOGRAPHY EQUIPMENT AND SERVICES

Shutterbugs love the atmosphere at Discount Camera (33 Kearny St between Geary and Post Sts; 415/392-1100; map:N3), a large downtown store that offers everything from same-day camera repair to advice on proper f-stop settings. It also has a full line of cameras, video cameras, binoculars, and more. For film developing within an hour, some locals prefer Wolf Camera, with several locations in the Financial District, including 650 Market Street between Second and Third Streets, 415/788-5950; and 700 Van Ness Avenue at Turk Street; 415/447-7395.

## POLICE AND SAFETY

In cases of emergency dial 911 from any phone. In nonemergency situations call the San Francisco Police Department (415/553-0123). San Francisco has a relatively good reputation for safety, though just as you would in any major urban area, keep your wits about you: Pickpockets have been known to strike on busy sidewalks and buses, and deserted streets and unattended bags can attract more aggressive thieves. Fortunately, the police department maintains a high-profile presence, and most officers are friendly and approachable.

## PUBLIC REST ROOMS

The City of San Francisco made a deal with a French company (and not without controversy) to put a handful of high-tech, advertisement-laden, self-cleaning public rest rooms in such well-trod spots as Market and First Streets, Fisherman's Wharf, and the cable car turnaround at Market and Powell Streets (look for the oval-shaped, olive-green kiosks covered with chic advertisements). It costs 25 cents to enter, with no time limit, but we don't recommend using the ones in the sketchier neighborhoods such as the Mission. Many parks and public buildings also have rest rooms, including the San Francisco Public Library (100 Larkin St at Grove St; map:M4), the San Francisco Shopping Centre (5th and Market Sts; map:M4), most museums, and major department stores.

## POST OFFICES

Call the 24-hour postal hotline (800/275-8777) for information on post office locations and hours, postal rates, sending valuables, and other mail-related questions. The main post office downtown is the Rincon Finance Station (180 Steuart St at Howard St; map:O2), open Monday through Friday 7am to 6pm, Saturday 9am to 2pm. The Chinatown Station (867 Stockton St at Clay St; map:N2) is open Monday through Friday 9am to 5:30pm, Saturday 9am to 4:30pm. Macy's at Union Square (180 O'Farrell St at Stockton St; map:N3) has a full-service post office in the store's lower level. It's the only post office in the city open on Sunday (11am to 5pm); Monday through Saturday hours are 10am to 5:30pm.

## SPAS AND SALONS

Nearly every spa and salon service you could imagine—and some you probably can't—is available in San Francisco, much of it at the finer hotels. Spa Nordstrom (San Francisco Centre, 865 Market St at 5th St; 415/977-5102; map:M4) and 77 Maiden Lane Salon & Spa (77 Maiden Ln btwn Grant and Kearny Sts; www.77maidenlane.citysearch.com; 415/391-7777; map:N3) are luxe establishments where you can get everything from a bikini wax to a Swedish massage (for more details on these spas, see Body Care in the Shopping chapter). At Zendo Urban Retreat (256 Sutter St, 2nd fl, btwn Kearny and Grant Sts; www.salonzendo.com; 415/788-3404; map:N2), a popular choice for personal relaxation and revitalization, services include hair and makeup styling, massage, and other body treatments. At the less expensive Kabuki Springs and Spa (1750 Geary Blvd at Fillmore St; 415/922-6000; map:K3) you can sink into a traditional Japanese group-style bath, have an exclusive hour-long private massage, or treat yourself to a facial, seaweed wrap, or salt scrub. The Kabuki's communal facilities are reserved for women only on Wednesday, Friday, and Sunday, and for men only on Monday, Thursday, and Saturday; on Tuesday it's coed.

# Local Resources

## BOOKSTORES (BIG ONES)

Borders Books & Music (400 Post St at Powell St; 415/399-1633; map:N3) is an enormous store near Union Square with four floors of books and music CDs—more than 200,000 titles—plus 2,000 CD-ROMs. There's also a great collection of periodicals from the United States and abroad, plus a cozy on-site cafe where you can sit and read them all. Perhaps the most celebrated bookstore in San Francisco is City Lights Bookstore (261 Columbus Ave btwn Broadway and Pacific Sts; 415/362-8193; map:N2), founded by Beat Generation icon Lawrence Ferlinghetti, who still reigns over the shop. The inventory is vast and varied, with an eclectic assortment of literary works by local and national authors, a comprehensive collection of political books, and of course everything ever written by Ginsberg, Kerouac, et al. The San Francisco outlet of Barnes & Noble (2550 Taylor St at Bay St; 415/292-6762; map:M1) has two floors of stacks featuring books in every imaginable category—125,000 titles in all. As with all Barnes & Noble stores, the staff encourages browsing, with numerous work tables and comfy chairs set out for your convenience.

## NEWSPAPERS

San Francisco is one of the few American cities that can still call itself a two-paper town. For years the **SAN FRANCISCO CHRONICLE** (901 Mission St at 5th St; 415/777-7000; www.sfgate.com; map:N3) has been the top daily morning paper, providing local coverage as well as the usual national syndicated news. The **SAN FRANCISCO EXAMINER** (988 Market St at 6th St; 415/359-2600; www.examiner.com), the first paper in the empire founded by famed media magnate William Randolph Hearst, used to be the afternoon daily, but it's now a morning paper as well. It's a bit more sensationalist but with a solid mix of national coverage and local flavor. A joint operating agreement crafted years ago has allowed the papers to share plant facilities and combine forces to publish a single (and massive) Sunday paper.

The city also supports two weeklies. The muckraking **SAN FRANCISCO BAY GUARDIAN** (520 Hampshire St at Mariposa St; 415/255-3100; www.sfbay.com; map:M6) has been a free source of lively political viewpoints and excellent nightlife and events coverage for decades; it's one of the largest and most respected alternative weeklies in the nation. **SF WEEKLY** (510/834-7717; www.sfweekly.com), although now owned by out-of-staters, still offers interesting features on controversial topics and an extensive entertainment and events section. The gay community is served by the magazine **Q SAN FRANCISCO** (415/764-0324; www.

qsanfrancisco.com), a glossy monthly with well-written articles on all aspects of gay and gay-related life, and the **BAY AREA REPORTER** (395 9th St at Harrison St; 415/861-5019; www.ebar.com; map:M4), a good paper featuring editorials, columnists, local news and arts coverage, and events listings. For in-depth business news and investigation, the weekly **SAN FRANCISCO BUSINESS TIMES** (275 Battery St, Ste 940, at Sacramento St; 415/989-2522; map:N2) is a trusted and widely read source.

## PUBLIC LIBRARIES

After more than a little controversy and extensive public debate, the San Francisco Public Library (100 Larkin St at Grove St; 415/557-4400; www.sfpl.lib.ca.us; map:M4), or the New Main, as it has come to be known, opened in 1996, just across the street from the Old Main. Love it or hate it, it's a sight to behold, a modernist temple of knowledge, with all the accoutrements in place for the ride into the 21st century. You enter the library through a breathtaking five-story spiraling atrium. The sleek hallways and various rooms are drenched in natural light, beckoning you to stay and feel at home. There's a 247-seat auditorium, a gallery, a cafe, and outdoor terraces. The book stacks contain special collections on subjects ranging from government and gay and lesbian history to music and environmentalism. There are sections on Chinese and African-American cultures and an area devoted entirely to San Francisco history. The New Main is as tech-savvy as any public library has ever been, with some 400 computer terminals, most offering free Internet access. And in a move lamented by a vocal group of traditionalists, much of the card catalog has been electronically converted, to be made available online at the library's website. Other sections worth noting are the Children's Center, which includes a computer education room; the Center for the Deaf and Hearing Impaired; the Library for the Blind and Print Handicapped; and the International Center, which contains materials for foreign language–speaking patrons. The New Main is open Monday 10am to 6pm, Tuesday through Thursday 9am to 8pm, Friday 11am to 5pm, Saturday 9am to 5pm, and Sunday noon to 5pm. Call 415/557-4400 to locate one of the 26 neighborhood library branches throughout the city.

## RADIO AND TV STATIONS

The radio dial is jam-packed in the Bay Area, with stations of every stripe squeezed in shoulder to shoulder. If the pop hit of the moment is what you seek, you can find it on no fewer than three major stations. The area is also home to one of the nation's first classic rock stations, KFOG, which continues to be a trendsetter in that genre. One of the first urban contemporary stations in the country, Berkeley's KBLX has spawned many an imitator from coast to coast. But for true diversity and a taste of local eccentricity, the lower end of the dial is the place to be. National Public Radio can be heard on two stations here (KQED and KALW), each emanating its own temperament in between national feeds. KPOO is one of the truly eclectic stations in the region, airing everything from gospel to Latin jazz as well as good locally produced shows on community and political affairs. The arbiter of independent programming has long been Berkeley's KPFA. Here's a quick guide to the radio dial.

## Radio Stations

**TALK / NEWS / SPORTS**

KPIX–FM / 95.7
KSFO–AM / 560
KNBR–AM / 680
KCBS–AM / 740
KGO–AM / 810
KFBK–AM / 1530
KPIX–AM / 1550
KLIV–AM / 1590

**PUBLIC / COLLEGE STATIONS**

KQED–FM / 88.5
KPOO–FM / 89.5
KZSU–FM / 90.1
KUSF–FM / 90.3
KALX–FM / 90.7
KALW–FM / 91.7
KPFA–FM / 94.1

**ROCK / CLASSIC ROCK / ALTERNATIVE**

KSJO–FM / 92.3
KLCQ–FM / 92.9
KUFX–FM / 94.5
KFOG–FM / 104.5
KITS–FM / 105.3

**URBAN / SOUL / HIP-HOP**

KBLX–FM / 102.9
KMEL–FM / 106.1
KDIA–AM / 1310

**JAZZ / URBAN CONTEMPORARY**

KSJS–FM / 90.7
KCSM–FM / 91.1
KJAZ–FM / 92.7
KKSF–FM / 103.7

**ADULT CONTEMPORARY**

KLLC–FM / 97.3
KIOI–FM / 101.3
KKIQ–FM / 101.7
KEZR–FM / 106.5

**OLDIES**

KBGG–FM / 98.1
KFRC–AM / 610

**COUNTRY**

KYCY–FM / 93.3
KSAN–FM / 94.9
KRTY–FM / 95.3

**CLASSICAL**

KKHI–FM / 100.9
KDFC–FM / 102.1
KDFC–AM / 1220

**SOFT HITS**

KOIT–FM / 96.5
KBAY–FM / 100.3

**SPANISH**

KZWC–FM / 92.1
KSOL–FM / 98.9
KBRG–FM / 104.9
KOFY–AM / 1050

## TV Stations

Fox–KTVU / 2
NBC–KRON / 4
CBS–KPIX / 5
ABC–KGO / 7

PBS–KQED / 9
WB–KBWB / 20
UPN–KICU / 36

## UNIVERSITIES

The University of San Francisco (USF) has a beautiful campus in the central part of the city and offers a full range of under- and postgraduate studies (2130 Fulton St at Parker St; www.usfca.edu; 415/422-5555; map:I3-J3). The University of California at San Francisco (UCSF), with campuses and hospital facilities throughout town, is part of the state's university program (505 Parnassus Ave; www.ucsf.edu; 415/476-9000). It's the only UC campus dedicated solely to graduate and professional study in the health sciences, and the school is world renowned for its scientific discoveries, research, and patient care. San Francisco State University (SFSU) is part of California's state college system, with a strong reputation for its psychology and business departments (1600 Holloway Ave at 19th Ave; www.sfsu.edu; 415/338-1111). The City College of San Francisco (main campus: 50 Phelan Ave at Ocean Ave; www.ccsf.org; 415/239-3000) has eight neighborhood campuses and offers a full range of courses leading to Associate of Arts and Science degrees, most of which meet the requirements of four-year colleges and universities. Free noncredit courses, such as English as a Second Language and Citizenship, are available as well. Golden Gate University (536 Mission St btwn 1st and 2nd Sts; www.ggu.edu; 800/448-4968; map:N3) has campuses throughout the city offering courses in law, business, and public affairs, among other fields.

# Important Telephone Numbers

| | |
|---|---|
| AAA CALIFORNIA (CSAA), MAPS AND ROAD INFO | 415/565-2012 |
| AAA EMERGENCY ROAD SERVICE (24 HOURS) | 800/222-4357 |
| AIDS HOTLINE | 800/367-2437 |
| AMBULANCE | 911 |
| AMERICAN RED CROSS (BAY AREA CHAPTER) | 415/427-8000 |
| AMTRAK | 800/872-7245 |
| ANIMAL CONTROL | 415/554-6364 |
| AUTO IMPOUND | 415/553-1235 |
| BETTER BUSINESS BUREAU | 415/243-9999 |
| BIRTH RECORDS | 415/554-2700 |
| BLOOD BANK | 415/567-6400 |
| CALIFORNIA HIGHWAY PATROL | 415/557-1094 |
| CHAMBER OF COMMERCE | 415/392-4520 |
| CHILD PROTECTIVE SERVICES | 800/856-5553 |
| CITY BOX OFFICE | 415/392-4400 |
| CITY OF SAN FRANCISCO INFORMATION | 415/554-4000 |
| COAST GUARD | 800/438-8724 |
| CONVENTION AND VISITORS BUREAU (SAN FRANCISCO) | 415/391-2000 |
| CUSTOMS (U.S.) | 415/782-9210 |

**33**

| | |
|---|---:|
| **DIRECTORY INFORMATION** | 411 |
| **DOMESTIC VIOLENCE HOTLINE** | 415/864-4722 |
| **EMERGENCIES** | 911 |
| **FBI** | 415/553-7400 |
| **FIRE** | 911 |
| **GREYHOUND BUS** | 800/231-2222 |
| **HIGHWAY CONDITIONS** | 800/427-7623 |
| **IMMIGRATION AND NATURALIZATION** | 800/375-5283 |
| **LOST PETS** | 415/567-8738 |
| **MARRIAGE LICENSES** | 415/554-4176 |
| **MISSING PERSONS** | 415/558-5500 |
| **MOVIE PHONE LINE** | 415/777-FILM |
| **MUNI BUS/RAILWAY INFORMATION** | 415/673-6864 |
| **PASSPORTS** | 415/538-2700 |
| **PLANNED PARENTHOOD** | 800/967-7526 |
| **POISON CONTROL** | 800/523-2222 |
| **POLICE** | 415/553-0123 |
| **POST OFFICE INFORMATION** | 800/275-8777 |
| **RAPE CRISIS/COUNSELING** | 415/647-7273 |
| **ROAD CONDITIONS** | 800/427-7623 |
| **SAN FRANCISCO DEPARTMENT OF PUBLIC HEALTH** | 415/292-1500 |
| **SAN FRANCISCO DEPARTMENT OF SOCIAL SERVICES** | 415/557-5000 |
| **SENIOR INFORMATION CENTER** | 415/626-1033 |
| **SUICIDE PREVENTION** | 415/781-0500 |
| **TICKETS (BASS)** | 510/762-2277 |
| **TIME** | 415/767-2676 |
| **TIX BAY AREA (DISCOUNT TICKETS)** | 415/433-7827 |
| **TOURIST INFORMATION** | 415/391-2001 |
| **TRANSIT INFORMATION (MUNI)** | 415/673-6864 |
| **WEATHER** | 831/656-1725 |
| **WESTERN UNION MONEYGRAM** | 415/325-6000 |
| **ZIP CODE INFORMATION** | 800/275-8777 |

# TOP 200 RESTAURANTS

# Restaurants by Star Rating

★★★★
Gary Danko
Masa's

★★★★
Aqua
Boulevard
Campton Place
The Dining Room at the
     Ritz-Carlton
Fifth Floor
Fringale
Hawthorne Lane
Jardinière
Kokkari Estiatorio
La Folie

★★★
Acquerello
Azie
Bizou
Cafe Kati
Delfina
Dine
Eliza's
Eos Restaurant & Wine Bar
Farallon
Fleur de Lys
42 Degrees
Isa
Jianna
Johnfrank
Kyo-ya
MC2
The Meetinghouse
One Market
Pacific
Pane e Vino
PlumpJack Cafe
Postrio
Rose Pistola
Rubicon
The Slanted Door
Thep Phanom
Tommy Toy's
Universal Cafe
Yank Sing
Zuni Cafe

★★★
Ana Mandara
Antica Trattoria
Aperto

bacar
Baker Street Bistro
Bix
Black Cat Cafe
Cafe Jacqueline
Cafe Marimba
Carnelian Room
Carta
Casa Aguila
Cha Cha Cha
Chez Nous
Citizen Cake
Ebisu
Elisabeth Daniel
Ella's
Firefly
Garibaldi's
Gordon's House of Fine Eats
Grand Café
Greens
Hayes Street Grill
Kabuto Sushi
Khan Toke Thai House
Le Colonial
Liberty Cafe
L'Osteria del Forno
Manora's Thai Cuisine
Mecca
Moki Sushi and Pacific Grill
Oritalia
Peña PachaMama
PJ's Oysterbed
Rumpus
Slow Club
South Park Cafe
Stars
Ti Couz
Timo's
Ton Kiang
2223 Restaurant and Bar
Woodward's Garden
Zarzuela
Zax

★★
A. Sabella's
Absinthe Brasserie and Bar
Ace Wasabi's
Avenue 9
Bacco
Betelnut Pejiu Wu
Bistro Aix
Blowfish Sushi to Die For

Brandy Ho's Hunan Food
Brasserie Savoy
Brazen Head
Cafe Bastille
Cypress Club
The Elite Cafe
Enrico's
Eric's
Fog City Diner
Foreign Cinema
Globe
Gold Mountain
Great Eastern
Harbor Village Restaurant
Harris'
Helmand
House of Nanking
Hyde Street Bistro
Il Fornaio
Indian Oven
Infusion Bar & Restaurant
Jackson Fillmore
Kan Zaman
La Taqueria
Le Charm
LuLu
Mario's Bohemian Cigar
     Store
Marnee Thai
Maykadeh
Millennium
Mom Is Cooking
Moose's
Mo's Gourmet Burgers
North Beach Restaurant
Park Chow
Pastis
Pauline's Pizza
Plouf
Red Herring
Scala's Bistro
Shanghai 1930
Straits Cafe
Suppenkuche
Swan Oyster Depot
Tadich Grill
Terra Brazilis
Thirsty Bear Brewing
     Company
Tokyo Go Go
The Waterfront
     Restaurant & Cafe
XYZ

Yuet Lee
Zazie
Zinzino

★⚡
Angkor Borei
AsiaSF
Balboa Cafe
Cafe Niebaum-Coppola
Cafe Pescatore
Caffe Macaroni
Caffe Sport
Capp's Corner
Chow
Dottie's True Blue Café
Firewood Cafe
Florio
Franciscan
Gordon Biersch Brewery
   Restaurant
The House

Kuleto's
Marcello's Pizza
Maya San Francisco
Mel's Diner
Miss Millie's
MoMo's
North Beach Pizza
Potrero Brewing Co.
R&G Lounge
Sears Fine Food
Sushi Groove
Tommaso Ristorante Italiano
Tú Lan
Zodiac Club

★
Alice's Restaurant
Beach Chalet Brewery &
   Restaurant
Brisas de Acapulco

Brother's Korean
   Restaurant
Cafe Claude
Charanga
Dol Ho
The Garden Court
Hard Rock Cafe
Indigo
Kate's Kitchen
La Villa Poppi
Lhasa Moon
Mifune
North Star
Rotunda
Sam's Grill & Seafood
   Restaurant
Sapporo-ya
Shalimar
Stinking Rose
Taqueria Cancun
Thai House

# Restaurants by Neighborhood

## BERNAL HEIGHTS
Liberty Cafe
Moki Sushi and Pacific Grill

## CASTRO
Chow
Firewood Cafe
Johnfrank
Marcello's Pizza
Mecca
Thai House
2223 Restaurant and Bar
Zodiac Club

## CHINATOWN
Dol Ho
Gold Mountain
Great Eastern
House of Nanking
R&G Lounge
Yuet Lee

## CIVIC CENTER
Jardinière
Millennium
Stars
Tú Lan

## COLE VALLEY
Eos Restaurant & Wine Bar
Zazie

## EMBARCADERO
Fog City Diner
Il Fornaio
Pastis
The Waterfront
   Restaurant & Cafe

## FINANCIAL DISTRICT
Aqua
Bix
Boulevard
Cafe Bastille
Cafe Claude
Carnelian Room
Elisabeth Daniel
Fifth Floor
The Garden Court
Globe
Gordon Biersch Brewery
   Restaurant
Harbor Village Restaurant
Kokkari Estiatorio
Kyo-ya
MC2
One Market
Plouf
Red Herring
Rubicon
Sam's Grill & Seafood
   Restaurant
Shanghai 1930

Tadich Grill
Tommy Toy's
Yank Sing

## FISHERMAN'S WHARF
A. Sabella's
Ana Mandara
Cafe Pescatore
Franciscan

## HAIGHT-ASHBURY
Cha Cha Cha
Indian Oven
Kan Zaman
Kate's Kitchen
Thep Phanom

## HAYES VALLEY
Absinthe Brasserie and Bar
Carta
Citizen Cake
Hayes Street Grill
Indigo
Suppenkuche
Terra Brazilis
Zuni Cafe

## MARINA/COW HOLLOW
Ace Wasabi's
Baker Street Bistro
Balboa Cafe
Betelnut Pejiu Wu

Bistro Aix
Brazen Head
Cafe Marimba
Greens
Isa
Lhasa Moon
Mel's Diner
Pane e Vino
PlumpJack Cafe
Zinzino

## MISSION DISTRICT

Angkor Borei
Blowfish Sushi to Die For
Brisas de Acapulco
Charanga
Delfina
Foreign Cinema
La Taqueria
La Villa Poppi
Mom Is Cooking
Pauline's Pizza
The Slanted Door
Taqueria Cancun
Ti Couz
Timo's
Tokyo Go Go
Universal Cafe
Woodward's Garden

## NOB HILL

The Dining Room at the
   Ritz-Carlton
Fleur de Lys
Masa's

## NOE VALLEY

Alice's Restaurant
Bacco
Eric's
Firefly
Miss Millie's
Thai House

## NORTH BEACH

Black Cat Cafe
Brandy Ho's Hunan Food
Cafe Jacqueline
Cafe Niebaum-Coppola
Caffe Macaroni
Caffe Sport
Capp's Corner
Cypress Club
Enrico's
Helmand
The House
Jianna

L'Osteria del Forno
Mario's Bohemian Cigar
   Store
Maykadeh
Moose's
Mo's Gourmet Burgers
North Beach Pizza
North Beach Restaurant
Peña PachaMama
Rose Pistola
Stinking Rose
Tommaso Ristorante
   Italiano
Zax

## PACIFIC HEIGHTS/ PRESIDIO HEIGHTS/ FILLMORE/ JAPANTOWN

Cafe Kati
Chez Nous
The Elite Cafe
Eliza's
Ella's
Florio
Garibaldi's
Hard Rock Cafe
Jackson Fillmore
The Meetinghouse
Mifune
Sapporo-ya
Polk Gulch
Swan Oyster Depot

## POTRERO HILL

Aperto
42 Degrees
Gordon's House of Fine
   Eats
North Star
Potrero Brewing Co.
Slow Club

## RICHMOND DISTRICT

Beach Chalet Brewery &
   Restaurant
Brother's Korean
   Restaurant
Kabuto Sushi
Khan Toke Thai House
Mel's Diner
Straits Cafe
Ton Kiang

## RUSSIAN HILL

Acquerello
Antica Trattoria

Gary Danko
Harris'
Hyde Street Bistro
La Folie
Sushi Groove
Zarzuela

## SOUTH OF MARKET (SOMA)

AsiaSF
Azie
bacar
Bizou
Dine
Fringale
Hawthorne Lane
Infusion Bar & Restaurant
Le Charm
LuLu
Manora's Thai Cuisine
Maya San Francisco
MoMo's
South Park Cafe
Thirsty Bear Brewing
   Company
XYZ

## SUNSET DISTRICT

Avenue 9
Casa Aguila
Ebisu
The House
Marnee Thai
Park Chow
PJ's Oysterbed

## TENDERLOIN

Dottie's True Blue Café
Shalimar

## UNION SQUARE

Brasserie Savoy
Campton Place
Farallon
Grand Café
Kuleto's
Le Colonial
Oritalia
Pacific
Postrio
Rotunda
Rumpus
Scala's Bistro
Sears Fine Food

# Restaurants by Food and Other Features

**AFGHAN**
Helmand

**ALL-NIGHT**
Mel's Diner

**AMERICAN**
Beach Chalet Brewery &
 Restaurant
Bix
Brazen Head
Cypress Club
Dine
Dottie's True Blue Café
Firewood Cafe
Fog City Diner
Globe
Gordon Biersch Brewery
 Restaurant
Gordon's House of Fine Eats
Hard Rock Cafe
Hawthorne Lane
Indigo
Johnfrank
Liberty Cafe
LuLu
Mel's Diner
The Meetinghouse
Miss Millie's
MoMo's
Moose's
Mo's Gourmet Burgers
North Star
One Market
PlumpJack Cafe
Potrero Brewing Co.
Rubicon
Sears Fine Food
Universal Cafe
The Waterfront
 Restaurant & Cafe
Woodward's Garden

**BAKERY**
Citizen Cake
Dottie's True Blue Café
Ella's
Greens
Il Fornaio
Liberty Cafe

**BARBECUE**
Brother's Korean
 Restaurant

**BREAKFAST**
Absinthe Brasserie and Bar
Baker Street Bistro
Beach Chalet Brewery &
 Restaurant
Brasserie Savoy
Cafe Pescatore
Campton Place
Citizen Cake
Dottie's True Blue Café
Ella's
The Garden Court
Grand Café
Il Fornaio
Kate's Kitchen
Kuleto's
Mel's Diner
Mom Is Cooking
Mo's Gourmet Burgers
Pacific
Postrio
Scala's Bistro
Sears Fine Food
South Park Cafe
Taqueria Cancun
Universal Cafe
XYZ
Zazie

**BREAKFAST ALL DAY**
Dottie's True Blue Café
Mel's Diner
Sears Fine Food

**BRUNCH**
Absinthe Brasserie and Bar
Avenue 9
Baker Street Bistro
Carnelian Room
Carta
The Elite Cafe
Ella's
Fog City Diner
The Garden Court
Gold Mountain
Greens
Kate's Kitchen
Liberty Cafe
The Meetinghouse
Miss Millie's
Moose's
Park Chow
Peña PachaMama

Postrio
Rotunda
Slow Club
Suppenkuche
2223 Restaurant and Bar
Universal Cafe
XYZ
Yank Sing
Zazie

**BURGERS**
Avenue 9
Balboa Cafe
Beach Chalet Brewery &
 Restaurant
Chow
Ella's
Enrico's
Fog City Diner
Hard Rock Cafe
Mel's Diner
Moose's
Mo's Gourmet Burgers
Park Chow
Slow Club
XYZ
Zuni Cafe

**CAJUN/CREOLE**
The Elite Cafe
PJ's Oysterbar

**CALIFORNIAN**
Alice's Restaurant
Aperto
Aqua
Avenue 9
Black Cat Cafe
Cafe Kati
Fog City Diner
The Garden Court
Garibaldi's
Gary Danko
Globe
Greens
Hayes Street Grill
Jardinière
Masa's
MC2
Postrio
Rumpus
Slow Club
Stars

Zax
Zodiac Club

**CAMBODIAN**
Angkor Borei

**CHINESE**
Alice's Restaurant
Brandy Ho's Hunan Food
Dol Ho
Eliza's
Eric's
Great Eastern
Gold Mountain
Harbor Village Restaurant
House of Nanking
R&G Lounge
Shanghai 1930
Tommy Toy's
Ton Kiang
Yank Sing
Yuet Lee

**COFFEE SHOP**
Dottie's True Blue Café
Kate's Kitchen
Mel's Diner
Sears Fine Food

**CONTINENTAL**
Absinthe Brasserie and Bar
Baker Street Bistro
Bistro Aix
Bizou
Boulevard
Brasserie Savoy
Cafe Bastille
Cafe Jacqueline
Campton Place
Fifth Floor
Fleur de Lys
Foreign Cinema
Fringale
Grand Café
Hyde Street Bistro
La Folie
Le Charm
Pastis
Plouf
South Park Cafe
Ti Couz
Zazie

**DESSERTS
(EXCEPTIONAL)**
Absinthe Brasserie and Bar
Acquerello

Aqua
Bistro Aix
Boulevard
Cafe Jacqueline
Campton Place
Citizen Cake
Cypress Club
Delfina
Eos Restaurant & Wine Bar
Farallon
Firefly
42 Degrees
Globe
Gordon's House of Fine Eats
Hawthorne Lane
Il Fornaio
Jardinière
Le Charm
Liberty Cafe
Masa's
The Meetinghouse
MoMo's
North Star
One Market
Pane e Vino
Postrio
Scala's Bistro
Ti Couz

**DIM SUM**
Dol Ho
Gold Mountain
Harbor Village Restaurant
Shanghai 1930
Ton Kiang
Yank Sing

**DINER**
Dottie's True Blue Café
Fog City Diner
Hard Rock Cafe
Mel's Diner
Miss Millie's
North Star
Sears Fine Food

**ECLECTIC**
AsiaSF
Carta
Firefly
Jianna
Mecca
2223 Restaurant and Bar
XYZ
Zodiac Club

**FAMILY-FRIENDLY**
Beach Chalet Brewery &
   Restaurant
Capp's Corner
Gold Mountain
Hard Rock Cafe
La Taqueria
Mel's Diner
Mifune
Mom Is Cooking
Mo's Gourmet Burgers
Sears Fine Food
Tommaso Ristorante
   Italiano
Yank Sing

**FIREPLACE**
A. Sabella's
Kokkari Estiatorio
Park Chow

**FRENCH**
Absinthe Brasserie and Bar
bacar
Baker Street Bistro
Bistro Aix
Bizou
Boulevard
Brasserie Savoy
Cafe Bastille
Cafe Claude
Cafe Jacqueline
Campton Place
Dine
The Dining Room at the
   Ritz-Carlton
Fifth Floor
Fleur de Lys
Foreign Cinema
42 Degrees
Fringale
Grand Café
Hyde Street Bistro
Isa
La Folie
Le Charm
Pastis
Plouf
South Park Cafe
Ti Couz
Zazie

**FUSION**
AsiaSF
Azie
Betelnut Pejiu Wu
Eos Restaurant & Wine Bar

The House
Infusion Bar & Restaurant
Oritalia
Pacific
Tommy Toy's
XYZ

### GERMAN
Suppenkuche

### GOURMET TAKE-OUT
Greens
Yank Sing

### GREEK
Kokkari Estiatorio

### GRILL
Brother's Korean Restaurant
Hayes Street Grill
Moki Sushi and Pacific
    Grill
MoMo's
Sam's Grill & Seafood
    Restaurant
Tadich Grill

### HEALTH-CONSCIOUS
Ace Wasabi's
Angkor Borei
Aqua
Blowfish Sushi to Die For
Chow
Ebisu
Gordon's House of Fine Eats
Greens
Kabuto Sushi
Kyo-ya
Millennium
Miss Millie's
North India Restaurant
Park Chow
Sapporo-Ya
Sushi Groove
Terra Brazilis
Tokyo Go Go
Zax

### INDIAN
Indian Oven
Shalimar

### ITALIAN
A. Sabella's
Acquerello
Antica Trattoria
Aperto
Bacco

Cafe Niebaum-Coppola
Cafe Pescatore
Caffe Macaroni
Caffe Sport
Capp's Corner
Delfina
Enrico's
Florio
Franciscan
Il Fornaio
Jackson Fillmore
Kuleto's
La Villa Poppi
L'Osteria del Forno
Marcello's Pizza
Mario's Bohemian Cigar
    Store
North Beach Restaurant
Pane e Vino
Rose Pistola
Scala's Bistro
Stinking Rose
Tommaso Ristorante Italiano
Zinzino

### JAPANESE
Ace Wasabi's
Blowfish Sushi to Die For
Ebisu
Kabuto Sushi
Kyo-ya
Mifune
Sapporo-Ya
Sushi Groove
Tokyo Go Go

### KITSCHY
Capp's Corner
Mel's Diner
Miss Millie's
Sears Fine Food

### KOREAN
Brother's Korean Restaurant

### LATE-NIGHT
bacar
Black Cat Cafe
Enrico's
Globe
Greens
Jardinière
Kan Zaman
Marcello's Pizza
Mecca
Mel's Diner
North Beach Pizza

Rose Pistola
Yuet Lee
Zodiac Club
Zuni Cafe

### LATIN
Cha Cha Cha
Charanga
Peña PachaMama
Terra Brazilis

### MEDITERRANEAN
Bizou
Chez Nous
Florio
42 Degrees
Garibaldi's
Kokkari Estiatorio
Zuni Cafe

### MEXICAN
Brisas de Acapulco
Cafe Marimba
Casa Aguila
La Taqueria
Maya San Francisco
Mom Is Cooking
Taqueria Cancun

### MICROBREWERY
Beach Chalet Brewery &
    Restaurant
Gordon Biersch Brewery
    Restaurant
Potrero Brewing Co.
Thirsty Bear Brewing
    Company

### OUTDOOR DINING
Baker Street Bistro
Betelnut Pejiu Wu
Bistro Aix
Cafe Bastille
Cafe Claude
Cafe Niebaum-Coppola
Cafe Pescatore
Enrico's
Foreign Cinema
42 Degrees
Il Fornaio
Isa
Khan Toke Thai House
Le Charm
Mario's Bohemian Cigar
    Store
MoMo's
Park Chow

Plouf
Potrero Brewing Co.
Rose Pistola
The Waterfront
   Restaurant & Cafe
Zazie
Zinzino

**OYSTER BAR**
Brasserie Savoy
The Elite Cafe
Farallon
Hayes Street Grill
Jianna
LuLu
PJ's Oysterbed
Red Herring
Swan Oyster Depot

**PAN-ASIAN**
Betelnut Pejiu Wu
The House
Moki Sushi and Pacific Grill
Pacific
Shanghai 1930
Straits Cafe

**PERSIAN**
Kan Zaman
Maykadeh

**PIZZA**
Cafe Niebaum-Coppola
Cafe Pescatore
Chow
Citizen Cake
Enrico's
Firewood Cafe
Il Fornaio
L'Osteria del Forno
LuLu
Marcello's Pizza
MoMo's
North Beach Pizza
Park Chow
Pauline's Pizza
Rose Pistola
Scala's Bistro
Tommaso Ristorante
   Italiano
2223 Restaurant and Bar
Universal Cafe

**PRIVATE ROOMS**
Azie
Boulevard
Carta

Ebisu
Johnfrank
Tadich Grill
Zarzuela

**ROMANTIC**
Absinthe Brasserie and Bar
Boulevard
Cafe Bastille
Cafe Jacqueline
Carnelian Room
The Dining Room at the
   Ritz-Carlton
Elisabeth Daniel
Fifth Floor
Fleur de Lys
Foreign Cinema
The Garden Court
Isa
Jardinière
Jianna
Khan Toke Thai House
La Folie
Masa's
The Meetinghouse
The Waterfront
   Restaurant & Cafe
Woodward's Garden
Zarzuela

**SEAFOOD**
A. Sabella's
Absinthe Brasserie and Bar
Ace Wasabi's
Aqua
Black Cat Cafe
Blowfish Sushi to Die For
Brasserie Savoy
Brisas de Acapulco
Cafe Pescatore
Ebisu
The Elite Cafe
Farallon
Franciscan
Great Eastern
Harbor Village Restaurant
Hayes Street Grill
Kabuto Sushi
Kyo-ya
Manora's Thai Cuisine
Moki Sushi and Pacific
   Grill
PJ's Oysterbed
Plouf
R&G Lounge
Red Herring

Rose Pistola
Sam's Grill & Seafood
   Restaurant
Sushi Groove
Swan Oyster Depot
Tadich Grill
Tokyo Go Go
Yuet Lee

**SOUP/SALAD/SANDWICH**
Chow
Citizen Cake
Dottie's True Blue Café
Ella's
Fog City Diner
Hard Rock Cafe
Mel's Diner
Park Chow
Rotunda
Sears Fine Food
Universal Cafe
Zazie

**SOUTHERN**
The Elite Cafe
PJ's Oysterbed

**SPANISH**
Timo's
Zarzuela

**STEAK**
Carnelian Room
Harris'
Sam's Grill & Seafood
   Restaurant

**SUSHI**
Ace Wasabi's
Blowfish Sushi to Die For
Ebisu
Kabuto Sushi
Kyo-ya
Mifune
Moki Sushi and Pacific
   Grill
Sushi Groove
Tokyo Go Go

**TAPAS**
AsiaSF
Cha Cha Cha
Charanga
Chez Nous
Enrico's
Fog City Diner
Isa
Slow Club

Thirsty Bear Brewing
    Company
Timo's
Zarzuela

**THAI**
Khan Toke Thai House
Manora's Thai Cuisine
Marnee Thai
Thai House
Thep Phanom

**TIBETAN**
Lhasa Moon

**UNIQUELY
    SAN FRANCISCO**
A. Sabella's
AsiaSF
Bix
Brazen Head
Enrico's
Franciscan
Gold Mountain
Kan Zaman
Kuleto's
L'Osteria del Forno
Mario's Bohemian Cigar
    Store
Moose's
North Beach Restaurant
Plouf
Rotunda

Sam's Grill & Seafood
    Restaurant
Swan Oyster Depot
Tadich Grill
Tommaso Ristorante Italiano

**VALUE, GOOD**
Bistro Aix
Brisas de Acapulco
Brother's Korean
    Restaurant
Capp's Corner
Chow
Dol Ho
Eliza's
Eric's
Gold Mountain
House of Nanking
Isa
Kate's Kitchen
La Taqueria
La Villa Poppi
Lhasa Moon
Manora's Thai Cuisine
Marcello's Pizza
Marnee Thai
Mifune
Mom Is Cooking
Park Chow
R&G Lounge
Sapporo-Ya
Sears Fine Foods
Shalimar
Taqueria Cancun

Tú Lan
Yuet Lee
Zarzuela

**VEGETARIAN**
Chow
Eric's
Greens
Lhasa Moon
Millennium
Miss Millie's
Park Chow

**VIETNAMESE**
Ana Mandara
Le Colonial
The Slanted Door
Tú Lan

**VIEW**
Beach Chalet Brewery &
    Restaurant
Boulevard
Carnelian Room
Franciscan
Greens
Red Herring
The Waterfront
    Restaurant & Cafe

**WINE BAR**
bacar
Eos Restaurant & Wine Bar
Liberty Cafe
Zinzino

# TOP 200 RESTAURANTS

## A. Sabella's / ★★

**2766 TAYLOR ST AT JEFFERSON ST; 415/771-6775**

One of the long-established Fisherman's Wharf restaurants, A. Sabella's has that old-time San Francisco feeling that attracts tourists and locals alike. The Sabella family has owned this restaurant for four generations, ever since 1887, when it was a fish market. The large dining room has floor-to-ceiling windows overlooking the wharf, and there's a massive fireplace in the lounge. With a remodel a few years ago, the restaurant traded in its 1960s decor for a sleeker, softer, less cavernous look, with slipcovered chairs and modern light fixtures. A 1,000-gallon saltwater tank harbors live Dungeness crab, abalone, and Maine lobster, which means you're guaranteed the freshest possible seafood in the traditional dishes such as cioppino, abalone dore, and bouillabaisse. Fortunately, the seafood has been updated along with the decor: The cioppino is fragrant, the clam chowder is fresh and light, and the petrale sole is enhanced with toasted capers and a nutty brown butter sauce. For an appetizer a whole cracked Dungeness crab hits the spot, and for dessert, try the Sabella specialty: New York–style cheesecake with a walnut–graham-cracker crust. *$$$; AE, DC, DIS, JCB, MC, V; no checks; lunch, dinner every day; full bar; reservations recommended; map:M1*

## Absinthe Brasserie and Bar / ★★

**398 HAYES ST AT GOUGH ST; 415/551-1590**

Stylish Absinthe, named for the green herbal liqueur so potent it was banned in turn-of-the-century France, re-creates the romance and mystery of the bygone Belle Epoque. The sumptuous decor begins at the entry with French rattan cafe chairs, copper-topped tables, and a mosaic checkerboard floor. Chef Ross Browne prepares a brasserie-style French and Italian menu with such starters as veal sweetbreads sautéed in a sweet marsala sauce, a delicious version of the classic pissaladière, and fluffy ricotta dumplings. A generous seafood platter loaded with Dungeness crab, shrimp, and mussels is a highlight. Entrees change daily and vary in consistency (much like, alas, the service). You'll find everything from roasted veal chops and seasonal risottos to inventive vegetarian creations. Desserts are more dependable: A Scharffen Berger chocolate pot de crème is sublime, as is the lavender crème brûlée. And while you won't find actual absinthe on the menu, professional bartenders mix a range of amusingly named cocktails, including one named after Hemingway's *Death in the Afternoon*—an unusual combination of Pernod and Champagne. *$$; AE, DC, DIS, MC, V; no checks; lunch Tues–Fri, dinner Tues–Sun, brunch Sat–Sun; full bar; reservations recommended; map:L4*

## Ace Wasabi's / ★★

**3339 STEINER ST AT CHESTNUT ST; 415/567-4903**

This sushi hot spot is a haven for the postcollege trust-fund society that has transformed the Marina into one of the most loved and loathed districts in the city. Owner Ken Lowe is savvy enough to know that in San Francisco, the food must come first, which is why he purchases only grade-A ingredients for his innovative Japanese dishes—and it shows. Saddle up to the bar for some sake bombers while a table frees up, then chow down on the wondrously tender calamari appetizer, the popular buckwheat-noodle/julienned-vegetable salad, the colorful Three Amigos roll (tuna, eel, and avocado), and the tasty Rock and Roll (unagi, avocado, and cucumber). The only drawbacks are the slow service and LOUD atmosphere on busy nights, but if you're into that kind of scene and sushi, you'll love Ace Wasabi's. *$$; AE, MC, V; no checks; dinner every day; full bar; reservations not accepted; www.acewasabis.com; map:K1*

## Acquerello / ★★★

**1722 SACRAMENTO ST BTWN VAN NESS AVE AND POLK ST; 415/567-5432**

Acquerello, which means "watercolor" in Italian, offers contemporary regional Italian cooking in a tranquil, refined setting. Co-owners Suzette Gresham and Giancarlo Paterlini worked together at Donatello during that restaurant's heyday, and they make a great team: Gresham in the kitchen turning out exceptionally flavorful and well-constructed *nuova cucina*; Paterlini in the 60-seat dining room pampering customers and offering expert advice on wines. The small, innovative menu changes often, but expect elegant dishes such as beef carpaccio with hearts of palm and black truffles to start, and pasta selections like triangular ravioli filled with swordfish in a light tomato-caper sauce. Entrees are beautifully presented and include such dishes as grilled quail with fresh oranges and sage or fillet of beef topped with Gorgonzola and walnuts. Gresham composes delicate dishes and light sauces, so you might have room for such knockout desserts as the chocolate "cloud cake" with pralines or the warm zabaglione scented with orange muscat. A converted chapel provides a serene setting for this stellar cuisine, with dramatic pointed archways, flower-filled planters, and a permanent collection of—what else?—watercolors. Jackets are suggested for gentlemen. *$$–$$$; AE, DC, DIS, MC, V; checks OK; dinner Tues–Sat; beer and wine; reservations recommended; gcp19@aol.com; www.acquerello.com; map:L3*

## Alice's Restaurant / ★

**1599 SANCHEZ ST AT 29TH ST; 415/282-8999**

Mention Alice's Restaurant to locals and you're likely to get a nice warm reminiscent smile and hear a tale of the great time they had at the place down the Peninsula. *That* Alice's, a ramshackle biker hangout in Woodside, has been a Bay Area staple since the 1920s. *This* Alice's, in the heart of Noe Valley, while younger, is recalled nearly as fondly by some who have eaten here. The understated, cheery corner restaurant serves fabulous and affordable Hunan and Mandarin specialties. The dishes are prepared artistically, with a California-cuisine flair. There are many house specialties: Among the best are Alice's spicy eggplant with chicken, shrimp, and chile peppers; the seafood delight, with prawns, scallops, fish, and fresh vegetables; and the Hunan smoked pork, with leeks, cabbage, and red and green chile peppers. The sweet-and-sour dishes and sizzling rice soups are also excellent. But the best part is that nothing on the menu is over $10. No wonder people like it so much. *$; MC, V; no checks; lunch, dinner every day; beer and wine; reservations not accepted; www.alicesrestaurant.citysearch.com; map:K8*

## Ana Mandara / ★★☆

**891 BEACH ST AT POLK ST; 415/771-6800**
It's pretty rare when a Fisherman's Wharf restaurant gets the locals' attention, but then again, it's not every day actor Don Johnson opens a restaurant in San Francisco. Ana Mandara ("beautiful refuge") is the city's newest, fanciest, and most expensive Vietnamese restaurant, a worthy showcase for Khai Duong, a highly trained and talented chef who hails from the village of Nha Trang on the south-central coast of Vietnam. The faux-bucolic setting—a large multi-level room filled with Asian artifacts, antiques, pottery, soft lighting, and tropical foliage—is meant resemble an upscale colonial facade. It's all very soothing and chic and a worthy complement to the drool-inspiring French-Vietnamese cuisine (no pho on *this* menu). A top-dish dinner starts with the crispy lobster ravioli with mango and coconut, followed by the banana blossom salad, the Chilean sea bass in miso sauce that's steamed in banana leaf, or the pan-seared Mekong basa (a whitefish) in spicy lemon sauce (both are amazingly good). And for dessert the creamy crème brûlée. The only complaints we have are the occasionally impolite service and the money-gouging sham of sending you to the bar first even if your table is ready when you arrive. *$$$; AE, DIS, MC, V; no checks; lunch Mon–Fri, dinner every day; full bar; reservations recommended; www.ana mandara.com; map:L1*

## Angkor Borei / ★☆

**3471 MISSION ST AT CORTLAND AVE; 415/550-8417**
In a dining room with pink walls, red carpet, and intricate carvings, this family restaurant serves exquisitely spiced Cambodian fare (which is similar to Thai food but less spicy) with surprising refinement and finesse. For an appetizer, try the crispy spring rolls stuffed with a variety of vegetables or the huge lacy crepes folded omelet-style over a juicy vegetable-nut filling. Cold main dishes might include a medley of bean sprouts,

chiles, basil, carrots, and julienned cucumbers, assembled over cold noodles and accompanied with a fragrant coconut-milk dipping sauce. For something hot and steamy, dip into the aromatic coconut-milk–laced curry with green Thai basil, lemongrass, Japanese eggplant, and straw mushrooms. A milder yet still complex red curry enhances a plate of sautéed shrimp nestled on a bed of spinach. Beautifully charred chicken, beef, or pork, highly spiced by long marinating, is served with fresh sliced vegetables and sweet dipping sauces to cool the palate. Many vegetarian dishes are available too. *$; AE, DC, MC, V; no checks; lunch Mon–Sat, dinner every day; beer and wine; reservations recommended for 5 or more; map:L8* &

## Antica Trattoria / ★★☆

**2400 POLK ST AT UNION ST; 415/928-5797**

Soon after Antica Trattoria opened its doors in 1996, the surrounding Russian Hill neighborhood was abuzz with talk of chef Ruggero Gadaldi's incredible Italian fare. Occupying a moderately busy corner on Polk and Union Streets, this simply decorated restaurant with dark wood floors and cream-colored walls has developed a deserved reputation as one of the city's best Italian trattorias. Appetizers might include a purée of potato and vegetable soup seasoned with bacon, or delicate (and divine) slices of beef carpaccio enhanced with capers, arugula, mustard, and Parmesan shavings. A recent rendition of the creamy risotto was prepared with pears and Taleggio cheese, while a memorable chestnut-flavored *fedelini* (angel hair pasta) was dressed with leeks and a smoked-chicken cream sauce. Main dishes might include a savory monkfish wrapped in pancetta, potatoes, and wild mushrooms, or a tomato risotto spiced with fennel sausage. Top it off with the terrific tiramisu. *$$; AE, DC, MC, V; no checks; dinner Tues–Sun; beer and wine; reservations recommended; map:L2* &

## Aperto / ★★☆

**1434 18TH ST AT CONNECTICUT ST; 415/252-1625**

One of the Potrero Hill neighborhood's best restaurants, Aperto is a homey, friendly place popular with locals. In a small dining room adorned with paintings by a local artist, patrons enjoy unpretentious service and generous portions of California-Italian cuisine. The changing menu emphasizes simple, honest peasant cuisine with innovative touches and might include a superior roast chicken with preserved lemon, fish and meat specials, and more than a half-dozen daily pasta dishes, such as penne with cumin-roasted eggplant, tomato, and goat cheese, or the popular spinach-ricotta tortellini with pistachio, pancetta, and sun-dried tomatoes in a cream sauce. The crab-cake salad garnished with a cucumber-and-chickpea purée is another good choice. For dessert, the warm chocolate soufflé is worth every calorie. Aperto doesn't take reservations, so you may have to stand in line for a table on weekend nights; once you settle in with a basket of house-made focaccia and a good glass of red wine, however, the wait will soon be forgotten. *$$; DC, MC, V; local checks only; lunch, dinner every day; beer and wine; reservations not accepted; map:N6* &

## Aqua / ★★★☆

**252 CALIFORNIA ST BTWN BATTERY AND FRONT STS; 415/956-9662**
When it opened in 1991, Aqua was the first restaurant in the city to elevate the humble seafood house to a temple of haute cuisine. Huge towering flower arrangements punctuate its spacious high-ceilinged dining room, where slipcovers on the chairs change with the seasons and the large mirrors and dramatic lighting reflect a well-heeled Financial District crowd. They're usually oohing and aahing over chef-owner Michael Mina's creations, which are marked by a refreshingly light touch with herbs and sauces. Some of our favorites are the roasted spot prawns stuffed with spicy crabmeat, black mussel soufflé, miso-marinated Chilean sea bass, lobster potpie, and grilled medallions of ahi tuna draped with a layer of foie gras in a pinot sauce. Segue into Hawaiian swordfish au poivre with pancetta-wrapped shrimp dumplings or cabbage-wrapped king salmon. If you're feeling flush, you could shell out 60 to 80 bucks for a parfait of Russian caviar. The dessert list is sure to include such delights as blackberry coffee cake, pumpkin cheesecake, and soufflés. A few non-seafood entrees are always available, and Mina demonstrates his tolerance for culinary landlubbers by offering a $55 vegetarian tasting menu alongside the regular $75 five-course and $95 eight-course tastings. *$$$–$$$$; AE, DC, DIS, MC, V; no checks; lunch Mon–Fri, dinner Mon–Sat; full bar; reservations recommended; map:N2*

## AsiaSF / ★★☆

**201 9TH ST AT HOWARD ST; 415/255-8889**
In a town filled with thousands of restaurants, it helps to have a gimmick. At AsiaSF, the draw is the wait staff—a half-dozen or so "gender illusionists" who work their tight butts off waiting on tables, then take turns every half-hour entertaining patrons with leggy lip-synched dance routines atop the bar. Really, these gals shake some serious booty, and if you weren't in on the gimmick, you might never know that she's a he. In between performances everyone's drinking fat martinis and munching on Asian-Californian dishes tapas-style. It's a hit-and-miss menu (it's more about the scene than the cuisine), but if you order the Asia-dilla (a tasty quesadilla stuffed with smoked duck, jack cheese, pepper, and scallions, topped with a sun-dried cherry crème fraîche), the chicken satay, the grilled shrimp and herb salad, and the banana beignet for dessert, you're set. And please don't kvetch about the spotty service—these men are women first, entertainers second, and waitresses a distant third. *$$; AE,*

*DC, DIS, MC, V; no checks; dinner every day; full bar; reservations recommended; www.asiasf.com; map:L5*

## Avenue 9 / ★★

**1243 9TH AVE BTWN LINCOLN WY AND IRVING ST; 415/664-6999**

Avenue 9 exudes energy, and a friendly, efficient wait staff serves a hefty offering of well-prepared Cal-Med fare at neighborhood prices. Tables line the right-hand wall of the restaurant, with a long banquette for seating; an exposed kitchen fills the rest of the room. A 10-seat bar allows patrons to view Jeff Rosen, the owner and head chef, busily working behind the stoves. Orange- and yellow-toned walls with just a bit of stainless steel and exposed pipe take the decor beyond the cafe look without getting mired in industrial chic. The menu is decidedly eclectic, with a strong California sensibility that's partial to local products. Petaluma duck breast is served with a mound of black mission figs and grilled *piadini*; a flatbread appetizer comes with house-cured salmon and Sonoma farmer's cheese. A lusty Tuscan salad of heirloom tomatoes, kalamata olives, and anchovies hits the mark, as does a caramelized onion and roasted-garlic pizzetta. Damn good cheeseburger and fries as well. For dessert try the gingerbread cake studded with caramelized walnuts—you won't be disappointed. A reasonably priced wine list offers mostly California selections and Rhône varietals, with more than 10 options by the glass. *$$$; AE, MC, V; no checks; lunch, dinner every day, brunch Sat–Sun; beer and wine; reservations recommended; www.avenue9. citysearch.com; map:H5*

## Azie / ★★★

**826 FOLSOM ST AT 4TH ST; 415/538-0918**

Chef-restaurateur Jody Denton wants to corner the culinary market on the up-and-coming scene on Folsom Street. By the looks of Azie, wedged in next door to his wildly popular LuLu, he's well on his way. This stylish restaurant bears its South of Market surroundings in mind, with 22-foot ceilings vaulted by four huge columns. The dining room is split-level; in the booths on the main level you can draw a set of curtains for a truly exclusive feel. The main level is also home to the exhibition kitchen, where Asian-inspired French cuisine such as roulade of monkfish, grilled veal medallions with sea urchin–wasabi butter, and aromatic oxtail bundles are beautifully arranged. Some of the most popular dishes are the boneless short ribs, roasted lobster in scallion-ginger cream, braised duck in red curry, and the Nine Bites appetizer, but if you have trouble making a decision, opt for the nightly tasting menu. Dining is also available at the bar, where a DJ plays oh-so-cool music nightly. *$$$; AE, DC, MC, V; no checks; dinner every day; full bar; reservations recommended; map:N4*

## bacar / ★★⯨

**448 BRANNAN ST BTWN 3RD AND 4TH STS; 415/904-4100**

You don't even want to know how much money was poured into this new triple-decker restaurant, the latest venture of Eos (see review) owner-chef Arnold Eric Wong and wine director Debbie Zachareas. The exposed brick-and-timber, warehoused-sized restaurant consists of a lower-level wine salon filled with couches, armchairs, and pretty people acting oh-so-cool, a high-energy (and loud) mezzanine bar, and a somewhat quieter dining area upstairs. While the service still has a few kinks to work out—expect to wait at the bar even if you have a reservation—Wong's French-bistro cuisine is garnering immediate kudos. Dishes like wild boar osso buco, duck and vegetable potpie, salt-cod cakes, and crispy thin-crust pizzas are expertly paired with Zachareas's mind-melting 1,000-bottle-long wine list, including 100 selections by the glass, as a 2-ounce sampler, or via decanter. Whether bacar can retain its new-restaurant popularity in a dying dot-com neighborhood is the $64K question, but for now it's the scene for being seen. Tip: bacar offers live jazz nightly after 10pm, and the kitchen stays open until 1pm. *$$$; AE, MC, V; no checks; dinner every day; full bar; reservations recommended; map:N4*

## Bacco (Ristorante Bacco) / ★★

**737 DIAMOND ST BTWN 24TH AND ELIZABETH STS ; 415/282-4969**

The enticing atmosphere of this modern Northern Italian–style trattoria, with its cheerful persimmon-colored dining rooms and small linen- and butcher-paper–covered tables, beckons to Noe Valley passersby on the lookout for a casual meal. Locals know it's the kind of neighborhood place where they can hang out with a plate of well-made pasta, authentic antipasti, and a decent Italian wine. Tables are perpetually full, service is smooth and efficient, and the food is fresh and tasty. Start with a terrine of eggplant, peppers, and goat cheese served with a green salad, or the excellent steamed clams and mussels seasoned with tomato and garlic. When it comes to pasta, the kitchen excels. Giant, thin ravioli are stuffed with chard and ricotta, drizzled with brown butter, and topped with crisp fried sage leaves. The classic bowl of orecchiette and slightly bitter broccoli rabe gets its zing from the anchovies, garlic, and red chile flakes. A couple of other good dishes are the grilled Italian sausages and polenta, served with a tomato and olive purée, and the tender broiled lamb chops dressed with garlic and rosemary. For dessert, dive into the opulent chocolate terrine with hazelnut custard sauce garnished with strawberries, or the espresso-infused tiramisu. *$$; MC, V; no checks; dinner every day; beer and wine; reservations recommended; map:K7* ⅄

## Baker Street Bistro / ★★☆

**2953 BAKER ST AT PRESIDIO AVE; 415/931-1475**

This small, quiet Union Street storefront bistro is the quintessential neighborhood cafe. In good weather, grab a seat outdoors and pretend you're in a Parisian arrondissement. Jacques Manuera opened Baker Street Bistro in 1991 after working as a chef in France and Washington, D.C. His excellent fare is—you guessed it—classically inspired French bistro. Expect such entrees as rabbit in mustard sauce, snails on a bed of angel hair pasta with mushroom sauce, osso buco, and New York steak with lemon butter and potatoes. This bistro is also the perfect place for a leisurely brunch of eggs Benedict, mimosas, and strong coffee. *$$; AE, MC, V; no checks; lunch, dinner Tues–Sun, brunch Sat–Sun; beer and wine; reservations recommended; map:J2* &

## Balboa Cafe / ★☆

**3199 FILLMORE ST AT GREENWICH ST; 415/921-3944**

The Balboa has had a long history as one of the main "meet-markets" in San Francisco, and the song remains the same. Co-owners Billy Getty (of *the* Getty clan) and San Francisco Supervisor Gavin Newsom run this joint as well as the PlumpJack Cafe up the street, which explains all the self-impressed politicos, gold diggers, DINKs (Dual Income No Kids), suits, and post-fraternity/sorority types hobnobbing around the handsome polished-wood-and-brass bar. Oh, and there's food served here as well. The menu offers a few upscale dishes such as citrus-braised short ribs with mashed potatoes, but they're all done better at PlumpJack (see review below) for about the same price. Instead, save a few dollars and order the kick-butt Niman Ranch Balboa Burger with house-made pickles or a Caesar salad, both of which are among the best in town. *$$; AE, MC, V; no checks; lunch, dinner every day; full bar; reservations recommended; www.plumpjack.com; map:K1*

## Beach Chalet Brewery & Restaurant / ★

**1000 GREAT HWY, AT WEST END OF GOLDEN GATE PARK NEAR FULTON ST; 415/386-8439**

Panoramic ocean-view restaurants are a rare commodity in the city, so hundreds of locals and tourists pack this American brewery/brasserie daily, enduring the so-so food and spotty service just to get some non-city scenery. You *can* have a perfectly wonderful time here, but you need to do it like this: arrive for lunch or well before sunset for dinner, beg for a window seat, order a pitcher of freshly brewed beer (the malty Churchyard Ale gets quite a buzz going) and a Niman Ranch burger with a side of onion rings as *soon* as the waiter arrives, and don't be in a hurry. For the kids, it's the same order with a real draft root beer brewed on site. On weekend nights (circa 10pm) the live surf music and jazz bands are worth the drive; on the way back to your car, be sure to spend a few minutes admiring the restored

WPA frescoes and historical displays on the ground floor. Tip: Skip the overpriced breakfast, and if the lot's full, park across the highway. *$$; AE, DIS, MC, V; no checks; breakfast, lunch, dinner every day; full bar; reservations accepted; www.beachchalet.com; map:C5*

### Betelnut Pejiu Wu / ★★

**2030 UNION ST BTWN BUCHANAN AND WEBSTER STS ; 415/929-8855**
A member of the Real Restaurants company (which includes such successes as Tra Vigne and Bix), this sumptuously decorated Asian "beerhouse" has the ever-so-slightly-tarty feel of an exotic 1930s Shanghai brothel. Named after a popular seed that is chewed throughout Asia for its intoxicating side effects, Betelnut became a huge success in a short time, and it's still on everyone's list of places to try (though, alas, the namesake nut is not offered here). Tall glass doors facing Union Street are opened on warm evenings to provide alfresco dining, and mechanized bamboo fans sway languorously above the busy bar. The mixed menu is pan-Asian, with an array of authentic dishes from Vietnam, Singapore, China, Thailand, Indonesia, and Japan. While the unusual concept entices diners, the reality is not always up to par. With more than a dozen cooks in the kitchen on busy nights, results can vary. Some dishes consistently get raves, including the spicy coconut chicken with eggplant, lemongrass, and basil; the crunchy tea-smoked duck; the succulent short ribs; and the sun-dried anchovies with peanuts, chiles, and garlic. But the green papaya salad gets mixed reviews, and Betelnut's dumplings can be downright disappointing. For dessert try the dreamy coconut tapioca. *$$; DC, DIS, MC, V; no checks; lunch, dinner every day; full bar; reservations recommended; map:K2*

### Bistro Aix / ★★

**3340 STEINER ST BTWN LOMBARD AND CHESTNUT STS; 415/202-0100**
French-trained chef and owner Jonathan Beard runs this trendy Marina District bistro frequented by stylish Gen-Xers and baby boomers. With its creamy lime-green walls decorated with black-and-white photos of Italy and France, Aix is a charming, casual restaurant that attracts patrons from all corners of the city. Part of the bistro's draw is the inexpensive early-bird fixed-price dinners served Sunday through Thursday  from 6pm to 8pm. Diners choose from three entrees, such as grilled top sirloin with roasted garlic, linguine with clams and tomatoes, or a juicy roasted chicken with a crusty golden skin. The main menu features cracker-crust pizzas with various toppings, such as goat cheese and grilled eggplant or wild mushrooms and truffle oil; sirloin burgers; grilled fish, like ahi tuna with black-trumpet mushrooms; and pastas such as an excellent orecchiette with spinach, pancetta, and a tangy tomato sauce. The wine list is reasonably priced and primarily Californian, peppered with European varietals. Desserts can be staggeringly rich, including the

warm macadamia-chocolate torte with espresso ice cream and caramel bananas. The dining room is small and sometimes cramped and noisy, so head for the heated back garden patio; it's romantically lit at night. *$$; AE, MC, V; no checks; dinner every day; beer and wine; reservations recommended; map:K1* &

## Bix / ★★☆

**56 GOLD ST BTWN SANSOME AND MONTGOMERY STS ; 415/433-6300**
Somehow the martini never seems to go out of fashion, and neither does Bix, one of the sexiest and most sophisticated supper clubs in the city (and rated Best Bar in *San Francisco Magazine*'s 2001 readers poll). It's modeled after a 1920s "New American" supper club, complete with massive silver columns, art deco–style lighting, and oodles of hand-carved Honduran mahogany. The restaurant's raison d'être, however, is the top-notch martinis that really sneak up on you. If you manage to make it to a dinner table (the ones on the intimate mezzanine are the best), it's de rigueur to order the crispy chicken hash, a Bix best-seller for more than a decade. Other popular choices include the crisp potato pan-cake with smoked salmon and caviar, classic steak tartare prepared table-side, day-boat scallops with black Périgord truffles pomme purée, and beluga caviar on toast for a mere $118 a pop (c'mon, live a little). Finish the feast in high fashion with another Bix specialty, the bananas Foster. *$$–$$$; AE, CB, DC, DIS, MC, V; no checks; lunch Mon–Fri, dinner every day; full bar; reservations recommended; map:N2*

## Bizou / ★★★

**598 4TH ST AT BRANNAN ST; 415/543-2222**
Bizou means "a little kiss" in French, but San Francisco foodies seem to have planted a big fat wet one on this lively bistro with the rustic Mediter-ranean menu. Since 1993, chef-owner Loretta Keller (formerly of Stars) has seduced even normally conservative diners into eating such exotica as braised beef cheeks, parsnip chips, cod ravioli, and house-cured anchovies (with the heads on, no less), winning them over with her deceptively simple, flavorful preparations. There are plenty of less adventurous items, to be sure, including a wonderful salad of pear, Gorgonzola, radicchio, frisée, and toasted walnuts; day-boat scallops with wild mushrooms, endive, and balsamic vinegar; stuffed young chicken with celeriac, grilled apples, and goat cheese; and desserts like French cream with persimmon and fig sauces and a Seville orange and Meyer lemon curd cake. Housed in a 1906 building, the corner storefront restaurant has an updated bistro feel, with window boxes, vintage light fixtures, weathered mustard-colored walls, large windows, and an oak bar. A few caveats, though: The tables are packed tightly together, the place can get very noisy, and the service can range from boffo to beastly. *$$; AE, MC, V; no checks; lunch Mon–Fri, dinner Mon–Sat; full bar; reservations recommended; map:N4*

## Black Cat Cafe / ★★☆

**501 BROADWAY AT KEARNY ST; 415/981-2233**

Black Cat is restaurateur Reed Hearon's (LuLu, Rose Pistola) latest venture, which plays on San Francisco's ethnic diversity by serving dishes from around the city: Chinese spareribs, North Beach pasta, Fisherman's Wharf seafood, and so on. Unfortunately, the mixed bag of menu items is getting mixed reviews, so you'll probably want to go with something that's hard to screw up, such as their big ol' T-bone steak for four or the great selection of fresh seafood and shellfish—lobster, crab, shrimp, mussels—served by the pound and prepared in five different ways (we prefer it grilled with garlic and hot pepper). Or hedge your bets and order an array of smaller dishes and dine family style, washing it all down with a few Black Cat sake-spiked martinis. As for the decor, subtle it ain't: Blazing red booths, checkered tablecloths, bright lighting, high ceilings, and more mirrors than Liberace's dressing room create an atmosphere of high-energy Parisian brasserie laced with classic San Francisco scenes. It's all still very popular with the local celebrities and CEOs, who always situate themselves in the dig-me booths so everyone can see how much fun it is to be wealthy. After dinner, take a gander at the soigné scene down in the Blue Bar jazz club below. Note: Black Cat is one of the few high-quality restaurants in the city that serves food until 2am. *$$–$$$; AE, DC, MC, V; no checks; lunch, dinner Mon–Sat; full bar; reservations recommended; map:N2* &

## Blowfish Sushi to Die For / ★★

**2170 BRYANT ST BTWN 19TH AND 20TH STS; 415/285-3848**

Japanese animation films play on two suspended television sets for the young and the hip who pack this place, lounging against a backdrop of velvet walls, techno dance music, and acid jazz. Clearly, Blowfish caters to a crowd that wants more than just good sushi. Located in the industrial northeast Mission District, the restaurant offers a combination of traditional and more adventurous sushi. For example, if you're intent on trying the infamously deadly blowfish, the Japanese delicacy otherwise known as puffer fish, expect to fork over about $30 if it's in season, and be prepared for a letdown: It's fairly bland. Move on to the mavericks: Maui Maki (tuna, mango, and macadamia nuts); double crab salad with soft-shell crab; tempura-battered asparagus maki wrapped in rice; and the restaurant's namesake, Blowfish Maki (a roll of yellowtail, scallions, and tobiko, draped with salmon—but, ironically, no blowfish). Non-fish-eaters also have choices: filet mignon with rosemary garlic butter, chicken pot stickers, or asparagus spring rolls with duck. Chef Ritsuo Tsuchida likes to tempt his regular customers with some of his more unusual creations: seared ostrich on portobello-mushroom tempura, anyone? Service is friendly and efficient. *$$–$$$; AE, DC, DIS,*

*MC, V; no checks; lunch Mon–Fri, dinner every day; full bar; reservations recommended; map:M6* ♿

## Boulevard / ★★★⯪

**I MISSION ST AT STEUART ST; 415/543-6084**

Nancy Oakes, a self-taught chef whose cooking career began in 1977 at a scruffy San Francisco saloon, teamed up with nationally renowned restaurant designer Pat Kuleto in 1993 and created this glittering jewel that sits squarely in the center of the city's culinary crown. Hailed as one of the nation's 10 best chefs by *Food & Wine* magazine, Oakes has come a long way from her days of dishing out saloon-style grub to an audience of longshoremen. At big, bustling Boulevard (rated Best Restaurant in *San Francisco Magazine*'s 2001 readers poll), she now serves hearty American-style cuisine with French and Italian influences. Before you indulge in her fabulous fare, feast your eyes on Kuleto's fantastic Parisian-inspired interior design, which he has dubbed "industrial art nouveau." After a spin through the revolving entrance door, you'll find yourself standing under an impressive domed brick ceiling offset by a dizzying array of details, including pressed-tin wainscoting, thousands of brightly colored mosaic tiles, and a sea of decorative ironwork that blends elegantly with the dark wood walls and chairs—it's all very romantic. Oysters, giant beluga caviar, and fresh sautéed Sonoma foie gras served on an apple and fig strudel top the extensive appetizer list. Main courses might include a boneless rabbit stuffed with fresh chicken-and-sun-dried-tomato sausages, roasted to perfection in the wood-fired oven; asparagus risotto accompanied by roasted prawns and shiitake mushrooms filled with herbed goat cheese; and oven-roasted northern halibut resting on a large bed of wilted baby spinach sprinkled with chanterelle mushrooms and a side of buttery potato-chive fritters. For dessert, the ganache-mousse tart with fresh raspberries or pecan pie topped with vanilla ice cream and chocolate sauce push the sated diner over a blissful edge. *$$$; AE, DC, DIS, MC, V; no checks; lunch Mon–Fri, dinner every day; full bar; reservations recommended; www. kuleto.com/boulevard; map:O3*

## Brandy Ho's Hunan Food / ★★

**217 COLUMBUS AVE AT PACIFIC AVE; 415/788-7527**

If you've never experienced good, hot Hunan cuisine, you're due for a visit to Brandy Ho's. It's located near the busy intersection of Broadway and Columbus and, ergo, does a lot of tourist business. That hasn't diminished the quality of its signature dishes: fried dumplings in ginger garlic sauce, cold chicken salad, fish-ball soup, Gon Pao chicken, and for your main course, Three Delicacies—a marvelous mix of scallops, shrimp, chicken, onion, bell peppers, and bamboo shoots, all seasoned with ginger, garlic, and wine and served with black-bean sauce. Unless you specify otherwise, most dishes come hot-hot-hot and require copious amounts of Chinese beer. The fancy black-and-white granite tabletops and large, open kitchen are a cut above the usual Chinese restaurant decor, but there's certainly no need to change out of your Levi's. It's not our favorite Chinese restaurant (Ton Kiang and Eliza's get our vote), but it's the best in the North Beach neighborhood. *$$; AE, DC, DIS, MC, V; no checks; lunch, dinner every day; beer and wine; reservations recommended; map:N2* &

## Brasserie Savoy / ★★

**580 GEARY ST AT JONES ST (SAVOY HOTEL); 415/441-2700**

Brasserie Savoy has long been a favorite pre- and après-theater dinner and cocktail scene, partly because the food is always consistently good and reasonably priced, and partly because it's just so Euro-cool. The atmosphere is pure French bistro, right down to the black-and-white marble floors and tables with matching woven chairs. The menu follows suit, serving such Franco classics as halibut steak rôti with preserved lemon, olives, basil, and tomato; a hearty bouillabaisse made with local seafood; and grilled rib eye with pommes frites and bordelaise sauce. A popular option is to sit at one of the banquettes or at the bar, order a glass of Alsace riesling, and nosh on seafood appetizers—mussels marinière, oysters in champagne sauce, fish soup—or a frisée salad. Darn good crème brûlée as well. *$$; AE, CB, DC, DIS, MC, V; no checks; breakfast every day, dinner Tues–Sun; full bar; reservations recommended; map:M3*

## Brazen Head / ★★

**3166 BUCHANAN ST AT GREENWICH ST; 415/921-7600**

If you already know about Brazen Head, you're probably a longtime local. This two-decade-old pub is a comfy, unpretentious (signless, even) little Cow Hollow neighborhood gem. You know the kind—dim lighting, burled wood paneling, framed portraits of poets and politicos, friendly blokes hanging out at the bar, a hearty hello from the proprietor, and nary a tourist in sight. The menu is heavy on meats and starches and butter and cheese and everything you shouldn't eat because it tastes so damn good. To do the Brazen Head right (à la my grandma), start with a cocktail (Grandma always has a Boodles gin & tonic), then order the Caesar salad with anchovies, and for the main dish choose either the pepper steak or lamb chops done medium rare, with a side of garlic mashed potatoes and a cheesecake chaser, followed by another cocktail (to aid the digestion, dearie). Sure, they serve the requisite fish and chicken, but it's the bloody steaks, chops, and Bob's-your-uncle atmosphere that everyone comes here for. *$$; cash only; dinner every day; full bar; reservations recommended; map:K2*

## Brisas de Acapulco / ★
**3137 MISSION ST AT CESAR CHAVEZ ST; 415/826-1496**

Among the mishmash of Mexican restaurants in the Mission District, this one stands out by offering dishes with a Salvadoran influence. Its friendly, no-frills, family-style approach is evident from the minute you walk in. And although the staff speaks little English, they are quick to point to their menu favorites. Specialties are seafood (in particular, the excellent shrimp dishes) and *sopa de pollo*, a hearty chicken soup that shouldn't be missed. If you are really hungry, order the Combinacion Brisas de Acapulco, which comes with snapper fillets, squid, shrimp, and clams. The *bistec salvadoreo*, a grilled steak in an onion-tomato sauce, is another highlight. Most dishes are under $10. *$; cash only; lunch, dinner every day; full bar; reservations not accepted; map:L7*

## Brother's Korean Restaurant / ★
**4128 GEARY BLVD BTWN 5TH AND 6TH AVES; 415/387-7991**

It's not much to look at—just a wood-paneled room with overhead ceiling fans and bright lights—but the folks who line up for dinner here aren't too concerned about aesthetics. They've come for a taste of home, and the many Korean expatriates who dine here are like a living testament to the great food. You can grill your own food at your table or, if you're not feeling so ambitious, have the kitchen do it for you. Either way, the marinated beef and pork are succulent and delicious, best when rolled into a lettuce leaf and consumed by hand. The kitchen also offers a range of authentic Korean fare, from beef soups to panfried fish to tempura. Entrees are served with side dishes including seaweed, kimchee, peanut sauce, and, of course, rice. Warning: Many of the dishes are so incredibly spicy that you might think the barbecue smoke in the air is coming from your mouth. *$; MC, V; no checks; lunch, dinner every day; beer and wine; reservations not accepted; map:H4*

## Cafe Bastille / ★★
**22 BELDEN PL, JUST E OF KEARNY ST BTWN PINE AND BUSH STS; 415/986-5673**

The narrow downtown alley known as Belden Place couldn't be a better spot for this ever-bustling Parisian-style cafe. Expats, Financial District workers, and in-the-know business folk seek out this cosmopolitan hangout for more than just the delicious crepes. Gregarious waiters, outdoor tables, and plenty of charm make Cafe Bastille a favorite lunchtime destination. During the day, sit outside and choose from sweet and savory crepes (the specialty here). Salads, croque monsieur sandwiches, and a variety of mussel dishes are also available. In the evening, listen to live jazz and enjoy the heartier dinner menu: roast chicken, boudin noir (black sausage) with sautéed apples, steak frites, or ratatouille. This inviting cafe's interior exudes a funky charm with its warm lighting, brightly tiled floor, and walls adorned with '50s French posters. Ask a friendly waiter for a recommendation from the moderately priced list of French and California wines, and take in the always-interesting scene. *$$; AE, MC, V; no checks; lunch, dinner Mon–Sat; full bar; reservations not accepted; map:N3*

## Cafe Claude / ★

**7 CLAUDE LN, OFF SUTTER ST BTWN GRANT AVE AND KEARNY ST; 415/392-3515**

Take a turn down tiny Claude Lane and it's as if you've accidentally encountered a little Parisian street. The lane is anchored by Cafe Claude, where tables are set out with umbrellas, servers are rude and abrupt, and everyone loves it as they sit and sip espresso and listen to the man playing the accordion in the corner. Actually, the service is never all that rude, but it definitely can be, shall we say, "Parisian." And that fits right in with the authentic cafe fare. The salads (including a great niçoise) and baguette sandwiches are popular choices at lunch. We recommend the daily pizza, which comes with any number of surprising toppings, from eggplant to artichoke hearts. At dinner, a hip crowd files in to hear live jazz by local trios (Thurs–Sat nights) and enjoy such reasonably priced plates (around $13) as roast Cornish hen with potatoes and aioli; beef braised in red wine with mushrooms; steamed mussels with garlic, tomatoes, and white wine; French shepherd's pie; and the soup du jour. Outdoor seating is available as well. *$; MC, V; no checks; lunch, dinner Mon–Sat; beer and wine; reservations recommended; www.cafeclaude.com; map:N3*

## Cafe Jacqueline / ★★★

**1454 GRANT AVE BTWN UNION AND GREEN STS; 415/981-5565**

Tucked along a narrow North Beach street filled with boutiques and Italian shops, Cafe Jacqueline is a small, romantic restaurant that serves one amazing dish: the soufflé. Inside the lace-draped storefront windows, a softly lit room holds about a dozen linen-covered tables topped with long-stemmed roses in vases, where you'll often see starry-eyed diners holding hands. This is also where you'll eat soufflé for dinner and soufflé for dessert. That's all there is, except for salad and soup appetizers. You won't care, however, because the soufflés are impeccably made by French-born Jacqueline Margulis. She says creating the soufflés is like painting—she never tires of creating them because each is one of a kind. Pick your own combinations: In a recent visit, the white corn, ginger, and garlic concoction balanced crisp, sweet corn against a creamy-rich base. The leek and chanterelle creation was technically perfect, but had no detectable mushrooms. The crab and the truffle soufflés are house specialties. For the grand finale, the sweet soufflés arrive with a fresh-fruit topping or a dusting of powdered sugar. A smooth white-chocolate version might contain pudding and cakelike bits. Many people come to Cafe Jacqueline solely for dessert, so if you're on a budget (the soufflés aren't cheap), go after dinner and add a glass of champagne or an espresso for a memorable evening out. *$$$; AE, DC, DIS, MC, V; no checks; dinner Wed–Sun; beer and wine; reservations recommended on weekends; map:N2* &

## Cafe Kati / ★★★

**1963 SUTTER ST BTWN FILLMORE AND WEBSTER STS; 415/775-7313**
Cafe Kati may not have the elbow room of some of San Francisco's other top restaurants, but there are few chefs on the West Coast who can match Kirk Webber—a California Culinary Academy graduate—when it comes to culinary artistry. Obscurely located on a residential block off Fillmore Street, this tiny, modest, 60-seat cafe has garnered a monsoon of kudos for Webber's weird and wonderful arrangements of numerous cuisines. Even something as mundane as a Caesar salad is transformed into a towering monument of lovely romaine arranged upright on the plate and held in place by a ribbon of thinly sliced cucumber. Fortunately, it tastes as good as it looks. Though the menu changes monthly, it always spans the globe: miso-marinated Chilean sea bass topped with tempura kabocha squash; pancetta-wrapped pork tenderloin bathed in a ragout of baby artichokes and chanterelle mushrooms; walnut-crusted chicken with Gorgonzola; crispy duck confit with sweet potato polenta and wild mushrooms. Complete the gustatory experience with the to-die-for butterscotch pudding. When making a reservation, request a table in the front room—and don't make any plans after dinner because the kitchen takes its sweet time preparing your objet d'art. *$$; AE, MC, V; no checks; dinner Tues–Sun; beer and wine; reservations recommended; katikwok@aol.com; www.cafekati.com; map:K3*

## Cafe Marimba / ★★☆

**2317 CHESTNUT ST BTWN SCOTT AND DIVISADERO STS; 415/776-1506**
This exuberant little restaurant sandwiched between shops in the Marina District is easy to miss, despite its vibrant sunset-purple facade and the seemingly endless stream of people who squeeze through its lime-green doors every evening. Step inside and you'll be bowled over by a profusion of more screaming colors—pink, turquoise, green, orange—not to mention a fiery-red, 10-foot-tall papier-mâché *diablo* towering above the room. The secret to eating at Marimba, which packs more people into a small space than an express Muni bus, is to make a reservation early in the evening so you won't have to wait long for a table. Once you're seated, immediately order the wonderful guacamole and chips. The restaurant has a changing repertoire of more than 50 salsas; the nightly selections might include roasted corn, avocado-tomatillo, or tomato with smoked chiles. Have a margarita to douse the flames, or sip a delicious fresh-fruit juice. Then move on to the sublime shrimp *mojo de ajo*, drenched in garlic, chiles, and lime; spicy snapper tacos with pineapple

salsa; or grilled chicken spiced with mild, smoky achiote seed. Even the more common fare has a twist: The seafood comes with a choice of five sauces, including garlic, caramelized onions, and fresh jalapeño sauces, or a combination of capers, olives, tomatoes, and jalapeños. Top it all off with the fantastic flan. *$$; AE, MC, V; no checks; lunch Wed–Sun, dinner every day; full bar; reservations recommended; map:J1*

## Cafe Niebaum-Coppola / ★★

**916 KEARNY ST AT COLUMBUS AVE; 415/291-1700**
Film director Francis Ford Coppola brought all the amenities of his hugely popular Napa Valley winery to the city and nestled them stylishly at the foot of the landmark Sentinel Building in North Beach. It may sound at first like a bit of a marketing ploy (and, in fact, it is), but once you sit down to eat you'll be convinced your stop was worthwhile. Coppola is known in these parts for his gourmet savvy, and it is reflected in the casual country Italian dishes served here—many are reportedly made from the director's favorite recipes. The pastas, pizzas, and panini are excellent, great for a light lunch or dinner. A large selection of Italian pastries is available early in the day, and the entire menu can be served outside. As you might expect, there are some 100 wines on the list, 24 of them available by the glass; many can be sampled at the wine-tasting bar. And who knows, after a couple of tastings, you may just talk yourself into buying a T-shirt. *$; AE, DC, MC, V; checks OK; lunch, dinner every day; full bar; reservations recommended; map:N2* ⅃

## Cafe Pescatore / ★★

**2455 MASON ST AT NORTH POINT ST; 415/561-1111**
It's hard to get a good meal at a fair price in the Fisherman's Wharf vicinity, which is why we're so fond of Cafe Pescatore. It's a modest yet attractively decorated trattoria-style restaurant that will leave you both stuffed and satisfied. The trick is to know what to order, which is basically anything cooked in the open kitchen's wood-fired oven. Our perennial favorites are the cioppino (a tomato-based seafood stew with crab, clams, mussels, fresh fish, and prawns), the oven-roasted sea bass in a pine-nut crust served with roasted veggies, the seared chicken with mushrooms and pine nuts in a sweet Madeira cream sauce, and any of the thin-crust pizzas. When the weather's warm the floor-to-ceiling windows are retracted, allowing for some very pleasant alfresco dining. *$$; AE, DC, DIS, MC, V; no checks; breakfast, lunch, dinner every day; full bar; reservations recommended; map:M1*

## Caffe Macaroni / ★★

**59 COLUMBUS AVE AT JACKSON ST; 415/956-9737**
Don't let the funky little facade or silly name fool you—Caffe Macaroni is one of the better Southern Italian restaurants in the city. It's so bloody

small you can't help but feel special, as if you've been invited to dine in some stranger's kitchen in Roma. (And if you think the main dining room is tiny, check out the one upstairs—bonk!) For such a diminutive kitchen, it churns out a surprising amount and variety of antipasti and pastas. The menu changes daily; we recently had an outstanding spinach-and-cheese ravioli dish served in a wild-mushroom sauce. Gnocchi fans will find happiness here as well. The soft polenta makes a good starter, and there's a wide selection of reasonably priced Italian wines. You'll adore the jovial and vivacious Italian waiters too—it's all part of the unique Macaroni experience. *$–$$; cash only; dinner Mon–Sat; beer and wine; reservations recommended; map:N2*

## Caffe Sport / ★★☆

**574 GREEN ST BTWN GRANT AND COLUMBUS AVES; 415/981-1251**
Since 1969 owner-chef Antonio Latona has been serving heaping plates of pasta and steaming hot bowls of cioppino to tourists and locals alike. Considered an institution by many (and antediluvian by as many), this lively North Beach restaurant serves lusty Sicilian dishes with more than a hint of the stinking rose on every plate. There's also often a heaping helping of attitude: The place is famous for service bordering on rude. Even so, reservations are a good idea, but Lord help you if you show up late. The best way to experience this unique slice of North Beach is to go with a group. Order large family-style portions of any of the pasta dishes; the pesto and the seafood combo are consistently rich and tasty. The copious amounts of garlic, unusual Sicilian paintings, decorative plates, hanging hams, and brusque waiters might all add up to sensory overload, but it's definitely an experience you won't soon forget. *$$; cash only; lunch, dinner Tues–Sat; beer and wine; reservations recommended; map:N2*

## Campton Place / ★★★☆

**340 STOCKTON ST BTWN POST AND SUTTER STS; 415/955-5555**
Just off the lobby of a small, European-style luxury hotel, Campton Place pairs an ambience steeped in serene, old-money traditionalism with a kitchen that delights in inventive, newfangled ideas. Since its unveiling in 1983, the pricey restaurant has been the proving ground for such noteworthy chefs as Bradley Ogden (who went on to Lark Creek Inn fame) and Jan Birnbaum (now the proud owner of Catahoula in Calistoga). Frenchman Laurent Manrique now wears the chef's toque, and has been wowing hard-to-please San Franciscans with his simple yet sophisticated Gascony cooking. Recommended dishes include his tomato and ham tartare crouton appetizer, the foie gras ravioli in a clear duck-Parmesan bouillon, the roasted monkfish Basquaise, and one of his signature dishes, poached chicken Aurelie. Desserts are as decadent as one would expect from this lush brand of cuisine. The service is quietly attentive,

and the decor is a study in understated elegance. Campton Place also serves a superb breakfast and lunch. *$$$–$$$$; AE, DC, DIS, MC, V; no checks; breakfast, lunch, dinner every day; full bar; reservations recommended; reservations@campton.com; map:M3* &

## Capp's Corner / ★★☆

**1600 POWELL ST AT GREEN ST; 415/989-2589**

Capp's Corner is everything most restaurants in San Francisco are not: a fun, friendly, slightly funky, family-style Italian-American mainstay where you feel immediately at home and it's OK to put your elbows on the table. Capp's is probably older than you are, and the brusque, matronly waitresses have been working there since the Nixon administration, so don't you dare cop an attitude or the gals will put you squarely in your place. Here's how it works: you walk in past the jukebox (which is invariably playing an oldies tune) and the old gruffs at the bar, sit down at one of the long tables set up family-style, sip wine from water glasses, and choose a main entree (such as spaghetti with meatballs, herb-roasted leg of lamb, osso buco with fresh polenta, or fettuccine with rock shrimp). And then the food starts coming on huge platters—bread, soup, salad, that main dish you ordered earlier, and dessert. Even if mediocre Italian comfort food isn't your favorite, Capp's is a great place to take the family or a group of pals and/or to make new friends, and the price is right: about $16 per person, $11 for kids. Tip: Validated parking is available at the Green Street Mortuary across the street. *$$; AE, DIS, MC, V; no checks; dinner every day; full bar; reservations recommended; www. cappscorner.com; map:N2*

## Carnelian Room / ★★★☆

**555 CALIFORNIA ST AT MONTGOMERY ST; 415/433-7500**

When it's time to treat yourself to the finer things in life, tell your diet and budget to bugger off and reserve a table at the Carnelian Room. One of our favorite high-rise restaurants, it's perched on the top floor of the Bank of America building—a giddy 52 floors above the streets of San Francisco. The combination of dark oak paneling, brass chandeliers, and enormous windows with captivating city views makes for a very romantic setting (particularly if you can score a windowside table). By day the Carnelian Room is the exclusive Banker's Club, accessible only to members or by invitation, but at night we little people can max out our Visas on Grand Cru burgundies, smoked sturgeon with caviar-whipped potatoes, and thick cuts of prime rib so tender you can cut them with a fork. (It's also a great place to have a drink and watch the sunset.) OK, so it's an old-school dinosaur in a city brimming with stylish restaurants, but red meat is back in style and few restaurants can make a thick-cut New York steak taste as sinfully pleasurable as this one. Our all-time favorite dish is the rack of lamb with port wine and rosemary sauce, best accompanied by a glass of Silver Oak cabernet sauvignon. Since the wine cellar houses some 36,000 bottles, it's a good idea to let the sommelier help find the right match for your meal. Of course there are several fish, fowl, and pasta dishes as well, but none compare to the kitchen's deft handling of premium-quality beef and lamb. The Sunday brunch is quite popular as well. *$$$; AE, CB, DC, DIS, MC, V; no checks; dinner every day, brunch Sun; full bar; reservations recommended; map:N2*

## Carta / ★★☆

**1760 MARKET ST BTWN OCTAVIA AND GOUGH STS; 415/863-3516**

Carta's ambitious concept showcases the dishes of a different country or region every other month, and surprisingly, it works quite well. Chef Rob Zaborny steps up to the challenge of creating remarkably good dishes from regions as diverse as Morocco, Russia, and the American Deep South. When Tuscany was the culinary destination not long ago, a sampling of small plates turned up deliciously prepared country-style rabbit stew infused with lovely hints of clove and red wine. A tart lemon vinaigrette perfectly complemented a salad of sweet figs, arugula, and shaved fennel. An eggy baked artichoke tart was disappointing, but a large plate of trout flamed with fresh herbs was cooked to perfection. Zaborny has converted a storefront on a nondescript block of Market Street to carry out his innovative vision. Wrought-iron light fixtures and brilliantly colored art hang from the sun-splashed yellow walls. A private dining area with a long banquette and a warm color scheme give the room a distinctly Mediterranean feel. Live piano music played Thursday through Saturday adds a soothing touch. There's a large and changing selection of varietals from around the world, with offerings by both the glass and the bottle. Curious diners can go online for a sneak preview of the cuisine to come. *$$$; AE, DC, MC, V; no checks; lunch Mon–Fri, dinner every day, brunch Sun; full bar; reservations recommended; map:L5* &

## Casa Aguila / ★★☆

**1240 NORIEGA ST BTWN 19TH AND 20TH STS; 415/661-5593**

Laura Esquivel's sensual novel *Like Water for Chocolate* comes alive in Casa Aguila. The minute a mountainous plate of wildly imaginative Mexican food arrives at your table, it's evident chef Luis Angeles Hoffman cooks anything but ordinary fare. Beautiful, robust dishes you would expect to find only in inland Mexico bring diners from all over the city to this small Outer Sunset District gem. Don't expect anything to happen quickly here. Once you sit down (an event that itself can be preceded by a long wait if you don't have a reservation), nibble on complimentary tamales and warm chips and salsa. If you're really hungry, try the zesty lime-marinated ceviche appetizer. But keep in mind that portions are enormous, so you may want to just pick one of the more than 20 enticing entrees. The *pollo ranchera* is a dizzying, aromatic mound of sweet potatoes, apples, and prunes topped with sweet marinated chicken breasts and wonderfully spiced whole sticks of cinnamon. For pork lovers, whole orange slices top a chop dish with apples, jicama, potatoes, and whole garlic cloves. If you have room for dessert, silky caramel-flavored flan is the perfect finish. At the end of the meal, you'll pay more than at your average taqueria, but everything here, including the tasty sangría, rates far above average. *$$; AE, MC, V; no checks; lunch, dinner every day; beer and wine; reservations recommended; map:G6* ⅃

## Cha Cha Cha / ★★★

**1801 HAIGHT ST AT SCHRADER ST; 415/386-5758**
**2327 MISSION ST BTWN 19TH AND 20TH STS; 415/648-0504**

When we're asked which San Francisco restaurants are our favorites (and we're asked all the time), one of the first we mention is Cha Cha Cha. It's fun, it's festive, the Caribbean food is very good, the prices are totally reasonable, the sangría is addictive, and every meal ends with a free Tootsie Roll. What's not to like? The cafe is wildly decorated with Santeria altars and such, which blend in perfectly with the varied mix of pumped-up patrons quaffing pitchers of sangría while waiting for a table (which often takes up to an hour on weekends, but nobody seems to mind). The tapas-style dishes we always start with: sautéed mushrooms, fried calamari, fried new potatoes (dig the spicy sauce), Cajun shrimp, mussels in saffron (order more bread for the sauce), and plantains with black-bean sauce. Check the specials board for outstanding seafood dishes as well, but skip the so-so steak. There's also a second branch in the Mission District, which serves exactly the same food in a much larger space; not only is the wait shorter (or nonexistent), but there's also a full bar. Still, the original is our favorite simply for the Cha Cha Cha experience. *$; MC, V; no checks; lunch, dinner every day; beer and wine; reservations not accepted; map:I5, map:L6*

## Charanga / ★

**2351 MISSION ST BTWN 19TH AND 20TH STS; 415/282-1813**

Chef Gabriela Salas left her post at the popular Cha Cha Cha restaurant (see review) after nine years to open her own place, named after a style of Latin music. And many people eagerly followed her to this outpost tucked behind an unassuming facade on Mission Street. She has provided San Franciscans with one of the few—and one of the best—restaurants in town serving cuisine from Costa Rica and the Caribbean. Ultimately, it's a tapas experience—which isn't to say the cuisine is the slightest bit like what you'll find anywhere else. Salas's spicy vegetable *empanaditas* are out of this world, served with a yogurt-pineapple-mint salsa that quickly cools the palate. The ceviche is another good selection, as are the mussels and the sautéed mushrooms. Charanga is relatively nondescript, but bring a large group, order a few pitchers of sangría, and you'll soon be creating your own atmosphere. *$; DC, DIS, MC, V; no checks; dinner Tues–Sat; full bar; reservations recommended; map:L6*

## Chez Nous / ★★☆

**1911 FILLMORE ST BTWN PINE AND BUSH STS; 415/441-8044**
Yes, it's a bit cramped, and yes, you'll probably have to wait for a table since they don't take reservations, but these are minor inconveniences for the opportunity to dine at Chez Nous, one of our favorite places to have a casual meal in the city. We like everything about this restaurant: the friendly staff, the erudite patrons, the energetic European ambience, the love-of-good-food esprit de corps, and particularly the tapas-style Mediterranean dishes. If you're a meat 'n' puhtatoes kinda guy, this isn't for you, but if you enjoy a multicourse sampling of light, clean, fresh dishes such as grilled asparagus, smoked squid with olives and frisée, potato gnocchi flavored with bits of prosciutto and mint, and lamb chops sprinkled with lavender salt, you'll become yet another Chez Nous repeat customer. The menu also offers a modest wine list and dessert selection (the lemon cake wins), and excellent bread from nearby Boulangerie Bay Bread, whose owners run this place as well. *$$; MC, V; no checks; lunch Wed–Sun, dinner Tues–Sun; beer and wine; no reservations; map:K3*

## Chow / ★☆

**215 CHURCH ST NEAR MARKET ST; 415/552-2469**
Chow, the first of Tony Gulisano's no-frills cafes serving bargain-priced food, regularly has Castro dwellers lining up. The warm, 80-seat dining room, with a long mahogany bar stretching the length of it, offers a casual and relaxed atmosphere—a good match for the inexpensive food. This no-reservations restaurant is known for its robust wood-fired pizzas with such toppings as fennel sausage with red onions or roast chicken with pancetta. 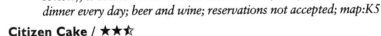 Vegetarians can easily find their way around the menu, with offerings like pasta with peppers and eggplant, grilled portobello mushrooms and polenta, or noodles with tofu and pesto. The desserts tend toward such classics as strawberry shortcake and a pie of the day. An impressive beer list includes several Belgian options and six microbrews on tap. A small list of wines by the glass is also available. A sister restaurant, Park Chow (see review), is located near Golden Gate Park. *$; MC, V; no checks; lunch, dinner every day; beer and wine; reservations not accepted; map:K5*

## Citizen Cake / ★★☆

**399 GROVE ST AT GOUGH ST; 415/861-2228**
Yet more proof that Hayes Valley is fast becoming the city's newest hip- ster hotspot is this chic little bakery and cafe. It is with much rejoicing to find such beautiful, architecturally fanciful confections on display in this once-seedy part of the city. When you're looking to impress with dessert, this is *the* place to get your cake and eat it too. Locals love Citizen Cake,

**65**

as much for its slick, modern feel—polished woods, gorgeous food displays, and terminally cool staff dressed in surgically clean white smocks—as for its magnificent baked goods, coffee drinks, seasonal ice creams, and gourmet cuisine, all made on premises using as much local organic produce as possible. Prices can be a bit steep, but that doesn't stop the underpaid Civic Center servants who line up at lunch for a crispy chicken out-of-the-pot-pie served with sweet white corn and Roma tomatoes; a BLT sandwich spiked with local king salmon; or a delicious thin-crust pizza. Dinner follows the same tantalizing tangent: seared Maple Leaf duck breast served with fresh grape preserves, Yukon Territory Arctic char atop jasmine rice, and our favorite, the roasted pork loin with housemade mustard spaetzle. Whatever you're in the mood for at any time of the day, Citizen Cake has it covered. *$–$$; MC, V; local checks only; breakfast, lunch, dinner Tues–Sun, brunch Sat–Sun; no alcohol; reservations not accepted; map:L4*

## Cypress Club / ★★

**500 JACKSON ST AT MONTGOMERY ST; 415/296-8555**

Reviews of the Cypress Club invariably begin with descriptions of its dining room, and for good reason: Everything in this sumptuous restaurant is over the top. Bulging archways are lined in hammered copper; glass light fixtures look like huge sundaes or a woman's breasts (you choose); low, serpentine partitions snake through the room; plump burgundy velvet covers booths and chairs; and columns resemble giant urns. It's almost as if a particularly impish animator, instead of an interior decorator, decided to fashion a luxury restaurant that would be right at home in Toontown. All this visual drama could easily overshadow the food, and in some cases it does, depending on who's the chef that month. Unfortunately, the Cypress Club suffers from a revolving-door turnover of chefs and other personnel, leaving it difficult for diners to know exactly what to expect. Entrees range from monkfish baked with heirloom pear tomatoes in a saffron lobster broth to herb-kissed loin of lamb with roasted baby beets and potato purée to a whole oven-roasted trout stuffed with lemon, sage, and foie gras. Dinner comes to a reliably rousing finale with temptations like warm lemon cake with white chocolate–poppyseed ice cream, dark chocolate and hazelnut timbale with Tahitian vanilla cream and chocolate sauce, and almond crème brûlée topped with honey-whipped cream. Be sure to scan the room as you dine, because you'll likely find yourself with some interesting dinner companions—everyone from TV talk-show host Conan O'Brien to actor Don Johnson has graced the Cypress Club's velvet-cushioned chairs. *$$–$$$; AE, DC, MC, V; no checks; lunch Mon–Fri (in Dec only), dinner every day; full bar; reservations recommended; map:N2* &

## Delfina / ★★★

**3621 18TH ST BTWN DOLORES AND GUERRERO STS; 415/552-4055**

Opening to rave reviews in 1998, this tiny Mission District neighborhood restaurant with a clean, modern design and pea-green walls has been packed ever since. Partners Anne and Craig Stoll have extensive pedigrees at other Bay Area restaurants, and chef Stoll's daily-changing creations showcase his skills for cooking Italian regional cuisine. Top-notch starters have included nettles-and-ricotta ravioli; a salad studded with fresh cracked crab, fennel, and grapefruit segments; and the far-from-ordinary fried Ribollita da Delfina minestrone. Entrees are hearty and include rich, braised meat dishes, excellent pastas, and fish. Pancetta-wrapped rabbit loin bursts with flavor, as do the buttermilk-battered fried onions and polenta served on the side. A textbook spaghetti with tomatoes, garlic, olive oil, and chile flakes has a little heat to warm the throat. Swordfish rests on a bed of soft leeks; salmon may be served with fresh vegetables and a tangy citrus dressing, and the salt cod is outstanding. Desserts are simply delicious: profiteroles stuffed with coffee ice cream, creamy buttermilk *panna cotta* (baked custard), and Gorgonzola with chestnut honey. Delfina's wine list is a well-edited one, with many moderately priced bottles among the offerings. And a tip for you romantics: Along with Best Italian, Delfina won Best Place for a First Date in *San Francisco* magazine's 2001 readers poll. *$$; MC, V; no checks; dinner every day; beer and wine; reservations recommended; map:K6*

## Dine / ★★★

**662 MISSION ST BTWN NEW MONTGOMERY AND 3RD STS; 415/538-3463**

Dine doesn't get a lot of press, but that doesn't stop fans of chef Julia McClaskey (Universal Cafe) from packing this big, sexy SoMa restaurant nightly. People peering in through the massive windows overlooking Mission Street witness quite the dining scene on a weekend night, particularly when the lively bar is packed with white-collar afterworkers. McClaskey's country French-American menu is both satisfying and filling (no chichi taster plates on *this* menu)—pot roast with root vegetables, chipotle-glazed short ribs with a side of citrus slaw, rack of lamb and fried green tomatoes, Tuscan bread-and-mussel stew, roasted chicken filled with Parmesan-flavored orzo—the kind of hearty upscale comfort dishes that have placed Dine among the city's best restaurants. Caveats? The noise level can get deafening, and service can suffer on busy nights. *$$$; AE, MC, V; no checks; dinner Mon–Sat; full bar; reservations recommended; map:N3*

## The Dining Room at the Ritz-Carlton / ★★★☆

### 600 STOCKTON ST AT CALIFORNIA ST; 415/773-6198

For those special occasions (or when the other person is buying), few restaurants go the extra distance to spoil you rotten like the Dining Room at the Ritz-Carlton hotel. No fewer than five tuxedoed wait staff are at your beck and call, surreptitiously attending to your needs as you bask in your evening of opulence. The setting is, as one would expect, sumptuous and regal, dripping with old-world charm. Cushy high-backed chairs, rich brocade, crystal chandeliers, elegant table settings, and live harp music provide a definite air of formality (though the servers will lighten up if you prod them with humor). Chef Sylvain Portay (a Frenchman from the famed Le Cirque restaurant in New York) continues the Ritz-Carlton tradition of using only the finest, freshest ingredients from around the world, though he brings a more modern style of French cooking to the table than have previous chefs. The seasonal menu is strictly prix fixe, offering a choice of three-, four-, or five-course dinners; optional wine pairings per course—chosen from one of the most extensive wine lists in the country—are offered by sommelier Stéphane Lacroix for a hefty additional fee. The menu offers such decadent dishes as frothy crayfish bisque, risotto with butternut squash and roasted squab, sweetbreads with scallions and bok choy, juicy roasted rack of Colorado lamb, and grilled John Dory (a New Zealand fish) spiked with basil and olives. For the finale, indulge in the ultimate French dessert: dark chocolate soufflé with bitter almond ice cream. The Dining Room also features a unique rolling cheese cart, laden with at least two dozen individually ripened cheeses. *$$$–$$$$; AE, DC, DIS, MC, V; no checks; dinner Mon–Sat; full bar; reservations required; www.ritzcarlton.com; map:M3*

## Dol Ho / ★

### 808 PACIFIC AVE BTWN STOCKTON AND POWELL STS; 415/392-2828

Some contend the mark of authenticity and quality at an ethnic restaurant is when people of that ethnicity are filling the place. Given that benchmark, Dol Ho must be one of the best places in town for dim sum. And it is. Despite lacking the polish and, well, cleanliness of the city's more popular dim sum parlors, this place serves dim sum that's quite fresh and delicious. What's more, it's considerably cheaper than you'll find almost anywhere else. The trays of shrimp and pork dumplings, fried eggplant, custard tarts, and other delights roll out from the kitchen every few minutes; as at all dim sum restaurants, just point at what you want when it passes. *$; cash only; dim sum every day 7am–5pm; beer and wine; reservations not accepted; map:N2*

## Dottie's True Blue Café / ★★☆

### 522 JONES ST AT O'FARRELL ST (PACIFIC BAY INN); 415/885-2767

Don't let the dicey neighborhood deter you from venturing to one of the best breakfast cafes in the city. Though Dottie's serves lunch, it's the all-day, all-American morning fare everyone lines up for, such as hefty portions of French toast, cornmeal pancakes, bacon and eggs, and omelets that look especially appealing against the blue-and-white checkerboard tablecloths. Because it's all made from scratch they don't mind taking special orders, and they do wonders with bean cakes that double as meatless sausage patties. The clincher, though, is the fantastic fresh-baked breads, muffins, or scones that accompany your order. It's a great place to start your day, and the kind of diner you wish was just around the corner from home. *$; DIS, MC, V; no checks; breakfast, lunch Thurs–Mon; beer and wine; reservations not accepted; map:M3*

## Ebisu / ★★☆

**1283 9TH AVE AT IRVING ST; 415/566-1770**
Known for its consistently fresh ingredients, this compact restaurant has been pleasing sushi-lovers with its exquisite creations for more than two decades. The best seat in the house at most sushi bars is the bar; that's true at Ebisu too, though you can opt for table seating or the tatami-covered private room as well. All will typically require a wait, so how hungry you are will usually determine where you decide to sit. If you're an adventurous eater, let the chef's recommendations be your guide. The tuna in every shape and form is always delicious: The buttery toro (or fatty tuna) is incredible, as are any of the nigiri-like maguro and hamachi. A number of whimsically named rolls are available; try the Tootsie Roll, made of tempura-fried salmon rolled in rice, or the Two Balls No Strikes—spicy tuna wrapped in thin avocado slices. Other Ebisu specialties include deliciously prepared chicken teriyaki and a unique and sumptuous seafood salad. *$$; AE, DC, MC, V; no checks; lunch, dinner every day; beer and wine; reservations not accepted; map:H5*

## Elisabeth Daniel / ★★☆

**550 WASHINGTON ST BTWN SANSOME AND MONTGOMERY STS; 415/397-6129**
The first thing you notice about this refined restaurant is the quiet. While the streets outside remind you that you're in the heart of a city, Elisabeth Daniel pampers you with the illusion that the world begins and ends within a few feet of your brocade-draped table. The intimate room holds only 16 of them, spaced so that your neighbors' conversations are almost inaudible. Meals are a leisurely affair; for lunch, a three-course meal and a five-course tasting menu compete for your favor. Dinner comprises six tantalizing courses, with three options for each. With alternatives like peppercorn-encrusted venison with spinach and a crisp potato galette; herb-scented black bass on a bed of lobster risotto; and a ragout of mushrooms, herbed gnocchi, and peas, the only disappointment is that you can't try them all. Portions are sized appropriately for the number of

## SAN FRANCISCO ON CELLULOID

As most film fans know, San Francisco's cinematic contributions are extensive. Time and time again, hotshot Hollywood producers and their entourages trek north to capture this seductive city on film. Here is a sampling of some of the more memorable movies made in the City by the Bay—just in case you didn't recognize her in her many glamorous poses.

American Graffiti
Another 48 Hours
The Bachelor
Basic Instinct
Birdman of Alcatraz
The Birds
Black Stallion II
Bullitt
Butterflies Are Free
The Candidate
Chan Is Missing
City of Angels
Class Action
The Conversation
Copycat
Crackers
Cujo
Dirty Harry
Dying Young
EDtv
Escape from Alcatraz
Flubber
48 Hours
Foul Play
George of the Jungle
The Graduate
Groove
Guinevere
Harold and Maude
High Anxiety
Interview with the Vampire
Invasion of the Body Snatchers
Jagged Edge
James and the Giant Peach
The Jazz Singer
The Joy Luck Club

The Killing Fields
Leonard VI
Love Story
Magnum Force
The Maltese Falcon
Mrs. Doubtfire
Murder in the First
The Net
The Night Before Christmas
Nine Months
1982
Nine to Five
Pacific Heights
The Parent Trap
Patch Adams
Patty Hearst Story
Phenomenon
Play It Again, Sam
Quicksilver
The Right Stuff
RoboCop II
The Rock
Shoot the Moon
Sister Act
Sister Act II
Sneakers
Star Trek IV
Sudden Impact
They Call Me Mr. Tibbs
Tucker
Vertigo
A View to a Kill
What Dreams May Come
When a Man Loves a Woman
Woman in Red

courses, leaving room for dessert (chilled tropical fruit soup with passion fruit sorbet, perhaps?). The only caveat here is the service, which ranges from professional to pathetic. *$$$–$$$$; AE, DIS, MC, V; no checks; lunch Mon–Fri, dinner Mon–Sat; wine only; reservations recommended; map:N2*

## The Elite Cafe / ★★

**2049 FILLMORE ST BTWN CALIFORNIA AND PINE STS; 415/346-8668**

In a city where new restaurant openings (and closings) are practically a daily event, the popular Elite Cafe (known as the E-light by many locals) has held its ground since 1981. A mostly local crowd comes to this bustling Fillmore institution for its fiery Cajun and Creole cuisine and fresh offerings from the oyster bar (be prepared to wait a while for a table, since reservations are not accepted). Handsome dark wood wainscoting and light-colored walls provide a comfortable, upscale setting for the gutsy Southern cuisine. Bountiful portions of thick and tasty gumbo, spicy baby-back ribs, and a signature blackened redfish will fill you to the gills. The à la carte seafood items, from oysters on the half shell and fried calamari to the divine creamy seafood chowder, consistently arrive fresh and generously portioned. For some of the best bread pudding in the city, try the Elite's version swathed in a rich bourbon sauce—it'll have you whistling *Dixie. $$$; AE, DC, DIS, MC, V; checks OK; dinner every day, brunch Sun; full bar; reservations recommended for 6 or more; map:K3*

## Eliza's / ★★★

**2877 CALIFORNIA ST AT BRODERICK ST; 415/621-4819**

Eliza's is not only one of our favorite Chinese restaurants in San Francisco, it's one of our favorite San Francisco restaurants period. Where else can you get such fresh, high-quality cuisine in an artistic setting for under $7 a dish? You'll either love or be confused by the decidedly anti-typical-Chinese-restaurant decor—resplendent with gorgeous handblown glassware, orchids, and modern accents create a rather curious ambience that works for some and appalls others, but it's neither here nor there once the food arrives. The menu offers a large array of classic Hunan and  Mandarin dishes, all served on beautiful Italian plates. Start with the assorted appetizer dish, which is practically a meal in itself for under $10. Three other recommended dishes are the kung pao chicken—a marvelous mixture of tender chicken, peanuts, chile peppers, hot sauce, and fresh vegetables—the sea bass in black-bean sauce, and the vegetable moo-shu (with sweet plum sauce). Regardless of what you order, you're likely to be impressed, and the lunch specials are a steal. The only drawback is the line out the door that often forms around 7pm, and the fact that they don't take reservations. *$; MC, V; no checks; lunch, dinner every day; beer and wine; reservations not accepted; map:N6*

## Ella's / ★★⯪

**500 PRESIDIO AVE AT CALIFORNIA ST; 415/441-5669**

If carbo-loading is your idea of a good time, Ella's—a sunny, charming corner cafe in Laurel Heights—won't disappoint. An in-house master baker whips up fabulous goodies, especially for breakfast and lunch: moist banana-nut–cinnamon coffee cake, sticky buns thick with pecans and orange zest, buttery sweet-potato–raisin muffins; and poached eggs that come on thick slices of yeasty house-made white toast. The buttermilk, pumpkin and pecan, or lemon and ginger oatmeal pancakes are airy and flavorful, the orange juice is fresh, and the omelets are bursting with sausages, roasted peppers, and provolone. Even the lunch menu is enlivened by hamburgers served on house-made buns and flaky potpies, along with salads, sandwiches, grilled fish, and specials such as pot roast with gravy. Dinner dishes are more substantial: beef stew, sautéed pork medallions, and lots of salads, vegetables, and homey American heartland–type entrees. Expect a madhouse at the weekend brunch, with lines of hungry folks wrapping around the corner starting at 8:30am. Service is courteous and efficient, despite all the hustle and bustle. Try to sit at the counter if a table isn't available—and on your way out, be sure to buy a loaf of bread to go. *$$; AE, MC, V; no checks; breakfast, lunch, dinner Mon–Fri, brunch Sat–Sun; beer and wine; reservations not accepted; www.ellassanfrancisco.com; map:J3*

## Enrico's / ★★

**504 BROADWAY AT KEARNY ST; 415/982-6223**

Like a phoenix rising from the ashes, Enrico's is back on bawdy Broadway and better than ever. This restaurant/bar/coffeehouse/jazz club is named after Enrico Banducci, who owned the famous hungry i nightclub during San Francisco's beatnik era and opened this eponymous place as well. (It was later closed in the '80s as the Broadway area went through a depression of sorts.) You can't help but love Enrico's, particularly when you're seated at the heated outdoor patio, sipping a cocktail, noshing on an array of tasty tapas, and listening to the cool jazz beat while a cross  section of the world's cultures walks by. The menu items change monthly, but you're bound to find something that appeals: brick-oven pizzas, Tuscan soups, fresh pastas, fresh seafood, and thick-cut steaks. When in doubt, opt for the juicy Niman Ranch hamburger served on focaccia with house-made condiments, which is offered until midnight on weekends. Enrico's is also the place to go for the best rum-and-mint mohitos anywhere (if you've never tried one, try this one—it packs a deceptive punch). A jazz band plays nightly with no cover charge, and valet parking is both available and necessary. *$$; AE, DC, DIS, MC, V; no checks; lunch, dinner every day; full bar; reservations recommended; map:N2*

## Eos Restaurant & Wine Bar / ★★★

**901 COLE ST AT CARL ST; 415/566-3063**

One of the most talked-about restaurants in the city, Eos has the tourists asking, "Where is Cole Valley?" It's not so much the menu—the Euro-Asian fusion theme is hardly original—as it is the portions (generous) and presentations (brilliant) that have brought throngs of visitors and residents to this once-little-known San Francisco neighborhood nestled near the southeast corner of Golden Gate Park. Owner-chef Arnold Wong, a California Culinary Academy graduate and a former architecture student, has taken the art of arrangement to a whole new level: Every dish is masterfully crafted to take full advantage of the shape, color, and texture of each ingredient. And—egad!—it's a desecration simply to dig in to such culinary artwork, though one's guilt is soon assuaged after the assault begins, particularly when it's upon the tender breast of Peking duck smoked in ginger-peach tea leaves and served with a plum-kumquat chutney. Other notable dishes are the almond-encrusted soft-shell crab appetizer dipped in spicy plum ponzu sauce, shiitake mushroom dumplings, blackened Asian catfish atop a bed of lemongrass risotto, five-pepper calamari, and red curry–marinated rack of lamb. Desserts are as fetching as the entrees, particularly the Bananamisu (akin to tiramisu) with caramelized bananas and the warm bittersweet chocolate soufflé cake. Unfortunately, a quiet, romantic dinner is out of the question here, since the stark deco-industrial decor merely amplifies the nightly cacophony. After dinner, adjourn to the restaurant's popular wine bar around the corner, which stocks more than 400 bottles—many at reasonable prices—from around the globe. Nearly 50 red and white wines are available by the glass, too. *$$$; AE, MC, V; no checks; dinner every day; beer and wine; reservations recommended; map:I5*

## Eric's / ★★

**1500 CHURCH ST AT 27TH ST; 415/282-0919**

The efficient service at this quaint, small corner Chinese restaurant in Noe Valley is mind-boggling. And while no one seems really hurried, the orchestration is actually essential to help expedite the feeding of Eric's Hunan specialties to the crowds lined up out the door. The mango beef and chicken are very good and come in sizable portions. Other good bets are Eric's soups, tiger prawns, and the five-taste chicken, battered and fried and served in a sweet-and-sour sauce. There are also some great vegetarian selections, including asparagus with black-bean sauce. And Eric's prices are incredibly reasonable—part of the reason this small spot packs 'em in. *$; MC, V; no checks; lunch, dinner every day; beer and wine; reservations not accepted; map:L8*

## Farallon / ★★★

**450 POST ST BTWN MASON AND POWELL STS; 415/956-6969**

Diving into the undersea world of chef Mark Franz (of Stars restaurant fame) and master designer Pat Kuleto can leave one breathless. In the fall of 1997, the two co-owners opened a dazzling $4 million, 160-seat restaurant offering seafood dishes that are as innovative as Kuleto's elegant aquatic-themed decor. Giant handblown jellyfish chandeliers with glowing tentacles seem to float beneath a sea-blue ceiling in the Jelly Bar cocktail lounge, where sculpted strands of kelp climb up illuminated pillars. Upstairs, the marine motif continues with huge sea-urchin chandeliers dangling from the arched, painted mosaic ceiling—all a dramatic but enchanting stage for Franz's excellent coastal cuisine. For starters, consider delectable asparagus bisque with cardamom cream; truffled mashed potatoes with crab and salmon caviar artfully stuffed into a real sea-urchin shell; Maine lobster and wild-mushroom gnocchi with a leek, tarragon, and champagne lobster sauce; or giant tiger prawns—the best thing on the menu. Entrees change daily and might include ginger-steamed salmon and sea-scallop pillows with a prawn mousse or sautéed gulf prawns with potato risotto, English peas, pearl onions, and truffle portobello coulis. While Franz's forte is fish, he also has a flair for meat dishes such as a juicy grilled filet of beef served with a portobello mushroom and potato galette, haricots verts, and black truffle aioli. The 300-item wine list fits in swimmingly with the menu (though prices are high), and about two dozen wines are available by the glass. The attentive staff helps make Farallon a deep-sea dine to remember. *$$$; AE, DC, DIS, MC, V; no checks; lunch Tues–Sat, dinner every day; full bar; reservations recommended; www.farallon.com; map:M3*

## Fifth Floor / ★★★☆

**12 4TH ST AT MARKET ST (HOTEL PALOMAR); 415/348-1555**

Chef George Morrone was much beloved in San Francisco when he presided over the stoves at Aqua. When he departed for New York to run Robert DeNiro's famed River Cafe, local foodies wept in unison. So it was with great anticipation that the city greeted the news he would return to open Fifth Floor, the chic restaurant atop the stylish new Palomar Hotel near Union Square. The zebra-print carpet and ebony wood paneling on the walls perfectly complement the combination of playfulness  and sophistication on Morrone's modern French menu. Start with the trio of tuna tartare (ahi, hamachi, and big-eye) or the decadent lobster consommé with lemongrass flan. Even the "simple salad" is prepared with 1970 Solera reserve sherry. The main-course choices are anchored by Morrone's signature tuna foie gras, a delicate, indulgent affair. Or if you're really feeling celebratory, order the whole Saint Pierre, poached in olive oil and carved and served tableside. The wine list is excellent, and the bar area is an elegant, hip alcove. *$$$; AE, MC, V; no checks; dinner Mon–Sat; full bar; reservations recommended; map:M3*

## Firefly / ★★★

**4288 24TH ST AT DOUGLASS ST; 415/821-7652**

Hidden in a cluster of homes on the west end of 24th Street is Noe Valley's best restaurant—just look for a giant metal sculpture of its namesake nocturnal insect perched above a lime-green and sizzling-yellow door. Inside, an eclectic array of modern art surrounds small tables laden with an equally eclectic display of food, which might include steaming bowls of bouillabaisse de Marseilles bubbling over with monkfish, prawns, scallops, and bass; shrimp-and-scallop pot stickers accompanied by a spicy sesame-soy dipping sauce (Firefly's signature appetizer); and a portobello mushroom Wellington served with linguine that's swirled with fresh vegetables. Co-owner–chef Brad Levy and co-owner Veva Edelson, both formerly of Embarko, dub it "home cooking with few ethnic boundaries." They also proudly announce on every menu that their meat comes from the well-known Niman Ranch, home of "happy, drug-free animals with an ocean view." The changing roster of desserts is as good as it looks, especially the not-too-sweet strawberry shortcake and the banana bread pudding with caramel anglaise. *$$–$$$; AE, MC, V; checks OK; dinner every day; beer and wine; reservations recommended; map:J7*

## Firewood Cafe / ★★

**4248 18TH ST AT DIAMOND ST; 415/252-0999**

Who says you can't get top-notch cuisine on a budget? Those who do have yet to visit Firewood, where you can satisfy your yen for such fresh fare as calamari with lemon-garlic aioli without breaking the bank. But just because the proprietors here are willing to save you money doesn't mean they don't bother to decorate: It's a handsome, comfortable dining room with enormous streetside picture windows. So what's the catch? No table service. Order at the counter and then retire to your seat. You'll quickly forget about the self-service once you sink your teeth into the succulent roast chicken and roasted new potatoes. Or try one of Firewood's gourmet pizzas. Salads here are large, fresh, and worthy of full-scale restaurants. The wine list is well edited and priced. By meal's end, if you haven't already gotten over the fact that there's no wait staff, you surely will when you walk out with your tip money in your pocket. *$; MC, V; checks OK; lunch, dinner every day; beer and wine; reservations not accepted; map:J6*

## Fleur de Lys / ★★★

**777 SUTTER ST BTWN JONES AND TAYLOR STS; 415/673-7779**

Fleur de Lys is definitely a "grand occasion" restaurant, with fantastic food, formal service, breathtaking decor, and a superb wine list. Trained by such French superstars as Paul Bocuse and Roger Vergé, chef and co-owner Hubert Keller displays a formidable technique—beautifully prepared ingredients accompanied by surprising garnishes and subtle sauces—and many of his contemporary French dishes are near-miracles. Recent standouts include the choucroute-crusted veal loin wrapped in applewood-smoked bacon, fresh Atlantic salmon baked in a tender corn pancake topped with imperial caviar and a watercress sauce, marinated loin of venison with a mustard-seed sabayon, and his four-course vegetarian feast, which prompted a flurry of favorable press when it debuted several years ago. Critics sometimes sniff that particular dishes are too complex, portions seem small, and prices loom large, but these are small dents in Fleur de Lys's mighty armor. The restaurant's decor matches the splendor of its food step for step: The romantic dining area is draped in a luxurious tentlike fashion with 700 yards of rich, red-and-gold hand-painted floral fabrics, and in the center of the room sits a spectacular crown of fresh flowers on a pedestal. Mirrored walls double this visual spectacle while simultaneously allowing you to admire yourself and your glitteringly attired companion. The wine list is strong if you stick to bottles; it's weak by the glass. Fleur de Lys isn't always crowded, but reservations are required; this is the sort of establishment that doesn't want to guess who's coming to dinner. Note: A recent small kitchen fire may result in some changes to the interior, which suffered smoke damage. *$$$–$$$$; AE, DC, MC, V; no checks; dinner Mon–Sat; full bar; reservations required; www.fleurdelyssf.com; map:M3*

## Florio / ★★☆

**1915 FILLMORE ST BTWN PINE AND BUSH STS; 415/775-4300**

This friendly, stylish, unassuming spot wasted little time becoming a Pacific Heights anchor, with several regulars among the clientele. With just 47 seats, the brasserie-style place always seems crowded. Many head for the bar area to have a glass from the excellent wine list. There are ownership ties here to the downtown supper club Bix (see review), and the service is on a par with that impeccable restaurant. The Italian-Mediterranean dishes are even-keeled—some very good, some less so. Try the lobster bisque or the steamed mussels for a taste of the chef's skill. Other dishes, such as classic steak frites or the roast chicken, are decent, but not so different from what you'd find at other San Francisco restaurants. Still, a unique experience is not what to look for when you visit Florio—a comfortable "insider" feeling is the ticket here. Just don't drive: Parking in these parts is notoriously tight. *$; AE, MC, V; no checks; dinner every day; full bar; reservations recommended; map:K3*

## Fog City Diner / ★★

**1300 BATTERY ST, AT LOMBARD ST ALONG THE EMBARCADERO; 415/982-2000**

The glimmering chrome, glass, polished woods, and neon decor à la master restaurant designer Pat Kuleto is sleek and sophisticated, but it does a poor job of absorbing the decibels when Fog City gets packed (which is often). Along with the upscale diner fare (gourmet cheeseburgers, ahi tuna sloppy joes, arugula and beet salad, and damn good onion rings), the kitchen offers a medley of savory "small plates" such as spicy crab cakes served with a side of fennel slaw, seared sirloin carpaccio with baby artichokes and truffle oil, and quesadillas heated with roasted Anaheim chiles. Full entrees are available as well, such as fresh fish, meat loaf, pork chops, cioppino, and pot roast, but the best bet is to nosh on the small plates tapas style. There's even a raw bar serving oysters on the half shell, clams, cracked crab, prawns, and clams. If you're feeling gluttonous, feast on Fog City's old-fashioned chocolate cake with a mandatory side of cold milk. On sunny days opt for one of the shaded sidewalk tables. *$$; B, DC, DIS, MC, V; no checks; lunch, dinner every day, brunch Sun; full bar; reservations recommended; www.fogcitydiner.cc; map:N1*

## Foreign Cinema / ★★

**2534 MISSION ST BTWN 21ST AND 22ND STS; 415/648-7600**

The concept behind this contemporary French restaurant is to combine dinner and a movie in a single location. Accessed through an unassuming door along Mission Street, the restaurant has an industrial-chic appearance, with deliberately unfinished walls, exposed mechanics in the ceiling, a stark open kitchen, and hard surfaces throughout. On one wall in a center courtyard, classic foreign films are projected in all their grainy black-and-white glory (early features included Fellini's *La Dolce Vita* and Bergman's *Seventh Seal*). Drive-in-movie–type speaker boxes are placed at each table so you can listen along as you dine—sort of like a movie-and-dinner date all rolled into one. But mostly the films are just an imaginative distraction from the main attraction: the food. The lobster and monkfish bouillabaisse is rich and decadent; the roasted Sonoma duck breast is tender and bursting with flavor; the rosemary-marinated lamb melts in your mouth; and for dessert it's the chocolate pot de crème. It's all quite a production, enough so that you may not even notice that some of the dishes seem a bit rushed and decidedly sub-par (read: Go with the wait staff's suggestions). *$$–$$$; MC, V; no checks; dinner every day; full bar; reservations recommended; www.foreigncinema.com; map:L6*

## 42 Degrees / ★★★

**499 ILLINOIS ST, 1 BLOCK OFF 3RD ST AT 16TH ST; 415/777-5558**

Like Caffe Esprit, the former occupant of this bayside site, 42 Degrees is popular with a relentlessly hip crowd of young professionals and boasts a spare, high-tech warehouse look, with a soaring ceiling and lots of concrete, metal, and glass. As night falls, however, candlelight, table linens, and strains of live jazz soften the effect, transforming the stark 100-seat space into an appealing supper club. The name refers to the latitude of

Provence and the Mediterranean Sea, and chef-owner James Moffat's ever-changing menu reflects this sun-splashed influence with starters like watercress salad with duck confit, walnuts, and pomegranates; Medjool dates with Parmesan and celery; and grilled artichokes with Meyer lemons. Entrees might include risotto with shaved truffles and mushrooms, pan-roasted chicken with lemon and black olive sauce, or grilled pancetta-wrapped salmon. Lighter eaters can look to the chalkboard for small plates such as pizzettas, Iberian blood sausage, and herb-roasted potatoes with aioli. Desserts include a sublime chocolate pot de crème, milk chocolate crème brûlée, and a warm apple napoleon with vanilla ice cream and huckleberry sauce. The service is courteous and professional, the mezzanine-level windows afford a view of the bay, and there's a large, pleasant courtyard patio for dining alfresco on warm days. Tip: free parking in the Esprit parking lot. $$–$$$; MC, V; *no checks; dinner Wed–Sat; full bar; reservations recommended; map:O5*

## Franciscan / ★★☆

### PIER 43½ AT FISHERMAN'S WHARF; 415/362-7733

This is one of the best restaurants on Fisherman's Wharf, with many pleasant surprises on its fresh seafood menu. The huge establishment has commanding views of the bay from most seats. Situated on three tiers, the tables in the dining room are mostly angled to face the massive floor-to-ceiling windows. The seafood is the best bet here, although the pasta dishes we've tried (such as the angel hair with rock shrimp) aren't bad. The roast Pacific snapper is tender and flaky, and the Maine lobster is super-rich. Portions are huge, served without a lot of fancy-shmancy flair. Kids will find much to like, too. Despite the throngs of tourists dining here, it's a pleasant respite from the madding crowd coursing through the wharf area outside. $$; AE, DC, MC, V; *no checks; lunch, dinner every day; full bar; reservations recommended; map:K1*

## Fringale / ★★★☆

### 570 4TH ST BTWN BRANNAN AND BRYANT STS; 415/543-0573

Chef–co-owner Gerald Hirigoyen, named one of the 10 best chefs in the nation by *Food & Wine* magazine, draws crowds to his tiny, boisterous 50-seat French restaurant tucked away in a charmless section of the city. Behind the cheery yellow facade, however, there's plenty of charm emanating from the casual, blond-wood–trimmed interior, petite curved bar, and friendly, largely French wait staff. Hirigoyen was born and raised in the Basque country of southwest France, and his origins serve as the abiding inspiration for his gutsy, flavor-packed—and reasonably priced—fare. Outstanding dishes include the frisée salad topped with a poached egg and warm bacon dressing, steamed mussels sprinkled with garlic and parsley, wild mushroom ravioli, rack of lamb, and his signature (and meltingly tender) pork tenderloin confit with onion and apple marmalade.

Hirigoyen was originally a pastry chef, and he flaunts his talents with his incredible crème brûlée and rich chocolate Basque cake topped with chocolate mousse. Fringale (French for "a sudden pang of hunger") is perpetually packed with famished folks at dinnertime, so expect a noisy crowd and a wait for a table, even if you've made a reservation. *$$; AE, MC, V; no checks; lunch Mon–Fri, dinner Mon–Sat; full bar; reservations recommended; bistro@aol.com; www.fringale.citysearch.com; map:O4*

## The Garden Court / ★

**2 NEW MONTGOMERY ST AT MARKET ST (PALACE HOTEL); 415/546-5010 OR 415/512-1111**

Dining at the Garden Court, showpiece of the grand 1875 Palace Hotel, is like entering a Victorian romance novel. One can almost picture scads of beauteous heroines perching straight-backed on the plush settees here, blushing as they avert their eyes from the steady gaze of roguish but tender-hearted young blades jostling each other near the potted palms. Ah, we digress—but you see what magic this incredibly romantic, old-fashioned room can work on you. Blame it on the soaring marble and gilt columns, the opulent furnishings, the mirrored doorways, or the rows of crystal chandeliers descending from the high, intricately patterned, domed ceiling of amber-stained glass. The food hasn't always lived up to the regal surroundings, but the management has made it a priority to improve the cuisine. Starters might include a French butter pear salad with Stilton cheese and a cracked-pepper vinaigrette or a velvety crab bisque; entrees range from grilled rack of lamb with sweet onions and basil mashed potatoes to freshwater prawns and rock shrimp served on a pumpkin risotto to grilled swordfish with Japanese sweet potato purée and ginger-butter sauce. In addition to lunch and dinner, the Garden Court serves an elegant afternoon tea to the strains of live harp and a lavish (and costly) Sunday brunch. *$$$; AE, DC, DIS, MC, V; no checks; breakfast, lunch every day, tea Wed–Sat, dinner Tues–Sat, brunch Sun and holidays; full bar; reservations recommended; www.sf palace.com; map:N3*

## Garibaldi's / ★★★

**347 PRESIDIO AVE BTWN SACRAMENTO AND CLAY STS; 415/563-8841**

Evocative of the great neighborhood-type restaurants in New York's Greenwich Village and SoHo, Garibaldi's seems like a place where everyone walked over from his or her house around the corner. The restaurant is small and the tables are jammed so close together that at times you feel like reaching over and trying something from your neighbor's plate. So it's a good thing the atmosphere is friendly and lively, if at times decidedly loud. The staff, polished yet down-to-earth, makes everyone feel like a regular. In fact, many people become regulars because the Italian-Mediterranean food is so good. The dishes are sophisticated without being highfalutin. The risottos (there are usually two on the menu, and sometimes one nightly special) are quite good. If you are looking to eat light but don't want to forsake robust flavor, try one of the entree salads, such as the grilled prawns marinated in charmoula. Among the entree highlights are a Mediterranean lamb dish and a generous cut of tender filet mignon. And don't miss the rich desserts: The signature sweet is a white-chocolate cheesecake with a crunchy cookie crust. Sunday brunches are very popular here, too. *$$; AE, MC, V; local checks only; lunch Mon–Fri, dinner every day, brunch Sun; full bar; reservations recommended; map:J3*

## Gary Danko / ★★★★

**800 NORTH POINT ST AT HYDE ST; 415/749-2060**

Award-winning chef Gary Danko (of San Francisco's Ritz-Carlton fame) created quite a stir among San Francisco's cognoscenti when he opened this highly anticipated restaurant on the northern slope of Russian Hill. The concept sounds simple, but is surprisingly difficult to achieve: fine French–New American cuisine combined with impeccable service. At Gary Danko, it seems to be working like a well-oiled machine, so much so that it won the James Beard Award for Best New Restaurant in 2000, was rated the #1 restaurant in *San Francisco* magazine's 2001 readers poll, and was awarded a rare Mobil five-star rating. In fact, Danko's goal from the outset was to create one of America's finest—though purposely austere—restaurants by offering seasonally fresh ingredients via a multi-course menu that is rooted in the classical school of high cuisine. In short, it's about the food: sweet glazed oysters with leeks, pearls of zucchini, and a dab of Osetra caviar; lightly seared foie gras with sweet peaches and caramelized onions; succulent roast Maine lobster with chanterelle mushrooms; tender mushroom and herb-crusted lamb loin; and a lobster risotto that will make your toes curl. Dinners are served in four tasting-menu formats: you choose either the three-, four-, or five-course meal from the various dishes on the right side of the menu, or lean left for Danko's "Seasonal Tasting Menu," a trust-the-chef arrangement of Danko's favorites. The decadence continues with a visitation from the temperature-controlled cheese cart, offering both local organic and European selections. Of course, nothing's perfect: The profusion of mirrors can't hide the fact that the 75-seat restaurant is a bit cramped, the over-abundance of glossy wood paneling only augments the noise level, and the smartly dressed staff is professional to a fault (they need to lighten up a little). The food and presentation, however, are flawless, so much so that you need to make reservations up to two months in advance. *$$$-$$$$; AE, DC, DIS, MC, V; no checks; dinner every day; full bar; reservations recommended; www.garydanko.com; map:L1*

## Globe / ★★

**290 PACIFIC AVE BTWN BATTERY AND FRONT STS; 415/391-4132**

With just 44 seats, this downtown restaurant sometimes seems to have at least twice that many people waiting for tables. The chic little spot, near the city's advertising and media offices, is the ultimate power-lunch venue, where deals are made and black is worn. The hipness of it all does not overshadow the food, though, which is probably the real reason Globe is enjoying such popularity. The menu changes weekly but usually includes variations on American and California classics: wood-fired roast lamb, pork chops with green-olive tapenade, excellent pastas, pizzas, salads, and the like. Hugely recommended is the tender T-bone steak for two. The wines, mostly from the Napa and Sonoma Valleys, are well chosen and priced. Desserts are to die for: The cheesecake will satisfy even the most stubborn purists. One more plus: Globe serves dinner later than a lot of spots in town (until 1am most nights), making it a popular hangout for the city's top chefs. *$$; AE, MC; local checks only; lunch Mon–Fri, dinner every day; full bar; reservations recommended; map:N1*

## Gold Mountain / ★★

**664 BROADWAY BTWN GRANT AVE AND STOCKTON ST; 415/296-7733**

Dining dim sum–style at Gold Mountain, a gymnasium-sized Chinese restaurant on the north side of Chinatown, is quite a scene on weekends between 8am and 3pm: hundreds of patrons sit at enormous round tables among glittering chandeliers illuminating gilded dragons and other won-drously gaudy decorations. Amid the cacophony, dozens of Chinese women push stainless steel carts loaded with small plates of exotic  foods—shrimp dumplings, pork buns, chicken feet, whole salted prawns,  chicken in foil—that invariably tempt you to point your chopsticks at a quasi-recognizable delicacy and say, "Oh, we'll have some of that as well." And even if you eat until you're ill, you'll never down more than $20 worth of food, making Gold Mountain a real bargain as well. Yes, Ton Kiang and Yank Sing serve better quality dim sum, but they're not real dim sum parlors; the experience just isn't the same, particularly when you're seated next to people who really know their dim sum and guide you through the event. It's a dining adventure you'll never forget. *$$; AE, MC, V; no checks; lunch Mon–Fri, dinner every day, dim sum brunch Sat–Sun; beer and wine; reservations not accepted; map:M2*

## Gordon Biersch Brewery Restaurant / ★☆

**2 HARRISON ST ALONG THE EMBARCADERO; 415/243-8246**

This modern, two-level brewery located at the foot of the Bay Bridge is one of the most popular après-work watering holes in the city. It's mostly a well-dressed 20s-to-late-30s crowd who come to catch a buzz, smoke on the front steps, and flirt (though you have to almost shout to be heard over the din). The lower level houses the shiny brewery equipment and horseshoe-shaped beer bar offering a variety of fresh lagers and ales. Upstairs is a full restaurant serving reasonably good bistro dishes such as a lemon-roasted half chicken with garlic mashed potatoes and baby-back ribs with garlic fries (our two favorites). Of course, each entree is paired with the proper brewski to wash it all down. If you're not up for a full meal, there's a wide array of smaller plates (try the crunchy calamari fritti appetizer) and salads. Unfortunately, the noise from below makes a quiet dinner for two out of the question. But if you like good beer, hearty food, and a high-energy environment, you'll like Gordon Biersch. *$$; AE, DC, DIS, MC, V; no checks; lunch, dinner every day; full bar; reservations recommended; map:O3*

## Gordon's House of Fine Eats / ★★☆

**500 FLORIDA ST AT MARIPOSA ST; 415/861-8900**
Longtime Real Restaurants chef Gordon Drysdale (Bix, Caffe Museo) has brought his many passions together under one big industrial-size roof with exhilarating results. This 110-seat restaurant sizzles with energy, and a genuine conviviality prevails. The converted 1930s bilevel warehouse space boasts plenty of exposed piping, concrete floors, and high-tech halogen lighting, but warm mahogany tables and colorful original artwork keep the industrial-chic elements in check. The downstairs bustles with activity around an open kitchen and a long concrete-faced bar; upstairs is slightly more quiet and relaxed. The menu or, more accurately, menus are wholly original and aim to please everyone. You can choose both appetizers and entrees from five categories: healthful, comfort, local favorites, luxury, and international. A healthful selection of smoky vegan pea soup is simply exquisite. The cornflake-fried chicken, a popular comfort selection, already has a following, though the more inventive pork osso buco with spaetzle and the ham steak with grilled pineapple and sweet-potato pie are better flavor-packed choices. Desserts, equally imaginative, include Gordon's doughnut plate, a playful combo of fritters, fried custard, and doughnuts, as well as frozen grasshopper pie that oozes with mint and chocolate—both are utterly unforgettable. And as if all that weren't enough, there's live music five nights a week. This is clearly Gordon's very full house of fine eats. *$$; DC, DIS, MC, V; no checks; lunch Mon–Fri, dinner every day, brunch Sun; full bar; reservations recommended; map:M6*

## Grand Café / ★★☆

**501 GEARY ST AT TAYLOR ST (ADJACENT TO THE HOTEL MONACO); 415/292-0101**
The Grand Café is one of the most beautiful restaurants in the city, a magnificent mix of art deco, art nouveau, and Beaux Arts (really, it's worth a detour). The Kimpton Hotel & Restaurant Group has done a brilliant job of refurbishing this turn-of-the-century grand ballroom into an objet

d'art highlighted with Parisian-style chandeliers, intricate murals, and amusing bunny-esque sculptures. It's a pleasure just being here, though you're bound to enjoy chef Victor Scargle's French-inspired, California-based cuisine as well. Be sure to start your experience with the rich, savory polenta soufflé and the confit of duck and arugula salad with roasted shallot-Dijon vinaigrette. Entrees we heartily recommend include the ultra-tender braised short ribs served with herbed barley and spring vegetables, the oven-roasted pork chop in peppercorn sauce, and the crispy sweetbread steak atop a wild mushroom ragout. For dessert it's the Chocolate Pudding Gateau, a devil's food cake filled with chocolate pudding and served with house-made cashew-toffee-brittle ice cream and coffee caramel sauce (ouch!). You'll enjoy the friendly, professional service as well. Note: The equally impressive bar and lounge has its own exhibition kitchen and menu, offering similar dishes for about half the price. The grilled marinated skirt steak with whipped potatoes and red-wine sauce is fantastic, as are the pizzas from the wood-burning oven. *$$$; AE, CB, DC, DIS, MC, V; no checks; breakfast, lunch, dinner every day; full bar; reservations recommended; www.grandcafe.city search.com; map:M3*

## Great Eastern / ★★

**649 JACKSON ST BTWN KEARNY ST AND GRANT AVE; 415/986-2500**
If you love seafood and Chinese food and have an adventurous palate, have we got a restaurant for you. The venerable Great Eastern restaurant in Chinatown is renowned for its hard-to-find seafood, yanked fresh from the huge fish tanks that line the back wall. If it swims, hops, slithers, or crawls, it's probably on the menu. Frogs, sea bass, soft-shell turtles, abalone, sea conch, steelhead, and Lord only knows what else are served sizzling on large, round, family-style tables. Check the neon board in  back to peruse the day's catch, which is sold by the pound. Our advice: Unless you're savvy at translating an authentic Hong Kong menu, order one of the set dinners (the crab version is fantastic) or point to another table and say, "I want that." (Don't expect much help from the harried servers.) The crystal chandeliers and glimmering emerald-and-black furnishings make an attempt at elegance, but it's the gaudy fish tanks filled with edible creatures that capture everyone's eye. *$$; AE, MC, V; no checks; lunch, dinner every day; beer and wine; reservations recommended; map:N2*

## Greens / ★★★

**FORT MASON CENTER, BLDG A, OFF MARINA BLVD AT BUCHANAN ST; 415/771-6222**
As Le Tour d'Argent in Paris is to the dedicated duck fancier and the Savoy Grill in London is to the roast beef connoisseur, so is Greens at Fort Mason to the vegetarian aesthete. Not only is the food politically

correct here, it's often so good that even carnivores find it irresistible. Part of the Greens treat is visual: Located in a converted barracks in the historic Fort Mason Center, the enormous, airy dining room is surrounded by huge windows with a spectacular view of the bay and the Golden Gate Bridge, and a gigantic sculpted redwood burl is a Buddhist-inspired centerpiece in the waiting area. Yes, Greens is owned and operated by the Zen Center—but this is a restaurant, not a monastery. The menu changes daily: Expect to see such dishes as mesquite-grilled polenta; phyllo turnovers filled with mushrooms, spinach, and Parmesan; pizza sprinkled with onion confit, goat cheese, and basil; and fettuccine with mushrooms, peas, goat cheese, and crème fraîche. Greens to Go, a takeout counter inside the restaurant, also sells baked goods, savory soups, sandwiches, and black-bean chili. An à la carte dinner menu is offered Monday through Friday; guests may order from the $45 prix-fixe five-course dinner menu only on Saturday. *$$–$$$; DIS, MC, V; local checks only; lunch Tues–Sat, dinner Mon–Sat, brunch Sun; beer and wine; reservations recommended; www.greensrestaurant.com; map:K1*

## Harbor Village Restaurant / ★★

**4 EMBARCADERO CENTER (LOBBY LEVEL), AT DRUMM ST BTWN SACRAMENTO AND CLAY STS; 415/781-8833**

A favorite of prosperous Pacific Rim businesspeople, middle- and upper-class Chinese-American families, and downtown office workers out for a lunchtime treat, this giant Hong Kong–style seafood and dim sum restaurant has great food, but it misses top honors because of minor inconsistencies in cooking and major flaws in service. Lunch is a state-of-the-art dim sum extravaganza, with master chefs from Hong Kong turning out plate after plate of sublime morsels in vast, interesting variety. At dinner you can choose from an enormous Cantonese menu that includes dishes rarely found on this edge of the Rim, among them prized varieties of shellfish, kept alive in tanks until the moment they're ordered and served with exquisite simplicity (albeit at an exorbitant cost). Many of the more affordable seafood dishes are just as marvelous, though some of the standard Chinese dishes suffer from perfunctory preparation, and all too often entire orders are piled simultaneously on the undersize tables by the standoffish staff. Still, the food and upscale decor (this is one of San Francisco's prettiest Chinese restaurants) might make you forgive these lapses. Note: The restaurant offers validated parking at the Embarcadero Center garage at the foot of Clay Street. *$$$; AE, DC, DIS, MC, V; no checks; lunch, dinner every day; full bar; reservations recommended; map:N2*

## Hard Rock Cafe / ★

**1699 VAN NESS AVE AT SACRAMENTO ST; 415/885-1699**

This San Francisco link in the Hard Rock chain is exactly what you would expect it to be: a loud, cavernous room filled with rock 'n' roll memorabilia, tourists, and a line for T-shirts. You'll have to speak up to be heard over the blaring rock music, but that's just part of the Hard Rock experience. Despite the often annoying ambience, the food is actually pretty good (not healthy, exactly, but good). The highlight of the menu is the Rock's juicy chicken sandwich, best accompanied with a side of addictive onion rings. Other diner-style menu items include fajitas, baby-back ribs, grilled fish, salads, sandwiches, and (of course) the all-American burger. Perhaps Hard Rock's strongest point, however, is that it's one of the few restaurants in the city that caters to teens and children. Otherwise, in a city with so many incredible restaurants, it's hard to justify a meal at the Hard Rock—particularly if you already have the shirt. *$–$$; AE, DC, DIS, MC, V; no checks; lunch, dinner every day; full bar; reservations recommended; map:L2*

## Harris' / ★★

**2100 VAN NESS AVE AT PACIFIC AVE; 415/673-1888**

Not just another steak house, Harris' is a living monument to the not-quite-bygone joys of guiltless beef-eating. You can even get a sneak preview of your meal by peering at the deep-pink slabs in the showcase window facing the street. The hushed, formal club setting boasts dark wood paneling, plush carpets, large brown tufted booths, well-spaced white-draped tables, and chairs roomy enough to accommodate the most bullish build. Jackets are appreciated (though no longer required). Choice midwestern beef, impeccably dry-aged for three weeks on the premises, bears the same relation to supermarket beef as foie gras bears to chicken liver; the tender steaks, grilled to order, can even be chosen by cut and by size. The larger bone-in cuts (such as the Harris' Steak and the T-bone) have the finest flavor, but the pepper steak and the rare prime rib are great, too. Those who prefer calf brains to these sanguine beauties will find a flawless version here. You might want to skip the usual steakhouse appetizers in favor of the excellent Caesar salad. For true-blue traditionalists, the exemplary martini—served in a carafe placed in a bucket of shaved ice—makes an excellent starter course. *$$$; AE, DC, DIS, MC, V; no checks; dinner every day; full bar; reservations recommended; map:L2*

## Hawthorne Lane / ★★★☆

**22 HAWTHORNE LN, OFF HOWARD ST BTWN 2ND AND 3RD STS; 415/777-9779**

When Hillary Rodham Clinton was in town to promote her book *It Takes a Village*, she ate a late dinner at Hawthorne Lane. Probably learned about it from hubby Bill, who supped here the year before and might have raved about the miso-glazed black cod with sesame spinach rolls, the special lobster tempura, the roasted Sonoma lamb with butternut squash and Parmesan risotto, or the house-made fettuccine with chanterelle mushrooms. Ever since it opened in 1995, Hawthorne Lane has been one of the city's hottest restaurants, its popularity fueled by its lovely design, its proximity to the happening SoMa scene, and the pedigree of owner-chefs David and Anne Gingrass (formerly of Spago and Postrio fame), who meld the cuisines of Italy, France, and Asia using the finest California foods. The dining room is a refined, beguiling space, with wrought-iron cherry blossoms, a massive skylight, giant urns with dazzling fresh floral displays, and light-colored woods creating an air of perennial spring. Hawthorne also wins raves for its varied selection of wonderful breads and desserts. If you can't get a reservation, snag one of the seats at the long, oval bar, where you can order from the dining room menu, or sign up for one of the many tables set aside for walk-ins. *$$$; DC, DIS, MC, V; checks OK; lunch Mon–Fri, dinner every day; full bar; reservations recommended; dcg@hawthornelane.com; www.hawthorne lane.com; map:O3*

## Hayes Street Grill / ★★☆

**320 HAYES ST AT FRANKLIN ST; 415/863-5545**

*San Francisco Examiner* restaurant reviewer Patricia Unterman, one of the nation's best food critics, is part owner and chef of this spartan yet venerable and reliable fish house that specializes in simple, perfectly prepared seafood. In a city where dining trends change monthly (and restaurants close weekly), the Grill is a citadel of consistency, offering impeccably fresh fish and straightforward preparations that highlight the quality of the ingredients. Whatever's the most fresh on the market is what's on the menu that day—Hawaiian swordfish, Alaskan king salmon, California red snapper—which is then prepared to your liking (mesquite grilled, lightly sautéed, braised), topped with a range of sauces (shallot butter, Sichuan peanut, tomatillo salsa), and served with a side of signature french fries cooked in peanut oil. Other seafood dishes are also available, such as savory fish soup, raw oysters on the half shell, and paella. Meat dishes are available as well: Niman Ranch rib-eye steak and pork chops, and house-made whiskey-fennel sausages. And don't miss the wicked crème brûlée for dessert. We highly recommend this Civic Center institution for a pre-opera/symphony/ballet meal, or anytime you crave fresh fish done well. *$$; AE, DC, DIS, MC, V; no checks; lunch Mon–Fri, dinner every day; full bar; reservations recommended; map:L4*

## Helmand / ★★

**430 BROADWAY BTWN MONTGOMERY AND KEARNY STS; 415/362-0641**
An oasis of good taste on Broadway's less-than-tasteful topless strip, Helmand serves delicious renditions of Afghan cuisine in a pretty room lit by brass chandeliers and small table lanterns. The restaurant's light and variously spiced house-made yogurts (a staple of Afghani cooking) dress several favorite appetizers, including *mantwo* (a house-made dumpling filled with sautéed onions and beef, topped with a carrot, yellow split pea, and beef sauce, and served on yogurt) and *kaddo borawni* (sweet baby pumpkin that's panfried, then baked, and tempered by a piquant yogurt-garlic sauce). For a main course try the *chowpan*—a tender, juicy half rack of lamb marinated like a fine Armenian shish kebab, then grilled and served with sautéed eggplant and rice pallow. Other fine choices include *sabzi challow* (a wonderfully seasoned mixture of spinach with lamb), *mourgh challow* (chicken sautéed with split peas and curry), and *koufta challow* (light, moderately spicy meatballs with sun-dried tomatoes, peppers, and peas), each served with a ramekin of flavorful fresh cilantro sauce and aromatic white or brown rice. Servers are personable (if sometimes slightly scattered), and the wine list is well chosen and well priced. Parking is scarce in this neighborhood, so take advantage of the validated parking (time is limited) at the lot down the block. *$$; AE, MC, V; no checks; dinner every day; full bar; reservations recommended; map:N2*

## The House / ★★☆

**1230 GRANT AVE AT COLUMBUS AVE; 415/986-8612**
**1269 9TH AVE BTWN IRVING ST AND LINCOLN WY; 415/682-3898**
Much is made of fusion cuisine in San Francisco, and it seems each month someone opens a new place to give it a whirl. But Larry Tse, chef-owner of The House in North Beach, has been quietly doing as well if not better than anyone else at creating fusion fare for years. Happily holding its own in a sea of Italian eateries, this little Asian-inspired restaurant is a wildly popular alternative. The dishes are fairly simple, given their East-meets-West concept. The Chinese chicken salad is one of the best-sellers, as is the Caesar, served with wok-seared scallops or spring rolls. The entree menu changes frequently; the daily specials are the safest bets. A ginger soy sauce–topped Chilean sea bass was a memorable recent selection. The wine list is interesting and well priced, though you might opt for a flavorful Chinese tea infusion to go with your fusion. The House has proved so popular that Tse and his wife opened another one on Ninth Avenue in the Inner Sunset. That is where he spends most of his time these days, leaving his brother-in-law at the helm on Grant Avenue. Be prepared for a noise level that can sometimes reach ear-splitting. *$; AE, MC, V; no checks; lunch Mon–Fri, dinner Mon–Sat (Grant Ave); dinner every night (9th Ave); full bar; reservations recommended; map:N2*

## House of Nanking / ★★

**919 KEARNY ST BTWN COLUMBUS AVE AND JACKSON ST; 415/421-1429**
This inconspicuous, greasy-looking little dive is one of San Francisco's worst-kept secrets. No joke: The dinnertime waiting line outside this wildly popular hole-in-the-wall starts at 5:30pm; by 6pm you may face a 90-minute wait for a cramped, crowded, itsy-bitsy table with a plastic menu that lists only half of the best dishes served here. Lunchtime crowds make midday eating just as problematic. Here's a solution: Arrive for a late lunch or a very early dinner (between 2:30pm and 5pm) and walk right in. When owner-chef-headwaiter Peter Fang can give you his full attention, he'll be glad to apprise you of the day's unlisted specials: perhaps succulent chicken or duck dumplings, an exotic shrimp-and-green-onion pancake with peanut sauce, or tempura-like sesame-battered Nanking scallops in a spicy garlic sauce. Or just take a look at what the diners sandwiched around you are eating and point to what looks good (it's hard to go wrong in this place). Nanking, Fang's hometown, is at the inland end of the Shanghai Railroad, making it an exchange point for foods from Sichuan, Peking, Guangdong, and the local coast; Fang is famous for concocting wily revisions of many traditional dishes. While the food is usually very good and the prices are some of the most reasonable in the city, the service is downright terrible (you may not get your beer until 10 minutes after you've started eating), and it's the main reason this restaurant doesn't earn three stars. *$; cash only; lunch Mon–Sat, dinner every day; beer and wine; reservations not accepted; map:N2*

## Hyde Street Bistro / ★★

**1521 HYDE ST BTWN JACKSON AND PACIFIC STS; 415/292-4415**
This little French bistro on Russian Hill sits next to a cable car line, and you'll hear the famous bells clanging right outside the door. Owned by chef Fabrice Marcon, Hyde Street Bistro is definitely a neighborhood haunt. You'll see Marcon charging in and out of the kitchen all night, talking with patrons, his baseball-capped head enthusiastically bobbing up and down. The best deal (available weekdays only) may be the well-priced Neighbor's Dinner, which includes an entree du jour served with a wine of Marcon's choice. His standard menu is small and reflects both regional French cuisine and Americanized versions. Sample dishes include a lyonnaise salad with smoked bacon and an optional poached egg; tender hanger steak drenched in a green peppercorn sauce; perfectly roasted honey-lavender–glazed duck confit (Marcon's specialty); and seared tuna au poivre. The eclectic wine list is heavy with French varietals but reasonably priced. Save room for the tarte Tatin floating on caramel sauce, or the warm and dense chocolate cake. *$$; AE, MC, V; checks OK; dinner Tues–Sun; beer and wine; reservations recommended; map:L2*

## Il Fornaio / ★★

**1265 BATTERY ST, IN LEVI PLAZA JUST OFF THE EMBARCADERO; 415/986-0100**

Il Fornaio began as a baker's school in Milan, a project started by the Veggetti family to collect regional recipes and save the disappearing art of Italian baking. In the late 1980s the Veggettis expanded their operation to include several retail bakeries, wholesale bakeries, and restaurants in California and other western states. The San Francisco and Palo Alto restaurants were the first to make it to these shores, and although the staffs occasionally suffer from a too-sexy-for-my-hat attitude, there's no denying that Il Fornaio serves fantastic baked goods and good Northern Italian food in an airy, stylish setting. Breads and breadsticks, served with pungent, extra-virgin olive oil, provide simple and unpretentious proof that bread is an art form. The antipasti are generally very good (give the grilled eggplant with goat cheese, sun-dried tomatoes, sweet onions, and capers a whirl), and the pizzas and calzones are universally delightful, crisp and smoke-flavored from the wood-burning oven. Interesting pasta choices include *ravioli di verdura* (pasta stuffed with spinach, Swiss chard, pine nuts, and basil in a rich baby artichoke and tomato sauce). The rotisserie meats are consistently well prepared. Dessert tortes, cakes, and cookies offer further proof of the skills of Il Fornaio's bakers. Many of the Il Fornaio restaurants in the Bay Area have pretty patios, and the San Francisco branch offers one of the most pleasant outdoor dining areas in the city. *$$; AE, DC, MC, V; no checks; breakfast, lunch, dinner every day; full bar; reservations recommended; www.ilfornaio.com; map:N1*

## Indian Oven / ★★

**233 FILLMORE ST BTWN HAIGHT AND WALLER STS; 415/626-1628**

In the culturally diverse Lower Haight, it isn't surprising to find the gamut of ethnic restaurants. What is surprising is to find one so very good and so very authentic. Indian Oven, a good-looking and affordably priced corner restaurant, gets both our vote—and *San Francisco* magazine readers' vote—as the best Northern Indian restaurant in the city. Roll up your sleeves and order the appetizer sampler plate: samosas (vegetable puffs stuffed with peas and potatoes), pakoras (deep-fried fritters filled with your choice of meat or vegetables), and pappadam crackers. The entrees are mostly outstanding, including a delicious *jheenga masala*—prawns sautéed in a spicy tomato sauce. The tandoori chicken and the chicken and lamb skewers are also good. When you've got to have your curry fix, there are few better places. *$; AE, DC, DIS, MC, V; no checks; dinner every day; beer and wine; reservations recommended; map:K4*

## Indigo / ★

**687 MCALLISTER ST AT GOUGH ST; 415/673-9353**

Surprisingly, in a town so keen on the symphony, opera, and ballet, there is a startling dearth of quality places near the Performing Arts Center for pre-performance dining. So when Indigo opened a while ago, there was a citywide standing ovation. All it had to do was perform. As the name might indicate, this restaurant is very blue, with elegant velvet booths and a gorgeous plaster sculpture running the length of one wall—very dramatic indeed. And the food follows suit, with dishes prepared from fresh local ingredients. The daily ravioli is usually quite good, but for something a bit heartier, the grilled pork chop with herb bread pudding is your best choice. The wait staff will even hasten your order if you're rushing to make a theater engagement. So far, the show here has been worthy of its favorable reviews. *$; AE, MC, V; no checks; dinner Tues–Sun; full bar; reservations recommended; www.indigorestaurant.com; map:L4*

## Infusion Bar & Restaurant / ★★

**555 2ND ST AT BRYANT ST; 415/543-2282**

Trendy, noisy, alcohol-oriented—these rather damning adjectives apply to Infusion, a SoMa bar and restaurant that nevertheless manages to establish itself as a place that's serious about good food. It was named after the house specialty, vodka-based infusions flavored with assorted fruits and vegetables, everything from jalapeño to pineapple, watermelon to cucumber (they have more than 50 flavors in stock). You can admire eight of them in their decanters behind the handcrafted Honduran mahogany bar that stretches along one side of the long, narrow room. The spare, modern furnishings stand in dramatic contrast to the intense, spicy complexity of the food. European, Asian, Mexican, and Caribbean influences add interesting grace notes to self-taught chef David Fickes's New American fare, with starters that range from guava empanadas with Brie to a ginger-cured tuna accented with wasabi-infused oil and tangerine essence. There are always a few imaginative pasta dishes, such as fusilli with chicken and chipotle chile sauce (Fickes has a fondness for chiles); entrees include a crisp walnut-crusted salmon with chardonnay-pear sauce and peppered filet mignon flamed with Wild Turkey. Fickes sometimes misses his mark with his innovative recipes, but when he hits it, he's incredible. Top off the fine feast with white-chocolate–bourbon mousse with pistachio shortbread or chocolate pecan pie. At 9:30pm Thursday through Saturday a band performs on the loft stage. *$$; AE, DC, MC, V; no checks; lunch Mon–Fri, dinner Mon–Sat; full bar; reservations recommended; infusn@aol.com; www.citysearch.com/sfo/infusion; map:O3*

## Isa / ★★★

**3324 STEINER ST BTWN CHESTNUT AND LOMBARD STS; 415/567-9588**

This modest Marina restaurant has the locals raving about tapas-style French dishes emanating from the tiny kitchen. It's a family-run affair (the owners, Luke and Kitty Sung, live upstairs—well, sleep upstairs, live downstairs), and the staff puts heart and soul into both the service and the à la carte–sized dishes. Typical of Marina restaurants, the long, narrow building has a few tables up front, but most everyone requests a table in the tent-covered and heated outdoor patio in back (*très romantique*). The menu only offers about 10 selections, all of which are enticing and carefully crafted using fresh, seasonal ingredients (and would cost  twice as much at a fancy French restaurant). The must-tries are the potato-wrapped sea bass in a caper, pepper, olive, and brown butter sauce (a mere $10); the roasted rack of lamb with ratatouille niçoise ($16); and the baked Laura Chenel goat cheese salad with fresh tomatoes, pine nuts, and basil ($6). Other dishes range from leek and potato soup with roasted scallops and white truffle oil ($5) to a ragout of veal sweetbreads and mushrooms ($14). The impressive wine list features numerous Europeans, including a few paired selections such as Muscadet with the Miyagi oysters or the Sauternes matched with the seared Hudson Valley foie gras. Really, you'll love this place. *$$; AE, DC, MC, V; no checks; dinner every day; full bar; reservations recommended; map:K2*

## Jackson Fillmore / ★★

**2506 FILLMORE ST AT JACKSON ST; 415/346-5288**

If you like to make an entrance, go to Jackson Fillmore, the minuscule trattoria on Fillmore that's so small, everyone in the dining room can't help but stop eating and turn their heads to the door when somebody walks in. And then be prepared to wait. But that's part of the fun at this bright neighborhood restaurant, where chef-owner Jack Kreitzman is usually the one to greet you, with a smile and a suggestion for a great glass of wine. Once seated, you are quickly served a helping of the fresh-made bruschetta with a mouthwatering aroma of garlic. From ricotta ravioli to roast chicken with garlic (highly recommended) to portobello mushrooms, the recipes here are fairly straightforward and skillfully executed. This is a great place for a couple to dine, but larger groups can also be accommodated. *$; AE, MC, V; no checks; dinner every day; beer and wine; reservations accepted for parties of 3 or more; map:K2*

## Jardinière / ★★★★

**300 GROVE ST AT FRANKLIN ST; 415/861-5555**

A native Californian, chef Traci Des Jardins worked in many notable restaurants in France, New York, and Los Angeles before co-opening Rubicon restaurant in San Francisco, which launched her culinary reputation nationwide. She won the prestigious James Beard Rising Star Chef of the Year award and was named one of *Food and Wine*'s Best New Chefs in America. With those kudos, it's no wonder that her own restaurant, Jardinière (pronounced zhar-dee-NAIR), was a smashing success as soon as the highly stylized glass doors swung open in 1997. With award-winning designer-restaurateur Pat Kuleto as her business partner, Des Jardins was assured of an impressive setting for her French-California cuisine. Formerly home to a jazz club, the two-story interior is elegantly framed with violet velvet drapes, and the focal point is the central oval mahogany and marble bar, frequently mobbed with local politicos and patrons of the arts (the symphony hall and opera house are across the street). Appetizers are Des Jardins's strong point, especially the flavor-packed lobster, leek, and chanterelle strudel and the delicate kabocha squash ravioli with chestnuts and sage brown butter. Some of her best entrees thus far have included the crisp chicken with chanterelles and applewood-smoked bacon, herbed lamb loin with cranberry beans and tomato confit, and pan-roasted salmon with lentils, celery root salad, and red-wine sauce. After your meal, consider the chef's selection of domestic and imported cheeses, which are visible in the temperature-controlled cheese room on the main floor. The live entertainment makes this restaurant ideal for a special night on the town. *$$$; AE, DC, DIS, MC, V; no checks; lunch Mon–Fri, dinner, late-night menu every day; full bar; reservations recommended; map:L4*

## Jianna / ★★★

**1548 STOCKTON ST BTWN UNION AND GREEN STS; 415/398-0442**

The dusty blue hues, fabric-covered walls, and sexy custom accents create a soothing jazz club–like ambience at this North Beach newcomer. The word on the street is that Jianna is stealing customers from the big boys (the Ritz, Masa's, Gary Danko—see reviews), a trend that has chef Marc Valiani elated. "Evolving American" is the style he's developed, a medley of Asian, European, and classic American cuisines that makes for a rather interesting menu: mushroom dumplings vs. fried green tomatoes; potato-leek lasagne vs. roasted rabbit; foie gras with peaches and cream vs. spice-encrusted ahi tuna. Tough choices like these explain the heavy rotation of repeat clientele, all of whom also appreciate the attentive service and subdued acoustics. Jianna also features a raw bar filled with fresh oysters, clams, mussels, and prawns, best accompanied with a glass of brut champagne. Strong wine list as well, with 15 selections by the glass. Tip: Valet parking for Jianna is available at Fior d'Italia at the corner of Union and Stockton Streets. *$$$; AE, DC, DIS, MC, V; no checks; dinner every day; full bar; reservations recommended; www. jianna.com; map:M2*

## Johnfrank / ★★★

**2100 MARKET ST AT 14TH AND CHURCH STS; 415/503-0333**

Yet another reason to visit the Castro is Johnfrank, an attractive, fashionable, I'm-wearing-black-tonight restaurant that's hugely popular with the local gay scene (in fact, service improves noticeably if there's a cute guy at your table). Clean lines, soothing pale earth tones, and a profusion of polished wood and steel offer welcome refuge from the busy intersection (good luck finding parking), and you'll need the leisure time to finish off chef Lance Dean Velasquez's generous portions of modern American-Californian cuisine. The seasonally changing menu is full of proven winners: molasses-glazed pork chop with herb spaetzle and butternut squash, potato gnocchi with bits of Serrano ham and English peas, roast steelhead salmon with braised wild mushrooms in a celery root puree. It's hearty, satisfying, and consistently well-prepared dishes like these that explain the nightly full house, so be sure to make reservations. Tip: The three-course prix-fixe dinner, which changes nightly, is a real bargain at $25. *$$; AE, MC, V; no checks; dinner every day; full bar; reservations recommended; www.johnfrankrestaurant.com; map:K5*

## Kabuto Sushi / ★★★

**5116 GEARY BLVD AT 15TH AVE; 415/752-5652**

In a town where hip sushi clubs are all the rage, Kabuto is something of a dinosaur. In fact, most people would never guess that this rather drab, unpretentious Japanese restaurant is run by one of the most talented and revered sushi chefs in the city: Sachio Kojima, San Francisco's godfather of sushi. It's a joy to sit at the small, semicircular sushi bar and watch his smooth yet swift technique as he prepares the standard seafood-and-rice delicacies—unagi, toro, spicy tuna roll, and such—in a whir of knives and bamboo rollers. But for the adventurous diner, the real fun begins when you say, "Mr. Kojima, surprise us!" and give him free rein to prepare some of his off-menu specialties that have made him so famous. Regardless of how much you order or how busy he is, Kojima usually finds time to sneak you a complimentary delicacy that never fails to amaze. If raw fish isn't your gig, classic tempura, teriyaki, and sukiyaki dinners are served in the adjoining dining room. Tip: If you prefer your wasabi deadly hot, ask for the stronger stuff Kojima serves on request. *$$; MC, V; no checks; dinner Tues–Sat; full bar; reservations recommended; map:G4*

## Kan Zaman / ★★

**1793 HAIGHT ST AT SHRADER ST; 415/751-9656**

Glass-beaded curtains lead into Kan Zaman, a favorite destination for grunge types who populate the Haight. Shed your shoes and gather around knee-high tables under a canopy tent—or snag the premier window seat—and recline on pillows while sampling the tasty, inexpensive hot and cold

Middle Eastern *meze* (appetizers). Before long you'll think you've been transported to (as Kan Zaman literally translates) "a long time ago." Traditional menu items include hummus, baba ghanouj, *kibbee* (cracked wheat with spiced lamb) meat pies, and various kebabs. Sample platters offering tastes of a little bit of everything are ideal for large parties. For a novel and truly exotic finish, puff on an *argeeleh* (hookah pipe) filled with fruity honey or apricot tobacco. Wine, beer, and spiced wine round out the beverage offerings. Another plus: Kan Zaman serves till midnight—a real find in this town. *$; MC, V; no checks; lunch Sat–Sun, dinner every day; beer and wine; reservations recommended; map:I5*

## Kate's Kitchen / ★

**471 HAIGHT ST AT FILLMORE ST; 415/626-3984**
It's almost standard procedure these days: Go to brunch on a weekend and wait an hour for a table. But at Kate's, which serves one of the best brunches in the Haight, the wait is well worth it. Perhaps no other restaurant in town serves Flanched Flarney Garney, a dish featuring delicious flaky biscuits topped with eggs. The ginger-peach pancakes are another favorite and can easily serve as your only meal of the day. The simple, rustic decor isn't much to look at, but once you've settled in with your newspaper and ordered a hot cup of coffee, the only thing you'll want to see is the giant omelet (try the one with red peppers and pesto) on your plate. *$; MC, V; local checks only; breakfast, lunch Mon–Fri, brunch Sat–Sun; no alcohol; reservations not accepted; map:K5*

## Khan Toke Thai House / ★★☆

**5937 GEARY BLVD BTWN 23RD AND 24TH AVES; 415/668-6654**
If you're in the mood for an exotic dining experience (or you just want to impress the heck out of your date), dine at the Khan Toke Thai House, the loveliest Thai restaurant in San Francisco. Following Thai tradition, you'll be asked to remove your shoes at the entrance, so be sure to wear clean (and hole-free) socks. You'll then be escorted through the lavishly decorated dining room—replete with carved teak, Thai statues, and hand-woven Thai tapestries—and seated on large pillows at one of the many sunken tables (or, if you prefer, at a table in the garden out back). Start with the appetizing *tom yam gong*, lemongrass shrimp with mushroom, tomato, and cilantro soup. Other delicious dishes include the prawns with hot chiles, mint leaves, lime juice, lemongrass, and onions; the chicken with cashew nuts, crispy chiles, and onions; and the ground pork with fresh ginger, green onion, peanuts, and lemon juice. For those dining family style, be sure to order the exquisite deep-fried pompano topped with sautéed ginger, onions, peppers, pickled garlic, and yellow-bean sauce. If the vast menu has you bewildered, opt for the multicourse dinner: appetizer, soup, salad, two main courses, dessert, and coffee. And if you're feeling frivolous after sipping a Singha beer or two, you might want to

engage your tablemate in a game of shoeless footsie—after all, how often do you get a chance to do that in public? *$$; AE, MC, V; no checks; dinner every day; beer and wine; reservations recommended; map:F4*

## Kokkari Estiatorio / ★★★☆

**200 JACKSON ST AT FRONT ST; 415/981-0983**
Kokkari's owners have done their best to invent a new category—upscale Greek with a California twist. And why not? It worked for Italian food. Indeed, Kokkari (pronounced koh-CAR-ee) works on many levels, so much so that it's one of our favorites: It's a beautiful, lavishly decorated restaurant (a $5 million investment) with a ritzy country-house ambience, thanks to the fire crackling in the oversize fireplace, the ornate rugs and plush chairs suitable for royalty, and the large windows and sun-bleached walls. This is a place to relax, soak up the atmosphere, and revel in executive chef Jean Alberti's California-style contemporary Hellenic cuisine. The front dining room feels the most luxurious. There's a second, larger dining room with exposed wood beams, an open kitchen, and cushy booths lining a walkway between the two dining areas. The usual Greek suspects play well here: avgolemono, the lemony egg, rice, and chicken soup; moussaka, the divinely spiced casserole of eggplant, lamb, and potato; and the quintessential Greek salad—no lettuce, just tomato, olive, red onion, and cucumber. Presentations are stunning, and the flavors are fresh and bright. For starters don't miss the whole crispy smelt and the octopus salad. The grilled lamb chops with fried potatoes are classic, as are the whole grilled fish. Thick Greek coffee is made in a multiple-step process that involves an elaborate urn of sand (you can even ask the wait staff for a demo). And be sure to leave room for dessert, in particular velvety *Kalithopita* chocolate cake, the luscious yogurt–granita duo (a dense chocolate cake with nougatine), or the rice pudding with a poached pear and black-currant sauce. *$$$; AE, DC, DIS, MC, V; no checks; lunch Mon–Fri, dinner Mon–Sat; full bar; reservations recommended; www.kokkari.com; map:N2*

## Kuleto's / ★★☆

**221 POWELL ST BTWN GEARY AND O'FARRELL STS (VILLA FLORENCE HOTEL); 415/397-7720**
If you're shopping in the Union Square area and you want to experience a classic high-energy San Francisco trattoria, follow the cable car down Powell Street to Kuleto's. Hanging prosciuttos, dried herbs, and peppers add a rustic note to an otherwise sleek, modern black-marble-and-mahogany hot spot where both tourists and locals squeeze in to be a part of the lively scene. Our usual modus operandi when dining here is to scout out the antipasto bar for some vacant stools, order a glass of chianti, nosh on antipasti and appetizers, and chat with the friendly wait staff. If you're hungry enough for a full meal, there's a wide array of main

courses as well. A few of our favorites include the penne pasta drenched in a tangy lamb-sausage marinara sauce, the clam linguine packed with fresh clams, or any of the fresh fish specials grilled over hardwoods. This isn't groundbreaking Italian cuisine, but it's not supposed to be; it's good, hearty Italian comfort food served in a beautiful, boisterous setting that has become a San Francisco institution. *$$; AE, CB, DC, DIS, MC, V; no checks; breakfast, lunch, dinner every day; full bar; reservations recommended; map:N3*

### Kyo-ya / ★★★

**2 NEW MONTGOMERY ST AT MARKET ST (PALACE HOTEL); 415/546-5090**
This elegantly austere restaurant in the Palace Hotel serves some of the best (and most expensive) sushi and sashimi in town. Catering to well-heeled business execs visiting from the other side of the Rim, Kyo-ya's food is fresh, authentic, and delicious. Sit at the sushi bar or settle into one of the dining room's black-lacquered chairs flanked by a glossy wood table set with a simple arrangement of fresh flowers. Order a decanter of sake (there are more than a dozen to choose from) and some toro (tuna belly), ebi (shrimp), hotate (scallops), or anything else on Kyo-ya's extensive list of sushi offerings—it's sure to be some of the finest you've ever had. While the sushi and nabemono (one-pot dishes cooked tableside) are undeniably expensive, several other dishes, including wonderful appetizers like steamed clams in sake and complete tempura and teriyaki dinners, are more reasonably priced. *$$$; AE, DC, DIS, MC, V; no checks; lunch Tues–Fri, dinner Tues–Sat; full bar; reservations recommended; map:N3*

### La Folie / ★★★☆

**2316 POLK ST AT UNION ST; 415/776-5577**
After a stingy San Francisco restaurateur fired him for spending too much on ingredients and serving overly generous portions, French-born chef Roland Passot decided to open his own restaurant where he could spend as much as he liked to make the food perfect. The paradisiacal result is the charming, small, family-run La Folie, now glistening after a much-needed interior refurbishing. The intimate, whimsical, theatrical dining room with white puffy clouds painted on the sky-blue ceiling now has  red-patterned carpeting, a colorful stained-glass entryway, and even marionettes from Lyon dangling from the wall—an appropriate stage for Passot's creative and exuberant but disciplined menu. His Roquefort soufflé with grapes, herbs, and walnut bread alone is worthy of a visit. Other memorable starters are the wonderful foie gras dishes; the potato blinis with golden osetra caviar, salmon, asparagus, and crème fraîche; the rabbit loin stuffed with exquisitely fresh vegetables and roasted garlic; the velvety corn-and-leek soup; the parsley and garlic soup with snails and shiitake mushrooms; and the lobster consommé. For an entree, choose whatever meat or fish suits your fancy, for it surely will be exquis-

itely prepared. To accommodate vegetarians, Passot has thoughtfully included a separate Vegetable Lovers' menu. And for those who can't make up their minds, the Discovery menu allows you to choose five courses à la carte (though it's pricey). For dessert, indulge in clafouti with chocolate sauce or croquettes of chocolate with orange zest sauce. The wine list is extensive, but the prices are steep. *$$$–$$$$; AE, DC, DIS, MC, V; no checks; dinner Mon–Sat; full bar; reservations recommended; map:L2*

## La Taqueria / ★★

**2889 MISSION ST BTWN 24TH AND 25TH STS; 415/285-7117**

Among colorful fruit stands, thrift shops, and greasy panhandlers lining bustling Mission Street sits La Taqueria, the Bay Area's best burrito factory. Its lackluster interior is brightened only by a vibrant mural depicting south-of-the-border scenes and a shiny CD jukebox pumping out merry Mexican music, all of which could mean only one thing: People come here for the food. Don't expect a wide variety, for the folks behind the counter just churn out what they do best: burritos, tacos, and quesadillas. It's all fresh, delicious, and guaranteed to fill you up—for little more than pocket change. The moist, meaty fillings include excellent *carnitas* (braised pork), grilled beef, sausage, beef tongue, and chicken (you won't find any rice in these burritos); and the *bebidas* vary from beer and soda to cantaloupe juice and even *horchata* (a sweet rice drink). Stand in line to place your order and pay, then take a seat at one of the shared, long wooden tables and wait for someone to bellow out your number (somehow they just know whether to say it in Spanish or English). *$; no credit cards; local checks only; lunch, dinner every day; beer only; reservations not accepted; map:L7*

## La Villa Poppi / ★

**3234 22ND ST BTWN MISSION AND BARTLETT STS; 415/642-5044**

Don't walk by too fast or you might miss this undiscovered gem wedged in among the lively Mission District restaurants and nightspots. La Villa Poppi is a cozy, tiny, but entirely charming spot. And the rustic Italian fare is delicious, if just a bit simplistic. The menu changes weekly, offering the characteristic pastas, soups, and salads as well as an antipasto plate. The house-baked breads are a tasty starter. You'll be hard pressed to find a wine on the list that costs more than $20. *$; AE, DC, MC, V; no checks; dinner Tues–Sat; beer and wine; reservations recommended; map:L7*

## Le Charm / ★★

**315 5TH ST BTWN FOLSOM AND HARRISON STS; 415/546-6128**

This classic, stylish, intimate French bistro south of Market Street offers some of the best values in French cuisine in the city. There aren't many places where you can find a three-course, expertly prepared, professionally served prix-fixe menu for about $24. The appetizers might include *fricasee d'escargot,* roasted quail stuffed with mustard greens, or a perfect French onion soup. For the entree your options might include duck confit, pan-roasted halibut, or the enormous leg of lamb. Desserts, which must be ordered in advance, are superb. The tarte Tatin and the chocolate roulades with coconut are showstoppers. Outdoor seating is available, making this a great place to enjoy a sophisticated lunch on a warm summer afternoon. *$; AE, MC, V; no checks; lunch Mon–Fri, dinner Mon–Sat; full bar; reservations recommended; map:N4*

## Le Colonial / ★★☆

**20 COSMO PL, OFF TAYLOR ST BTWN POST AND SUTTER STS; 415/931-3600**

The once-popular Trader Vic's restaurant thrived for many years on this tiny, tucked-away side street near the Tenderloin and Union Square. Today this hideaway is the home of Le Colonial, which serves excellent Vietnamese food that is much more expensive than what you'll find at the usual Asian restaurants around town. But this is no typical Asian restaurant: It's a place to be seen, dress up, and pose along with the other pretty people who arrive here after work to schmooze and flirt. Fashioned after a 1920s Vietnamese plantation, complete with wicker, fans, and rich wood, Le Colonial offers a blend of French and Vietnamese cooking. Upstairs in the lounge, relax with a drink on the cozy couches and choose from an extensive list of appetizers. The dinner menu also offers a wide selection, and most dishes are a tantalizing blend of sweet, spicy, sour, and aromatic flavors. Dishes can be ordered individually as entrees or served family style. Some good choices include the steamed sea bass wrapped in a banana leaf (their best dish), coconut-curry prawns with mango and eggplant; wok-seared beef tenderloin with watercress and onion salad; cold beef salad with tender chunks marinated in lime; ginger roast duck; and the crispy Vietnamese spring rolls. *$$$; AE, DC, MC, V; no checks; dinner every day; full bar; reservations recommended; map:M3*

## Lhasa Moon / ★

**2420 LOMBARD ST BTWN SCOTT AND DIVISADERO STS; 415/674-9898**

If you can't hike the Himalayas, you can at least trek to the Marina District to experience the food of Tibet. This is San Francisco's only Tibetan restaurant and one of the few on the West Coast. Restaurant creator Tsering Wangmo, Tibetan born and raised in a Tibetan refugee settlement  in South India, revives the dishes she learned to cook from her mother. She's eager to introduce people to both the cuisine and the culture from whence it came. The menu is curious and amazing, with such dishes as *churul* (a pungent cheese and minced beef soup) and *phing alla* (a crepe filled with bean thread, vegetables, and mushrooms). A highlight is the *momo*, a dim sum–like array of juicy dumplings filled with anything from chopped beef to mint-flavored vegetables. Among the intriguing and flavorful main dishes, the *kongpo shaptak* (spicy cheese-flavored beef and chile peppers) and *jhasha shamdeh* (curry-marinated chicken in yogurt and herbs) are two standouts. Several vegetarian dishes are available as well. *$; AE, MC, V; no checks; lunch Thurs–Fri, dinner Tues–Sun; beer and wine; reservations recommended; map:J1*

## Liberty Cafe / ★★☆

**410 CORTLAND AVE AT BENINGTON ST; 415/695-8777**

The neighborhood of Bernal Heights is fast becoming known as the last bastion of affordable housing in the city. And as residents move in, the restaurants are springing up to feed them. The Liberty Cafe is the best one so far. The big draw is its traditional (though pricey) chicken potpie, with lots of juicy chicken, potatoes, carrots, pearl onions, and other tasty treats. The seasonally changing menu often has a pleasant surprise or two, including a fantastic tamale dish on a recent visit. The desserts, anchored by juicy, delicious fruit pies, get their own space in a cottage next door. The bakery/wine bar has a couple dozen more seats; here you can have an appetizer while you wait for your table. Reservations are not accepted, and the wait can sometimes be long. *$$; AE, MC, V; no checks; lunch Tues–Fri, dinner Tues–Sun, brunch Sat–Sun; beer and wine; reservations not accepted; map:L8*

## L'Osteria del Forno / ★★☆

**519 COLUMBUS AVE BTWN GREEN AND UNION STS; 415/982-1124**

Don't let the touristy Columbus Avenue location fool you: This eight-table cafe attracts legions of locals who brave lousy parking for anything that comes out of the brick-lined oven, such as fantastic focaccia sandwiches, freshly made pizzas and pastas, kick-butt cipolline, and a wondrously succulent roast pork braised in milk (everyone's all-time favorite). Small baskets of warm focaccia and Italian wine served by the glass tide you over until the entree arrives. The kitchen is run by two charming Italian women who have combined good food with a homey Italian-bistro atmosphere. Ergo, expect a warm welcome and authentic Italian food at low prices. Darn good espresso, too. *$–$$; cash only; lunch, dinner Wed–Mon; beer and wine; reservations not accepted; map:M2*

## LuLu (Restaurant LuLu) / ★★

**816 FOLSOM ST AT 4TH ST; 415/495-5775**

LuLu may not enjoy the legendary status it once commanded, but it's still one of the most energetic and popular restaurants in San Francisco and yet another feather in the chef's cap of Reed Hearon (who has since gone on to fry bigger fish). It's easy to see why LuLu was and remains a hit. As soon as you enter, you're pleasantly assaulted with divine aromas emanating

## BIG-CITY STREET PARKING TIPS

Driving around San Francisco presents a formidable challenge. The combination of hills, traffic, aggressive drivers, and a notable lack of parking will tax your driving skills and patience. To avoid runaway cars on steep hills, *curb your wheels!* Turn the tires *away* from the curb and toward the street when facing uphill, and *toward* the curb when facing downhill—otherwise your car may find itself on a surprise journey or, at best, slapped with a parking ticket. Also, tow-away zones and time limits proliferate, and parking regulations (particularly on street cleaning days) are strictly enforced. The best way to chalk up tickets is to either ignore parking signs or assume any degree of flexibility. In fact, the city relies on parking citations to augment the government coffers (we're talking *millions* of dollars annually).

As for all those multicolored curbs, here's what the parking department is trying to tell you: a *red* curb means no stopping or parking ever, not even for a second; *blue* curbs are reserved for drivers with disabilities who have a California-issued disabled plate or a placard; a *white* curb means there's a 5-minute limit *if* the business it fronts is open; *green* indicates a 10-minute limit during business hours; and *yellow* and *yellow-black* curbs are for commercial vehicles only during the day.

Ultimately, the best way to see the city is on your feet or via public transportation. Taxis are few and far between, so much so that locals joke that there are only four or five cabs in the whole town—which doesn't seem so far-fetched when you try to find a free one on a Friday night. Instead, buy a bus map and a day pass and take Muni, our unreliable but essential public transport system of buses, streetcars, and cable cars. For information about the Muni system, including rates and routes, call 415/673-6864 or visit the Muni website at www.sfmuni.com.

from the massive open kitchen, which overlooks the cavernous yet stylish dining room where a hundred or more diners are feasting family style and creating such a din that the kitchen staff has to wear two-way headsets (it's quite a scene). The sine qua non starter is the sputtering iron-skillet–roasted mussels served with drawn butter. Essentially everything that comes from the twin wood-burning ovens is superb, particularly the pork loin rubbed with fennel, garlic, and olive oil and served with mashed potatoes; the rosemary-infused chicken and warm potato salad; and the thin, crisp pizzas topped with first-rate prosciutto, pancetta, and other savory toppings. Everything is served on a large platter to facilitate sharing. For dessert, go for the gooey chocolate cake served with a scoop of gourmet ice cream. *$$; AE, DC, MC, V; no checks; lunch, dinner every day; full bar; reservations recommended; www.restaurantlulu.com; map:N4*

## Manora's Thai Cuisine / ★★☆

**1600 FOLSOM ST AT 12TH ST; 415/861-6224**
There are dozens of Thai restaurants in the city, but this SoMa institution has always managed to stand out as one of the best. That explains the crowded seating arrangement, the noisy atmosphere, and the guaranteed wait during the peak dining hours, but the food is so incredibly flavorful and reasonably priced that no one sweats these little things. Be sure to start the feast with the chicken satay, followed by the fresh stuffed mint rolls (divine). The menu has a vast array of Thai-style curries, tangy soups, meats, and vegetarian plates, but it's the seafood dishes that really shine, particularly the exotic deep-fried crab shell stuffed with fresh pork, shrimp, crab, herbs, vegetables, and spices. If you plan on going out after dinner, finish the meal with Manora's addictively sweet, caffeine-laden Thai iced tea or coffee. *$–$$; MC, V; no checks; lunch Mon–Fri, dinner every day; full bar; reservations recommended; map:N4*

## Marcello's Pizza / ★★☆

**420 CASTRO ST AT MARKET ST; 415/863-3900**
Every neighborhood has to have one: a late-night pizza-by-the-slice standby that's always there for you when you leave the party bombed and starving. In the Castro that place is Marcello's, which must make a small fortune serving a wide array of slices to a very eclectic crowd until 1am Sunday through Thursday, and until 2am Friday and Saturday. Both thick- and thin-crust pizzas with a wide array of toppings are enticingly set behind the glass counter, and it usually takes only one big slice to do the trick. Chicken wings, calzones, salads, and sandwiches are also available, but most everyone sticks with the thick, gooey, God-this-tastes-good pizza. Beer and wine are available as well. There are only about half a dozen stools in the cramped and narrow pizzeria, but the crowd moves quickly. *$; cash only; lunch, dinner every day; beer and wine; reservations not accepted; map:K6*

## Mario's Bohemian Cigar Store / ★★

**566 COLUMBUS AVE AT UNION ST; 415/362-0536**
You can't consider yourself a San Franciscan unless you've had a focaccia sandwich at this century-old North Beach Italian institution that, in a previous incarnation, really was a cigar store. It's an adorable little low-key cafe in a prime location across from Washington Square. Both tourists and locals squeeze themselves into the well-worn bar or a windowside table overlooking the park, order a cappuccino or a glass of chianti, watch the foot traffic, and ponder the old black-and-white photos of longtime regulars. There are several kinds of sandwiches to choose from, but the best are the hot meatball and the eggplant, both made with fresh focaccia (direct from Liguria Bakery right across the square), topped with melted Swiss cheese, and cut into triangles for easy pickings.

*$; cash only; lunch, dinner every day; beer and wine; reservations not accepted; map:M2*

## Marnee Thai / ★★

**2225 IRVING ST BTWN 23RD AND 24TH AVES; 415/665-9500**

Some very clever thinking went into the design of Marnee Thai, one of San Francisco's best Thai restaurants. The walls and A-shaped ceiling consist of woven palm-frond mats with bamboo framing, creating the illusion that you're a guest dining in a remote Thai village. Then there's May, the owner, an attractive—and assertive—woman who, dressed in beautiful Thai clothing, runs the always-crowded restaurant with logistical precision (she's also a psychic who has the ability to tell your fortune by the shape of your face). But all is for naught unless the food is good, right? Well, it is. In fact, it's wonderful. One bite of the spicy angel wings (crispy chicken wings sautéed with fresh chile, garlic, and crispy sweet basil) or the fried corn cakes and you're hooked. Recommended entrees include the *chan pad poo* (spicy crab noodles), the *pad ginger* (chicken sautéed with fresh ginger, onions, and dried mushrooms), the whole deep-fried pompanoa fish, and any of the Thai curries (shrimp in red curry is our favorite). For dessert don't miss the fried bananas with coconut ice cream. *$–$$; AE, MC, V; no checks; lunch, dinner every day; beer and wine; reservations recommended; map:F6*

## Masa's / ★★★★

**648 BUSH ST BTWN POWELL AND STOCKTON STS (HOTEL VINTAGE COURT); 415/989-7154 OR 800/258-7694**

No one just drops in for dinner at Masa's. Not only do you have to make a reservation at least three weeks in advance, but it may take that long to arrange the financing: This is probably San Francisco's most expensive restaurant. That said, the prices accurately reflect the precious ingredients, generous portions, stunning presentations, and labor-intensive nature of the elegant French-California cuisine invented by the late Masataka Kobayashi and carried out flawlessly by Iron Chef winner Ron Siegel. Along with the new chef (lured from Charles Nob Hill by a fat paycheck and a customized kitchen), Masa's also has a new, trendy look to go with its new $60 three-, $75 six-, and $105 nine-course tasting menus. By all accounts Masa's continues to impress its cultivated clientele with its inviting atmosphere (neither glitzy nor snobbish), professional service (never intimidating), and unremittingly stellar cuisine. To get an idea of Masa's idea of indulgence, take a gander at the offerings from a typical ménu dégustation: sautéed Bellwether Farm baby lamb chops accompanied with potato gnocchi and spring onions; farm-raised Davenport abalone served with hand-cut linguine; lobster ravioli with fava beans and beech mushrooms in a lobster cream sauce; and potato-crusted Japanese halibut served with cinnamon cap mushrooms and baby leeks. The excellent wines are even more exorbitantly priced than the food; moreover, if you want to bring a special bottle of your own, you should know that the corkage fee is equal to the retail value of a top-flight chardonnay. *$$$$; AE, DC, DIS, MC, V; checks OK; dinner Tues–Sat; full bar; reservations required; www.masas.citysearch.com; map:M3*

## Maya San Francisco / ★★☆

**303 2ND ST BTWN HARRISON AND FOLSOM STS; 415/543-2928**
The food at Maya is something of a gourmet spin on traditional Mexican dishes prepared with regional touches and presented with unprecedented flair. What's more, there are many dishes that simply are not served in most local Mexican restaurants. The corn chowder is delicious—and probably impossible to find short of inviting yourself into a Mexican family's home. Other highlights include the chiles rellenos, pan-roasted Chilean sea bass, the chicken tamale in chipotle sauce, the chicken mole, and grilled pork tenderloin. The sauces are a specialty in themselves. The dining room makes the most of its windswept, mall-like location with warm, earth-toned walls and subtle ambient lighting. *$; AE, DC, MC, V; no checks; lunch Mon–Fri, dinner every day; full bar; reservations recommended; map:N4*

## Maykadeh / ★★

**470 GREEN ST BTWN KEARNY ST AND GRANT AVE; 415/362-8286**
For many centuries, Persia (now Iran) was the culinary capital of the world; its enduring influence penetrated court cuisines from the Middle East to India and Iberia. At Maykadeh you can sample the fare of medieval princes for a less-than-princely sum. A meal at this cheerful, comfortable restaurant begins with a complimentary *sabzi* plate—a refreshing snack of feta cheese, onions, fresh basil, and mint meant to be tucked into warm pita bread. The most venturesome appetizers are the tender lamb tongue in a creamy sauce, and the succulent mesquite-grilled calf brains with a saffron-scented lemon butter. Main-course choices are primarily stews and kebabs, which are well marinated and tender, but culinary explorers may enjoy the exotic *ghorme sabzi* (lamb shank braised in an assertive sauce of onions, red beans, fried lime, leeks, chives, and mysterious Persian herbs). Entrees are served with basmati rice and a ramekin of tart crimson sumac powder (made from a Middle Eastern berry) for seasoning your dishes. End the adventure with a dish of lush, rose-perfumed ice cream. *$$; MC, V; no checks; lunch Fri–Sat, dinner every day; beer and wine; reservations recommended; map:N2*

## MC² / ★★★

**470 PACIFIC AVE BTWN MONTGOMERY AND SANSOME STS; 415/956-0666**
One of the best-looking restaurants in the city, this sleek, modern establishment has earned awards and acclaim as much for its architecture as

for its food. Built into a historic brick warehouse from the Barbary Coast era, the room features wood ceilings, brick walls, and exposed beams, a stylish aesthetic that threatens to make the meals here a second act. The exhibition kitchen exports light, flavorful contemporary California-French cuisine that is among the best in town, particularly the appetizer of seared tuna and tuna tartare with shiitake mushrooms, and the dinner entrees of roasted day-boat scallops and shiitake-crusted filet of beef with root vegetables. The Sonoma duck breast with caramelized turnip tart and foie gras sauce is also outstanding. The massive wine list can be a bit daunting, but the sommelier is friendly and quick with a perfect recommendation. Service is generally flawless but can be distant. *$$$; AE, DC, MC, V; no checks; lunch Mon–Fri, dinner Mon–Sat; full bar; reservations recommended; map:N2*

## Mecca / ★★☆

**2029 MARKET ST BTWN DOLORES AND CHURCH STS; 415/621-7000**

Mecca is a magnet for those who want an abundance of sexy atmosphere with hearty American bistro fare—and this silver supper club lined with chocolate-brown velvet drapes delivers. Start with one of the sassy cocktails (how about She's-a-Bad-Girl-Mecca-rita with Cuervo, Cointreau, and lime?) at the slick, zinc-topped bar inset with multicolored fiber-optic lights, and enjoy the moody music, which is often provided by jazz and R&B ensembles on the small stage. Executive chef Mike Fennelly, who made *Food & Wine* magazine's list of Best New Chefs in 1993, specializes in contemporary American cuisine with an emphasis on influences from Asia and the American Southwest. His signature dishes are the oysters on the half shell with red chile ponzu sauce, barbecued oysters with crispy pancetta, and ahi tuna spring rolls with balsamic and soy vinaigrette. Fennelly's talent also shines through when it comes to pastas and meats: Sicilian sausage penne in a wonderful rosemary and cream sauce spiked with tomatoes and fava beans; thick-cut Jamaican jerked grilled pork chop with a side of potato and sweet onion hash; and tamarind-glazed Muscovy duck breast served with mustard-braised French fingerling potatoes and snow peas. Yes, it's as good as it reads. Unlike most San Francisco restaurants, the glamorous Mecca serves dinner until midnight Thursday through Saturday, making it the perfect stop during those late-night benders. *$$$; AE, DC, MC, V; no checks; dinner every day; full bar; reservations recommended; www.sfmecca.com; map:K5*

## The Meetinghouse / ★★★

**1701 OCTAVIA ST AT BUSH ST; 415/922-6733**

In 1996 owner-chefs John Bryant Snell and Joanna Karlinsky converted an old apothecary space into one of the very best restaurants in San Francisco. Custard-yellow walls, dark green trim, wood ceiling fans, and hardwood floors make this warm, intimate space utterly inviting. To add to the charm, one entire wall still boasts the remnants of an earlier identity—hundreds of tiny built-in drawers that formerly held medicinal potions. This dinner-only establishment offers superb seasonal American cuisine served by an exceptionally professional staff. Baskets of warm biscuits and homemade breads arrive at your table immediately. A small seasonal menu typically boasts no more than five enticing entrees. A fall offering included a marvelous rock shrimp and scallion johnnycake appetizer with a sweet-pepper relish, and an exquisite tomato salad drizzled with a lightly sweetened balsamic vinaigrette and toasted pine nuts. Unforgettable entrees have included a grilled pork loin chop with applesauce served with braised baby greens; a pan-seared Chilean sea bass in a sumptuous red-wine jus; and braised short ribs smothered in a sweet barbecue sauce. For dessert, try the utterly delectable strawberry shortcake with sweet berries nestled in a cloud of whipped cream atop a strawberry and wine purée. A carefully selected, reasonably priced list of primarily California wines is perfectly matched with the extraordinary American cuisine. *$$$; AE, DC, MC, V; checks OK; dinner every day, brunch Sat–Sun; beer and wine; reservations recommended; map:L3*

## Mel's Diner / ★★☆

**2165 LOMBARD ST AT FILLMORE ST; 415/921-3039**
**3355 GEARY BLVD AT STANYAN ST; 415/387-2244**

When you're in the mood for a cheeseburger, greasy fries, and a chocolate shake, there's no place that does it better than Mel's. Modeled after an *American Graffiti*–style '50s diner, the place is replete with glimmering stainless steel, large comfy booths, and nickel jukeboxes at each table. Some toe-tappin' hit from the '50s or '60s is bound to be playing, and the staff even dresses for effect in spotless short-sleeve white shirts and  hats. Along with the diner standards—hot dogs, cheese sandwiches, hot fudge sundaes—are a half-dozen "blue-plate specials" such as a turkey dinner complete with stuffing and mashed potatoes, and meat loaf just like Mom (or somebody's mom) used to make. A classic American breakfast is served each morning as well. Mel's two best attributes, however, are that it's open late (till 3am Sunday through Thursday and 24 hours Friday and Saturday) and it's one of the few restaurants in the city that caters to kids and teens. *$; cash only; breakfast, lunch, dinner every day; beer and wine; reservations not accepted; map:K2, map:I4*

## Mifune / ★

**1737 POST ST AT FILLMORE ST; 415/922-0337**

 "It's OK to slurp your noodles," says a note on Mifune's menu. And that's a good thing, because you are likely to do just that at this spartan restaurant in the Upper Fillmore area. When a noodle fix is what you require, there is no better place than Mifune. Choose either an udon (broad, flat) or a soba (thin, buckwheat) base, then select from more than

50 toppings. Whether it's beef, chicken, tempura, or plain old miso, you won't be disappointed. The lunch special, with noodles, sushi, salad, and tea for less than about $7, is a real bargain. You'll also find a few tempura and sushi selections, but don't waste your time. Noodles are the order here. Just raise the bowl to your chin, shovel in the goodies with your chopsticks, and slurp, slurp, slurp! *$; AE, DC, DIS, MC, V; no checks; lunch, dinner every day; beer and wine; reservations recommended; map:K3*

## Millennium / ★★

**246 MCALLISTER ST BTWN HYDE AND LARKIN STS (ABIGAIL HOTEL); 415/487-9800**

When Millennium opened a few years back, it seemed as if it wouldn't live to see the new century, simply because upscale vegetarian/vegan restaurants rarely do well. But executive chef Eric Tucker has proved the critics wrong with his wonderfully creative and inventive meatless menu (if you've ever tried cooking vegan, you know how difficult it can be). Set in a narrow Parisian bistro–style dining room in the city's Civic Center district, Millennium enjoys a strong repeat clientele. They come for Tucker's egg-, butter-, and dairy-free dishes, which even meat and dairy eaters concede are delicious (most of the time). Two of our favorite main courses from the weekly-revised menu are the ragout of wild mushrooms, leeks, and butternut squash inside a flaky phyllo purse, and the artichoke enchiladas served in a poblano pecan crème with pickled nopale cactus and chipotle rhubarb salsa. The sautéed portobello mushrooms and rosemary polenta are also quite good, and Tucker's meat substitutes made with seitan are astonishingly similar to the real thing. Occasionally he can really muddle some daily specials, though, so be sure to query the friendly wait staff for a recommendation. *$$; DC, MC, V; no checks; dinner every day; beer and wine; reservations recommended; www. millenniumrestaurant.com; map:M4*

## Miss Millie's / ★★☆

**4123 24TH ST BTWN CASTRO AND DIAMOND STS; 415/285-5598**

When you want comfort in Noe Valley, stop by to see Miss Millie. The welcoming, 1930ish diner first opened as a strictly vegetarian restaurant, but has evolved into one of the best places in the area for brunch. The brunch menu is huge, with flavorful takes on recognizable favorites. Try the lemon-ricotta pancakes with blueberry syrup or the spinach and goat-cheese omelet for something you won't soon forget. Dinners are also a treat. The roasted chicken risotto and the grilled red snapper are terrific. The menu is still heavily vegetarian, but the fare is so hearty that carnivores will feel right at home. And that's the whole point at Miss Millie's: to make everyone feel at home. *$$; MC, V; no checks; dinner Tues–Sun, brunch Sat–Sun; beer and wine; reservations not accepted for brunch; map:K7*

## Moki Sushi and Pacific Grill / ★★★

**830 CORTLAND AVE AT GATES AVE; 415/970-9336**

Everyone in town has a favorite sushi spot, and everyone argues over which is the best. The folks in Bernal Heights have argued in favor of Moki since the day it opened, and we couldn't agree more. Besides serving some of the best sushi and rolls we've *ever* had, this place also excels where the others try and fail: with selections from the grill. Try the Thai-style crab cakes in red curry sauce or the Vietnamese-style rice paper rolls stuffed with shrimp and avocado and you'll see what we mean. On the sushi side, the aptly named Ecstasy Roll is the specialty, with white and red tuna, avocado, tobiko, and green onions. The Outrigger Roll with tempura shrimp and creamy avocado is another good choice. Sure, it's probably out of the way, and you might have to wait a bit for a table, but if you're a sushi fanatic, hoo boy is it worth it. *$–$$; DC, MC, V; no checks; dinner every day; beer and wine; reservations recommended; map:L8*

## Mom Is Cooking / ★★

**1166 GENEVA AVE AT MAPLE ST; 415/586-7000**

For three decades this friendly family-style restaurant has provided the Excelsior district with some of the best, most authentic Mexican food in San Francisco. Mom is Abigail Murillo, who hails from Mexico City and spends most of her time in the kitchen. That's good for us, because Mom's cooking is mouthwateringly delicious and well worth making the trip to the outskirts of the city to enjoy. The tamales are second to none, and no matter which enchilada you choose (succulent pork, juicy chicken) you won't be disappointed. The breakfasts are also worth getting up early for. *Huevos* (eggs) come in some 10 variations, and the breakfast burritos are gigantic. Most everything is made from scratch—and the mole sauce is unbelievable! On top of all this, it seems as if the prices haven't gone up since the place opened. At the bar, tequila reigns, with countless varieties available for sipping or mixing into a zesty margarita. This is one of the best Mexican restaurants in town. *$; cash only; breakfast, lunch, dinner Tues–Sun; full bar; reservations recommended; map:J5*

## MoMo's / ★★

**760 2ND ST AT KING ST; 415/227-8660**

When plans for San Francisco's new baseball stadium were announced, business owners in the surrounding South of Market area licked their chops in anticipation of the commercial windfall to follow. The spacious, modern-looking MoMo's was first to pounce, and although the scene is a bit too L.A.-ish for most locals, it's still going strong. The kitchen staff is adept at utilizing their wood-fired grill, situated in the center of the enormous open kitchen. The classic dishes—from braised short ribs to roast to chicken and New York steak—are served in large portions, each bursting with flavor. Granted, the kitchen never really hits anything out of the park here, but they're a solid team and surprisingly consistent given the giant size of the dining room. Desserts are another plus, especially the delicious banana bread pudding. Heated outdoor patio seating is available, and there's another, larger heated patio in front where after-work white-collar revelers jostle for tables, cocktails, and appetizers (go with the onion rings and ahi salad) every night of the week. But beware: This place is a zoo during baseball season. *$$; AE, MC, V; no checks; lunch, dinner every day; full bar; reservations recommended; map:O4*

## Moose's / ★★

**1652 STOCKTON ST BTWN FILBERT AND UNION STS; 415/989-7800 OR 800/28-MOOSE**

Every major city has a place where the prime movers-and-shakers hang out, and ours is Moose's. Run by well-respected San Francisco restaurateur Ed Moose, the lively, ever-so-friendly establishment facing Washington Square in San Francisco's North Beach district is abuzz every night with lawyers, politicians, and local celebrities who come to sup and schmooze within the spacious, high-energy dining room. The exhibition kitchen offers a monthly-changing menu of upscale American dishes that have garnered many a favorable review. The most recommended dishes  are anything that's cooked in the wood-burning oven, particularly the famous tender grilled veal chop served with a potato galette or the center-cut pork loin chop served with creamy yellow grits. When in doubt, stick with the roasted chicken or the legendary Caesar salad and juicy Mooseburger combo, washed down with a glass of spicy zinfandel and followed by the butterscotch pot de crème. There's always a jazz combo playing nightly, and the adjacent bar—separated from the main dining room by a frosted-glass partition—stays busy long after the kitchen closes. Moose's hosts a popular weekend brunch as well. *$$–$$$; AE, CB, DC, JCB, MC, V; no checks; lunch Thurs–Fri, dinner every day, brunch Sat–Sun; full bar; reservations recommended; www.mooses.com; map:M2*

## Mo's Gourmet Burgers / ★★

**1322 GRANT AVE BTWN VALLEJO AND GREEN STS; 415/788-3779**

How do you make the perfect hamburger? Well, if you're a grillmaster at Mo's Gourmet Hamburgers, you use only the best-quality center cut chuck (properly aged, of course), ground fresh daily and hand-formed into big, thick patties. Next, you ignite the volcanic rock underneath the custom-made rotating grill, slap those puppies on, grill 'em exactly to the customer's liking, cover them with soft yet crusty buns, and serve them with a host of accoutrements such as fresh tomatoes, onions, lettuce, and house-made mayonnaise. Voilà! Mo's "Best Burger." Other variations include the BBQ, Bacon, Mushroom, Tex-Mex, California (with avocado), Western (with applewood-smoked bacon), Belly Buster (with cheddar and carmelized onions), and the Alpine (with Swiss Gruyère)—all accompanied with a side of french fries, black beans, Spanish rice, or cabbage. Steak, pork chops, chicken, and a few vegetarian dishes are also on the menu, but it's the burgers that draw carnivores from around the city to this North Beach bastion for beefaholics. Oh, and don't pass on the mocha shake, served thick and tall in a shimmering steel container. *$; MC, V; no checks; breakfast Sat–Sun, lunch, dinner every day; beer and wine; no reservations; map:N2*

## North Beach Pizza / ★☆

**1499 GRANT AVE AT UNION ST (AND BRANCHES); 415/433-2444**
San Franciscans as a whole despise any intrusion of "chain" restaurants on our hallowed soil, so it is with a touch of smugness that we order our pizzas not from Domino's but from the sine qua non of San Francisco pizza—North Beach Pizza. Not unlike burritos, no one can seem to agree which pizzeria makes the best pie in the city, but North Beach Pizza is certainly ranked among the best. Toppings tend to be sparse, but it's that heavenly layer of gooey whole-milk mozzarella that wins people over, as does the hand-spun dough with thick, chewy edges. Besides pizzas there's a huge assortment of pastas, poultry, sandwiches, and salads, but 98 percent of the orders are for 12-, 14-, or 16-inch pies of paradise. Either create your own pizza from their list of 20 fresh ingredients (sausage with black olives is killer), or choose from the house's 10 specialties, such as the San Francisco Special—clams, garlic, cheese, and one mighty fine case of halitosis. Fast, free delivery is available at all locations, which are usually open until 3am on the weekends. *$; AE, DC, DIS, MC, V; no checks; lunch, dinner every day; beer and wine; no reservations; www. northbeachpizza.com; map:N2*

## North Beach Restaurant / ★★

**1512 STOCKTON ST BTWN GREEN AND UNION STS; 415/392-1700**
A staple of the largely Italian neighborhood for two decades, North Beach Restaurant is elegant, classic, and refined. The kitchen doesn't toil in trends, offering instead straightforward interpretations of such dishes as eggplant Parmesan, veal scaloppine, and calamari. The cioppino, a house specialty, comes shelled so you don't have to make a mess to enjoy it. The sand dabs are also highly recommended. Everything here is well executed, and the service follows suit. If you don't see anything you like on the menu, the kitchen takes requests—but allow some extra time if you opt for that route. All desserts are made on the premises, and the tiramisu and cheesecake are presented in classic large and unfettered form. North Beach Restaurant also has one of the best wine cellars in town, with nearly 100 cabernets as well as some 75 grappas and 25 California white wines, not to mention vintages from 20 regions of Italy. For an unforgettable North

Beach experience, this is the place. *$$$; AE, MC, V; no checks; lunch, dinner every day; full bar; reservations recommended; map:M2*

## North Star / ★

**288 CONNECTICUT ST AT 18TH ST; 415/551-9840**

The multimedia types who work in the area populate the chic, comfortable room of North Star at lunch, while dinners are a relaxed affair, with casual, friendly service and lively conversation. The menu is rooted largely in American classics, from meat loaf in wild mushroom gravy to barbecued pork chops to tasty fried chicken. A few unusual items set this place apart from the usual glorified diner, such as deep-fried maki tempura. The desserts come from the Little Dipper Bakery next door—and be sure to save room, because they're a true highlight. *$; MC, V; no checks; lunch every day, dinner Tues–Sun; beer and wine; reservations recommended; map:N6*

## One Market / ★★★

**1 MARKET ST AT STEUART ST; 415/777-5577**

If you enjoy dining in large, high-energy, big-city restaurants—we're talking seating for 220 among a sea of stylish banquettes, polished mahogany, and floor-to-ceiling windows—then you'll really like this one. When it first opened, the fare at One Market was surprisingly inconsistent, bringing both bravos and boos from major restaurant critics. But the ratings improved rapidly when rising star executive chef Adrian Hoffman took over the open kitchen, presiding over an ever-changing menu that makes the most of California's abundance of farm-fresh products. "Rooted in the classics but prepared in a contemporary style" is how Hoffman describes his cuisine, which translated into deeds comes out as crispy spiced softshell-crab stew, sausage-corn griddle cakes in a sherry honey, whole-roasted snapper stuffed with sausage and fennel in an olive jus, mustard-crusted pork tenderloin in a port-plum glaze with fava bean bread pudding, slow-braised beef shoulder encircled by pearl onions, and similar hunger-inducing dishes. The 300-bottle American wine list is one of the city's best, and live jazz piano music filters through the cavernous dining room every evening. *$$$; AE, DC, MC, V; no checks; lunch Mon–Fri, dinner Mon–Sat; full bar; reservations recommended; map:O2*

## Oritalia / ★★☆

**586 BUSH ST AT STOCKTON ST; 415/782-8122**

Oritalia is an amalgamation of "Oriental" and "Italian," which is precisely what the menu delivers at this plush and popular downtown restaurant. Actually, the flavors of Italy, China, Korea, France, and Southeast Asia are all represented in various combinations on the sophisticated menu, often with outstanding results (go with the wait staff's recommendations). The restaurant's decor—silk chandeliers, Oriental rugs, curtained booths—offers both artistry and intimacy, but the most attractive items are on the dinner plate, such as the heavenly satsuma potato gnocchi made with sautéed Maine lobster, asparagus, and lime beurre blanc. Other dishes that are simply incredible are the sake-steamed sea bass with Chinese black-bean sauce, and the five-spice duck confit and frisée salad. End the world tour with a slice of dreamy passion-fruit cheesecake. *$$–$$$; AE, CB, DC, MC, V; no checks; dinner every day; full bar; reservations recommended; map:N3*

## Pacific / ★★★

**500 POST ST AT MASON ST (PAN PACIFIC HOTEL); 415/771-8600**
Ensconced within the Pan Pacific Hotel is one of San Francisco's best and least-known haute cuisine restaurants. Perhaps its lack of an off-street entrance is the reason it hasn't quite caught on, but anyone who samples Erik Oberholtzer's terrine of fresh Sonoma foie gras will become a die-hard fan of this immensely talented chef. The beautiful mezzanine-level dining room, stellar wine list, and professional yet unpretentious service are certainly appreciated, but it's Oberholtzer's mastery with seasonally inspired dishes that brings us back again and again. Dishes we strongly recommend include the sweet-potato gnocchi with foraged mushrooms and pineapple sage, roasted beef tenderloin on braised leeks, and mashed potatoes with a crispy oxtail and root vegetable strudel. Tip: The hotel offers free four-hour valet parking for diners. *$$$; AE, DC, MC, V; no checks; breakfast, lunch, dinner every day; full bar; reservations recommended; map:M3*

## Pane e Vino / ★★★

**3011 STEINER ST AT UNION ST; 415/346-2111**
Well hidden on the outskirts of posh Pacific Heights, this dark-wood–trimmed trattoria framed by a cream-colored awning is a local favorite. The two tiny, simply furnished dining rooms with small white-clothed tables fill up fast, and as waiters spouting rapid-fire Italian dart back and forth between the kitchen and their customers, folks waiting for a table are often left frantically searching for a place to stand out of the way. It's all enchantingly reminiscent of the real ristorante scene in Italy, which is perhaps one of the reasons people keep coming back. Newcomers unaccustomed to the hustle and bustle may be a bit disconcerted at first, but after a sip or two of wine and a bite of rustic Italian fare everything becomes rather entertaining. Do yourself a favor and indulge in the amazing chilled artichoke appetizer, stuffed with bread and tomatoes and served with a vinaigrette—it's divine! Follow that lead with one of the perfectly prepared pastas, ranging from the simple but savory capellini tossed with fresh tomatoes, basil, garlic, and extra-virgin olive oil to the zesty bucatini (hollow straw pasta) smothered with pancetta, hot pep-

pers, and tomato sauce. The excellent entrees vary from rack of lamb marinated in sage and rosemary to the whole roasted fresh fish of the day. Before you raise your napkin to your lips for the last time, dive into the delightful dolci: A luscious crème caramel, assorted gelati, and a terrific tiramisu are the standouts. *$$; AE, MC, V; no checks; lunch Mon–Sat, dinner every day; beer and wine; reservations recommended; map:K2*

## Park Chow / ★★

**1240 9TH AVE BTWN IRVING ST AND LINCOLN WY; 415/665-9912**

There just aren't enough good things to say about Park Chow, one of our all-time favorite places to eat in the city. First of all, it's cheap (you get hefty servings of quality food for around $10 to $13), it's consistently good, the service is fast and friendly, the atmosphere is lively and fun, and you always leave feeling satisfied. The restaurant, which is fashioned after a rustic ski lodge, is located in the Inner Sunset District near Golden Gate Park and caters mostly to a local clientele. Sample Park Chow's outstanding braised short ribs served with fresh greens and mashed potatoes, the giant portobello mushroom cap served with creamy polenta, and the linguine with calamari, mussels, clams, and shrimp. Burgers, chicken, salads, and a reasonably good wine-by-the-glass list are on the menu as well. While you're waiting for a table (they're always busy and don't take reservations), order a glass of wine from the bar and snuggle with your honey by the fireplace. On sunny days, request a table in the roof garden. Brunch is served until 2:30pm on weekends. If you're in the Castro, check out the sister restaurant, Chow (see review). *$–$$; MC, V; no checks; lunch, dinner every day, brunch Sat–Sun; beer and wine; reservations not accepted; map:H5*

## Pastis / ★★

**1015 BATTERY ST BTWN UNION AND GREEN STS; 415/391-2555**

Named after the anise-flavored apéritif, Pastis continues co-owner Gerald Hirigoyen's tradition of hearty brasserie fare at reasonable prices. Like Fringale (see review), his other top-flight San Francisco restaurant, this is a classy little bistro. Inside, there's an industrial feel, with tile floors, hardwood banquettes, brick walls, a beamed ceiling, and a curved concrete bar. The French-American fusion fare comes across as sophisticated and European. For starters, try the tender spinach salad with crisp pieces of bacon and hard-cooked eggs; generous slices of crisp foie gras with grapes and verjuice (a tart grape juice); or prawns marinated in pastis, garlic, and thyme. Entrees might include a tender rack of lamb served in a soup plate over a bed of meaty beans mixed with a tomato broth, a steak with Roquefort and basil butter, and baked halibut with quinoa risotto and papaya. End your meal with the sophisticated warm chocolate tart topped with purple-basil ice cream. Portions are moderate, as they are in Paris, but you'll get value for your dollar and you'll dine in style. *$$; AE, MC, V; checks OK; lunch Mon–Fri, dinner Mon–Sat; full bar; reservations recommended; map:N2*

## Pauline's Pizza / ★★

**260 VALENCIA ST BTWN DUBOCE AVE AND 14TH ST; 415/552-2050**

Pauline's has been quietly churning out what very well could be the "chosen pizza" for years. The bright yellow building on Valencia Street is as unassuming as the restaurant's reputation, but patrons come from around the city to sit and enjoy the basic meal: pizza and salad. Don't bother looking for anything else, because you won't find it—and you won't want it. There's plenty to hold your interest on the toppings menu, from French goat cheese to spiced pork shoulder to house-spiced chicken. It all goes on Pauline's handmade thin-crust dough. The eclectic salads are prepared from certified organic, handpicked lettuces and vegetables, accented with herbs from the restaurant's own local gardens. Also, the service here always comes with a welcoming smile. *$–$$; MC, V; checks OK; dinner Tues–Sat; beer and wine; reservations recommended; map:L5*

## Peña PachaMama / ★★★

**1630 POWELL ST BTWN UNION AND GREEN STS; 415/646-0018**

The moment you walk past the neon-orange–clad figure of Kusillo at the door, you are folded into the musical family of Sukay. This Andean ensemble, which has been performing together for more than 20 years, opened Peña PachaMama (Mother Earth, in the ancient Quechua language) to create a center for Bolivian food and music in San Francisco. The Nuevo Latino cuisine—a fusion of traditional Bolivian dishes with the lighter, organic California sensibility—is the perfect opening act for the show; Friday and Saturday nights, the cozy restaurant gets even cozier as the group plays an invigorating, nonamplified collection of traditional and Bolivian music on a stage next to the dining room. Peña PachaMama's engaging warmth gives it the feel of a neighbor's house, but the kitchen creates savory concoctions that your next-door neighbor might never imagine. Appetizers include Bolivian Rock Soup—a purée of corn tortillas, roasted peppers, tomatoes, and spices—and a wonderful green salad with a dab of ground nut and a drizzle of mango-lime sauces. For the main course, Pacha Pollo is a succulent pan-seared chicken with Andean spices, a purée of Peruvian potatoes (they're purple!), and organic greens. Vegetarians can happily put themselves in Canter's hands with the Chef's Vegetarian Selection. An evening here is a full night out on the town—food, culture, and entertainment—all for the very reasonable price of dinner. *$$; AE, MC, V; checks OK; dinner every day, brunch Sat–Sun; beer and wine; reservations recommended; www.pena pachamama.com; map:M2*

## PJ's Oysterbed / ★★☆

**737 IRVING ST BTWN 8TH AND 9TH AVES; 415/566-7775**

For a taste of Mardi Gras, just head to PJ's. Step into this perennially packed, festively decorated hot spot, feel the loud rhythms of zydeco music, breathe the intoxicating smells of spicy Cajun cookin', and get ready to take it all in. The all-you-can-eat crawfish is a favorite, and the hearty plates of spicy jambalaya or shrimp gumbo are some of the best San Francisco has to offer. Several exotic offerings for the adventurous diner include alligator eggs or double-trouble alligator nuggets. Either sit in the bustling dining room or at the oyster bar, which provides an entertaining view of the kitchen. Or if you've come without a reservation, order a drink or two from PJ's well-stocked full bar and enjoy the festivities while you wait. *$$$; AE, DC, DIS, MC, V; checks OK; dinner every day; full bar; reservations recommended; map:H6*

## Plouf / ★★

**40 BELDEN ST, JUST E OF KEARNY ST BTWN PINE AND BUSH STS; 415/986-6491**

Walk down the chichi little alley called Belden Street in the Financial District, and you'll swear you'd just stepped into a Parisian street full of curbside cafes. Forbidden to cars, Belden Street is filled with umbrella-topped outdoor tables and folks who come for the European ambience and cuisine. One of the restaurants gracing the alley is Plouf, which is onomatopoeic for "splash." It's a hybrid California-French seafood bistro specializing in mussels. An oversize steel door leads to a fun, Euro-modern interior with a long steel bar and booths of polished wood. Don't pass up the huge bowl of mussels served with your choice of seven sauces (ranging from escargot butter to a bold crayfish and tomato sauce), designed to be sopped up with bread. If you like fries, order a bowlful—they're salty and crisp here. The main courses are stylish as well as delicious: monkfish with cabbage, pearl onions, and bacon; tuna with black pepper, served over ratatouille; sea bass with fennel and a ginger-port sauce; steamed salmon with braised leeks and mushrooms and a mustard-tarragon sauce. There are also pork, chicken, lamb, and steak entrees for non–seafood-lovers. *$$; AE, DC, MC, V; no checks; lunch Mon–Fri, dinner Mon–Sat; full bar; reservations recommended; map:N3*

## PlumpJack Cafe / ★★★

**3127 FILLMORE ST BTWN FILBERT AND GREENWICH STS; 415/563-4755**

Co-owned by Bill Getty (son of billionaire Gordon Getty) and wine-connoisseur-cum-politician Gavin Newsom, this exotic California-Mediterranean bistro is one of San Francisco's leading restaurants, with consistently excellent food and (thanks to its companion wine store a few doors away) a surprisingly extensive wine list featuring fine bottles offered at near-retail prices. The appetizers are often the highlight of the menu, particularly the bruschetta, topped with roasted beets, goat cheese, and garlic one night, and eggplant, sweet peppers, and goat cheese the next. Don't miss the remarkable risottos, richly flavored with artichokes, applewood-smoked bacon, and goat cheese, or perhaps smoked salmon and shiitake mushrooms. Other recommended dishes include the superbly executed roast herb chicken breast with foie gras, hedgehog mushrooms, and spinach and the roast duck breast and leg confit with French green lentils, barley, parsnip chips, and a sour cherry jus. While the restaurant's highly stylized, handcrafted interior design is unique—gold-leafed lights, chairs with medieval-shield–shaped backs, curved metal screens at the windows—the unpretentious taupe and olive color scheme ensures that what really stands out is the food. *$$$; AE, MC, V; no checks; lunch Mon–Fri, dinner Mon–Sat; full bar; reservations recommended; www.plumpjack.com; map:K2*

## Postrio / ★★★

545 POST ST BTWN MASON AND TAYLOR STS (PRESCOTT HOTEL); 415/776-7825

Owned by Southern California superstar chef Wolfgang Puck and the Kimpton Hotel & Restaurant Group, Postrio is a splashy slice of Hollywood set in the heart of San Francisco, with superglitzy decor à la restaurant designer Pat Kuleto, delightful culinary combinations, and the perpetual hope of catching sight of some celeb at the next table. One enters through a spiffy street-level bar that serves tapas and little Puckish pizzas to the unreserving; from there a grand sculpted-iron-and-copper staircase—on which everybody can at least *play* the star role—descends dramatically into a crowded, pink-lighted dining room ringed with paintings and plants. It's a lovely, sophisticated setting for some terrific food, prepared by chefs Mitchell and Steven Rosenthal, who proved themselves capable successors when founding chefs Anne and David Gingrass jumped ship to open Hawthorne Lane in '95. Working closely with Puck, the brothers Rosenthal have crafted an exciting hybrid of California-Asian-Mediterranean cuisine that includes such creations as grilled quail accompanied by spinach and a soft egg ravioli with port wine glaze; sautéed salmon with plum glaze, wasabi mashed potatoes, and miso vinaigrette; Chinese duck with mango sauce; and roasted leg of lamb with garlic potato purée and niçoise olives. Tempting choices, indeed, but pastry chef Christine Law's dessert menu has its own array of showstoppers—from the potato-pecan pie to the caramel pear tart with Grand Marnier crème fraîche. The wine list is excellent, the service professional, and reservations essential—make them several weeks in advance. *$$$; AE, DC, DIS, MC, V; no checks; breakfast, lunch Mon–Fri, dinner every day, brunch Sat–Sun; full bar; reservations recommended; www. postrio.com; map:M3*

## Potrero Brewing Co. / ★★

**535 FLORIDA ST AT 18TH ST; 415/552-1967**

These days it seems so many places are brewing their own beer. The microbrew restaurant trend has been good to San Francisco, but this one may be the best so far. Built into an old mayonnaise plant in the newly trendy section between the Mission District and Potrero Hill, the Potrero Brewing Co. retains its industrial charm, right down to the two gigantic brewing tanks out front. Inside, the huge place unspools before you as if you're on a factory tour. From the front downstairs bar, packed with the high-tech after-work (out of work?) crowd, move upstairs, grab a pint, and shoot a game on one of the three pool tables. Beyond that is a massive outdoor patio with tables warmed by heat lamps. The outstanding beers include a crispy pale ale, a robust porter, a rich stout, an authentic ESB, a tangy IPA, and a flavorful wheat. They also make seasonal brews and handcraft their own sodas. And when you get hungry? The risotto cakes, crispy calamari, and pan-roasted clams are good starters. Among the dinner selections, the braised brisket with spinach and green onion mashed potatoes is a perfect complement to the beer. Other menu highlights include the fried lemon buttermilk chicken and the enormous double-cut pork chop served with horseradish mashed potatoes. Clearly, this is well beyond your typical pub grub. *$$; AE, DC, MC, V; no checks; lunch, dinner every day; full bar; reservations recommended; map:M6*

## R&G Lounge / ★★

**631-B KEARNY ST AT CLAY ST; 415/982-7877**

Situated in limbo between the edge of Chinatown and the edge of the Financial District, the two-story R&G Lounge attracts a mixed crowd of tourists, businesspeople, and local Chinese residents. The restaurant has a loyal following of diners who champion the fresh Cantonese seafood dishes and good prices. The main downstairs dining room has all the charm of a cafeteria, with glaring fluorescent lights and Formica tables. It's harder to get a table in the formal upstairs dining room, where the lighting is a little easier on the eyes. Each dining room offers the same menu, half in English, half in Chinese. Not everything is on both menus, so ask your server for recommendations, or order what we order every time: the very greasy but rich deep-fried salt and pepper crab, the tangy R&G Special Beef, the savory roast duck, seafood in a clay pot, and for dessert the adzuki bean pudding finale. Most delicious. *$$; AE, DC, MC, V; no checks; lunch, dinner every day; full bar; reservations not accepted; map:N2*

## Red Herring / ★★

**155 STEUART ST BTWN MISSION AND HOWARD STS; 415/495-6500**

Fittingly located near the city's Embarcadero with some spectacular bay views, Red Herring serves what it calls New American seafood. That's not to say all the fish is American, or even exactly local, but the waterfront makes for a scenic backdrop while you're enjoying the fresh and imaginative fare. The restaurant, long and narrow (a bit dark in the middle section), reels in the finicky locals with a "Bait Bar," which serves oysters on the half shell, cracked crab, and the like. The menu features a delightful lobster and mango salad and a decadent Dungeness crab chop—a crab cake fashioned to resemble a pork chop. If you'd rather get "out of the water," the spit-roasted chicken or dry-aged New York strip are good choices as well. Tip: Request a table in the back overlooking the bay. *$$; AE, DC, MC, V; no checks; lunch Mon–Fri, dinner every day; full bar; reservations recommended; map:D2*

## Rose Pistola / ★★★

**532 COLUMBUS AVE BTWN UNION AND GREEN STS; 415/399-0499**

A star has been born in North Beach, and her name is Rose Pistola. The brainchild of Midas-like chef-restaurateur Reed Hearon (who launched the reputations of LuLu and Cafe Marimba), this sleek and sexy addition to the Columbus Avenue promenade is as pleasing to behold as it is to dine in (it's actually named after a popular octogenarian North Beach restaurateur). If you prefer to oversee the preparation of your meal, sit at the counter overlooking the grill; however, the family-style meals are best enjoyed in the large dining room's comfy booths (and tables on the sidewalk offer an alfresco option). The food is rustic Italian with a California flair (less fats, more flavors), inspired by the cuisine of Liguria: roast rabbit with fresh shell-bean ragout and polenta, pumpkin-filled ravioli, or roast pork chop with *panzanella*, an Italian bread salad infused with onions, basil, and tomatoes. The pastas, wood-fired pizzas, and antipasti are also very well prepared, but the fish dishes (particularly the whole roasted fish) are Hearon's specialty. A late-night menu is served until 1am on weekends. *$$–$$$; AE, DC, MC, V; no checks; lunch, dinner every day; full bar; reservations recommended; map:M2*

## The Rotunda Restaurant at Neiman Marcus / ★

**150 STOCKTON ST AT GEARY ST (NEIMAN MARCUS); 415/362-4777**

Popular with the ladies who lunch, the Rotunda is a sophisticated respite from the throngs of shoppers below on Union Square. This restaurant within the Neiman Marcus department store, which anchors one corner of the square, is a light, comfortable room with natural light streaming through a historic stained-glass dome overhead. Specialties are the lobster club sandwich, the fresh pastas, fish, and salads, and the popular house-made popovers with berry-flavored butter. The room's circular design makes for lots of privacy, and the mood always seems quiet. It's just what you need to send you back out into the square, where shopping is a competitive sport. A formal tea service is offered each afternoon. *$$; AE, DC, MC, V, Neiman Marcus store cards; local checks only; lunch Mon–Sat, brunch Sun; beer and wine; reservations recommended; map:N3*

## Rubicon / ★★★

**558 SACRAMENTO ST BTWN SANSOME AND MONTGOMERY STS; 415/434-4100**

Thanks to Rubicon's star-studded cast of financial backers—Robert De Niro, Robin Williams, and Francis Ford Coppola—this Financial District restaurant received so much advance publicity that San Franciscans were setting dates to eat here long before the seismic reinforcements were bolted to the floorboards. Chances are slim that you'll see any Tinseltown talent at the table next to you, but one bite of the foie gras with caramelized rhubarb compote and you couldn't care less who walks in. Other highlights on executive chef Dennis Leary's monthly-changing menu might include butter-poached Alaskan halibut, seared scallops in a sweet onion purée, venison chops over barley, and roulades of steelhead under a crisp herbal crust. Leary has also been known to send out a little unexpected treat now and then, a nice complement to the already stellar service. The excellent, extensive, and expensive wine list is literally one of the nation's best. Because of its Financial District location it does a brisk power-lunch business, so for a more relaxed meal opt for dinner. *$$$; AE, DC, MC, V; no checks; lunch Mon–Fri, dinner Mon–Sat; full bar; reservations recommended; map:N2*

## Rumpus / ★★☆

**I TILLMAN PLACE BTWN POST AND SUTTER STS; 415/421-2300**

Located in a small cul-de-sac off Grant Avenue near Union Square, Rumpus is well known among San Francisco's cognoscenti for serving upscale California-bistro fare in an attractive, modern, and fuss-free setting. It's very popular among weekend shoppers, who stop in for lunch or dinner before heading home; many a business lunch takes place here as well. The menu offers a reasonably priced array of high-quality dishes ranging from crispy pan-roasted chicken atop fluffy mashed potatoes to a thick cut of New York steak, smoked chicken ravioli, and seasonal fresh fish. However, the most popular menu item is the puddinglike chocolate brioche cake (in fact, it's worth dining here just for the brioche). If you're a connoisseur of wine, you'll enjoy sifting through Rumpus's award-winning wine list. The only caveat is the noise level, which can get bothersome when the restaurant is full. *$$; AE, DC, MC, V; no checks; lunch Mon–Sat, dinner every day; full bar; reservations recommended; map:N3*

## Sam's Grill & Seafood Restaurant / ★

**374 BUSH ST BTWN MONTGOMERY AND KEARNY STS; 415/421-0594**

 If you want to take a trip back in time to an old-school San Francisco dining institution, head to Sam's Grill, one of the last remaining steak and seafood houses in the city. It's everything you would expect from a Raymond Chandler novel: resplendent with polished mahogany, dark wood wainscoting, velvet, brass, and high-backed booths with privacy curtains and buzzers for summoning the appropriately brusque tuxedo-clad waiters. It's hugely popular with Financial District heavies, who have been coming here to conduct power lunches since 1967. Eschewing all that fancy-shmancy fusion stuff, the kitchen sticks to the same basics it's been serving for more than three decades: charbroiled fish, thick-cut steaks, fresh shellfish, and stiff pours of single-malt scotch. Start with a bowl of clam chowder followed with the sand dabs or veal porterhouse, a side of creamed spinach, and for dessert, French pancakes anisette. If you're not a fan of heavy sauces, ask for yours on the side. If you're romantically bent (or you need to fire somebody gracefully), request a curtained booth. *$$; AE, CB, DC, MC, V; no checks; lunch, dinner Mon–Fri; full bar; reservations recommended; map:N3*

## Sapporo-ya / ★

**1581 WEBSTER ST AT FILLMORE ST; 415/563-7400**

Located at one end of the Japantown shopping center, Sapporo-ya is a great place for a big, heaping bowl of soba or ramen on a Saturday afternoon. The charming little room does noodles and they do them right: The ancient noodle-making machine on display at the entrance pays homage to the house specialty. Some 10 versions of ramen are available, served with lots of tasty additions, including fresh vegetables, barbecued pork, and tempura. The noodles come in large clay bowls, piping hot and swimming with bamboo shoots, carrots, egg, and spinach. Given the quick, efficient service, you might want to stop here before taking in a movie at the Kabuki movie complex on Japantown's opposite end. *$; AE, MC, V; no checks; lunch, dinner every day; beer and wine; reservations not accepted; map:K3*

## Scala's Bistro / ★★

**432 POWELL ST BTWN POST AND SUTTER STS (SIR FRANCIS DRAKE HOTEL); 415/395-8555**

Opened in 1995, Scala's Bistro immediately won an enthusiastic following by offering exceptional rustic Italian and country French cooking in a lovely, welcoming setting. Co-owners Donna and Giovanni Scala, who operate Napa's hugely popular Bistro Don Giovanni, installed a golden bas-relief ceiling, amber walls, and lead-pane windows, along with brass wall sconces and Craftsman-type chandeliers that cast a warm glow reminiscent of a Mediterranean sunset. (A remarkable transformation indeed, considering this spot in the Sir Francis Drake Hotel used to be a dingy sports bar with the singularly unappetizing name of Crusty's.) Standout appetizers include grilled portobello mushrooms, crispy "Earth and Surf" calamari, and sautéed veal sweetbreads. Pastas range from a dynamite persillade tagliatelle with artichokes, wild mushrooms, and truffle oil to rigatoni with veal meatballs in an oregano and tomato sauce. The seared salmon fillet with buttermilk mashed potatoes, the tender duck-leg confit, and the grilled pork loin with Yukon Gold mashed potatoes and rosemary oil are three highly recommended entrees; risottos, salads, and thin-crust pizzas round out the menu. Portions are generous, but do try to save room for dessert such as the Chocolate I.V. (layers of chocolate ice-cream cake and mousse encased in a toasted butter-pecan crust) and the Bostini cream pie (creamy vanilla custard topped with orange chiffon cake and a warm chocolate glaze). Night owl tip: Scala's takes reservations until midnight. *$$; AE, DC, DIS, MC, V; no checks; breakfast, lunch, dinner every day; full bar; reservations recommended; map:M3*

## Sears Fine Food / ★★☆

**439 POWELL ST BTWN POST AND SUTTER STS; 415/986-1160**

Sears is your classic San Francisco–American coffee shop, where the decor and the staff haven't changed since the Nixon administration. Story has it that Sears first opened in 1938 when Ben the Clown decided to retire from the circus and open his own restaurant. His Swedish wife,  Hilbur, chipped in her family's secret recipe (still a secret to this day) for Swedish pancakes (18 silver dollars to a serving), and there's been a line out the door every weekend morning since. Some might call it tacky, but there's something comforting about the matronly waitresses in their pink uniforms and the booths covered with pink vinyl tablecloths. If pancakes aren't your thing, try the crispy dark-brown waffles or sourdough French toast. The fresh fruit cup marinated in orange juice is also quite popular. Lunch is served as well, but it's the classic breakfast experience that makes Sears worth the wait. *$; cash only; breakfast, lunch every day; no alcohol; reservations accepted; map:M3*

## Shalimar / ★

**532 JONES ST BTWN GEARY AND O'FARRELL STS; 415/928-0333**

If you're searching for truly authentic Indian fare, and you don't mind venturing into an area that is a bit beyond unsavory, Shalimar is for you. It's located right in the heart of the Tenderloin, and that may be the only reason it hasn't been overrun by yuppies. Because when it comes to tandoori lamb and chicken and beef skewers, Shalimar does it with a skill  that can be learned only from the homeland. The flatbreads are warm and delicious, but the place really is all about the food: Linoleum and glaring lights dominate the decor, and service is strictly from the counter. Yet from the minute you step inside, the aroma will be your reward for braving the neighborhood. And what they save on interior design, they pass on to you: Some items are less than $3! *$; cash only; lunch, dinner every day; no alcohol; reservations not accepted; map:M3*

## Shanghai 1930 / ★★

**133 STEUART ST BTWN MISSION AND HOWARD STS; 415/896-5600**

Experience the cosmopolitan and exotic lifestyle of pre–Communist China at Shanghai 1930. A deco entrance leads to this below-street-level restaurant. You'll walk past a packed bar with a jazz band; behind the bar is a dazzling 40-foot backlit aquamarine mirror, with rows of silhouetted bottles. This classy restaurant serves upscale Chinese food in beautiful presentations: minced duck in lettuce with water chestnuts, celery, mushrooms, and (a Mediterranean twist) kalamata olives in plum sauce; stacked baskets of dim sum—little pillows of pork, chopped scallops, and shrimp, with three dipping sauces; rock cod garnished with fresh red grapes and a red-wine-and-soy reduction sauce; chicken breast stir-fried with fresh lily bulbs in a black-bean sauce; and pretty prawns cooked in a bright red-bean chile sauce. Decadent desserts are both Western- and Chinese-style—from warm chocolate cake to fried banana flambé—and change seasonally. Owner George Chen also started Betelnut (see review), a popular pan-Asian beer house on Union Street, and the Long Life Noodle Co. & Jook Joint in the SoMa area. Shanghai 1930 is his most glamorous restaurant so far, with service and cuisine to match. *$$$; AE, MC, V; no checks; lunch Mon–Fri, dinner Mon–Sat; full bar; reservations recommended; map:O3*

## The Slanted Door / ★★★

**584 VALENCIA ST AT 17TH ST; 415/861-8032**

Thank goodness chef Charles Phan abandoned his original plan to build a crepe stand in San Francisco, because otherwise we never would have had the opportunity to sink our teeth into his superb green papaya salad or stir-fried caramelized shrimp. When Phan and his large extended family discovered a vacant (and affordable) space on a slightly run-down stretch of Valencia Street, they ditched the crepery plan in late 1995 and transformed the high-ceilinged room into a small, bilevel restaurant specializing in country Vietnamese food. Phan's design talents (he's a former UC Berkeley architecture student) are evident from the moment you enter the stylish, narrow dining room and take a seat at one of his green-stained wood tables. But even more impressive is Phan's unique fare, based on his mother's recipes, which attracts droves of people for lunch and dinner. The dinner menu changes weekly to reflect the market's offerings, but look for the spring rolls stuffed with fresh shrimp and pork; crab and asparagus soup; caramelized shrimp; curried chicken cooked with yams; "shaking" beef sautéed with onion and garlic; any of the terrific clay pot dishes; and, of course, Phan's special Vietnamese crepes. When business is booming the service gets slow, but if you order a pinot gris from the very good wine list, you won't mind so much. For dessert, the hands-down favorite is the all-American chocolate cake. Go figure. *$$; MC, V;*

*no checks; lunch, dinner Tues–Sun; beer and wine; reservations rec-
ommended; eat@slanteddoor.com; map:L6*

## Slow Club / ★★☆

**2501 MARIPOSA ST AT HAMPSHIRE ST; 415/241-9390**

Though small, Slow Club, with its cool cement floors, metal railings, and
stark design, exudes urban chic. And this isn't the only thing that draws
a loyal following: The California cuisine is top-notch. Lunch and dinner
are equally good. During the day the juicy Niman Ranch burgers and
oven-roasted potatoes served with aioli are favorites. The crisp Caesar
salad also hits the mark. You can also choose from an ever-changing
selection of consistently fresh and tasty tapaslike small plates. Prices at
dinner are higher, but the food remains impeccably fresh and well prepared. Various roasted chicken dishes, succulent pork chops served with
seasonal ingredients, and rosemary-infused leg of lamb might be typical
fall offerings on the daily-changing menu. This still-hip neighborhood
spot is well worth a visit, even if only for a cocktail and appetizers at the
small bar. *$$; MC, V; no checks; lunch Mon–Fri, dinner Mon–Sat,
brunch Sat–Sun; full bar; reservations not accepted; map:M6*

## South Park Cafe / ★★☆

**108 SOUTH PARK ST BTWN 2ND AND 3RD STS AND BRANNAN AND
BRYANT STS; 415/495-7275**

If you're fond of Parisian-style cafes you'll adore the South Park Cafe,
one of our favorite lunch spots in the city. Located on the north side of
South Park—a small patch of grass in the heart of SoMa's Internet com-
munity—this popular cafe with its pale yellow walls, French-accented
wait staff, copper-lined bar, and assortment of French newspapers
hanging on racks has a distinct European ambience to complement the
authentic French cuisine. Popular dishes range from steamed mussels
sautéed in white wine to roasted duck breast with lavender sauce, grilled
steak served with thin pommes frites, and (but of course) grilled rabbit—
all at moderate prices. One caveat: The noisy lunch crowd gets rather
thick from about 12:30pm to 2pm. *$$; AE, MC, V; no checks; breakfast, lunch Mon–Fri, dinner Mon–Sat; full bar; reservations recom-
mended; map:O4*

## Stars / ★★☆

**555 GOLDEN GATE AVE BTWN VAN NESS AVE AND POLK ST; 415/861-7827**

Celebrity chef Jeremiah Tower opened this restaurant years ago and saw
that it lived up to its name. The local luminati—politicos, movie stars,
socialites—packed the place. The star faded, however, and Tower left for
more glamorous pastures. But he left behind the restaurant's name, and the
subsequent owners have been quick to capitalize on that, giving the place
a sleek, modern update, with clean lines and low-slung fixtures that provide great sight lines. The bar (purportedly the longest in the city) is once

again a high-profile gathering spot, and the restaurant is also regaining its luster. The massive open kitchen churns out rustic, Italian-inspired dishes from the wood-burning grill, rotisserie, and oven. The menu changes seasonally, but usually features good spit-roasted chicken and pork loin and a delicious grilled fish of the day. The soups, pastas, and small plates (including an excellent duck confit) are a good bet as well. The wine list is lengthy and well arranged; several selections are offered by the glass. *$$$; AE, DC, MC, V; no checks; lunch Mon–Fri, dinner every day; full bar; reservations recommended; www.starsrestaurant.com; map:L4*

## Stinking Rose / ★

### 325 COLUMBUS AVE BTWN VALLEJO ST AND BROADWAY; 415/781-7673

"We season our garlic with food," boasts the menu at the Stinking Rose, one of the most popular tourist restaurants in North Beach. Everything, from the ice cream to soup to pizzas, salads, pastas, and meats, is given a healthy infusion of garlic. It's a high-energy, festive place decorated with black-and-white checkered floors, large windows overlooking the street, and lots of hanging strands of garlic. Actually, you can smell the Stinking Rose before you can see it: The garlicky aroma wafting down Columbus Avenue has become a North Beach fixture. As with most theme restaurants, the cuisine doesn't strive for greatness, but we have ferreted out a few favorites, including the garlic-steamed clams and mussels, the garlic pizza, the 40-clove garlic chicken, and the Stinking Special, braised rabbit served with garlic mashed potatoes (naturally). If you're into this sort of dining experience, you'll love the place; if not, then head down the road to L'Osteria del Forno (see review). *$$; AE, DC, JCB, MC, V; no checks; lunch, dinner every day; full bar; reservations recommended; www.thestinking rose.com; map:N2*

## Straits Cafe / ★★

### 3300 GEARY BLVD AT PARKER ST; 415/668-1783

There are a handful of restaurants worth venturing all the way out to the Richmond District for, and Straits is definitely one of them. Owner-chef Chris Yeo delivers a knockout combination of authentic and fantastic Singaporean dishes (a combination of Indian, Malaysian, Indonesian, and Chinese cuisines) in a kitschy yet clever setting that resembles a Singapore village. Burlap palm trees, pastel-painted murals, faux balconies, and clotheslines strung across the walls set the stage for Yeo's multicultural meal. It takes several trips to Straits to become even remotely familiar with the menu, but the white-jacketed wait staff is adept at deducing your culinary tolerance. A recommended starter is the *murtabak* (Indian bread stuffed with spiced onion and beef), and if you like hot and spicy food then try the *ikan pangang* (fish stuffed with a chile paste) or the even-hotter *sambal udang* (prawns sautéed in chile-shallot *sambal* sauce). Other popular dishes are the salmon wrapped in banana leaves and the fried rice with prawns and mixed vegetables. Start the feast with a tropical drink and end it with the *sago* tapioca pudding or the *bo bo cha cha* (taro root and sweet potato in sweetened coconut milk). *$$; AE, DC, MC, V; no checks; lunch, dinner every day; full bar; reservations recommended; map:I4*

## Suppenkuche / ★★

### 601 HAYES ST AT LAGUNA ST; 415/252-9289

Smack in the middle of the hip and trendy Hayes Valley is a little slice of Deutschland, a German *wursthaus* whose authenticity runs from the bratwurst to the beers to the volume level. Everything here is large and hearty. Favorites include the potato soup and the potato pancakes to start, then the Wiener schnitzel and the Gebratene Rehmedaillions (venison medallions in red-wine plum sauce). Brunches are very popular and include massive omelets with a plateful of potatoes and roast pork sausages in an egg scramble. But the biggest draw has to be the beer, served in giant-size steins and running the gamut from Hefe (three kinds) to Pils (four varieties) to Bock (two types). It's all served on tap, and there are also a couple of Belgian and English brands just to keep things even. *$; AE, MC, V; no checks; dinner every day, brunch Sun; full bar; reservations recommended; map:L4*

## Sushi Groove / ★★☆
## Sushi Groove South / ★★☆

### 1916 HYDE ST BTWN UNION AND GREEN STS; 415/440-1905
### 1516 FOLSOM ST AT 11TH ST; 415/503-1950

It's hard to decide which looks better here: the restaurant or the clientele. While you might think a place that takes its appearance so seriously (chic, modern, well-lit) could never follow through on substance, the sushi is fresh, well cut, and nicely presented. All the requisite rolls and pieces are on the menu; a few good variations do exist, however, such as the jungle roll (yellowtail tuna and papaya) and the monkey roll (sea urchin with eel and avocado). A nice selection of fine sakes is available, too. Service is friendly, welcoming, and typically as good-looking as the clientele. *$$; AE, CB, DC, MC, V; no checks; dinner every day; full bar; reservations recommended; map:L2, map L5*

## Swan Oyster Depot / ★★

### 1517 POLK ST BTWN CALIFORNIA AND SACRAMENTO STS; 415/673-1101

You won't find white linen tablecloths at this oyster bar—in fact, you won't even find any tables. Since 1912, loyal patrons have balanced themselves on the 19 hard, rickety stools lining the long, narrow marble counter cluttered with bowls of oyster crackers, fresh-cut lemons, napkin holders, Tabasco sauce, and other seasonings. On the opposite side stands a quick-shucking team of some of the most congenial men in town, always ready and eager to serve. Lunch specialties include Boston clam chowder, sizable salads (crab, shrimp, prawn, or a combo), seafood cocktails, cracked Dungeness crab, Maine lobster, and smoked salmon and trout. If you want to take home some fish for supper, take a gander at all the fresh offerings in the display case: salmon, swordfish, delta crawfish, red snapper, trout, shrimp, lingcod, and whatever else the boat brought in that day. Truly, this is a classic San Francisco experience that you shouldn't miss, even if the line's long (it moves fast). *$$; no credit cards; checks OK; lunch Mon–Sat (open 8am–5:30pm); beer and wine; reservations not accepted; map:L3*

## Tadich Grill / ★★

**240 CALIFORNIA ST BTWN BATTERY AND FRONT STS; 415/391-1849**
The Tadich Grill is one of the most venerated and venerable seafood restaurants in California and, along with Sam's Grill & Seafood Restaurant, one of the last "Old San Francisco" restaurants left in the city. It's supposedly been open in one form or another since 1849 and claims to be the very first to have broiled seafood over mesquite charcoal, back in the early 1920s. The original mahogany bar still remains, as do the classic private booths, dim lighting, and crusty old white-jacketed waiters (expect brusque service—that's their job). It's hugely popular with both  tourists and Financial District heavies, and is a refreshing change from all the trendy restaurants that surround it. The best dishes are the ones that forgo the heavy sauces, such as the shrimp or prawn Louis salad, the seafood cioppino and clam chowder, the panfried sand dabs, or the best-selling charcoal-broiled petrale sole with butter sauce. If you're not counting calories, feast on the baked casserole of stuffed turbot with crab and shrimp à la Newburg. Most dishes come with a side of fried potatoes and—but of course—sourdough bread. *$$; MC, V; no checks; lunch, dinner Mon–Sat; full bar; reservations not accepted; map:N2*

## Taqueria Cancun / ★

**2211 MISSION ST AT VALENCIA ST (AND BRANCHES); 415/550-1414**
In spite of itself, this taqueria has a huge, loyal following. It does little to keep people coming back other than offer incredibly flavorful Mexican dishes à la carte and at bargain-basement prices. Its location, on a decidedly unseemly stretch of Mission Street, makes for some unusual characters coming through the doors, but that's part of the Cancun experience, second only to the incredible carne asada burritos and tacos, veggie burritos, and hot, fresh-made salsas (the green salsa is dynamite). The *carnitas* are another reason it's worth putting up with the occasional dining-room argument that can ignite in this place. They also have branches at 1003 Market Street at Sixth Street (415/864-6773) and 2288 Mission Street at 19th Street (415/252-9560). *$; cash only; breakfast, lunch, dinner every day; beer only; reservations not accepted; map:L6*

## Terra Brazilis / ★★

**602 HAYES ST AT LAGUNA ST; 415/241-1900**

At this contemporary restaurant that sits beneath a senior citizens center, chef-owner Alberto Petrolino endeavors to take Brazilian cuisine to tastier, healthier heights. The small place, bound on two sides by huge windows, its walls hung with original work by local artists, has become enormously popular in its relatively short existence. This is mostly due to Petrolino's skill at such dishes as curried shellfish stew with prawns and baby clams, as well as his use of *vatapa* sauce, a Brazilian mainstay made with peanuts and curry spices. The wine list is excellent, with lots of Spanish varietals, and the wait staff is knowledgeable enough to make informed recommendations. There is also a full bar, though it seats only three at a time. *$$; AE, MC, V; no checks; dinner Tues–Sun; full bar; reservations recommended; map:L4*

## Thai House / ★
## Thai House Bar and Cafe / ★

**151 NOE ST AT 15TH ST; 415/863-0374**
**2200 MARKET ST AT SANCHEZ ST; 415/864-5006**

The very popular Thai House restaurant has a loyal following in its Noe Valley neighborhood. The atmosphere is friendly and while the fare is a bit predictable, it's also predictably good: The kitchen regularly turns out tasty spicy shrimp rolls, a savory sirloin served with spinach and peanut sauce, excellent chicken satay, and delicious panfried shrimp. A satellite outlet, the Thai House Bar and Cafe on Market Street in the Castro district, offers the same menu with less consistency but in a more sociable environment. *$; MC, V; no checks; dinner every day (Noe St); lunch, dinner every day (Market St); beer and wine (Noe St); full bar (Market St); reservations not accepted; map:K6, K5*

## Thep Phanom / ★★★

**400 WALLER ST AT FILLMORE ST; 415/431-2526**

Thailand's complex, spicy, cosmopolitan cuisine has always been adaptive, incorporating flavors from India, China, Burma, Malaysia, and, more recently, the West. San Francisco boasts dozens of Thai restaurants; virtually all of them are good, and many (including Khan Toke Thai House and Manora's Thai Cuisine) are excellent. Why, then, has Thep Phanom alone had a permanent line out its front door for the last 14 years even though it takes reservations? At this restaurant, housed in a grand Victorian, a creative touch of California enters the cultural mix, resulting in sophisticated preparations that have a special sparkle. The signature dish, *ped swan*, is a boneless duck in a light honey sauce served on a bed of spinach—and it ranks with the city's greatest entrees. Tart, minty, spicy *yum plamuk* (calamari salad), *larb ped* (minced duck salad), coconut chicken soup, and the velvety basil-spiked seafood curry served on banana leaves (available Wednesday and Thursday only) are superb choices, too. Service is charming and efficient; the tasteful decor, informal atmosphere, eclectic crowd, and discerning wine list are all very San Francisco. *$$; AE, DC, DIS, MC, V; no checks; dinner every day; beer and wine; reservations recommended; www.thaitaste.com/thepphanom;map:K5*

## Thirsty Bear Brewing Company / ★★

**661 HOWARD ST BTWN 2ND AND NEW MONTGOMERY STS; 415/974-0905**
Stupid name, yes, but great house-made microbrews and authentic Spanish tapas have made Thirsty Bear one of SoMa's most popular afterwork hangouts for the late 20- to 30-something crowd of artists, techies, and brokers. The split-level restaurant/brewery is housed in a high-ceilinged brick warehouse that's been given an industrial-chic makeover with little regard to sound dampening (during happy hour it can get really noisy in here). Our preference is to sit at the bar and order from the dinner menu, though we always know what we want well ahead of time: the paella Valenciana, a sizzling combo of chicken, shrimp, sausage, shellfish, and saffron-laden rice served in a cast-iron skillet, and a *tortilla de patatas* appetizer to tide us over. Other recommended dishes emanating from the open kitchen are the *escalivada* (roasted vegetables served at room temperature), the *espinacas à la Catalana* (spinach sautéed with garlic, pine nuts, and raisins), and the fish cheeks. If you're visiting the San Francisco Museum of Modern Art, we highly recommend you walk around the corner and stop in here for a light meal and a tall, cool glass of India Pale Ale. *$$; AE, DC, MC, V; no checks; lunch Mon–Sat, dinner every day; full bar; reservations recommended; map:N3*

## Ti Couz / ★★★

**3108 16TH ST AT VALENCIA ST; 415/252-7373**
Other restaurants offer crepes, but none compare to what this popular Mission District establishment does with the beloved French pancake. Ti Couz—French for "the old house" and pronounced "tee cooz"—serves delectable, Brittany-style sweet and savory crepes in a homey setting that feels very much like an old French inn. Don't be overwhelmed by the menu: Though countless ingredients are listed so you can create your own *crêperie bretonne*, the menu (in French and English) lists several suggested combinations: ham and cheese, mushroom-almond, and more. A ratatouille-and-cheese creation bursts with flavor, and a hearty sausage-filled pancake won't disappoint. But be forewarned: The large buckwheat crepes are *très énormes!* And you must leave room for dessert. The sweet wheat-flour crepes, fluffier than the savory buckwheat versions, are ideal for luscious fillings such as apples, ice cream, and caramel, or fresh berries à la mode. Complete the meal with a choice of several hard ciders served in bowls—the fruity flavors complement this unique and tasty fare like nothing else. You can also choose from a list of French wines or

Celtic beers, as well as French-style coffees and cocktails. Open until midnight Friday through Saturday. *$; MC, V; no checks; lunch, dinner every day; full bar; reservations not accepted; map:L6*

## Timo's / ★★★☆

**842 VALENCIA ST BTWN 19TH AND 20TH STS; 415/647-0558**

Tapas bars are plentiful these days, but despite the growing competition, Timo's remains one of San Francisco's best. The exuberant food matches the vibrancy of the purple-and-orange-painted walls, and the happenin' Valencia Street location draws a varied crowd, from Mission hipsters to Marina-ites. These "little plates" of food go especially well with Timo's popular sangría, or you can choose from a small list of Spanish wines. Start with a sampling of both hot and cold plates and be sure to try Spain's best-known tapa, the *tortilla Española*, a simple dish of layered potatoes and onions. A delicious Catalán-style spinach tapa brimming with pine nuts, raisins, and apricots combines incredible flavors and textures. The mushroom preparations are always enjoyable, especially the hot grilled mushroom plate with a hearty dose of garlic. Other favorites include potato decadence—creamy Yukon Gold potatoes layered with earthy mushrooms—and ahi ceviche with avocado. A flamenco guitarist adds a festive note on Thursday evenings to this already lively hot spot. *$$; AE, MC, V; no checks; dinner every day; full bar; reservations recommended; www.timos.com; map:L6*

## Tokyo Go Go / ★★

**3174 16TH ST BTWN VALENCIA AND GUERRERO STS; 415/864-2288**

This is not your typical sushi joint. Ken Lowe, the owner of Ace Wasabi's in the Marina District, figured the success he's had there could surely be duplicated in the Mission. So he opened Tokyo Go Go and gave it a retro-futuristic Jetsons look, with quirky fixtures and smooth surfaces. His Marina loyalists followed, but they quickly gave way to residents of the area, who now populate this hip, lively spot. Fun is the order of the day here. The sushi is fresh and flavorful and you'll find all the standard selections, but the kitchen likes to cut loose, too, and if you are willing to experiment, you'll find some pleasant surprises. The Go Go Roll places cooked shrimp over a roll of cucumber that wraps a garlic crouton. The Tuscan Roll features salmon, cucumber, sun-dried tomatoes, basil, and capers rolled with rice in a cone of seaweed—hard to imagine, easy to eat. Or try the Flying Kamikaze: spicy tuna and asparagus topped by albacore tuna and ponzu sauce. Premium sakes such as the dee-licious Momokawa are served in martini glasses garnished with cucumber slices. *$; MC, V; no checks; dinner Tues–Sun; full bar; reservations recommended; map:L6*

## Tommaso Ristorante Italiano / ★★☆

**1042 KEARNY ST AT BROADWAY; 415/398-9696**

Because it's sandwiched in between "adult entertainment" arcades just off the main Broadway strip, it's at first surprising to find that Tommaso's comes highly recommended for family dining. But the small, cozy place with wooden booths and no windows regularly has folks of all ages lining up at the door. The restaurant has endeared itself to locals by consistently turning out amazingly delicious traditional-style pizzas, available with any of 19 different toppings and baked in an oak-burning brick oven. While pizzas are the main draw, the hearty Italian classics such as chicken cacciatore and a super-cheesy lasagne should not be overlooked. Order a bottle of chianti for the table and you're in business. Service is quick, efficient, and downright neighborly. A true San Francisco treasure. *$; AE, DC, DIS, MC, V; local checks only; dinner Tues–Sun; full bar; reservations not accepted; map:N2*

## Tommy Toy's / ★★★

**655 MONTGOMERY ST AT COLUMBUS AVE AND WASHINGTON ST; 415/397-4888**

Tommy Toy's is so lavish in every manner that it's almost surreal. It's sort of a cross between a plush men's club, a fancy Chinese restaurant, and a four-star French restaurant. The $1.5 million dining room was fashioned after a 19th-century empress dowager's reading room, complete with dimly lit candelabras, museum-quality artwork, and oodles of opulence. The stellar service is equally impressive, but of course such niceties don't come cheap. Expect to pay about $50 per person for Tommy's signature dinner: a prix-fixe, six-course, French-Chinese fusion feast of minced squab in lettuce leaves, lobster bisque served in a coconut shell and topped with puffed pastry, a whole lobster sautéed with peanuts and mushrooms, Peking duck carved tableside and served with lotus buns and plum sauce, medallions of beef, and a coup de grâce dessert of peach mousse. Dining at Tommy's isn't something one does with regularity, but it's certainly worth a visit if only to experience that rarest of the rare— haute Chinese. *$$$; AE, DC, DIS, JCB, MC, V; no checks; lunch Mon–Fri, dinner every day; full bar; reservations recommended; map:N2*

## Ton Kiang / ★★☆

**5821 GEARY BLVD BTWN 22ND AND 23RD AVES; 415/387-8273**

Ton Kiang has established a solid reputation in San Francisco as one of the best Chinese restaurants in the city, particularly when it comes to dim sum and Hakka cuisine (a mixture of Chinese cuisines, sometimes referred to as "China's soul food," developed by a nomadic Chinese tribe). Ton Kiang's dim sum is phenomenal—fresh, flavorful, and not the least bit greasy (tip: On weekends ask for a table by the kitchen door to get first dibs from the dim sum carts). Other proven dishes on the regular menu are the ethereal steamed dumplings, chicken wonton soup, house special beef and fish-ball soup (better than it sounds), fried spring rolls, steamed salt-baked chicken with a scallion and ginger sauce (a famous though quite salty Hakka dish), and any of the stuffed tofu or clay pot dishes (a.k.a. Hakka casseroles). Seriously, this place is worth the drive and the wait. *$$; AE, DC, DIS, MC, V; no checks; lunch, dinner every day; beer and wine; reservations recommended; map:G4*

## Tú Lan / ★★☆

### 8 6TH ST AT MARKET ST; 415/626-0927

If you're a fan of hole-in-the-wall ethnic dives in seedy locations that serve top-notch food at bargain prices, have we got a gem for you. Located in one of the sketchiest and foulest-smelling parts of the city, Tú Lan is a greasy, grimy little Vietnamese diner that, unless you are hip to the secret, you would neither find nor frequent. Which makes it all the more bewildering that a drawing of Julia Child's unmistakable face graces the cover of the greasy menus, but apparently she's one of Tú Lan's biggest fans. And once you try the light, fresh imperial rolls served on a bed of rice noodles, lettuce, peanuts, and mint, you'll become one too. Other recommended dishes include the lemon beef salad, the fried fish in ginger sauce, and the pork kebabs, though pointing at whatever looks good on the Formica counter works just as well. Note: The faint-of-heart may want to order to go, and definitely do not use the upstairs bathroom (that's a dare, of course). *$; cash only; lunch, dinner Mon–Sat; beer and wine; reservations not accepted; map:M4*

## 2223 Restaurant and Bar / ★★★

### 2223 MARKET ST BTWN SANCHEZ AND NOE STS; 415/431-0692

Also known as the No Name, this popular Castro district spot has been packing in the crowds because it's one of the first upscale restaurants in the area that offers serious food, friendly and professional service, and a terrific bar scene. You'll see only the restaurant's address on the outside of the building, so look for a red exterior and a lively crowd visible through large storefront windows. A long bar flanked by a mural dominates one side of the restaurant. You'll probably end up waiting there for a table, which will give you time to enjoy the great cosmopolitans and martinis. Across the room, the narrow dining area has wood tables, bistro chairs, and cushioned banquettes. The menu is as eclectic as the crowd—mostly American-Mediterranean, with Southwestern and Southeast Asian touches. The romaine salad is a great Caesar variation, with capers, thinly sliced cornichons, and smoky onions. Try one of the pizzas, such as the pancetta, onion confit, Teleme cheese, marjoram, and sun-dried tomato pesto version. For entrees, the kitchen serves generous portions of comfort food: juicy pan-roasted chicken with garlic mashed potatoes, double-cut pork chop served with a side of chayote squash, grilled salmon with lemon-caviar fondue, and sliced lamb sirloin fanned on a ragout of fava beans and fresh artichoke hearts. Indulge in the Louisiana crème brûlée with pecan pralines for dessert. Despite the noise from the bar, 2223 is a terrific neighborhood spot—especially if you can find a nearby parking place. *$$; AE, DC, MC, V; local checks only; dinner every day, brunch Sun; full bar; reservations recommended; www.2223restaurant.com; map:K5*

## Universal Cafe / ★★★

### 2814 19TH ST AT BRYANT ST; 415/821-4608

The Universal Cafe is the kind of place you would kill to have on your block. First off, the industrial-art decor is extremely sleek, suave, and chic and the staff is refreshingly sans attitude. Second, you can actually find parking in this quiet section of the Inner Mission. And third, the food is both fantastic and reasonably priced. Truly, this is one of those out-of-the-way gems that either you discover by accident or someone sends you to. For lunch, try the salmon sandwich on focaccia (outstanding), gourmet thin-crust pizza, or one of the wickedly good salads. Dinner from the daily-changing menu gets more serious: braised duck leg on a bed of creamy polenta; sea bass served with risotto, spinach, and caramelized onions; pot roast with lumpy mashed potatoes and fresh veggies; braised Sonoma rabbit in mustard sauce with caramelized cabbage (yum, now we're hungry). If your dish doesn't come with it, ask for a side of the addictive mashed potatoes. Trust us—if you're anywhere near the Mission or Potrero Hill, seek this place out and join the converted. *$$; AE, DC, MC, V; no checks; breakfast Tues–Fri, lunch, dinner Tues–Sun, brunch Sat–Sun; beer and wine; reservations recommended; map:L6*

## The Waterfront Restaurant & Cafe / ★★

### PIER 7, ALONG THE EMBARCADERO NEAR BROADWAY; 415/391-2696

In a city that has some of the most spectacular vistas in the world, it's surprising how few restaurants there are with grand views of the bay. Let's rephrase that: how few *good* restaurants there are with grand views of the bay. In its previous life the Waterfront was just another lousy tourist restaurant, but after a $3 million-plus makeover in 1997 and a new menu, it's now one of the darlings of the waterfront restaurant scene. On the bottom floor is the nautical-themed cafe, which offers a wide selection of choices (at far lower prices than the fancier restaurant upstairs) for lunch and dinner: excellent salads and pizzas, wood-fired grill items, Maine blue crab cakes, grilled apricot-glazed quail, and house favorites such as falafel-crusted sea bass and sautéed chicken breast with herbed polenta and rosemary pan sauce. For a more romantic dining experience, head upstairs to the high-ceilinged sleek 'n' chic dining room. It offers a more upscale (read: expensive) menu—things like Kasu-marinated filet of beef with taro gnocchi, tatsoi and shiitake relish, and soy consommé; roasted squab with potato and wild rice galette and Bing cherry chutney; and Sonoma lamb carpaccio—but the head chef seems to change weekly, so it's a hit-and-miss dining experience. If ambience isn't crucial, stick with the lower-priced cafe for now, and be sure to arrive before sunset to admire the view. Oh, and don't pass up the free valet parking. *$$$; AE, DC, MC, V; no checks; lunch Mon–Fri (cafe every day), dinner every day; full bar; reservations recommended; map:N2*

## Woodward's Garden / ★★☆

**1700 MISSION ST AT DUBOCE AVE; 415/621-7122**
In what is arguably one of the least desired commercial spaces in the city stands what is certainly one of the Bay Area's better restaurants. Woodward's Garden is tucked under a busy highway overpass on a gritty, windy, noisy corner. But that doesn't deter those who reserve one of the diminutive restaurant's 11 tables at least a couple of weeks in advance for a weekend night (there are four seatings per night). To say Woodward's Garden has an open kitchen is putting it mildly—the kitchen takes up at least half the room and the handful of tables are lined up around it. Not only can you see and smell your food being prepared, but you can feel the heat of the flames! Chef-owners Margie Conard (from Postrio) and Dana Tommasino (from Greens) offer an American/Mediterranean–influenced menu featuring five appetizers and five entrees. The menu changes weekly; a recent visit started with a savory sweet-potato–ginger soup with a dollop of crème fraîche, smoked-trout bruschetta with Romesco sauce and arugula, and perfectly sautéed scallops served with endive, Meyer lemon beurre blanc, and caviar. The entrees were equally delightful: A fork-tender lamb shank braised with fennel and orange was nestled on a bed of saffron risotto with asparagus and Reggiano, and a duck breast was roasted to perfection and paired with grilled polenta, a cherry-onion marmalade, and braised chard. Bravo! *$$$; MC, V; checks OK; dinner Tues–Sun; beer and wine; reservations required; map:L5*

## XYZ / ★★

**181 3RD ST AT HOWARD ST (W HOTEL); 415/817-7836**
The W Hotel was the first ground-up hotel to open in San Francisco in more than a decade. The restaurant inside, cleverly named XYZ, has been wildly popular with visitors and locals alike, all of whom seem to resemble characters from whatever urban-setting sitcom is currently tops in the ratings. The place itself is adequately chic and stylish, and the service is never as austere as you'd expect given the rarefied surroundings. The menu offers light, flavorful dishes with French and Asian accents. Good dinner choices might include the peppered ahi on mushroom potatoes, the sweetbread tortellini in pepper sauce, or the broiled Chilean sea bass. The entree selection is a bit limited, however, so you

may opt to order from among the many excellent soups, salads, and pastas instead. (To be honest, it's more about the scene here than the cuisine.) Tip: If you're staying at the W, order breakfast here—which actually offers the best menu of the three meals. Another tip: If the menu prices have you gasping, sit at the bar and order the fantastic burger and fries combo—that's what we do. *$$; AE, CB, DC, DIS, MC, V; no checks; breakfast, lunch Mon–Fri, dinner Mon–Sat, brunch Sat–Sun; full bar; reservations recommended; map:N3*

## Yank Sing / ★★★

**101 SPEAR ST BTWN MISSION AND HOWARD STS (1 RINCON CENTER); 415/957-9300**
**49 STEVENSON ST BTWN MARKET AND MISSION STS; 415/541-4949**

Yank Sing's fare is as good as any dim sum you'll get in Hong Kong, and the prices (and service) are much better than in nearby Harbor Village Restaurant (see review). Numerous servers wander past your table with carts bearing steamer baskets, bowls, and tureens. If you want some, just nod. Yank Sing serves more than 90 varieties of dim sum, including such standards as pot stickers, spring rolls, plump shrimp dumplings (deelicious!), stuffed crab claws, fried eggplant, and *bao* (steamed buns stuffed with aromatically seasoned minced meat). The barbecued chicken is a house specialty, although some find it too sweet; other favorites are Peking duck (served by the slice), minced squab in lettuce cups, and soft-shell crab. Make reservations or prepare to wait and wait and wait, especially for a weekend brunch. Takeout is available, too, and it costs much less. *$$; AE, DC, MC, V; no checks; lunch every day, brunch Sat–Sun; beer and wine; reservations recommended; www.yanksing.com; map:N2, N3*

## Yuet Lee / ★★

**1300 STOCKTON ST AT BROADWAY; 415/982-6020**

Looks like a dive. Smells like a dive. So must be a dive, right? Well, yes and no. While the ambience scores a solid 1 on the 1 to 10 scale (both inside and out), the seafood dishes can range anywhere from a 5 to a 9. In fact, a few are downright outstanding, such as fresh-roasted pepper and salt squid, crab sautéed in ginger and green onions, pepper and salt prawns in the shell, clams in black-bean sauce, and salt-and-pepper spareribs. As you might have guessed, seafood is the specialty here, served fast and brusque at cheap Formica tables in a dining room that is as ugly—and fishy smelling—as they come in Chinatown (the lime green exterior is quite heinous, too). But it's all part of the Yuet Lee experience, and the food's usually so good that everything else is forgivable. You can't miss it; just look for the glowing corner restaurant one block east of the Broadway tunnel. Tip: Every seasoned party-hound in the city knows that Yuet Lee stays open until 3am. *$–$$; cash only; lunch, dinner Wed–Mon; beer and wine; no reservations; map:M2*

## Zarzuela / ★★★

**2000 HYDE ST AT UNION ST; 415/346-0800**

You can't miss it—nobody passes by the huge yellow awning out front without noticing. You also can't park here: The crowded Hyde Street location means nobody should even try to drive to Zarzuela. But this excellent tapas restaurant atop Russian Hill has been popular from day one. Drenched in soothing colors, this is an elegant, sophisticated spot for well-priced Spanish cuisine such as tender roast pork stuffed with chorizo and Castilian-style oxtail stew. Fresh bread and Spanish olives are whisked to your table as soon as you sit down, and from there the noshing begins. The tapas recipes are not extraordinarily original—grilled prawns, fried squid, poached octopus, *tortilla Española*—but they *are* prepared with fresh ingredients and a liberal use of seasonings that sets them apart from the usual tapas fare. The paella is excellent, arguably the best in town; it's available only for two or more and requires a 30-minute wait—but it's more than worth it. Zarzuela takes its name from one of the menu's dishes, a traditional Catalan seafood stew that has become this restaurant's trademark. *$$; MC, V; no checks; dinner Tues–Sat; full bar; reservations not accepted; www.zarzuela.es.vg; map:M1*

## Zax / ★★★

**2330 TAYLOR ST BTWN COLUMBUS AVE AND FRANCISCO ST; 415/563-6266**

If you're a lover of fresh and stylish food, you'll rejoice over many of the creations at Zax, a sophisticated California-Mediterranean restaurant tucked away in North Beach. Owned by husband-and-wife duo Barbara Mulas and Mark Drazek, who met at the California Culinary Academy, Zax offers a chic but understated interior and a charming blend of casual, often excellent cuisine. The small, seasonal menu changes monthly, but it's always healthy and well balanced, with an emphasis on quality and flavor as opposed to heavy sauces. The house-specialty appetizer is the warm, puffy, and golden-brown twice-baked goat-cheese soufflé—don't miss it. The simple but savory salads range from tomato, feta, and olives with oregano-flecked olive oil to romaine leaves dressed with anchovies, lemon, garlic, and Romano cheese. The half-dozen main courses might include lamb stew with grilled rosemary polenta and roasted tomatoes, sweet roasted Sonoma duck breast with a grilled-fig vinaigrette, and spicy short ribs with horseradish mashed potatoes. *$$$; MC, V; no checks; dinner Tues–Sat; beer and wine; reservations recommended; map:M1*

## Zazie / ★★

**941 COLE ST BTWN PARNASSUS AND CARL STS; 415/564-5332**

Catherine Opoix's cheery French bistro, with its inviting dining room, checkerboard floors, and light and airy ambience, serves tasty (if somewhat inconsistent) fare. Breakfast is served daily until 2:30pm; a reliable favorite is the gingerbread pancakes served with roasted pears and a tangy lemon curd. The egg dishes, though decent, sound better than they taste; they range from eggs valence (fried eggs served atop grilled eggplant and chèvre) to a changing omelet option, accompanied by slightly bland potatoes. Lunch features such simple plats du jour as a grilled tuna sandwich, salade niçoise, or a tomato-fennel soup. Dinner specialties include a Provençal fish soup of mussels and snapper topped with Gruyère cheese; a hearty coq au vin; and pork medallions with honey-braised cabbage and fresh plum sauce. To add to Zazie's European-style charm, opera singers and jazz musicians perform on Sunday evenings. In temperate weather, the patio offers some of the best outdoor dining in the city. *$$; MC, V; no checks; breakfast, lunch, dinner every day, brunch Sat–Sun; beer and wine; reservations not accepted; map:I5*

## Zinzino / ★★

**2355 CHESTNUT ST AT DIVISADERO ST; 415/346-6623**

It's always a huge gamble opening up yet another trendy Italian restaurant in the Marina District, but there's no better recipe for success than exceptional food and reasonable prices, and that's exactly what the staff at Zinzino has accomplished. The long, narrow trattoria is smartly arranged for such a small space (it used to be a laundromat). At the entrance is a small wine bar, followed by the main dining room, the exhibition kitchen, and a cute little heated patio in the back. Though the menu changes seasonally, there are a few dishes that we hope they'll never take off the menu, such as the wood-fired, fennel-seed–laden sausage pizza (the pizzas here *rock*), the shaved-fennel-and-mint salad, and the roasted jumbo prawns wrapped in crisp pancetta and bathed in a tangy balsamic reduction sauce. The wood-fired oven is put to good use, particularly with the roasted half chicken—one of the most tender and flavorful we've ever tasted—and the accompanying goat-cheese salad and yellow potato frisée are the perfect sides. Zinzino also offers weekly rotating specials such as oven-roasted half lobster, roasted shellfish platter, and baby lamb chops. *$$; AE, DC, MC, V; no checks; dinner every day; beer and wine; reservations recommended; www.zinzino. com; map:J1*

## Zodiac Club / ★☆

**718 14TH ST BTWN CHURCH AND SANCHEZ STS; 415/626-7827**

Get lost in space at this trendy restaurant and nightspot in the Upper Market/Duboce Triangle area. Living up to its name, the club has a celestial theme, and many of the folks who frequent it certainly do look like stars. The California-inspired menu changes with each astrological phase, and each sign gets its own dish (on one visit, the Libra special was grilled skewers of scallops and beef). The food is generally good if just a bit fussy and far-reaching (do we really need to see paella and linguine on the same menu?). But the main attraction is the atmosphere, dark and textural, with a nightly crowd of see-and-be-seen types who come for late-night suppers—served until midnight on Friday and Saturday—and to sip such inventive cocktails as the Leo Drop (Absolut Citron, fresh lemon juice, and lemon-zest sugar) and the Scorpion (Meyer's Platinum Rum, brandy, fresh-fruit juices, and a hint of almonds); and if you've yet to sample a trendy Cosmopolitan, the Zodiac makes the best. But beware: Cocktail prices are similarly stratospheric—the Scorpion is $8! *$$; MC, V; no checks; dinner Mon–Sat, cocktails only on Sun; full bar; reservations recommended; map:K5*

## Zuni Cafe / ★★★

**1658 MARKET ST AT FRANKLIN ST; 415/552-2522**

Before it got famous, Zuni was a tiny Southwestern-style lunch spot in a low-class neighborhood. When Chez Panisse alumna Judy Rodgers came on board as chef and co-owner, the cafe became so popular it had to more than double its size. Today, with its copper-topped bar, grand piano, and exposed-brick dining room, it's nearly as quintessential a San Francisco institution as Dungeness crab and sourdough bread (though many loyal patrons miss the days when it was little more than a hole in the wall). It wouldn't be stretching the truth to say that one reason the neighborhood started improving was Zuni's Mediterranean-influenced upscale food, as divinely simple as only the supremely sophisticated can be. Picture a plate of mild house-cured anchovies sprinkled with olives, celery, and Parmesan cheese; polenta with delicate mascarpone; a terrific Caesar salad; a small, perfectly roasted chicken for two on a delicious bed of Tuscan bread salad (perhaps the best chicken you've ever tasted); a grilled rib-eye steak accompanied by sweet white corn seasoned with fresh basil. At lunchtime and after 10pm, you can get some of the best burgers in town here, too, served on focaccia with aioli and house pickles (and be sure to order a side of the great shoestring potatoes). Service is first-rate for regulars and those who resemble them. Tip: Dinner is served until midnight Tuesday through Saturday. *$$$; AE, MC, V; no checks; lunch, dinner Tues–Sun; full bar; reservations recommended; map:L5*

# LODGINGS

# LODGINGS

## Campton Place Hotel / ★★★☆

### 340 STOCKTON ST AT POST ST; 415/781-5555 OR 800/235-4300

Almost as soon as Campton Place reopened after an extensive restoration in 1983, its posh surroundings, stunning objets d'art, superlative service, and elegant accommodations began swaying the patrons of the carriage trade away from traditional San Francisco hotels. The lobby, reminiscent of a gallery with its domed ceiling, miles of marble, crystal chandeliers, and striking Asian art, alone is worth the visit. The 110 guest rooms are very comfortable, and the custom-built chairs and handsome desks lend a pervasive air of luxury. The limestone bathrooms are equipped with telephones, bathrobes, hair dryers, and French-milled soaps. For the best views ask for one of the larger deluxe corner rooms on the upper floors. The view from Room 1501, which overlooks Union Square, is particularly stunning. For help with your laundry, dry cleaning, a shoe shine, or even baby-sitting, just pick up the phone and you'll be accommodated, tout de suite. The concierge will make any and all of your arrangements (a reservation for the hotel's limo, perhaps?), and 24-hour room service will deliver whatever you're craving from the menu at the well-regarded Campton Place restaurant, one of the city's prettiest—and priciest—dining establishments (see review in the Restaurants chapter). *$$$–$$$$; AE, DC, MC, V; checks OK; reserve@campton.com; www.camptonplace.com; map:M3*

## The Clift / ★★★☆

### 495 GEARY ST AT TAYLOR ST; 415/775-4700 OR 800/652-5438

San Francisco's opulent turn-of-the-19th-century hotel has been given a decidedly 21st-century makeover by celebrity hotelier Ian Schrager, the man behind L.A.'s Mondrian, Miami's Delano, and NYC's Royalton and Paramount. What it all means is that this isn't your grandparents' favorite hotel anymore; rather, it is now the hippest, most trendsetting hotel in the city, and will probably remain so for the next decade. With the help of designer Philippe Starck, Schrager has transformed this stately old gal into functional modern art. Behold the lobby: hand-painted Italian plaster walls, Italian limestone floors, an 18-foot bronze fireplace mantel by French sculptor Gerard Garouste, a concierge desk by renowned 20th-century French designer Jean Nouvel, and even a bronze and marble coffee table by Salvador Dalí. The 375 guest rooms are equally gilded: massive sleigh beds made from English sycamore on a polished chrome base, 400-thread-count Italian percale bedding, oversized bathrooms with a dressing area and vanity table, custom-made cabinetry housing state-of-the-art entertainment centers, custom night tables made from vivid orange Plexiglas, and floor-to-ceiling mirrors. But wait, there's more: The stodgy old Redwood Room cocktail lounge has been transformed into a monochromatic masterpiece where the city's dig-me crowd watches flat-screen TVs playing digital works by avant-garde digital artists, and the same lavish theme is carried over to the hotel's new Asian-Cuban fusion restaurant, Asia de Cuba. Other additions include a 24-hour business center with computer workstations, 24-hour concierge service, a 24-hour gymnasium with private trainers and fitness classes, and all the requisite big-hotel services. You'll appreciate the location as well—in the Theater District, a mere 2 blocks from Union Square. *$$$$; AE, DC, MC, V; checks OK; www.clifthotel.com; map:M3*

## Commodore Hotel / ★★
**825 SUTTER ST AT JONES ST; 415/923-6800 OR 800/338-6848**
The 110-room Commodore Hotel is a surprisingly fun and affordable lodging. The management actually helps guests explore the city by offering a free staff-created tour book highlighting San Francisco's top insider attractions; if after reading it you're still baffled about what to do next in this city of plenty, spin the gimmicky but fun Wheel of Fortune located in the hotel's sexy lobby and let it choose an only-in-San-Francisco activity for you. The hotel's lower Sutter Street location means that all the hot tourist spots—Chinatown, Union Square, the Financial District—are within walking distance. And after a day of exploring you can cool your tired dogs here at the wickedly hip Red Room, a dazzling bar

and cocktail lounge that reflects no other spectrum of light but ruby red. Also adjoining the lobby is an art deco–style diner serving inexpensive buckwheat griddle cakes, big burgers, tofu sandwiches, and similar fare. If you're on a tight budget, stick with the plain but pleasant rooms on the first two floors; otherwise, break out an extra Jackson and live it up near the top, where the interiors echo the neo-deco theme. All guest rooms feature a large walk-in closet, a tub and shower, coffeemaker, iron/ironing board, hair dryer, cable TV, and a phone with a data port. There's also access to a full-service health club, room service via Waiters on Wheels (a company that delivers from numerous restaurants in the city), and nearby parking for an extra fee. *$$–$$$; AE, DC, MC, V; no checks; www.thecommodorehotel.com; map:M3*

## Golden Gate Hotel / ★★

**775 BUSH ST BTWN POWELL AND MASON STS; 415/392-3702 OR 800/835-1118**

The Union Square area has a slew of small, reasonably priced European-style hotels housed in turn-of-the-century buildings, and the Golden Gate Hotel is one of the best. It's a family-run affair, owned by John and Renate Kenaston and managed by their daughter, and these kind folks will bend over backward to make sure you have an enjoyable stay. The guest rooms are individually decorated with antique and wicker furnishings, quilted bedspreads, and sweet-smelling fresh flowers; all have phones and TVs as well. If you like a good soak, request a room with a claw-footed tub. A complimentary afternoon tea is served daily from 4pm to 7pm, a good time to chat with the Kenastons. The location is great—2 blocks from Union Square and Nob Hill, and a stone's throw from the cable car stop for Fisherman's Wharf and Chinatown. *$–$$; AE, CB, DC, MC, V; no checks; www.goldengatehotel.com; map:M3*

## Grand Hyatt San Francisco on Union Square / ★★★

**345 STOCKTON ST BTWN POST AND SUTTER STS; 415/398-1234 OR 800/233-1234**

Union Square exudes big-city excitement, and right in the thick of it is the Grand Hyatt, the alpha mother of San Francisco's three Hyatt hotels. She's a big one, too: 685 rooms within 36 floors of steel, marble, and glass, and surrounded by some of the best shopping and restaurants on terra firma. Waltz past the doorman into the gilded lobby with its museum-quality Asian objets d'art and take the speedy elevator to your high-rise room with its stunning view of the city. OK, so decor-wise it's not the Ritz-Carlton (though it's just as expensive), but the guest rooms are pleasantly decorated and spacious and come with such luxury amenities as TVs in the bathroom, telephones with computer hookups, and access to the hotel's extensive health club. For a reasonable fee you can upgrade to the Regency rooms, which are slightly larger and include continental breakfast and evening hors d'oeuvres, or the Business Plan rooms, which come with a private fax machine and 24-hour access to a host of business services. The 36th-floor Grandviews Restaurant (appropriately named) serves breakfast, lunch, and dinner every day and features live jazz most evenings. *$$$–$$$$; AE, DC, DIS, JCB, MC, V; checks OK; www.sanfrancisco.grand.hyatt.com; map:N3*

### Hotel Diva / ★★★

**440 GEARY ST BTWN MASON AND TAYLOR STS; 415/885-0200 OR 800/553-1900**

Ever since it opened in 1985, Hotel Diva has been the prima donna of San Francisco's modern hotels, winning Best Hotel Design from *Interiors* magazine for its suave, ultramodern design. The hotel's facade is still a veritable work of art, a fashionable fusion of cement, steel, and glass that radiates the aura of a 1920s posh ocean liner. But the high style doesn't stop here: Even the 115 guest rooms are works of art, decorated with cobalt blue carpets, sculptured steel furnishings and fireplaces, and haute-design metal headboards fashioned after ocean waves. Standard luxury amenities in each room include invigorating bath products, a remote-control television with interactive multimedia and VCR, designer bathrobes, CD player, two telephones with extra-long cords, global Internet data ports, and voice mail. Guest services include a complimentary breakfast of fresh fruit, breads, yogurt, coffee, and orange juice delivered to your boudoir, as well as room service, a concierge, a 24-hour Cardio Workout Room, four Internet-access guest lounges, and a business center offering free use of computers, software, and a laser printer. Best of all, the Diva is in a prime location, just around the corner from Union Square. Insider tip: Reserve one of the rooms ending in "09," which have extra-large bathrooms with vanity mirrors and makeup tables, and be sure to ask the concierge for Diva's "SF Hot Spots" checklist. *$$$; AE, DC, DIS, MC, V; checks OK; www.hoteldiva.com; map:M3*

### Hotel Monaco / ★★★☆

**501 GEARY ST AT TAYLOR ST; 415/292-0100 OR 800/214-4220**

"Wow!" is a common exclamation among first-time guests at Hotel Monaco, one of the hottest hotels in a city brimming with top-notch accommodations. After a $24 million renovation, Monaco opened in June 1995 and has received nothing but kudos for its sumptuous, stunning decor. Expect a melding of modern European fashion with flourishes of the American Beaux Arts era—the trademark of award-winning designer Cheryl Rowley, who envisioned the 201-room hotel as a "great ship traveling to the farthest reaches of the world, collecting exotic, precious treasures and antiquities." Hence the guest rooms replete with canopy beds, Chinese-inspired armoires, bamboo writing desks, old-fashioned decorative luggage, and a profusion of bold stripes and vibrant colors. The entire hotel is truly a feast for the eyes, particularly the Grand Café with its 30-foot ceilings, cascading chandeliers, plethora of stately columns, and many art nouveau frills—all vestiges of its former incarnation as the hotel's grand ballroom. A chic see-and-be-seen crowd typically fills the impressive dining room, noshing on trendy California-French cuisine (see review in the Restaurants chapter). And of course there are the requisite hotel toys (health club, steam room, whirlpool spa, sauna), services (massages, manicures, valet parking, business and room service), and complimentary perks (newspaper delivery, morning coffee, afternoon tea and cookies, evening wine reception). Hotel Monaco is conveniently located in the heart of San Francisco's Theater District, a mere 2 blocks from Union Square and the cable cars. *$$$–$$$$; AE, DC, DIS, MC, V; no checks; map:M3*

## Hotel Rex / ★★★

**562 SUTTER ST BTWN POWELL AND MASON STS; 415/433-4434 OR 800/433-4434**

The Joie de Vivre hotel company has created another winner with the 94-room Hotel Rex, the latest addition to its cadre of fashionable yet affordable accommodations. The hotel's sophisticated and sensuous lobby lounge is cleverly modeled after a 1920s library, meant to create a stylish sanctuary for San Francisco's arts and literary community (hence the adjoining antiquarian bookstore). To keep costs—and rates—down, many imported furnishings of the site's former Orchard Hotel have been retained, which adds a bit of authenticity to the European boutique hotel–style ambience. All of the spacious (for a downtown hotel) guest rooms feature CD players, two-line telephones with voice mail and data port, and an electronic key-card system. The rooms in the back not only are quieter but also overlook a tranquil, shaded courtyard. Perks include room service, same-day laundry/dry cleaning, complimentary newspaper, an evening wine hour, concierge service, and morning car service to the Financial District. The hotel is in a key location as well, within walking distance of Union Square and surrounded by first-rate galleries, theaters, and restaurants. *$$$; AE, DC, MC, V; no checks; map:M3*

## Hotel Triton / ★★★

**342 GRANT AVE AT BUSH ST; 415/394-0500 OR 800/433-6611**

The Hotel Triton has been described as modern, whimsical, sophisticated, chic, vogue, neo-baroque, ultrahip, and retro-futuristic—but words just don't do justice to this unique hostelry-cum-art-gallery that you'll simply have to see to appreciate. The entire hotel, from the bellhop's inverted pyramid–shaped podium to the iridescent throw pillows on the beds and the ashtrays ringed with faux pearls, is the original work of four imaginative (some might say wacky) San Francisco artisans. For a preview of what's behind the bedroom doors, peek into the lobby, where you'll see curvaceous chairs shimmering in gold silk taffeta, an imposing duo of floor-to-ceiling pillars sheathed in teal, purple, and gold leaf, and a pastel mural portraying mythic images of sea life, triton shells, and human figures—all that's missing are Dorothy, Toto, and the ruby slippers. Add to this visual extravaganza the amenities you'd find in any luxury hotel, including a concierge, valet parking (essential in this part of town), room service, complimentary wine and coffee, business and limousine services, and even a fitness center. The 140 rooms and designer suites (designed by such celebs as Carlos Santana, Graham Nash, and the late Jerry Garcia) continue the modern wonderland theme: Walls are splashed with giant, hand-painted yellow and blue diamonds, king-size beds feature navy-and-khaki-striped camelback headboards, and armoires that hide remote-control TVs are topped with golden crowns. The tree-hugger in all of us can embrace the EcoFloor, the Triton's environmentally conscious seventh floor, where almost everything is made from recycled, biodegradable, or organically grown materials, and the air and water are passed through fancy filtration systems. Heck, the Triton is so utterly hip, even the elevator swings to Thelonious Monk. *$$$; AE, DC, DIS, MC, V; checks OK; www.hotel-tritonsf.com; map:N3*

## Pan Pacific / ★★★⯪

### 500 POST ST AT MASON ST; 415/771-8600 OR 800/533-6465

While most other Union Square hotels are bending to the winds of fashion, the Pan Pacific remains a cornerstone of class, style, and awe-inspiring architecture. Even if you're not staying here, it's worth a few minutes of your time to take a ride up the glass elevator to marvel at the sky-rise's 18-story atrium-style interior, a marvel of engineering and architectural art. The lobby is located on the third floor, as is the cozy piano lounge and highly recommended Pacific restaurant—note the rather risqué marble fountain with the four nude dancing figures (see review in the Restaurants chapter). The 329 spacious, immaculate guest rooms seem rather ordinary at first, but it doesn't take long to appreciate the quality of the fabrics and furnishings and the soothing shades of sage and brown. All the usual first-class offerings are here, including big marble-laden bathrooms with mini-TVs, three phones with voice mail, plush bathrobes, in-room safes, and fax machines. Of course, luxury hotel services are also available, including baby-sitting, a health club, a business center, secretarial services, complimentary Rolls-Royce transportation in the city, newspaper delivery, and in-room massage. The Pan Pacific may not be fashionable, but it's still one of our favorites. *$$$$; AE, DC, DIS, JCB, MC, V; no checks; www.panpacific.com; map:M3*

## Petite Auberge / ★★

### 863 BUSH ST BTWN TAYLOR AND MASON STS; 415/928-6000

Located a few blocks from Union Square, the Petite Auberge is a romanticized version of a French country inn with terra-cotta tile floors, Pierre

Deux fabrics, oak furniture, lace curtains, and dried floral wreaths adorning the walls. You'll also see lots of teddy bears on parade, vintage children's toys on shelves and mantels, and a carousel horse cantering in the lobby—not everyone's taste, for sure. The 26 rooms are small but sweet, with inviting window seats; most have fireplaces. (Rooms on the upper floors toward the back tend to be the quietest.) Honeymooners should splurge on the Petite Suite, which has its own private entrance, deck, and spa tub. Guests are supplied with plush terry-cloth robes; nightly turndown service includes the proverbial chocolate on the pillow, and you'll wake up with the morning paper. A generous buffet breakfast is served downstairs in a quaint breakfast room with French doors that open onto a small garden. In the afternoon you may sip tea or wine and snack on hors d'oeuvres in a lounge where a horde of teddy bears on gingham-checked couches face off with a row of rabbits in front of the fireplace. Guests who need to work may use the business services at the White Swan Inn (owned by the same people), just two doors away. *$$$; AE, DC, MC, V; checks OK; map:M3*

## The Prescott Hotel / ★★★

**545 POST ST BTWN MASON AND TAYLOR STS; 415/563-0303 OR 800/283-7322**

Opened in 1989 by the late San Francisco hotel magnate Bill Kimpton, the Prescott has put pressure on Union Square's neighboring luxury hotels by offering first-rate accommodations at a fairly reasonable price. This, combined with dining privileges at one of the city's most popular restaurants (the adjoining Postrio; see review in the Restaurants chapter), superlative service from an intelligent, youthful staff, and a prime location in the heart of San Francisco, places the Prescott at the top of the Union Square hotel list. The rooms, decorated with custom-made cherry-wood furnishings, black-granite–topped nightstands and dressers, and silk wallpaper, have rich color schemes of hunter green, deep purple, cerise, taupe, and gold. The Prescott offers 166 rooms, including numerous suites and a wildly posh penthouse complete with a grand piano, a rooftop Jacuzzi, a formal dining room, and twin fireplaces. For a few additional "fun tickets" you can gain "Club Concierge Level" status, which grants you access to a plush lounge (complete with a complimentary premium bar), an hors d'oeuvres reception, and a continental breakfast, as well as a host of other privileges—not a bad investment for 30 bones. Standard perks include limo service to the Financial District, overnight shoe shine, valet parking, laundry service, a daily newspaper delivered to your room, and access to the adjacent and newly renovated fitness facility. *$$$; AE, DC, DIS, MC, V; checks OK; map:M3*

## Savoy Hotel / ★★

**580 GEARY ST BTWN TAYLOR AND JONES STS; 415/441-2700 OR 800/227-4223**

Originally built in 1913 for the Panama-Pacific International Exposition, this seven-story hotel is a posh French Country–style inn with a gorgeous facade of richly veined black marble, beveled glass, mahogany, and polished brass. It's ideally located in the center of the Theater District, just 2½ blocks from Union Square. The 83 guest rooms and suites are small but beautifully appointed, with reams of *toile de Jouy* fabrics, heavy French cotton bedspreads, imported Provençal furnishings, plump feather beds, goose-down pillows, two-line telephones with modem jacks, and minibars. A few of the suites come with Jacuzzi tubs. The most tranquil rooms are on the northeast corner (farthest from the traffic noise) facing a rear courtyard. Guests are nurtured with a continental breakfast and afternoon tea and sherry; a full breakfast is also available. Additional amenities include an overnight shoe shine and room service from the hotel's popular Brasserie Savoy (see review in the Restaurants chapter). This restaurant is a replica of an authentic French brasserie, right down to the zinc bar, black-and-white marble floors, comfy banquettes, woven-leather chairs, and staff clad in long, starched white aprons. Its air of casual sophistication, reasonable prices, and generally very good food—foie gras, filet mignon with truffle sauce, crispy sweetbreads, duck confit—make it a reliable bet, especially for a meal before show time (ask about the well-priced three-course dinner special offered from 5pm to 8pm daily). *$$; AE, DC, DIS, MC, V; no checks; www.thesavoyhotel.com; map:M3*

## Sir Francis Drake Hotel / ★★★

**450 POWELL ST AT SUTTER ST; 415/392-7755 OR 800/227-5480**

While nowhere near as resplendent as the nearby Westin St. Francis, the 21-story Sir Francis Drake gives us ordinary folks a reasonably priced opportunity to stay in one of San Francisco's grande dames. A $5 million renovation in 1999 spruced up the 417 rooms a bit, but there's still a little wear around the edges. No matter—it's listening to the sounds of Union Square wafting through your window that makes staying here an enjoyable experience. Then there's Tom Sweeny, the legendary and ever-jovial Beefeater doorman who has graced more snapshots than any other San Franciscan; the top-floor Harry Denton's Starlight Room, one of the most fun and fashionable cocktail-dance lounges in the city; Scala's Bistro on the lower level, an upscale yet affordable restaurant we guarantee you'll enjoy (see review in the Restaurants chapter); and all the requisite big-hotel services such as room service, newspaper delivery, business services, baby-sitting, in-room massage, and laundry. So considering that you can get a standard room here for about half the price of rooms at the St. Francis—and with far better eating, drinking, and dancing—the Drake

## TOM SWEENY

That weirdly dressed guy standing in front of the Sir Francis Drake Hotel at Union Square is Tom Sweeny, who for the past 20 years has been the hotel's head doorman and San Francisco's only living historical monument (literally). The traditional beefeaters costume he's wearing can be yours for a mere $1,400, but with it comes a heavy responsibility— posing for an average 200 photos per day and pressing flesh with every president since Gerald Ford.

is definitely worth looking into. *$$$–$$$$; AE, DC, DIS, MC, V; no checks; www.sirfrancisdrake.com; map:M3*

### Westin St. Francis / ★★★☆

**335 POWELL ST BTWN GEARY AND POSTS STS; 415/397-7000 OR 800/WESTIN-1**

San Francisco's first world-class hotel still attracts a legion of admirers; most of them can't afford the steep room rates but are content with lounging in the lobby just to soak up the heady, majestic aura of this historic hotel. The "who's who" of the world have all checked in at one time or another, including Queen Elizabeth II, Mother Teresa, Emperor Hirohito, the Shah of Iran, King Juan Carlos of Spain, and all the U.S. presidents since Taft. Just strolling through the vast, ornate lobby with its century-old hand-carved redwood paneling is a treat in itself. To keep up with the times, the adjacent 32-story Tower was added in 1972, which  doubled the capacity (1,194 rooms total) and provided the requisite banquet and conference centers. The older rooms of the main building vary in size, but have more old-world charm than the newer rooms. The newly renovated Tower rooms, however, have better views of the city from the 18th floor and above. In 1999 the Westin dumped a staggering $60 million into renovations, replacing the furniture, carpeting, and bedding in every guest room, as well as enhancing the lobby and restoring the facade. A $2 million fitness center has been added too. And if there's one thing you must do while visiting San Francisco, it's high tea (3pm to 5pm) at the hotel's Compass Rose cafe and lounge, one of San Francisco's most enduring and pleasurable traditions. *$$$$; AE, DC, DIS, JCB, MC, V; checks OK; map:M3*

### White Swan Inn / ★★

**845 BUSH ST BTWN TAYLOR AND MASON STS; 415/775-1755 OR 800/999-9570**

Perhaps the only hotel in San Francisco more adorable than the White Swan is its nearby sister inn, Petite Auberge. The theme here also harks back to a cozy English-garden bed-and-breakfast, embellished with teddy bears piled on steps, shelves, and couches, as well as a colorful carousel horse in the small lobby. The 1903 building with curved bay windows has 26 rooms with fireplaces and private bathrooms, and each chamber is charmingly decorated with elegant fabrics, comfy armchairs, antiques, and floral-print wallpaper. Some rooms have inviting bay windows where you can sit and read or gaze out at the garden, and each has a fireplace, refrigerator, TV, phone, and wet bar. For peace and quiet, ask for a room in the back overlooking the sunny, tree-lined courtyard. If you have business matters to tend to, data ports, a fax machine, and a conference room with audio/video machines are available. Guests are treated to a big breakfast, morning newspaper, afternoon tea, and home-baked cookies. The cozy library, often warmed by a roaring fire, is an ideal spot to curl up and read a novel in the company of—surprise!—more teddy bears. *$$$; AE, DC, MC, V; checks OK; map:M3*

# Financial District

## Mandarin Oriental / ★★★★

**222 SANSOME ST BTWN PINE AND CALIFORNIA STS; 415/276-9888 OR 800/622-0404**

The rooms at the Mandarin Oriental—currently the *only* Mobil Five Star–rated hotel in the city—offer some of the most remarkable views in the city. Because it's perched high in the sky (on the top 11 floors of the 48-story 345 California Center Building, San Francisco's third-tallest skyscraper), not only are you guaranteed a bird's-eye view of the city, but you'll be gazing at the entire Bay Area, including the Golden Gate Bridge, Alcatraz, and Coit Tower. The 158 guest rooms are comfortable and deceptively austere. Well hidden among the simple blond-wood furniture and fine Asian artwork are all the latest deluxe amenities: three two-line speakerphones with fax hookups, cordless phones, Internet access, remote-control televisions with access to video and DVD, fully stocked minibars, binoculars, and CD players, as well as jumbo marble bathrooms with stall showers and extra-deep soaking tubs (you can even admire the city's skyline from the hotel's signature bathrooms, which feature floor-to-ceiling windows next to the tub). Once settled in your room, you'll be treated to complimentary jasmine tea service and your choice of either Thai silk or terry-cloth slippers. Contrary to the policy of many other hotels, the room rates at the Mandarin don't vary according to scenery, so request one of the corner rooms (numbers ending with 6 or 11) or the Signature rooms (04 or 14) for the best views. Additional perks include access to numerous business services, valet parking, a continental breakfast and afternoon tea served in the lounge, complimentary shoe shines, concierge, 24-hour room service, and a state-of-the-art fitness center. The hotel's award-winning restaurant, Silks, may be the Maytag repairman of luxury restaurants: It's all gussied up and eager to serve, but a tad lonely and underappreciated. Chances are you won't be disappointed if you choose to dine here, but do bring plenty of money. *$$$–$$$$; AE, DC, DIS, MC, V; checks OK; reserve-mosfo@mohg. com; www.mandarinoriental.com; map:N2*

## The Palace Hotel / ★★★

**2 NEW MONTGOMERY ST AT MARKET ST; 415/512-1111 OR 800/325-3535 (RESERVATIONS ONLY)**
Reminiscent of more romantic times, this opulent hotel built in 1875 has housed such luminaries as Thomas Edison, D. H. Lawrence, Amelia Earhart, and Winston Churchill, as well as 10 American presidents and numerous aristocrats and royalty from around the world. Hoping to attract a similarly high-class clientele in the future, the management closed the Palace in 1989 for 27 months and poured $170 million into restoring it to its original splendor. And splendid it is. The downstairs decor is truly breathtaking, from the multiple sparkling Austrian-crystal chandeliers, the double row of white Italian marble Ionic columns, and the 80,000-pane stained-glass dome of the Garden Court, to the three grand ballrooms and early-19th-century French tapestry gracing the walls. Unfortunately, all this impressive glitz comes to a screeching halt when you open the door to one of the 551 guest rooms. Although comfortable and attractive, the rooms are more akin to gussied-up generic hotel rooms than to any palace chamber. However, this place does offer all the perks you'd look for in a luxury hotel, including a concierge, 24-hour room service, valet parking, and an elaborate business center, plus a new, palm-embellished health club with an exercise room, coed sauna, whirlpool, and stunning white-tiled lap pool capped by a dome of clear glass. Restaurants include the Garden Court, famous for its elaborate breakfast buffet and elegant afternoon tea (see review in the Restaurants chapter); Kyo-ya, a rather austere Japanese dining room serving the best (and most expensive) sushi and sashimi in town; and the Pied Piper Bar, which is dominated by a stunning, $2.5 million, 1909 Maxfield Parrish painting of the Pied Piper of Hameln leading a band of 27 children. Even if you don't have the resources to recline or dine here, this place, like most palaces, is worth a self-guided tour. *$$$$; AE, DC, DIS, MC, V; checks OK; www.sfpalace.com; map:N3*

## Park Hyatt San Francisco / ★★★★

**333 BATTERY ST AT CLAY ST; 415/392-1234 OR 800/HYATT-CA**
It may not look it from the outside, but this is one of San Francisco's best first-class business hotels. Located in the heart of San Francisco's Financial District, the 26-story Park Hyatt (which is about half the size of Hyatt's typical megahotels) has a rather ordinary exterior, but the interior is all class: Australian lacewood paneling, handmade custom carpets

from China, polished Italian granite, and opalescent Spanish alabaster chandeliers adorn the gilded lobby. The 360 rooms are more understated but equally impressive. Each comes loaded with Italian wood furnishings, wondrously comfortable beds, large bathrooms, and extraordinary views of the city. If it's on the company's tab, request one of the corner suites on the upper floors, which also come with outdoor balconies or a Jacuzzi tub—a tough choice. Complimentary exercise cycles and rowing machines can be delivered to your room, or you can use the on-site health center. Other pluses include complimentary service via the house Mercedes-Benz to anywhere within the downtown area, and every business service you could possibly need. The hotel's restaurant, the Park Grill, serves California-Continental cuisine in an elegant setting; more casual alfresco dining is available on the Outdoor Terrace. Be sure to check out the sexy sake bar as well. *$$$$; AE, DC, JCB, MC, V; checks OK; www.sfpalace.com; map:N2*

# SoMa (South of Market Street)

## Harbor Court Hotel / ★★★

165 STEUART ST BTWN MISSION AND HOWARD STS; 415/882-1300 OR 800/346-0555

On the southwest edge of the Financial District, this low-key, high-style hotel caters mainly to business travelers, but will equally impress the weekend vacationer. It's larger and less expensive than the adjacent Hotel Griffon (see below), and it was once a YMCA, but don't let that dissuade you: The high-quality accommodations, gorgeous views of the bay, and complimentary use of the adjoining fitness club—complete with indoor Olympic-size swimming pool—add up to one sweet deal. Each of the 131 guest rooms is nicely equipped with soundproof windows, half-canopy beds, large armoires, and writing desks. Amenities include limited room service to secretarial services, laundry and dry cleaning, evening wine reception, newspaper delivery, valet service, and car service to the Financial District. When the sun drops, slip on down to the bar at Boulevard and mingle with the swinging yuppie singles (see review in the Restaurants chapter). *$$$–$$$$; AE, DC, MC, V; no checks; www.harbor courthotel.com; map:O2*

## Hotel Griffon / ★★★

155 STEUART ST BTWN MISSION AND HOWARD STS; 415/495-2100 OR 800/321-2201

This is one of our favorite small luxury hotels, a 62-room sleeper that does a brisk repeat-customer business. It's in an ideal location, on the south end of the Embarcadero at the foot of San Francisco's historic waterfront. The guest rooms are beautifully decorated with whitewashed

## INTERNET CAFES

Postcards are out, e-mails are in. Here's where you need to go to tell everyone what a great time you're having in San Francisco. The following Internet-enabled cafes offer access to the web so you can check your e-mail for free at websites such as www.mail2web.com (simply plug in your e-mail address and password): **Brainwash** (1122 Folsom St btwn 7th and 8th Sts; 415/861-3663); **Cafe.com** (970 Market St btwn Mason and 6th Sts; 415/922-5322); **Chat Cafe** (498 Sanchez St at 18th St; 415/626-4700); and **The Crepe House** (1755 Polk St at Washington St; 415/441-2421). Rates range from $1.25 per 10 minutes to $10 an hour, and some cafes (such as Chat Cafe) offer free access with food purchase. Don't forget to pack a list of your friends' e-mail addresses.

brick walls, contemporary cherry-wood furnishings, marble vanities, high ceilings, window seats, and art deco–style lamps. You have to pay extra for the beautiful Bay Bridge view, but it's definitely worth it (believe it or not, it used to be a view of a freeway overpass). And for a small hotel, the Griffon offers a lot of big-hotel amenities, including room service, secretarial services, concierge, in-room massage, free access to a nearby health center, and complimentary Town Car service to the Financial District. The adjacent restaurant, Red Herring (see review in the Restaurants chapter), is worth your money as well. *$$$–$$$$; AE, DC, DIS, MC, V; no checks; www.hotelgriffon.com; map:O2*

## San Francisco Marriott / ★★☆

### 55 4TH ST BTWN MARKET AND MISSION STS; 415/896-1600 OR 800/228-9290

It's your call: either an architectural masterpiece or the world's biggest parking meter. Opinions sway both ways about the San Francisco Marriott, one of the largest buildings in the city and a definite eye-catcher with its numerous fantails and thousands of glimmering windows. The massive hotel, completed in 1989, does a brisk convention business (the Moscone Convention Center is 2 blocks away), but hundreds of visitors pass through daily simply to gape at the panoramic view of the city and bay from the View Lounge on the 39th floor (best seen when the fog rolls in from below). For a corporate citadel, its 1,500 rooms are surprisingly attractive and cozy, with extra-large bathrooms, big comfy beds, and—of course—extraordinary views (ask for a room overlooking Yerba Buena Gardens). Within the hotel are an indoor pool, spa, and health club (complimentary use, of course), as well as a Japanese teppanyaki restaurant and sushi bar (Kinoko), the Garden Terrace restaurant, and two cocktail lounges on the top floor where live entertainment plays nightly. *$$$–$$$$; AE, DC, JCB, MC, V; checks OK; www.marriotthotels.com/sfodt/; map:N3*

## W Hotel / ★★★

**181 3RD ST BTWN MISSION AND HOWARD STS; 415/777-5300 OR 877/W-HOTELS**

Hip hotels are all the rage now, and the Starwood Hotels & Resorts corporation has capitalized on the craze with a San Francisco version of the popular W Hotel in New York. Art, technology, service, and sex appeal are all applied in force from the moment you walk into the lobby. In fact, you don't even know you're in a 31-story hotel at first, because the first person to greet you is the bartender (brilliant). To your right is a gaggle of hip, young, beautiful people lounging in the ever-so-chic lobby, and to the left is XYZ, the latest SoMa restaurant hot spot (see review in the Restaurants chapter). The room decor mimics the overall theme—bold colors, soft fabrics, sensual curves—almost enough to make you not notice how small they are. No matter: Dive onto the thick, luscious goose-down comforter and you won't ever want to leave. High-tech toys include a 27-inch TV with Internet service, CD player, and modem jacks for your laptop. The location is fantastic as well, smack-dab in the smoking-hot SoMa district and literally sharing real estate with the beautiful San Francisco Museum of Modern Art and Yerba Buena Gardens. The verdict? If you want to play with San Francisco's in crowd, W is the place to be (at least for now). *$$$$; AE, DC, JCB, MC, V; checks OK; www.whotelscom; map:N3*

# Nob Hill

## Fairmont Hotel & Tower / ★★★☆

**950 MASON ST AT CALIFORNIA ST; 415/772-5000 OR 800/527-4727**

The Fairmont is another one of San Francisco's grand old hotels that are part hotel, part tourist attraction. Few hotels in the world have such a fabulous entrance: massive Corinthian columns of solid marble, vaulted ceilings, velvet smoking chairs, enormous gilded mirrors, and a colossal wraparound staircase. Heck, they even have a harpist posted near the entrance. All that's lacking is your top hat and coattails. And thanks to a recent $85 million renovation, the impressive decor applies to the guest  rooms as well, all of which are tastefully decorated with shiny new furnishings and oodles of luxury: goose-down pillows, large walk-in closets, multiline phones with private voice mail, and electric shoe buffers. Hefty room rates help pay for the 24-hour concierge and room service, complimentary morning limousine to the Financial District, free shoe shine, business center, and baby-sitting services. Within the hotel there's a beauty salon, barbershop, shopping arcade, and even a pharmacy (yes, this place is big). There are several restaurants and bars as well, including the famous Polynesian-style Tonga Room bar and restaurant, fine dining at Masons, and the top-floor Crown Room restaurant and bar, which has a spectacular panoramic view of the city. *$$$$; AE, CB, DC, DIS, MC, V; checks OK; www.fairmont.com; map:M3*

## Huntington Hotel / ★★★

**1075 CALIFORNIA ST BTWN MASON AND TAYLOR STS; 415/474-5400 OR 800/227-4683**

The small, modest lobby of this imposing Nob Hill landmark belies its lavish interior. The Huntington is graced with a remarkable array of antiques, plush sofas, and museum-quality objets d'art; the doorman is subdued and genteel but always seems delighted to see you; the staff maintains a professional attitude and at the same time treats you like a favored guest. These things—along with superb security—explain why the Huntington has long been a favorite of many of San Francisco's visiting dignitaries and celebrities, from Archbishop Desmond Tutu to Robert Redford. The 12-story hotel's 140 rooms are spacious and lavish, with imported silks, 17th-century paintings, and stunning views of the city and the bay. The rooms are individually decorated, and some are so handsome they have been featured in *Architectural Digest*. Several flaunt gold velvet sofas and fringed, tufted hassocks surrounded by antiques, while others boast modern leather couches, faux-leopard-skin hassocks, and marble bars. Guests are treated to a formal afternoon tea and complimentary sherry, nightly turndown service, and a morning paper. Valet parking and room service are also available, along with a full range of business services and access to the Nob Hill Club, a top-of-the-line fitness center 1 block away. Yes, Virginia, it's expensive, but offers such as the Romance Package (including free champagne, sherry, and limousine service) make the Huntington worth considering for that special occasion. *$$$$; AE, DC, DIS, MC, V; checks OK; www.huntingtonhotel. com; map:M3*

## Nob Hill Inn / ★★

**1000 PINE ST AT TAYLOR ST; 415/673-6080**

Any well-appointed bed-and-breakfast ought to have a resident ghost. This elegant establishment—housed in a four-story Edwardian mansion built in 1907—has a winsome lass who wanders through the inn's Louis XIV– and Louis XV–style decor at whim. Take the etched-glass English elevator upstairs to the 21 antique-filled guest rooms. The low-end rooms are quite small, so splurge on a spacious suite. Downstairs, ceiling fans turn slowly above the wicker furniture in the parlor and sun room, where a continental breakfast is served among the wine racks in the atmospheric wine cellar. Add to this an afternoon tea and nightly turndown service, and it's little wonder that even the ghosts don't want to leave. *$$–$$$; AE, DC, MC, V; checks OK; map:M3*

## The Ritz-Carlton San Francisco / ★★★★

**600 STOCKTON ST BTWN PINE AND CALIFORNIA STS; 415/296-7465
OR 800/241-3333**

In 1991, after a four-year, multimillion-dollar renovation, this 1909 17-columned neoclassical beauty—formerly the Metropolitan Life Insurance Company building—reopened as the Ritz-Carlton hotel. Since then it's been stacking up heady accolades, making *Conde Nast Traveler's* "Gold List" for seven consecutive years, and earning a "#1 in the World" ranking in the 2001 issue of *Institutional Investor* magazine. The hotel's lobby is breathtaking, with a series of enormous high-ceilinged lounges, gigantic floral arrangements, an abundance of museum-quality paintings and antiques, and crystal chandeliers at every turn. The spectacular Lobby Lounge is the place to mingle over Afternoon Tea or sushi, and live piano performances perk up the scene every day. The 336 guest rooms are also luxury personified: sinfully plush and loaded with high-society amenities such as spiffy Italian-marble bathrooms, 300-thread-count sheets, fully stocked honor bars, thick terry-cloth robes, high-speed Internet access, and in-room safes. Some (though not many) have wonderful views of the city and the bay, but your best bets are the quieter rooms overlooking the landscaped courtyard. Business travelers should book one of the Club rooms on the upper floors, which come with a dedicated concierge, elevator-key access, and complimentary meals throughout the day. The hotel's ritzy fitness center has an indoor lap pool, whirlpool, sauna, fully equipped training room, and massage services. Two restaurants are located in the hotel: the formal Dining Room at the Ritz-Carlton (see review in the Restaurants chapter) and the more casual Terrace, serving excellent Mediterranean fare and sensational desserts in a pleasant dining room adorned with handsome oil paintings. *$$$$; AE, DC, DIS, MC, V; no checks; www.ritzcarlton.com; map:N2*

# North Beach

## Hotel Bohème / ★★

**444 COLUMBUS AVE BTWN VALLEJO AND GREEN STS; 415/433-9111**

Hopelessly chic is perhaps the best way to describe the Hotel Bohème, one of the sexiest small hotels in the city and a favorite retreat of visiting writers and poets. Hovering two stories above Columbus Avenue—the Boulevard Saint-Michel of San Francisco streets—the Bohème artfully  reflects North Beach's bohemian flair dating from the late 1950s and early '60s. The time trip starts with a gallery of moody black-and-white photographs lining the hallways and segues into the 16 guest rooms decorated in soothing shades of sage green, cantaloupe, lavender, and black. The rooms feature handmade light fixtures crafted from glazed collages of jazz sheet music, Ginsberg poetry, and old menus and headlines, as well as black iron beds with sheer canopies, European armoires, bistro tables, wicker chairs, and Picasso and Matisse prints. Modern amenities abound, including private baths, remote-control cable TV, and telephones with modem jacks. A couple of minor caveats: Most rooms are quite small, and those facing Columbus Avenue aren't kind to light sleepers (though views of the ever-bustling cafes and shops are entrancing). Otherwise, Hotel Bohème's engaging amalgamation of art, poetry, and hospitality will forever put you off America's cookie-cutter corporate hotels. $$; AE, DC, DIS, MC, V; no checks; mail@hotel boheme.com; www.hotelboheme.com; map:M2

## San Remo Hotel / ★

**2237 MASON ST AT CHESTNUT ST; 415/776-8688 OR 800/352-REMO**
Hidden in a quiet North Beach neighborhood between bustling Washington Square and Fisherman's Wharf, the San Remo is within easy walking distance of San Francisco's main attractions, including Chinatown, the Embarcadero, Pier 39, and one of the main cable car stations. Combine the locale with an inexpensive price tag, and you have one of the best room bargains in the city. This well-preserved, charming three-story Italianate Victorian building originally served as a boardinghouse for dockworkers displaced by the great fire of 1906. Space was at a premium, so the hotel's 63 rooms are rather small, the bathrooms are shared, and the walls are thin. If you can live with these minor inconveniences, however, you're in for a treat. The rooms are reminiscent of a European pensione, modestly decorated with brass or iron beds, pedestal sinks, wicker furniture, and oak, maple, or pine armoires; all have ceiling fans. Rooms 42 and 43, which overlook Mason Street, are the favorites. The old-fashioned bathrooms, spotlessly clean and restored to their original luster, have brass pull-chain toilets with oak tanks, showers, and claw-footed tubs. The penthouse suite, one of the best deals in town, offers a private bath, a small deck, and a 360-degree view of the city. The hotel's lobby and hallways are awash with antiques, leaded-glass windows, and plants bathed by sunlight filtering through stained-glass skylights. You can count on the friendly, city-savvy staff to help you plan your day touring San Francisco's abundant attractions. $; AE, DC, DIS, MC, V; checks OK; info@sanremohotel.com; www.sanremohotel.com; map:M1

## The Washington Square Inn / ★★

**1660 STOCKTON ST BTWN FILBERT AND UNION STS; 415/981-4220 OR 800/388-0220**
The Washington Square Inn's prime location in the middle of the historic North Beach district—just a short walk from Fisherman's Wharf, Ghirardelli Square, the Embarcadero, and Chinatown—is its best asset. And behind the inn's plain, inconspicuous facade is a delightful European-

style bed-and-breakfast. The 15 comfortable, modest rooms are furnished with European antiques, bright flower-print drapes and matching bedspreads, and vases of fresh flowers. The least expensive rooms have a private bath across the hall; the priciest units are the larger corner rooms with private baths and bay windows where you can sit and watch the hustle and bustle in the tree-lined square. In the morning you'll find a local newspaper waiting outside your door. The expanded continental breakfast can be served in your room or in front of the lobby fireplace, although you may want to stroll over to one of the many nearby Italian cafes for a frothy cappuccino or latte instead. Guests are treated to freshly baked cookies and tea every afternoon, as well as wine and hors d'oeuvres in the evening. Parking in North Beach is virtually impossible, so take advantage of the hotel's valet parking services. *$$$; AE, DC, DIS, MC, V; checks OK; map:M2*

# Fisherman's Wharf

## Sheraton Fisherman's Wharf / ★

**2500 MASON ST BTWN BEACH AND NORTH POINT STS; 415/362-5500 OR 800/325-3535**

If there's no room at the Tuscan Inn, your second-best option for Fisherman's Wharf lodging is the Sheraton Fisherman's Wharf. It's a rather unsightly, boxy brown three-story building (notice that its facade doesn't appear on the brochure), built in the mid-'70s and completely renovated in 1999. The 525 rooms are exactly as you'd expect them to be—clean, comfortable, and boring—but at least there are no unpleasant surprises. Which is just as well, because if you're looking for lodging near Fisherman's Wharf, it's probably because you have the kids along (even so, we recommend that you stay somewhere with more authentic San Fran-cisco appeal, such as North Beach or Pacific Heights). All the usual big-chain amenities are available, such as 24-hour room service, evening turndown, access to a nearby health club, a business center, a car-rental desk, dry cleaning and laundry, and newspaper delivery. There's also Chanen's Restaurant, serving standard American fare for breakfast, lunch, and dinner daily. One of the best perks about the Sheraton (and why we recommend it for families) is that it's one of the few reasonably priced hotels in the city that has an outdoor heated swimming pool. Tip: Another good Fisherman's Wharf family-friendly hotel is the Wharf Inn (2601 Mason St; 415/673-7411 or 800/548-9918), which offers quality rooms starting at $100 and has free parking as well. *$$$–$$$$; AE, DC, DIS, MC, V; checks OK; www.sheratonatthewharf.com; map:M1*

### Tuscan Inn at Fisherman's Wharf / ★★

**425 NORTH POINT ST AT MASON ST; 415/561-1100 OR 800/648-4626**

With its location in the heart of Fisherman's Wharf, just a skip away from Ghirardelli Square, the Embarcadero, and the cable car lines, it's no wonder the low-key Tuscan Inn is the favored hideout of many of Hollywood's actors and producers. You won't find the glitz of San Francisco's downtown hostelries or even a terrific view here, but the Tuscan's 211 attractive guest rooms (including 12 deluxe suites) offer every creature comfort one could need. Burgundy floral-print bedspreads, armchairs, writing desks, honor bars, remote-control TVs, direct-dial phones, and private bathrooms are standard features of every room. And as is typical of a Kimpton Group hotel, a room at the Tuscan comes with a plethora of complimentary services: a concierge, coffee and biscotti served in the lobby every morning, weekday limousine service to the Financial District and the Moscone Convention Center, an evening wine reception, room service, valet parking, and same-day laundry service. The Tuscan also offers guest privileges at several popular San Francisco fitness centers, including a 24-Hour Nautilus just a block away. Adjoining the hotel is the glittering Cafe Pescatore, a classic Italian trattoria serving very good fresh fish and pasta dishes as well as a variety of pizzas baked in a wood-fired oven (see review in the Restaurants chapter). When weather permits, the Pescatore opens its floor-to-ceiling windows to allow for prime people-watching and quasi-alfresco dining. *$$$; AE, DC, DIS, MC, V; checks OK; www.tuscaninn.com; map:M1*

# Civic Center and Japantown

### The Archbishop's Mansion / ★★★

**1000 FULTON ST AT STEINER ST; 415/563-7872 OR 800/543-5820**

This stately Belle Epoque mansion, built in 1904 for San Francisco's archbishop, is an exercise in Victorian splendor and excess: A three-story staircase winds beneath a gorgeous, 16-foot-tall stained-glass dome, and the surrounding redwood Corinthian columns, crystal chandeliers, Oriental carpets, and gorgeous antiques create an aura of almost papal  splendor. The 15 large rooms and suites, each named after a famous opera, are decorated with lush fabrics, embroidered linens, and 19th-century antiques. All have partial canopied beds and private baths with stacks of plush towels and French-milled soaps. Many rooms have a fireplace, a Jacuzzi tub, and a view of Alamo Park, and some have a parlor and sitting area. The posh, rose-colored Carmen Suite has a claw-footed bathtub in front of a fireplace, a comfortable sitting room with yet another fireplace, and another pretty park view. The ultraluxurious Don

Giovanni Suite boasts a cherub-encrusted antique four-poster bed imported from a French castle, as well as a parlor with a palatial fireplace and a lavish seven-head shower in the bathroom. You may breakfast in bed on scones and croissants; then, after spending the day strolling through the park admiring the neighborhood's cherished Victorian homes, return in the afternoon for wine in the French parlor, which is graced by a grand piano that once belonged to Noël Coward. *$$$; AE, DC, MC, V; checks OK; www.archbishopsmansion.com; map:K4*

## Hotel Majestic / ★★★
**1500 SUTTER ST BTWN OCTAVIA AND GOUGH STS; 415/441-1100 OR 800/869-8966**
A pillar of Victorian grandeur, this five-story 1902 Edwardian building, located in a residential neighborhood near Japantown, was one of San Francisco's earliest grand hotels. Granite steps and ornate leaded-glass doors open onto a magnificent yet cozy lobby featuring dark green marble pillars, plush sofas, chairs and pillows cloaked in silk-tasseled brocades, a white marble fireplace topped with a precious 19th-century bronze clock, and numerous antique fixtures. Upstairs, the 58 guest rooms and luxury suites are individually decorated in old-world elegance, incorporating soft tones of teals, camels, creams, and golds with custom-made matching furniture in French, Greek, and Italian styling (you literally get your choice). Of course, the rooms all have modern amenities such as televisions, private baths, direct-dial phones, and individually controlled thermostats. For maximum charm, request a deluxe room or suite; these rooms have wonderful semicircular bay windows as well as fireplaces and queen-size beds. Concierge services, 24-hour room service, a Club Room with honor bar, business facilities, valet service, a morning limousine service, and valet parking are also available. The adjacent Perlot restaurant is in the midst of nailing down a more permanent chef, but it consistently wins annual reader awards for its oh-so-romantic setting. After dinner, sip a digestif at Avalon, the Majestic's handsome 19th-century French mahogany bar, and note the fascinating framed butterfly collection displayed on the dark turquoise walls. *$$$–$$$$; AE, DC, MC, V; no checks; www.hotelmajestic.com; map:L3*

## Phoenix Hotel / ★★
**601 EDDY ST AT LARKIN ST; 415/776-1380 OR 800/248-9466**
What do the Red Hot Chili Peppers, Johnny Depp, Ziggy Marley, Pearl Jam, Linda Ronstadt, and Arlo Guthrie have in common? At one time or another they've all checked into the Phoenix Hotel. Why? Because it's cool. Not hip, mind you, or lavish or discreet or exclusive. In fact, at first glance you wouldn't think much of it, except for the heated outdoor pool with its paisley mural by artist Francis Forlenza and the modern-sculp-

ture garden surrounding it. And you definitely won't think highly of the seedy Tenderloin location. But this retro 1950s-style hotel is the primo pick of visiting rock bands, writers, filmmakers, and celebrities, partly because the Phoenix is the best thing San Francisco has to offer for Southern Californians seeking a Palm Springs–style hotel. The 44 bungalow-style guest rooms are uniquely decorated with bamboo furnishings, an assortment of tropical plants, and original local artwork. VCRs and movies are available on request, as well as an on-call massage therapist. Heck, there's even free parking (if the limos and tour buses haven't hogged the lot). Adjoining the hotel is Backflip, an aqua-blue cocktail lounge serving tapas and Caribbean-style appetizers to a young, hip crowd. *$$–$$$; AE, DC, MC, V; no checks; www.sftrips.com; map:L4*

## Queen Anne Hotel / ★★★

**1590 SUTTER ST BTWN GOUGH AND OCTAVIA STS; 415/441-2828 OR 800/227-3970**

The Queen Anne is one classy hotel. In fact, it was once a grooming school for upper-class young women, and has since been converted into a fabulous re-creation of San Francisco's turn-of-the-century inns. The "Grand Salon" lobby, for example, is draped with rich burgundy fabrics and replete with English oak paneling and period antiques. The rooms are equally opulent, each decorated with marble-top dressers, beautiful armoires, and a various assortment of Victorian-era antiques. They also have a wide array of niceties: Some have a separate sitting area, while others have corner turret bay windows, reading nooks, and fireplaces. All rooms have two telephones (one's in the bathroom), voice mail, Internet data ports, a television, and extensively renovated bathrooms with quality bath products. Guests can also retire to the parlor with its fluted columns and floor-to-ceiling fireplace, or to the hotel's library. Luxury amenities include morning newspaper delivery, complimentary expanded continental breakfast and afternoon tea and sherry, room service, complimentary local Town Car service, and access to an off-premises health club with a lap pool. *$$$; AE, DC, DIS, MC, V; checks OK (in advance); www.queenanne.com; map:L3*

# Pacific Heights

## The Bed and Breakfast Inn / ★★

**4 CHARLTON CT BTWN BUCHANAN AND LAGUNA STS; 415/921-9784**

San Francisco's first bed-and-breakfast maintains the convincing illusion that it's a charming old English inn in a picturesque mews somewhere in Cornwall. The main difference, of course, is that you're not surrounded by verdant countryside dotted with horses and sheep munching on grassy meadows and wildflowers. Instead, this B&B tucked into a cul-de-sac is just steps away from the popular boutiques, bars, and restaurants lining Union Street, one of the city's most popular shopping areas. The three adjoining green Victorian buildings—graced with twining ivy, window boxes bursting with bright red geraniums, and a birdhouse bobbing from a tree out front—offer 13 enchanting guest rooms, each individually decorated with family antiques, floral prints, and appealing personal touches (ask for a room that opens directly onto the alluring back garden). The least expensive rooms have shared baths. Of the two sunny penthouses, the Mayfair offers a living room, kitchen, latticed balcony, and spiral staircase leading to a bedroom loft with a king-size bed; the Garden Suite, popular with groups of four, has a king-size bed in the master bedroom, a double bed in the loft, a fully stocked kitchen, a living room with a fireplace, two bathrooms (one with a Jacuzzi tub), and French doors leading to a private atrium and garden. You may enjoy your simple continental breakfast in your room, the garden, or the diminutive English tearoom. *$$–$$$; AE, CB, DC, DIS, MC, V; checks OK; map:K2*

## Edward II Inn & Pub / ★★

**3155 SCOTT ST AT LOMBARD ST; 415/922-3000 OR 800/473-2846**
The best part about this three-story faux English country inn is that it has a guest room to match most anyone's budget, ranging from one of the pensione-style rooms with shared bathrooms (starting at $75) to one of the $235-a-night luxury suites complete with living room, kitchen, and whirlpool bathtub. The inn was originally built to house visitors to the 1915 Panama-Pacific International Exposition, and now it's the pride and joy of innkeepers Denise and Bob Holland, a friendly couple who have put together a fine hotel that does a lot of repeat business. Regardless of the rate, all the guest rooms are spotlessly clean and comfortably appointed with antique furnishings. Light sleepers will want to request a room that doesn't face busy Lombard Street; the hotel is also close to a wealth of great shops and restaurants along Union and Chestnut Streets. Perks include a complimentary breakfast and evening apéritifs, served in the adjoining pub (naturally). *$–$$$; AE, MC, V; no checks; www.edwardii.com; map:J1*

## Hotel Drisco / ★★★

**2901 PACIFIC AVE AT BRODERICK ST; 415/346-2880 OR 800/634-7277**
If you're a fan of San Francisco's Ritz-Carlton, you'll adore Hotel Drisco. The five-story structure, perched on one of the most coveted blocks in the city, was built in 1903 as a boardinghouse for neighborhood servants. After surviving the great fire of 1906, it was converted into a hotel in the mid-'20s but eventually fell into major disrepair. Combining the financial might of hotelier Tom Callinan (Meadowood, the Inn at Southbridge) and the interior design skills of Glenn Texeira (Ritz-Carlton,

Manila), Hotel Drisco's proprietors transformed years of blood, sweat, and greenbacks into one of the finest small hotels in the city. The 24 rooms and 19 suites are bathed in soothing shades of alabaster, celadon, and buttercup yellow and feature rich fabrics, quality antiques, and superior mattresses. Standard amenities include a two-line phone with a modem hookup, a CD player, a discreetly hidden TV with a VCR, and a minibar; suites include a handsome sofa bed, an additional phone and TV, and terrific views. The spacious marble-clad bathrooms are equipped with hair dryers, plush robes, and (in most units) bathtubs. Room 404A—a corner suite with an extraordinary view of Pacific Heights mansions and the surrounding neighborhood—is a favorite. An extended continental breakfast is served in one of the three quiet, comfortable common rooms. *$$$; AE, DC, DIS, MC, V; no checks; www.eldrisco hotel.com; map:J2*

### Jackson Court / ★★

**2198 JACKSON ST AT BUCHANAN ST; 415/929-7670**

Tucked away behind a brick archway and a white-trellised garden courtyard, this three-story brownstone is set in the heart of the exclusive Pacific Heights residential neighborhood. The living room of the sedate manse is comfortably grand, with Oriental carpeting, gilt-framed mirrors, and a striking, oversize fireplace adorned with figures of wind sprites and storm gods. All 10 blissfully quiet guest rooms have handsome architectural details, pleasantly spare high-quality antiques, telephones, cable television, and private baths; two rooms have fireplaces. Particularly noteworthy is the luxurious Garden Court suite, originally the mansion's dining room, which boasts handcrafted wood paneling and cabinets, an antique chandelier, period furnishings, a king-size bed, and a private garden patio. After dining downstairs on the expanded continental breakfast, spend the day browsing the numerous boutiques along bustling Union Street, and return in time for the late afternoon tea served in the living room. *$$$; AE, MC, V; checks OK; map:K2*

### Marina Inn / ★★★

**3110 OCTAVIA ST AT LOMBARD ST; 415/928-1000 OR 800/274-1420**

If you don't really care where you stay in San Francisco and you want the most for your money, book a room here; we checked out all the inexpensive lodgings in the city and none have come close to offering as good a deal. The building, located on busy Lombard Street (the only caveat), is a handsome 1924 four-story Victorian, and the guest rooms are equally impressive: two-poster beds with cozy comforters and mattresses, rustic pine-wood furnishings, attractive wallpaper, and a pleasant color scheme of rose, hunter green, and pale yellow. You'll especially appreciate the high-class touches that even many of the city's expensive hotels don't include, such as full bathtubs with showers, remote-control televisions discreetly hidden in pine cabinetry, and nightly turndown service à la chocolates on your pillow. How much for all these creature comforts? As little as $65 a night, and that includes complimentary continental breakfast and afternoon sherry. It's in a good location as well—within easy walking distance of the shops and restaurants along Chestnut and Union Streets, and right on the bus route to downtown. *$–$$; AE, MC, V; no checks; map:L1*

## The Sherman House / ★★★★

**2160 GREEN ST BTWN WEBSTER AND FILLMORE STS; 415/563-3600 OR 800/424-5777**

Once the home of musical-instrument magnate and opera buff Leander Sherman, this 1876 Victorian mansion has housed such luminaries as Lillian Russell and Enrico Caruso, who sang to privileged guests in the house's private three-story recital hall. The stunning decor is based on a French Second Empire motif, with fine antiques and choice custom replicas, richly upholstered sofas and chairs, and gorgeous carpets covering polished hardwood floors. The huge, sky-lit recital hall still has a grand piano, but now the room serves as a luxurious lobby guarded by a bevy of musically minded finches. Most of the eight guest rooms and the six one-bedroom suites feature gilded bronze chandeliers, brocaded bed hangings, rich tapestries, and beautifully crafted wainscoting. Four rooms have Roman-style baths, while the rest have Jacuzzi tubs. A few rooms even have such extras as a private garden, bay view, and rooftop deck, and all but one have a wood-burning marble fireplace (ask for one of the upstairs rooms, which have broad bay windows, plush window seats, and views of the bay). If you prefer more contemporary surroundings, the Carriage House contains three luxury suites decorated with silk floral fabrics and French Country furnishings. The concierge, butler, valet parking, and 24-hour room service are superb. Guests are also given exclusive seating at the Sherman House Restaurant—a grand dining establishment that, unfortunately, is closed to nonguests. *$$$–$$$$; AE, DC, MC, V; checks OK; www.integra.fr/relaischateaux/sherman; map:K2*

## Union Street Inn / ★★

**2229 UNION ST BTWN FILLMORE AND STEINER STS; 415/346-0424**

Owners Jane Bertorelli and David Coyle have lent such a pleasant personal touch to the period decor, and the staff is so convivial, that this delightful bed-and-breakfast wins a prize for overall ambience. Although the two-story Edwardian mansion is situated amid the bustle of trendy Union Street, it's set high above the traffic at the top of a steep set of stairs. The five large guest rooms and a deluxe carriage house across the garden have private baths (some feature Jacuzzis), king- or queen-size beds, telephones, terry-cloth robes, fresh-cut flowers, and televisions (for those who can't survive the Edwardian era without one). Each room has its

## CITYPASS: AN E-TICKET TO RIDE

If you plan on doing a lot of sightseeing in the city for more than a couple of days, do yourself a favor and purchase a San Francisco CityPass. Not only does it include unlimited public transportation—including cable cars, Metro streetcars, and the entire bus system—but you also get 50 percent off admission fees at 24 of the city's major attractions, including the M. H. De Young Memorial Museum, the Asian Art Museum, the California Academy of Sciences, and the Japanese Tea Garden (all in Golden Gate Park); the Museum of Modern Art; Coit Tower; the Exploratorium; the zoo; the National Maritime Museum and Historic Ships (where you can visit the USS *Pampanito* and the SS *Jeremiah O'Brien*); and a Blue & Gold Fleet bay cruise or Alcatraz tour. You can buy a CityPass at the San Francisco Visitor Information Center, the Holiday Inn Civic Center, and the TIX Bay Area booth at Union Square, among other outlets. Current rates are $33.75 for adults, $26.75 for seniors 65 and older, and $24.75 for kids 5 to 17. For more information visit the CityPass website at www.citypass.net or send an e-mail to info@citypass.com. For recorded information call 707/256-0490.

own theme and color scheme, enhanced by bay windows, patterned wallpaper, Oriental carpets, antiques, and comforters. The best rooms, such as the Wildrose, face the flourishing back garden. The parlor downstairs is furnished with a fireplace, a beguiling range of period finds, and a 24-hour coffee/tea/buffet station. Start your day with a full breakfast in the beautiful English garden, in the parlor, or in bed; spend the afternoon strolling through Union Street's ever-popular boutiques, bars, and cafes; then return by 5pm for a predinner snack of wine and cheese. *$$–$$$; AE, DIS, MC, V; checks OK; www.unionstreetinn.com; map:K2*

# Haight-Ashbury

## Red Victorian Bed Breakfast & Art / ★★

### 1665 HAIGHT ST BTWN CLAYTON AND COLE STS; 415/864-1978

The Red Vic, located smack-dab on an exciting stretch of Haight Street, is one of the most eclectic and groovy lodgings in the city. You'll have the quintessential Haight-Ashbury experience staying in any of the 18 colorfully decorated rooms, all with great names such as the Flower Child Room, the Peace Room, and the Redwood Forest Room, each with its own '60s Summer of Love heritage theme. For example, the luxury Peacock Suite features stained-glass windows, a canopied king-size bed, and a bathtub in a mirrored window alcove looking into the sitting room. Economy double rooms include the Earth Charter Room and Summer of

Love Room. Eight of the guest rooms have private baths, while the remaining rooms share four "theme" bathrooms down the hall. In fact, Sami will *suggest* that you take the time to explore the shared Aquarium Bathroom (where goldfish swim in the toilet tank), the Starlight Bathroom, the Love Bathroom, and the Infinity Bathroom (how could one resist such an offer?). A complimentary breakfast is served family style in the breakfast salon at 9am each morning, offering an opportunity to meet the other guests (and what an interesting lot it is) and discuss the social and environmental needs of the planet. Founder and artist-in-residence Sami Sunchild owns and runs this one-of-a-kind tribute to the '60s, and you couldn't dream up a more dedicated, gracious host. So c'mon, inject a little peace, love, and happiness into your travels and give Ms. Sunchild a call. *$–$$$; AE, DIS, MC, V; checks OK; www.redvic.com; map:I5*

## Stanyan Park Hotel / ★★
### 750 STANYAN ST AT WALLER ST; 415/751-1000

If you're interested in the historic Haight-Ashbury area but aren't willing to forgo the creature comforts you've grown accustomed to over the years, you'll appreciate what the Stanyan Park Hotel has to offer. The stately three-story Victorian has been in operation since 1904, long enough to put it on the National Register of Historic Places. Hence the Victorian theme throughout: Victorian furnishings, bedding, wallpaper, curtains, and carpets, all tastefully done. You'll like the bathrooms as well: Each has a tub-shower with a massaging showerhead and scented soaps. Standard guest rooms start at about $125. The hotel also has a bevy of suites starting at $260 that include full kitchen, dining room, and living room and can comfortably sleep up to six. A complimentary continental breakfast is included, as is a tea service each afternoon and evening. *$$–$$$$; AE, DC, DIS, MC, V; no checks; info@stanyan park.com; www.stanyanpark.com; map:I5*

# The Castro

## Dolores Park Inn / ★★
### 3641 17TH ST BTWN CHURCH AND DOLORES STS; 415/621-0482

Rumor has it that celebrities such as Robert Downey Jr. and Tom Cruise stay at this beautiful two-story 1874 Victorian inn to avoid their fans. Either that, or they just like staying here, which is easy to understand.  First off, it's in a great location—adjacent to popular Dolores Park and just a short stroll to the numerous Castro district shops, cafes, and clubs. Owner Bernie Vielwerth (this guy's a real character), who bought the mansion over two decades ago, has spent a lot of time and money restoring and decorating it. The guest rooms are beautifully sumptuous, each individually decorated with beautiful antiques and queen-size beds. The most popular room is The Suite, which has a 20-foot sun deck overlooking Twin Peaks as well as a four-poster bed and kitchen. Both breakfast, served outside on a patio behind the kitchen, and afternoon wine are included in the room rate. A two-night minimum stay is required, though we guarantee you'll want to stay longer. Note: Both gay and straight couples are equally welcome here. *$$–$$$; MC, V; checks OK; map:L6*

## Inn on Castro / ★★

### 321 CASTRO ST AT MARKET ST; 415/861-0321

This convivial bed-and-breakfast, catering to the gay and lesbian community for nearly two decades, has developed an ardent following—hence the intriguing collection of more than 100 heart-shaped boxes on the sideboard in the hallway, trinkets left behind by a legion of wistful patrons who can say they left their hearts in San Francisco. The restored Edwardian exterior is painted in a pleasing medley of blue, rose, and green, with gilded details and dentils. The interior is equally festive, with contemporary furnishings, original modern art, exotic plants, and elaborate flower arrangements. There are eight individually decorated guest rooms ranging from a small single to a suite with a deck; every room has a private bath, cable TV, and a direct-dial phone. Avoid the sunny but noisy rooms facing Castro Street. An elaborate breakfast, served in the dining room, may feature a fresh fruit salad, house-made muffins, fruit juice, and scrambled eggs, French toast, or pancakes. After your repast, relax in the cozy living room with its fireplace and deeply tufted Italian couches, or head out for a stroll in the colorful, ever-bustling Castro. Note: For longer stays, the inn also rents three corporate apartments. *$$; MC, V; checks OK; www.innoncastro2.com; map:K6*

# Airport Area

## Comfort Suites / ★

### 121 E GRAND AVE, SOUTH SAN FRANCISCO; 650/589-7100 OR 800/228-5150

The midpriced Comfort Suites is recommended for families who want to be well situated for an early departure. There's the outdoor hot tub for Mom and Dad to relax in while the kids duke it out on the Nintendo  game system or watch one of the pay-cable channels. As the name says, each room is a suite, and comes with a king-size bed, queen-size sleeper sofa for the kids, microwave, and a refrigerator, as well as a hair dryer, iron and board, and the requisite coffeemaker. The rooms are clean, comfortable, and ordinary—exactly what you'd expect. It's the free perks that make this hotel attractive, such as complimentary continental breakfast,

## THE BEST VIEWS OF SAN FRANCISCO AND THE BAY

Few people forget seeing their first sunset at **Ocean Beach.** Whether viewed from the water's edge or over cocktails at the Cliff House or the Beach Chalet, the sight of the scarlet and purple tones slowly deepening into darkness as the sun slips below the horizon is something that resists adequate description. Check the weather section of the daily papers for the time the sun will be setting, and get there a little early for the full effect. It's easy to get to Ocean Beach: just take Geary Boulevard west all the way to the ocean. There's plenty of prime parking along the beach, and you can stay warm and dry in your car to watch the show.

The crest of **Dolores Park**, where the Mission gradually blends into Noe Valley, offers a breathtaking view of the city, with the downtown section in view and the hills of the East Bay glimmering in the distance. Sunny weekends find the park strewn with sun-bathers, and some marriages are performed here with the city serving as a beautiful backdrop to the wedding photographs. It's located on Dolores Street (off upper Market Street) between 18th and 20th Streets.

But the sine qua non of grand San Francisco views is at **Twin Peaks**, the two rounded hills jutting out below the giant red-and-white-striped Sutro Tower on the southwest side of the city. A drive to this popular lookout area gives you a full 360-degree view that is particularly lovely as the fog drifts in, adding a hint of mystery and romance (particu-larly at night). It's reachable via Market Street—just keep heading southwest on Market until you reach the top of the hill (just past Clipper Street) and turn left on Twin Peaks Road, which leads to the top.

**Other good viewpoints:** the Golden Gate Bridge, Coit Tower, Angel Island, the Embarcadero just north of the Bay Bridge, the road to the Marin Headlands, and any of the top-floor high-rise cocktail lounges (see "San Francisco's Swankiest Hotel Bars" in the Nightlife chapter).

evening soup-and-bread bar, and airport shuttle service. *$$; AE, DC, DIS, MC, V; no checks; map:KK5*

## Embassy Suites / ★★☆

**250 GATEWAY BLVD, SOUTH SAN FRANCISCO; 650/589-3400 OR 800/362-2779**

Your best pick—and most expensive—of the airport chain hotels is Embassy Suites, which does its darnedest to make you forget you're in the middle of dreary, industrial South San Francisco. It's almost as if you're in Las Vegas, what with the spewing fountains, numerous palm trees, and indoor pool, whirlpool, and sauna. The guest rooms are all two-room suites and come with all the standard deluxe amenities such as two TVs, two phones, microwave, fridge, wet bar, coffeemaker, hair dryer, iron, and so on. A cooked-to-order breakfast (delivered to your door upon request) is included in the room rate. Shuttle service to SFO is complimentary as well. *$$$; AE, DC, MC, V; checks OK; www. embassy-suites.com; map:KK5*

## Holiday Inn (San Francisco Airport North) / ★

**275 S AIRPORT BLVD (OFF HWY 101), SOUTH SAN FRANCISCO; 650/873-3550 OR 800/HOLIDAY**

If you prefer to go with who you know, there's the Holiday Inn next to the airport. The guest rooms are Holiday Inn standard: spotless, inoffensively decorated, with all the usual amenities such as minibars, coffeemakers, hair dryers, movie channels, and such. There's also a health spa (sauna, gym, Jacuzzi, and tanning bed) to keep you entertained until your flight leaves, as well as a gift shop, full business services, and Rookie's Sports Bar & Grill and the City Cafe, which serves American-style breakfast, lunch, and dinner daily. The rates are surprisingly reasonable for all the perks included, starting at only $85 per night. *$$–$$$; AE, DC, DIS, MC, V; no checks; map:KK5*

## San Francisco Airport North Travelodge / ★

**326 S AIRPORT BLVD (OFF HWY 101), SOUTH SAN FRANCISCO; 650/583-9600 OR 800/578-7878**

If you've got kids in tow and a limited budget, the Travelodge near SFO is your best choice for a quick morning departure. All of the rooms are at or under $100, but the real clincher is the hotel's large heated pool, where the kids can play Marco Polo all day while the parents relax in the  typically warm South San Francisco weather. The list of free amenities includes a complimentary copy of *USA Today*, in-room coffee and tea, free HBO, and voice mail. There's a so-so American-style restaurant adjacent to the hotel, though we recommend you walk to Rookie's Sports Bar & Grill at the Holiday Inn down the street. The hotel's 24-hour complimentary shuttle will get you to SFO in about five minutes. *$$; AE, DC, DIS, MC, V; no checks; www.sfotravelodge.com; map:KK5*

# EXPLORING

# EXPLORING

## Top 25 Attractions

### 1) ALCATRAZ ISLAND

**Access from Pier 41 near Fisherman's Wharf; 415/705-5555** This tiny land mass in the middle of the San Francisco Bay was first "discovered" in 1775 by Spaniard Juan Manuel Ayala, who named it after *los alcatrazes* (the pelicans) that populated this coastal area. After the United States annexed California, the island served as a military post for 80 years. The first lighthouse on the West Coast was built here in 1854, and in the 1860s the island held prisoners from the Civil War. From 1870 to 1890, during the western Indian Wars, captured Native Americans were held on the island as well.

But Alcatraz is undoubtedly most famous as a federal penitentiary that harbored the 20th century's most villainous gangsters. From 1934 to 1963, "the Rock" was home away from home for the likes of Al Capone, Machine Gun Kelly, and legendary "birdman" Robert Stroud. The icy waters of the bay made escaping alive all but impossible. Frank Morris and the Anglin brothers, whose attempt to do so was turned into the Clint Eastwood blockbuster *Escape from Alcatraz,* did manage to leave the island, but whether they made it across the frigid bay is still the subject of debate. In 1963, shortly after their departure, the prison was closed permanently (though primarily for financial rather than security reasons, because all supplies—including water—had to be shipped in). The masks they used as decoys to trick the guards are on display at the Maritime Museum (see Attraction 19).

In 1972 the island was made part of the Golden Gate National Recreation Area, and it has since become one of San Francisco's must-see tourist spots. But Alcatraz isn't for everyone. The park can get extremely crowded during summer months and weekends, so it's not recommended for those averse to sharing their day with a pack of strangers. If the crowds don't deter you, then perhaps the steep quarter-mile climb to the prison or the chilly bay winds will. For those eager to see the Rock first-hand, warm clothing and comfortable shoes are strongly recommended, as are advance tickets.

Self-guided tours let you wander at your own pace, while the excellent audio tours (narrated by actual former prisoners) offer a fantastic account of what it was like being a prisoner here—definitely worth the small additional fee. Park rangers lead crowds off the ferry and up the hill, recounting colorful stories about the island's former residents and critiques of Hollywood's various attempts to translate prison life to the silver screen. Reservations during peak season are mandatory, and if you

## TOP 25 ATTRACTIONS

1) Alcatraz Island
2) Cable cars
3) Fisherman's Wharf
4) Pier 39
5) Golden Gate Bridge
6) Union Square
7) Lombard Street
8) Golden Gate Park
9) Coit Tower
10) The Presidio
11) Ghirardelli Square and The Cannery
12) The Exploratorium and the Palace of Fine Arts
13) San Francisco Museum of Modern Art
14) Yerba Buena Center for the Arts–Yerba Buena Gardens–Metreon
15) Pacific Bell Park
16) Golden Gate National Recreation Area
17) Embarcadero Center
18) Alamo Square Historical District
19) San Francisco Maritime National Historical Park–Maritime Museum–Hyde Street Pier
20) California Palace of the Legion of Honor
21) Cliff House
22) Fort Mason Center
23) Mission Dolores
24) City Hall
25) Grace Cathedral

don't plan your tour early, you may be shut out. You can buy tickets in advance from the Blue & Gold Fleet ticket office on Pier 41, via the web at www.blueandgoldfleet.com, or over the phone (415/705-5555) using American Express, MasterCard, or Visa; a $2.25-per-ticket service fee is charged on phone orders. The Blue & Gold Fleet, which operates the tour, also offers evening tours of the island, which include a sunset view of the city (fog permitting). *Admission charge for adults and children 5 and older; open every day 9:15am–4:15pm in summer; open every day 9:30am–2:15pm in winter. Ferries depart every half hour at 15 and 45 minutes after the hour on weekends, and every 45 minutes Mon–Fri. Arrive at least 20 minutes before departure time; map:K1 (ferry)* &

## 2) CABLE CARS

**Hyde-Powell and Powell-Mason cable car lines begin at Powell and Market Sts; the California line begins at Market and Drumm Sts** The once-extensive network of cable cars that traversed San Francisco's steep streets was the brainchild of Andrew Smith Hallidie, a London-born mechanic turned entrepreneur. Like so many others, he came to California in 1852 to make his fortune. Instead of digging for gold, however, he developed a transport system for gold mining, and his patented wire ropes were soon hauling more than nuggets.

Necessity being the mother of invention, Hallidie's inspiration occurred while watching a team of overworked horses haul a heavily laden carriage up a steep San Francisco slope. One horse slipped and the car rolled back, dragging the team with it. At that moment, Hallidie resolved that he would invent a mechanical contraption to replace such horses; the many residents who lived along the hill's steep inclines also welcomed the idea of a cable car in their neighborhood and invested in Hallidie's Clay Street Hill Railroad. Just four years later, on August 1, 1873, the first engineless cable car made its maiden run from the top of Clay Street at Jones Street down to Kearny Street and, to the surprise of many an onlooker, back up again. A San Francisco icon was born.

Skeptics ridiculed the engineless invention as "Hallidie's Folly," but slowly the cable car was embraced by the city as a much-improved—not to mention cleaner—alternative to horse-drawn cars (particularly since horses were often injured trying to climb the brutally steep hills). Soon there were eight lines running in Pacific Heights, the Castro, Russian Hill, and Nob Hill. Popular as they were, however, their star was soon eclipsed by the electric trolley. By 1893 many cable car lines were already being replaced. In the 20th century, buses and budget concerns brought the elimination of several more lines. Concerned citizens fought hard to preserve the California, Hyde-Powell, and Powell-Mason lines—these three existing lines comprise the world's only surviving system of cable cars—and, in 1964, they were added to the National Register of Historic Places. Such landmark status ensures that the cable cars will run well into the 21st century.

How do they work? Each cable bar, weighing in at about 6 tons, is hauled along by a steel cable that is enclosed under the street in a center rail (if you peer straight down into the crack, you can see—and hear—the cable, which is powered by huge generators at the Cable Car Barn at Washington and Mason Streets). The car moves when the gripper pulls back a lever that closes a pincerlike "grip" on the moving cable, which always moves at a steady 9½ miles an hour. To learn more about these amazing machines, be sure to visit the fascinating Cable Car Barn Museum, which houses the engine rooms and repair shops (see the Museums section).

The two types of cable cars in use—which hold a maximum of 90 and 100 passengers, respectively—are so popular with tourists that the Hyde-Powell and Powell-Mason lines are almost impossible to get on unless you wait in the unbelievably long line near the bottom of Powell at Market or at the Hyde Street Pier. Locals, however, still use the California line to commute to and from the Financial District. This less popular trip offers great views with a shorter waiting time. Tip: Early risers will find that the lines are usually quite short during the first run, which is often the most beautiful. *The cable car system operates from approximately 6:30am to 12:30am; map:M3 (Hyde-Powell and Powell-Mason), N2 (California)*

## 3) FISHERMAN'S WHARF

**Jefferson St btwn Grant and Van Ness Aves** Fisherman's Wharf, one of the most popular tourist destinations in the world, has had a long and varied history. During the heady Gold Rush years, this bustling waterfront area—known then as Meigg's Wharf—was a major shipping port. Around the beginning of the 1900s, however, construction of new, larger port facilities along the Embarcadero forced the city's Italian immigrant fishermen to move their fleet here from east of Telegraph Hill.

And so Fisherman's Wharf remained a bastion for San Francisco's fishing fleet until, in the late '50s and '60s, two concurrent forces changed the face of this bustling waterfront for better or worse: A boom in tourism and a drop in commercial fishing. Cost Plus Imports opened here in 1958 while waterfront real estate was still within affordable reach. The **GHIRARDELLI SQUARE** shopping complex rose like a phoenix in 1968, the same year the **CANNERY** overhaul was completed (see Attraction 11). **PIER 39** opened to the public in 1978. As with many of San Francisco's historic districts, tourism forever changed the look and feel of this once working-class neighborhood. But remnants of San Francisco's commercial fishing industry can still be found—arrive in the early morning hours to see the small fishing fleet at the foot of Taylor Street bring their catch onto the docks.

Today, sidewalk stalls that once served up fish stew to local fishermen now sell steaming Dungeness crabs to tourists from Tallahassee to Tokyo. It's not a place you'll find many locals, but the amusement-park atmosphere that dominates Jefferson Street between Taylor and Mason attracts millions each year from around the world.

After 30 years, **RIPLEY'S BELIEVE IT OR NOT! MUSEUM** (415/771-6188; www.ripleysf.com) still draws the curious tourist looking for jaw-dropping proof that the world is full of the unbelievable and the bizarre. Robert LeRoy Ripley made his career assembling a museum full of oddities such as a shrunken human torso, a two-headed calf, and other outlandish freaks of nature.

Where else would the likes of Fidel Castro, Michael Jackson, Count Dracula, Marilyn Monroe, and George Bush mingle but within the walls of a wax museum? In the style of Madame Tussaud's more notorious London venture, San Francisco's **WAX MUSEUM** (415/202-0400; www.waxmuseum.com) offers an up-close and personal experience with the likenesses of the world's most famous people, monsters, and the like. Some 240 figures in 50 settings already crowd the waterfront, with more recent favorites such as Leonardo DiCaprio and Will Smith being added regularly.

Of course, numerous restaurants cater to the crowds; most are Italian, offering moderately priced pasta and seafood (all served with sourdough bread, naturally). The oldest restaurant on the wharf is **ALIOTO'S**, at Fisherman's Wharf and Taylor Street (415/673-0183), said to be the premier place to enjoy the famous cioppino seafood stew that's

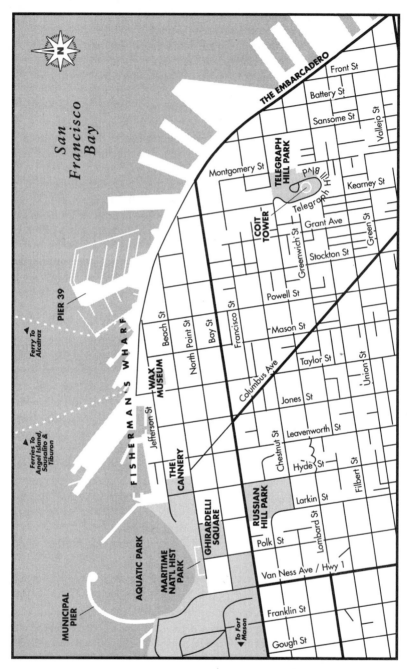

FISHERMAN'S WHARF

a city favorite. **A. SABELLA'S** (415/711-6775), at 2766 Taylor Street at Jefferson Street, was founded in 1920 by the Sabella family, Sicilian immigrants. Eighty years and three generations later, they've added a touch of Asian flavor to their Italian seafood dishes. After dinner, try **LOU'S PIER 47 CLUB** (415/771-5687), at 300 Jefferson Street at Jones Street, which offers live music nightly. For a touch of history and a pick-me-up cocktail, slip into the **BUENA VISTA CAFE** (415/474-5044), at 2765 Hyde Street at Beach Street, where the first Irish coffee was served in the United States in 1952. Fisherman's Wharf is open year-round. There's no charge for wandering around, but the surrounding parking lots fill quickly and charge a small fortune, so consider taking public transportation. *Free; open every day; map:L1* ♿

### 4) PIER 39

**The Embarcadero at Beach St; 415/981-PIER** The goal of Pier 39's developers was to re-create the genteel boardwalk culture of the 19th century. The 4½-acre multilevel waterfront complex was constructed atop an abandoned cargo pier and opened to the public in 1978, offering more than 100 stores, 10 restaurants, a massive arcade, a two-tiered Venetian carousel, and beautiful bay views. But although Pier 39 is certainly a spectacle, it bears no resemblance to anything remotely genteel. Then again, it's hard to get an overall impression of the architecture while elbowing through throngs of tourists. Reportedly the third-most-visited tourist site in the world (Walt Disney can claim the first two), this place is not recommended for the claustrophobic or anyone who loathes overly contrived tourist attractions.

The Pier's restaurants are known for fun atmosphere rather than quality food, and the shops are more kitsch than classic, but with so many wares and attractions, it endeavors to offer something for everyone, particularly families. **PUPPETS ON THE PIER**, the **NFL SHOP**, **SF TEA & COFFEE COMPANY**, and **VICTORIAN SHOPPE** are among the schlocky stores vying for tourist dollars. Restaurants include the greasy **BUBBA GUMP SHRIMP CO.** (415/781-4867), **NEPTUNE'S PALACE** (415/434-2260), and **YET WAH** (415/282-0788). The 707,000-gallon, $38 million **AQUARIUM BY THE BAY** (888/SEA-DIVE or 415/623-5300; www.aquariumofthebay.com) entertains visitors with a menagerie of finned creatures including sharks and stingrays. Additionally, the big-screen **CINEMAX THEATER** provides visitors with an informative 35-minute movie about San Francisco, perfect for first-timers.

Pier 39 offers countless places to drop your cash (and credit), but the best attraction is free: The boisterous California **SEA LIONS** that call the actual pier home. Since the winter of 1990, hundreds of the barking pinnipeds have claimed the marina for their own, much to the annoyance of the property owners, who would prefer to rent the space to paying customers. Safeguarded by the federal Marine Mammal Protection Act, the sea lions are here to stay—at least until they decide to find other digs. On the weekends from 11am to 5pm, volunteers from the Marine Mammal Center give informative talks about the sea lions. The noisy herd summers in the Channel Islands, so if you're visiting anytime from June to August, you may miss out. *Free; open every day 10:30am–8:30pm; www.pier39.com; map:M1* &

## 5) GOLDEN GATE BRIDGE

**Hwys I/101, btwn San Francisco and Marin County; 415/921-5858** The successful marriage of engineering, design, and necessity has transformed the highway bridge linking San Francisco and Marin County into one of the most recognizable—and most photographed—landmarks in the world. Designed by engineer Joseph P. Strauss and architect Irving F. Morrow, the mile-long Golden Gate Bridge was built by a crew of hundreds, a number of whom gave the ultimate sacrifice. The 887,000-ton bridge, which opened in May 1937, took a mere 52 months to complete, but cost a then-riveting $35 million. The tollbooths, designed by Donald MacDonald to complement the original art deco feel, were added in 1982; the charge is now $3 for southbound traffic.

Though it's more than 60 years old, the Golden Gate Bridge's numbers are still impressive. The art deco twin towers rise 746 feet into the sky like a ladder—each rung a slightly different dimension—narrowing as the eye rises. The daring 4,200-foot span between the two towers held the record for the longest span of a suspension bridge for more than 20 years. The bridge boasts 7,650 feet of cables from anchorage to anchorage; the maximum side sway of the center span is 27.7 feet.

But don't take our word for it, because if there's one thing everyone should do at least once in their life, it's walk across the world-famous Golden Gate Bridge. Simply driving across won't work; to feel the bridge swaying under your feet as you peer 260 feet down to certain death— now that's living. It's a 1¼-mile stroll across and takes about an hour round-trip. Pedestrians and bicyclists must use the path on the east side of the bridge, which is open daily from 5am to 9pm (bicyclists have to use the west side on weekends). Free parking is available at both ends of the bridge, though the lots usually fill up fast on summer weekends (late arrivals will have to park in the Presidio and walk). The vista point on the Marin side provides a perfect place to stop and reflect on the sheer beauty of this architectural and engineering wonder. Be sure to dress warmly or you'll be sorry: The weather is windy and cold most of the year. *www.goldengate.org; map:G1*

## 6) UNION SQUARE

**Bounded by Geary, Post, Stockton, and Powell Sts** The area around Union Square was once home to fashionable turn-of-the century houses, synagogues, and churches. In 1847, civil engineer Jasper O'Farrell designed a spacious open square as a refuge in the growing city. During the American Civil War, San Franciscans—influenced by the elegant oratory of preacher Thomas Starr King—took a decidedly pro-Union stance, a momentous decision that eventually swayed the entire state. The square was named to commemorate this historic position. At the center of the square a bronze statue of Victory stands atop a granite Corinthian column, commemorating Admiral Dewey's exploits in the Spanish-American War. (The model for Victory was a young art student named Alma de Bretteville, who went on to marry the heir to the Spreckels sugar fortune. Decades later, she would help fund the creation of the California Palace of the Legion of Honor.)

Union Square was soon surrounded by the by-product of San Francisco's economic boom: Businesses and stores blossomed in the decades following the Gold Rush and statehood. In 1876, I. Magnin opened its doors at the corner of Geary and Stockton (sadly, the store has since closed). In 1896, the City of Paris (now Neiman Marcus) went up across the street. The famed St. Francis Hotel (now the Westin St. Francis) was not far behind, bursting on the scene in 1904. Soon after, the great earthquake and fire struck, leveling the entire area.

Undaunted by Mother Nature, San Franciscans continued their building boom and the square was soon in business again. Only a few of the older establishments, such as **BULLOCK & JONES** and **SHREVE & COMPANY**, remain. Most of the postquake buildings have been either demolished or taken over by newer, trendier tenants such as **NIKETOWN**, **MACY'S**, and **SAKS FIFTH AVENUE**. Gone are the days of crinoline-clad ladies promenading with parasols to protect themselves from the sun, but Union Square, like New York's Fifth Avenue, is still the historic heart of San Francisco shopping. A major renovation of the square is purportedly in the works, but it will be years before it's completed. *Map:M3*

## 7) LOMBARD STREET

**1000 block of Lombard St btwn Hyde and Leavenworth Sts** One curvaceous block of Lombard between Hyde and Leavenworth has given the street the title "the Crookedest Street in the World." In actuality, the majority of Lombard is wide and straight and filled with motels. But this little Russian Hill block with its eight switchbacks is certainly circuitous. What it isn't, however, is San Francisco's crookedest, let alone the world's. Vermont Street on Potrero Hill takes the honor for curves, but tourists still flock to Lombard in droves to wend their way down the world-renowned one-way street.

Perhaps it's the terraced gardens filled with hydrangeas, the beautiful brick-lined road, or the picturesque, carefully manicured hedges that attract such attention. What is certain is that block-long lines of cars queue up to witness this urban wonder during the summer weekends, causing some major congestion in a once-peaceful neighborhood (and boy, do the neighbors complain—but to little avail). While the best photo opportunities are from the bottom of the hill, most people linger at the top to take in the stunning vistas to the east. The view of the bay from this spot is truly breathtaking.

Lombard used to be a simple cobblestone street back in the early part of the 20th century. The hill's steep 27 percent grade led one inventive resident to propose a series of curves to make the area accessible to the increasingly popular automobile. Engineer Clyde Healy designed the present configuration, which transformed the steep grade to a mere 16 percent. The city paid for the initial work, but the residents chipped in for the fancy brickwork and agreed to tend their gardens. Talk of privatizing the street has been heard on and off for years, but city funds keep the site open to tourists. If you don't have a car, you can still walk the block via curve-free staircases on either side of the street.

Unfortunately for residents and tourists alike, this small stretch of Lombard simply can't handle all the traffic it attracts. If you plan to drive it on the weekend, expect long lines, detours, and potential overheating as you crawl up the steep incline that leads to the crooked block. It's a lot of work for a few seconds of fun, but hey—when in Rome. . . . *Map:L1*

## 8) GOLDEN GATE PARK

**Bounded by Stanyan St and the Great Hwy, Fulton St and Lincoln Wy; 415/391-2000 or 415/831-2700** Although the idea of converting this-barren, sandy land into a park was conceived in the 1860s, it wasn't until a Scot named John McClaren arrived in 1887 that landscaping of the park began. Part botanist and part landscaper, McClaren had developed a new strain of grass called sea bent, which he had planted to hold the sandy soil along Scotland's Firth of Forth. Presented with the same challenge at the windswept tip of this peninsula, he planted sea bent grasses to anchor the sandy soil and built the two windmills (both of which still stand today) on the western edge of the park to pump water for irrigation. After this was accomplished, McClaren spent the next 40 years building a natural retaining wall out of bundled sticks to keep the ocean from eroding the western fringe of the park.

The end result was (and still is) a masterpiece of park design. The main playground for an entire city, Golden Gate Park encompasses 1,017 acres of beautiful, lush grounds dotted with lakes, forested groves, gardens, and ponds, as well as dozens of miles of trails for hikers, bikers, and horses. For a good introduction to the park's attractions, join one of the free guided walking tours held every weekend from May through October; call the Friends of Recreation and Parks (415/263-0991 or 415/750-5105) for more information.

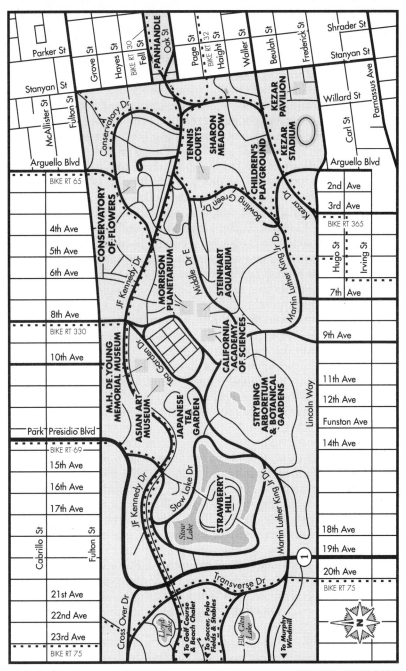

GOLDEN GATE PARK

Park highlights include the **CALIFORNIA ACADEMY OF SCIENCES** (off Middle Dr E, btwn John F. Kennedy and Martin Luther King Jr. Drs; 415/750-7145). While tourists flock to Fisherman's Wharf and Pier 39, locals often head in the other direction to the extraordinary California Academy of Sciences, where under one roof you'll find the **NATURAL HISTORY MUSEUM**, which traces the course of 3½ billion years of evolution, from the earliest life forms to the present day, via dozens of fantastic exhibits; the **MORRISON PLANETARIUM**, offering guided tours through the universe via its 65-foot domed ceiling (with such evocative titles as "The Universe Unveiled" and "Star Death: The Birth of Black Holes") and related cosmos exhibits in the adjacent Earth and Space Hall; and the superb **STEINHART AQUARIUM**, which contains one of the most diverse collections of aquatic life in the world—about 14,500 specimens, including seals, dolphins, penguins, and alligators, in nearly 200 displays such as the hands-on California tide pool (a big hit with kids), the living coral reef, and the 100,000-gallon Fish Roundabout. *Admission charge for adults and children 4 and older; free for everyone the first Wed of each month. Planetarium/Laserium shows are $2.50 for adults and $1.25 for children under 18 and seniors 65 and over; open every day; www.cal academy.org; map:H5*

**STRYBING ARBORETUM AND BOTANICAL GARDENS** (near 9th Ave and Lincoln Wy; 415/661-1316). At this botanist's paradise, more than 7,000 plant and tree varieties are on display, including a grove of California redwoods, numerous rare species, and ancient plants growing in the "Primitive Garden." *Open Mon–Fri 8am–4:30pm, Sat–Sun 10am–5pm; docent tours begin at 1pm every day.*

**CONSERVATORY OF FLOWERS** (John F. Kennedy Dr near Conservatory Dr; 415/641-7978). Built for the 1894 Midwinter Exposition, this Victorian fairyland hothouse—modeled on the famous glass house at Kew Gardens in London—was full of tropical flora until massive storms destroyed most of its glass-paneled glory in 1995. It's still an architectural beauty worth admiring from the outside, but is closed until enough money can be acquired to pay the lofty repair bill (the latest rumor is that it won't be totally repaired until 2004). To the right of the entrance, in the center of what was once a carriage roundabout, is the colorful **DAHLIA GARDEN**, the most beautiful flower garden in the park (particularly spring through fall).

**STOW LAKE** West of the Conservatory of Flowers off John F. Kennedy Drive is serene Stow Lake, where you can rent rowboats, paddleboats, and electric boats daily from 9am to 4pm and circle the 430-foot-high artificial island known as **STRAWBERRY HILL**, the highest peak in the park (and a very romantic picnic spot). Highlights include the hill's waterfall and Chinese moon-watching pavilion, as well as the numerous turtles and ducks that live on the serene lake; call 415/752-0347 for boat rental information.

**JAPANESE TEA GARDEN** (415/752-1171). Located off Martin Luther King Jr. Drive in Golden Gate Park (near the Strybing Arboretum), this is the oldest Japanese-style park in the United States. The Garden, which first opened its gates in 1894 for the Midwinter Exposition, is a real crowd-pleaser, particularly when the cherry blossoms and azaleas bloom in late March and April. On weekdays and rainy afternoons it's a peaceful, relaxing experience to wander along the winding paths and high-arched bridges through groves of cherry trees and sculptured bonsai. Highlights include the massive bronze Buddha (cast in Japan in 1790 and donated by the Gump family), the Shinto wooden pagoda, and the Wishing Bridge, which appears as a complete circle when reflected in the water. The story goes that the original curators, the Hagiwara family, invented the fortune cookie to be served here with tea (though the Golden Gate Fortune Cookies factory makes the same claim). *Free; open every day Nov–Feb 8:30am–5pm, Mar–Oct 8:30am–6pm. For more information, call 415/752-1171.*

**CHILDREN'S PLAYGROUND** If you have youngsters in tow, be sure to take them to the Children's Playground, located at the intersection of Martin Luther King Jr. and Kezar Drives. The highlight here is the dazzling, restored 1912 carousel (the oldest one in a public park), which is guaranteed to thrill younger kids and bring back fond memories to the older folks.

**CAR-FREE SUNDAYS** Every Sunday, Golden Gate Park's main drag, John F. Kennedy Drive, is closed to auto traffic so hundreds of skaters and joggers can recreate on the wide tree-lined street. Skate rentals are readily available on Fulton Street and on Haight Street. *Map:D5–I5*

## 9) COIT TOWER

**I Telegraph Hill Blvd; 415/362-0808** A childhood rescue from a fiery blaze left Lillie Hitchcock forever fascinated with firefighting and firemen. Legendary for her saucy behavior, this 19th-century socialite liked to hang out at the Engine Company Number 5 and, according to legend, often dressed in firemen's uniforms. (It was the undressing that made society cringe.)

In spite of her brazen past, she married Howard Coit, a wealthy businessman, and when she died in 1929 she left $125,000 to the city "to be expended in an appropriate manner for the purpose of adding to the beauty of the city which I have always loved." The Coit Advisory Committee, after much haranguing, settled on a memorial tower. In 1933 a 180-foot fluted pillar was erected high atop a hill amid the trees of Pioneer Park, one of the city's oldest parks. Designed by architect Arthur Brown Jr. of City Hall fame, this still-controversial tower is said to resemble a fire hose. Off-color comparisons have also been made over the years, but the tower remains a landmark on the city's skyline nonetheless.

In 1934 President Franklin Roosevelt's Works Progress Administration provided funding for local artists to embellish the tower lobby with a series of frescoes that paid homage to the men and women who labored to make California great. Twenty-five master artists and 19 apprentices worked on the murals for 8½ months; each received $94 a month for their efforts. Ray Boynton's *Animal Force and Machine Force* juxtaposes fishermen pulling their catch in from the sea with a hydroelectric dam. *California,* by Maxine Albro, highlights the importance of agriculture to the state. One of the most controversial murals is by John Langley Howard: His *California Industrial Scenes* depicts the harsh reality of the country's laboring poor—migrant workers, miners, and construction workers toiling in dangerous, stressful conditions for little pay.

While many visitors are content to admire the view from the circular parking lot, the small admission fee to view the murals includes an elevator ride to the top of the tower, offering spectacular views of the North Bay, including the Golden Gate Bridge, and of the hills of Contra Costa County to the east. Better yet, stroll up at sunset on a clear San Francisco day and be rewarded by the sight of the magical lights of the skyscrapers, bridges, and the sailboats floating on the bay. To get here, head east on Lombard Street, which takes you directly to Coit Tower. *Admission charge (to view the inside of the tower) for adults and children 5 and older. Open every day 10am–7pm; map:N1*

## 10) THE PRESIDIO

**Entrances via Lombard St, Marina Blvd, Arguello Blvd, Presidio Ave, and Lincoln Blvd; 415/561-4323** For more than 200 years the Presidio served as San Francisco's principal military outpost, originally commandeered for its strategic importance and later retained for its private golf course. Founded in 1776 by Spaniard Jose Joaquin Moraga, it was occupied from 1822 to 1835 by the Mexican government when the region  was known as Alta California. When California's gold-filled upper half was annexed by the United States, the Presidio remained a military base. During the rough-and-tumble Gold Rush years, added fortifications were built to protect the city. During the war with Spain in 1898, thousands of troops camped in tent cities awaiting shipment to the Philippines, and soon afterward, the Presidio proved strategically important as the United States stretched its interests west across the Pacific to Hawaii and beyond.

In 1914, troops under the command of General John Pershing left here to pursue Pancho Villa and his men. Crissy Army Airfield, the first of its kind on the West Coast, was established here in the 1920s. After the attack on Pearl Harbor and the ensuing U.S. involvement in World War II, the Presidio became the headquarters for the Western Defense Command, and more than a million soldiers passed through it on their way to war. The base hospital served 72,000 sick and wounded during that era.

In the 1950s, the Presidio served as the headquarters for the Sixth U.S. Army and a missile defense post, but in 1972 sections of the 1,480-acre installation were turned over to the Golden Gate National Recreation Area (GGNRA) and opened to the public as part of the largest network of urban parkland in the world. In 1989 the Pentagon decided to close the post, and the entire area—consisting of coastal scrub, prairie grasslands, sand dunes, a variety of rare plants, and more than 150 species of birds—became part of the GGNRA (though many army officers' homes and barracks still remain, as does the national cemetery). With miles of biking and hiking trails and a first-class golf course, the Presidio remains a verdant oasis in the urban jungle.

As you drive through the Presidio, you'll see numerous signs of its military past, including dozens of recessed bunkers and many war memorials. One of the most poignant is the tribute to the men of the USS *San Francisco*. Sections of the actual bridge of the warship—riddled with enormous holes from enemy gunfire—flank a series of bronze plaques depicting the sad, heroic story of the 107 men lost in one of the fiercest close-quarter battles in naval history. The shrine is located at the end of El Camino del Mar, one block up from the Cliff House Restaurant and gift shop.

To inquire about the wide array of free guided tours of the Presidio's highlights—everything from bike rides to pier crabbing and cemetery walks—call the **PRESIDIO VISITOR CENTER AND ARMY MUSEUM** for information (415/561-4323). The top tour pick is **FORT POINT**, which was constructed in 1853 to protect the narrow entrance to the harbor. It was built to house 500 soldiers manning 126 muzzle-loading cannons, but by 1900 it became obsolete, and only the solidly built brick edifice remains. Currently it's open Friday through Sunday from 9am to 5pm, and park rangers clad in authentic Civil War garb give guided tours and smooth-bore cannon demonstrations at the site once or twice daily, depending on the time of year (that explains the strange booming sound you'll hear if you're anywhere near the fort). For more information, call 415/556-1693.

After the tour, take a bayside walk along the **GOLDEN GATE PROMENADE**, the most popular and scenic jogging route in the city. The 4-mile path, which starts (or ends) at Fort Point, leads past the windsurfers off Crissy Field, around the Yacht Harbor, and along the Marina Green toward Fort Mason and Aquatic Park. Note: Navigating your way into, through, and out of the Presidio is almost comically confusing. Even locals get temporarily turned around as they attempt to negotiate the maze of winding roads, dead ends, and maddening loops, so don't even attempt the trip without a map. The smartest approach is to head due west on Geary Boulevard to the end, stop by the GGNRA Visitors Center (415/556-8642) behind the Cliff House Restaurant, and plunk down

$2.50 for *The Official Map & Guide to the Presidio. Open every day 10am–5pm; map:G1-3–J1-3*

## 11) GHIRARDELLI SQUARE AND THE CANNERY

**900 North Point St btwn Polk and Larkin Sts; 415/775-5500, 2801 Leavenworth St at Beach St; 415/771-3112** Domingo Ghirardelli (pronounced "gear-ar-DELI"), the Italian-born founder of San Francisco's signature chocolate company, came to California in 1849 to search for gold, but he had better luck selling sweets. He set up shop in Jackson Square and was so successful that his sons later expanded the business. In 1893 they purchased land in a then-remote northern district of the city for a new factory. The Ghirardelli family hired architect William Mooser Sr., an important player in the development of turn-of-the-century San Francisco, to design a modern complex that would span an entire block of the waterfront. The famous Clock Tower office building, a derivation of the French Château de Blois, was the final edifice to go up.

Along with the glowing Ghirardelli sign that lit the harbor at night, the Clock Tower became a treasured jewel in the skyline. When the plant could not keep up with technology and was abandoned for a newer, sleeker East Bay property, fear grew that the landmark would be demolished. Enter another San Francisco entrepreneur, William Roth, heir to the Matson shipping fortune. In order to preserve the city's now-famous waterfront silhouette, he bought the property and decided to transform it.

His vision was not some staid museum, but a 10-level shopping complex with 50 stores and 20 restaurants of various stripes. Dozens of architects and artists worked on the project, which attempted to capture the spirit of the old factory while offering a modern touch. Today it is one of the more tasteful spots in the frenetic maze of consumerism that has overwhelmed the wharf.

From July to September, historic walking tours of the square are offered by guides dressed in period costume. The 20-minute tour includes historic information about Domingo Ghirardelli and his family, his chocolate empire, the eight buildings within Ghirardelli Square, and Andrea, the controversial mermaid fountain sculpture. Guests receive chocolate treats at the end of the tour.

Dozens of boutiques make Ghirardelli Square a fun destination for shopping enthusiasts. **CARLO BARON LEATHER** features a good selection of leather fashions. **GORDON BENNETT** specializes in furnishings for home and garden. The **HAT GENERATION** has a collection of unique headgear, both playful and serious. The nationally known **NATURE COMPANY** sells gifts, books, music, and toys with an environmental focus. A wide array of glass art and decorative items are available at **THE GLASS SCULPTORS. PEARL OF THE ORIENT** offers a fine collection of pearl jewelry.

Three art galleries call Ghirardelli home. The **MARK REUBEN GALLERY**, on the first floor of the Cocoa Building, focuses on sports-related works and history legends. Works by contemporary American artists fill the **MUD, WIND, AND FIRE GALLERY**, on the first floor of the Mustard Building. The Woolen Mill Building is home to the **WHITE BUFFALO GALLERY**, which specializes in American Indian art and jewelry.

Several fine restaurants are located in the complex. The **MANDARIN RESTAURANT** (900 North Point St btwn Polk and Larkin Sts; 415/673-8812), in the Woolen Mill Building, has long offered one of San Francisco's finest Peking-Sichuan dining experiences. **MCCORMICK & KULETO'S** (900 North Point St btwn Beach and Larkin Sts; 415/929-1730), in the Wurster Building, features classic seafood dishes with a spectacular view of the bay. The city's most elegant Indian food can be found at **GAYLORD INDIA RESTAURANT** (900 North Point St btwn Polk and Larkin Sts; 415/771-8822), on the third and fourth floors of the historic Chocolate Building. Recently opened in the spot formerly held by Long Bar is **ANA MANDARA** (891 Beach at Polk St; 415/771-6800; see review in the Restaurants chapter); located in the Power House Building, this French-Vietnamese restaurant is owned in part by actor Don Johnson and sometimes appears on his TV show, *Nash Bridges*.

## THE CANNERY

The brick facade is all that remains of architect William M. Mooser Sr.'s 1907 fruit canning plant, cleverly named the Cannery (2801 Leavenworth St at Beach St; 415/771-3112). The building's entrails were completely gutted in the late 1960s when enterprising developers converted the structure into a mall with more than 50 different shops on three floors. For stability, a reinforced concrete structure was carefully inserted into the existing brick building. The result is a serene blend of old and new, where hundred-year-old olive trees mingle with modern cafes and trendy vendors in a central courtyard. On the top floor, **JACK'S CANNERY BAR** (415/931-6400) boasts more than 110 beers on tap, a national record (try a glass of the locally made Foghorn barley wine—it really packs a wallop). *Free; open every day 10am–9pm in summer, 10am–6pm in winter; map:L1*

## 12) THE EXPLORATORIUM AND PALACE OF FINE ARTS

**3601 Lyon St at Marina Blvd; 415/563-7337 or 415/561-0360 for recorded information, 3301 Lyon St at Bay St; 415/563-6504** Founded by Frank Oppenheimer, brother of the inventor of the A-bomb, the  Exploratorium has been called the finest science museum in the United States by *Scientific American* magazine. But to call it a museum is misleading. While more than 100,000 square feet of science-related objects are on display (you could spend all day here and still not see everything), visitors aren't expected to look from a distance: Touching is definitely encouraged. The Exploratorium offers 400 hands-on displays where children and adults alike can create fog, experience a face-morphing screen, design bubbles, touch a tornado, or step inside an optical illusion. Visitors are invited to explore the wondrous world of science through displays that explain the phenomena behind light, electricity, motion, sound, and weather.

A visit to the **TACTILE DOME**—a series of lightproof, soundproof chambers that visitors navigate using only their sense of touch—requires making reservations. **PLAYSQUARE** offers younger children (accompanied by an adult) the chance to use their imaginations as they try out motor skills and social skills.

The Exploratorium's unique appeal draws visitors from all over the globe, including such notables as President Bill Clinton and science author Oliver Sacks. The gift shop, chock-full of educational tools and toys, is well worth a visit (great for high-quality stocking stuffers). A small cafe serves sandwiches, salads, and various coffee drinks. Parking is free. *Admission charge for adults and children 3 and older; free the first Wed of each month. Memorial Day–Labor Day and holidays: Mon–Tues and Thurs–Sun 10am–6pm, Wed 10am–9pm. Rest of the year: Tues and Thurs–Sun 10am–5pm; Wed 10am–9pm; www.exploratorium.edu; map:J1* &

## PALACE OF FINE ARTS

Architect Bernard Maybeck's mock-Roman ruin and reflecting pool, an ode to classical art and architecture, is all that remains of the Panama-Pacific International Exposition, held along San Francisco's marina in 1915. The event was more than an international fair; it was a chance for San Francisco to celebrate its renaissance after the devastation of the then-recent earthquake and fire. In a spirited show of decadence, a mile-long stretch of the marina was lined with neoclassical buildings to form a mock city, with the Palace of Fine Arts its glowing centerpiece. Since officially the party was meant to celebrate the opening of the Panama Canal, the Tower of Jewels re-created that engineering feat, complete with movable parts and electric lights.

The party lasted 288 days, and when it was over many locals didn't want the fabulous centerpiece destroyed. Maybeck's design was saved and used as a recreation area. Later it housed ammunition during World War II. After the war the building fell into ruin (actual this time, not re-created). In 1962 Walter Johnson, a wealthy Marina District resident, offered to help refurbish the Beaux Arts structure. With matching funds from the government in hand, William Merchant was enlisted to bring the beauty back to life. It took 13 years and $7 million, but the central rotunda with its sea of rosy Corinthian columns now resides permanently at the corner of Lyon and Bay Streets. The swan-filled waters and verdant grounds provide an ideal setting for picnicking (bring bread crumbs), strolling, and the ever-popular wedding photos.

Part of the city-owned space has been converted into a theater. Originally built for ballet performances, the Palace of Fine Arts Theatre's 75-foot-wide stage houses not only stage productions but also film festivals, concerts, local graduation ceremonies, and, when he's in town, David Letterman's *Late Show.*

## 13) SAN FRANCISCO MUSEUM OF MODERN ART

**151 3rd St btwn Mission and Howard Sts; 415/357-4000** The San Francisco Museum of Modern Art (SFMOMA), housed in a $62 million modernist building designed by internationally acclaimed Swiss architect Mario Botta, offers more than 17,000 works of art, including gems by Picasso, Matisse, O'Keeffe, Rivera, Pollock, Warhol, Klee, De Forest, and Lichtenstein, to name just a few. Some contend that the museum's exhibition space plays second fiddle to the dramatic black-and-white central tower that climbs out of Botta's impressive sienna brick building. The interior architecture is equally impressive. Natural light falls through the circular skylight, illuminating the central atrium and a few of the nearby galleries. A catwalk stretches high above the atrium, offering museum-goers a touch of adventure along with their culture.

After whisking David Ross away from his position at the helm of New York's Whitney Museum, SFMOMA went on a buying spree, acquiring 23 new works by leading 20th-century artists, including Louise Bourgeois, Marcel Duchamp, Alberto Giacometti, Anselm Kiefer, Brice Marden, Piet Mondrian, Robert Motherwell, Barnett Newman, Robert Rauschenberg, and Wayne Thiebaud. (Ross then left San Francisco for greener pastures in 2001.) SFMOMA was also one of the first to recognize photography as a major art form; its extensive collection includes more than 9,000 photographs by such notables as Ansel Adams, Henri Cartier-Bresson, and Edward Weston.

In addition to its growing permanent collection, the museum has become the West Coast stop for many ambitious traveling shows. Exhibition subjects run the gamut from Jasper Johns and René Magritte to contemporary Japanese textiles and the 19th-century landscape photographs of Carleton Watkins. Docent-led tours take place daily; times are posted at the admission desk. Call for current details of upcoming special events, or visit the website below.

Even if you don't tour the museum, be sure to visit the adjoining **MUSEUMSTORE**, which carries a fantastic collection of modern-chic art, books, jewelry, desk toys, and other stylish gift items (in fact, it's one of the best shops in the city for tasteful souvenirs). The museum also has an excellent, inexpensive, and oh-so-trendy cafe, **CAFFE MUSEO**, located to the right of the museum entrance. Even 9-to-5ers come here daily for the fresh soups, sandwiches, salads, and coffee drinks. *Admission charge for adults and children 13 and older; half-price for all Thurs 6–9pm; free*

*the first Tues of each month; open Mon–Tues, Fri–Sun 10am–6pm,*
*Thurs 10am–9pm; www.sfmoma.org; map:N3* &

## 14) YERBA BUENA CENTER FOR THE ARTS—YERBA BUENA GARDENS—METREON

**701 Mission St at 3rd St; 415/978-2700 or 415/978-ARTS for box office**
After 20-plus years of politics, Yerba Buena Center for the Arts opened in 1993 and instantly provided a welcome addition to the burgeoning South of Market (SoMa) District. Across Third Street from the San Francisco Museum of Modern Art, and set amid a peaceful park, the center hosts artists from the worlds of theater, dance, plastic arts, and performance art. Unlike most museums, Yerba Buena has no permanent collection, but strives instead to offer exhibition opportunities to a broad range of artists.

Built by the San Francisco Redevelopment Agency, the high-tech center fills two buildings: a theater and a visual arts space. The **GALLERIES AND FORUM**, designed by Japanese architect Fumihiko Maki, feature works by local, national, and international artists. Recent exhibitions include *Nothing but Ways* by filmmakers Lynn Kirby and Trinh T. Minh-Ha, and new ceramic works by Robert Hudson and Richard Shaw. The theater space, designed by James Stewart Polshek, features a 45-foot-deep stage and a 44-foot proscenium and seats 755 people. The space is rented out to dance and theater companies. *Admission charge for adults and children 6 and older; free the first Tues of each month; open Tues–Wed, Sat–Sun 11am–6pm, Thur–Fri 11am–8pm; www.yerbabuenaarts.org; map:N3* &

### YERBA BUENA GARDENS

In the heart of the city (Mission St btwn 3rd and 4th Sts), across from the San Francisco Museum of Modern Art, is Yerba Buena Gardens. This 5-acre park in the middle of SoMa features an Esplanade Garden with restaurants and cafes, a sculpture garden, and inviting stretches of wide-open grassy space. A beautiful memorial to Martin Luther King Jr. sits partially hidden behind a glistening 50-foot-high waterfall. The memorial's multiple panels feature odes to peace and tolerance written in a number of languages. Bands play regularly during lunch, making this a popular spot for a noontime picnic.

Newly added is the $56 million **ROOFTOP AT YERBA BUENA**, devoted to youth recreation; the highlight is a 93-year-old hand-carved carousel. Originally from San Francisco's infamous Playland-at-the-Beach, the carousel returned to the city after having spent 20 years in Southern California. Also at the Rooftop is an NHL-regulation-size **HOCKEY RINK**, which serves hockey teams and figure skaters and sports a breathtaking view of the San Francisco skyline. The rink is the home of former Olympian Brian Boitano's Youth Skate, which provides free ice time and skating lessons to area kids. Children can also enjoy a **12-LANE BOWLING ALLEY**, a technology and arts center called **ZEUM** (415/777-

2800; www.zeum.com), and an interactive play and learning garden for and by kids. Tours of Yerba Buena Gardens are available by appointment for a nominal fee; for more details, call 415/541-0312. *Map:N3*

### METREON

Metreon (4th and Mission Sts at Yerba Buena Gardens; 415/369-6000 or 415/369-6200) is a South of Market megaplex entertainment center that is billed as one of the most forward-looking play/shop environments in existence. It certainly blows the movie competition out of the water: a 350,000-square-foot complex with 3,900 stadium-style seats and "the most advanced digital cinema sound in the world today." The **IMAX THE-ATRE**—with the largest screen in North America—features 3-D headsets that bring the screen action "into" the audience.

Metreon also offers a number of shops to peruse before or after the show. **MICROSOFT SF** and **SONYSTYLE** sell a predictable array of their own gadgets. More interesting is the **DISCOVERY CHANNEL STORE**, sure to be a hit with devotees of animal documentaries. At **WILD THINGS**, kids are encouraged to make up and perform in their own adventures with a crew of creative monsters modeled after those in Maurice Sendak's book. The **METREON GATEWAY** hosts a lively marketplace that aims for a street-fair feel; local artists sell original art, clothing, and gift items.

A few new dining venues endeavor to draw picky San Franciscans to the complex. **JILLIAN'S** claims to be the ultimate in entertainment with food, drinks, pool tables, videos, live music, and a DJ. **MONTAGE** (415/369-6111) cooks up California cuisine with an emphasis on fresh seafood. You can order movie tickets while you dine, and they're even brought to your table. And a cantina in a garage?? That's **MALVINA'S**, tucked into the bizarre world of Jean "Moebius" Giraud's fictional work *The Airtight Garage*. Maurice Sendak is on display here, too; his artistry is the inspiration for this diner-style restaurant. Don't expect a crew of hovering waiters, though—this is a do-it-yourself spot.

In addition to new eateries, Metreon offers spin-offs from five of the city's favorites: SoMa's **LONG LIFE NOODLE CO. & JOOK JOINT** offers unique and inexpensive Asian cuisine; the Castro's **FIREWOOD CAFE** features salads and pizza; Marin's venerable **BUCKHORN** specializes in grilled meats; **SANRAKU** re-creates the Japanese favorites popular at its lower Nob Hill location; and **LUNA LOCA** offers south-of-the-border fare. And of course, there's the ever-present **STARBUCKS**. *www.metreon.com; map:N3*

## 15) PACIFIC BELL PARK

**3rd and King Sts; 415/972-2000** The best thing to happen to San Francisco in a long time is the completion of the magnificent new Pacific Bell Park, praised by sportswriters as one of the finest ballparks in America. Even if you're not a baseball fan, you'll still be impressed by the old-school design and bayside location of the $319 million ballpark, located at the southeast corner of the South of Market District, at the south end of the Embarcadero. Do whatever it takes to score yourself some tickets if the Giants are in town—it's the best and biggest (the 13-acre ballpark seats 40,800) party in town.

There's only one problem: During the Major League season—which runs from April through October—tickets to the game are usually hard to come by, and expensive when you can find them. You can try to obtain them through BASS Ticketmaster (510/762-2277), or you can join the "Bleacher Bums" by purchasing one of the 500 bleacher-seat tickets sold every day before the game. Even that is no simple task, however: You have to show up at the ballpark four hours early to get a lottery number (you'll see the line on the north side of the building along Third St), then come back two hours before the game to get your tickets (maximum four per person). The payoff for your trouble is that the tickets are only $8.50 to $10. If the bleacher seats are sold out, you can still watch the game by joining the "Knothole Gang," the group of fans who stand at the Port-walk (located behind right field) to catch a free glimpse through cut-out portholes that look into the ballpark. In the spirit of sharing, Portwalk peekers are encouraged to take in only an inning or two before giving way to fellow fans.

One sure way to get into the ballpark is to take a guided tour. The **PACIFIC BELL PARK TOURS**, which run seven days a week every hour starting at 10am, with the last tour leaving at 2pm, take you where even the most diehard fans have never been, including the dugout (no spitting), visitors' clubhouse, press box, a luxury suite, and more. *Admission charge for the tour; no tours on game days, and limited tours on the day of night games; www.sfgiants.com or www.pacbellpark.com; map:O4*

### 16) GOLDEN GATE NATIONAL RECREATION AREA

The Golden Gate National Recreation Area (GGNRA) encompasses some of the Bay Area's (and Northern California's) most beautiful real estate and is a recreational outlet for the 20 million visitors who play here each year. At nearly 80,000 acres, it's the largest urban park in the world, twice the size of San Francisco itself. The late San Francisco Congressman Philip Burton, an early environmentalist, was responsible for drafting the legislation that preserves lands vacated by the military for public use. The National Park Service protects these lands against developers, whose mouths must salivate at the thought of all the potential million-dollar lots that line the coast.

While the GGNRA is the modern protector of this vast land, it is really the military we have to thank for the preservation of so much open space. Even before statehood, the Marin Headlands and San Francisco coast were sequestered for strategic military installations; their presence has long kept developers at bay. Today these now-decommissioned installations provide some of the most beautiful views found anywhere in the world.

In San Francisco, the GGNRA consists of the **PRESIDIO, FORT POINT, CRISSY FIELD,** the **SAN FRANCISCO MARITIME NATIONAL HISTORICAL PARK, OCEAN BEACH, BAKER BEACH, CHINA BEACH,** and **LAND'S END,** along with the shoreline between Fort Mason and the Golden Gate Bridge. (Most of these areas are covered elsewhere in this chapter; see index for specific page numbers.) **ALCATRAZ ISLAND** falls under GGNRA jurisdiction as well. The paths and trails leading from Fort Mason to Fort Point are ideal for walking, jogging, or cycling, and you can even do in-line skating along some stretches.

Across the bay in Marin, the GGNRA oversees still more land. The **MARIN HEADLANDS** are an outpost of sanity for many San Franciscans. A mere bridge away from the hustle of urban life, the headlands are a verdant paradise for hikers, bikers, and horseback riders. Spend a day hiking around **MOUNT TAMALPAIS** or soaking up the sun on **TENNESSEE BEACH.** One of the most popular Marin Headlands attractions is the **MARINE MAMMAL CENTER** (415/289-SEAL), a volunteer-run hospital for injured and abandoned mammals of the sea. Signs list each animal's adopted name, species, stranding site, and injury—the latter of which, sadly, is usually human-caused. The center, located at the east end of Fort Cronkhite near Rodeo Lagoon, is open daily from 10am to 4pm; admission is free, but a donation is appreciated.

At Rodeo Beach, stop by the **MARIN HEADLANDS VISITORS CENTER,** housed on another decommissioned army base, for maps and information on this amazing area. Back in the city at Fort Mason, the GGNRA official headquarters (415/556-0560; www.nps.gov/goga) is the place to go for maps, information, and a free copy of the quarterly publication *Park Events,* listing activities and events throughout the GGNRA.

## 17) EMBARCADERO CENTER

**Bordered by Drumm, Sacramento, Clay, and Battery Sts; 415/772-0500** Developer David Rockefeller and architect John C. Portman Jr. turned a 10-acre downtown area into a modern shopping complex filled with a number of impressive works of art, including Louise Nevelson's *Sky Tree* and Jean Dubuffet's *La Chiffonniere.* With more than 120 shops, this three-level, four-block outdoor shopping complex endeavors to provide a happy compromise between the San Francisco Shopping Centre's enclosed mall world and the genteel shops along Post and Geary in Union Square. Bordered by Battery and Drumm west to east and Clay and Sacramento north to south, the busy center offers office workers a convenient place to shop and eat during the lunch hour and also attracts tourists from all over the world. They come for the popular names in fashion like **BANANA REPUBLIC, TALBOT'S, GAP, VICTORIA'S SECRET,**

ANN TAYLOR, and ENZO ANGIOLINI and housewares giants such as WILLIAMS-SONOMA and POTTERY BARN. But the center also houses a number of smaller boutiques with an indie feel, like EDWARD'S LUGGAGE and EARTH'S SAKE.

Small soup-and-sandwich cafes cater to the eat-and-run crowd, while tried-and-true favorites like CHEVY'S (415/391-2323) and PIZZERIA UNO (415/397-8667) provide a more festive dining atmosphere. For a more elegant meal, try SCOTT'S SEAFOOD (415/981-0622), HARBOR VILLAGE (415/781-8833), or SPLENDIDO (415/986-3222).

A welcome addition to the complex is the EMBARCADERO CENTER CINEMA (415/352-0810). The five screens occasionally show blockbuster titles, but the focus is definitely on foreign and independent features. Map:N2

## 18) ALAMO SQUARE HISTORICAL DISTRICT

**Hayes and Steiner Sts; 415/292-2009** Alamo Square, named for the poplar trees that lined the area in the 1860s (*alamo* is Spanish for "poplar"), is a quiet hilltop park bounded by Steiner, Fulton, Webster, and Grove Streets. Home to San Francisco's famous row of Victorian homes known as the PAINTED LADIES, the park is one of the most visited and photographed spots in the city. Built between 1892 and 1896 by Irish-born carpenter Matthew Cavanaugh, the seven Queen Anne–style homes lining Steiner Street feature similar three-story design with bay windows, decorative wood trim, and steeply angled roofs. Cavanaugh lived in number 722 with his family, but he built the others as spec houses. Most people pass through the area on their way to Japantown or the Haight, taking a few snapshots of the colorful houses and continuing on their way. But the park deserves a longer look. A leisurely picnic allows time to admire the views of the renovated City Hall down Fulton Street and reflect on the turn-of-the-century elegance of the surrounding Victorian homes (a handful have been turned into bed-and-breakfasts).

The ARCHBISHOP'S MANSION (1000 Fulton St at Steiner St; 415/563-7872), which opened as a bed-and-breakfast in 1982, was built in 1904 as the residence for the Catholic Archbishop of San Francisco. In 1980, Jonathan Shannon and Jeffrey Ross began renovating the Second Empire–style mansion. After the walls and woodworking were overhauled, furnishings were gathered from sources around the world in an attempt to capture the feeling of the 19th-century French Belle Epoque. From the foyer, a three-story staircase sweeps upward to the guest rooms and suites, named after leading characters in famous operas. A 16-foot-wide stained-glass dome miraculously survived the 1906 earthquake. It's open to the public, so feel free to pop in and take a look.

Built in 1865 by the Baum family, the ALAMO SQUARE BED & BREAKFAST (719 Scott St at Fulton St; 415/922-2055) is a 15-room mansion designed by German-born architects Kenitzer and Barth. Constructed during a transitional period in San Francisco architecture, the Baum house incorporates three different styles: Queen Anne, neoclassical, and Colonial Revival. The roofline and cantilevered circular corner bay window are Queen Anne style, while the exterior ornamentation and oval window are neoclassical. The interior architecture boasts 12-foot ceilings and floors made of quarter-sawn oak. Also part of the Alamo Square Bed & Breakfast club is the Tudor-revival house next door. Constructed in 1896 by the firm of Knox and Cook, the building features elaborate half-timbering along its stucco finish. The interior of the home still retains the original unpainted redwood paneling with butterfly joints, as well as built-in window seats, cabinetry, and bookcases.

A third restored treasure is **CHATEAU TIVOLI** (1057 Steiner St at Golden Gate Ave; 415/776-5462). Built in 1892 by architect William H. Armitage, it was restored a century later at a cost of more than a million dollars. Today the 22-room historic landmark is also a bed-and-breakfast. *Map:K4*

## 19) SAN FRANCISCO MARITIME NATIONAL HISTORICAL PARK—MARITIME MUSEUM—HYDE STREET PIER

**Beach St at Polk St; 415/561-7100**   A few blocks west of Fisherman's Wharf is the San Francisco Maritime National Historical Park, which consists of the Maritime Museum and Hyde Street Pier tourist attractions. Perched at the foot of Aquatic Park, the **MARITIME MUSEUM** is a beautiful white ship-shaped building that houses one of the finest collections of maritime artifacts and memorabilia in the world. On display are figureheads, nautical instruments, and minutely detailed model ships. Photographs (including an 1851 image of hundreds of abandoned ships that were deserted en masse by crews rushing off to participate in the Gold Rush) and naval memorabilia pay tribute to the history of the seafaring vessels around the world. For bibliophiles, the **PORTER SHAW LIBRARY** has more than 14,000 volumes, back issues of some 500 periodicals, and an extensive bibliographic file on maritime-related works. The oral history collection preserves more than 400 interviews with salty sailors and some 100 sea chantey recordings. The library even offers classes in oar-making and chantey singing. *Maritime Museum open every day 10am–5pm. Admission charge for adults and children 12–17; free for seniors over 62; www.nps.gov/safr/sparks.html.*

Two blocks east of the museum is the **HYDE STREET PIER**, where several historic ships are now moored and open (boardable, even) to the public. Before the completion of the Golden Gate Bridge, the Hyde Street Pier served as a terminal for ferry service to Marin County and Berkeley. Today it draws crowds of cable car riders and historic ship enthusiasts (kids love this imaginative place as well). Among the vessels of yesteryear docked here are the following:

**THE BALCLUTHA:** A 256-foot square-rigger and one of the last great 19th-century sailing ships, she was built in Glasgow, Scotland, in 1886, and was used to carry grain from California at a near-record speed of 300 miles a day.

**THE C. A. THAYER:** This black-hulled, three-masted, 156-foot schooner was built in 1895 for transporting Pacific Northwest lumber to the carpentry shops of California.

**THE 1890 EUREKA:** The last of 50 paddle-wheel ferries that regularly plied the bay between San Francisco and Sausalito. The 300-foot side-wheeler made its final trip in 1957 and has since been restored to its original splendor at the height of the ferryboat era (even its cargo deck is loaded with antique cars and trucks).

Other historic ships on display include the **1907 HERCULES**, a 135-foot oceangoing steam tug; the two-masted **ALMA**, a 59-foot, flat-bottomed cargo-carrying sailboat used for bringing hay to the horses of San Francisco; and a 100-foot paddle tug called the **EPPLETON HALL**, built in England in 1914 to operate on London's River Thames. At the pier's small-boat shop, visitors can follow the restoration progress of historic boats from the museum's collection (the shop is behind the maritime bookstore on your right as you approach the ships). *Hyde Street Pier open every day 10am–6pm; museum closes at 5pm. Admission charge for adults and children 12–17; free for seniors over 62; www.nps.gov/safr.*

Also at the park is the **USS PAMPANITO**, located at Pier 45. This veteran submarine, built in 1943, sank five Japanese ships in the Pacific during World War II. Now a National Historic Landmark, it has been restored and is open to the public. Don't forget to duck as you explore the sub's torpedo room, control room, crew's quarters, and fully operational galley. World War II submarine captain Edward Beach narrates the self-guided audio tour, providing an insider's perspective on the underwater world of war (415/775-1943). *USS Pampanito open Mon–Thurs 9am–6pm, Fri–Sun 9am–8pm. Admission charge for adults and children ages 6 and older; map:L1*

## 20) CALIFORNIA PALACE OF THE LEGION OF HONOR

**Legion of Honor Dr at 34th Ave and Clement St in Lincoln Park; 415/750-3600 or 415/863-3330 for recorded information** Perched on a hilltop along San Francisco's rugged coast is one of the world's most dramatically situated museums. Closed for three years for seismic work and general renovation (which unearthed the bones of more than 1,000 pioneers buried in what was the old Golden Gate Cemetery), the museum reopened on November 11, 1997. Founded in 1924 by Alma de Bretteville Spreckels (wife of the sugar magnate) and Adolph Bernard, the

California Palace of the Legion of Honor stands as a monument to the soldiers who fell in France during World War I. The museum's neoclassical style and the triumphal arch were designed by George Applegarth and modeled after the Legion of Honor in Paris.

The Legion is home to one of the finest collections of **RODIN SCULPTURES** outside Paris. Several imposing statues fill the grounds as well; these include equestrian bronzes of El Cid and Joan of Arc, and one of only five original castings of Rodin's *The Thinker*. One of the most controversial works of art on the lawn is George Segal's *The Holocaust*. White plaster figures writhe on the ground while a solitary figure watches from behind a barbed-wire fence. The juxtaposition of this intense suffering with the natural beauty of the surrounding landscape renders the artwork even more disturbing—as was intended.

The Legion was originally devoted exclusively to French art but recently expanded its collection. Today the museum's holdings span 4,000 years of art. The 20 galleries on the museum's upper level are devoted to European art from the 14th to the 20th century. Key artists include El Greco, Rubens, Cellini, Rembrandt, Manet, Rodin, Monet, and Cézanne. Period rooms feature furniture and decorative arts from various eras, and include a dramatic Mudejar ceiling from medieval Spain. The lower level houses English and European porcelain and ancient Assyrian, Greek, Roman, and Egyptian art. Also on the lower level is the collection of the Achenbach Foundation for Graphic Arts, which has the largest holdings of graphic art in the West. The museum's collection of 70,000 works on paper has been digitized to make these fragile pieces available to the public.

The **LEGION CAFE** has a garden terrace with a spectacular view of the Golden Gate Bridge. Parking here is limited, so be prepared to walk up the hill from the surrounding streets. *Admission charge for adults and children 12 and older; free the first Tues of each month. Open Tues–Sun 9:30am–5pm; www.legionofhonor. com; map:E4*

## 21) CLIFF HOUSE

**1090 Point Lobos Ave at the west end of Geary Blvd; 415/386-3330** If 19th-century photographs of this shoreline establishment have lured you out to Ocean Beach, prepare to be disappointed. The famous seven-story structure built by Adolph Sutro in 1896 was actually the second incarnation of the Cliff House; the original, built in 1863, was destroyed in a fire in 1894. Sutro seized the opportunity to create something truly extraordinary. His architectural wonder, designed by C. J. Colley and F. S. Lemme, was lavish even by Victorian standards. Often compared to a gingerbread house, the building, sadly, was destroyed in a fire in 1907, though it lives on in photographs, postcards, and the memories of those who were alive during its heyday. The present Cliff House, the fifth incarnation, is a sad shadow of its former self. What used to be an architectural treat is now a boring box—albeit a box with great views. Design aside, the lack of truly spectacular waterfront dining in this city by the bay ensures that the Cliff House will draw crowds for decades to come.

If you're feeling adventurous, consider a tour through the ruins of the SUTRO BATHS—the famous bathing area that once drew hundreds to the shore. In 1886, Adolph Sutro completed the baths at a cost of $250,000. The complex spread over 3 acres and included fresh- and saltwater tanks, three restaurants, history exhibits, art galleries, and an amphitheater. Phenomenally popular in its early years, the bath complex was struggling financially by the 1930s. A skating rink was attempted, but that too failed. In 1966 the site was sold to land developers, but before their high-rise apartments were completed, a fire destroyed the property. Today the ruins of the baths are part of the Golden Gate National Recreation Area.

In what feels like an attempt to make up for the Cliff House's subpar exterior, visitors can choose from no less than three dining options. The most casual atmosphere is on the bottom level at PHINEAS T. BARNACLE (or PTB), where soups, sandwiches, and bar-food favorites like nachos and deep-fried calamari are available (along with magnificent ocean views in the fireside cocktail lounge next door). The SEAFOOD &

## FAMILY ATTRACTIONS

With its incredible selection of restaurants, bars, and museums, San Francisco is a great playground for adults, but it also has a number of kid-friendly venues. Top among them is the **Exploratorium** (415/563-7337 or 415/561-0360 for recorded information). Located at the Palace of Fine Arts in the Marina District, the Exploratorium, rated the number one museum in the West by *FamilyFun* magazine, offers youngsters a chance to experience science firsthand—literally. There are dozens of fun and fascinating exhibitions kids can touch and play with and experiments they can take part in. Other family favorites include the **San Francisco Zoo** (Sloat Blvd at 45th Ave; 415/753-7061); it may not rank among the nation's biggest, but the koalas, gorillas, and lions are certainly a hit with children. Younger kids will love the Children's Zoo—a 4-acre park featuring the Insect Zoo and barnyard area, where kids can pet and feed the animals. The herd of bison that makes **Golden Gate Park** its home offers a rare chance for kids and adults to see this historic beast up close. One of the neatest sites in the city for kids is the **Rooftop at Yerba Buena Gardens** at Fourth and Howard Streets. With a skating rink, children's museum, bowling alley, and kid-run garden to explore, your young ones can spend the entire day (and well into the evening) at this downtown oasis.

**BEVERAGE COMPANY** features oysters on the half shell, crab cakes, and a long list of fresh fillets and shellfish along with its beautiful view. A more elegant atmosphere is available at **UPSTAIRS AT THE CLIFF HOUSE,** where brunch is served on Sundays and traditional Continental cuisine—lobster, rack of lamb, and pasta—is dished up nightly. The ocean view and candles add a bit of romance to the otherwise unremarkable meal.

Also located here is the **NATIONAL PARK SERVICE INFORMATION CENTER** (open every day 10am–5pm; 415/556-8642), where you can pick up maps for exploring the Presidio, Marin Headlands, and the entire Golden Gate National Recreation Area. *Map:C4*

## 22) FORT MASON CENTER

**Marina Blvd and Buchanan St; 415/441-3400** The city of San Francisco has benefited time and time again from obsolete military real estate, and Fort Mason is perhaps the most inventive case. An important western command post for the U.S. Army in the second half of the 1800s and later a major military depot during World War II, the Fort Mason Center is now part of the Golden Gate National Recreation Area (GGNRA). Since 1977 the vast complex of waterfront warehouses has housed more than 50 nonprofit arts, advocacy, and environmental groups.

Fort Mason's military history spans two centuries. In 1797 Spanish soldiers built a small fortification here and called it Bateria San Jose. When the Yankees claimed the area in the mid-1800s, they inherited the existing battery and renamed it Black Point. In 1853, during the presidency of Millard Fillmore, the fort became a major army headquarters in the ongoing Indian wars. In 1882 the name was changed to Fort Mason in honor of Colonel Mason, the military governor of California from 1847 to 1849. During World War II, more than 1.5 million U.S. soldiers embarked for the Pacific theater from Fort Mason.

In somewhat of an ironic fate, today the ex–military base's focus is on culture. The center publishes a free monthly paper, *Fort Mason Center,* to keep locals and visitors abreast of the myriad events, exhibitions, and classes offered here. A number of museums and galleries bring the art world to the waterfront. **MUSEO ITALO-AMERICANO** is devoted to contemporary works by Italian and Italian-American artists. The **SAN FRANCISCO CRAFT AND FOLK ART MUSEUM** exhibits handicrafts from around the world and offers many distinctive items for sale. And the **AFRICAN-AMERICAN HISTORICAL AND CULTURAL SOCIETY** features a library, gallery, and exhibitions of African art.

The Center's five theaters include **LIFE ON THE WATER THEATRE** (Building B), the family-oriented Young Performers Theatre, the **MAGIC THEATRE** (Building D), which has premiered works by such playwrights as Sam Shepard, and **COWELL THEATER** (Pier 2), which hosts larger productions and the weekly radio program *West Coast Live*. International art exhibitions, crafts shows, and music events like the Celtic Music & Dance Festival are featured here throughout the year. **GREENS** (Building A; 415/771-6222) offers brilliant bay views along with award-winning vegetarian cuisine (see review in the Restaurants chapter).

A fairly demanding stairway leads from the waterfront to upper Fort Mason, where you'll find the **GREAT MEADOW**. This wide stretch of rolling green is perfect for picnics, Frisbee, or a nap in the sun (or fog). Alongside the meadow, former officers' quarters now house a youth hostel and the headquarters for the GGNRA, which provides information about its extensive park system. *Map:K1*

## 23) MISSION DOLORES

**3321 16th St at Dolores St; 415/621-8203** Mission San Francisco de Assis (better known as Mission Dolores) is the sixth of Father Junípero Serra's 21 California missions, as well as the oldest standing structure in San Francisco. The adobe building, designed by Father Francisco Palou, was begun in 1782 and completed in 1791. Miraculously, the edifice survived a period of neglect during the middle of the 19th century and then two major earthquakes, one in 1868 and the infamous one in 1906. Architect Willis Polk began the restoration of the site in 1918.

The original mission is a compact structure standing a mere 22 feet wide and 114 feet long. The original 4-foot-thick adobe walls have since been coated with cement to protect them from erosion, but several original details remain untouched. A trio of bronze bells brought from Mexico in the early 1800s decorate the chapel's interior. The hand-wrought ironwork along the font and altar is also original. Various statues and paintings record the rich Spanish Baroque tradition brought over to the New World by the conquistadores and later absorbed by Mexico.

The purpose of the many missions that run up and down the Camino Real from San Diego to Sonoma was to Christianize the Native Americans of the California frontier. The basket-weave designs of converted Costanoan Indians decorate the ceiling of the 175-seat chapel, where mass is still held at 7:30am on weekdays and 5pm on Saturdays.

For a $3 admission fee ($5 for a 45-minute audio tour), visitors can wander at a leisurely pace through the chapel and into the neighboring museum, which is filled with religious artifacts from Spanish America, including gifts to the mission from Father Serra. Also on display is a glass window that provides an interesting look at the building's underlying adobe.

One of the mission's best features is its cemetery (old movie buffs may recognize the spot from Alfred Hitchcock's *Vertigo*). Gravestones from three centuries fill this small parcel of land, but what you can't see are the markers for the more than 5,000 Costanoans who are reportedly buried here. Prominent figures from the days when Mexico ruled the land rest in peace here—among them Francisco de Haro, the first mayor of San Francisco, and Captain Luis Antonio Arguello, the first Mexican governor of Alta California. Not far away is the grave of mission architect Father Palou.

The larger, multidomed basilica next to the chapel was built in 1913. It can accommodate up to 1,100 parishioners and is used for three masses on Sunday as well as numerous weddings. *Open every day 9am–4:30pm; map:K5* &

## 24) CITY HALL

**1 Dr. Carlton B. Goodlett Pl at Polk St; 415/554-4858** San Francisco earthquakes have certainly taken their toll on City Hall. The old City Hall was devastated by the catastrophic events of 1906. In a drive to rebuild the city, newly elected Mayor "Sunny Jim" Rolph called for architects to bid on the new project. The front-runner was Chicago architect Daniel Burnham, who envisioned a complete overhaul of the entire Civic Center. The idea appealed to many in government who wanted to bring the city back to its prequake stature. Surprisingly, the job went to the local firm of Bakewell and Brown, with Arthur Brown Jr. in charge of designing the building. (Brown also designed the Opera House, Coit Tower, and Berkeley's City Hall.)

The striking Beaux Arts design was favored by Americans educated at the Ecole des Beaux Arts in Paris. The granite-and-marble edifice was topped by a massive dome (the world's fifth tallest), modeled after St. Peter's in Rome and the Capitol building in Washington, D.C. At 306 feet, it actually stands taller than the latter (which measures 288 feet). Over the Polk Street entrance, Renaissance-style sculptures by Henri Crenier symbolize Labor, Industry, Truth, Learning, Wisdom, and the Arts.

The doors to the 83-year-old City Hall reopened to the public in January 1999 after a four-year, $300 million renovation. The money was used to repair damage done by the 1989 Loma Prieta earthquake. In order to be completely retrofitted, the building was lifted off its base and placed on top of 600 vulcanized rubber and stainless steel base isolators, designed to insulate against tremors. About 1,200 tons of steel near the top of the dome were intended to help it sway in the event of another quake. Other renovations were more cosmetic, like the dome's $400,000 gold-leaf detailing and the enlarged atrium that accommodates more visitors.

The glory of City Hall is still the oak, marble, and limestone rotunda and the vast, fanning marble staircase. To the north is the City Store, filled with San Francisco memorabilia; a coffee bar is open during the week from 11am to 5pm. To the south is *Icons of San Francisco,* an exhibition filled with historical artifacts and tchotchkes. The second floor holds the offices of Mayor Willie Brown, the board of supervisors, the sheriff, and other officials. The massive building, which spans two full city blocks, serves a workforce of more than 1,000 people. Free docent tours are available seven days a week. *Free; open Mon–Fri 8am–8pm, Sat–Sun noon–4pm; map:M4 &*

## 25) GRACE CATHEDRAL

**1100 California St at Taylor St; 415/749-6310** The former site of railroad tycoon Charles Crocker's mansion is now the seat of the Episcopal Church in San Francisco. The Crocker family donated their block of real estate to the church after the fire of 1906 demolished their homes. Inspired by the Gothic architecture of Notre Dame in Paris, this neo-Gothic edifice was designed by Lewis Hobart in the late 1920s; it took 53 years to complete. Although the church appears to be made of stone, it was actually constructed using reinforced concrete that was beaten to achieve a stonelike effect. Ralph Adams Cram added to Hobart's original plan, and the building was finally consecrated in 1964.

In a thoroughly 20th-century fashion, the cathedral pays tribute to various artistic styles. The many stained-glass windows are fairly modern creations—yes, those are glass images of Robert Frost, Thurgood Marshall, and Albert Einstein—but they recall the medieval mastery of Saint-Chapelle in Paris. The heavy bronze doors are copies of Lorenzo Ghiberti's Renaissance masterpiece *Gates of Paradise* in Florence. A modern black and bronze stone sculpture of St. Francis by Beniamino Bufano welcomes visitors with outstretched arms. Also part of the church are the 44-bell carillon and a series of religious frescoes completed in the 1940s by Polish artist John de Rosen.

Grace is perhaps most renowned for its brilliant rose window, a 25-foot-wide stained-glass wonder made in Chartres, France, at the Gabriel Loire studios in 1964. The design depicts St. Francis of Assisi's 13th-century Canticle of the Sun. Featured at the center is Brother Sun. Surrounding the sun are Chi Rho (Greek symbols for Christ), Sister Moon, Sister Earth, Sister Death, Sister Water, Brother Fire, and Brother Wind.

Another popular attraction is the re-creation of a 13th-century **LABYRINTH AT CHARTRES**. A purple and beige carpet sits near the entrance to the church past the baptismal font. Take your shoes off and join the silent walkers as they meditate through the quarter-mile maze. A similar labyrinth sits in the cathedral's outer courtyard. In 1995, an AIDS Interfaith Chapel was opened as a memorial to the countless lives lost to the disease. A Keith Haring sculpture and panels from the AIDS Memorial Quilt comfort those who have lost loved ones.

Soaring architecture and room for 1,300 people make Grace an ideal spot for concerts. From uplifting church choirs and organ recitals by John Fenstermaker (the cathedral's organist and choir master) to jazz jam sessions, music is frequently heard within these walls. Other cultural events held here include weekly forums on spiritual, social, and political issues, as well as silent films.

The **GRACE CATHEDRAL GIFT SHOP** sells mugs, T-shirts, religious books, and artistically rendered copies of religious icons. There's also a small cafe. *Free; open Sun–Fri 7am–6pm, Sat 8am–6pm; www.grace cathedral.org; map:M2*

# Neighborhood Districts

## FINANCIAL DISTRICT

More than 200,000 people make the pilgrimage to the Financial District—a sea of glass and steel skyscrapers bordered by Washington Street, Market Street, Montgomery Street, and the bay—every Monday through Friday to work, work, work. They come from as far away as Sacramento and Sebastopol and arrive by bridge, BART, Muni, ferry, train, bike, or on foot. From seven in the morning to six at night the streets are filled with people, cars, and buses, and the air is filled with a cacophony of horns, the clanging of construction equipment, and the tell-tale bells of the cable cars. In fact, the only people who aren't in perpetual motion are the newspaper vendors and the homeless.

It wasn't always thus. The Financial District, like the Marina, is built on landfill. Over a century ago, before the city went mad with the news of gold, the waters of Yerba Buena Cove rose and fell at the foot of Rincon, Telegraph, and Nob Hills. There was no flat, gentle entryway into the city; rather, it was hilly and inhospitable. But then the Gold Rush began. Once a simple bayside beach town, San Francisco was soon transformed into a bustling metropolis. The influx of fortune seekers, and of savvy businessmen ready to make money off them, was unprecedented.

But the men who made the most money weren't panning for gold; they were sitting behind the desks at fledgling banks that supported the city's rapid growth. A. P. Giannini founded the Bank of Italy primarily to help newly arrived immigrants like his parents, who could not get loans from more established banks. During the early hours of the 1906 earthquake and subsequent fire, Giannini personally secured his holdings and was among the first to lend money to rebuild the city. Several years later, he also helped back the building of the Golden Gate Bridge, an adventure considered foolhardy by many. By then his company had been renamed Bank of America to coincide with the institution's growing power and Giannini's phenomenal wealth.

Today, two little-known downtown museums celebrate the city's chaotic growth during the 19th century. They are the **WELLS FARGO HISTORY ROOM** (800/411-4932) at 420 Montgomery Street at California Street, which has hundreds of genuine vestiges from the company's Wild

West days—pistols, posters, photographs, mining equipment—and the **MUSEUM OF THE MONEY OF THE AMERICAN WEST** in the massive Bank of California building at 400 California Street at Kearny Street.

Nowadays, firms specializing in banking, telecommunications, power, engineering, insurance, and oil make their headquarters here in the neighborhood's massive skyscrapers. The most distinct of the Financial District's many high-rises is the quartz-aggregate **TRANSAMERICA PYRAMID**, located at 600 Montgomery Street between Clay and Washington Streets. Designed by William Pereira and Associates, and built from 1970 to 1972, this 48-story, 853-foot-tall structure is the highest office building in the city. Adjacent to the Pyramid is **REDWOOD PARK**, a lush, tranquil oasis amid the downtown hubbub planted with 80 redwood trees imported from the Santa Cruz Mountains.

One of the most striking buildings on the San Francisco skyline is the 52-story **BANK OF AMERICA** building at 555 California Street. Built in 1969, the entire edifice is encased in carnelian marble and stands 779

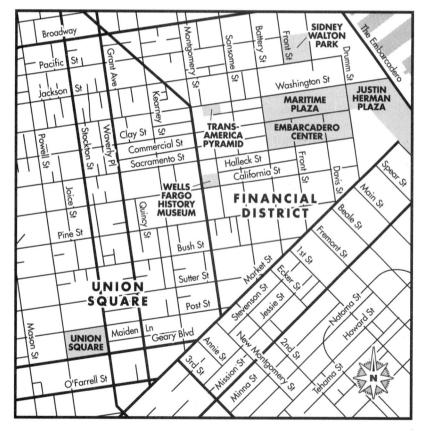

feet tall. At the main plaza is a black granite sculpture that somewhat resembles a misshapen jelly bean. The creator, Japanese architect Masayuki Nagare, named it *Transcendence,* but locals prefer its nickname, "The Banker's Heart." Other stand-out buildings: Aglow with a cluster of bright lights during the winter holiday season, the four highrises of **EMBARCADERO CENTER** offer hundreds of shops to peruse in a modern, multilevel complex; for spectacular views, try the **CARNELIAN ROOM** on the 52nd floor of the Bank of America building.

Along the actual Embarcadero, the **FERRY BUILDING**, built in 1903, survived the quake and fire thanks to the heroic efforts of many. In its heyday, before bridges linked San Francisco to the mainland, it was the second-busiest transportation terminal in the world; more than 150 ferries carried commuters across the bay and back each day. Today the Ferry Building holds no such records, but stands as a landmark welcoming visitors nonetheless. Recently, Pier 7 received a face-lift; decked out with new benches and fancy lampposts, it is now a popular public promenade and a great place to watch the day draw to a close.

**JACKSON SQUARE**, in the Financial District's northwest corner, was once smack in the middle of the infamous Barbary Coast. Today it's a protected historic district filled with antique shops and restaurants. As legend has it, this was the place to go during the city's uncivilized boom years for drinking, dancing, gambling, and whoring. Even murder was commonplace along these streets (though there were patches of respectability). Mickey Finn, a chemist who worked in the area, apparently sold a powerful drug used to knock out the unsuspecting—a devilish trick that later bore his name.

Before you leave the Financial District, be sure to visit the lively **FARMERS MARKET** held along the Embarcadero on Saturday mornings. Local restaurants offer breakfast snacks and coffee, but the real stars here are the Northern California farmers and ranchers who fill the market with fabulous fresh produce, organic meats, local oysters, and olive oils. *Map:N2–O3*

## CHINATOWN

Chinatown has long been a blend of tacky and traditional. As early as 1893, Baedeker's *Guide to the United States* was advising travelers that "the Chinese Quarter is one of the most interesting and characteristic features of San Francisco and no one should leave the city without visiting it." In the early 1900s, when the city was recovering from the quake and fire, there was a movement afoot to rebuild the neighborhood with its original "ethnic" attributes. (Even back then, it seems, Chinatown was good for tourism.) After the 1906 earthquake, Anglo architects designed Edwardian buildings and then added chinoiserie detailing to the architecture to give the area an Asian feel. One prime example is the elaborate facade at 745

Grant Avenue, built in 1920—the result bore no resemblance to the architecture of Asia yet became a distinctly San Francisco phenomenon.

The Chinese who first settled into this cramped neighborhood in the early 1800s hailed from two main regions in China. The wealthier, more prosperous immigrants came from the province of Guangzhou. They learned English and succeeded as city merchants and cultural ambassadors to the predominantly European city. The majority of Chinese, however, were neither well educated nor wealthy. Rather, they were laborers who hailed from Toishan County and spoke a Chinese dialect unintelli-

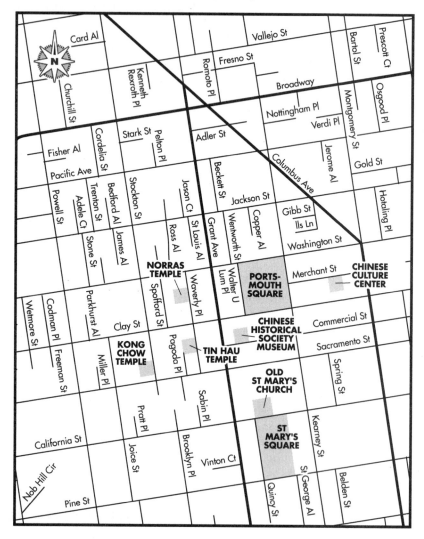

gible to their more affluent neighbors. They had no desire to learn the local language or customs; most intended to stay only long enough to make a small fortune in the gold mines and then return to China, though most ended up as overworked and underpaid railroad workers.

The Chinatown of the Gold Rush years was predominantly male. Because of growing prejudice, the Chinese Exclusion Act of 1882 was passed, which outlawed immigration for 10 years and restricted it until 1943. Hence, there was little chance of the area becoming a family-oriented neighborhood. The Chinese were also denied the opportunity to buy homes outside the Chinatown ghetto until the 1950s, so the lonely, isolated men were forced to remain in the city. Few were ever able to afford a return voyage to China. Opium dens helped many cope with their loneliness and the growing racism of the outside world.

Today, San Francisco has the second-largest community of Chinese in the United States (about 33 percent of the city's population), and Chinatown spreads from Union Square toward North Beach and the Financial District. More than 80,000 people live in Chinatown, making it one of the most densely packed neighborhoods in the country—second only to Harlem. Its boundaries are generally regarded as Broadway, Taylor, Bush, and Montgomery Streets. The popular dragon-crowned portal at Bush and Grant welcomes visitors into another world. Grant Avenue has changed since Chinatown's early days, when it was known as Dupont Street and catered to an underworld culture of gambling and drugs. Today, kitsch shops prevail (if you spend more than $10 for three T-shirts, you're paying too much). Stores crammed full of poorly made luggage and trinkets rub elbows with those selling elegant jade jewelry. The schlock shops go on for blocks except on the more interesting streets, like Sacramento or Clay.

A more authentic Chinatown experience can be had along Stockton Street. The sidewalks are crammed full of tourists and locals alike, all moving at a snail's pace past lively fishmongers and produce markets bursting with durian, Asian pears, lychees, Chinese broccoli, and baby bok choy. Other markets specialize in packaged goods like dried shiitake mushrooms, jasmine tea, and crispy rice snacks. Herbalists trained in the art of Chinese medicine sell bulk curatives to faithful customers who prefer the old ways to Western medicine. Stop by a shop and watch as a merchant measures out the gnarled ginseng root or haggles with a customer over fresh armadillo meat. Though not on Stockton Street, another must-see is the **GOLDEN GATE FORTUNE COOKIES** factory (56 Ross Alley at Washington St; 415/781-3956), which sits amid cloistered sweatshops on Ross Alley. Said to be the birthplace of the fortune cookie, the factory is open to tourists.

In keeping with the traditional Chinese culture are the neighborhood's many Buddhist temples. Lanterns, incense, and burnt offerings await visitors to the **TIN HAU TEMPLE**, on the fourth floor of a nondescript building on Waverly Place. A few doors down sits the **NORRAS TEMPLE**, run by the Buddhist Association of America. Chanting monks and the gentle tinkle of bells lend a sense of calm to the building, which also houses Chinese cultural associations. The oldest Buddhist temple in the country, the **KONG CHOW TEMPLE**, is located at 855 Stockton Street at Sacramento Street (415/788-1339) above a post office. The modernized exterior offers little hint of the carved, gilded altars and elaborate furnishings within. Another religious enclave in this bustling neighborhood is the **GOLD MOUNTAIN MONASTERY** (800 Sacramento St at Grant Ave; 415/421-6117).

**PORTSMOUTH SQUARE** (Washington and Kearny Sts) was the town square of San Francisco's original Spanish settlement, known as Yerba Buena. Back in the 18th century the surf swelled up onto Montgomery Street—once the shoreline of that fledgling village before the shallow waters were filled in to make room for the growing Financial District. Today this seemingly forgotten square serves as a gathering spot for many elderly Chinese. In the morning, large groups congregate to practice the ancient art of tai chi, while mahjong is a popular afternoon activity.

After immigration restrictions were relaxed in the 1960s, recently arrived Chinese immigrants didn't settle in Chinatown, but instead moved out into the city's more spacious western neighborhoods. New Chinatowns have sprung up along Clement Street in the Richmond District and Taraval Street in the Sunset District. But the downtown neighborhood is still the key to the past for many second- and third-generation Chinese Americans. The **CHINESE HISTORICAL SOCIETY MUSEUM** (965 Clay St at Washington St; 415/391-1188) and the **CHINESE CULTURE CENTER** (750 Kearny St btwn Washington and Merchant Sts; 415/986-1822) both feature regular exhibitions celebrating the cultural heritage of the area. Photos and artifacts from the Gold Rush era speak of the important role the Chinese community played in the growth of San Francisco and the state.

Food is one of the highlights of any Chinatown visit, and the number of dining options seems endless. Cantonese food is the local specialty, but Sichuan, Hunan, and Mandarin restaurants are also easy to find. A fun alternative to a standard Chinese meal is dim sum. These tiny dumplings filled with pork, shrimp, scallops, and vegetables are ordered in plates of three and four and arrive at the table in bamboo baskets. Pork spare ribs, roast duck, and a variety of vegetable dishes also feature prominently in any dim sum service. Neighborhood eateries fill to capacity with locals during the weekend lunch hour, the traditional time to eat dim sum, attesting to the popularity of this unique dining experience. *Map:M2–N3*

## NORTH BEACH

Long a neighborhood of immigrants, today North Beach is famous for its Italian food and sidewalk cafes. So charismatic is the area—bordered by Columbus Avenue, Washington and Beach Streets, and the Embarcadero—that few notice that there isn't even a beach here. There was one about a hundred years ago, until it was filled in to make room for factories and waterfront activity. During the Gold Rush years, immigrants from all over the globe flocked here to live near the wharves and factories. They worked as fishermen and toiled in canneries along the then-industrial waterfront. Over the years the Italian community grew and soon outnumbered other ethnic groups. By the early 1930s more than 50,000 Italian Americans were living and working in North Beach, and five Italian-language newspapers were published locally.

Tourism keeps the Italian community here employed, but the Little Italy portion of North Beach is shrinking as Chinatown continues to expand. The citywide rise in rents and real estate prices has made it difficult for many small, family-owned businesses to stay afloat. Many area merchants have joined together to protest the arrival of chain stores like Starbucks and Rite Aid that would take away the historic look and feel of

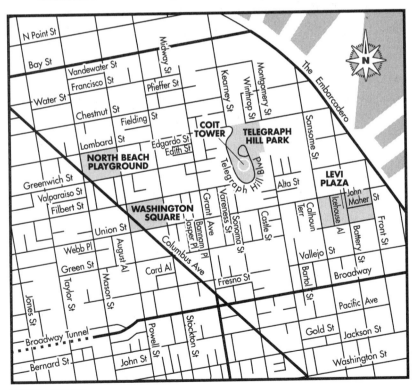

NORTH BEACH

the neighborhood. So far they have succeeded in keeping the chains at bay, but it may be only a matter of years before the area's charm is lost forever.

At the corner of Columbus and Union Street is **WASHINGTON SQUARE PARK**, a haven for tai chi practitioners and sunbathers, painters, and panhandlers. At the north end of the park stands the **SAINTS PETER AND PAUL ROMAN CATHOLIC CHURCH**. Designed in 1922 by Charles Fantoni, this Romanesque building, with its distinctive twin spires and animal statuary, provides a picturesque backdrop for a Sunday picnic or impromptu soccer game. It's also known as the church of the fishermen, and processions depart from here each October for the annual blessing of the fleet. Once an Italian-language church, it now also offers services in English.

In the late 1950s a group of young artists and writers made North Beach their late-night hangout and changed the path of American culture. Legendary Bay Area columnist Herb Caen called them beatniks, but to many fans they will forever be known as the founders of the Beat movement. Allen Ginsberg, Lawrence Ferlinghetti, Jack Kerouac, and their coterie of poet and writer friends haunted the bars and cafes of North Beach, holding poetry readings and drinking late into the night. For lovers of this area's bohemian heritage, a visit to **CITY LIGHTS BOOKSTORE** (261 Columbus Ave at Broadway; 415/362-8193) is a must. Ferlinghetti, poet, publisher, and champion of free speech, opened the store in 1953. Famous for publishing poet Ginsberg's controversial work, City Lights was also the nation's first all-paperback bookstore. Ferlinghetti, still the proprietor, is alive and well and is often spotted in and around the shop. To relive the Beat years, visit **VESUVIO CAFE** (255 Columbus Ave at Broadway; 415/362-3370) or **TOSCA CAFE** (242 Columbus Ave btwn Broadway and Pacific Ave; 415/986-9651), where not much has changed since Jack Kerouac drank here.

In the evening this quaint neighborhood is transformed into a boisterous block party where entertainment options abound. Postprandial coffee can be had at one of the numerous cafes along Columbus. Or head to **CLUB FUGAZI** (678 Green St btwn Powell St and Columbus Ave; 415/421-4222) for a raucous good time at a performance of the city's famous *Beach Blanket Babylon*, a cabaret show that spoofs current politics and pop culture. Listen to music at **GRANT & GREEN BLUES CLUB** (1371 Grant Ave at Green St; 415/693-9565) or swing dance at the **HI-BALL LOUNGE** (473 Broadway btwn Kearny and Montgomery Sts; 415/397-9464). If it's X-rated entertainment you're looking for, the neon lights along Broadway east of Columbus advertise a seemingly endless array of topless bars and "adult" clubs and shops. *Map:N1*

## TELEGRAPH HILL

Back in the pre-boom 1800s, living high atop San Francisco's hills was considered a curse, not a sign of wealth and success. After all, what's a "million-dollar" view when you have to schlep your aching body back up the hill each night? As a result, fishermen and their families were once the primary residents of now-exclusive Telegraph Hill.

This neighborhood, which got its name from a nearby Morse code signal station, is best known as the home of **COIT TOWER** (see Top 25 Attractions). The 1934 monument was named after its benefactor, Lillie Hitchcock Coit, a 19th-century socialite who left money to the city to memorialize her beloved firefighter friends. Designed by Arthur Brown of City Hall fame, the narrow tower offers amazing views of the city and also houses numerous murals documenting Depression-era San Francisco.

The completion of Coit Tower gave Telegraph Hill a new, spiffed-up image around town. Most of the rough-and-tumble cottages gave way to fancy new houses and elegant apartment buildings. Gentrification brought better streets and garbage service and meant increased rents for many dockworkers. As cottages were razed to make way for architectural dream homes, some San Franciscans foresaw the end to a piece of the city's history. A concerned group of residents formed the Telegraph Hill Historic District in 1986 to ensure preservation of the existing cottages.

Today, a hike up the **FILBERT STEPS** is rewarded with a peek at these time capsules from another era, as well as numerous weathered benches, plush gardens, and amazing views. Some of the gems along the way include 228 Filbert Street, a Gothic Revival cottage built in 1873. At 10 Napier Lane stands an Italianate house from 1875. Down the lane at number 21 is an 1885 cottage that epitomizes the simple working-class housing that covered the hillside before it was home to the well heeled. Another set of still-steeper steps leads down to Greenwich Street and the waterfront area below.

A walk along Montgomery Street offers another pair of architectural treats. Bogie and Bacall's *Dark Passage* was filmed at 1360 Montgomery, a splendid example of art deco design built in 1936 by Irving Goldstine. Down the street at 1541 sits **JULIUS' CASTLE** (415/392-2222); its crenellated edifice was built in 1921 by Italian architect Louis Mastropasqua. The restaurant's tight location proved so difficult to drive in and out of that a turntable was installed back in the 1920s to enable large cars to come and go (they now provide valet parking). *Map:N1*

## NOB HILL

The staggering wealth of railroad and silver barons had a significant impact on the history and development of San Francisco. The Big Four, as they were called, left their personal mark all over the city in the last half of the 1800s, particularly on the city peak called Nob Hill, where the city's first cable car started operating in 1873. Sacramento power brokers Leland Stanford, Collis Huntington, Charles Crocker, and Mark Hopkins joined forces to create the Central Pacific Railroad, which connected the rest of the country to California. These nabobs amassed an amazing fortune in the bustling days before the earthquake and fire, and they sank their money into ostentatious mansions high atop Nob Hill. Only the **FLOOD MANSION** (1000 California St at Mason St), now the exclusive Pacific Union Club, remains. It was built between 1885 and 1886 for James Clair Flood, who went from working as a bartender to being one of the city's wealthiest men thanks to a wise investment in the Comstock Lode. The house cost $1.5 million to build, and the wrought iron fence alone cost $30,000. For a look back into the past, cross the street and visit the Big Four Restaurant in the Huntington Hotel (1075 California St btwn Mason and Taylor Sts; 415/771-1140), which showcases memorabilia and photographs from the era.

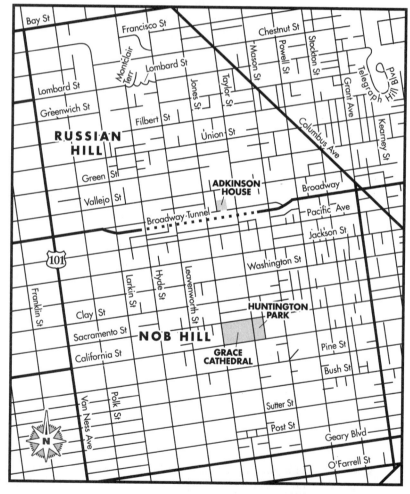

NOB HILL/RUSSIAN HILL

Even though the original architecture was destroyed in 1906, the summit of Nob Hill still reflects that golden era of unbridled wealth. The **FAIRMONT, MARK HOPKINS, STANFORD COURT,** and **HUNTINGTON** hotels are bastions of antique opulence. The manicured lawns, sandbox, swings, and central Tortoise Fountain attract tourists and locals alike to **HUNTINGTON PARK,** donated to the city in 1915 by the widow of Collis Huntington. **GRACE CATHEDRAL**'s 20th-century Gothic architecture creates an impressive profile on the corner of California and Taylor. With its popular meditative labyrinth, stained-glass windows, quilt panels from the AIDS-related Names Project, and formidable bronze doors, this house of worship offers something for even the most ardent atheist.

Though not known for its nightlife, Nob Hill does offer a few places to let your hair down. The Fairmont Hotel's ode to the South Seas, the **TONGA ROOM** (950 Mason St at California St; 415/772-5278), is the perfect spot for a campy night out. For more civilized drinking, **JOHN BAR-LEYCORN** (1415 Larkin St at California St; 415/771-1620) serves up Bass and Guinness and has a cozy fireplace. On a clear day, the famous **TOP OF THE MARK** (999 California St at Mason St; 415/616-6916) offers beautiful sunset views and live music in the evening.

In addition to majestic hotels, Nob Hill also offers architectural indulgences for residents. In 1907, Julia Morgan, the architect of Hearst's San Simeon castle, redesigned the circa-1881 brick structure at 920 Sacramento Street at Stockton Street (415/781-0401), now the **DONAL-DINA CAMERON HOUSE.** She also drew up the plans for the shingle-and-stucco building at 1202–1206 Leavenworth Street at Sacramento Street. Prominent San Francisco architect Willis Polk lent his architectural talent to the row of town houses along Mason Street (numbers 831 to 849). The impressive 1924 **BROCKLEBANK APARTMENTS** at 1000 Mason Street at Sacramento Street may look familiar to *Vertigo* fans—Kim Novak's character lived here. *Map:M2*

## RUSSIAN HILL

To the north of Nob Hill lies Russian Hill, another sought-after address and one where it's uncommonly hard to find a parking space. The neighborhood earned its name from the Russian explorers and trappers who arrived in the early 1800s to trade with the Spanish and Native Americans in the San Francisco Bay. The rough voyage from Fort Ross up north and exposure to the New World diseases proved too much for many sailors, who did not live to make the journey back home. They were buried high atop the hill that overlooked the harbor, their graves marked by black crosses with Russian inscriptions. For years the gravestones were all that distinguished this uninhabited hill.

As the city grew, so did the demand for a room with a view. Cable car lines made living in this uphill district possible. Soon the summit of what came to be called Russian Hill—the neighborhood between Van Ness and Columbus Avenues, Broadway and Fisherman's Wharf—drew businessmen, architects, and the literati. Mark Twain, Frank Norris, Jack London, Robert Louis Stevenson, and Ambrose Bierce all belonged to Russian Hill's literary circles. Photographers Dorothea Lange and Imogen Cunningham lived and worked here as well. Decades later, Jack Kerouac drew inspiration from the neighborhood's slopes and magnificent views while crashing at Neal Cassady's tiny attic on Russell Place. Most recently, Macondray Lane has been immortalized in Armistead Maupin's *Tales of the City.*

Head to Nob Hill and Pacific Heights for grand Victorian mansions, but for historic architecture on a more livable scale, Russian Hill is second to none. The Reverend Joseph Worcester, an amateur architect, was the creative force behind the Bay Area shingle style; his creations at 1034 and 1036 Vallejo are the oldest remaining examples in the area. High atop the summit at 1023 Vallejo sits a 1917 Julia Morgan–designed home done in the Bay Area shingle-style tradition popular in the early 1900s. Morgan reworked the 1866 Italianate home at 1055 Green Street into a Beaux Arts wonder. A few doors down at 1067 Green stands another San Francisco landmark, the **FEUSIER OCTAGON HOUSE**, built from 1857 to 1859 for George Kenny (a friend of Leland Stanford and Mark Twain); the mansard roof and cupola were added in the late 1880s. Willis Polk's Spanish Revival houses, built around 1916, sit at 1, 3, 5, and 7 Russian Hill Place.

Shops along Russian Hill's busy stretch of Polk Street come and go, but **ROSE PAOLI'S CITY DISCOUNT** (2436 Polk St btwn Filbert and Union Sts; 415/826-6660) has been around for decades. Come to this little-known gem for ramekins, cast-iron skillets, mammoth jars of marinated artichoke hearts, and olive oil. At 1903 Hyde Street at Green Street, up away from the Polk Street melee, is **ATELIER DES MODISTES** (415/775-0545), a fashionable boutique for women. Ice cream lovers shouldn't miss the original **SWENSEN'S** (415/775-6818) at the corner of Union and Hyde. This old-time parlor has been family owned since 1948. *Map:L2*

## CIVIC CENTER

Politics, highbrow culture, and homelessness all mingle at the Civic Center. The mayor's office and the board of supervisors' chambers are housed in the beautiful Beaux Arts **CITY HALL** (see Top 25 Attractions) designed in 1916 by Arthur Brown. Its magnificent dome measures 306 feet, a full 18 feet higher than the Capitol dome in Washington, D.C., and is a visible landmark from many points in the city.

The Civic Center borders the city's infamous red-light district, the Tenderloin, where many homeless live on the streets. While this has long been a neighborhood to avoid, an influx of Vietnamese, Laotian, and

Cambodian families has changed the area over the years. And while it's still not for the faint-hearted, it now has a number of good ethnic markets and many excellent—though bare-bones—eateries. If you're looking for kaffir lime leaves or galangal (and who isn't?), this is the place to come.

In the Civic Center area itself, the newly remodeled City Hall and cultural buildings are well worth a visit. The **WAR MEMORIAL OPERA HOUSE**—another Arthur Brown design—stretches along Van Ness Avenue, the city's widest thoroughfare. The site where the United States and Japan signed their peace treaty after World War II, today it hosts San Francisco's ballet and opera seasons, which run from January to May and September to July, respectively. Built in 1932 to honor the soldiers of World War I, the **VETERAN'S BUILDING** contains the Herbst Theatre, home to the City Arts and Lectures series, which has welcomed such noted writers as Saul Bellow, Stephen King, Jane Smiley, and Frank McCourt, as well as San Francisco Performances, which highlights classical soloists, duets, trios, and quartets.

**LOUISE M. DAVIES SYMPHONY HALL**, built in 1981 on the corner of Van Ness Avenue and Gough Street, houses the largest concert-hall organ in North America—so massive that the instrument's 9,235 pipes are played with the aid of a computer. The symphony season runs from September through May. Also of note is the **SAN FRANCISCO PERFORMING ARTS LIBRARY AND MUSEUM** at the corner of Grove and Gough Streets. Devoted to the local arts scene, this building houses more than 4,000 books on theater, dance, opera, and music from the city's beginnings to the present, as well as a wealth of theater posters, playbills, and newspaper clippings.

The old Main Library, which closed in 1995, was replaced by a brand-new building right across the street. The new **SAN FRANCISCO PUBLIC LIBRARY** (100 Larkin St at Grove St; 415/557-4257) opened in 1996 to mostly rave reviews, although its less-than-inviting exterior received more than a few boos. The Beaux Arts architecture of the government buildings is complemented by the library's entrance on Larkin and Fulton Streets. The Grove and Hyde Street facades offer a dramatically modern design. The highlight of the equally modern interior is a five-story atrium that fills much of the building with natural light. Three large-scale art installations add drama to the interior. Mounted on the wall behind the grand staircase is Nayland Blake's *Constellation,* a collection of 160 illuminated glass ovals bearing the names of authors among the library's holdings.

On Market Street between Seventh and Ninth Streets, the **UNITED NATIONS PLAZA** commemorates the charter meeting of the organization, held in June 1945 at the War Memorial Opera House. Today it is the site of a twice-weekly farmers market. Fulton and Market Streets bustle on Wednesdays and Sundays with predominantly Asian purveyors whose tables overflow with fresh fruits and vegetables at reasonable prices.

The **CALIFORNIA CULINARY ACADEMY** (625 Polk St at Turk St; 415/771-3500) is a training ground for many of the city's chefs. The school offers a 16-month course for those interested in a career in the kitchen, as well as continuing education for the less dedicated gourmet. The Academy opens its doors to the general public at the **CAR'ME ROOM** (415/771-3536), a restaurant with glass walls that provide views of the students preparing your food in the kitchen. Another restaurant downstairs, the **ACADEMY GRILL** (415/292-8229), offers reasonably priced burgers and blue-plate specials. *Map:L4*

## PACIFIC HEIGHTS

Pacific Heights, one of San Francisco's most exclusive neighborhoods, is bordered by Van Ness Avenue, Broadway, and Divisadero and Pine Streets. After transportation was extended to the outer districts of the city, the elite moved west, away from the noise of downtown. They sought quiet streets and bigger lots on which to build their grand mansions. Many of those still stand today; a few are even open to the public.

The **HAAS-LILIENTHAL HOUSE** (2007 Franklin St btwn Washington and Jackson Sts; 415/441-3000) is one of them. While much of the surrounding architecture burned in the 1906 blaze, this jewel, designed by Peter Schmidt in 1886 with a Queen Anne circular tower and bay windows, survived. A bigger threat was the subsequent bulldozing of single-family houses to make way for large apartment buildings. But the owners preserved their home as a testament to the glory of Victorian San Francisco. The house, now a museum run by the Foundation for San Francisco's Architectural Heritage, has been furnished with period pieces, many from the Haas-Lilienthal family.

For another look at the grand homes of Victorian and Edwardian San Francisco, visit the **WHITTIER MANSION** at 2090 Jackson Street at Laguna Street. Once the director of the present-day Pacific Gas and Electric Company (PG&E), Whittier came to California from Maine in 1854. After making his fortune, he built a state-of-the-art San Francisco home complete with steel-reinforced brick walls, hydraulic elevator, and central heating. Accordingly, the house survived the events of 1906. Now run by the California Historical Society, this 1896 mansion, designed by Edward Swain, is open to the public for visits and tours. Lavish interiors are paneled with rich mahogany, birch, and oak and filled with late-19th-century furnishings.

The **JAMES FLOOD MANSION**, designed in 1913 by Bliss and Faville, is now one of three impressive buildings that constitute the Convent and Schools of the Sacred Heart, which educate the city's elite. Built with an unlimited budget, the mansion resembles a hotel in scale and accommodations. Located at 2222 Broadway at Webster Street, the magnificent red brick mansion features the finest stonework in San Francisco. Spiraled Corinthian columns and Tennessee marble add to the majesty of this palatial estate. Also among the buildings of the Sacred Heart are the 1910 **JOSEPH DONOHOE GRANT MANSION** at 2200 Broadway and the 1905 **ANDREW HAMMOND MANSION** at 2252 Broadway.

Other fine buildings worth a look are the **SPRECKELS MANSION** (now home to romance novelist Danielle Steel) at 2080 Washington Street, designed by George Applegarth—better known as the architect of the California Palace of the Legion of Honor—and the **BOURN MANSION** at 2250 Webster Street. Designed by Willis Polk for mining baron William Bourn in 1896, this building features a unique tunnel entrance. Two luxury apartment buildings of note are 2006 Washington Street, a 10-story salmon-colored building, and 2000 Washington, a 7-story Beaux Arts building, both designed by C. A. Meussdorffer in 1925 and 1922, respectively.

No architectural tour of Pacific Heights would be complete without a look at two of the area's distinctive houses of worship: the **TEMPLE EMANU-EL** on Arguello Boulevard and Lake Street and the **SWEDEN-BORGIAN CHURCH** on Lyon and Washington Streets. The temple, Northern California's largest synagogue, was designed by Arthur Brown after Union Square construction swallowed up the original downtown structure. Its magnificent 150-foot dome was influenced by the Haggia Sophia in Istanbul. In 1927, a year after its completion, Temple Emanu-El was selected as the finest piece of architecture in Northern California by the American Institute of Architects. The Swedenborgian Church, originally called the Church of New Jerusalem, stands in stark contrast to the opulence of neighboring mansions with its refined rustic interior and fireplace. Built in 1894 by a group of architects and artists committed to the American Craftsman movement, the church features carved wooden beams, stained-glass windows, handcrafted chairs, and a wood-burning fireplace.

Two beautiful parks offer greenery in this otherwise cramped neighborhood. Landscape architect John McLaren, who designed Golden Gate Park, also left his mark on **ALTA PLAZA PARK**, a small patch of land bordered by Clay, Steiner, Jackson, and Scott Streets. The park's terraced landscape was modeled after the Grand Casino in Monte Carlo. The uppermost level affords spectacular vistas in all directions. A few blocks to the east, **LAFAYETTE PARK** sits at the corner of Laguna and Sacramento Streets. The four square blocks of open space offer views of Twin Peaks and the bay to the north. *Map:K2–L3*

## THE MARINA

With spectacular views of the Golden Gate Bridge, Alcatraz, and the bay, the Marina (see map) is desirable real estate for the young and affluent.

A middle-class Italian neighborhood until the 1960s, the Marina now houses some of that community's wealthiest families, who live in the elegant homes that line the waterfront. Cozy art deco flats and stucco houses with Mediterranean-tiled roofs sit on quiet streets only steps away from waterfront activities.

At the turn of the century, the Marina was virtually underwater. The marshland was filled in when it was chosen as the site of the 1915 Panama-Pacific International Exposition, which celebrated the opening of the Panama Canal. Today the Palace of Fine Arts, located at Baker and Beach Streets, serves as a beautiful reminder of that festive event.

Within a few blocks of home, Marina residents often spend their weekends at the **EXPLORATORIUM** and the **PALACE OF FINE ARTS**, the historic Presidio, and the Marina Green, popular with joggers, in-line

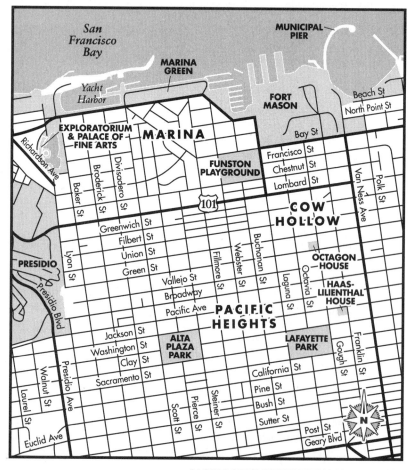

PACIFIC HEIGHTS/MARINA/COW HOLLOW

skaters, sunbathers, kite flyers, and outdoor sports enthusiasts of all kinds. **FORT MASON** (Marina Blvd and Buchanan St), a former military outpost turned into a cultural center, houses the Museo Italo-Americano, the San Francisco Craft and Folk Art Museum, and a number of theaters and nonprofits. On Saturdays, Sedge Thomson's radio show *West Coast Live* is taped before a live audience at the Cowell Theater. For a picnic lunch, pop into the Marina Safeway, a legendary pickup spot for local singles. (For more information on these sites, see Top 25 Attractions.)

The heart of the Marina is **CHESTNUT STREET** between Fillmore and Divisadero Streets. Once a quaint shopping district, Chestnut was permanently altered by the 1989 earthquake. Extensive damage forced a number of small businesses to close. It was only a matter of months before big-name chains and high-end boutiques set up shop (an unwelcome citywide trend that sticks in the gullet of many San Franciscans). Today it's a yuppie shopping haven, complete with Gap Kids, Pottery Barn, and Williams-Sonoma. One welcome newcomer is **HEAVEN DAY-SPA & CENTER FOR WELLNESS** (2209 Chestnut St at Pierce St; 415/749-6414), which offers body wraps, acupuncture, yoga, and full salon services. *Map:J1–K2*

## COW HOLLOW

In the 19th century, numerous dairies populated the rural valley between Pacific Heights and the Marina. Springs gurgled up from underground and provided farmers with natural irrigation for their acres of grazing pasture. Bucolic as that sounds, the dairies were banned in the 1880s when the board of health declared that cows were a health risk to the growing population. In 1891 the animals that gave Cow Hollow its name were shipped off to farms and slaughterhouses.

Bordered by Broadway, Lyon, and Lombard Streets and Van Ness Avenue (see map), Cow Hollow is one of the city's most attractive neighborhoods—for those able to pay the expensive rents. Single, white-collar professionals and double-income families settle here to enjoy the nearby shops, Marina Green, and the Presidio.

Nearby attractions include **OCTAGON HOUSE** (2645 Gough St at Union St; 415/441-7512), one of only two remaining eight-sided houses in the city. Built in the mid-19th century, when such houses were considered good luck, it is now open as a museum filled with antiques and decorative arts from the colonial and Federal periods. Among the many treasures is a collection of autographs by the signers of the Declaration of Independence.

**UNION STREET**, especially between Van Ness Avenue and Steiner Street, is Cow Hollow's most obvious claim to fame. Every day thousands of locals and tourists visit its numerous restaurants, bars, cafes, boutiques, and galleries. Big names like Bebe, Armani Exchange, and Kenneth Cole share the sidewalks with independent boutiques. **FUMIKI**

(2001 Union St at Buchanan St; 415/922-0573) sells fine Asian art, antiques, and some furniture. **GIRLFRIENDS** (1824 Union St at Octavia St; 415/673-9544) caters to women who want youthful fashions. **CASA COLLECTION** (3656 Sacramento St at Locust St; 415/346-5008) offers an eclectic collection of armoires, chairs, chests, and tables.

Cow Hollow has also earned a reputation for its raucous bar scene and is known as a prime pickup spot for young singles. Back in the '80s the **BALBOA CAFE** (415/921-3944), the **CITY TAVERN** (415/567-0918), and the former **BAJA CANTINA** (now occupied by Eastside West), all located at the intersection of Fillmore and Greenwich Streets, formed a sort of Bermuda Triangle, from which on any given Friday or Saturday night patrons probably didn't often make it home alone or remotely sober. It's still quite the singles scene, but today's crowds are somewhat better dressed and behaved. Another boisterous spot is the **UNION ALE HOUSE** (1980 Union St at Buchanan St; 415/921-0300), located in a restored Victorian and featuring 19 microbrews on tap. Down the street a bit, the **BUS STOP** (1901 Union St at Laguna St; 415/567-6905) offers sports fans a friendly place to sip a beer, watch a ball game, and shoot some pool. *Map:J1–L2*

## JAPANTOWN

Located in what is variously known as the Western Addition and lower Pacific Heights, Japantown disappoints many tourists who come expecting to find a Japanese version of Chinatown. In truth, this small neighborhood enclosed by Geary Boulevard and Sutter, Laguna, and Fillmore Streets is more a monument to the cultural and historical importance of San Francisco's Japanese community than a true ethnic neighborhood. Like their Chinese-American neighbors, Japanese Americans live in many different districts throughout San Francisco. Japantown is what remains of a postquake community torn apart by racism and war.

Japanese immigration to San Francisco was minimal during much of the 1800s. It was only after enforcement of the Chinese Exclusion Act of 1882 that the Japanese arrived in greater numbers. They mainly were employed in agriculture and proved to be hardworking and successful farmers. Many saved money and bought land of their own. Japanese immigrants settled in Chinatown alongside the Chinese and also in the industrial area south of Market Street. After the 1906 earthquake and fire, the Chinese were encouraged to rebuild Chinatown because it had become a tourist attraction, but many Japanese could not afford to rebuild and instead took to the outer reaches of the city west of Van Ness Avenue, settling in what is now known as Japantown. By 1940 the area had spread to 30 blocks.

The Japanese community was growing and thriving, but soon a number of racist, protectionist policies would hamper that prosperity. In

1913 the Alien Land Law was passed, which deprived Japanese Americans of the right to buy farmland. The only way Japanese immigrants could hold on to their property was to turn the title over to their nisei, or American-born children. But after the bombing of Pearl Harbor, even that tactic was no longer viable. During World War II Japanese-American bank accounts were frozen. With the signing of Executive Order 9066, 112,000 Japanese Americans, "aliens and citizens alike," were taken from their homes and sent to camps in California, Utah, and Idaho. For a brief period Japantown became a ghost town; then its houses, apartments, and stores were occupied by a new wave of immigrants—Southern blacks.

When the Japanese Americans were released from internment camps in 1945, they returned to find that their old neighborhood had moved on without them. Many tried to reestablish businesses and pick up the pieces of their former lives, but most resettled in the avenues of the Richmond and Sunset Districts.

Today, Japantown is most famous for the five-tiered **PEACE PAGODA**, designed by world-renowned Japanese architect Yoshiro Taniguchi "to convey the friendship and goodwill of the Japanese to the people of the United States." It's located in the heart of the Japan Center, an Asian-oriented shopping mall anchored by the 14-story Radisson Miyako Hotel and occupying three square blocks bounded by Post, Geary, Laguna, and Fillmore Streets. The mall is crammed with sushi and noodle restaurants, teahouses, and dozens of shops featuring everything from kimonos and tansu chests to Japanese books and bonsai. For traditional Japanese ceramics, rice steamers, and sushi knives, visit **SOKO HARDWARE** (1698 Post St at Buchanan St; 415/931-5510). Another reason to visit is the **KABUKI SPRINGS AND SPA** (1750 Geary Blvd at Fillmore St; 415/922-6002), a traditional Japanese public bathhouse open to men and women on alternate days of the week; on Tuesdays it's co-ed. *Map:K3*

## HAIGHT-ASHBURY

The Summer of Love lasted a mere three months, but 30 years later tourists and nostalgic San Franciscans still flock to the Haight to experience the flavor of the late '60s. Once home to Janis Joplin, the Grateful Dead, and myriad hippies, Haight-Ashbury has long since lost the uplifting spirit of that infamous summer, but drugs, alcohol, and tie-dye remain. As old-timers from several nearby rehabilitation centers struggle to overcome their drug-filled past, a new generation of street urchins zones out along the storefronts of the neighborhood, playing guitars, stringing beads, boldly demanding "Spare a buck for a beer?" or mumbling "Kind bud" (Translation: "Want to buy some pot?") to random passersby.

Bordered by Stanyan, Fulton, Divisadero, and Waller Streets, the Haight went through several ups and downs in the years before it became world famous. In the 1800s it was part of the far-reaching Outside Lands, a 17,000-acre sand dune west of Divisadero—a desolate area home only to a squadron of squatters hired by local businessmen with designs on developing the area. The lands lay in limbo until an 1865 Supreme Court decision ruled that the City of San Francisco was the legitimate heir to the area acquired from the Yerba Buena pueblo settled by the Mexican government. Frank McCoppin, a city supervisor, represented the area that included the Outside Lands. His grand plan for the area included a massive public park. In 1866, he became mayor and decided to secure his plan by organizing the claimants and negotiating a deal. Eventually all parties agreed to an arrangement whereby claimants would cede some 10 percent of their stake to the city in return for official rights to develop their remaining land. The protected 10 percent would soon become Golden Gate Park, while the remaining 90 percent was developed and became Haight-Ashbury and later the avenues. Neighborhood streets are named after city supervisors Haight, Ashbury, Cole, Clayton, Stanyan, and Shrader.

**STANYAN PARK HOTEL** (750 Stanyan St at Waller St; 415/751-1000), built in 1904, dates back to the days of early development, when

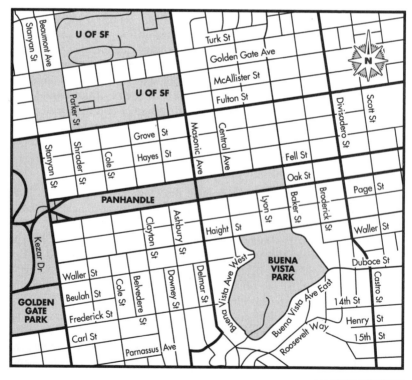

HAIGHT-ASHBURY

an amusement park and baseball field brought tourists out to this area. The events of 1906 further spurred a building boom. Displaced by the earthquake and fire, up-and-coming immigrants flocked to the area. They included Germans, Irish, Swedes, Jews, Scots, French, and Japanese. A large number of African Americans also settled here. The postquake development brought a wealth of Queen Anne homes to the neighborhood; many still stand today.

This once-prosperous enclave took a turn for the worse two decades later. In 1928, a tunnel was built through Buena Vista Park that carried middle-class residents from downtown out to the Sunset District, bypassing Haight-Ashbury completely. The Depression of the 1930s brought still more decline. The grand homes were simply too big to heat and maintain, and subdivision soon followed. Today, large single-family dwellings are few and far between, and most of the opulent Victorians have been converted to condos and apartments.

Economically, Haight-Ashbury, or the Upper Haight, as it is also known, has cashed in on its illustrious past. Commerce has replaced free love: Stores dedicated to the hippie legacy sell tie-dyed shirts, psychedelic posters, incense, pot paraphernalia, and used records. The **RED VICTO-RIAN BED, BREAKFAST & ART** (1665 Haight St at Clayton St; 415/864-1978) dedicates its entire lower level to '60s and '70s memorabilia. Tattoo parlors and pipe shops draw alternative crowds, but the majority of people parading down Haight Street are tourists. Hundreds flock here each day to witness the nonstop freak show this street has become. When Jerry Garcia died in 1995, the neighborhood became a meeting place for the bereaved. His former home, at 710 Ashbury Street at Waller Street, has long been part of the Haight pilgrimage.

As a sign of the times, the Gap now holds down the fort at the infamous corner of Haight and Ashbury; across the street is the hippie-capitalist bastion Ben & Jerry's. Trendy boutiques selling space-age shoe designs and retro fashions line the street from Masonic to Stanyan, along with a plethora of used clothing shops, leather stores, used bookstores, and head shops.

For residents, one of the main draws of the neighborhood is its proximity to so many parks. The city's gargantuan **GOLDEN GATE PARK**, the eight-block Panhandle, and the little-known **BUENA VISTA PARK** offer many options for parkgoing, including hiking, breathtaking views of the Pacific, and lying in the sun. *Map:I4–J5*

## THE CASTRO

Once part of the 4,000-acre ranch belonging to Jose de Jesus Noe, former alcalde of Mexican San Francisco, the Castro area underwent a huge transformation when the Yankees moved into town. In 1854, John Horner bought the undeveloped stretch of ranch land and planned a neighborhood along a rigid grid pattern that didn't take into account the area's steep grades. Originally called Eureka Valley, the land was parceled out in the 1860s, though few were adventurous enough to establish a home here, as the area was isolated from downtown.

Around the turn of the century, the Market Street Cable Railway was extended to Castro Street, opening the area to middle-class families. The 1920s were boom years for the newly developed neighborhood. Built in 1922, the Castro Theatre stood as the elegant centerpiece of this growing community (and still does). Eureka Valley remained a peaceful lower- and middle-class neighborhood for about 50 years; then the dynamic area we know today began to take shape.

In the 1970s, a large number of gay men moved into the area, renovated weathered Victorians, and gave the neighborhood a general facelift. The Castro came alive again, this time as the epicenter of gay pride. The neighborhood rejoiced in 1977 when local camera store owner Harvey Milk was elected to the board of supervisors, becoming the nation's first openly gay elected city official. A year later, the community suffered a devastating blow when Supervisor Milk and Mayor George Moscone were gunned down in City Hall by former supervisor Dan White. Today, Harvey Milk Plaza at Castro and Market Streets is a popular meeting place for marches and political rallies. The dozens of rainbow-striped flags gracing the neighborhood attest to its current status as the capital of gay America.

AIDS, understandably, is one of the neighborhood's most uniting causes. Hospices and crisis centers have sprung up to support the sick and their caregivers. The Names Project office, anchored at Castro and Market Streets, houses the famous **NAMES QUILT**, a powerful array of more than 30,000 panels, each representing a casualty of AIDS.

The Spanish Renaissance–style **CASTRO THEATRE** (429 Castro St near Market St; 415/621-6120) draws crowds for its innovative and retro movie offerings as well as its landmark architecture. Another plus is the restored Wurlitzer on which an organist plays "San Francisco, Open Your Golden Gate" before each show (the organ then sinks into the floor by way of a hydraulic lift—very cool). Also unique to the neighborhood are the painted vintage streetcars that run through here from lower Market Street. A fairly recent addition to Muni's old-time F line, these trains were imported from faraway cities like Beijing, Milan, Lisbon, and Baltimore. It was such a costly endeavor that it spawned talk of reverting to the standard trains, but by then these little gems had become so popular that huge protests squashed the proposal.

The neighborhood's main shopping areas are on Market, Castro, and 18th Streets. **DOES YOUR FATHER KNOW** (528 Castro St at 18th St; 415/241-9865), or DYFK, sells gay-themed greeting cards. **A DIFFERENT**

**LIGHT BOOKSTORE** (489 Castro St btwn 18th and Market Sts; 415/431-0891) stocks a large collection of books by, for, and about gays and lesbians. The gourmet chocolates of **JOSEPH SCHMIDT CONFECTIONS** (3489 16th St btwn Sanchez and Church Sts; 415/861-8682) can be found at high-end stores around the city, but he started in the Castro—chocolate lovers shouldn't miss his store.

For after-dinner drinks and a chance to soak up the local color, head toward **METRO** (3600 16th St at Market St; 415/703-9750), where you

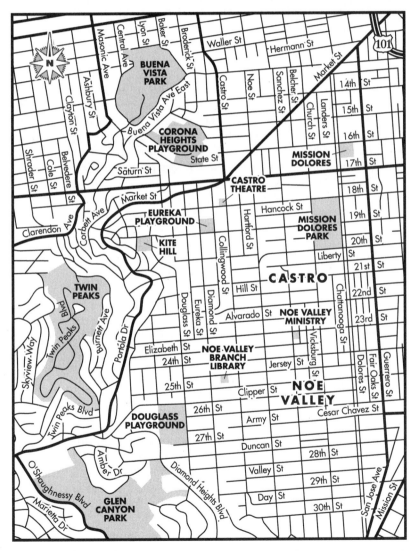

CASTRO/NOE VALLEY

can watch the locals stroll by from the wraparound balcony. If you're feeling more adventurous and aren't intimidated by male meat markets, a drink at **DETOUR** (2348 Market St near Castro St; 415/861-6053) comes complete with go-go dancers. An eclectic crowd flocks to **CAFE DU NORD** (2170 Market St btwn Church and Sanchez Sts; 415/861-5016) for live salsa, swing, jazz, and blues. Dance classes are offered before some shows. *Map:K6*

## NOE VALLEY

Long before 24th Street was lined with fashionable shops and cruised by young parents pushing strollers, the sunny patch of land known as Noe Valley was home to San Francisco's last Mexican mayor, Jose de Jesus Noe. Noe built a ranch on the 4,443 acres given to him in 1834 by Spanish governor Pio Pico. His holdings extended from Twin Peaks to Daly City, but today only a street and this quiet neighborhood, bounded by 22nd and 30th and Dolores and Castro Streets, bear his name. When Alta California was annexed by the United States, the land was purchased and developed by John Horner, who mapped out a grid of blocks that stretched from Castro to Valencia and from 18th to 30th Streets. Today many streets are still named after prominent Mexican ranchers from the alcalde's era.

In the early 1900s, improved public transit opened the neighborhood to working-class families, who flocked here for the quiet streets and warm weather. Noe Valley and the Mission District were collectively known as the Emerald Enclave when the Irish began to settle here in large numbers. German, Scandinavian, and Mexican Americans flocked to the valley as well. Before the housing crunch of the 1990s, it was one of the city's last bastions of affordable housing because while it offers some sweeping hilltop panoramas, it lacks those sought-after bay views.

Twenty-Fourth Street was an active commercial district even before the turn of the century. The 1906 earthquake and fire stopped at 20th and Church Streets, sparing most of Noe Valley. Today it's a bustling community with a large commercial street and an amazing number of beautifully maintained houses.

A plethora of interesting shops and good cafes line 24th Street from Castro to Church Streets. **COMMON SCENTS SOAPS AND LOTIONS** (3920-A 24th St at Sanchez St; 415/826-1019) is a popular store, as is **ASTRIDS RABAT** (3909 24th St at Sanchez St; 415/282-7400), which sells shoes and accessories. For the little one in your life, **SMALL FRYS** (4066 24th St btwn Noe and Castro Sts; 415/648-3954) offers a selection of baby things. One of the best stores in Noe Valley is the **REAL FOOD COMPANY** (3939 24th St btwn Noe and Sanchez Sts; 415/282-9500), which sells organic veggies and bulk items.

In addition to the shops and charming homes, other attractions include the **NOE VALLEY MINISTRY** (1021 Sanchez St at 23rd St; 415/282-2317), a Stick-style church designed by Canadian Charles Geddes and completed in 1889. Restored in the late 1970s, it today serves not only as a place of worship but as a community center offering day care, senior programs, lectures, and exercise classes. Another worthwhile stop is the **NOE VALLEY BRANCH LIBRARY** (451 Jersey St btwn Castro and Diamond Sts; 415/695-5095), built in 1916 with money from Andrew Carnegie. *Map:K7*

## MISSION DISTRICT

Known as one of the sunniest and most diverse neighborhoods in the city, the Mission District stretches across a huge swath of land roughly bounded by Market, Cesar Chavez (Army), and Dolores Streets and Potrero Avenue. The site of San Francisco's original Spanish settlement, Mission Dolores, the Mission District owes much to the Mexican ranchers who bought up large tracts of land during the pre–Gold Rush days when Alta California belonged to Mexico.

During the early 1900s, a large number of immigrants settled here. The first wave of immigration included Irish, Germans, Scandinavians, and Jews. During the second half of this century the majority of new faces have been Latino and Asian. But the Mission isn't merely a home to recent arrivals. For decades artists, students, and blue-collar workers of all stripes have flocked here for sunshine and affordable housing. Today, a large lesbian population vies for housing with Silicon Valley transplants and first- and second-generation Mexican and Salvadoran immigrants.

To experience the heart of the Mission's Latino culture, head down to 24th Street, where **CASA LUCAS MARKET** (2934 24th St btwn Alabama and Florida Sts; 415/826-4334) sells delicious sweet-corn tamales along with scores of Latin American staples. **GALERIA DE LA RAZA** at 24th and Bryant honors the neighborhood's cultural heritage with exhibitions, movies, and classes. Off 24th and Harrison, the murals along Balmy Alley draw visitors from all over the world.

The Mission is known more for its lively energy than for its architectural wonders, but it has a number of historic buildings. Head to **LIBERTY STREET** at Dolores for a look at 40 years of architectural design. Styles include Italianate (#159), Craftsman (#151–153), Queen Anne (#123), and Stick-style Victorian (#121–121A, 117–119, and 111–115).

The streets are filled with shopping opportunities. Bookstores and thrift shops abound, and recently the area has attracted a slew of home furnishings stores. The Irish-owned **HARRINGTON BROS. ANTIQUES** (599 Valencia St at 17th St; 415/861-7300) is one of the oldest neighborhood businesses and sits on what has recently become prime real estate. **THERAPY** (415/861-6213) has stores at 545 and 1051 Valencia

Streets (at 16th and 21st Streets, respectively) where you can find vintage furniture and collectibles as well as clothing. **RAYON VERT** (3187 16th St at Guerrero St; 415/861-3516) carries furniture as well as decorative items like lamps, dishware, and candles.

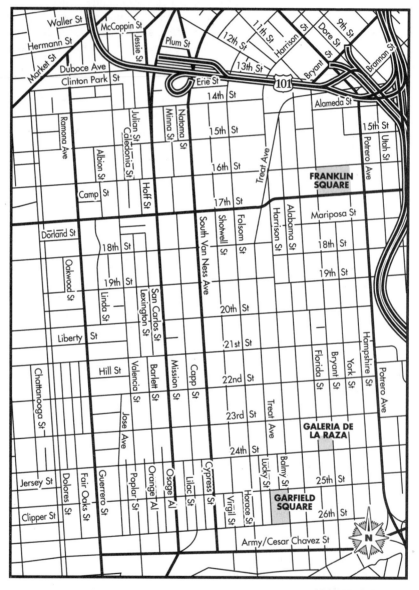

MISSION DISTRICT

If you're hungry, the stretch of Mission between 21st and 24th Streets bursts with produce stands selling inexpensive fruits and vegetables, including hard-to-find ethnic items like plantains, yucca, and nopales. **LUCCA RAVIOLI COMPANY** (1100 Valencia St btwn 21st and 22nd Sts; 415/647-5581) sells delicious fresh pasta and sauces. A few blocks down, at 548 Valencia Street at 16th Street, is **BOMBAY BAZAAR** (415/621-1717), an Indian market filled with imported spices, groceries, and yummy ice cream.

Nightlife in the Mission is as varied as the people who live here. The **ELBO ROOM** (647 Valencia St btwn 17th and 18th Sts; 415/552-7788) has long been a hot spot for live music. An older crowd flocks to the **LONE PALM** (3394 22nd St at Guerrero St; 415/648-0109) for occasional live jazz and a comfortable ambience. Nightly drag shows at **ESTA NOCHE** (3079 16th St btwn Valencia and Mission Sts; 415/861-5757), a Latino gay bar, bring the Castro crowd down to the Mission. Lesbians have made a place for themselves at the **LEXINGTON CLUB** (3464 19th St btwn Mission and Valencia Sts; 415/863-2052).

The heart of experimental, cutting-edge culture in the city, the Mission offers a wealth of options for an evening's entertainment. **THE MARSH** (1062 Valencia St btwn 21st and 22nd Sts; 415/641-0235) showcases new and offbeat performance work; Mondays offer an opportunity for aspiring actors, comedians, and playwrights to hone their craft. The **ROXIE CINEMA** (3117 16th St at Valencia St; 415/863-1087), a slightly ramshackle but well-loved 275-seat repertory theater, features offbeat feature films and documentaries. **INTERSECTION FOR THE ARTS** (446 Valencia St btwn 15th and 16th Sts; 415/626-2787), with its cement walls and bleacher seats, is located in an unsavory part of the Mission, but has long been a prime venue for performance artists, dancers, writers, and dramatic artists. *Map:L5–N7*

## SOMA (SOUTH OF MARKET STREET)

Until just recently, much of the South of Market area (known by the acronym SoMa) had long been a bastion of affordable—albeit ramshackle—housing; even in the early days of the Gold Rush, it was home to a tent city of newly arrived immigrant 49ers. As San Franciscans prospered on Gold Rush fever, the area around South Park—now the heart of Multimedia Gulch—evolved into a gated community surrounded by opulent mansions. Though the mansions have since vanished, a bit of old-world charm remains: at 615 Third Street, a plaque marks the site where Jack London was born in 1876 (the original structure was destroyed in the 1906 quake).

When the city rebuilt after the devastation, industrialists took hold of the area, putting up warehouses, factories, and train yards. All that remains of SoMa's affluent patches are the historic **WPA MURALS** at the

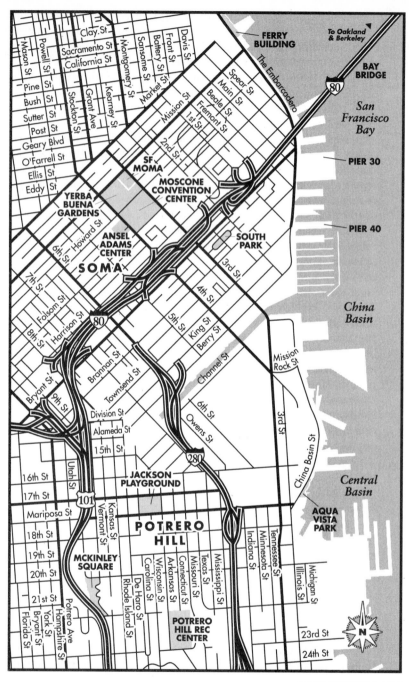

SOMA/POTRERO HILL

former Rincon Hill post office (now Rincon Center, 99 Mission St at Spear St). A gem from the more recent past is the **PACIFIC BELL TELE-PHONE BUILDING,** a 1925 skyscraper that provides a dramatic backdrop to the San Francisco Museum of Modern Art.

In the 1800s, SoMa was known as South of the Slot because of the cable car slots that ran down Market Street. Eventually the area became the transportation hub of San Francisco, and it remains so today. The CalTrain station, the Southern Pacific train depot, the Greyhound bus terminal, and the Transbay Terminal are all located here. The intercity system known as BART tunnels beneath the waters of the bay, delivering throngs of passengers daily to four underground stations along Market Street. The Bay Bridge (Interstate 80/101), connecting San Francisco and Oakland, channels thousands of cars into the area each day.

Ironically, it was **MOSCONE CONVENTION CENTER**—completed in 1981 and named after former mayor George Moscone, who was slain in 1978—that brought the first injection of tourist money into the area. Since then, numerous apartment complexes have sprung up along the waterfront, along with dozens of high-tech work lofts. For many older businesses, this urban renewal is a mixed blessing. Many of SoMa's outlet stores are closing as rents continue to rise. Cheap hotels along Third and Fourth Streets were razed to make room for the new buildings. And parking? Fuhggetaboutit, particularly when the Giants are playing ball at the new PacBell baseball stadium.

It was the unveiling of Swiss architect Mario Botta's **SAN FRAN-CISCO MUSEUM OF MODERN ART** in 1995 that solidified SoMa's repu-tation as the artistic heart of the city, attracting visitors from all over the world. On the heels of the museum's completion came the **YERBA BUENA CENTER FOR THE ARTS,** which hosts diverse exhibitions ranging from avant-garde video and installation art to the more conventional *Impres-sionists in Winter.* Surrounding the center is **YERBA BUENA GARDENS,** a 5-acre public oasis that includes a Martin Luther King Jr. Memorial—etched glass panels displayed behind a long, shimmering cascade of water—as well as other sculptures. (See Top 25 Attractions.)

Museums and restaurants may be the focus for much of the day (there are a number of destinations for serious diners in SoMa), but around midnight, the club scene takes center stage. Hip clubs continue to come and go. Eleventh Street, with **SLIM'S** (333 11th St at Folsom St; 415/522-0333) and **PARADISE LOUNGE** (1501 Folsom St at 11th St; 415/861-6906), is the center of mainstream nightlife, but alternatives exist in abundance. Depending on the night of the week, your favorite club could be something entirely unexpected. **THE END UP** (401 6th St at Harrison St; 415/357-0827) becomes "The Fag" on Fridays, with beau-tiful boys dancing into the wee hours, but on Thursdays it's the "Kit Kat

Club" and caters to both gay and straight night owls. "Bondage à Go-Go" happens at the **CAT CLUB** (1190 Folsom St at 8th St; 415/431-3332) on Wednesday nights. Come in your fetish gear and get a discount at the door. On Fridays, Latin tunes, funk, and soul fill the Cat Club as it morphs into Ibiza. On Fridays, **THE STUD** (399 9th St at Harrison St; 415/863-6623), normally a gay bar, becomes the Dollhouse, a meeting place for lesbians looking for a wild night out. The Stud's Saturday incarnation is more inclusive; it becomes Sugar and welcomes the ultrahip het set as well as the usual gay crowd. In short, whatever it is you're into, chances are it's taking place South of Market. *Map:M3–O4*

## POTRERO HILL

The area south of 16th Street between Potrero Avenue, Highway 280, and Cesar Chavez Boulevard, Potrero Hill is a quiet, sunny neighborhood with views of the downtown skyline, the industrial side of the bay, and Daly City. Once called Goat Hill, this former home to grazing herds is now an up-and-coming residential area. Infamous for its low-income housing known as "the projects" (O. J. Simpson grew up here), the sunny hillside was once one of the last bastions of affordable housing in the city. Word has since got out and it's affordable no longer (though patches of sketchy neighborhoods definitely remain, so be aware). Local architecture varies from modern condos and airy lofts to Victorian and Edwardian remodels and nondescript stucco buildings.

**MCKINLEY SQUARE**, bounded by Vermont, 20th, and San Bruno Streets, offers great views and a fantastic playground for kids. The portion of Vermont Street leading down to 22nd Street is actually more crooked and steep than the famous stretch of Lombard Street. **POTRERO HILL RECREATION CENTER** (415/695-5009) at 22nd and Arkansas Streets may be a small city park, but it has big, big views. It also offers facilities for baseball, tennis, and barbecues.

Over the years a cadre of design firms and antique shops has grown in the area around 16th and Division Streets on the border of SoMa, but for the most part Potrero is still a quiet neighborhood for shopping. Also known as the Teddy Bear Factory, the **BASIC BROWN BEAR FACTORY** (444 De Haro St at Mariposa St; 415/626-0781 or 800/554-1910) manufactures 30 different styles of bears, and you can even stuff your own. Tours are offered daily by reservation; prices start at $12 for stuff-your-own bears. Connoisseurs of fresh seafood should head down by the water to **NIKKO FISH CO.** (699 Illinois St at 18th St; 415/864-5261), where glistening slabs of fresh ahi tuna sit waiting to be sliced into sushi, and fresh oysters can be had for a song. Beer lovers shouldn't miss the tour at the **ANCHOR BREWING CO.** (1705 Mariposa St at De Haro St; 415/863-8350)—the only brewery in the country handcrafting quality steam beers. Free weekday tours cover the company's history and brewing techniques and also offer the chance to sample each of Anchor's seven brews. Reservations are difficult to obtain, however, so be sure to call as far in advance as possible.

Potrero's eclectic nightlife offers something for everyone. The **BOTTOM OF THE HILL** nightclub (415/621-4455), at 17th and Missouri Streets, draws crowds from all over the city to listen to its up-and-coming musical lineup. Once you get past the surly barkeeps at **BLOOM'S SALOON** (415/861-9467) at 1318 18th Street at Texas Street, head to the back deck, where a spectacular view of the city awaits. Located at 1830 17th Street at DeHaro Street, the **METRONOME BALLROOM** (415/252-9000) offers a variety of dance classes and also opens as a nightclub on Friday, Saturday, and Sunday nights from 7:30pm to midnight. *Map:N5–N7*

## THE RICHMOND AND SUNSET DISTRICTS

The Richmond and Sunset neighborhoods, which sit at the western end of the city and stretch from Arguello Boulevard out to the ocean, are collectively known as "the avenues" (as opposed to SoMa and the Mission District, which are referred to as "the streets"). This area first became popular at the end of the 1800s, when Adolph Sutro created two crowd-pleasing attractions in the city's western reaches. The first and foremost in the city's memory was the seven-story Victorian masterpiece called the **CLIFF HOUSE** (Sutro was responsible for its second and most splendid incarnation). The second was the ambitious **SUTRO BATHS**, a compilation of a half-dozen indoor ocean-water swimming pools. Sadly, neither attraction remains standing today—at least not as conceived by Sutro—but in their heyday they helped to bring the growing city out west.

Many present-day landmarks still draw tourists and San Franciscans alike to the **RICHMOND DISTRICT**. Perhaps the most dramatic are the rocky cliffs that loom over the pounding surf at Land's End. At the end of Clement Street and 34th Avenue, Lincoln Park is home to the **CALIFORNIA PALACE OF THE LEGION OF HONOR** art museum (see Top 25 Attractions) and the 18-hole **LINCOLN PARK GOLF COURSE**, which skirts the Golden Gate. One of the Richmond's unique sites is the Neptune Society's **COLUMBARIUM** (415/752-7892). The only remnant of the old Odd Fellows cemetery, this neoclassical edifice was built in 1898 and houses urns and ashes of prominent San Franciscans. Located on Loraine Court off Anza, the building is open weekdays from 10am to 4pm and weekends from 10am to 2pm.

In recent decades, thousands of Russian, Irish, and Chinese immigrants have landed in the Richmond. They've settled in the bland stucco-covered houses that stretch from just past Pacific Heights to the Pacific Ocean, making this one of the most international neighborhoods in the city. Although the Richmond is located miles from the city center, Geary Boulevard and 19th Avenue provide easy links to the rest of the city. The parallel commercial streets of Geary and Clement provide locals with most major conveniences.

San Francisco's large Irish community also has a strong presence in the Richmond. The **IRISH CULTURAL CENTER** is located at 2700 45th Avenue between Sloat Boulevard and Wawona Street (415/661-2700). **PAT O'SHEA'S MAD HATTER** (3848 Geary Blvd at 3rd Ave; 415/752-3148) and the **PLOUGH & STARS** (116 Clement St at 2nd Ave; 415/751-1122) are among a number of Irish pubs that make the neighborhood a busy area for evening revelry (and the place to be on St. Patrick's Day).

The **SUNSET DISTRICT** is the neighborhood that runs south of Golden Gate Park to Sloat Boulevard, and west from Stanyan Street to Ocean Beach. The broad streets slope gently toward the sea and are lined with Mediterranean-style stucco homes. These ubiquitous, boxy tunnel houses (two-bedroom homes with a bay window over the garage) sprang up after World War II, when the economy mandated smaller lots and simple architecture.

The neighborhood is divided into the Inner Sunset, the area just east of 19th Avenue, and the Outer Sunset, the area past 19th toward the ocean. The Sunset has long frightened away newcomers due to its infamous fog, but proximity to the beach is still a strong draw for many. On Friday and Saturday nights, bonfires light up the coast of **OCEAN BEACH** (burning permits are not required). **STERN GROVE, LAKE MERCED**, and the **SAN FRANCISCO ZOO** are other nearby attractions.

Predominantly working class with lots of families, the Sunset is ethnically split between whites and Asians. The presence of the **UNIVERSITY OF CALIFORNIA MEDICAL CENTER** on Parnassus Street has brought many students to the neighborhood, as has San Francisco State University, located in the southwestern end of the city past Sloat Boulevard. *Map:C3–I5 (Richmond), C5–H7 (Sunset)*

## TWIN PEAKS

When the Spaniards arrived in San Francisco in the 1700s, they set up a mission, fortified the area, and began naming the countryside's geographical points of interest. This pair of hills in the center of the city was named Los Pechos de la Choca, or "Breasts of the Indian Maiden," a name that testifies to the loneliness of frontier life. Many of San Francisco's place names have survived from that earlier period but, for obvious reasons, Breasts of the Indian Maiden didn't cut it with the Victorians. Ergo, the more PC moniker Twin Peaks.

Though Mount Davidson, at 928 feet, is the highest point in the city, it's Twin Peaks that draws the visitors. On a clear day, tourists flock here for truly spectacular panoramic views of the city, the bridges, the East Bay, and beyond. Marin's Mount Tamalpais and the Campanile clock tower at UC Berkeley are both visible, weather permitting. Much of the hillside is undeveloped, making it a perfect venue for urban naturalists. Challenging terrain and clusters of wildflowers reward those willing to tackle Twin Peaks on foot.

It wasn't until the 1920s that daring developers decided to have a go at the area. Even then, steep hillsides and limited public transportation deterred many from snatching up the new housing. Boring, boxy apartment buildings make up much of the east side of the neighborhood, but attractive, affluent areas can be found in the sections of Clarendon Heights, Forest Knolls, Miraloma Park, and Parnassus Heights. Today more than 10,000 people reside along the steep, circuitous streets of Twin Peaks. It has become a desirable area for both gay and straight couples as well as for a few families.

Though stunning views abound here, many locals must also live in the shadow of the controversial Sutro Tower. Visible from most points in the city, this enormous red-and-white-striped television antenna is a familiar San Francisco landmark (and a godsend for anyone without cable), but so far it hasn't won over locals the way Coit Tower and the Transamerica Pyramid did.

One neighborhood gem is **TOWER MARKET** (415/664-1600), at 635 Portola Drive and Woodside Avenue. Beautiful produce, a fine deli, and a wide selection of affordable wines attract more than just the locals. Another asset is the **RANDALL MUSEUM** (415/554-9600). Hidden at the top of Roosevelt and Masonic Streets, this fantastic children's museum offers hands-on nature exhibits, an activity center with ceramics and woodworking classes, and a small art gallery. *Map:J7*

# Museums

*Note:* Galleries for established San Francisco artists are located primarily on lower Grant Avenue and near Union Square, while up-and-coming artists tend to exhibit in the SoMa (South of Market Street) area. For current art and gallery listings, check the *San Francisco Chronicle*'s "Datebook" in the Sunday paper, or visit www.bayarea.citysearch.com and click on "The Arts" link.

**ANSEL ADAMS CENTER / 655 Mission St btwn 3rd and New Montgomery Sts; 415/495-7000** Photography buffs can marvel at the work of the master himself, as well as that of Imogen Cunningham, Dorothea Lange, and many other notable contemporary and historical photographers. The photos are showcased in the center's five exhibition galleries, one of which is dedicated solely to displaying the works and exploring the legacy of Ansel Adams. *Admission is $7 for adults, $4 for students and seniors, free for children 12 and under; open every day; www.friends ofphotography.com; map:N3*

**ASIAN ART MUSEUM / 200 Larkin St at McAllister St; 415/379-8800**
The Asian Art Museum is one of the largest museums in the Western world devoted exclusively to Asian art. After 35 years in Golden Gate Park, the museum has moved to a new earthquake-proof building that once housed the city's main library—a loss for the park but a gain for the Civic Center. World-class artworks on exhibit include more than 12,000 sculptures, ceramics, paintings, bronzes, and decorative objects spanning 6,000 years of history from more than 40 Asian countries. The museum's free daily guided tours are highly recommended as well; call for times. *Admission is $7 for adults, $5 for seniors 65 and over, $4 for youths 12–17, free for children 11 and under; free the first Wed of each month; open Tues–Sun; www.asianart.org; map:G5*

**BAY AREA DISCOVERY MUSEUM / Fort Baker, Sausalito (directions below); 415/487-4398** Located on the other side of the Golden Gate Bridge in Sausalito, the Bay Area Discovery Museum is a wonderland of  hands-on science, art, and multimedia exhibits designed for kids from toddlers on up. To get there, head north across the bridge, exit at Alexander Avenue, and follow the signs to East Fort Baker and the museum. *Admission is $7 for adults, $6 for children 1–18; open Tues–Sun; www.badm.org; map:FF6*

**CABLE CAR BARN MUSEUM / 1201 Mason St at Washington St (all cable cars stop near here); 415/474-1887** Housed in a brick building at the corner of Mason and Washington Streets, the San Francisco Cable Car Museum is one of the best and most interesting museums in the city. Although it was built for the Ferries and Cliff House Railway in 1887,  the familiar hum of the cables moving underfoot is your first clue that this is not merely a memorial to the past. More than a century later, it still serves as the powerhouse and repair shop for the entire cable car system, and in 1984 underwent an $18 million reconstruction to restore its original gaslight-era look, add a museum of San Francisco transit history, and install an amazing spectators' gallery—a cleverly designed room that allows visitors to actually watch the sheaves (giant iron wheels) that power and regulate the cables. An amazingly simple feat of engineering propels the cars a consistent 9½ miles per hour around town.

If you can pull yourself away from the gears and pulleys, the museum also features vintage photographs and cable car memorabilia, including a cross section of cable. (You may not want to ride the cars again once you find out all that's keeping you from screaming down Hyde Street.) Placards explain that the cables last between 100 and 300 days depending on which line they serve, the Powell-Mason line being the most demanding. A demonstration car explains how the gripman and brakeman control the cars, including the bells that are used to communicate. One of the highlights is Car No. 8 from Andrew Hallidie's original 1873 Clay Street cable car. Saved from the 1906 fire because it was on loan to the city of Baltimore for an exhibition in 1905, the car has been restored and, along with two 1876 cars from the old Sutter Street line, stands as a monument to one of the city's best-loved legacies. A gift shop sells the usual tourist paraphernalia: postcards, key chains, coffee cups, etc. *Free; open every day; www.cablecarmuseum.com; map:M2*

**CALIFORNIA ACADEMY OF SCIENCES / Golden Gate Park, off Middle Dr E, btwn John F. Kennedy and Martin Luther King Jr. Drs; 415/750-7145** Three extraordinary and mind-expanding museums under one roof, and so entertaining that even the locals visit regularly. See Top 25 Attractions for more information. *Map:H5*

**CALIFORNIA PALACE OF THE LEGION OF HONOR / Legion of Honor Dr at 34th Ave and Clement St; 415/863-3330** Witness the finest collections of Rodin sculptures outside Paris, as well as many other works of art, at this beautiful neoclassical monument. See Top 25 Attractions for more information. *Map:E4*

**COIT TOWER FRESCOES / 1 Telegraph Hill Blvd; 415/362-0808** Inside the base of the tower are a series of murals titled *Life in California, 1934,* which were completed by more than 25 artists—many of whom studied under Mexican muralist Diego Rivera—as part of the New Deal. See Top 25 Attractions for more information. *Map:N1*

**EXPLORATORIUM / 3601 Lyon St at Marina Blvd in the Palace of Fine Arts; 415/563-7337 or 415/561-0360 for recorded information** Don't miss what *Scientific American* calls "the best science museum in the world." See Top 25 Attractions for more information. *Map:J1*

**HAAS-LILIENTHAL HOUSE / 2007 Franklin St btwn Washington and Jackson Sts; 415/441-3000** Built in 1886, this Queen Anne Victorian housed the Haas-Lilienthal family from 1886 until 1972. Peter Schmidt's lavish design for the 24-room mansion cost $18,500 to build. The interior architecture features a yellow sienna marble fireplace and a red Namidian marble hearth, redwood paneling, dormer windows, flying cupolas, and oak wainscoting. A 1920s update by Gardner Daily  brought modern conveniences such as a stove and elevator. What's the story? It all has to do with Alice Haas-Lilienthal, who grew up—and passed away—in this historic home. While much of the neighboring area was being sold to developers eager to build profitable apartment buildings, she held on to her family legacy and lived there until her death in 1972. In 1974, her heirs donated the house to the Foundation for San Francisco's Architectural Heritage. This nonprofit organization decided to open the doors of the amazing landmark to the public. It's a one-of-a-kind opportunity to glimpse the pristine interior of one of San Francisco's world-famous Victorians. *Admission is $3–$5; tours Wed noon–3pm and Sun 11am–4pm; map:L1*

**MARITIME MUSEUM / 900 Beach St at Polk St; 415/556-3002** Peruse the dignified array of spectacular photos, ship models, and displays at this world-class museum dedicated to the ships of yesteryear. See Top 25 Attractions for more information. *Map:L1*

**MEXICAN MUSEUM / Yerba Buena Center for the Arts; 701 Mission St at 3rd St; 415/202-9700** The city has several terrific folk-art museums, most notably the Mexican Museum—the first museum in the country to focus on the arts of Mexico and Mexican Americans. With a permanent collection of more than 10,000 objects ranging from pre-conquest artifacts to popular, modern, and contemporary Mexican and Chicano art, the museum presents the complexity and richness of Latino art throughout the Americas. Revolving exhibits range from the art of New Mexican women to Mexican surrealism. (Note: The museum's new location at the Yerba Buena Center is not expected to open until late 2003; for more information, visit www.mexicanmuseum.org.)

**MISSION DOLORES / 3321 16th St at Dolores St; 415/621-8203** Ponder the old tombstones and religious artifacts from Spanish America at this authentic Spanish mission. See Top 25 Attractions for more information. *Map:K5*

**MUSÉE MÉCANIQUE / Cliff House, 1090 Point Lobos Ave at the west end of Geary Blvd; 415/386-1170** You'll marvel at this collection of antique mechanical amusement machines that actually work. See Cliff House in Top 25 Attractions for more information. *Map:C3*

---

### THE MARVELOUS MUSÉE MÉCANIQUE

If there was ever a museum that was truly "fun for all ages," it's the Musée Mécanique, a glorious old trove of antique mechanical amusement machines that actually work (providing you have a pocket full of quarters). Watch the small children cower in fear as Laughing "Fat Lady" Sal—of San Francisco's Playland-at-the-Beach fame—gives her infamous cackle of a greeting, or see what Grandmother the Fortune Teller has to say about your future. Most older kids congregate around the far less imaginative video games in back. Behind the arcade museum is the **Camera Obscura,** a replica of Leonardo da Vinci's invention that reflects and magnifies an image of nearby Seal Rocks and Ocean Beach on a giant parabolic mirror. Both are located directly below the Cliff House Restaurant at 1090 Point Lobos Avenue at the west end of Geary Boulevard, and are open daily from 11am to 7pm (open earlier on weekends); 415/386-1170.

**OCTAGON HOUSE / 2645 Gough St at Union St; 415/441-7512** Maintained by the National Society of Colonial Dames of America, this eight-sided, cupola-topped house dates from 1859 and is now a small museum displaying Early American antiques—furniture, ceramics, portraits—and historic documents such as signatures of 54 of the 56 signers of the Declaration of Independence. The architectural features are extraordinary as well. *Free; open only on the second Sun and second and fourth Thurs of each month, noon–3pm (closed Jan); map:L2*

**PRECITA EYES MURAL ARTS CENTER / 2981 24th St btwn Harrison and Alabama Sts; 415/285-2287** Fantastic murals decorate many public spaces in the city, particularly in the Mission District, the city's vibrant, primarily Hispanic neighborhood. At the Precita Eyes Mural Arts Center, you can pick up maps outlining self-guided walks, or opt for the very informative 1¾-hour guided tour of 85 murals in an eight-block walk. Tours are conducted on Saturday at 11am and 1:30pm, Sunday at 1:30pm, and every day during Mural Awareness Month (usually May). If you don't have time for a tour, at least stroll down narrow Balmy Alley (near Harrison and 25th Streets), which is lined with about 30 incredibly colorful murals and is the birthplace of mural painting in San Francisco. *Admission to the center is free; call for tour rates; open every day; map:M7*

**RIPLEY'S BELIEVE IT OR NOT! MUSEUM / 175 Jefferson St at Fisherman's Wharf; 415/771-6188** Witness freaks of nature that stymie our perception of reality (that, and get totally grossed out). See Fisherman's Wharf in Top 25 Attractions for more information. *www.ripleysf.com; map:M1*

**SAN FRANCISCO MUSEUM OF MODERN ART / 151 3rd St, btwn Mission and Howard Sts; 415/357-4000** More than 17,000 works are housed in this $62 million monument to modern art. See Top 25 Attractions for more information. *Map:N3*

**WAX MUSEUM / 145 Jefferson St at Fisherman's Wharf; 415/202-0400** Sure, it's a cheesy, kitschy tourist trap, but it's still loads of creepy fun for both kids and adults. See Fisherman's Wharf in Top 25 Attractions for more information. *Map:M1*

**YERBA BUENA CENTER FOR THE ARTS / 701 Mission St at 3rd St; 415/543-1718** Witness cutting-edge multimedia shows and computer-generated art at this stylish high-tech art center. See Top 25 Attractions for more information. *Map:N3*

# Parks, Beaches, and the
# San Francisco Zoo

Scenic spots abound in San Francisco, and views can be had all over the city. Some wonderful parks include **GLEN CANYON PARK**, which has a playground, on Bosworth Street and O'Shaughnessy Boulevard (map:J8); the lush **STERN GROVE**, on Sloat Boulevard at 19th Avenue (map:G9); and **LAKE MERCED**, off Harding Road between Highway 35 and Sloat Boulevard, near the zoo (map:E9).

Riptide-ridden and blustery **OCEAN BEACH**, a long, sandy stretch located off the Great Highway, is a haven for seasoned surfers as well as for families, dog-walkers, joggers, and strolling lovers (map:D2–D9). On warm days, sun worshippers prefer to bask at **BAKER BEACH** while gazing at the beautiful view of the Golden Gate (as at most of the city's beaches, however, swimming is unsafe here). The east side of the beach is a popular gay hangout, where sunbathers bare all; take 25th Avenue west to the end, bear right, and then look for signs to Baker Beach (map:F1–F2).

In the southwest corner of the city, near the ocean and Lake Merced, is the popular **SAN FRANCISCO ZOO** (45th Ave and Sloat Blvd; 415/753-7080; www.sfzoo.org; map:D9). Launched in 1889 with a grizzly bear named Monarch that was donated by the *San Francisco Examiner,* the zoo now sprawls over 65 acres and attracts more than a million visitors each year. Highlights include the famed **PRIMATE DISCOVERY CENTER**, where several rare species of apes and monkeys live in glass-walled condos; Penguin Island, home to a large breeding colony of Magellanic penguins; the Koala Crossing and Australian Walkabout exhibit, filled with koalas, kangaroos, emus, and wallaroos; and Gorilla World, one of the world's largest exhibits of gorillas. The zoo also has rare Sumatran and Siberian tigers, African lions (visit during their mealtimes), a children's petting zoo, and even an insect zoo. A free, informal walking tour of the zoo is available on weekends at 11am, and the Zebra Zephyr train tour takes visitors on 30-minute zoo tours daily (weekends only in winter). The zoo is open daily from 10am to 5pm; admission is $9 for adults, $6 for seniors and youths 12–17, $3 for children 3–11, and free for children under 3. Note: Free the first Wed of each month except for the children's zoo.

If you want to get out on the bay, but Alcatraz isn't your cup of tea, head to **ANGEL ISLAND**, a 740-acre state park with a few interesting sights and a lot of hiking and biking trails (map:FF5). Before the Spaniards "discovered" the island, it was a fishing and hunting spot for the local Miwok Indians. For almost 100 years, from the Civil War to the cold war, the island housed a variety of military installations. It also played a major role in the settlement of the West, serving as both a Public Health Service quarantine station and an immigration station. State park volunteers lead **TOURS** of Angel Island's historic immigration station, Camp Reynolds, and Fort McDowell on the weekends between 10am and 4pm, and by appointment during the week. Tours and admission to the park are free, though donations are accepted. Ferries land at Ayala Cove, the perfect site for a family picnic. Call the Blue & Gold Fleet (415/705-5555; recorded information, 415/773-1188; www.blueand goldfleet.com) for ferry service and rates from San Francisco.

# Organized Tours

## BUS TOURS

**GRAY LINE** (800/826-0202 or 415/558-9400), San Francisco's largest bus-tour operator, offers several ways to see San Francisco. Its **DELUXE CITY TOUR** wheels past the Civic Center, Mission Dolores, Twin Peaks, Golden Gate Park, Cliff House, Vista Point North, and Golden Gate Bridge. The 3½-hour tour concludes at Fisherman's Wharf. The fare is $37 for adults, $18.50 for children ages 5–11. Tours run daily: 9am, 10am, 11am, 1pm, 2pm (3:30pm seasonal). Gray Line also offers this tour with a bay cruise option for an additional $12. An added trip to Alcatraz Island runs an extra $15. Reservations are required for most tours, which are available in several foreign languages. Offices are located at the Transbay Terminal, First and Mission Streets, and Pier 39; and a free pickup and return service runs between centrally located hotels and departure locations.

For a different perspective on the city, try **SAN FRANCISCO FIRE ENGINE TOURS & ADVENTURES** (415/333-7077). One-hour tours on an old-fashioned open-top fire engine cover the Golden Gate Bridge, the Presidio, and Union Street; or Fisherman's Wharf, the Embarcadero, and North Beach (everyone on this trip always looks as if they're having a ball). The fire engine can also be chartered for a custom tour.

## BOAT TOURS

One of the most fun and scenic ways to explore the Bay Area is by ferry. In addition to the popular ride over to Alcatraz, a number of options for cruising the bay are available. The **BLUE & GOLD FLEET** (415/705-5555; www.blueandgoldfleet.com) offers ferry service to Alcatraz, Angel Island, Sausalito, and Tiburon, as well as **NARRATED BAY CRUISES** throughout the week year-round via its 400-passenger sightseeing boat, complete with a cafe and bar. All tours depart from Pier 39's West Marina

## SAN FRANCISCO'S SUNDAY MORNING SENSATION

Ever since the Reverend Cecil Williams took the helm of the **Glide Memorial Church** nearly four decades ago, San Franciscans of every color, tax bracket, and lifestyle have joined together on Sunday mornings to celebrate life in one of the most high-energy, roof-raising renditions you'll ever witness. As Glide's new reverend, the first thing Williams did was remove all overt religious icons in order to establish a nondenominational church. He then assembled a 120-member choir accompanied by a blues-style band, and opened the doors to literally every type of person—poor, famous, homeless, wealthy, crazy—of every religion, raising their spirits with uplifting sermons and songs about hope and love.

Since then, the Reverend Williams's efforts to help the homeless and poor of the Tenderloin (one of the city's most poverty-stricken neighborhoods) have attracted nationwide fame. Luminaries either on the stage or in the audience have included San Francisco local Sharon Stone, Bobby McFerrin, Robin Williams, Maya Angelou, Oprah Winfrey, and Bill Clinton. Even if you're an ardent atheist who has never been to church before, go: you'll be glad you did. Just be sure to arrive a little early to get a first-floor seat (the balcony's view is limited). The church is located at 330 Ellis Street at Taylor Street, west of Union Square (415/771-6300; www.glide.org). Services take place every Sunday at 9am and 11am.

beginning at 10am in summer and 11am in winter; call or visit the website for the latest schedules and rates.

Also located on Fisherman's Wharf is the **RED & WHITE FLEET** (877/855-5506 or 415/447-0597; www.redandwhite.com). The tour company offers a one-hour Golden Gate Bridge Cruise that takes in all the city's waterfront sites and also cruises under the Golden Gate Bridge, along the Marin Headlands, and past Sausalito, Angel Island State Park, and Alcatraz Island. Also offered is a 45-minute "Round the Rock" cruise that circles Alcatraz. It's based at Pier 43 on Fisherman's Wharf; call or visit the website for schedules and rates.

### WALKING TOURS

Celebrating San Francisco's folklore, history, and diversity is the goal of **CITY GUIDES,** an affiliate program of the San Francisco Public Library that employs 200 volunteers who lead free themed walking tours covering just about every corner of the city. Architecture buffs might take the Art Deco Marina or Pacific Heights Mansions tours. Fans of the Barbary Coast period of San Francisco history will enjoy the Brothels, Boardinghouses & Bawds tour. The alphabet soup of tours covers everything from Alamo Square to the Zakheim Mural. Call 415/557-4266 for schedules, or pick up a brochure at the San Francisco Visitor Information Center, on the lower level of Hallidie Plaza (900 Market St at Powell St; 415/391-2000; map:N3), or at any branch of the San Francisco Public Library.

**CHINATOWN TOUR:** For an expert tour of Chinatown, try **WOK WIZ CHINATOWN WALKING TOURS & COOKING CENTER** (654 Commercial St btwn Kearny and Montgomery Sts; 415/981-5588). Author and cooking instructor Shirley Fong-Torres and her well-trained staff lead a number of tours throughout the neighborhood that cover the history, culture, folklore, and food of Chinatown. Tours are conducted daily from 10am to 1:30pm and can include a dim sum lunch (optional). Groups are generally held to a maximum of 15, and reservations are essential. Prices (including lunch) are $39 for adults, $35 for seniors 62 and older, and $37 for children under 12. For the perpetually hungry, Shirley also operates an I Can't Believe I Ate My Way Through Chinatown tour (most Saturdays; $65 per person) and a Walk & Wok tour, in which you shop for food in Chinatown and then cook and eat it together at Shirley's Cooking Center (most Saturdays; $75 per person). For more information, visit www.wokwiz.com.

**NORTH BEACH TOURS:** Feeling low on energy? Get a buzz with the brisk **JAVAWALK**, a 2-hour tour tracing the vein of caffeine in San Francisco history. Coffee lover and self-described "coffeehouse lizard" Elaine Sosa shares colorful stories of North Beach and Jackson Square while exploring cafes, a coffee roastery, and a shop that sells—what else?— espresso machines. Javawalk is offered on Saturdays only at 10am. The price is $20 per person, and kids are half price. For more information, call 415/673-WALK or visit www.javawalk.com. Reservations are required.

Food writer GraceAnn Walden offers her own **MANGIA NORTH BEACH!** tour, which includes behind-the-scenes looks at bakeries, pubs, truffle makers, and restaurants, as well as visits to Italian book and ceramic stores. For more information, call 415/397-8530.

Lest you get the impression that San Franciscans think only about food, tactileHeart (415/721-1763; www.tactileheart.com) offers the **FOOTNOTES STREET THEATER LIVING LITERATURE TOUR**, a performance walk through North Beach, following in the footsteps of local authors such as Jack Kerouac and Maya Angelou.

**HAIGHT-ASHBURY TOUR:** Rachel Heller leads a guided promenade through the psychedelic past of the **UPPER HAIGHT**. During the 2½-hour tour, you'll be introduced to Janis Joplin's former house, the Grateful Dead's old crash pad, and the Haight's rich history, including, of course, the Summer of Love. Tours are offered on Tuesdays at 9:30am and Saturdays at 9:30am; $15 per person; 415/863-1621.

**VICTORIAN HOME TOURS:** If you're a fan of Victorian architecture, you'll really enjoy the **VICTORIAN HOMES HISTORICAL WALKING TOUR**

led by San Francisco local Jay Gifford (415/252-9485; www.victorian walk.com). The leisurely (and tour bus–free) 2½-hour tour wanders through the Pacific Heights and Cow Hollow neighborhoods and covers everything you ever wanted to know about San Francisco's Victorian architecture and history. The tour passes about 200 restored Victorians— including the ones where *Mrs. Doubtfire* and *Party of Five* were filmed— and ends with a trolley bus ride back to Union Square, passing through North Beach and Chinatown. Tours start at 11am in the lobby of the Westin St. Francis Hotel on Union Square and are offered daily year-round; $20 per person. Reservations are required.

Another tour option is the **VICTORIAN AND EDWARDIAN PACIFIC HEIGHTS WALK** (415/441-3000), led by guides from the Foundation for San Francisco's Architectural Heritage. The 2-hour stroll costs only $5 and covers the area's many turn-of-the-century mansions, family homes, and row houses. Tours meet daily at 2007 Franklin Street (map:L3). Saints and Sinners (415/922-7181), led by Footprints on the Pavement, is a 2½-hour tour through the Victorian mansions, row houses, churches, and hotels of the Cathedral Hill area. Cost is $25 per person and includes lunch; reservations are required.

**MISSION DISTRICT TOUR:** Precita Eyes Mural Arts Center (2981 24th St btwn Harrison and Alabama Sts; 415/285-2287; map:N7) offers walking tours to view the Mission District's many murals. The 1¾-hour guided tours, which cover 85 colorful, vibrant murals during an eight-block walk, are conducted on Saturday at 11am and 1:30pm, Sunday at 1:30pm, and every day during Mural Awareness Month (usually May). Tour prices are $10 for adults, $8 for students with ID, $5 for seniors, and $2 for children under 18.

**CASTRO TOUR:** For a closer look at the exciting Castro neighborhood, **CRUISIN' THE CASTRO** (400 Castro St; 415/550-8110; map:K6) takes off from Harvey Milk Plaza (where many gay rights marches and protests begin) and includes brunch at Caffe Luna Piena. Tours are led by Trevor Hailey, who was involved in the development of the Castro in the 1970s, and begin at 10am Tuesday through Saturday and most holidays. The cost is $40 per person and reservations are required; for more information, visit www.webcastro.com/castrotour.

# SHOPPING

# SHOPPING

## Major Shopping Areas

### UNION SQUARE

Of all the great shopping destinations in San Francisco, none matches the high-energy sophistication of Union Square. Named for Union supporters who gathered here before the Civil War, this area at the turn of the century was a favorite with white-gloved society ladies who lunched at the St. Francis Hotel. The first Union Square department store opened in 1896. Today the newly expanded Macy's, genteel Saks Fifth Avenue, and luxe Neiman Marcus anchor the area, with retail theaters such as Niketown and Disney adding a glitzy modern twist. And the latest feather in Union Square's cap is the New York–based Bloomingdale's, which is now slated to open in 2002.

Just off the square is the Parisian-style alleyway known as **MAIDEN LANE**. Originally called Morton Street and lined with bordellos, it got a name change (and started attracting a different clientele) in 1922. These days you'll find chic couturiers such as Chanel and Jil Sander commingling with fine home and accessory shops. Take a short walk east down Post Street to the beautiful **CROCKER GALLERIA** (50 Post St btwn Montgomery and Kearny Sts; open Mon–Fri 10am–6pm, Sat 10am–5pm; www.shopatgalleria.com), modeled after Milan's Galleria Vittorio Emmanuelle. This elegant glass-domed pavilion features three tiers of shops, including big names like Nicole Miller, Versace, and Polo Ralph Lauren, with plenty of cafes and tea shops for a pleasant mid-shopping break. Go west down Market Street and you'll come to the skylit, nine-story **SAN FRANCISCO SHOPPING CENTRE** (865 Market St at 5th St; open Mon–Sat 9:30am–8pm, Sun 11am–6pm; www.sanfrancisco centre.com), one of a handful of vertical malls in the nation, with more than 100 shops, including Abercrombie & Fitch, Enzo Angiolini, Club Monaco, and J. Crew. The unique spiral escalator circles all the way up to Nordstrom's fourth floor. If you can't find what you're looking for there, head back east toward the bay to the **EMBARCADERO CENTER** (bordered by Battery and Drumm Sts, Sacramento and Clay Sts; open Mon–Fri 10am–7pm, Sat 10am–6pm, Sun noon–5pm). Here amid the towers of the Financial District is a four-tower complex with restaurants, award-winning gardens, and more than 130 shops and restaurants, from Pottery Barn and Crabtree & Evelyn to the Gap, Banana Republic, Liz Claiborne, and much more.

### FISHERMAN'S WHARF

Yes, it's touristy, but there's more retail to this area than T-shirt shops. The three-level red-brick **CANNERY** (Leavenworth and Beach Sts; open

Mon–Sat 10am–6pm, Sun 11am–6pm), built at the turn of the century as a Del Monte fruit-packing plant, now holds a variety of restaurants, outdoor vendors, and stores purveying kitchenware, shoes, and fine local food and wine. The Museum of the City of San Francisco is on the third floor, and from the walkways and balconies you can look down to a tree-shaded courtyard where performers entertain daily. A stone's throw away is **GHIRARDELLI SQUARE** (900 North Point St btwn Larkin and Polk Sts; open Mon–Sat 10am–9pm, Sun 10am–6pm), site of a former mill and chocolate factory; nowadays retailers such as Ann Taylor, Benetton, The Sharper Image, a shoe store, and an architectural book-store coexist cheek by jowl with the famous chocolate shop. Another restoration success—or monstrosity, depending on one's point of view—is **PIER 39** (The Embarcadero at Beach St; open every day), a converted pier lined with more than 100 restaurants and novelty shops.

## SOUTH OF MARKET AREA (SOMA)

This former industrial warehouse district is now a hot spot for hip restau-rants, nightclubs, and bargain and discount stores. Most of the action takes place on Brannan, Second, Third, Howard, and Townsend Streets. Though markdown outlets come and go, **BURLINGTON COAT FACTORY** (899 Howard St at 5th St; 415/495-7234; www.coat.com; map:N4)—carrying more than coats—is one of the stalwarts. The **SAN FRANCISCO FLOWER MART** (640 Brannan St at 6th St; 415/392-7944; www.sf flmart.com; map:N5) is another great destination, where early risers can pick up well-priced fresh and dried flowers from wholesale merchants who also sell to the public. A relative newcomer to SoMa is **METREON** (150 4th St at Mission St; open every day 10am–11pm; map:N4). Inside are four floors of retail spectacle, including a Maurice Sendak–themed restaurant, a movie multiplex with an IMAX theater, a Discovery Channel store, a Microsoft store, a shop called Sony Style, a marketplace devoted to works by local retailers and artists, and more.

## SHOPPING BY NEIGHBORHOOD

San Francisco's neighborhoods are rewarding retail therapy in them-selves. Near the Marina District is an area known as **COW HOLLOW**, named after the cattle that grazed freely in this area in the mid-1800s; these days shoppers consider it good grazing for trend-setting clothing and home decor. Apparel stores on **UNION STREET** (between Van Ness Ave and Steiner St) tend toward European designs or the sporty, casual look; many shops and restaurants are housed in old Victorians or tucked down picturesque courtyards and alleys. **CHESTNUT STREET** (between Laguna and Lombard Sts) is the Marina's main artery; on weekends in-line skaters and baby-boomers-with-strollers share the sidewalks, stop-ping at everything from old-fashioned delis and edgy boutiques to chain stores such as Williams-Sonoma and the Gap. Another upscale/hip enclave of high-end antiques, furnishings, and more can be found on **FILLMORE STREET** (from Pine St to Jackson St) in Pacific Heights; here you'll rub elbows with the city's elite, many of whom live in huge mansions a few blocks away. A dozen or so blocks down Fillmore Street on **SACRAMENTO STREET** (near Presidio Ave), amid a peaceful residential neighborhood of tree-shaded Edwardians, the antique dealers share the sidewalks with chic clothing boutiques such as Sarah Shaw and decorator treasure trove Sue Fisher King.

Across town, between Douglas and Dolores Streets, is **24TH STREET**, Noe Valley's version of the Chestnut Street shopping area in the Marina, only with a cozier flavor. Here you'll find lots of family-run retailers purveying toys, children's apparel, handicrafts, and books, plus loads of cafes and bakeries where you can recharge yourself after taking it all in. A short drive away down Castro Street is the **CASTRO**, the heart of the gay community, always packed with shoppers checking out the mainstream and offbeat (sometimes downright risqué) clothing and novelty shops, along with the historic Castro Theatre.

If it's ultra-*ultra*-hip you want, head toward the Civic Center area to **HAYES STREET**, which was a run-down strip of bars and liquor stores before forward-thinking merchants moved in. Today you'll find a pedestrian-friendly setting to browse for avant-garde clothes, shoes, books, and funky furniture finds.

Some neighborhoods are worth shopping in just for their ethnic or subcultural flavor. In the Richmond District, **CLEMENT STREET** between Arguello and Park Presidio Boulevards is chockablock with every imaginable Asian restaurant and produce market, and also boasts terrific consignment shops and bookstores. **HAIGHT STREET**, even more threadbare these days but still with its heart in the '60s, has loads of stores hawking vintage clothing, Grateful Dead posters, and tie-dyed T-shirts. And **JAPANTOWN** (between Post and Buchanan Sts) is the place to go for imported Japanese textiles, ceramics, and silk.

It's hard to believe picturesque **JACKSON SQUARE** (between Columbus Ave and Sansome St) was once part of San Francisco's rough-and-tumble Barbary Coast. The Depression of the '30s closed the saloons and brothels, leaving vacant buildings; in the '50s, interior decorators and architects moved in. Today it's a delightful enclave of gaslamp-lit alleys and Victorian storefronts housing antique shops with superb European, Continental, and Asian furniture and decorative arts.

Follow Jackson Street to Columbus Avenue and you'll reach **NORTH BEACH**, the old Italian neighborhood that the Beat Generation made famous. Bookstores and clothing shops still cater to bohemian (and upscale) tastes, and the area around Filbert Street houses Italian craft shops, delis, and bakeries galore.

## GOLDEN GATE BRIDGE BY THE NUMBERS

| | |
|---|---|
| Length: 8,981 feet | Cable thickness: 36½ inches |
| Span: 6,450 feet | Cable length: 7,650 feet |
| Cost: $35 million | Steel used: 83,000 pounds |
| Completion date: May 28, 1937 | Concrete used: 389,000 cubic yards |
| Date paid in full: July 1971 | Miles of wire cable: 80,000 |
| Engineer: Joseph B. Strauss | Gallons of paint annually: 10,000 |
| Road height: 260 feet | Color: International Orange |
| Tower height: 746 feet | Rise, in cold weather: 5 feet |
| Swing span: 27 feet | Drop, in hot weather: 10 feet |
| Deepest foundation: | Traffic: 3 million vehicles per month |
| 110 feet under water | Toll: $3 (southbound only) |

And finally there's **CHINATOWN**, with its big green metal dragon-and lion-flanked Grant Avenue gate. Home to one of the largest Asian populations in North America, it's a fun place to pick up kitschy imported trinkets, porcelains, and silks. Or join locals haggling over already bargain-priced produce, poultry, and meats.

## OUTLYING MALL

South down 19th Avenue in the foggy Sunset District is **STONESTOWN GALLERIA** (3251 20th Ave at Winston Dr; 415/759-2626; open Mon–Sat 10am–9pm, Sun 11am–6pm; www.stonestowngalleria.com; map:G9)—a bit of a trek, but worth it for the terrific selection of stores under one roof. Besides Nordstrom and Macy's there's Eddie Bauer, the Gap, Banana Republic, and lots of small jewelry, shoe, and accessory boutiques, plus an enormous sunlit food court and—egad!—plenty of free parking.

## DEPARTMENT STORES

**MACY'S UNION SQUARE / 170 O'Farrell St btwn Powell and Stockton Sts; 415/397-3333** After a major remodel and expansion, Macy's Union Square is now the third-largest department store in the world (following Harrod's of London and Macy's New York): 700,000 square feet, including the separate men's store across the street. The refurbished eight-story building includes a six-story glass window overlooking the square. Inside you'll find departments representing mid- to high-end apparel, accessories, cosmetics, and housewares. "Shoes on Two" is the biggest footwear department on the West Coast, and the sportswear floors stock more than 80,000 pairs of jeans from all major makers. There's a terrific selection of furniture, kitchenware, bedding, and linen, including designer sheets and accents. Edibles sold in the Cellar range from healthy snacks at Jamba Juice to gourmet deli entrees by celebrity chef Wolfgang Puck. *Open Mon–Sat 10am–8pm, Sun 11am–7pm; www.macys.com; map:N3*

**NEIMAN MARCUS / 150 Stockton St at Geary St; 415/362-3900** The elegant Dallas-headquartered department store with its Philip Johnson–designed facade boasts a giant atrium with a stunning stained-glass ceiling—all that remains of the historic City of Paris store that once occupied the site. Thierry Mugler, Escada, and St. John are some of the high-end designers represented in the haute-couture boutiques. The main level boasts an excellent selection of fragrances and cosmetics. The accessories and gourmet food departments are also superb. During the holidays shoppers flock to Neiman's to see its gaily decorated three-story tree. *Open Mon–Sat 10am–7pm, Thurs 10am–8pm, Sun noon–6pm; www.neimanmarcus.com; map:N3*

**NORDSTROM / San Francisco Centre, 865 Market St at 5th St; 415/243-8500** What started as a family-run Seattle shoe store has become one of the most popular shopping destinations in the West. In the San Francisco Centre store, a spiral escalator—one of only two in the country—accesses Nordstrom's different levels. In addition to more than 100,000 pairs of shoes you'll find fine jewelry, gift items, cosmetics, and high-end fashion from Oscar de la Renta, Valentino, and others. Services include a beauty spa, four restaurants, personal shoppers, a concierge, live piano music while you shop, and even valet parking (at the 5th St entrance). *Open Mon–Sat 9:30am–9pm, Sun 10am–7pm; www.nordstrom.com; map:M4*

**SAKS FIFTH AVENUE / 384 Post St at Powell St; 415/986-4300** The West Coast branch of this New York–based retailer is renowned for its designer boutiques and high-end cosmetics and jewelry. A central escalator links five floors, and there's a cafe on the top floor overlooking the square. *Open Mon–Wed, Fri 10am–7pm, Thurs 10am–8pm, Sat 11am–6pm, Sun noon–6pm; www.saks.com; map:N3*

**SAKS FIFTH AVENUE MEN'S STORE / 220 Post St btwn Stockton St and Grant Ave; 415/986-4300** Art deco detailing, wood paneling, a fireplace, and a bar in the fitting room add up to one of the classiest men's shopping destinations in town. Five floors feature sportswear, accessories, and traditional and contemporary attire. The fourth floor is modeled after a New York City penthouse to showcase fashions from Armani, Gucci, Prada, and others. *Open Mon–Wed, Fri–Sat 10am–7pm; Thurs 10am–8pm; Sun noon–7pm; www.saks.com; map:N3*

# Shops from A to Z

## ANTIQUES

**ARGENTUM–THE LEOPARD'S HEAD / 414 Jackson St btwn Sansome and Montgomery Sts; 415/296-7757** If you're looking for that elegant trinket to spruce up the table, then this is the place. Taking up the second floor of a historic building, Argentum specializes in English, Scottish, Irish, and American silver from the early 18th to late 19th century. The selection is dazzling, from flatware and trivets to knife rests and platters. Most items are food related: urns, soup tureens, sauceboats, salvers (small servants' trays used to hold drinks), and more. The array of silver wine accoutrements is one of the best in the country. If you're a serious collector, don't miss Paul Storr's creations or the coffee services and tea caddies by Hester Batemen, one of the first female silversmiths. *Open Mon–Fri 9:30am–5pm, Sat 10am–4pm; www.argentum-theleopard.com; map:N2*

**BUTTERFIELD & BUTTERFIELD / 220 San Bruno Ave off 16th St; 415/861-7500** What was founded as a clearinghouse for surplus goods has become one of the most successful auction houses in the world. Established in 1865 on the site of the Transamerica Pyramid, the company moved to larger quarters south of Market Street when it expanded to represent antiques, fine art, and furnishings. Estate sales are held monthly, and the main gallery auctions are on Sundays. Catalogs are available for a fee. Absentee bids can be made by telephone, by mail, or online at www.butterfields.com. *Open Mon–Fri 9am–5pm; www.butterfields.com; map:N5*

**COLLECTIVE ANTIQUES / 701 Bayshore Blvd at Industrial St; 415/656-0300** Collective Antiques is a 6,600-square-foot space with more than 27 dealers (many of them decorators) showcasing higher-end English Continental, American-influence, and Italian and French artifacts. Merchandise must be pre-1950 and in excellent condition. A full-time designer oversees the displays, which are arranged so you can see how the antiques might look in your home. The decorative elements alone are worth the trip; they run the gamut from French magazine stands and Victorian laptop desks to fabulous old lanterns and globes. *Open Mon–Sat 10am–5pm, Sun noon–5pm; www.collectiveantiques.citysearch.com; map:N5*

**DILLINGHAM & COMPANY / 431 Jackson St btwn Montgomery and Sansome Sts; 415/989-8777** Gaylord Dillingham is a dealer in the old-fashioned sense. He specializes in one area: authentic English and Continental furniture from the 18th to the 19th century. With more than 25 years of experience and a degree from the Victoria & Albert Museum in London, Dillingham keeps his gallery well furnished with authentic

Chippendale, William & Mary, and Regency pieces, most found on his buying trips to Europe. *Open Mon–Fri 9am–5pm, Sat 11am–3pm; www.dillinghamandcompany.com; map:N2*

**ED HARDY ANTIQUES / 188 Henry Adams St btwn 14th and 15th Sts; 415/626-6300** A longtime veteran of San Francisco's antiques community, Ed Hardy had his business in the heart of downtown before building this gorgeous Palladian-style building with 15-foot ceilings, a Renaissance stone fireplace, and 16th-century Italian red marble columns. The merchandise, as elegant and eclectic as the surroundings, includes 16th- to 20th-century decorative items from Italy, England, and France. A fountain courtyard showcases antique garden furniture and statuary. Can't find what you're looking for? Ask the staff. Chances are it's hidden in one of the numerous nooks or crannies. *Open Mon–Fri 9am–5pm; www.edhardysf.com; map:N5*

**EVELYN'S ANTIQUE CHINESE FURNITURE / 381 Hayes St at Gough St; 415/255-1815** Disney executive Michael Eisner is one of the many celebrities whose home is decorated with antiques from this shop. Evelyn's is the largest importer of pre-1850 Chinese antiques in the nation, and it's been a well-kept secret of designers and collectors since it opened in 1987. The selection appears small at first glance (the Chinese custom is to show a little at a time), but in the back are a storeroom and restoration workshop jam-packed with Ming chairs, lohan beds (designed for Buddhist sages), altar tables, baskets, and pots. *Open Mon–Sat 10:30am–6:30pm; map:L4*

**FOSTER-GWIN, INC. / 38 Hotaling Place btwn Montgomery and Sansome Sts; 415/397-4986** Bring money. Lots of money. Foster-Gwin caters to the well heeled, who make frequent pilgrimages to the gallery for its splendid furnishings from the Renaissance to the early 19th century. Located on an alley named for a distiller and real-estate baron, the space served as a livery in days gone by. Stairs to the second floor were horse ramps to the stalls, though the feed troughs have long since been replaced with ornate consoles and tapestries from 17th-century Belgium and France. *Open Mon–Fri 9am–5pm, Sat 10am–3pm; map:N2*

**INTERIEUR PERDU / 340 Bryant St at 2nd St (inside a big round building); 415/543-1616** This is one of our favorite destinations for the French Country look. The owners scour small villages and old farmhouses to keep the warehouse filled with rustic hutches, bistro tables and chairs, and antique daybeds and cribs. Adorable wooden goat carts are ideal for filling with pots of geraniums or ivy and placing next to Parisian park benches in your garden. You'll also find old farm tables, wire egg baskets, and enamel coffeepots and cups. *Open Mon–Sat 11am–6pm; map:O3*

**JOHN DOUGHTY ANTIQUES, INC. / 619 Sansome St btwn Washington and Jackson Sts; 415/398-6849** Those looking for fine 18th- and 19th-century furniture, oil paintings, and decorative accessories need look no further than John Doughty, who purchases most of his inventory on buying trips to his native England. The shop was founded in 1963 and still serves many of its original clients. *Open Mon–Fri 9:30am–5pm; map:N2*

**MURETA'S ANTIQUES / 2418 Fillmore St btwn Washington and Jackson Sts; 415/922-5652** Lifetime collector Gary Mureta runs this neighborhood shop in posh Pacific Heights, where society matrons allow him access to estate sales before other dealers. Mureta keeps the place pleasantly cluttered with silver, crystal, and china that befits a mansion as well as more humble abodes. *Open Tues–Sun noon–6pm; map:K2*

**THOMAS LIVINGSTON / 414 Jackson St at Sansome St; 415/296-8150** What was once a tram barn for storing streetcars is now home to a shop specializing in 18th- and 19th-century English and American antiques. Former University of California at Berkeley professor Thomas Livingston switched to dealing antiques more than 25 years ago and has developed a stunning array of fine Georgian and Regency pieces, in addition to wonderful decorative items such as delftware, clocks, lamps, and chandeliers. *Open Mon–Fri 9am–5pm, Sat 10am–4pm; map:N2*

## APPAREL

**A/X ARMANI EXCHANGE / 2090 Union St at Webster St; 415/749-0891** This branch of the nationwide chain, a casual, more affordable arm of Armani, carries sportswear and work wear geared to the chic but casual California lifestyle. You'll find a great selection of jeans, trousers, shirts, sweaters, jackets, skirts, and dresses at prices that won't cost a month's pay. Also look for leather totes, hats, and socks. *Open Mon–Sat 10am–8pm, Sun 11am–6pm; map:L2*

**ANN TAYLOR / 240 Post St btwn Stockton St and Grant Ave (and branches); 415/788-0716** Ann Taylor is a big favorite with career women, who love its selections of well-made suits, silk blouses, evening dresses, and sweaters, as well as the Taylor accessory line of jewelry, scarves, fragrances, belts, and shoes. You'll see a few trendier touches among the sportswear knits and denims. Other branches include the San Francisco Shopping Centre (415/543-2487), 3 Embarcadero Center (415/989-5355), and Ghirardelli Square (415/775-2872). *Open Mon–Sat 10am–6pm, Sun noon–6pm; map:N3*

**BANANA REPUBLIC / 256 Grant Ave at Sutter St (and branches); 415/788-3087** The flagship store of this hip national chain takes up an entire city block. Inside are several levels of casual men's and women's slacks, shorts, T-shirts, and dresses in de rigueur black, white, and khaki, plus whatever other colors are in this season. Fabrics lean toward linen, wool, cotton, cashmere, velvet, suede, and silk. Other branches include 2 Embarcadero Center (415/986-5076) and the Stonestown Galleria (415/753-3330). *Open Mon–Sat 9:30am–9pm, Sun 11am–6pm; www.bananarepublic.com; map:N3*

**BARCELINO / 498 Post St at Mason St; 415/781-5777** If you're looking for impeccable Italian-made men's suits and apparel, this is the place. Catering to the fashion-conscious male, Barcelino features sport jackets, ties, shirts, shoes, hats, and ascots—all adding up to that dapper, well-polished look. Barcelino for Ladies is located just two doors down at 476 Post Street (415/912-5700). *Open Mon–Wed, Fri–Sat 10am–7pm; Thurs 10am–8pm; Sun 11am–6pm; map:N3*

**BEBE / 21 Grant Ave at O'Farrell St (and branches); 415/781-2323** Don't expect bows or ruffles at Bebe: This boutique chain attracts younger career women who go for the drop-dead sleek and snug European fit. Clothes are trendy, but stylish enough to go straight from the office to dinner. Expect lots of black, olive, and brown, with the occasional flash of burgundy or hot pink. Other branches include the San Francisco Shopping Centre (415/543-2323) and 2133 Fillmore Street (between California and Sacramento Sts; 415/563-6895). *Open Mon–Fri 10am–7pm, Sat–Sun 10am–6pm; www.bebe.com; map:N3*

**BROOKS BROTHERS / 201 Post St btwn Grant Ave and Kearny St; 415/397-4500** The 180-year-old New York–founded clothier still specializes in traditional button-downs and pinstripes as well as classic sweaters and accessories for both women and men. Though known for the ultraconservative Ivy League look, Brooks now has a trendier collection of sportswear and weekend wear. *Open Mon–Sat 9:30am–6pm, Sun noon–5pm; www.brooksbrothers.com; map:N3*

**CAROL DODA'S CHAMPAGNE & LACE LINGERIE BOUTIQUE / 1850 Union St #1, btwn Laguna and Octavia Sts; 415/776-6900** Legendary North Beach topless star Carol Doda, former queen of the Condor club, owns and operates this sliver of a shop featuring unique bras, panties, chemises, teddies, bustiers, and other not-so-basic "foundations" not often found in department stores. Most are sexy, slinky, and ultratransparent. Bridal corsets and garments in hard-to-find sizes are another reason to visit. There are also silk thongs and boxers for men. Ooh la la! *Open every day 12:30–6:30pm; map:L2*

**CELINE PARIS BOUTIQUE / 233 Geary St at Stockton St; 415/397-1140** This is one of only four Celine boutiques in the nation carrying the complete line of women's ready-to-wear clothing and accessories from design superstar Michael Kors. Heavy on gray, black, white, and red, Kors sportswear uses luxe fabrics such as silk, suede, cashmere, and fur. *Open Mon–Sat 10am–7pm, Sun noon–5pm; map:N3*

**CHANEL / 155 Maiden Ln btwn Grant Ave and Stockton St; 415/981-1550** Coco would be proud to know the little black dress still reigns supreme at her namesake boutique. Today Chanel fashions come under the Karl Lagerfeld label in a variety of fabrics, including tweeds and silks. The store also sells the signature quilted handbags, costume jewelry, and wraparound glasses. *Open Mon–Sat 10am–6pm, Sun noon–5pm; www.chanel.com; map:N3*

**CIELO / 2225 Fillmore St btwn Sacramento and Clay Sts; 415/776-0641** This Euro-boutique, the sister store of L'Uomo, imports avant-garde fashions for women. Miu Miu is one of the popular labels. Colors tend toward neutral beige, blacks, and browns, and there are accessories to complement separates or ensembles. *Open Mon–Sat 11am–7pm, Sun noon–6pm; map:K3*

**DAVID STEPHEN MEN'S / 50 Maiden Ln btwn Grant Ave and Kearny St; 415/982-1611** One of the oldest men's stores in the city, David Stephen specializes in high-end, hand-tailored suits and sportswear from Italian designers such as Pal Zileri, Canali, and Ermenegildo Zegna. Along with jackets and shirts, you'll find sports coats, exquisite handmade cashmere sweaters and robes, and accessories. On-site tailoring is available, and there's a good selection of men's grooming products. *Open Mon–Sat 9:30am–5:30pm; www.davidstephen.com; map:N3*

**DIESEL / 101 Post St at Kearny St; 415/982-7077** Diesel's West Coast flagship store is packed with trendy denim fashions. Browse for Italian-made jeans, sportswear, and a huge selection of denim skirts, vests, and jackets. More than 3,000 pairs of the signature boot-cut denims are in stock, as well as sunglasses and accessories. *Open Mon–Fri 10am–8pm, Sat 10am–7pm, Sun noon–6pm; www.diesel.com; map:N3*

**EDDIE BAUER / 250 Post St at Stockton St; 415/986-7600** The canoes hanging from the ceiling are a big tip-off: This huge three-level store for men and women stocks stylish but functional outdoor and leisure wear. The emphasis is on well-made shirts, T-shirts, casual pants, shorts, and outerwear, in traditional colors. There's also a line of dress sportswear called AKA Eddie Bauer and an Eddie Bauer Home collection. *Open Mon–Fri 10am–8pm, Sat 9:30am–8pm, Sun 11am–6pm; www.eddie bauer.com; map:N3*

**EMPORIO ARMANI / 1 Grant Ave at O'Farrell St; 415/677-9400** The elegant marble setting is the perfect showcase for Armani's suits, sports-wear, formal wear, and accessories. The style is professional and classy, yet more affordable than other big-name boutiques. Some home furnishings are available. For a break from shopping, have an espresso or lunch at the classy cafe. *Open Mon–Fri 10am–7pm, Sat 10am–6pm, Sun noon–6pm; map:N3*

**FOG CITY LEATHER / 2060 Union St btwn Buchanan and Webster Sts; 415/567-1996** A San Francisco tradition, Fog City Leather carries a large selection of premium (read: expensive) leather goods including custom-made jackets, belts, wallets, and accessories. *Open Tues–Sat 11am–6pm, Sun noon–5pm; www.fogcityleather.com; map:K1*

**JESSICA MCCLINTOCK / 180 Geary St at Stockton St; 415/398-9008** Ever since San Francisco designer Jessica McClintock introduced her demure country-print Gunne Sax dresses in the early 1960s, young girls have been flocking to her boutiques in search of the romantic, feminine look. This shop is heavy on elegant wedding gowns and bridesmaid's dresses, plus luxurious long dresses for formal occasions. Purses and shoes are available to complete the ensemble. *Open Mon–Fri 10am–7pm, Sat–Sun 11am–6pm; map:N3*

**LEVI STRAUSS / 300 Post St at Stockton St; 415/501-0100** Where else can you sit in a shrink-to-fit tub? Levi's latest gimmick in its new 24,000-square-foot store is a two-person tub, where shoppers can take a quick dip into the water while wearing a new pair of pants; the pants are quickly dried so the wearers can make sure the pants really fit. Baby boomers can get jeans adorned with "Flower Power" and other '60s touches. Besides jeans, there are khaki and cargo pants, shirts, belts, and jackets. FYI, the original Levi Strauss made his fortune selling his tough blue jeans to the '49ers. *Open Mon–Sat 10am–8pm, Sun 11am–6pm; www.levi.com; map:N3*

**L'UOMO / 352 Sutter St at Stockton St; 415/397-3633** Look for Vestimenta, Luciano Barbera, Gravati, and Ferragamo at this Union Square atelier, which imports fine Italian fashions and accessories for men. In-house tailoring is complimentary and finished in two days. *Open Mon–Sat 10am–6pm, Sun noon–5pm; map:N3*

**METIER / 355 Sutter St at Stockton St; 415/989-5395** Locals love this boutique for its California and international labels from designers such as Peter Cohen, Rebecca Taylor, Souchi, and Alberto Biani. The store offers classic career apparel and separates, as well as contemporary evening dresses and coordinating accessories. Don't miss Cathy Waterman's jewelry. *Open Mon–Sat 10am–6pm; map:N3*

**TOUJOURS / 2484 Sacramento St at Fillmore St; 415/346-3988 or 888/621-9397** Owner Beverly Weinkauf keeps this tidy boutique packed with romantic lingerie from high-end names such as Calida and Wolff. She also carries Wolford's deluxe hosiery. For the bride-to-be there are bustiers and merry widows to wear under the gown, plus lacy leg garters for the ceremonial postnuptial toss. Toujours also has a mail-order catalog. *Open Mon–Sat 11am–6pm, Sun noon–5pm; www.toujours lingerie.com; map:K3*

**WILKES BASHFORD / 375 Sutter St btwn Grant Ave and Stockton St; 415/986-4380** Local haberdasher Wilkes Bashford has dressed three generations of San Franciscans—including such prominent politicos as Willie Brown—in fine Italian suits, sportswear, cashmere sweaters, and imported leather shoes. The six-level shop features top designers Brioni, Gautier, and Wilson & Dean, among others. *Open Mon–Sat 10am–6pm, Thurs 10am–8pm; map:N3*

## BAKERIES

**THE BAGELRY / 2139 Polk St btwn Broadway and Vallejo St; 415/441-3003** Located on a rapidly gentrifying stretch of Polk Street, the 25-year-old Bagelry produces what are quite possibly the best bagels in the city. Boiled before they are baked, in the authentic New York style, the bagels come out lightly crusted with a dense, chewy center. Flavors are mostly traditional: sesame, onion, garlic, poppy, plain, and salt, plus cinnamon-raisin, along with onion bialys and seeded bagel sticks. A refrigerator stocks cream cheese, lox, and other accoutrements to round out your nosh. *Open Mon–Tues, Thurs–Sat 6:30am–5pm; Wed 6:30am–noon; Sun 7am–4pm; map:L2*

**BOUDIN SOURDOUGH BAKERY & CAFÉ / Fisherman's Wharf, 156 Jefferson St btwn Mason and Taylor Sts (and branches); 415/928-1849** This place put sourdough bread on the San Francisco food lover's map. In 1849 French refugee Isidore Boudin combined sourdough starter with the French bread-making technique and opened the French Bread Bakery where, as legend has it, locals and panhandlers lined up each morning for a loaf of her famous sourdough bread. Today you can still see the bakers at work through a rear window in the bakery's Fisherman's Wharf location. Each bakery has an adjoining cafe dishing up fresh soups, salads, and specialty sandwiches. Tops on this list are the turkey havarti, "turkey berry," and the house-made clam chowder served in a mini–gold miner's loaf. There are more than 40 Boudins throughout the city, including at 120 O'Farrell Street (at Stockton St; 415/296-7372) and 67 Fifth Street (at Jessie St; 415/543-8304). *Open every day 7:30am–9pm; www. boudinbakery.com; map:M1*

**CITIZEN CAKE / 399 Grove St at Gough St; 415/861-2228** Former pastry chef Elizabeth Falconer whips up innovative sweets and baked goods with unusual shapes at this artisan bakery in Hayes Valley, an ultrahip shopping district near the Civic Center and Davies Symphony Hall. Signature desserts include the After Midnight devil's food cake, made with a moist buttermilk base and Scharffen Berger chocolate mousse and ganache filling, and the Rosebud brûlée tart. Also don't miss the Retro Tropical Shag, made with creamy passion-fruit mousse layered between a buttery génoise and slathered with a rum buttercream frosting. Falkner also makes melt-in-your-mouth Mexican wedding cookies and chewy date-pecan tartlets. Afternoon tea is served daily with assorted savories and a choice of tea or champagne. See also the review in the Restaurants chapter. *Open Tues–Fri 7am–7pm, Sat–Sun 9am–2pm; map:L4*

**EPPLER'S / Laurel Village Shopping Center, 3465 California St at Laurel St (and branches); 415/752-0825** Every neighborhood should have an Eppler's, and in San Francisco, almost every one does. From first thing in the morning to closing, customers keep the staff busy ordering the European-style pastries, coffee cakes, breads, and delicate cookies made with rich creamery butter. Scones come laden with apricots, raspberries, raisins, or blueberries. The cakes are artfully crafted and include lemon, cheesecake, cappuccino, chocolate raspberry, and pudding; the Sacher tortes are created from an old Austrian recipe. The immaculate setting is a perfect place to indulge in a cup of fresh-brewed coffee and a napoleon or custard eclair. *Open Mon–Fri 6am–7pm, Sat 6am–5pm, Sun 7am–3pm; map:J3*

**I LOVE CHOCOLATE / 397 Arguello Blvd at Clement St; 415/750-9460** Locals have been queuing up for pastries at this neighborhood bakery since it opened seven years ago. Owner Mary Brinkmann studied cooking in Paris and makes everything from scratch. Sure, there are the usual cookies and muffins, but the real lure is the blow-your-diet I Love Chocolate Cake with its famous white and semisweet chocolate mousse filling and chocolate truffle frosting. A close second is the Cookies 'n' Cream Cake, oozing with vanilla buttercream and a crushed Oreo cookie center. Mary's croissant recipe comes from the cooking school where she studied in Paris. *Open every day 6:30am–5pm; map:I3*

**JUST DESSERTS / 3735 Buchanan St btwn North Point and Beach Sts (and branches); 415/922-8675** Everything really is just right at Just Desserts. Founded in 1974 by Elliott Hoffman to market his rich homemade cheesecake, the popular cafe has expanded to offer chocolate mousse cake, carrot cake, fudge cake, triple lemon cake, and the beloved chocolate Weekend Cake with chocolate buttercream frosting. All items are made from scratch daily. Muffins and coffee cake are available for early-bird patrons. Other branches are at 248 Church Street near Market Street (415/626-5774) and 3 Embarcadero Center at Sacramento and Drumm Sts (415/421-1609). *Open Mon–Thurs 7am–8pm, Fri 7am–10pm, Sat 8am–10pm, Sun 8am–8pm; www.justdesserts.com; map:K1*

**LA NOUVELLE PATISSERIE / 2184 Union St at Fillmore St; 415/931-7655, San Francisco Centre, 865 Market St at 5th St; 415/979-0553** Forget counting calories when you shop at this tidy bakery, owned by a Frenchman who crafts rich French-style pastries he calls edible Van Goghs. Specialties include fresh fruit tarts (apple, pear, raspberry, and plum) and a variety of cakes: chocolate charlotte cake, opera cake, napoleons, and a three-mousse cake with white, dark, and milk chocolate smushed between chocolate sponge layers. The President's Cake alternates layers of rich hazelnut buttercream and chocolate hazelnut cake. *2184 Union St: Open Mon–Thurs 7am–10pm, Fri–Sat 7am–11pm, Sun 7am–8pm; map:K2, map:M3.*

**LIGURIA BAKERY / 1700 Stockton St at Washington St; 415/421-3786** You'll be hard-pressed to find a better focaccia than what comes out of this North Beach institution. Known as Ligurian pizza bread, the focaccia is slowly baked night to morning in an old-fashioned Italian brick oven dating back to 1911. The focaccia comes plain, topped with raisins, or sprinkled with olive oil and salt. Come early and buy a large slab; the bread always sells out soon after it comes out of the oven. *Open Mon–Fri 8am–4pm, Sat 7am–4pm, Sun 7am–noon; map:N1*

**STELLA PASTRY & CAFFE / 446 Columbus Ave btwn Green and Vallejo Sts; 415/986-2914** This North Beach landmark is known for its *sacripantina* (sponge cake with maraschino liqueur and zabaglione), cannoli, tiramisu, and Italian rum cake. But Stella's also makes delicious butter cookies and biscotti, ideal for dunking in a good strong espresso from one of the neighboring cafes. *Open Mon–Tues, Sun 7:30am–6pm; Wed–Thurs 7:30am–10pm; Fri–Sat 7:30am–midnight; map:N2*

**VICTORIA PASTRY CO. / 1362 Stockton St at Vallejo St; 415/781-2015** Yes, the St. Honoré Cake is the most popular, but others vying for top honors include the *fedora* (a sponge cake with chocolate custard and whipped-cream filling), chocolate truffle, mocha butter, lemon custard, and gâteau Antoinette (devil's food with whipped-cream filling and fudge topping). Don't miss the cookies; there are dozens to choose from. Pick up extras to freeze and serve when your great-aunt comes to tea. *Open Mon–Sat 7am–6pm, Sun 8am–5pm; www.victoriapastry.com; map:N2*

## BODY CARE

**BARE ESCENTUALS / 3 Embarcadero Center, Davis St btwn Sacramento and Clay Sts (and branches); 415/391-2830** Started 25 years ago in a San Francisco suburb, this family-run purveyor of custom-blended scents has grown to 20 outlets nationwide. While the all-natural body products are still a big draw, the makeup line is fast gaining favor and has even made the fashion magazines. Employees give complimentary makeovers, then show patrons how to mix and match on their own. A mail-order department will keep you well stocked if there isn't a store in your town. Other San Francisco branches include Pier 39 (415/781-0631) and 2101 Chestnut Street at Steiner St (415/441-8348). *Open Mon–Fri 10am–7pm, Sat 10am–6pm, Sun noon–5pm; www.bareescentuals.com; map:N2*

**ELIZABETH ARDEN RED DOOR SALON & SPA / 126 Post St at Kearny St, 4th fl; 415/989-4888** Most people come here for the legendary day of pampering and beauty treatments—makeovers, facials, massage, and the famous Red Door Manicure—but you can also buy the complete line of skin-care products and cosmetics. *Open Mon, Sun 9am–6pm; Tues–Wed, Sat 9am–7pm; Thurs–Fri 9am–8pm; www.reddoorsalon. com; map:N3*

**JACQUELINE PERFUMERY / 103 Geary St btwn Grant Ave and Stockton St; 415/981-0858** One of the first boutiques devoted exclusively to perfume, this place now has a loyal clientele from around the world. Its incredible selection includes many hard-to-find scents. Crystal atomizers and gift items are also for sale, along with a small array of European skin-care products, including Stendahl. Refills by mail or by phone. *Open Mon–Sat 9:30am–6pm; map:N3*

**SEPHORA / 1 Stockton St at Ellis St; 415/392-1545** It was just a matter of time before hands-on shopping hit the beauty biz, and who better than Europe's largest cosmetic company to take on this turf? Shopping is self-service, and the innovative displays include a fragrance wall and a lipstick rainbow with one shade for each day of the year. Besides carrying well-known French labels from Dior, Guerlain, and Yves St. Laurent, Sephora also stocks lesser-known brands such as Stila and Club Monaco. *Open Mon–Sat 10am–8pm, Sun 11am–7pm; www.sephora.com; map:N3*

**77 MAIDEN LANE SALON & SPA / 77 Maiden Ln btwn Grant Ave and Kearny St, 2nd fl; 415/391-7777** Celebs who have frequented this joint include Sharon Stone, Sean Connery, and Nicolas Cage. Though famous for its hair coloring, the salon also offers manicures and massages, plus a full line of eco-friendly hair and skin care. *Open Mon–Wed, Fri–Sat 9am–6pm; Thurs 9am–8pm; Sun 10am–6pm; www.77maidenlane salon.citysearch.com; map:N3*

## BOOKS AND MAGAZINES

**BARNES & NOBLE / 2550 Taylor St at Bay St; 415/292-6762** One of the now ubiquitous breeds of megabookstores, Barnes & Noble stocks more than 170,000 titles on everything from psychology and tai chi to cooking and gardens. The wood-and-brick interior makes this branch feel cozier than others, and you can peruse your potential purchase over a snack in the literary cafe. *Open every day 9am–9pm; www.barnesandnoble. com; map:M1*

**BOOKS INC. / Laurel Village Shopping Center, 3515 California St at Laurel and Spruce Sts (and branches); 415/221-3666** This place feels like one of those old-fashioned neighborhood bookstores where you can while away an afternoon browsing for a good mystery or novel. There are three branches in the city, but they all have good sections for children and travelers. Don't miss the sale table, always piled high with great deals on last season's best and worst sellers. Other branches include 2251 Chestnut Street (415/931-3633) and 864 Market Street (415/864-6777), the latter of which devotes a large area to gay-and-lesbian literature. *Open Mon–Thurs, Sun 9am–11pm; Fri–Sat 9am–midnight; map:I3*

**BORDERS BOOKS & MUSIC / 400 Post St at Powell St; 415/399-1633** A bibliophile's Eden, stocking more than 200,000 titles, plus a dazzling array of music and videos. The espresso bar and cafe overlooks Union Square and is a pleasant place to have coffee and a snack while you browse. *Open Mon–Thurs 9am–11pm, Fri–Sat 9am–midnight, Sun 9am–9pm; www.borders.com; map:N3*

**CAFE DE LA PRESSE / 352 Grant Ave at Bush St; 415/398-2680** Located across from the Chinatown gate, this Euro-cafe attracts an international crowd with its fabulous array of European magazines and periodicals. Sip an espresso or *bière* while catching up on *Le Monde*, the *International Herald Tribune*, or the *London Times*. You'll feel like you're in Paris. *Open every day 7am–11pm; map:N3*

**CALIFORNIA HISTORICAL SOCIETY / 678 Mission St btwn 3rd and New Montgomery Sts; 415/357-1860** Quite simply, this is one of the best places to find authoritative books on local and western history. Housed inside the new California Historical Society near the Yerba Buena Center for the Arts, this well-organized bookstore features topics that run from wild women of the West to the Gold Rush and the Barbary Coast. Paintings, cards, and photographs are also for sale, and lectures are occasionally held. *Open Tues–Sat 11am–5pm; map:N3*

**CITY LIGHTS BOOKSTORE / 261 Columbus Ave at Broadway; 415/362-8193** If Allen Ginsberg were alive, he'd still be hanging out at this decidedly unconventional North Beach bookstore opened in 1953 by Beat bard Lawrence Ferlinghetti. Once a mecca for Beat poets and writers, who scrawled their stuff at nearby cafes, the store now attracts book lovers who peruse works on art, poetry, philosophy, politics, and fiction, including some by counterculturalists Kerouac, Ginsberg, and other icons of that bohemian age. *Open every day 10am–midnight; www.city lights.com; map:N2*

**A CLEAN, WELL-LIGHTED PLACE FOR BOOKS / 601 Van Ness Ave at Golden Gate Ave; 415/441-6670** This is literally a clean, well-lighted place to shop for books, located in Opera Plaza near the Civic Center.

The shop's name is taken from an Ernest Hemingway short story; inside you'll find shelves filled with his works, as well as other classic and general fiction and nonfiction. The staff is knowledgeable and helpful, and author signings are regularly scheduled. *Open Mon–Sat 10am–11pm, Sun 10am–9pm; www.bookstore.com; map:L4*

**GREEN APPLE BOOKS AND MUSIC / 506 Clement St at 6th Ave; 415/387-2272** You'll find the largest used books selection in the city at this neighborhood gem, which has more than 100,000 used titles as well as 60,000 new books. The entire stock of used fiction, along with music CDs, is housed in an annex a few doors down. One employee is an authority on graphic novels and comics, another specialty of the store. You can bypass a visit by buying online, but half the fun of Green Apple is sharing good reads with fellow bookworms and the knowledgeable staff. *Open Mon–Thurs, Sun 10am–10:30pm; Fri–Sat 10am–11:30pm; www.greenapplebooks.com; map:H3*

**HAROLD'S NEWSSTAND / 454 Geary St btwn Mason and Taylor Sts; 415/441-2665** Harold's old-fashioned newsstand offers an incredible array of national and international newspapers and magazines. *Open Mon–Thurs, Sun 8am–8pm; Fri–Sat 8am–11pm; map:M3*

**MODERN TIMES / 888 Valencia St at 20th St; 415/282-9246** Alternative and not-so-alternative thinkers flock to this Mission District bookstore, voted the Best Independent Bookstore by locals for its comprehensive selection of literary reviews and magazines. Books in Spanish are well represented, along with general fiction, women's studies, and books on anarchism and other social issues. Author readings and cultural events are held weekly. *Open Mon–Sat 10am–9pm, Sun 11am–6pm; www. mtbs.com; map:L6*

**RAND MCNALLY MAP & TRAVEL STORE / 595 Market St at 2nd St; 415/777-3131** A must-stop for the inquisitive traveler in search of a tremendous selection of travel guides, maps, globes, atlases, language tapes, and videos. *Open Mon–Fri 9am–7pm, Sat 10am–6pm, Sun 11am–5pm; www.randmcnallystore.com; map:N3*

**RICHARD HILKERT BOOKSELLER / 333 Hayes St at Franklin St; 415/863-3339** This delightful jewel is reminiscent of those old-fashioned bookstores you find on a side street of London. Classical music plays in the background, and floor-to-ceiling shelves are jam-packed with tomes on gardening, interior design, art, and music. Hilkert, the son of an Ohio haberdasher and music teacher, is a bespectacled charmer who welcomes each customer personally, believing that the shop is an extension of his home. *Open Mon–Fri 9am–5pm, Sat 11am–5pm; map:L4*

**RIZZOLI / 117 Post St btwn Kearny St and Grant Ave; 415/984-0225** A stunning Union Square setting for perusing fine books from the popular

New York–based publisher. The first floor is devoted to literature, the second floor has the famous architecture and coffee-table books, and the third level stocks a variety of greeting cards, music, and CDs. An extensive selection of *libris Italia* pays tribute to the Italian owner and founder. *Open Mon–Sat 10am–7pm, Sun 10:30am–6pm; map:N3*

**STACEY'S / 581 Market St at 2nd St; 415/421-4687** The city's oldest and largest independent bookstore is a mecca for professionals seeking reference books on computers, medicine, management, finance, and other technical subjects. A broad range of general books and fiction also draws in customers. *Open Mon–Fri 8:30am–7pm, Sat 10:30am–7pm, Sun 10:30am–6pm; www.staceys.com; map:N3*

**THOMAS BROS. MAPS & BOOKS / 550 Jackson St at Columbus Ave; 415/981-7520 or 800/969-3072** The retail outlet for the famed mapmaker stocks possibly the best selection of maps in the city. Look for atlases, travel guides, and local and international hiking and street maps, which will take you from San Francisco to Sydney. *Open Mon–Fri 9am–6pm; www.thomas.com; map:N2*

**WILLIAM K. STOUT ARCHITECTURAL BOOKS / 804 Montgomery St btwn Jackson and Pacific Sts; 415/391-6757** Explore the granddaddy of architectural bookstores, housing more than 20,000 titles in a 1,500-square-foot space. Stout, an architect, started collecting early in his career, but when his collection numbered in the thousands he opened the shop. Today there are more than 20,000 titles covering architecture, interior design, and modern art, plus rare and out-of-print books. A must-see for lovers of design and architecture tomes. *Open Mon–Fri 10am–6:30pm, Sat 10am–5:30pm; www.stoutbooks.com; map:N2*

## CANDY AND CHOCOLATES

**CHOCOLATE COVERED / 3977 24th St at Noe St; 415/641-8123** "Anything good is better covered with chocolate" is the slogan at this tiny shop, which packs an incredible assortment of sweets into 200 square feet. Owner Jack Epstein looks for emerging and undiscovered candy makers with superior products. A favorite is Richard Donnelly, who crafts French chocolate bars, then adds coconut, hazelnut toffee, or macadamia nuts double-dipped with white chocolate. DeGroot is another small confectioner who makes gorgeous Belgian chocolate truffles with tequila, Rémy Martin, or Jack Daniel's fillings. Epstein custom-packages the chocolates in appealing hand-covered tins, which he designs and fabricates himself. *Hours are "as early as we can make it, as late as we can take it," but generally from 11am to 7pm every day; map:K7*

**CHOCOLATE HEAVEN / Pier 39 at Beach St; 415/421-1789** The name says it all. Buy in bulk or pick up souvenir gift boxes with San Francisco icons such as cable cars on the wrappers. The store also carries hard-to-find Guylian and novelty shapes like Band-Aids, motorcycles, and miniature bottles of Kahlua. *Open every day 9:30am–10pm; www.chocolate heaven.com; map:M1*

**CONFETTI LE CHOCOLATIER / 525 Market St at 1st St (and branches); 415/543-2885** A family-owned gem of a place to indulge in old-fashioned caramels and gooey nut clusters, plus chocolates from Neuhaus, Joseph Schmidt, Ghirardelli, and Gaston as well as an array of fine flavored coffee. Other branches are at 4 Embarcadero Center (at Drumm and Sacramento Sts; 415/362-1706); at the Cannery, 2801 Leavenworth Street (at Jefferson St; 415/474-7377); and in Macy's, 120 O'Farrell Street (at Stockton St; 415/296-4228). *Market St: Open Mon–Thurs 7am–6pm, Fri–Sun 10am–6pm; other branches: Open Mon–Sat 10am–6pm; map:N3*

**GHIRARDELLI CHOCOLATE SHOP / Ghirardelli Square, 900 North Point St at Larkin St; 415/474-3938** This San Francisco institution has supplied locals and visitors with sweets since it was founded by Domingo Ghirardelli in 1861. The headquarters is at Fisherman's Wharf, where visitors are treated to an old-fashioned soda fountain selling the famous Ghirardelli hot-fudge sundae. Don't miss the small chocolate factory, which still uses the original equipment. A retail shop carries the full line of chocoholic products. *Open Mon–Thurs 9am–11:30pm, Fri–Sat 9am–midnight; www.ghirardelli.com; map:L1*

**GODIVA / San Francisco Shopping Centre, 865 Market St at 5th St; 415/543-8910** Can you imagine? A shop devoted just to Godiva! Fillings include Key lime, nuts, buttery caramel, and nougat. Gift baskets can be custom made to fit individual budgets and tastes. *Open Mon–Sat 9am–8pm, Sun 11am–6pm; www.godiva.com; map:M4*

**JOSEPH SCHMIDT CONFECTIONS / 3489 16th St btwn Sanchez and Church Sts; 415/861-8682** Former pastry chefs Joseph Schmidt and Audrey Ryan hand-sculpt Belgian chocolate into Transamerica buildings, windmills, tulips, and cable cars (including a five-foot car made for Queen Elizabeth on her last visit). During the holidays you'll find adorable nutcrackers, toy soldiers, Santa's, and sleds, and at Easter there are chocolate bunnies and eggs. Year-round, shelves are always well stocked with at least 20 varieties of truffles, including Grand Marnier and Earl Grey tea. The chocolate teddy bears are enormously popular as gifts. *Open Mon–Sat 10am–6:30pm; www.jsc.com; map:K6*

**TEUSHER CHOCOLATES / 75 O'Farrell St at Stockton St; 415/781-2601** Imported from Switzerland, Teusher specializes in obscenely decadent champagne truffles and *gandugja*, a variety of ground hazelnut with chocolate. *Open Mon–Sat 10am–6pm; www.teusherusa.com; map:N3*

## CHILDREN'S CLOTHING

**DOTTIE DOLITTLE / 3680 Sacramento St at Locust St; 415/563-3244**
For more than two decades Dottie Dolittle has dressed little girls and
boys for birthdays, baptisms, weddings, and holidays. Sizes range from
infant to preteen, with apparel made of satin, linen, cotton, and tulle.
Play attire, swimwear, nighties, and blankets are also for sale, plus
charming shoes, purses, and jewelry. *Open Mon–Sat 9:30am–6pm, Sun
noon–5pm; map:I3*

**KINDER SPORT / 3566 Sacramento St btwn Locust and Laurel Sts;
415/563-7778** Bring your aspiring Chris Evert to this children's sportswear shop for the ultimate in chic tennis wear and gear, including tennis
skirts, shorts, rackets, and shoes for newborns to preteens. Come winter,
skiwear takes over the rounders, with complete lines and separates from
names such as Spider, Marker, Balance, and Snowbird. Kinder Sport is
also a must-visit for its pint-size sleeping bags, rain gear, snorkeling
equipment, and hats. *Open Mon–Sat 10am–5pm, Sun noon–5pm
(closed on Sun in summer); www.kindersport.com; map:I3*

**MUDPIE / 1694 Union St at Gough St; 415/771-9262** Grandmothers
love shopping at this Union Street boutique, packed with dainty white
lace gowns and matching straw bonnets. In addition, there are rompers,
jumpsuits, and overalls in solids and prints, as well as colorful galoshes,
toys, and games. A Mudpie furniture store at 1750 Union Street
(415/673-8060) carries bunk beds, rockers, high chairs, and chests.
*Open Mon–Sat 11am–5pm, Sun 11am–6pm; map:L2*

**SMALL FRYS / 4066 24th St btwn Castro and Noe Sts; 415/648-3954**
Owned by a former Levi Strauss marketing manager, this place is chock-
full of fun T-shirts, shorts, and dresses, as well as OshKosh overalls and,
of course, loads of Levi jeans and jackets to fit babies and small children.
Besides apparel you'll find whimsical stuffed animals, baby dishes, quilts,
and sandbox toys tucked away in corners and on shelves. *Open
Mon–Thurs 10am–6pm, Fri 10am–7pm; www.sssmallfrys.com; map:K7*

## COFFEE AND TEA

**COFFEE ROASTERY / 950 Battery St at Vallejo St (and branches);
415/956-9772** This local roastery has kept neighborhood mugs topped
off with its full-flavored coffee since it opened in 1979. There are more
than 30 varieties to choose from, including the signature Plantation, a
blend of four types of beans. A full espresso bar offers desserts, fresh pastries, and house-roasted peanuts and granola. Lunch is also served in
some locations, featuring tasty focaccia sandwiches, quiches, soups,
salads, and daily pizzas by the slice. *Open Mon–Fri 5:30am–6pm, Sat
9am–6pm; map:N2*

## COFFEEHOUSE CULTURE

Decades before there was a Starbucks on every American street corner, there was a coffeehouse culture in San Francisco. In the '50s a group of freethinkers descended on the North Beach area and created a social phenomenon centered around open expression, art, red wine, and, of course, coffee. The Beats, led by Allen Ginsberg, Neal Cassady, Lawrence Ferlinghetti, and Jack Kerouac, were drawn to San Francisco in general because it was known to be a cosmopolitan city, far from the social constraints of Middle America. And North Beach in particular was a desired destination because of its European atmosphere and abundance of coffeehouses and taverns with great entertainment.

San Francisco has been home to many alternative thinkers and takes great pride in being the supportive hot spot where these minds can flourish. So take a notebook or a sketch pad down to one of the many cafes on Columbus Avenue—perhaps **Caffe Trieste, Vesuvio Cafe, Caffe Greco,** or **Tosca Cafe**—have a few shots of espresso, and feel your creative spirit emerge in a way it never would in the slick chrome confines of a franchise.

**GRAFFEO COFFEE ROASTING CO. / 735 Columbus Ave at Filbert St; 415/986-2429 or 415/986-2420** You'll know you've arrived when you smell the beans. Graffeo is a North Beach institution purveying some of the best coffee in the city. Beans are roasted daily in four styles: Italian light, dark, light-and-dark blend, and a Swiss water-process decaf. While it mainly sells wholesale to restaurants, the shop accommodates walk-ins (though it doesn't serve coffee) and does a large mail-order business. *Open Mon–Fri 9am–6pm, Sat 9am–5pm; map:M1*

**PEET'S COFFEE & TEA / 1156 Chestnut St at Pierce St (and branches); 415/931-8302** This favorite San Francisco gourmet roastery is known for its very intense European-style coffee developed by Alfred Peet, who grew up in the business in Europe and learned firsthand how to buy and roast beans. Peet introduced his blends to San Francisco in 1966. Today there are more than 30 roasts, including the ever-popular Major Dickason's, developed 27 years ago by a retired Army officer and longtime Peet's fan. Seasonal and organic beans are also for sale. In addition to coffee you'll find premium tea, espresso makers, mugs, and teakettles. Other branches include 2197 Fillmore Street (at California St; 415/563-9930) and 235 Montgomery Street (at Bush St; 415/421-8420). *Open every day 6am–7pm; mailorder@peets.com; www.peets.com; map:J1*

**TEN REN TEA CO. / 949 Grant Ave btwn Jackson and Washington Sts; 415/362-0656** Located in the heart of Chinatown, this shop stocks 50 imported teas, mostly from China and Taiwan. Guests are offered a cup to sip while browsing the shelves, which also feature ginseng, herbs, and tea accoutrements, including pots and infusers. Mail order is available if you get hooked on a favorite. *Open every day 9am–9pm; map:N2*

## DISCOUNT

**ESPRIT OUTLET STORE / 499 Illinois St at 16th St, 1 block E of 3rd St; 415/957-2550** This popular Esprit store is located in a warehouse setting and offers great bargains on seconds and discontinued apparel from the youthfully hip San Francisco–based label. You'll find loads of shoes, belts, and accessories at up to 70 percent off retail. Call for details on future special promotions and sales. Note: There's a retail Esprit store in the Stonestown Galleria (415/759-2626). *Open Mon–Fri 10am–8pm, Sat 10am–7pm, Sun 11am–6pm; map:O6*

**GOODBYES / 3464 Sacramento St btwn Laurel and Walnut Sts; 415/346-6388** Bargain hunters love this consignment shop for its incredible finds on men's and women's styles from Donna Karan, Armani, Polo/Ralph Lauren, and more. You'll find accessories and accents, too, and all are in excellent condition. A second Goodbyes store filled with women's fashions is located across the street at 3483 Sacramento Street. *Open Mon–Wed, Fri–Sat 10am–6pm, Thurs 10am–8pm, Sun 11am–5pm; map:J3*

**JOANIE CHAR / 527 Sutter St btwn Powell and Mason Sts; 415/399-9867** Local designer Joanie Char built her fashion empire in the 1970s, when her clothes were carried at high-end stores nationwide. Now she sells her silk, wool, cotton, and rayon creations exclusively at this store. Prices are close to wholesale, and lower for off-season styles. *Open Mon–Sat 10am–6pm, Sun noon–6pm; map:N3*

**LOEHMANN'S / 222 Sutter St btwn Grant Ave and Kearny St; 415/982-3215** A fabulous find, the granddaddy of discount fashion stores, Loehmann's still offers great prices on designer lines, plus career apparel, shoes, lingerie, hosiery, fragrances, accessories, and swimwear. Labels are removed, so you're buying for quality and style (not brand names). Personal shopping service is available, too. *Open Mon–Fri 9am–8pm, Sat 9:30am–8pm, Sun 11am–6pm; map:N3*

**THE NORTH FACE OUTLET / 1325 Howard St at 9th St; 415/626-6444** This South of Market outlet gets a supply of surplus goods from the North Face factory and sells them at a substantial discount of 20 to 70 percent. Inventory changes quickly, but outerwear and daypacks are almost always in stock. Sometimes you'll also find tents, backpacks, and sleeping bags. Their retail store stocks current goods and equipment (see the Sports and Outdoor Gear section). *Open Mon–Wed 10am–6pm, Thurs–Sat 10am–7pm, Sun 11am–6pm; www.thenorthface.com; map:M4*

## ETHNIC AND SPECIALTY FOODS

**A. G. FERRARI / 468 Castro St btwn 18th and Market Sts; 415/255-6590, 3490 California St at Locust St; 415/923-4470** A third-generation Italian family runs these upscale gourmet stores, well stocked with goodies inspired by old family recipes. The Castro branch is an especially warm setting in which to browse for homemade pesto as well as sauces, porcini mushrooms, and a huge array of pastas, tortas, frittatas, and bite-size arancini (ricotta balls). Spiedini (skewered chicken), *tramezzini* (finger sandwiches), and *formaggi* (cheese and grissini) are other customer favorites. The sliced meats and cheeses are ideal for picnics or casual dinners. *Open Mon–Sat 10am–8pm, Sun 11am–6pm; www.ag ferrarifoods.com; map:K6, H5*

**ANDREW ROTHSTEIN FINE FOODS / 2238 Polk St at Green St; 415/447-4094** Until a few years ago caterer Andrew Rothstein made his name supplying gourmet shops with his innovative salads. These days his namesake store features at least 18 of his signature creations, all tastefully displayed in clean, modern cases. Favorite salads are the wonton salad, Russian potato, brussels sprouts with almonds, Roman chicken, and roasted-vegetable ravioli. Ask for a free sample. Want something hot? There's salmon *en croute*, stuffed rolled turkey breast, or fruited pork loin in Madeira. Mashed celeriac potatoes, pumpkin soup, and balsamic glazed beets are some of the mouthwatering sides. For dessert, try the lemon tart or tiramisu. *Open Mon–Fri 11am–9pm, Sat 11am–8pm; map:L2*

**BOMBAY BAZAAR / 548 Valencia St btwn 16th and 17th Sts; 415/621-1717** Stock up on everything you need to cook an Indian dinner. Besides dals and freshly ground spices, Bombay Bazaar has chutneys, fresh ginger, and an amazing array of kari leaves, basmati rice, and teas. Everything is neatly arranged on shelves or in bins. This is also a good destination for traditional *thali* plates and Indian cookware. *Open Tues–Sun 10:30am–7:30pm; map:L6*

**LA PALMA MEXICATESSEN / 2884 24th St at Florida St; 415/647-1500** Hand-patted corn tortillas are the big draw at this 20-year-old Mission District shop—or you can pick up some fresh-ground masa to make your own. You'll also find an arsenal of chiles, chili powder, home-fried chips, tamale leaves, and authentic Mexican vanilla for baking cookies and flan. Hot tacos and burritos are made daily and ready to eat. *Open Mon–Sat 8am–6pm, Sun 8am–5pm; map:M7*

**LITTLE CITY MEAT MARKET / 1400 Stockton St at Vallejo St; 415/986-2601** Savvy cooks make the trek to this North Beach butcher for the superb locally raised veal. Buy it cut as scaloppine or thick chops, or as shanks to make osso buco. Rolled breast of veal comes ready to stuff.

Flavorful Kansas-raised beef and pork ribs for grilling are another reason to visit. *Open Mon–Fri 8am–6pm, Sat 8am–5:30pm; map:M2*

**LUCCA DELICATESSEN / 2120 Chestnut St btwn Pierce and Steiner Sts; 415/921-7873** The Bosco family has been carrying on the family business since their Lucchesi grandfather opened this Marina District deli in 1929. Be prepared for a wait: The queue starts early as locals pop in for a succulent Lucca chicken, handmade ravioli, or freshly made sandwich. Shop shelves are jam-packed with Italian olive oil, condiments, and other imported goodies, along with Berkeley's incomparable Acme bread. *Open Mon–Sat 9am–6:30pm, Sun 9am–6pm; map:K2*

**MOLINARI DELICATESSEN / 373 Columbus Ave at Vallejo St; 415/421-2337** Opened in 1896, this North Beach fixture is one of the few remaining old-fashioned Italian delis in town. It carries the requisite Italian meats and sausages, as well as homemade ravioli, tortellini, semolina, arborio rice, and Italian cheeses, including fresh mozzarella. Complete the meal with a bottle of Italian wine, a loaf of bread, and a fine Tuscan olive oil. *Open Mon–Fri 8am–6pm, Sat 7:30am–5:30pm; map:N2*

**SAY CHEESE / 856 Cole St at Carl St; 415/665-5020** Though known for its French regional chèvres, this Cole Valley treasure carries more than 200 other cheeses, including the hard-to-find Brillat-Savarin (a triple-cream cheese named for an 18th-century food writer) and a rare Italian sheep's-milk cheese with porcini mushrooms and black truffles. Caviar and tortes are a must-buy for the gourmet, as are the 12 kinds of pâtés, including venison and pheasant. *Open Mon–Sat 10am–7pm, Sun 10am–5pm; map:I5*

**TSAR NICOULAI CAVIAR / 144 King St btwn 2nd and 3rd Sts; 800/952-2842** The Tsar offers a no-frills setting in a no-frills neighborhood where you can stock up on mega-sizes of imported Russian caviar. There's beluga, osetra, American sturgeon, and salmon; the Tsar line of beluga is popular for its rich, robust flavor. This is also one of the few places you'll find California-farmed osetra, which tastes just like the imported version but is organically raised. To avoid waiting, call ahead so that your order is ready when you arrive. *Open Mon–Fri 8am–5pm; www.tsar nicoulai.com; map:O4*

**24TH STREET CHEESE CO. / 3893 24th St at Sanchez St; 415/821-6658** It's hard to believe, but there are close to 400 cheeses in this tiny Noe Valley shop. You'll find at least 20 goat cheeses, plus fresh Camembert from Normandy, cheddars, imported Goudas, and cheese for grating. It's one-stop shopping if you also need bread and wine. *Open Mon–Fri 10am–7pm, Sat 10am–6pm, Sun 10am–5pm; map:K7*

**VIVANDE PORTA VIA / 2125 Fillmore St at California St; 415/346-4430**
Squeezed in between an apartment complex and a cafe on a bustling, upscale stretch of Fillmore Street, this neighborhood institution is owned by superchef Carlo Middione, who prepares mouthwatering dishes either for sit-down dining or to go. Try the signature eggplant sandwiches and chicken hand pies or daily pastas and fresh-broasted meats. The terrines, homemade sausages, and tortas are other good bets. *Open every day 10am–7pm; map:K3*

## FLOWERS AND PLANTS

**FIORDELLA / 1920 Polk St at Jackson St; 415/775-4065** San Franciscans pay dearly for Fiordella's innovative creations—and the arrangements are worth it. Custom work is a specialty, and the designers use unusual and hard-to-find flowers. The store also sells accents, furnishings, and trinkets in case you need to pick up a gift. *Open Mon, Wed, Fri 9am–6pm; Tues, Thurs, Sat 10am–6pm; map:L2*

**FIORI / 2314 Chestnut St btwn Scott and Divisadero Sts; 415/346-1100** Specializing in lush English garden–style arrangements, this neighborhood shop uses only high-quality flowers—no mums, gladiolas, carnations, or baby's breath. Choose from hydrangeas, dahlias, lilacs, or whatever is in season. Worldwide shipping is available. *Open Mon–Sat 8am–7pm, Sun 9:30am–5:30pm; map:J1*

**FRENCH TULIP / 3903 24th St at Sanchez St; 415/647-8661** This Noe Valley flower stand could have been plucked from a side street of Paris. The specialty is European-style bouquets, loosely wrapped as if just picked from the garden. Arrange in a white porcelain pitcher or jug and you have a fetching centerpiece for the table. The Market Street location has staff designers who can craft more sophisticated arrangements. *Open Mon–Sat 8am–8pm, Sun 9am–7pm; www.frenchtulip.com; map:K7*

**LIVING GREEN / 3 Henry Adams St at Kansas St; 415/864-2251** This jewel of a garden and interior landscape shop is filled with a jungle of exotic palms, bushy ferns, and towering ficus artfully displayed around antiques from Indonesia, Greece, China, and the Philippines. Smaller plants are tucked in corners and around tables. The staff is a joy to deal with and happily shares tips on caring for your purchase. *Open Mon–Fri 9am–5pm, Sat 11am–5pm; map:N5*

**PODESTA BALDOCCHI / 508 4th St at Bryant St; 415/346-1300** One of the city's best-known florists creates simple and artistic arrangements, from fairy-tale centerpieces for weddings to themed creations for Christmas, Easter, or Halloween. *Open Mon–Fri 8am–5pm, Sat 8am–4pm; map:N4*

**SMEDLEY HERRERA / 511 Laguna St at Fell St; 415/864-2506** Smedley
Herrera is known for its wild and bountiful Parisian-style bouquets. The
flower selection includes lavender, roses, and gladiolas, among others.
Locals pop in for colorful arrangements to brighten up the workplace or
home. *Open Wed–Sat 11am–6pm, Sun noon–4pm; map:L4*

## FURNITURE

**HARVEST INTERIORS / 3349 Sacramento St at Presidio Ave; 415/922-
3622** Baby boomers love the American Country furnishings at this Pacific
Heights shop. The cozy showroom is chock-full of end tables, dining
tables, armoires, and hutches, available in more than 30 wood finishes.
Spiff up existing dressers and bureaus with the old-fashioned door pulls
and hardware. With the reasonable prices, you get a lot of style for your
dollar. *Open every day 10am–6pm; map:I3*

**LIMN / 290 Townsend St at 4th St; 415/543-5466** Sleek, modern furniture from more than 900 vendors, including Cappellini, Cassina, B&B
Italia, and Herman Miller, can be found at this cavernous gallery. High-
end Bulthaup kitchens from Germany come complete with cabinetry,
islands, and all the appliances. Agape does the same for the bath. Accents
are fashioned from a cutting-edge mold, and there's a complete lighting
gallery with obscure lamp shades shaped as umbrellas and asymmetrical
globes. The Limn Art Gallery showcases modern works from a variety
of artists. *Open Mon–Fri 9:30am–5:30pm, Sat–Sun 11am–5:30pm;
www.limn.com; map:O3*

**THE MAGAZINE / 528 Folsom St btwn 1st and 2nd Sts; 415/777-4707**
A glass-walled loft is home to this atelier showcasing modernist reproductions from Le Corbusier, Mies van de Rohe, and other designers.
Most furnishings are chrome, glass, or upholstered leather in vibrant
reds, blues, and yellows. A reproduction Eames chair made of molded
plywood is one of the big sellers. *Open Mon–Sat 10am–6pm, Sun
noon–4pm; www.themagazine.org; map:O3*

**MIKE FURNITURE / 2142 Fillmore St at Sacramento St; 415/567-2700**
Michael Moore takes designs by legends such as Billy Baldwin, Michael
Taylor, and Jean-Michael Frank and gives them a contemporary twist.
His Chanel sofa is the living-room couch on the TV series *Frasier*. There
are dozens of living- and dining-room sets, plus armchairs and ottomans
available in a slew of fabrics and patterns. Pieces are custom made in the
factory, including lamps, pillows, and decorative items. *Open Mon–Sat
10am–6pm, Sun noon–5pm; www.surfmike.com; map:K3*

**ZONAL / 568 Hayes St btwn Octavia and Laguna Sts (and branches);
415/255-9307** Walking into Zonal is like taking a trip back in time to
your great-grandmother's farm. The floors hold a panoply of painted pie
safes, jelly cupboards, and old porch gliders with the original weathered

patina. Owner Russell Prithard scours the Midwest to keep the store well stocked, and he's recently added armchairs upholstered in leather as well as faded florals to fit an old-fashioned parlor. Antique linens from France are in a back nook, along with Bella Notte's beautiful velvet shams and duvets to dress up that vintage four-poster bed. *Open every day 11am–6pm; www.zonalhome.com; map:L4*

## GIFT AND SPECIALTY SHOPS

**ARCH / 99 Missouri St at 17th St; 415/433-2724** Arch is stocked to the rafters with high-quality supplies for the architecture trade, as well as portfolios, photo albums, and loads of first-rate vellums in funky patterns and colors. You'll also find spiral paper clips, unusual pens, classy clocks, designer paperweights, clever cards, toys, and other intriguing small treasures ideal for gift-giving or that occasional splurge. *Open Mon–Fri 9am–6pm, Sat noon–5pm; map:N6*

**BELL'OCCHIO / 8 Brady St btwn Franklin and Gough Sts; 415/864-4048** Tucked down an alleylike street just off Franklin and Market Streets, Bell'occhio ("beautiful eye" in Italian) is a charming place to browse for imported linens, ribbons, and trimmings, including 18th-century "point de beauvais" needlepoint and heavy silk bands for decorating purses, garters, and hats. The store's black-and-white ribbon graced Kate Winslet's gloves in *Titanic*. Don't miss the private-label lotions and makeup, pretty French pottery, jewelry, handmade boxes, and prints. *Open Tues–Sat 11am–5pm; www.bellocchio.com; map:L4*

**BRITEX / 146 Geary Blvd btwn Stockton St and Grant Ave; 415/392-2910** Family-owned and -operated since 1952, Britex is a New York–style fabric store with four floors of well-organized textiles and trimmings for both home and fashion. Expect to find every fabric imaginable, from English men's suiting to imported woolens, chiffons, and couture designs. On the second floor the home-decorating department has an array of upholstery and sheers for slipcovers and curtains. The third floor is popular with bargain hunters for its discounted remnants. The fourth floor houses an amazing assortment of tassels, trims, ribbons, collars, and more than 30,000 new and antique buttons. The knowledgeable staff collectively speaks more than 19 languages, including Chinese and Persian. *Open Mon–Wed, Sat 9:30am–6pm; Thurs–Fri 9:30am–7pm; www.britexfabrics.com; map:N3*

**CANDELIER / 33 Maiden Ln btwn Grant Ave and Kearny St; 415/989-8600** Candelier is a pleasant place to purchase all manner of candles, including long-burning paraffin and hand-dipped beeswax. There's an assortment of holders, plus gift frames, pillows, vases, and porcelain. The coffee-table books are other good bets. *Open Mon–Sat 10am–6pm; map:N3*

**DANDELION / 55 Potrero Ave at Alameda St; 415/436-9500** Dandelion is an all-time favorite stop for its lovely interior setting and selection of accents and gifts. Furnishings range from Japanese tansus edged in leather to pottery and ceramics. You'll also find an appealing array of barware, books, and toys. The Zen-like second floor has slate tabletop fountains, bamboo place mats, and screens. *Open Tues–Sat 10am–6pm; map:M5*

**FLAX ART & DESIGN / 1699 Market St at Valencia St; 415/552-2355** More than 20,000 square feet of handmade papers, custom stationery, artist's tools, and blank journals keep people rolling into this 60-year-old store. There are literally thousands of graphic supplies for kids of all ages. The Flax Gallery showcases work by local artists, and a gift department includes Venetian masks, vases, Zen fountains, handsome picture frames, desk accents, and an array of greeting cards. Flax also has a mail-order catalog. *Open Mon–Wed, Fri–Sat 9:30am–6pm; Thurs 9:30am–7pm; www.flaxart.com; map:L5*

**GUMP'S / 135 Post St btwn Grant and Kearny Sts; 415/982-1616** No trip to San Francisco would be complete without a visit to this premier destination for antiques and objets d'art. Founded in 1861 by Solomon Gump as a mirror and framing shop, Gump's is now housed in a light, airy building down the street from its original site. Jade, Baccarat, Steuben crystal, and antiques are still specialties of the house; you'll also find contemporary crafts, bedding and towels, and garden ornaments and accessories. Another big draw is the artistic glass from Italian-born Lino Tagliapietra, known for his playful spiral shapes. Traditional glassware and china comes in some 400 patterns. *Open Mon–Sat 10am–6pm; www.gumps.com; map:N3*

**JAPONESQUE / 824 Montgomery St btwn Jackson and Pacific Sts; 415/391-8860** This handsome gallery of Asian arts, crafts, and antiques stocks a good supply of rice-paper books, stone sculptures, porcelain bowls, and other treats from the East. Well-heeled New Yorkers often stop by in between business meetings when they feel the urge to splurge on a new treasure for the home or office. *Open Tues–Fri 10:30am–5:30pm, Sat 11am–5pm; map:N2*

**MUSEUMSTORE / San Francisco Museum of Modern Art, 151 3rd St at Mission St; 415/357-4035** Locals as well as tourists flock here for the incredible selection of contemporary gifts. Perennial favorites are Finnish architect Alvar Aalto's fine glass angular vases and the specially designed MOMA dinnerware. Then, of course, there's the huge selection of art and architecture books, including a sale nook with markdowns of up to 70 percent. *Open Mon–Wed, Fri–Sun 10am–6:30pm; Thurs 10am–9:30pm; www.sfmoma.org; map:N3*

**ZINC DETAILS / 1905 Fillmore St btwn Pine and Bush Sts; 415/776-2100** This charming little shop is filled with contemporary interpretations of minimalist '50s designs, including beech consoles that double as dining tables, birch chests, rice-paper lamps, colorful dishware, and glasses mouth-blown by local artists. The famous Zinc bud vase is still available in a full palette of colors. *Open Mon–Sat 11am–7pm, Sun noon–6pm; www.zincdetails.com; map:K3*

## HEALTH-FOOD STORES

**RAINBOW GROCERY / 1745 Folsom St btwn 13th and 14th Sts; 415/863-0620** This health-food supermarket has a dazzling array of natural baked goods, organic produce, herbs, spices, and aromatherapy bath and body care products. No meats are sold here, but you'll find a good selection of hormone-free milk, butter, and cheese, including fresh goat's- and sheep's-milk ricotta and imports from Africa and France. A good source for hard-to-find items such as chestnut flour, organic linguine, seaweed, and masa harina. *Open Mon–Sat 9am–9pm; map:M6*

**THE REAL FOOD COMPANY / 2140 Polk St btwn Broadway and Vallejo St; 415/673-7420, 3060 Fillmore St at Filbert St; 415/567-6900** These neighborhood health-food stores stock bulk grains and flours, pesticide-free fruits and veggies, dairy products, and fresh bread from top bakers. The small butcher counter in back has hormone-free poultry and meats. Vitamins, supplements, and skin-care products are well represented upstairs in the Polk Street store's "vita-loft." *Open every day 8am–9pm; map:L2, K2*

## HOME ACCESSORIES

**BROWN DIRT COWBOY / 2406 Polk St at Union St; 415/922-9065** Named for an Elton John song, this shop with a picturesque entry resides in a restored Victorian on Russian Hill. Brown Dirt Cowboy started out selling refurbished wood armoires, chests, and decorative items, but has expanded to include reupholstered chairs from the '20s and '30s and a line of custom children's furniture painted with whimsical storybook characters. Colorful pots, ceramic tiles, unique kitchen gadgets, and towels are other treasures to check out. *Open Mon–Sat noon–7pm, Sun noon–6pm; www.browndirtcowboy.com; map:L2*

**CITY DISCOUNT / 2436 Polk St btwn Filbert and Union Sts; 415/771-4649** This tidy neighborhood shop has kept cooks well supplied with discounted pots, pans, and culinary gadgets for more than a decade. In addition to loads of mashers and basters, there are pie tins, pans, steamers, and griddles galore. One section is devoted entirely to barware and stacks of the white plates and platters used in French restaurants and bistros. Another features gourmet goodies from around the world. *Open Mon–Sat 10am–6pm, Sun 11am–7pm; map:L2*

**COOKIN'** / **339 Divisadero St at Oak St; 415/861-1854** Cookin' is a funky little gem crammed to the rafters with recycled and obscure gourmet trinkets and tools. Look for Jell-O molds, cast-iron skillets, roasters, and old-fashioned casseroles for making macaroni and cheese. French pastry bags, measuring cups, and rolling pins are also for sale. Most of the secondhand goods are in excellent condition and bring back warm memories of watching Grandma or Grandpa make breakfast or Thanksgiving dinner. *Open Tues–Sat noon–6:30pm, Sun 1pm–5pm; map:K6*

**FILLAMENTO** / **2185 Fillmore St at Sacramento St; 415/931-2224** There are imitators, but few stores of its kind can rival Fillamento for quality and style. Housed in a restored three-level Edwardian, this gallery of chic domesticity stocks everything from contemporary dinnerware and goblets to traditional Limoges platters and old-fashioned tassels. The table linens and textiles are top quality and include Ann Gish's exquisite handmade pillows. A bath department stocks luxe towels and accents, and there's a huge array of furniture for living areas and the home office. *Open Mon–Sat 11am–7pm, Sun noon–6pm; www.fillamento.com; map:K2*

**GORDON BENNETT** / **Ghirardelli Square, 900 North Point St at Larkin St; 415/351-1172** English expatriate Ian Johnson scours his native countryside to keep Gordon Bennett a treasure trove of unusual knickknacks and gifts. Antique pots, terra-cotta urns, birdhouses, and French metal buckets are scattered about. The staff will help you track down that perfect accent or trinket. If you're buying for the gardener, ask about the custom-made grab bags, which come with colorful rubber gloves, Farmer's Friend hand salve, miniature soaps, and a tiny garden trowel. *Open Mon–Sat 10am–9pm, Sun 10am–7pm; www.gordonbennett. com; map:L1*

**HOMECHEF** / **Laurel Village Shopping Center, 3527 California St at Locust St; 415/668-3191** What started as a cooking school in owner Judith Ets Hokin's kitchen has grown to one of the city's most popular kitchenware stores. Shelves are neatly arranged with well-edited essentials, along with entertaining accessories and gourmet foods. Familiar brands include Emile Henry, All-Clad, and Calphalon, plus the Home-Chef house label. Still part cooking school, HomeChef also hosts classes and workshops led by well-known industry professionals. *Open Mon–Sat 9:30am–6:30pm, Sun 11am–5pm; www.homechef.com; map:I3*

**MA MAISON HOME ACCENTS** / **592 3rd St at Brannan St; 415/777-5370** Owners John and Isabelle Karatzas import direct to keep prices down on their objets d'art from South Africa and France. In addition to champagne flutes, pewter cutlery, and Limoges porcelain, the store features Italian cast-metal culinary tools, handmade frames, velvet pillows, and bedding. *Open Mon–Fri 10am–5pm, Sat 10am–5:30pm; www.ma-maison.com; map:O4*

**SCHEUER LINENS / 340 Sutter St btwn Grant Ave and Stockton St; 415/392-2813** Established in the 1930s, family-run Scheuer's is known for superb linens and table coverings imported from all over the world. What sets the store apart, however, is how the sales staff gives customers a hands-on education in the various weaves and thread counts. There are loads of colors and prints to choose from, and the selection of towels and gift items is worth a stop in itself. More than 40 kinds of soap from 40 countries are available, including Palais Royale's wildly popular triple-milled soap imported from Scotland. Embroidery and monogramming services are available. *Open Mon–Sat 9:30am–5:30pm; www.scheuer linens.com; map:N3*

**SUE FISHER KING / 3067 Sacramento St btwn Broderick and Baker Sts; 415/922-7276** This shop is a longtime favorite for elegant gifts, lamps, pillows, and imported sheets from Italy in creamy damasks or Egyptian cotton. The bath/spa boutique has fluffy white towels and plush mats and robes. King takes buying trips to Europe to keep the lineup fashionable and fresh. During the holidays she fills shelves with ornaments from more than 30 countries. *Open Mon–Sat 10am–6pm; map:J3*

**SUR LA TABLE / 77 Maiden Ln at Grant Ave; 415/732-7900** Founded in Seattle more than 25 years ago, Sur La Table features two floors jam-packed with everything a cook could need for a well-equipped kitchen. Fulfill any fantasy: Bakers will find dozens of cookie cutters in fanciful shapes as well as rosette molds to create doves, snowflakes, and roses. One area has place mats and napkins; another features teapots, teacups, and sushi-dipping bowls and trays. There's a slew of barbecue items, including sturdy mitts, aprons, and chips for the fire along with those hard-to-find gadgets such as cornichon slicers and claw-shaped lobster crackers. You'll also find hundreds of cookbooks on everything from vegan cooking to baking with figs. The lower level holds an 800-square-foot cooking school and demonstration kitchen. *Open Mon–Sat 10am–6pm, Sun noon–5pm; www.surlatable.com; map:N3*

## IMPORTED GOODS

**CANTON BAZAAR / 616 Grant Ave btwn California and Sacramento Sts; 415/362-5750** Canton Bazaar showcases a wide assortment of arts and crafts from China and other Asian cultures. Antique treasures are hidden among ubiquitous Chinatown wares. This is a good place to browse for that quirky trinket or beautiful jade amulet or bracelet. *Open every day 10am–10pm; map:N2*

**COTTAGE INDUSTRY / 4068 24th St btwn Castro and Noe Sts; 415/821-2465** This basement shop specializes in gorgeous adult and children's clothing, bags, and purses made from Guatemalan cotton, which is also sold by the yard. Don't miss the rayon batiks from Indonesia and silver earrings from Nepal. Refurbished furniture from India is carried at a sister location at 2326 Fillmore Street (at California St; 415/821-2465). *Open Mon–Sat 11am–7pm, Sun 11am–6pm; map:K7*

**FOLK ART INTERNATIONAL–BORETTI AMBER–XANADU TRIBAL ARTS / 140 Maiden Ln btwn Stockton St and Grant Ave; 415/392-9999** Housed in a historic Frank Lloyd Wright–designed building, this upscale gallery is actually three in one, each carrying museum-quality imported art and antiques. Works range from neolithic pots circa 3,000 B.C. to Panama basketry and hand-loomed wool from Kashmir. Check out the Bwami hats made of fiber, buttons, and elephant hair. *Open Mon–Sat 10am–6pm; www.folkartintl.com; map:N3*

**MA-SHI'-KO FOLK CRAFT / Japan Center, 1581 Webster St at Post St, 2nd fl; 415/346-0748** Though its specialty is pottery from Ma-Shi'-Ko, the oldest pottery village in Japan, this shop also carries delicate handmade sake cups and teacups, Akita Masome cedar chopstick rests, and beautiful chestnut and cypress bowls and trays. *Open Mon–Sat 11am–6pm, Sun 11am–5pm; map:K3*

**SILKROUTE / 3119 Fillmore St at Filbert St; 415/563-4936** Step into Silkroute for its mammoth collection of more than 2,000 old and new floor coverings from around the world, including Oriental carpets, tribal rugs, and kilims from China, Turkey, Persia, Morocco, India, Pakistan, and Afghanistan. The shopkeepers also buy, trade, clean, and repair carpets. *Open Mon–Sat 10:30am–6:30pm, Sun noon–5pm; map:K2*

**TOUCH OF ASIA / 1784 Union St at Octavia St; 415/474-3115** Beautiful black lacquer cabinets and tansu chests are among the decorative items found in this upscale shop, dealing in both antiques and reproductions from China, Japan, Korea, and Thailand. Standouts include a gold satsuma fish bowl and a pair of custom cloisonné lamps. *Open Mon–Sat 11am–6pm, Sun noon–5pm; map:L2*

**XELA IMPORTS / 3925 24th St at Sanchez St; 415/695-1323** The Italian owner of this small outlet imports rayons and cottons from Indonesia and India and turns them into stylish clothes. Handprinted cotton T-shirts are especially popular with locals. Gift items include Sri Lanka moonstone jewelry, amber from Poland, Balinese mirrors, and gauze sarongs. *Open every day 10:30am–7pm; map:K7*

## JEWELRY AND ACCESSORIES

**ALFRED DUNHILL / 250 Post St btwn Grant Ave and Stockton St; 415/781-3368** The San Francisco outpost purveys the same high-quality accessories as its mother store in England (founded in London in 1893), including watches, cuff links, jewelry, and ties. A back room does a brisk business in humidors, pipes, tobacco, and imported cigars—despite the city's strict anti-smoking regulations. Personal services include monogramming, polishing, and wardrobe advice. *Open Mon–Sat 10am–6pm, Sun noon–5pm; map:N3*

**AMIR H. MOZAFFARIAN / 155 Post St btwn Kearny St and Grant Ave; 415/391-9995** A fourth-generation family of jewelers runs this elegant shop, first established in the late 1800s. Look for names like Fabergé, Piaget, and Harry Winston, whose designs fill the display cases and shelves. Along with opulent diamonds and sapphires, there are rubies, emeralds, and a stunning selection of gold bracelets and rings. *Open Mon–Sat 10am–5:30pm; map:N3*

**BULGARI / 237 Post St btwn Stockton St and Grant Ave; 415/399-9141** What started more than 300 years ago as a silversmith in Rome has become one of the world's most famous jewelers. Bulgari still handcrafts works out of gold, platinum, or a mix of gems and metals. Rings are hand-set on prongs in the time-honored tradition. Designs tend to be bold with lots of intricate detail, but understated enough to fit most occasions. *Open Mon–Sat 10am–5:30pm; www.bulgari.com; map:N3*

**CARTIER / 231 Post St btwn Stockton St and Grant Ave; 415/397-3180** This shop carries elegant jewelry from the famous French designer, including the hallmark Tank ring, bracelets, and earrings, plus luxury gift items such as scarves, leather accessories, pens, crystal, and perfume. *Open Mon–Sat 10am–5:30pm; www.cartier.com; map:N3*

**LANG ANTIQUES AND ESTATE JEWELRY / 323 Sutter St btwn Stockton St and Grant Ave; 415/982-2213** If you're looking for antique watch fobs or stickpins, here's the spot. Founded by Czech native Jarmilla Lang, the shop has an incredible selection of estate and hard-to-find jewelry, such as vintage bracelets, cuff links, and old-fashioned cameo pendants. Don't miss the window displays, which change daily to showcase the latest antique treasures. *Open Mon–Sat 10:30am–5:30pm; map:N3*

**MRS. DEWSON'S HATS / 2050 Fillmore St at California St; 415/346-1600** The colorful Ruth Dewson owns this funky little gem, brimming with sophisticated and fun hats for both sexes. For women there are '40s-style cocktail hats trimmed in silk or rosettes. Men can choose from old-fashioned boaters, bowlers, Biltmores, and Panamas. The famous "Willie" fedora is named for a famously flamboyant San Francisco mayor, Willie Brown. Most hats are handmade and hand-dyed. *Open Mon–Sat 11am–6pm, Sun noon–4pm; www.mrsdewsonhats.com; map:K3*

**PEARL EMPIRE / 427 Post St at Dowell St; 415/362-0606** The name says it all—this is a veritable empire of pearls, in all colors, sizes, and shapes, that can be turned into rings, pendants, or pins. Burma jadeite—the finest in the world—is sold here as well. Many of the staff have worked in the store since it opened in 1957 and will help you develop a jewelry wardrobe to fit your budget and lifestyle. *Open Mon–Sat 9:30am–5:30pm; www. pearlempire.com; map:N3*

**SHREVE & CO. / 200 Post St at Grant Ave; 415/421-2600** Founded in 1852, and one of the city's oldest retailers, Shreve is located in a historic building with a gorgeous marble-and-wood interior where its famous jewelry, silver, crystal, and gifts are showcased. There's a Mikimoto pearl boutique as well as a watch boutique carrying Patek Philippe and Chopard. *Open Mon–Sat 10am–6pm, Sun noon–5pm; www.shreve.com; map:M3*

**TIFFANY & CO. / 350 Post St btwn Powell and Stockton Sts; 415/781-7000** Beautiful people shop at this beautiful store, established in 1837 in New York and immortalized by Audrey Hepburn in the movie *Breakfast at Tiffany's.* Along with designs from Jean Schlumberger, Elsa Peretti, and Paloma Picasso, there are scarves, crystal, silver, and the Tiffany perfume. All come wrapped in the signature blue box with white bow. *Open Mon–Sat 10am–5:30pm; www.tiffany.com; map:N3*

**UNION STREET GOLDSMITH / 1909 Union St at Laguna St; 415/776-8048** This is the place to buy custom jewelry made on-site by Bay Area designers. The specialty is rose, yellow, or white gold creations in 14, 18, and 22 karats. Display cases also feature designs from Italian, German, and other European jewelers. *Open Mon–Sat 11am–5:45pm, Sun noon–4:45pm; unionstreetgoldsmith@yahoo.com; map:K2*

## MUSIC (CDS, RECORDS, AND TAPES)

**AMOEBA MUSIC / 1855 Haight St at Stanyan St; 415/831-1200** This bustling music emporium is as popular for people-watching as it is for buying, selling, or trading CDs, videos, and tapes. Located in the Haight-Ashbury district, the store is jammed with an eclectic mix of tattooed Gen-Xers and baby boomers browsing the 500,000 new and used discs. The store is well organized and represents every type of music imaginable, from hip-hop to rap to experimental. One section is devoted to old 45rpm records. *Open Mon–Sat 10:30am–10pm, Sun 11am–9pm; www.amoebamusic.com; map:I5*

**MEDIUM RARE RECORDS / 2310 Market St btwn Noe and Castro Sts; 415/255-7273** This cozy music shop specializes in show tunes, lounge music, and pop stars from the past. You'll find vocals by Sophie Tucker, Bing Crosby, Doris Day, Judy Garland, Peggy Lee, Liza Minnelli, and many others. There are both CDs and LPs. The store also has a good

**275**

## SAN FRANCISCO'S STREET FAIRS

Combine beer gardens, live music, diverse neighborhoods, and San Francisco's screw-the-fog-let's-party mentality, and you've got the right combination for a full season of lively street fairs to choose from. Each fair takes place in a different neighborhood about every other week, resulting in a wide range of crafts, food, and cultural expression. The Folsom Street Fair, for example, is a lusty, leathery celebration of homosexuality, whereas the North Beach Fair is heavy into jazz and blues bands.

The fair season runs from late spring, when the weather starts warming up, to the middle of fall. Pray for sunshine, but bring a light jacket just in case, and good luck finding parking, so take Muni. Here's a rundown on a few of the most popular fairs; for more info on San Francisco's street fairs and festivals, log onto SFGate's fairs and festivals webpage at www.sfgate.com/traveler/events/fairsfestivals.shtml.

### Haight Street Fair

The Summer of Love may be a long-gone if fondly recalled memory, but the Haight Street Fair attempts a resuscitation each June, right at the fabled intersection of Haight and Ashbury Streets. The art for sale tends toward the psychedelic, the T-shirts toward tie-dye, and wandering artists offer face painting to some of the fair's 80,000 to 100,000 attendees at a reasonable price. Just like in the old days, there's music in the streets: ex–Grateful Dead crony Merle Sanders traditionally closes out the two days of festivities on the main stage at Haight and Stanyan Streets. More than 20 food booths help hold the munchies at bay: standbys such as burritos, pizza, and cheese steaks share the stalls with delicacies of China, Thailand, and Ghana in West Africa (try the yummy fried bananas). The merchandise for sale at all the city's street fairs is of a handcrafted, individually manufactured sort—no ready-mades.

### North Beach Street Fair

Another two days in June brings the North Beach Street Fair, which usually draws 60,000 to 70,000 people to the still heavily Italian neighborhood that is also proud to proclaim itself the home of the Beat Generation (Allen Ginsberg began working on his groundbreaking *Howl* at 1010 Montgomery Street, above Broadway). In keeping with finger-snapping '50s cool, there's a strong jazz current on at least two musical stages, but North Beach has over the years also become something of a home to the blues. Three blues-oriented bars (the Grant & Green Blues Club, the Lost and Found, and the Saloon) showcase a rotating talent roster, from the down-home acoustic to the slick-and-swinging-with-a-horn section.

### Carnaval

In the heavily Roman Catholic cultures of Latin America, the traditional Carnaval is pegged to Lent as a final burst of indulgence in all the things the devout are soon going to be expected to give up. Judging from the annual Carnaval Parade and Festival, a massive one-day street party at the end of May, this includes some of the skimpiest costumes this side of an arrest for indecent exposure—which may explain why attendance has been known to reach several hundred thousand. In recent years the palette of the festival has broadened to include tastes and sounds not strictly Latin. The same is true of the food: In addition to tacos and pupusas and mouthwatering roasted corn, you can feast on Caribbean-style jerk chicken and Cajun sausage, Thai and Chinese foods, gyros, and gumbo. There are more than 50 crafts booths to choose from, with merchandise ranging from art to handbags, and a children's area.

## Cinco de Mayo Festival

Commemorating the defeat of the French at the Battle of Puebla on May 5, 1862, which forever spelled the end of French designs on Mexico, the Cinco de Mayo Festival is an expression of national pride. Three music stages feature sounds from the traditional *norteñas* and *rancheros*, *conjuntos*, and *corridas* to the hip-hop favored by the up-and-coming. The food from the 20-or-so booths similarly runs the gamut, from tasty tacos to Thai noodles. The 30-plus crafts booths offer clothing, jewelry, candles, paintings, and religious artifacts (the Virgin of Guadalupe is a major figure in Mexican folklore). Attendance for this one-day event generally tops out at 50,000 to 60,000.

## Folsom Street Fair

In the market for a studded dog collar for your significant other? Then head on down to the fetish-heavy Folsom Street Fair, thrown during the last week in September. The leather scene that once called Folsom Street its home is slowly waning (mostly due to skyrocketing real-estate rates), but once a year the faithful gather for a celebration of their highly ritualized vision of bearded, burly masculinity. There are 20 or so food booths—falafel, gyros, and barbecue—and two stages featuring live music of a most cutting-edge variety. But the real attraction here is the crafts booths, if for no other reason than that you don't often find a good pair of leather chaps at other street fairs. This is probably not the best fair to take the kids to, and not just because there's no children's area—it might be tough to explain why the teddy bears for sale are adorned with metal spikes.

## Castro Street Fair

The first Sunday in October brings revelers, on average more than 100,000 of them, to the Castro Street Fair to bid farewell to the last of the great summer weather. Jammed but mellow, the fair features some 30 food booths, with fare such as falafel, ice cream, and barbecue as well as beer and wine; more than 50 crafts booths, where you can get outfitted in anything from shirts to sandals and see real men having serious discussions about their earrings; and a huge music stage at the corner of Castro and Market Streets, where DJs keep the beat going between live acts.

selection of international film soundtracks. *Open Mon–Thurs, Sun 11am–7pm; Fri–Sat 11am–9pm; map:K6*

**TOWER RECORDS / 2525 Jones St btwn Bay and Columbus Sts (and branches); 415/885-0500** Tower Records is always hopping, partly due to its convenient (and free) parking lot. Fans of rock, soul, and country also gravitate to the store for its huge selection of CDs and cassettes. There's a splash of easy listening, pop vocals, soundtracks, Latin, blues, and New Age—even folk and gospel. Across the street is an annex catering to the classical set. Other branches are at Market and Noe Streets (415/621-0588) and in the Stonestown Galleria (415/759-2626). *Open every day 9am–midnight; www.towerrecords.com; map:M1*

**VIRGIN MEGASTORE / 2 Stockton St at Market St; 415/397-4525** With three levels of listening stations and music for just about every taste, Virgin is indeed a megastore. Cruise the racks for that perfect CD, cassette, or DVD. The store carries every genre, even film soundtracks and comedy. It's heaven for classical music lovers, who have a separate room to themselves. The store also has loads of magazines, books, and computer games focusing on music and musicians. Consider buying a cool Virgin T-shirt, sweatshirt, or jacket as a souvenir. *Open Mon–Thurs 9am–11pm, Fri–Sat 9am–midnight, Sun 10am–11pm; www.virgin mega.com; map:N3*

## SEAFOOD

**NIKKO FISH CO. / 699 Illinois St at 18th St; 415/864-5261** For more than a decade Tadanory Chiyo has run this unpretentious fish market, selling possibly the freshest fish in town. Oysters are available by the bag, and there are live crabs, giant prawns, halibut, salmon, and fresh tuna. Imported caviar is available by special request. *Open Mon–Sat 9am–6pm; map:O6*

**SWAN OYSTER DEPOT / 1517 Polk St at California St; 415/673-1101** Half oyster bar, half fish counter, Swan's is a neighborhood landmark, serving fresh oysters and shellfish since it opened in 1912. Four Danish brothers operated it for more than three decades before selling it in 1946 to Sal Sancimino, a fifth-generation fisherman whose five very friendly grandsons, Steve, Vince, Tom, Jim, and Phil, now run the counter. Locals make this place a regular pilgrimage for the convivial service and to pick up the day's catch for dinner. Don't miss the famous Boston clam chowder. *Open Mon–Sat 8am–5:30pm; map:L6*

**YUM YUM / 2181 Irving St at 23rd Ave; 415/566-6433** The retail outlet for Nikko Fish Co. (see above), this tiny shop purveys fresh filleted fish, ranging from halibut and haddock to snapper and yellowfin tuna. The quality is consistent, and there's fresh sushi to go if you don't want to make it yourself. *Open Tues–Sun 10:30am–7:30pm; map:G6*

## SHOES

**THE ALDEN SHOP / 201 Kearny St at Sutter St; 415/421-6691** Opened in 1884, this is one of the nation's oldest men's shoe stores, carrying an incredible selection of well-made dress and casual footwear in a variety of styles and hard-to-find sizes. The oxfords, cap-toes, and loafers are especially popular with the white-collar crowd. *Open Mon–Sat 10am–6pm; www.aldenshoes.com; map:N3*

**ARTHUR BEREN SHOES / 222 Stockton St btwn Geary and Post Sts; 415/397-8900** If you've been to Arthur Beren but not lately, you're in for a surprise. The ultraconservative men's and women's footwear store has now given way to high-fashion designs from Robert Clergerie, YSL, Emanuel Ungaro, Stuart Weitzman, Arche, Bruno Magli, and others. Shoes are finely crafted from leather, stretch fabric, and an occasional exotic skin (a pair of crocodile loafers fetches $1,300). A must-stop if your feet are especially narrow or wide. *Open Mon–Fri 9:30am–7pm, Sat 9:30am–6pm, Sun noon–5pm; map:N3*

**BALLY OF SWITZERLAND / 238 Stockton St at Geary St; 415/398-7463** The well-heeled are well-shod in the soft, supple styles of this century-old chasseur. Pumps, strappy '40s-style sandals, and slingbacks are some of the styles for women, while men can choose from two-tones, classic lace-ups, and the signature calfskin loafers with gold tassels. Prices are high, but so is the quality. *Open Mon–Sat 10am–6pm, Sun noon–5pm; www. bally.com; map:N3*

**BIRKENSTOCK SAN FRANCISCO / 42 Stockton St at O'Farrell St; 415/989-2475** Once an icon for the fashionably unfashionable, Birkenstock now attracts mainstream buyers with its two floors of footwear in more than 350 colors and styles. You'll find the familiar hippie sandals sharing space with wedges, black patent flats, kids' shoes, and clogs. A new line of dressy footwear is ideal for business or that special occasion. *Open Mon–Sat 10am–8pm; Sun 11am–6pm; www.birkenstock.com; map:N3*

**BULO MEN, BULO WOMEN / 437-A Hayes St btwn Gough and Octavia Sts; 415/864-3244, 418 Hayes St btwn Gough and Octavia Sts; 415/255-4939** *Bulo* is Perugian for "hip," which describes the selection of shoes at these tiny Hayes Valley and Fillmore boutiques. Italian imports from OXS, Krizia, Roberto del Carlo, and Enzo Romanelli fill the shelves and include mules, platforms, slip-ons, and boots. Textures such as leather, canvas, and mesh keep changing with new shipments to keep the inventory fresh. *Open Mon–Sat 11am–6:30pm, Sun noon–6pm; www.buloshoes.com; map:L4*

**CHURCH'S ENGLISH SHOES / 50 Post St btwn Montgomery and Kearny Sts; 415/433-5100 or 888/99-SHOES** This branch of the century-old

English shoemaker offers veddy proper gentlemen's shoes, such as wingtips, brogues, two-tones, and boots. Styles are featured in burgundy, black, and brown. *Open Mon–Fri 10am–6pm, Sat 10am–5pm; www. churchsshoes.com; map:N3*

**GIMME SHOES / 416 Hayes St btwn Gough and Octavia Sts; 415/864-0691** Shoppers who want to stay one step ahead of the trends make regular pilgrimages to this avant-garde salon to check out edgy footwear from European makers such as Dries Van Noten, Prada, Espace, and Miu Miu. Geared to the shoe hound who believes footwear makes a loud statement about the wearer, Gimme Shoes stocks everything from fur slip-ons to orange-and-white polka-dot pumps. *Open Mon–Sat 11am–6:30pm, Sun 11am–6pm; www.gimmeshoes.com; map:L4*

**KENNETH COLE / San Francisco Shopping Centre, 865 Market St at 5th St (and branches); 415/227-4536** Styles by this hip New York designer, who launched his career selling boots from a trailer, are now carried by major retailers as well as in his own boutiques. Most shoes—for men and women—have the familiar masculine square toe; many are modern remakes of classic leather loafers, oxfords, mules, and Mary Janes. He has expanded his line to include gorgeous leather and cashmere jackets, sweaters, handbags, belts, and eyewear. Other branches include a flagship store at 166 Grant Avenue (at Kearny St; 415/981-2653) and a smaller store at 2078 Union Street between Webster and Buchanan Streets (415/346-2161). *Open Mon–Sat 9:30am–8pm, Sun 11am–6pm; www. kencole.com; map:N3*

**TUFFY'S HOPSCOTCH / 3307 Sacramento St at Presidio Ave; 415/440-7599** The pitter-patter of little feet is a familiar sound in this Sacramento Street shop, catering to tots with European footwear from Brakkies, Elefanten, Aster, and Mod 8. There's a wonderful array of colors and styles in play shoes and dressy styles for christenings, the first day of school, and other special occasions. *Open Mon–Sat 10am–6pm; map:J3*

## SPORTS AND OUTDOOR GEAR

**ANY MOUNTAIN–THE GREAT OUTDOOR STORE / 2598 Taylor St at Bay St; 415/345-8080** Conveniently located at Fisherman's Wharf, Any Mountain provides hikers and campers with apparel, boots, and gear. The friendly and well-informed staff is quick to help in selecting the appropriate tent, sleeping bag, or other outdoor essentials. Swimsuits and water gear are for sale in summer, snowboards and skis in winter. Sundog bags and Eagle Creek travel accessories are carried year-round. *Open Mon–Wed 10am–7pm, Thurs–Fri 10am–9pm, Sat 10am–6pm, Sun 11am–6pm; www.anymountaingear.com; map:M1*

**COPELAND'S SPORTS / 901 Market St at 5th St; 415/495-0928, Stonestown Galleria, 3251 20th Ave; 415/759-2626** Copeland's is packed with apparel and gear for just about every sport: baseball, basketball, football, soccer, golf, tennis, running, skating, skiing, bicycling, swimming, skateboarding, bodyboarding, snowboarding—you name it. Fitness freaks will find a section devoted to exercise machines and weight-lifting equipment. Casual wear and men's and women's athletic and golf shoes are also in stock. *Open Mon–Fri 9am–8pm, Sat 10am–7pm, Sun 9am–6pm; www.shopsports.com; map:M4*

**DON SHERWOOD GOLF AND TENNIS WORLD / 320 Grant Ave at Sutter St; 415/989-5000** Established in 1961, this store is for the serious golf and tennis enthusiast. Merchandise is organized by floor: tennis rackets in the basement, men's and women's apparel and shoes on the lower level, and golf equipment on the two upper floors. The golf staff conducts a computer analysis of each golfer's swing before fitting him or her with a club shaft. Don't miss the tennis tunnel, where you can try out a racket before buying. *Open Mon–Sat 10am–6:30pm, Sun noon–5pm; map:N3*

**G&M SALES, THE GREAT OUTDOORS STORE / 1667 Market St at Gough St; 415/863-2855** Highly regarded by locals, G&M carries an extensive selection of camping and backpacking supplies, including a large array of tents, sleeping bags, pads, backpacks, duffels, stoves, cook kits,  coolers, freeze-dried foods, and fishing poles. Unbreakable wineglasses and enamel espresso cups are also for sale. This is where city slickers come for everything from a mosquito headnet to a "Luggable Loo." Plus, tents, bags, stoves, lanterns, coolers, and fishing poles are available to rent at reasonable rates. *Open Mon–Fri 10am–7pm, Sat 10am–5pm, Sun 11am–4pm; www.gmoutdoors.com; map:L4*

**LOMBARDI SPORTS / 1600 Jackson St at Polk St; 415/771-0600** This spacious store stocks a variety of sports apparel, shoes, and gear, and the specialty is backpacking and bicycling equipment, which takes up the second floor. There's a good array of water accessories, including suits, goggles, snorkels, and masks, plus in-line skates from Rollerblade, Salomon, and K2. Women runners and joggers will appreciate the large selection of running shoes and bras, including the Champion line. *Open Mon–Wed 10am–7pm, Thurs–Fri 10am–8pm, Sat 10am–6pm, Sun 11am–6pm; www.lombardisports.com; map:L2*

**NIKETOWN / 278 Post St at Stockton St; 415/392-6453** Here's the very hip, very cool place to shop for the Nike brand of clothing and shoes. Goods are grouped by sport—basketball, soccer, running, tennis, golf, et cetera—with the exception of kids' wear, which has its own section. Videos and multimedia displays entertain you while you shop. *Open Mon–Sat 10am–8pm, Sun 11am–7pm; www.nike.com; map:N3*

**THE NORTH FACE / 180 Post St btwn Grant Ave and Kearny St; 415/433-3223** "Never stop exploring" is the mantra of this top-notch climbing store. Whether the goal is scaling El Capitan, Mount Everest, or simply the nearest indoor climbing wall, North Face can outfit you with no-nonsense expedition apparel, tents, packs, backpacks, and sleeping bags. Subzero jackets, bodysuits, and layered outerwear are ideal for hard-core mountaineering enthusiasts, and rock climbers shouldn't miss the quick-drying and lightweight Tekware line. The store hosts monthly lectures and events about climbing. Their outlet in SoMa has fantastic deals on their trademark goods and equipment (see the Discount section). *Open Mon–Sat 10am–8pm, Sun 11am–7pm; www.the northface.com; map:N3*

**PATAGONIA / 770 North Point St btwn Hyde and Leavenworth Sts; 415/771-2050** Patagonia manufactures outdoor clothing for men, women, and children, including the well-known line of windbreakers and fleece jackets. The soft organic cotton knit and flannel shirts for men and women and the multipocket mesh vests for fishers and photographers are especially great finds, as is the Capilene underwear in pretty pastels and muted colors. Patagonia surfboards are sold here as well. *Open Mon–Tues, Fri–Sat 10am–6pm; Wed–Thurs 10am–7pm; Sun 11am–5pm; www.patagonia.com; map:L1*

## TOYS

**ARK / 3845 24th St btwn Church and Sanchez Sts; 415/821-1257** For nearly two decades this store has been selling high-quality European and American crafts and toys. Besides an incredible selection of musical instruments, including steel drums, accordions, tambourines, and kazoos, you'll find hand-carved ships, piggy banks, rideable trucks, and playful walking ducks with webbed feet. *Open Mon–Sat 10am–6pm, Fri 10am–7pm, Sun 10am–5pm; map:K7*

**BASIC BROWN BEAR FACTORY / 444 De Haro St at Mariposa St; 415/626-0781 or 800/554-1910, The Cannery, 2801 Leavenworth St at Jefferson St; 415/931-6670** This is one of the few remaining stuffed-animal factories in the nation. Bears and bear-themed toys are designed by Merrilee Woods and handmade at the factory. Drop-in tours are held daily at 1pm and include behind-the-scenes demonstrations of how bears are designed and made. Then you get to stuff your own bear, dragon, bunny, or reindeer as a souvenir of your visit. *Open Mon–Sat 10am–5pm, Sun 11am–5pm; www.basicbrownbear.com; map:N6, L1*

**DISNEY STORE / 400 Post St at Powell St; 415/391-6866** The Disney store sells everything from oversize Mickey Mouses and Donald Ducks to cartoon clothing, backpacks, games, videos, and accessories. The helpful sales staff will steer you to merchandise commemorating your favorite Disney personality. And if that's not enough, a high-end gallery features art based on popular Disney cartoon figures, but expect to find five-figure price tags attached. *Open Mon–Fri 10am–8pm, Sat 10am–6pm, Sun 11am–6pm (extended summer and holiday hours); www.disneystore.com; map:M3*

**FAO SCHWARZ / 48 Stockton St at O'Farrell St; 415/394-8700** This three-story upscale toy store was made famous by actor Tom Hanks when he danced on a giant toy piano in the popular movie *Big*. A small version of the now-famous piano is located on the third floor. Allow lots of time to linger here—kids of all ages love browsing through flamboyant Barbie World, oogling over the giant plush animals, and testing the flashy toy race cars and trains. *Open Mon–Sat 9:30am–7pm, Sun 11am–6pm; www.fao.com; map:N3*

**IMAGINARIUM / Laurel Village Shopping Center, 3535 California St btwn Locust and Spruce Sts; 415/387-9885** At Imaginarium, young-sters can play with many of the toys while you shop. Look for old favorites such as Gumby, as well as modern storybook characters, Raggedy Ann and Andy dolls, trains, educational books and cassettes, and the store's own entertaining line of learning games. *Open Mon–Fri 9:30am–7pm, Sat 9:30am–6pm, Sun 11am–6pm; map:I3*

**JONATHAN KAYE / 3548 Sacramento St btwn Laurel and Locust Sts; 415/563-0773** A delightful emporium of tiny-tyke toys and games. Play with Babar, Madeline, Curious George, and other childhood pals; there's also a huge array of adorable handcrafted and painted furnishings. The rocking horses and puppet theaters are especially popular with kids, and the doll cradles can be custom ordered in pink or blue with fanciful moon and star designs. *Open Mon–Fri 10am–6pm, Sat 10am–5:30pm, Sun noon–5pm; www.jonathankaye.com; map:I3*

## VINTAGE CLOTHING

**AARDVARK'S ODD ARK / 1501 Haight St at Ashbury St; 415/621-3141** The atmosphere is more thrift store than boutique, but the sheer quan-tity of mostly '50s and '60s shirts, skirts, pants, and leather jackets makes  Aardvark's, a Haight Street institution, one of San Francisco's most pop-ular vintage clothing stores. The real treasures are buried in the back room, where intrepid shoppers will find perfectly preserved zoot suits and silk smoking jackets from the '30s and '40s. *Open every day 11am–7pm; map:J5*

**AMERICAN RAG COMPANY / 1305 Van Ness Ave at Sutter St; 415/474-5214** Located in a former auto showroom, this cavernous store offers both new and vintage clothing, shoes, and accessories for men and women. The new clothes, many from European designers, are cutting-edge trendy and expensive. The huge selection of vintage clothes, mostly from the '40s through the early '70s, seems to go on and on; it's a bit pricey, but in good condition. This is where you'll find the city's largest selection of little black dresses. *Open Mon–Sat 10am–9pm, Sun noon–7pm; map:L3*

**DEPARTURES FROM THE PAST / 2028 Fillmore St btwn Pine and California Sts; 415/885-3377** Owner Stephen "Spig" Spigolon aptly describes his filled-to-the-rafters store as a "wacky Woolworth's." The emphasis here is on '50s and '60s costumes, with all the accessories— wigs, hats, sunglasses, jewelry, purses, and shoes—to complete the look. Don't miss the knockout silk pajamas and other great vintage lingerie. The store also carries some new items patterned after vintage styles. *Open Mon–Sat 11am–7pm, Sun noon–6pm; map:K2*

**GUYS AND DOLLS / 3789 24th St btwn Church and Dolores Sts; 415/285-7174** Tucked away in Noe Valley, Guys and Dolls is a cheerful, well-lit shop purveying a young, hip look. Lounge music complements the '30s, '40s, and '50s fun day wear, which includes straight skirts, beaded sweaters, Hawaiian shirts, and swimsuits, all in good condition. The store also carries new sunglasses, jewelry, and other accessories in older styles, plus a few collectibles, such as Reglor lamps (around $500) and harlequin wall hangings. The friendly owners hand-select all items and change merchandise seasonally. *Open Mon–Fri 11am–7pm, Sat 11am–6pm, Sun noon–6pm; map:L7*

**LA ROSA / 1711 Haight St at Cole St; 415/668-3744** A thickly carpeted floor, soothing plum-colored walls, and votive candles floating in champagne glasses set the mood at La Rosa, one of the Bay Area's best high-end vintage clothing stores. Most of the merchandise dates back to the '40s and earlier, though there's a large selection of men's suits from the '50s and '60s. Items range from a spectacular rhinestone cowgirl outfit (boasting a $2,000 price tag) to gorgeous silk robes and old-fashioned doctors' satchels. A nice touch: Each garment comes with a tag noting the approximate year it was manufactured, along with its fabric content, condition, and care instructions. *Open Mon–Fri noon–midnight, Sat 11am–7pm, Sun noon–6pm; map:I5*

**THIRD HAND ROSE / 1839 Divisadero St at Pine St; 415/567-7332** At the same address since 1967, Third Hand Rose is San Francisco's oldest vintage clothing store, and certainly one of its best. The merchandise will appeal not just to vintage aficionados but also to anyone who appreciates well-made, one-of-a-kind styles. From elegant Victorian gowns to early '70s "trash," this smallish store offers museum-quality items, including hard-to-find flapper dresses, exquisite lace blouses, sumptuous brocade jackets, and even dyed turkey feather vests. Specialties include well-priced bridal gowns (both antique and new) and vintage ethnic wear from the Middle East and Asia. *Open Mon–Sat noon–6pm; map:J3*

**WASTELAND / 1660 Haight St at Cole St; 415/863-3150** Located in a converted vaudeville and silent-movie palace, Wasteland is a vast emporium of clothes dating from the Victorian era to the present—8,000 items in 5,000 square feet. Prices are a bit inflated, but the store's colorful gargoyles, famously loud and obnoxious music, and outrageously attired salespeople add up to one of the best shows in town. *Open Mon–Thurs, Sun 11am–7pm; Fri–Sat 11am–8pm; www.thewasteland.com; map:I5*

## WINE, BEER, AND SPIRITS

**CALIFORNIA WINE MERCHANT / 3237 Pierce St btwn Chestnut and Lombard Sts; 415/567-0646** A 25-year-old neighborhood institution, California Wine Merchant offers hard- and not-so-hard-to-find West Coast wines. Though tiny, the shop packs floor-to-ceiling racks with well-edited bottles of boutique and esoteric wines, such as Lewis, Peter Michael, and Au Bon Climat. It leans slightly more toward reds in keeping with the trend; there's a good selection of California-style Rhônes. The knowledgeable staff can suggest a wine to fit any occasion. *Open Mon–Sat 11am–7pm, Sun noon–5pm; map:K1*

**CANNERY WINE CELLARS / 2801 Leavenworth St btwn Beach and Jefferson Sts; 415/673-0400** Here amid the touristy shops of Fisherman's Wharf is an incredibly sophisticated array of wines, beers (more than 300 labels), and liquor, including the West Coast's largest selection of single-malt scotch. The store ships all over the world, and offers one-stop shopping for wine gadgets and gifts. *Open every day 10am–8pm; www.cannerywine.com; map:M1*

**JUG SHOP / 1567 Pacific Ave at Polk St; 415/885-2922** Besides boasting the best selection of Australian and New Zealand wines in the country, the Jug Shop stocks more than 400 brands of beer and loads of spirits, especially scotches. Wines range from limited releases to big-name producers. Savvy shoppers stop here on the way home to pick up a bottle for guests coming to dinner. The tasting bar is open Thursday through Saturday. *Open Mon–Fri 10am–7pm, Sat 10am–6pm, Sun 10am–5pm; map:L2*

**PLUMPJACK WINES / 3201 Fillmore St at Greenwich St; 415/346-9870** Named for a Shakespearean character, this Marina District hot spot sells well-priced and well-edited California and imported wines, especially lesser-known labels. Service is a big reason customers make PlumpJack a repeat destination. *Open Mon–Sat 10am–8pm, Sun 11am–7pm; www. plumpjack.com; map:K1*

**WINE CLUB / 953 Harrison St btwn 5th and 6th Sts; 415/512-9086 or 800/966-7835** Serious wine connoisseurs peruse the Wine Club's shelves for bargain prices on more than 1,000 local and imported labels. Markups are just above wholesale, and most collectors buy in quantity to take advantage of the savings. Though heavy on burgundies, including rare vintages, the stock also includes loads of reds and whites from France, Italy, Germany, Spain, and Australia. Phone orders are shipped for a fee. *Open Mon–Sat 9am–7pm, Sun 11am–6pm; www.thewineclub. com; map:N4*

# PERFORMING ARTS

# PERFORMING ARTS

## Theater

Purists lament that San Francisco lacks a theater scene worthy of the city's global acclaim. But in reality the theater culture here is world class. Only a dreamer or a fool would compare it to the stages of London or New York, but as long as such lofty examples remain in sight, Bay Area producers and performers will continue to improve on what is already a polished, wide-ranging collection of offerings for the stage. Sure, a provincial texture persists, evident in the excitement generated whenever a major touring production from the Best of Broadway series arrives and unloads its trucks. But resident houses such as the beloved American Conservatory Theater, the Magic Theatre, and the New Conservatory Theatre Center routinely unleash a dramatic torrent that creates national waves. And it's in the work of these local houses—from mainstream repertory to leading-edge fringe, from traditional drama to lesbian-themed musicals—that the true flavor of San Francisco theater resides. The following are some of the best groups currently performing innovative theatrical works.

**ACTOR'S THEATRE / 533 Sutter St at Powell St; 415/296-9179** Tucked away on Sutter Street above Union Square, away from the main theater district, the Actor's Theatre produces high-quality productions on a minimal budget for appreciative audiences, many composed of fellow actors. The theater has fewer than 100 seats, and there's not really a bad one in the house. Much of the fare is chosen to show off the actors' abilities—so expect to see lots of Tennessee Williams and heavy American drama. *www.angelfire.com/ca5/actorstheatresf/; map:M3*

**AMERICAN CONSERVATORY THEATER (ACT) / Geary Theater, 415 Geary St at Mason St (performances); 30 Grant Ave (office); 415/749-2228** ACT is one of the best established resident theater groups, not only in San Francisco but in the nation. From its home stage at the historic 1910 Geary Theater, the company presents polished interpretations of the classics as well as important contemporary U.S. and world premieres.  ACT is known as much for its stage presentations as for its tradition of thespian teaching: It has earned Tony Awards for both outstanding theatrical performance and training. Actors the world over have studied here, and alums include Annette Bening, Denzel Washington, John Turturro, and Winona Ryder. The season runs from September to midsummer and is punctuated by lectures, audience discussions, and special student plays. A local favorite is the holiday production of Dickens's *A Christmas Carol*. In spite of all its accomplishments and national

## TICKETS TO SHOWS

OK, so we may not have New York City's big-time Broadway productions, but we also don't have NYC's big-time ticket lines. In fact, for most performances a phone call and a credit card is all it takes to score a primo seat. Chances are the ticket you're in need of is available at one of these three main ticket providers:

**TIX Bay Area:** Your best source for both full-price and half-price tickets to most performance halls, concerts, sporting events, and clubs. Half-price tickets are sold only on the day of the show (except for Sunday and Monday events, which are sold on Saturday), and only cash or traveler's checks are accepted, but it's a fantastic bargain. A service charge of $1 to $3 is levied on all tickets; Visa and MasterCard are accepted for full-price tickets. Tix is open Tuesday to Thursday 11am to 6pm, and Friday and Saturday 11am to 7pm, and is located inside the Union Square Garage at Geary and Powell (enter the garage on Geary St and turn right); 415/433-7827.

**BASS Ticketmaster:** Hefty service charges have ticked off thousands of concertgoers, so we don't recommend using BASS unless you absolutely have to. Downtown BASS Ticketmaster ticketing offices are located at Tix Bay Area (see above) and Wherehouse Records stores throughout the city, such as the one at 30 Powell St. Call 510/762-2277 for over-the-phone ticket sales.

**City Box Office:** Located at 153 Kearny St, Ste 402 (415/392-4400), CBO sells tickets to most theater and dance events over the phone via your MasterCard, Visa, or American Express card.

renown, ACT is refreshingly unstuffy, making both veteran theatergoers and first-timers feel at home. *www.act-sfbay.org; map:M3*

**BAY AREA PLAYWRIGHTS' FESTIVAL / 470 Florida St btwn 17th and Mariposa Sts; 415/399-1809 or 415/263-3986** A regular in San Francisco's fall arts season, the Bay Area Playwrights' Festival was founded in 1976 as one of the nation's first writer-focused theater festivals. It has garnered national kudos, developing the work of such award-winning playwrights as Sam Shepard, Anna Deavere Smith, Holly Hughes, and David Henry Hwang. A creative haven for writers that stays out of the limelight most of the year, the festival usually opens its doors to the public in early September or late October to provide a glimpse of participants' new work. *www.bayareaplays.org; map:M6*

**BAY AREA THEATRESPORTS (BATS) / Bayfront Theater, Fort Mason Center, Bldg B, 3rd fl, Marina Blvd at Buchanan St; 415/474-8935**  When it comes to improv comedy, Bay Area Theatresports does it so well it's like playing a game. In fact, it is a game. This company of actors and comedians produces a highly dynamic summer improv series, in which "teams" of performers compete on a stage, much to audiences' delight. It's one of the top improv festivals in the Bay Area. BATS also offers an assortment of fun and inventive acting classes for all skill levels. Free parking, too. *www.improv.org; map:K1*

**BERKELEY REPERTORY THEATRE / 2025 Addison St at Shattuck Ave, Berkeley; 510/845-4700 (performances) or 510/204-8901 (informa-tion)** Although a fairly small company, this dramatic magnet across the bay has a huge impact on national theater circles and won the 1997 Tony Award for outstanding regional theater. The Berkeley Rep, founded in a storefront amid the counterculture hubris of 1968, has grown to become a mature theater company, though no less socially or politically aware. Works range from inventive updates on the classics to premieres of spe-cially commissioned pieces by top playwrights. The annual seven-play season begins in September and runs through midsummer. *www.berkeleyrep.org; map:FF2*

**BRAVA THEATER CENTER / 2781 24th St at York St; 415/641-7657** Since 1986 Brava for Women in the Arts has produced, commissioned, and presented some of America's most gutsy and aggressive theater. The company's latest move was to purchase a dilapidated old movie house in a run-down part of the city's Mission District and convert it into a  13,000-square-foot training facility—including a 250-seat theater—where more than 300 budding actors, playwrights, and stage techni-cians are enrolled each year. Brava's penchant for politically motivated and mostly feminist-, lesbian-, and Latina-oriented fare has earned it quite a following in San Francisco. Plays are usually small in scale, but always adventurous. *www.brava.org; map:N7*

**COWELL THEATER / Fort Mason Center, Bldg D, Marina Blvd at Buchanan St; 415/441-3687** One of a few charming theaters in the expansive Fort Mason Center, Cowell plays host to everything from new dance works by experimental ensembles to monologues by Spalding Gray to the annual season of San Francisco's New Pickle Circus. The high stage lends itself to big spectacles, although the moderate size (about 450 seats) keeps the feeling intimate. Another factor that makes it a favorite venue with San Franciscans: lots of free parking! *www.fortmason.org/theaters; map:K1*

**CURRAN THEATRE / 445 Geary St at Mason St; 415/551-2000** Many lose sight of the fact that this gorgeous 1,665-seat theater has hosted all manner of dramatic fare on its stage since 1922. That's because for six years starting in 1993 it was home to the wildly popular production of Andrew Lloyd Webber's *Phantom of the Opera*. Producers poured money into the place to accommodate the special theatrics, a renovation that restored the building's original grandeur and added modern lighting and technical updates. Since *Phantom*'s closing, the Curran has provided another great venue for several hit Broadway plays. *www.bestof broadway-sf.com; map:M3*

**EUREKA THEATRE / 215 Jackson St btwn Front and Battery Sts; 415/788-7469 (info) or 415/392-4400 (tickets)** The Eureka Theatre was long known for its intimate staged readings, playwright development, and lively, socially relevant, community-based theater. Then in 1992, the company premiered Tony Kushner's *Angels in America*—and, willy-nilly, had to grow up with that play's skyrocketing success. Now in a beautiful permanent home in a renovated old movie house, the Eureka continues to foster innovative theater under a more structured administration. The theater still hosts staged readings and works-in-progress, in addition to more fully developed productions by the likes of the multimedia performance group AWD. Another recent success was the audience-interactive, continuously developing, and increasingly wacky live soap opera performed by San Francisco's own Liquid Soap. *Map:N2*

**42ND STREET MOON / New Conservatory Theatre Center, 25 Van Ness Ave at Market St; 415/861-8972 (performances) or 415/281-5868 (information)** This is one of only a few theater companies in the nation devoted entirely to the revival of "lost" musicals. Founded in 1993, the company got its name from a 1920s song about the bright lights of Broadway. It focuses on lesser-known gems from the golden age of American musical theater—from Cole Porter and Gershwin to Rodgers and Hammerstein—and each year presents them anew in the intimate New Conservatory Theatre Center. Past seasons (beginning in October) have included *One Touch of Venus, Let's Face It, Hollywood Pinafore, Once in a Blue Moon,* and the U.S. premiere of Rodgers and Hammerstein's *Three Sisters. www.capybara.com/42ndStMoon; map:L4*

**GOLDEN GATE THEATRE / 1 Taylor St at Market St and Golden Gate Ave; 415/551-2000** Despite its proximity to one of the less attractive stretches of Market Street, the Golden Gate packs 'em in from all over town, usually showing the latest blockbuster from the Best of Broadway series. The large 1920s theater was once a two-screen movie house owned by RKO. It has been a stage theater since 1979, hosting such productions as *Chicago, Carousel,* and *Rent. www.bestofbroadway-sf.com; map:M4*

**MAGIC THEATRE / Fort Mason Center, Bldg D, 3rd fl, Marina Blvd at Buchanan St; 415/441-8822** One of the best and most popular companies in San Francisco, the Magic once had a policy of staging only world-premiere works. It has since lightened up, but the quality is still evident in season after season of works by new and emerging American playwrights. Founded in 1968, the Magic is perhaps best known as the theatrical birthplace of playwright Sam Shepard (his Pulitzer Prize–winning play, *Buried Child,* had its premiere here, as did a more recent production of Shepard's *The Late Henry Moss* starring Nick Nolte,

**291**

Sean Penn, and Woody Harrelson), but has certainly earned notoriety for works beyond that, including its debut of the specially commissioned *Pieces of the Quilt*, an evening of AIDS-related one-acts by Tony Kushner and Lanford Wilson. Another Magic world premiere was Michelle Carter's *Hillary and Soon-Yi Shop for Ties*. The theater is divided into two spaces, one seating 156, the other 160. *www.magic theater.org; map:K1*

**THE MARSH / 1062 Valencia St btwn 21st and 22nd Sts; 415/641-0235** The Marsh bills itself as a "breeding ground for new performance" and does a pretty good job of living up to the claim. The company presents more than 300 performances a year in its three venues: the main stage, the Mock Cafe, and the Marsh Studio. Audience members, many from the Mission District neighborhood, like being surprised by the eclectic bill of fare. Various local acting, dance, and music ensembles perform here; works-in-progress are a common occurrence, as are solo shows and longer runs of full-fledged original plays. Tickets are usually cheap—well under $20. *www.themarsh.org; map:L6*

**NEW CONSERVATORY THEATRE CENTER (NCTC) / 25 Van Ness Ave at Market St; 415/861-8972** The New Conservatory Theatre Center hosts the annual gay-themed Pride Season of original musicals, comedies, and dramatic plays. A recent season included the world premiere of the gay comedy *Key West* by Jack Heifer and Ed Decker. Another NCTC offering was Karen Finley's one-woman show *Shut Up and Love Me*, part of the theater's Celebrating Women Festival. The company also hosts a matinee series for kids on Tuesday and Saturday mornings, as well as productions by local ensembles. The NCTC is located in an office building near the Civic Center, and it's home to 42nd Street Moon's annual season of "lost musicals" (see 42nd Street Moon review). *www.nctcsf.org; map:L4*

**ORPHEUM THEATRE / 1192 Market St at Hyde St; 415/551-2000** With a whopping 2,200 seats and an enormous stage, the Orpheum may be the most grandiose theater space in the city. Accordingly, it gets to host the big shows. A massive remodel of the 1926 building brought the technical facilities into the 21st century, and they were used to full effect when the theater was home to the popular touring production of *Miss Saigon*. The Orpheum usually presents large-scale productions from the Best of Broadway series. *www.bestofbroadway-sf.com; map:M4*

**SAN FRANCISCO FRINGE FESTIVAL / 156 Eddy St at Taylor St, and other venues; 415/673-3847** Started in 1991, this festival is a celebration of uncensored, uncurated, fly-by-the-seat-of-your-pants theater. Held each September in various Union Square–area venues (primarily the Exit Theatre and the Exit Stage Left at 156 Eddy Street), the Fringe features strange, offbeat, and obscure performances by actors, comedians, jugglers, poets, clowns, and experimentalists of all kinds. The 2001 festival featured about 250 performances over an 11-day period by 55 local, national, and international theater companies. Locals have elevated "fringing" to an art form, bouncing from performance to performance, taking in only what they like. It's easy to do, since most shows last less than an hour, and you can sometimes see five different performances within 30 minutes. *www.sffringe.org; map:M3*

**SAN FRANCISCO MIME TROUPE / 855 Treat St at 21st St; various venues; 415/285-1717** Each summer in city parks, the renowned San  Francisco Mime Troupe presents free shows that address burning political and social issues, ranging from neighborhood gentrification to racism to the ills of the Information Age. Alumni of the Tony Award–winning troupe include Peter Coyote, Sharon Lockwood, and Arthur Holden. *www.sffringe.org; map:M6*

**SAN FRANCISCO SHAKESPEARE FESTIVAL / Golden Gate Park, and other venues; 415/422-2222** Since 1983, this beloved theater group has been producing its annual Free Shakespeare in the Park series each September in Golden Gate Park and other locales. A performance is often a whimsical update of the Bard's classics, transplanted to such environs as 1950s Italy, a contemporary Maine fishing village, or the Roaring '20s. The festival is also known for its inventive youth theater programs, including Midnight Shakespeare. Be sure to bring a picnic lunch. *www.sfshakes.org; map:D5–H5*

**THEATRE ON THE SQUARE (TOTS) / 450 Post St at Mason St; 415/433-9500** In a 740-seat space originally built as a hotel ballroom, TOTS typically stages long-running, very popular productions of dance theater, musical revues, or small plays that earn big reviews. One of its longest runs was Steve Martin's *Picasso at the Lapin Agile*. *www.theatreonthe square.com; map:N3*

**THEATER RHINOCEROS / 2926 16th St at South Van Ness Ave; 415/861-5079** Its motto is "We're Here, We're Queer, We Do Plays," and indeed, this is the nation's oldest lesbian and gay theater. Founded in 1977, it still produces some of the most relevant and engaging fare in the genre. The  productions endeavor not just to preach to the choir, however, but to gain a voice in the mainstream. As a result of the company's world renown, it has hosted many premieres and special commissions; a recent season included the West Coast premiere of the controversial play *Shopping and Fucking*, a hit on London's West End. *www.therhino.org; map:L5*

**A TRAVELING JEWISH THEATRE / 470 Florida St btwn 17th and Mariposa Sts; 415/399-1809** Although this acclaimed actor-led ensemble, true to its name, has traveled to perform in some 60 cities, it was happy to establish a permanent home in the Mission District not long ago. A Traveling

Jewish Theatre is one of the city's most skilled and challenging theater groups. Founded in Los Angeles in 1978 (it moved here officially in 1982), the group produces Jewish-themed pieces that examine the condition of all humanity. In 1990 it was one of the first American theaters to tour post–Warsaw Pact Eastern Europe. Deep, thought-provoking, poignant, and funny, the original works are inspired by everything from the legends of Hasidism to Yiddish poetry. The company's 23rd season opens with the premiere of *Isaac* by David Schulner, a bold new look at the story of the sacrifice of Isaac, followed by the world premiere of Albert Greenberg's eagerly awaited new Ladino (the language of Spanish Jews) musical-theater work *Una Noche de Suenos vidi Flores (A Dream of Flowers)*. *www.atjt.com; map:M6*

# Cabaret

**BEACH BLANKET BABYLON / Club Fugazi, 678 Green St btwn Powell St and Columbus Ave; 415/421-4222** North Beach's Club Fugazi is the exclusive home to this campy and very San Francisco cabaret extravaganza, which has been playing to sold-out audiences for more than 25 years. In the early '70s Steve Silver created a show of fantastic characters with kooky costumes and stage sets. Silver died in 1994, but his everlasting freak show parties on. The main story of the comedic musical revue remains the same, but it gets a periodic shot in the arm with  updated spoofs on whatever happens to be in the news at the moment, so it's a little different every time you go. The performers can really belt out the tunes, but the real showstoppers are the phenomenal hats, which can weigh up to 100 pounds and are engineered to pull off some amazing special effects. This show is extremely popular with locals and tourists, so advance ticket purchase is highly recommended. Tickets designate seating in a certain area, but within that area seats are first-come, first-served, so line up early with the rest of the crowd to get a good spot. Drinks are served at all but the Sunday matinee performances, where patrons under 21 are allowed. A photo ID is required for the evening shows. Call for box office hours and show times. *www.beachblanket babylon.com; map:N2*

---

# Classical Music and Opera

San Franciscans take their classical music very seriously and enjoy it with fervor. The San Francisco Symphony, one of the world's top-notch orchestras, is led by the colorful Michael Tilson Thomas, one of the world's most touted and talented musical directors. Next door to the symphony is the world-renowned **SAN FRANCISCO OPERA**, the oldest continuously running opera company in the United States. At the smaller end of the spectrum, groups like the **POCKET OPERA** perform less traditional but no less significant fare. The **SAN FRANCISCO GAY MEN'S CHORUS** (415/865-3650) and the **LESBIAN/GAY CHORUS OF SAN FRANCISCO** (415/861-7067) are only two of the groups that harmoniously coexist on the choral music scene. Concerts at **GRACE CATHEDRAL** (415/749-6310) feature the popular **CHOIR OF MEN AND BOYS** as well as guest performers ranging from the Slavyanka Russian Chorus to pianist George Winston. And if it's festivals you want, you'll find plenty of those too, including the popular **MIDSUMMER MOZART** (415/292-9620). Here are some of the major music makers in town.

**KRONOS QUARTET / Yerba Buena Center for the Arts, 701 Mission St at 3rd St; 415/978-2787** One of the world's leading-edge chamber ensembles, the Kronos Quartet has spent two and a half decades stretching, bending, and contorting the conventions of contemporary music for the string quartet. Ensemble members Jennifer Culp, Hank Dutt, John Sherba, and David Harrington are formally trained and firmly rooted in tradition. Kronos commissions several new works each season and performs more than 100 concerts a year, visiting an average of 15 countries and more than a dozen U.S. states. Since its inception in 1973, the quartet has performed more than 600 works and recorded about 30 albums. The list of composers who have created works especially for Kronos reads like a who's who of the music world: from John Adams, Peter Apfelbaum, and Frank Zappa to Mr. Bungle, John Coltrane, and Thelonious Monk. The home season usually begins in September. *www.kronosquartet.org; map:N3*

**OLD FIRST CHURCH CONCERTS / 1751 Sacramento St at Van Ness Ave; 415/776-5552** With a truly active congregation, this 1911 Romanesque church is known for its lively and warm Presbyterian prayer services as well as its impressive calendar of recitals and choral and chamber music concerts. The acoustics are outstanding. *www.oldfirst.org; map:L3*

**PHILHARMONIA BAROQUE ORCHESTRA / Herbst Theatre, 180 Redwood St, Ste 200, btwn Van Ness Ave and Polk St, and other venues; 415/252-1288** Symphony director Michael Tilson Thomas may command the classical spotlight, but Nicolas McGegan, musical director of the Philharmonia Baroque, is a quiet powerhouse in his own right. The Cambridge- and Oxford-trained conductor is one of the world's foremost Handel interpreters. He and his 40-piece ensemble perform refined and perfectly balanced renditions of early music, from Handel to Bach to Vivaldi, more than 30 times per season throughout the Bay Area. The company started in 1987 with two concerts, and today is acclaimed by the *New York Times* as "the country's leading early music orchestra." In San Francisco it plays primarily in Herbst Theatre. The season, which usually includes a program of Handel's *Messiah* during the holidays, begins in October. *www.philharmonia.org; map:L4*

**POCKET OPERA / Palace of the Legion of Honor, Lincoln Park, 34th Ave and Clement St, and other venues; 415/575-1102** Fear of the Viking-helmeted fat lady is all too common, but for anyone remotely curious about the grandeur of opera—especially young ones—Donald Pippin's Pocket Opera is a great place to start. Pippin, who leads the singers and chamber orchestra on piano, has said that "if you don't know the opera's story on the way to the theater, you won't know it on the way home either." With that in mind, he began creating translations of classic operas and presenting them in a North Beach bar; soon the show was so popular he took it on the road. Now the Pocket performs throughout the Bay Area with a regular season that runs from December till spring. Programs are sung in English (translated to convey the thrust of the story) and are scaled down with minimal costumes and usually no formal set. It's great fun for families. Some performances are adaptations of complete operas, such as *The Marriage of Figaro* or *La Traviata*; others are inventive originals by Mr. Pippin, like the local favorite *Alice in Operaland. www.pocketopera.org; map:E3*

**SAN FRANCISCO BACH CHOIR / Various venues; 415/922-1645 (performances) or 415/441-4942 (information)** The oldest community choir in the western states, this group has spent the past 63 years introducing Northern Californians to the works of J. S. Bach. Since 1981 it has been led by music scholar and accomplished concert organist David Babbitt. Performances are usually held from fall through late spring in churches and temples throughout the Bay Area. *www.sfbach.org*

**SAN FRANCISCO CONSERVATORY OF MUSIC / 1201 Ortega St at 19th Ave; 415/564-8086** Founded in 1917 as a piano school, the conservatory is now a world-renowned learning institution. The school is kept deliberately small; the study is intense, but less rigid than at many well-known European conservatories. In addition to academics, the school presents

296

concerts by students, the Conservatory Orchestra, and distinguished visiting musicians. Most events are free or very low priced. Each Christmas the conservatory holds its *Sing-It-Yourself Messiah* at Davies Symphony Hall (301 Van Ness Ave), an audience-participation sing-along to Handel's beloved masterwork. *www.sfcm.edu; map:G7*

**SAN FRANCISCO CONTEMPORARY MUSIC PLAYERS / Yerba Buena Center for the Arts, 701 Mission St at 3rd St; 415/978-2787 (performances) or 415/252-6235 (information)** The San Francisco Contemporary Music Players is the oldest contemporary chamber music ensemble on the West Coast and one of the top ensembles of its kind in the country. It's also a five-time winner of the national ASCAP/Chamber Music America Award for Adventurous Programming of Contemporary Music. Special commissions include works by such composers as John Adams, John Cage, Chen Yi, and Julia Wolfe. The six-concert season usually begins in September; formats vary from 6 to 18 performers. *www.sfcmp.org; map:N3*

**SAN FRANCISCO OPERA / War Memorial Opera House, 301 Van Ness Ave btwn McAllister and Grove Sts; 415/864-3330 (performances), Ticket and Patron Services, 199 Grove St at Van Ness Ave; 415/864-3330 (information)** San Francisco's opera company, currently the country's second largest, was founded in 1923; on September 26 of that year locals were treated to a lively performance of *La Bohème* in the Civic Auditorium. The auditorium couldn't hold the burgeoning company for long, however, and in 1932 the opera moved into the opulent, Arthur Brown Jr.–designed, Beaux Arts–style War Memorial Opera House—the anchor of the city's performing-arts complex today. The building was christened with a performance of Puccini's *Tosca*—and 75 years later reopened with yet another *Tosca* after an extensive $50 million retrofit (in the wake of the 1989 earthquake). The renovation not only restored the building to its original glory but added 21st-century technical innovations. These days the company is on an adventurous yet well-scripted path; the repertory season undertakes the classics (the 2002 season includes such favorites as Puccini's *Madama Butterfly* and *Carmen,* and Verdi's *Rigoletto)* and new, often specially commissioned works, including André Previn and Philip Littell's acclaimed adaptation of *A Streetcar Named Desire*. The season begins in September and lasts until late spring. Traditionally, the company follows opening night with a free concert in Golden Gate Park. Operas are performed in their native language and presented with English supertitles. The Merola Opera Program, one of the nation's top training grounds for young singers, performs in the summer. *www.sfopera.org; map:L4*

## CUT-RATE CULTURE

San Francisco is one of the costliest cities in the country to visit (and live in), but that doesn't mean you can't get some of your kicks for free. Here are numerous top attractions that are gratis either all the time or at least once in a while:

**City Guides** There are over 20 different walking tours of San Francisco offered; tours start at various points throughout the city. Call for locations and times. Free: always. Tours offered year-round; 415/557-4266; www.walking-tours.com/cityguides.

**Fort Point** A National Historic Site under the south end of the Golden Gate Bridge; off Lincoln Blvd at Long Ave. Free: Fri–Sun. Open every day; 415/556-1693; www.nps.gov/fopo.

**Golden Gate Park** Main entrance: Stanyan St at Fell St; maps are available at the San Francisco Visitor Information Center (415/391-2000) and at park headquarters in McLaren Lodge, Stanyan St at Fell St. Free: always. Open every day; www.nps.gov/goga.

**The Presidio** In the northwest corner of the city, near the Marina District and the foot of the Golden Gate Bridge. Free: always. Open every day; 415/561-4323; www.nps.gov/prsf/.

**San Francisco Zoo** At Sloat Blvd and 45th Ave. Free: 1st Wed of the month. Open every day; 415/753-7080; www.sfzoo.org.

**Sigmund Stern Grove** Various music concerts are held outdoors throughout the summer; in Stern Grove at Sloat Blvd and 19th Ave. Free: always. Held on select summer weekends, rain or shine; 415/391-2000 (San Francisco Visitors Bureau).

**California Academy of Sciences, Steinhart Aquarium, and Natural History**

**SAN FRANCISCO PERFORMANCES / Various venues; 415/398-6449** This nonprofit group, founded in 1979 by a former administrator with the San Francisco Opera, is dedicated to the cultivation of the arts in San Francisco by presenting classical and chamber music, jazz, dance, and solo recitals in intimate settings (many shows are held at Herbst Theatre or at Yerba Buena Center for the Arts). The repertoire has grown from 7 to more than 180 programs, along with educational and community outreach activities. San Francisco Performances kicks off its season in October and features the likes of the Lincoln Center Jazz Orchestra or perhaps violinist Anne-Sophie Mutter. Your ticket to the show often includes a chance to meet the performers. *www.sfperf.org*

**SAN FRANCISCO SYMPHONY / Davies Symphony Hall, 201 Van Ness Ave at Grove St; 415/864-6000 (box office) or 415/552-8000 (information)** San Franciscans are so fond of their symphony that even during the Great Depression, when hard times for all threatened to put an end

**Museum** On the Music Concourse at Golden Gate Park. Free: 1st Wed of the month. Open every day; 415/750-7145; www.calacademy.org.

**California Palace of the Legion of Honor** In Lincoln Park, 34th Ave and Clement St. Free: 1st Tues of the month. Open Tues–Sun; 415/750-3600; www.legionofhonor.com.

**Exploratorium** In the Palace of Fine Arts, 3601 Lyon St at Marina Blvd. Free: 1st Wed of the month. Open every day in the summer, Tues–Sun the rest of the year; 415/561-0360; www.exploratorium.edu.

**Cable Car Barn Museum** 1201 Mason St at Washington St. Free: always. Open every day; 415/474-1887; www.cablecarmuseum.com.

**Maritime Museum** In Aquatic Park, at the northernmost end of Polk St. Free: always. Open every day; 415/556-3002; www.nps.gov/safr/sparks.html.

**San Francisco Museum of Modern Art (SFMOMA)** 151 3rd St between Mission and Howard Sts. Free: 1st Tues of the month. Open Thurs–Tues; 415/357-4000; www.sfmoma.org.

**Wells Fargo History Museum** 420 Montgomery St btwn California and Sacramento Sts. Free: always. Open Mon–Fri; 415/396-2619; www.wellsfargohistory.com/museums.

**Yerba Buena Center for the Arts** 701 Mission St at 3rd St. Free: 1st Thurs of the month 11am–6pm. Open Tues–Sun; 415/978-2700; www.yerbabuenaarts.org.

**Musée Mécanique** 1090 Point Lobos Ave at the W end of Geary Blvd below the Cliff House Restaurant). Free: always. Open every day; 415/386-1170; www.musee mecanique.citysearch.com/.

to the music, citizens passed a bond measure to save it. Founded in 1911, the San Francisco Symphony quickly played its way into the hearts of locals and went on to capture kudos from critics and fans all over the world. It's since become one of the finest classical acts around, acclaimed for both its performances and its numerous Grammy Award–winning recordings. The distinguished list of music directors has included Henry Hadley, one of the top American composers of his era; Alfred Hertz, who led many important American premieres at the Metropolitan Opera; and Pierre Monteux, who introduced the world to *Le Sacre du Printemps*; as well as Josef Krips, Seiji Ozawa, and Herbert Blomstedt. Michael Tilson Thomas (also known as "MTT"), who took the helm in 1985, continues to lead the company into new and interesting terrain, with intensely eclectic programs that suit many tastes. A season schedule might include anything from a classic such as Prokofiev's *Romeo and Juliet* to Copland's *The Modernist*, with guest performers ranging from violinist

Itzhak Perlman to soprano Lisa Vroman and guest conductors such as Sir Georg Solti. Concerts at the technically topflight Louise M. Davies Symphony Hall are routinely packed, and the season opener each September is one of the city's biggest cultural fetes. Other highlights include the annual "Night in Old Vienna," a holiday-themed program of waltzes and operettas, and the Summer in the City pops series with such guest artists as Arlo Guthrie and Roberta Flack. The San Francisco Symphony Chorus, always a treat, performs several times a year. Community programs are another company focus, including performances in local schools, educational and outreach offerings for kids, the award-winning San Francisco Youth Symphony, frequent free open rehearsals, and occasional free outdoor concerts. In 1989, not long after the Loma Prieta earthquake rattled nerves around the bay, the symphony gave a gratis performance of Beethoven's Ninth Symphony in Golden Gate Park; 20,000 people turned out to reaffirm their civic pride. *www.sfsymphony. org; map:L4*

**THE WOMEN'S PHILHARMONIC / Yerba Buena Center for the Arts, 701 Mission St at 3rd St; 415/978-2787 (performances) or 415/437-0123 (information)** Founded in 1981 to help boost the representation of women in the classical music world, the Women's Philharmonic is now known the world over and is the winner of several national music awards. It has presented the work of more than 150 female composers, including 35 specially commissioned pieces. Artistic director and conductor Apo Hsu, an accomplished musician, has worked with an impressive list of artists, including Andre Watts, Gil Shaham, Sarah Chang, Tony Bennett, and Judy Collins. Programs usually feature newer works, with the occasional earlier composition by Amy Beach or Mabel Daniels. The season begins in October and continues through May. *www.womens phil.org; map:N3*

# Dance

San Francisco enjoys a vibrant and varied dance community that includes the world-famous San Francisco Ballet as well as some of the nation's foremost modern dance troupes. The city is also home to numerous wonderful smaller groups, including the **MARGARET JENKINS DANCE COMPANY** (415/826-8399), the **STEPHEN PELTON DANCE THEATER** (415/241-0111), and a variety of ethnic dance troupes ranging from Rosa Montoya's **ARGENTINIAN BAILES FLAMENCOS** (415/824-1960) to the **CHINESE FOLK DANCE ASSOCIATION** (415/834-1359).

**ETHNIC DANCE FESTIVAL / Palace of Fine Arts, 3301 Lyon St btwn Bay St and Richardson Ave; 415/474-3914** Presented annually by World

Arts West for more than 20 years, the Ethnic Dance Festival is now a highly anticipated San Francisco cultural event. In fact, it's so popular that the auditions, held in January, now draw nearly as many people as the June festival itself. The festival features dance and music from Africa, Latin America, China, Japan, India, Ireland, Eastern Europe, and many other countries. World Arts West also puts on educational programs for children, low-income groups, and seniors, including a great puppet theater show and a summer dance workshop. *www.worldartswest.org; map:J1*

**JOE GOODE PERFORMANCE GROUP / Yerba Buena Center for the Arts, 701 Mission St at 3rd St; 415/978-2787 (performances) or 415/646-4848 (information)** Quirky, whimsical, and athletic—that's Joe Goode, a true Bay Area treasure and one of the nation's most intriguing modern choreographers. The city has turned out en masse to see his ensemble present visually stunning works that are often multimedia performances, usually political, and always artistic and avant-garde. Headquartered in San Francisco since 1979, the Joe Goode Performance Group has also become a sensation on the road. A recent program, the critically acclaimed *Deeply There*, examined the unlikely relationships born within the shadow of the AIDS epidemic. The home season starts in June. *www.joegoode.org; map:N3*

**LAWRENCE PECH DANCE COMPANY / Yerba Buena Center for the Arts, 701 Mission St at 3rd St; 415/978-2787** Worldwide patrons of ballet know the name Lawrence Pech. He studied under Mikhail Baryshnikov and has worked with such illustrious choreographers as George Balanchine, Martha Graham, Twyla Tharp, and Jerome Robbins. Now based in San Francisco, Pech works outside the confines of traditional ballet; his namesake ensemble, founded in 1995, has quickly established itself as an innovative force in the dance world. Pech has choreographed and premiered more than a dozen original ballets; most are rooted in classical movement but have decidedly contemporary dramatic threads and scores. The two-part performance season usually takes place in the spring and fall. *www.lpdance.org; map:N3*

**LINES CONTEMPORARY BALLET / Yerba Buena Center for the Arts, 701 Mission St at 3rd St; 415/978-2787 (performances) or 415/863-3040 (information)** Alonzo King has a firm reputation as an innovator, challenging the conventions of traditional movement while crafting ballets that fall well within the framework of classical dance. He has created works for a wide range of companies, from the Dance Theater of Harlem to the Joffrey Ballet. In 1982 he established LINES Contemporary Ballet, a national touring company of 12 to 15 dancers, and turned it into an integral part of the national dance vernacular. He also helped transform the San Francisco Dance Center, the company's home, into one of the largest training facilities on the West Coast. King's work mines the rich quarries of classical music as well as traditional African music and avant-jazz—it's one of the most eclectic repertoires in modern dance. The home season begins in May. *www.linesballet.org; map:N3*

**ODC–SAN FRANCISCO / 3153 17th St at Shotwell St; 415/863-6606** Its high-flying acrobatics and extraordinary energy set this ensemble well apart from the pack. With a well-deserved international reputation, ODC is one of the country's top modern dance companies, fueled by the tireless creativity and commitment of its three resident choreographers, Brenda Way, K. T. Nelson, and Kimi Okada. Way, who trained in New York under George Balanchine, founded the company in 1971; it moved to San Francisco in 1976 and became one of the first established modern dance companies to flourish outside the Big Apple. ODC was also the nation's first modern dance company to establish its own resident facility, where it now houses a dance school, theater, and gallery. The group performs its impressive original and collaborative repertoire for about 50,000 people a year. Programs are presented in the namesake facility, but one of the company's biggest events is Dancing Downtown, held each spring at Yerba Buena Center for the Arts. Another popular ODC work is the holiday production of *The Velveteen Rabbit*. *www.odcdance.org; map:L6*

**ROBERT MOSES' KIN / Theatre Artaud, 450 Florida St at 17th St, and other venues; 415/621-7797 or 415/252-8384** An excellent dance ensemble, Robert Moses' Kin is one of a select few in the city that's rooted in the African-American aesthetic. Founded in 1995 to explore such issues as race, class, and gender through dance, the company features more than 30 original works by artistic director Robert Moses, who also collaborates with such artists as jazz composer Marcus Shelby and the a cappella ensemble SoVoSo. The pieces are complex and provocative. Most performances are held at Theatre Artaud in the Mission District or at Yerba Buena Center for the Arts. *www.robertmoseskin.org; map:M6*

**SAN FRANCISCO BALLET / 455 Franklin St at Fulton St; 415/865-2000 (performances) or 415/861-5600 (ticket and information)** Founded in 1933 as the San Francisco Opera Ballet, the city's ballet is the oldest, and now one of the three largest, professional ballet companies in the United States. It got off to an auspicious start by presenting America's first full-length productions of *Coppélia* and *Swan Lake*. And it wasn't long before the company, renamed the San Francisco Ballet, had established itself as a leading force in American dance. The ballet presented the national premiere of *The Nutcracker* in 1944, and in 1951, under artistic director Lew Christensen, the company began touring the world to international acclaim. In 1972 the ballet started staging its annual season in

San Francisco's War Memorial Opera House, where it still performs today. Not so long ago the company fell on hard times, teetering toward financial failure. San Franciscans, of course, would have none of that, and a grassroots effort called "Save Our Ballet" managed to bring the company back from the brink. Helgi Tomasson, the company's artistic director since 1985, has taken it to new heights. With a roster of 65 dancers, the company presents its home season (usually about six programs) from January to May. Its training program, the San Francisco Ballet School, annually draws some 300 students from far and wide to the company's $13.8 million facility; graduates are now dancing in some of the world's best ballet companies. *www.sfballet.org; map:L4*

**SMUIN BALLETS–SF / Yerba Buena Center for the Arts, 701 Mission St at 3rd St, and other venues; 415/665-2222** The company's namesake, Michael Smuin, is a former director of the San Francisco Ballet. Founded in 1994, this group quickly stirred the passions of local lovers of dance. Smuin, who has won a Tony Award and several Emmys, imbued his debut program, *Dances with Songs*, with languid, athletic movement and set it to the classic pop hits of Willie Nelson, Elvis Presley, and Nat King Cole. The following year he introduced the city to what would become its newest holiday tradition, *The Christmas Ballet*, a 180-degree departure from the traditional *Nutcracker* that includes a wild mix of traditional takes on J. S. Bach's *Magnificat* and obscure, whimsical pieces with titles like *Santa Got a DWI*. The group also premiered the world's first ballet set to mambo music, *Frankie and Johnny*. More recently it has taken to the road, performing in select U.S. cities. The home season starts in May; *The Christmas Ballet* is usually performed in early December. *Map:N3*

# Film

San Francisco is one big film festival. If locals aren't stumbling over each other to attend a first-run documentary or an international premiere, they're stumbling over cables strewn across sidewalks by movie crews filming on location. These days, of course, the Bay Area is also a haven for independent filmmakers shunning the trappings of Tinseltown. And while the mighty multiplex has definitely reared its head here, there are still a few single-screen holdouts. At the **UNITED ARTISTS VOGUE** (3290 Sacramento St at Presidio Ave; 415/221-8183; map:J3), an intimate movie house with a postage stamp–size lobby, you can see first-run pictures produced by its parent company. The **UNITED ARTISTS CORONET** (3575 Geary Blvd at Arguello Blvd; 415/752-4400; map:H3) may host a lot of blockbusters, but it's still a grand old stadium-style theater in the best moviegoing tradition. In the Marina District are two thriving throwbacks:

# THE BARBARY COAST

In 1849 San Francisco boomed as thousands of people headed west to find gold. What was once a small town of about 1,000 soon became an international port city of nearly 100,000. Those who came to find their fortunes were named forty-niners after the year they arrived (a few months after gold was discovered in the Sierra foothills). Most of the arrivals weren't what you'd call proper gentlemen, and with so many of these unsavory characters descending upon the city a district was soon formed to cater to their carousing. That area-where parts of the Embarcadero, Chinatown, and North Beach neighborhoods now exist-was called the Barbary Coast after the infamous region of the same name in North Africa.

The Barbary Coast remained the seedy nightlife epicenter of San Francisco for close to 70 years, evolving from the raucous haunts of miners and prostitutes to the more refined-yet still illegal-speakeasies of Prohibition. It was this underground legacy that drew the social misfits of the '50s-the Beats and their followers, the beatniks-to North Beach. While there are still some strip clubs along the main drag of Broadway, most of the area shows little sign of its bawdy past-unless you look closely.

Some of the bars in North Beach pay homage to the denizens of the Barbary Coast. Stop in at the **San Francisco Brewing Company** (155 Columbus Ave at Pacific St; 415/434-3344) and ask for an Emperor Norton brew, named after the self-proclaimed emperor whose eccentricities endeared him to San Franciscans. This microbrewery is housed in what is believed to be one of the last standing Barbary Coast saloons. Look down at the tiled trough running along the base of the bar, which once funneled off tobacco spit . . . and other liquids. (These troughs are present in some other area bars, but are usually covered with a wood plank.)

Other small glimpses of the past can be had at the **Saloon** (1232 Grant Ave at Columbus Ave; 415/989-7666), one of the oldest bars in the city. While mostly a local hangout, it's still a good place for visitors to stop for a drink and see what a Barbary Coast saloon looked like in its heyday (there's that trough again). Off Columbus Avenue near Broadway, down a tiny alley, you'll find **Specs' Twelve Adler Museum Cafe** (12 Saroyan Pl off Columbus Ave; 415/421-4112). Specs' has gone through many transformations since its inception as a bordello, and proudly displays artifacts of all its past lives-including a certain whale appendage. It may have been a century and a half ago, but it takes just a moment in one of these haunts to feel the presence of the revelers of the old Barbary Coast.

CINEMA 21 (2141 Chestnut St btwn Steiner and Pierce Sts; 415/921-6720; map:J1), with its balcony and enormous curved screen, and the PRESIDIO THEATER (2340 Chestnut St btwn Scott and Divisadero Sts; 415/922-1318; map:J1). In Pacific Heights, the CLAY (2261 Fillmore St at Clay St; 415/352-0810; map:K3), built in 1910, is the oldest continuously operating movie house in town and, together with smaller complexes such as the EMBARCADERO and OPERA PLAZA CINEMAS, is now owned by Landmark Theaters, the largest exhibitor of first-run international and art-house films in the country.

For a funkier repertory experience, the ROXIE (3117 16th St at Valencia St; 415/863-1087; map:L5) screens and distributes original works of all kinds, and it has one of the most eclectic lineups around. You never know what you'll find, but it's usually worth checking out—anything from a controversial documentary to the revival of Bruce Lee's *Enter the Dragon*. Another old chestnut is in the Mission District: the ornate 1908 VICTORIA THEATRE (2961 16th St at Mission St; 415/863-7576; map:M6), with orchestra, mezzanine, and balcony seating. And then there's the king of all the San Francisco movie palaces, the gorgeous 1922 Timothy Pflueger–designed CASTRO THEATRE (469 Castro St near Market St; 415/621-6120; map:K6)—as vital today as it ever was, screening everything from special revivals and director's cuts to touring art-house flicks. To get the full effect of this place, arrive well before showtime to hear the organist pump out a rousing rendition of "San Francisco, Open Your Golden Gate" on the vintage pipe organ. Of course the Haight-Ashbury district has its own funky film house called the RED VIC (1727 Haight St between Cole and Shrader Sts; 415/668-3994; www.redvicmoviehouse.com), a worker-owned movie collective that specializes in independent releases and contemporary cultish hits. For the really serious cinema hound, YERBA BUENA CENTER FOR THE ARTS (701 Mission St at 3rd St; 415/978-2787; www.yerbabuenaarts. org; map:N3) screens films geared to artistic, sociocultural, and academic perspectives—not snobbish symposia on dead French directors but curated series on such esoteric themes as bizarre violence or women in prison.

## FILM FESTIVALS

CINE ACCIÓN FESTIVAL / 346 9th St at Folsom St, 2nd fl, and other venues; 415/553-8140 For a few days in September San Francisco hosts one of the country's top celebrations of Latino cinema, highlighting full-length features, shorts, and other top-notch efforts from the United States, Latin America, and beyond. *www.cineaccion.com; map:N3*

FILM ARTS FOUNDATION FESTIVAL OF INDEPENDENT CINEMA / 346 9th St, 2nd fl, at Folsom St, and other venues; 415/552-8760 "Where independent film is still independent" is the motto of the Film Arts Foundation, and this event, held in November, lives up to the claim. It's a treasure trove of new, inventive, and locally grown cinema, presented by a nonprofit organization for Bay Area film- and video-makers. Since its inception the festival has launched such films as the Oscar-nominated *Complaints of a Dutiful Daughter*, *For Better or for Worse*, and *Waldo Salt*. Screenings are often held at the Roxie and Victoria theaters. The Film Arts Foundation of Independent Cinema also offers film- and video-related seminars and workshops, and an excellent magazine. *www.film arts.com; map:N3*

**SAN FRANCISCO ASIAN AMERICAN FILM FESTIVAL / 346 9th St, 2nd fl, at Folsom St, and other venues; 415/863-0814** Presented in early March by the National Asian American Telecommunications Association (NAATA), this event in the past 18 years has become the largest of its kind. More than 100 films and videos from more than a dozen countries are screened, from North America, the Pacific, and all Asian areas of the globe. Among the many works that have premiered here are the Academy Award–winning feature documentary *Maya Lin: A Strong Clear Vision*, Deepa Mehta's *Fire*, and Kayo Hatta's *Picture Bride*. Throughout the year, NAATA also presents several sneak previews, including local premieres of films such as *Shanghai Triad*, *The Wedding Banquet*, and *Farewell My Concubine*. *www.naatanet.org/festival; map:N3*

**SAN FRANCISCO INTERNATIONAL FILM FESTIVAL / 1521 Eddy St at Fillmore St, and other venues; 415/561-5000** This 43-year-old salute to cinema, presented by the prestigious San Francisco Film Society each April and May at the Kabuki, the Castro, and other Bay Area locations, is one of the best on the film-festival circuit. The opening gala is a star-studded event, bringing out such locally based luminaries as Sean Penn, Francis Ford Coppola, and Nicolas Cage, as well as Steven Spielberg or any other industry bigwigs who happen to be in town. Featured are new films by both well-known and up-and-coming filmmakers from around the world. The enormous list of works that have debuted here includes *A Hard Day's Night*, *Gigi*, and *Scarface*. Special screenings of Bay Area–made films are a regular highlight and have unearthed such gems as *Regret to Inform*, an Oscar-nominated Vietnam documentary by Barbara Sonneborn. Each event features special tributes to actors and directors, many of whom accept the honor in person and discuss their work. *www.sfiff.org; map:K4*

**SAN FRANCISCO INTERNATIONAL GAY & LESBIAN FILM FESTIVAL / 346 9th St, 2nd fl, at Folsom St, and other venues; 415/703-8650** The world's oldest, largest, and best festival of its kind celebrated its 24th year in 2000. Each year it screens more than 200 films, videos, and documentaries at the Castro, Roxie, and Victoria theaters. The event is one of the most talked about in the city; selections shown here often win national and international acclaim. Notable films from previous festivals included Jim Fall's hit comedy *Trick* and the U.S. premiere of the Swedish lesbian love story *Show Me Love*. Special appearances by directors and stars are always part of the fun. The festival promotes environmentally friendly modes of transportation and even offers valet-parking services for your bicycle if you ride it to a screening. *www.frameline.org; map:N3*

**SAN FRANCISCO JEWISH FILM FESTIVAL / 346 9th St, 2nd fl, at Folsom St, and other venues; 415/621-0556** Each July and August in the Bay Area the San Francisco Jewish Film Festival screens a diverse range of films that address the subjects of Jewish identity and history—some but not all of them by Jewish filmmakers. At about 20 years old, it's the longest-running celebration of Semitic cinema in the country. A typical lineup includes approximately 40 works, from Russian- and German-language films to heartrending documentaries to French features such as *Mina Tannenbaum. www.sfjff.org; map:N3*

# Literature

There's much more to San Francisco's literary legacy than Danielle Steel. This is a decidedly writerly town, home to scribblers famous and unknown, highbrow, lowbrow, and everything in between. *Maltese Falcon* author Dashiell Hammett, who wrote most of his grittier mysteries here, put the city on the book lover's map when he placed Sam Spade's Continental Detective Agency in the Flood Building on Market Street (where Hammett worked a part-time day job at Pinkerton's Detective Agency in real life). The city returned the favor by naming a street after him—an honor it also bestowed on many other literary native sons and daughters. Cruising the city's streets you'll come across signs bearing the names of Jack London, Mark Twain, Ambrose Bierce, Frank Norris, William Saroyan, and, of course, Kerouac and Ferlinghetti of Beat Generation and **CITY LIGHTS BOOKSTORE** fame. The bookstore lives on in North Beach, as do former Beat hangouts like Vesuvio Cafe.

The bohemian trappings have changed, but today's San Francisco is still home to author readings, signings, and literary happenings galore. Several cafes hold scheduled or spontaneous poetry slams, and you'll find a full literary lineup at all the major (and most smaller) chain and independent bookstores in town, including **STACEY'S** (581 Market St at 2nd St; 415/421-4687; map:N3), the city's largest independent bookstore; the **BOOKSMITH** (1644 Haight St between Clayton and Cole Sts; 415/863-8688; map:I5) in the Haight-Ashbury neighborhood; and **MODERN TIMES BOOKSTORE** (888 Valencia St btwn 19th and 20th Sts; 415/282-9246; map:L6) in the Mission District, which showcases local, socially conscious writers and young poets from California schools. And once a year, you can get it all in one place: Every July the Northern California Independent Booksellers Association (415/927-3937) presents **BOOKS BY THE BAY**, an outdoor festival with publishers' booths, author readings and signings, poetry fests, and activities for kids. Year-round, here's where to look for other literary events.

**CITY ARTS & LECTURES / Herbst Theatre, 401 Van Ness Ave at McAllister St; 415/392-4400** Discussing everything from literature and criticism to science and performing arts, stellar intellects conduct enlightened conversations and monologues on the Herbst Theatre stage. Recent guests have included Jane Smiley, Stephen King, Jamaica Kincaid, Saul Bellow, and Richard Price—all in the span of a month. Many programs benefit nonprofits such as the California Academy of Sciences, Friends of the San Francisco Public Library, and California Poets in the Schools. *Map:L4*

**CITY LIGHTS BOOKSTORE / 261 Columbus Ave at Broadway; 415/362-8193** The Beat goes on here, with poet-proprietor Lawrence Ferlinghetti still leading the charge. In the '50s Ferlinghetti started a small press at this Columbus Avenue address to publish the works of comrades Allen  Ginsberg, Jack Kerouac, and others. Today the shop has virtually everything ever written by those folks, along with an incredibly large selection of poetry and local writers' works. While you're not likely to stumble across any impromptu *Howl*s, the store holds occasional signings and readings and is probably the best-known and best-loved bookstore in town. *www.citylights.com; map:N2*

**A CLEAN WELL-LIGHTED PLACE FOR BOOKS / 601 Van Ness Ave at Golden Gate St; 415/441-6670** A favorite writers' hangout, this bookstore has shelf after shelf of literary journals, plus excellent fiction and nonfiction sections; many of the featured authors appear for book signings and discussions. *www.bookstore.com; map:L4*

**A DIFFERENT LIGHT BOOKSTORE / 489 Castro St btwn Market and 18th Sts; 415/431-0891** The inventory here is entirely "by, about, or of interest to" gays and lesbians, the proprietors say. The small shop, run by a friendly staff, has a patio with a garden where readings are held. *www.adlbooks.com; map:K6*

# NIGHTLIFE

# Nightlife by Feature

**ALTERNATIVE**
Bottom of the Hill
Cafe du Nord
The Cat Club
Elbo Room
The Fillmore
Great American Music
  Hall
Make-Out Room
Paradise Lounge
Slim's
Warfield Theatre

**BLUES**
Bimbo's 365 Club
Biscuits & Blues
Blue Lamp
The Fillmore
Grant & Green Blues Club
Great American Music
  Hall
John Lee Hooker's Boom
  Boom Room
Lou's Pier 47
Pier 23 Cafe
San Francisco Brewing
  Company
Storyville
Warfield Theatre

**COCKTAIL LOUNGES**
Backflip
Bimbo's 365 Club
Bix
Bubble Lounge
Cafe du Nord
Cafe Mars
Club Deluxe
15 Romolo
Hi-Ball Lounge
Julie's Supper Club
Marina Lounge
Martuni's
Royal Oak
Tosca Cafe

**COMEDY**
Cobb's Comedy Club
Punchline Comedy Club

**DANCING/
  DANCE FLOORS**
Backflip
Bimbo's 365 Club

Bottom of the Hill
The Cafe
Cafe du Nord
The Cat Club
Club Deluxe
Elbo Room
The End Up
Fiddler's Green
The Fillmore
Grant & Green
Great American Music
  Hall
Hi-Ball Lounge
John Lee Hooker's Boom
  Boom Room
Make-Out Room
Nickie's BBQ
Paradise Lounge
Pier 23 Cafe
Slim's
Sound Factory
Storyville
The Stud
1015 Folsom
The Top
Warfield Theatre

**DIVE BARS**
Li Po
Specs' Twelve Adler
  Museum Cafe

**DRINKS WITH A VIEW**
Buena Vista Cafe
Pier 23 Cafe

**FOLK/ACOUSTIC**
Caffe Trieste
Fiddler's Green
Paradise Lounge

**GAY/LESBIAN BARS**
The Cafe
The Eagle Tavern
The End Up
Lexington Club
Martuni's
The Stud
Twin Peaks Tavern

**IRISH/CELTIC**
Fiddler's Green
Harrington's Bar and Grill
O'Reilly's Irish Bar

**JAZZ**
Bimbo's 365 Club
Bix
Blue Bar
Cafe du Nord
Club Deluxe
Elbo Room
Enrico's
Gold Dust
Jazz at Pearl's Restaurant
  & Bar
Rasselas Jazz Club and
  Ethiopian Cuisine
San Francisco Brewing
  Company
Storyville
Up & Down Club

**OUTDOOR SEATING**
Backflip
Blondie's Bar & No Grill
Bottom of the Hill
The Cafe
Cafe Mars
The Eagle Tavern
The End Up
Enrico's Sidewalk Cafe
Fiddler's Green
Harrington's Bar and Grill
O'Reilly's Irish Bar
Pier 23 Cafe
San Francisco Brewing
  Company

**PIANO BARS**
Gold Dust
Lone Palm
Martuni's

**POOL TABLES/
  BILLIARDS**
Blondie's Bar & No Grill
Blue Lamp
Bus Stop
Cafe du Nord
Cafe Mars
Chalkers Billiard Club
Crow Bar
The Eagle Tavern
Elbo Room
The End Up
Fiddler's Green
Greens Sports Bar
Marina Lounge

Nickie's BBQ
Paradise Lounge
Sound Factory
The Stud
The Top

**PUBS/ALE HOUSES**
Fiddler's Green
Harrington's Bar and Grill
O'Reilly's Irish Bar
San Francisco Brewing
    Company
Toronado

**REGGAE/SKA/
    WORLDBEAT**
Elbo Room
The End Up
Great American Music
    Hall
Nickie's BBQ
Paradise Lounge
Pier 23 Cafe
Warfield Theatre

**ROCK**
Bimbo's 365 Club
Blue Lamp
Bottom of the Hill
Cafe du Nord
Elbo Room
The Fillmore
Grant & Green Blues Club
Great American Music
    Hall
Make-Out Room
Paradise Lounge
Pier 23 Cafe
Slim's
Warfield Theatre

**ROMANTIC**
Bimbo's 365 Club
Enrico's
Hayes and Vine Wine Bar
Jazz at Pearl's Restaurant
    & Bar
Lone Palm
Martuni's
Rasselas Jazz Club and
    Ethiopian Cuisine

Tosca Cafe

**SPORTS BARS**
Bayside Sports Bar and
    Grill
Bus Stop
Greens Sports Bar

**SWING**
Bimbo's 365 Club
Cafe du Nord
Club Deluxe
Hi-Ball Lounge

**UNDERAGE/NO
    ALCOHOL**
Cobb's Comedy Club
The Fillmore
Great American Music
    Hall
Punchline Comedy Club
Slim's
Warfield Theatre

# Nightlife by Neighborhood

**CASTRO**
The Cafe
Cafe du Nord
Cafe Flore
Twin Peaks Tavern

**CHINATOWN**
Li Po

**FINANCIAL DISTRICT**
Bix
Harrington's Bar and Grill
London Wine Bar
Pier 23 Cafe
Punchline Comedy Club

**FISHERMAN'S WHARF**
Buena Vista Cafe
Cobb's Comedy Club
Lou's Pier 47

**LOWER HAIGHT**
Nickie's BBQ
Storyville
The Top
Toronado

**UPPER HAIGHT**
Club Deluxe

**HAYES VALLEY**
Hayes and Vine Wine Bar

**MARINA/COW HOLLOW**
Balboa Cafe
Bayside Sports Bar and
    Grill
Bus Stop
Comet Club
Marina Lounge

**MISSION DISTRICT**
Alfred Schilling
    Restaurant, Chocolate,
    and Pastry
Beauty Bar
Blondie's
Dalva
Elbo Room
Lexington Club
Lone Palm
Make-Out Room
Martuni's
Muddy Waters Coffee
    House

**NOB HILL**
Skylark

**NORTH BEACH**
Bimbo's 365 Club
Blue Bar
Bubble Lounge
Caffe Greco
Caffe Puccini
Caffe Trieste
Crow Bar
Enrico's
Fiddler's Green
15 Romolo
Finocchio's
Grant & Green
Hi-Ball Lounge
Jazz at Pearl's Restaurant &
    Bar
The North End
O'Reilly's Irish Bar
San Francisco Brewing
    Company
Specs' Twelve Adler
    Museum Cafe
Steps of Rome
Tosca Cafe
Vesuvio Cafe
Zero Degrees

## PACIFIC HEIGHTS
The Fillmore
John Lee Hooker's Boom
  Boom Room
Rasselas Jazz Club and
  Ethiopian Cuisine

## POTRERO HILL
Bottom of the Hill

## THE RICHMOND
Joe's Ice Cream
Toy Boat Dessert Cafe
Trad'r Sam

## RUSSIAN HILL
Greens Sports Bar
Royal Oak

## SOUTH OF MARKET
  (SOMA)
Cafe Mars
The Cat Club
Chalkers Billiard Club
The Eagle Tavern
The End Up
Julie's Supper Club
Paradise Lounge
Slim's
Sound Factory

The Stud
1015 Folsom
Up & Down Club

## TENDERLOIN
Backflip
Blue Lamp
Great American Music
  Hall

## UNION SQUARE AND
  DOWNTOWN
Biscuits & Blues
Gold Dust
Warfield Theatre

# NIGHTLIFE

## Music and Clubs

Because San Francisco is such a cosmopolitan city, a lot of the club trends surface here before the rest of the country (well, aside from New York) gets wind of them. Recently the sound reverberating through many of the hottest clubs was "drum and bass," but who knows when the next wave is going to hit? Most of the dance clubs are in the South of Market area (that's SoMa for you out-of-towners) and in the Mission District. But don't be surprised if you walk into a club that someone told you was just your kind of scene only to find it's completely not. Most clubs change the style of the party every night. For example, a club might be gay on Thursday, a rave on Friday, techno on Saturday . . . well, you get the point. If there's a particular club you're set on visiting, call first and find out what's doing that night.

For more information on what's going on in the city, you can also check the entertainment listings in the tabloid-size **SAN FRANCISCO BAY GUARDIAN** or **SF WEEKLY**. Both are free weeklies that come out every Wednesday and can be found all over the city in newspaper racks or coffeehouses. Two good online resources are **SAN FRANCISCO CITYSEARCH** (www.bayarea.citysearch.com) and **WWW.SFSTATION.COM** (click on "clubs"). For even more up-to-the-minute info you just can't get in the papers, call the **BE-AT LINE** (415/626-4087) and listen to a recording of daily updates on the hip-hop, house, and acid jazz scenes; **HOUSEWARES** (415/281-0125) for the rave and techno action; or the **CLUB LINE** (415/339-8686; www.sfclubs.com) for the more mainstream dance clubs. The following is a list of venues and clubs that will most likely be around for your next night on the town, but definitely phone before you go to make sure.

**BACKFLIP / 601 Eddy St at Larkin St; 415/771-3547** The Phoenix Hotel houses this ultracool aqua-blue cocktail lounge that's supposed to resemble a swimming pool, complete with a deep end (a few shots of the hard stuff helps the illusion—though there *is* a pool off the courtyard). In the middle of the seedy Tenderloin neighborhood, it's an oasis of trendy nightlife. On weekends the hiply dressed crowd of twentysomethings waits in line to drink and pseudo-dance (it's too crowded to let loose) to anything from ambient to techno music spun by an international set of visiting DJs. There is a menu of "small plates" of cocktail-type food. On a rare warm night you'll want to sit out by the real pool, which was designed by Andy Warhol. *AE, MC, V; no checks; open Tues–Sun; full bar; map:M4*

# THE SCENES OF SAN FRANCISCO

For a relatively small city (46 square miles), San Francisco is jam-packed with cool places to go and entertaining things to do. No matter what kind of action you're in the mood for, chances are you'll find it here. Following are general descriptions of some city neighborhoods and the kind of vibe you're likely to encounter there when the sun goes down:

**North Beach:** Something for everyone. Late-night cafes with outdoor seating, live music and dancing, cool old joints and hip new bars.

**Mission District:** (Valencia Street): Young hipsters and poseurs, trendy but cool bars, and music spots in a not-quite-safe neighborhood. Gay, straight, and whatever mix it up.

**Upper Haight:** (close to Golden Gate Park): Young, alternative, and hip crowd mixed in with some old hippies and young runaways on the street.

**Lower Haight:** (away from Golden Gate Park): Young, edgy crowd in bars and dance spots in a somewhat dicey area.

**Castro:** Some of the world's best gay bars and hangouts.

**South of Market (SoMa):** Live music and dance club mecca in an industrial-type area. A mostly young crowd. Not entirely safe, but OK on weekend nights.

**The Marina and Cow Hollow:** Young urbanites and the trendy postcollegiate set party hard in the many bars on Union and Chestnut Streets.

**Pacific Heights:** One of the more affluent neighborhoods, quiet but fun local bars, a couple of jazz clubs, and some sidewalk cafes for young and old alike.

**Hayes Valley:** Chic shops, restaurants, and wine bars in a working-class neighborhood. Getting trendier by the day.

**Union Square and Downtown:** Tourist central. The theaters and shops keep people coming to this area even though it borders on a seriously seedy part of town called the Tenderloin. A few cool old-school bars make the surroundings tolerable.

**Yerba Buena:** A hopping cultural center by day, but at night there isn't much besides chain restaurants catering to a conventioneer crowd.

**Financial District:** After-work business types belly up to one of the many bars for a few drinks before going home or on to another area. For the most part, very quiet after about 9pm.

**Chinatown:** Dive bars and late-night Chinese restaurants abound.

**Fisherman's Wharf:** Touristy, mostly chain-type sports bars, though there are a few places worth checking out, such as Ana Mandara or Lou's Pier 47.

**Russian Hill (Polk Street):** Young to middle-aged mellow crowd hangs at the neighborhood bars.

**Nob Hill:** Big hotels house some fancy, expensive bars with great views in this quiet area.

**BIMBO'S 365 CLUB / 1025 Columbus Ave at Chestnut St; 415/474-0365**
No, this isn't a great place to pick up empty-headed, silicone-implanted
babes. Bimbo's has been owned by the same family since it opened in
1931 and is named after the family patriarch. Through the years and
ever-changing styles this wonderful North Beach club has kept its swanky
interior intact, including the tiers of red vinyl booths and oodles of velvet
(think Lucy and Ricky). The naughty paintings of large-busted mermaids
and the nude girl riding the giant goldfish on your cocktail napkin remind
you of a simpler, less politically correct time. The powder room attendant
makes even a 21st-century woman feel like Holly Golightly. The kind of
crowd varies with the live entertainment for the evening, and that could
be anything—country, rock, jazz, R&B—you name it. Call for the
schedule. *cash only; dates depend on shows; full bar; www.bimbos365
club.com; map:M1*

**BISCUITS & BLUES / 401 Mason St at Geary St; 415/292-2583** Just off
Union Square you'll find this underground supper club serving good
Southern food and live blues. Some of the best local and national blues
players perform here nightly. Chances are whatever night you come,
you're in for a good show. The candlelit tables and the New
Orleans–speakeasy theme set the mood. When things get cooking here it
gets loud and conversations stop, so order up some fried chicken and
tasty biscuits (of course), sit back, and groove. Tip: Their happy hour
deal (Monday through Friday from 5pm to 7pm) includes drink specials,
cheap apps, recorded blues, and no cover charge. *AE, MC, V; no checks;
open every day; full bar; map:M3*

**BLUE BAR / 501 Broadway at Kearny St; 415/981-2233** Downstairs
from Reed Hearon's Black Cat Restaurant is a dark, cozy little jazz club.
The plush decor of crushed velvet and a blue backlit bar make this a
swanky stop for the "in" 30- to 40-something crowd. North Beach used
to be famous for its jazz; the music scene is now having a renaissance with
new clubs opening all over. The Blue Bar even hosts some jazz and poetry
nights (Jack Kerouac's rolling in his grave). You can order from the club
menu (a shortened version of the restaurant's pricey offerings) until 1am.
*AE, MC, V; no checks; open every day; full bar; map:N2*

**BLUE LAMP / 561 Geary St at Jones St; 415/885-1464** It's small, dark,
and dusty and it's covered in red-velvet-flocked wallpaper—how much
cooler can a place get? It also has a great bar, a pool table, and a foosball
table, and it rocks every night with loud live music. The neighborhood is
a weird mix of the Tenderloin homeless and hoity-toity theatergoers, but
once you're inside the bar, the crowd is mostly music-and-beer-loving
locals. Weekends are usually for rock bands, with a special blues jam session on Sundays. *cash only; open every day; full bar; map:M3*

**BOTTOM OF THE HILL / 1233 17th St at Missouri St; 415/621-4455** This Potrero Hill live music venue is out of the way but worth the trip. There's not much else out in these parts, but once you get into the club for a good night of local indie music there's no reason to leave. Aside from the occasional aging rocker such as Joan Jett, you've probably never heard of the bands that play here—it's a small place, and once a band makes it big it moves on to larger clubs, so this is a great opportunity to listen to the newest cutting-edge music. There's an outside patio area to get a breath of fresh air and give your ears a rest, as well as a pool table. Most Sundays from 4pm to 7pm there's an incredibly cheap all-you-can-eat barbecue with live music included. *MC, V; no checks; open every day; full bar; www.bottomofthehill.com; map:O6*

**THE CAFE / 2367 Market St at Castro St; 415/861-3846** This Castro-area gay and lesbian dance club is all about having a good time. There's no cover, and the place gets packed and sweaty as the mostly young, hip crowd shimmies their booties off to the extremely danceable sounds of techno, house, '80s, and disco. There's a patio outside to take a breather and a few tables near the back. Earlier in the evening locals come by for a more mellow scene of beer drinking and pool playing. But when the music starts the party begins, and goes on and on until last call. Even then the fun continues with everybody spilling out into the street, where the pickup scene is at its spiciest. *cash only; open every day; full bar; map:K6*

**CAFE DU NORD / 2170 Market St btwn Church and Sanchez Sts; 415/861-5016** When you know you're in a club that used to be a speakeasy, it just makes you feel a little naughtier. Cafe du Nord has been a hot spot for a few years now, attracting a young, hip crowd to this old-world-cozy yet slightly lurid club. The place does serve dinner, but most of the people are here for the nightlife. The front area consists of a beautiful, long carved-wood bar and a dining room where the club patrons chill in intimate alcoves when dinner hours are through. The back room is the cabaret area, where musicians play swing, rock, pop, soul, R&B, jazz, salsa, and the occasional experimental to a packed house. Tip: On Sunday evenings there are usually free dance lessons. *AE, DC, MC, V; no checks; open every day; full bar; www.cafedunord.com; map:K6*

**THE CAT CLUB / 1190 Folsom St at 8th St; 415/431-3332** The Cat Club caters to a mixed crowd, and everyone's welcome here regardless of sexual (or any other) orientation. There are two dance floors; DJs spinning from up above the masses turn up anything from techno to funk. The Cat Club's most famous night is Bondage à Go-Go, a leather-and-latex, ravelike, whip-and-chain fetish fest held every Wednesday night from 9pm to 3am that even the bridge-and-tunnel crowd can appreciate (that is, it won't have you cringing unless you're a major prude or scar easily). In fact, if you don't dress the part you'll be charged extra to get in. *AE, MC, V; no checks; open every day; full bar; map:N4*

**CHALKERS BILLIARD CLUB / One Rincon Center, 101 Spear St at Mission St; 415/512-0450** Chalkers is the city's snazziest pool hall, a cross between a men's smoking club and a big ol' billiards joint. Both pool sharks and hapless hipsters play it cool among the 27 gleaming pool and snooker tables, so don't sweat it if you suck. Unlike most pool joints, there's a full bar here, as well as an American Grill menu and tableside service. There's also a pro shop featuring 200 custom cues, along with cue lockers, private and group lessons, billiards books, videos, clothing, and accessories. And this being California, there's even a nonsmoking playing area. On weekdays Chalkers offers a happy hour from 5pm to 7pm. Note: Only those 21 and older are allowed inside. *AE, DC, DISC, MC, V; no checks; open every day; full bar; www.chalkers.com; map:O2*

**CLUB DELUXE / 1511 Haight St at Ashbury St; 415/552-6949** Many people say the '90s cocktail-lounge craze started here at the Deluxe. It sounds right when you first walk up to the silver metal exterior and through that art deco door. It hits home even harder when you hear owner Jay Johnson crooning away in his special tribute to the Chairman himself on Frank Sinatra Night. This small Haight Street bar gets packed every weekend, with swingers and their dolls at every table and lining the bar in their slick duds. During the week it's still popular but a little mellower. The only drawback: There's no space to really dance to the hot tunes of the live bands. Oh well, just throw back another Manhattan and tap those toes to the swingin' beat. *cash only; open every day; full bar; map:I5*

**COBB'S COMEDY CLUB / The Cannery, 2801 Leavenworth St at Beach St; 415/928-4320** Housed in the Cannery building near Fisherman's Wharf, Cobb's features mostly mainstream comedians and the occasional national headliner such as Jake Johannsen and Pam Stone. With its wharf location, it caters to a largely tourist crowd; ergo, the comics usually make jokes about different nationalities and San Franciscans. A comedy show is featured every night, including a 15-comedian, three-hour marathon, All-Pro Monday showcase. The place is windowless yet intimate, and when a good comedian is onstage that intimacy can really work (hence all the couples on first and second dates). Tip: If you don't want to get picked on by the comic, sit in the back. There's a two-drink minimum per person and some bar-type food available (chicken wings and the like), and it's open to those 18 and over (and occasionally to kids 16 and 17 if they are accompanied by a parent or legal guardian, but call ahead first). Cajun-Creole food is served from adjoining Belle Roux

Louisiana Kitchen (415/771-5225), and they even offer validated parking. *MC, V; no checks; open every day; full bar; www.cobbs comedy.com; map:M1*

**ELBO ROOM / 647 Valencia St btwn 17th and 18th Sts; 415/552-7788** This bohemian joint in the Mission houses a comfortable bar with pool tables, a jukebox downstairs, and a kind of rec-room-live-music bar upstairs. It's purposely dim and moody and caters to a young, casual crowd. The live music ranges from jazz to hip-hop to funk. Both the upstairs and downstairs bars have some good beers and pour a strong drink. Check out the photo booth and get a few snaps of yourself and a buddy. *cash only; open every day; full bar; www.elbo.com; map:L6*

**THE END UP / 401 6th St at Harrison St; 415/357-0827** This hard-core club is mainly for the after-hours set and not for the faint of heart. The DJ music scene changes nightly but mostly caters to the gay club crowd. On Mondays and Wednesdays the End Up houses Club Dread, a mellow reggae club; on Thursdays it's the Kit Kat Club, a swinging singles mecca;  Fag Friday draws hundreds of muscular young men; and on Saturdays the lesbian crowd takes over for G-Spot. On Sunday at about 5:30am gay clubbers come from all the other late-night spots to "end up" at the Sunday T Dance, which lasts until 2 Monday morning. Needless to say, the crowd here looks like the slightly warmed-over living dead at certain times, but there's no shortage of interesting people-watching. *cash only; open every day; full bar; www.theendup.com; map:N4*

**FIDDLER'S GREEN / 1333 Columbus Ave at Beach St; 415/441-9758** This Irish pub in the wharf area on the outskirts of North Beach is of two minds. There's the downstairs bar where most of the crowd is throwing back pints and listening to a guitar player sing Irish folk songs and U2 covers, and then there's the upstairs bar, which packs in a crowd of European tourists and a few locals dancing to the DJs spinning Euro-cool rave and house tunes. It's a young bunch upstairs, especially in summer when the college kids come over with their student visas. Downstairs is a mixed bag, where the locals grudgingly share the bar with the lowly tourists and by the end of the night everyone has become friends. Ah, the power of a few pints of Guinness. Fiddler's also sports a great pub menu. *MC, V; no checks; open every day; full bar; map:N2*

**THE FILLMORE / 1805 Geary Blvd at Fillmore St; 415/346-6000** The historic Fillmore started out its life as a dance hall in the early 1900s but became world famous when promoter Bill Graham turned the space into the epicenter of live music concerts in the late '60s. Jimi Hendrix, Janis Joplin, the Grateful Dead, and every other important band of that era played here at one time or another. The Fillmore still hosts most of the big-name acts that come into the city, and even though the capacity is about 1,000, it feels intimate when you go to a show. Check out the poster room upstairs for a psychedelic journey through the days of flower power. On your way out grab a free apple, a tradition started by Graham in the '60s that survives to this day. *AE, MC, V; call for show dates; full bar; www.thefillmore.com; map:K3*

**GRANT & GREEN BLUES CLUB / 1371 Grant Ave at Green St; 415/693-9565** This medium-size joint in the heart of North Beach presents local blues acts every night. The dress and attitude are casual, and the crowd is a strange mix of cool locals, red-nosed old-timers, and the occasional overdressed couple from the burbs. The blues bands rock *loudly*, and the noise reverberating down the block is what draws all these different types in—it just sounds like there's too much fun going on in there. Tip: If you don't like the band here, walk down the street to the Saloon (1232 Grant Ave at Columbus Ave; 415/989-7666), a classic North Beach dive that claims to be the oldest bar in the city and hosts live blues band nightly. *cash only; open every day; full bar; map:N2*

**GREAT AMERICAN MUSIC HALL / 859 O'Farrell St btwn Polk and Larkin Sts; 415/885-0750** This ornate Victorian beauty housed a bordello and restaurant in the early 1900s. Now it's a live music venue, and fortunately no one ever tried to change the decor over the years. You can't help but marvel at the marble columns holding up the massive balcony below the elaborately frescoed ceiling. It's one of the coolest San Francisco experiences to sit and listen to some band that you really dig in the middle of this amazing old building where the city's finest illicit night-lifers once reigned. But besides being a historic treasure, it also books some great music acts running the gamut from alternative to rock to country. *MC, V; no checks; open every day; full bar; www.musichallsf.com; map:L3*

**HI-BALL LOUNGE / 473 Broadway btwn Kearny and Montgomery Sts; 415/397-9464** When you look up *retro* in the dictionary, the caption should read "see Hi-Ball Lounge." It's a small space but smartly arranged, with comfy red banquettes lining the walls and intimate tables in between. There's a small dance floor in front of a red-velvet-draped stage where local and visiting bands play to the young swingers nightly. Some nights the dancers are out-of-control hot, but most of the time you won't feel too stupid joining them. There are lessons early in the evening on certain nights; call to find out when. There's a dress code, so don't arrive wearing a baseball cap, tennis shoes, T-shirt, or ripped jeans. *MC, V; no checks; open every day; full bar; www.hiball.com; map:N2*

**JAZZ AT PEARL'S RESTAURANT & BAR / 256 Columbus Ave at Broadway; 415/291-8255** Pearl's is an elegant, old-time North Beach jazz club with exposed brick walls hung with old pictures of jazz legends. This is the place to go in San Francisco to hear the local talent, which plays

**319**

every night of the week. The intimate tables are a great place for couples to gaze into each other's eyes. While there is no cover, there's a two-drink minimum, and the bar specializes in froufrou-type drinks. *AE, MC, V; no checks; open every day (call for Sun); full bar; map:N2*

**JOHN LEE HOOKER'S BOOM BOOM ROOM / 1601 Fillmore St at Geary Blvd; 415/673-8000** The now-deceased John Lee Hooker bought this neighborhood hangout a couple of years back and renovated it into one of the best blues clubs in the city. When a big-name act plays here—such as the Rolling Stones, who showed up for an unannounced jam session—it can get cramped and steamy, just like a blues club should. It's a great place to grab a few drinks before a show at the Fillmore (see review), then come back after a show lets out early. The neighborhood isn't the city's finest, so be sure to park at the underground lot across the street. *cash only; open every day; full bar; www.boomboomblues.com; map:K3*

**LOU'S PIER 47 / 300 Jefferson St at Jones St; 415/771-5687** Lou's Fisherman's Wharf location draws in the tourists, who are lured here by the blues bands that blast away upstairs (you can hear them down the block) all night long. It's a New Orleans–style joint, with a so-so seafood restaurant downstairs (with sidewalk seating) and an open-air blues club upstairs. While no self-respecting local would admit to ever coming here, everyone always seems to be having a great time dancing and drinking until the wee hours (of course, most everyone here is on vacation). There's no cover for the first band, which plays nightly from 4pm to 8pm, but when the second band plugs in at 9pm it'll cost you at least $5. *AE, MC, V; no checks; open every day; full bar; map:M1*

**MAKE-OUT ROOM / 3225 22nd St btwn Mission and Valencia Sts; 415/647-2888** Right now this Mission District spot is a hipster haven, but by the time you finish reading this sentence who knows what it will be. Either way it's a cool dive with an even cooler name, although there's not as much spit-swapping as you'd expect with that moniker. It's basically a large room with a huge oak bar and a couple of booths, decorated with some deer heads. Local indie bands play on the small stage a couple of times a month, and it can get crowded on weekends. *cash only; open every day; full bar; map:L6*

**NICKIE'S BBQ / 460 Haight St btwn Fillmore and Webster Sts; 415/621-6508** If you like your dance clubs small, intimate, and sweaty, then Nickie's is your place. A young crowd of every ilk and lifestyle comes to this Lower Haight club to get down, and man, do they ever. The small dance area is packed every night, and each night is a different DJ scene, from Grateful Dead Jam early in the week warming up to high-energy funk and old-school disco by the weekend. Note: Be careful when coming

## SAN FRANCISCO'S SWANKIEST HOTEL BARS

Hotel bars aren't just for tourists anymore. Many of the nicer ones are frequented by locals who come for the great view, some campy fun, or just a stiff drink and good music. If that's what you're looking for, be sure to check out these choice hotel bars:

**Harry Denton's Starlight Room** (450 Powell St at Sutter St; 415/395-8595) on the 21st floor of the Sir Francis Drake Hotel. The superswanky retro-style penthouse lounge atop this Union Square hotel is run by San Francisco's ultimate party maker. A mixed crowd of snappily dressed young and old enjoy the velvet booths and great bands performing big band and swing. Bring cash for the cover.

**The Red Room** (827 Sutter St at Jones St; 415/346-7666) in the Commodore Hotel. Although not the hot spot it was a couple of years ago, this no-other-color-but-ruby-red lounge is still a sight to see. A crowd of 20- to 30-something hipsters hangs out here sipping kick-yo-butt Cosmos, but tourists are always popping in for a look at the David Lynch–esque interior.

**The Redwood Room** (495 Geary St at Taylor St; 415/775-4700) in the Clift Hotel. Previously one of the city's most beloved classic piano bars, the Redwood Room is now a modern interpretation of itself (sans the piano and old-world class) since famed hotelier Ian Schrager took over the reins. Despite the too-trendy atmosphere, the room's claim to fame—the beautifully paneled interior allegedly created from a single, enormous, 2,000-year-old redwood tree—is still a stunning backdrop for a classic cocktail.

**Tonga Room** (950 Mason St at California St; 415/772-5278) in the Fairmont Hotel. Tiki mania is the theme in this ultracampy Polynesian lounge. Have a tropical drink (try the Scorpion) and a huge plate of appetizers while listening to the island music. Be prepared for stormy weather—the indoor fountain shoots jets of water periodically.

**XYZ** (181 3rd St at Howard St; 415/777-5300) in the W Hotel. XYZ is on the cutting edge of hotel bars. It's in a great part of the South of Market area—close to the San Francisco Museum of Modern Art—so it draws a cool crowd that appreciates avant-garde art.

in and out of Nickie's since the neighborhood is a little sketchy. *cash only; open Mon–Tues, Thurs–Sun; full bar; www.nickies.com; map:L5*

**PARADISE LOUNGE / 1501 Folsom St at 11th St; 415/861-6906** Live music is the focus for this SoMa club. It's a huge industrial structure that has four different stages and multiple bars. The Blue Room is the main venue with its dance floor, elevated stage, and balcony seating. Adjacent is the lounge, where lesser-known bands strive to be heard, and upstairs is Above Paradise, where acoustic bands play and a pool room shares space with the bar. Next door the Transmission Theater hosts indie bands in an old garage that is attached to Paradise through a side door. The age range can be from early 20s to late 40s depending on the entertainment that evening, and the crowd tends to be pretty casual and laid back. *MC, V; no checks; open every day; full bar; map:M5*

**PIER 23 CAFE / Pier 23, The Embarcadero at Greenwich St; 415/362-5125** This is where postcollegiate overgrown frat boys and the girls who love them go to get lucky. Pier 23 is prime property with its heated deck right on the water and great views of the Bay Bridge. When a good reggae, Latin, or soul band plays, the crowd really heats up on the small dance floor. Expect to wait in line on weekends. The Long Island Iced Tea is frickin' expensive but hoo-boy good. *MC, V; no checks; open every day; full bar; map:N1*

**PUNCHLINE COMEDY CLUB / 444 Battery St btwn Washington and Clay Sts; 415/397-7573** This downtown comedy club is usually packed on weekends and—believe it or not—is a great place to meet people. The tables seat four, and if you come with a friend you'll be seated with another twosome. Top names in comedy—Rosie O'Donnell, Ellen DeGeneres, Chris Rock, Drew Carey, Dana Carvey—have performed here for the last 20 years, and there are also nights devoted to local rising stars (or not). It's a small, intimate theater where almost all the seats have a good view of the stage. Most shows are for ages 18 and over and require a two-drink minimum per person (nonalcoholic for those under 21, of course). FYI, local hero Robin Williams got his start here. *AE, MC, V; no checks; open Tues–Sun; full bar; www.punchlinecomedyclub.com; map:N2*

**RASSELAS JAZZ CLUB AND ETHIOPIAN CUISINE / 2801 California St at Divisadero St; 415/567-5010** Rasselas is a casually comfortable jazz club consisting of small tables and overstuffed couches occupied by people looking to hear local jazz bands. It's not pretentious or trying to be any-thing it's not. Rather, it's local San Franciscans hanging out and listening to some cool tunes. Mellow, baby. The bands that play here aren't usually famous, but they are quality musicians and always entertaining. The dining room next door serves authentic Ethiopian meals. *AE, CB, DC, MC, V; no checks; open every day; full bar; map:J3*

**SLIM'S / 333 11th St at Folsom St; 415/522-0333** One of the best local venues for live music, Slim's brings in some of the finest rock and alternative bands. The club is co-owned by musician Boz Scaggs, who sometimes takes the stage under the name "Presidio Slim." The combination of a smokin' sound system, big dance floor, high ceilings, and expansive bar makes this a great place to enjoy good music. The crowd is usually casually dressed and friendly, and ranges in age depending on the entertainment. There's a pretty good pub menu for those who arrive early and can manage to get a table. *MC, V; no checks; call for show dates; full bar; www.slims-sf.com; map:M5*

**SOUND FACTORY / 525 Harrison St at 1st St; 415/339-8686** With new clubs opening all the time, it's amazing that people are still lining up to get into the aging Sound Factory, but they are. It's a gigantic behemoth of a club that's been divided into a bunch of different miniclubs, with something for everyone—live music, DJs, techno, drum and bass, and more. There's one giant main dance area, another smaller (but still pretty big) dance area called the Conga Room, and yet another dance floor called the Blue Room. Scattered throughout are busy bars selling over-priced water and drinks. There's also a pool room and a sky lounge (where you can look down on the dancers), and little rooms here and there where you can chill out and people-watch. *cash only; open Fri–Sat; full bar; map:N3*

**STORYVILLE / 1751 Fulton St at Masonic Ave; 415/441-1751** Storyville started out as a classic jazz club but has loosened its description to include some other varieties such as acid jazz, drum and bass, and ambient sounds. It's a refreshingly trend-free club with a mostly local crowd in front listening to live jazz or blues in a cool dark setting. In back the bigger names play, or DJs come in to spin for a dancing crowd. There's no cover, but there is a two-drink minimum of well-poured cocktails. *AE, CB, DC, DIS, MC, V; no checks; open Tues–Sat; full bar; map:J4*

**THE STUD / 399 9th St at Harrison St; 415/863-6623** This famous gay and lesbian hangout has been around for over 30 years. A laid-back crowd plays pool and pinball or dances to DJ music while the cute bar-tenders keep the liquor flowing. There are always some people standing around outside waiting to get in, but it's usually not long before you're in the door. The welcoming atmosphere and the casual clientele make this bar great for first-timers to the gay bar scene. "Trannyshack" is one of the most popular nights due to the amateur drag show. *cash only; open every day; full bar; map:M4*

**1015 FOLSOM / 1015 Folsom St at 6th St; 415/431-1200** 1015 (say "ten-fifteen") is a SoMa after-hours dance club mainstay. Its popularity comes and goes with the local clubbers, but on weekends it's always packed. The three-story multiroom structure houses one of the city's largest dance floors, with international DJs spinning techno and house. There are smaller rooms with music ranging from light and danceable to mellow and ambient; the basement hosts the more experimental DJs. There are six bars, so it's easy to refresh yourself between sweaty dance sessions. Every Sunday (except the first one of the month) it's home to Spundae, the infamous techno party for those who just can't let their weekend end. *cash only; open Wed–Sun; full bar; www.1015.com; map:N4*

**THE TOP / 424 Haight St at Webster St; 415/864-7386** This is not a place to bring a date or anyone else you are interested in talking to. This is a place to shut up and dance to the superloud sounds of the DJ-spun techno, house, and disco music on a crowded dance floor of young ravers. It's cheap, it's fun, and it's loud. They also have pool tables, but you've got to play early, before the crowds show up. It's a great singles scene, although you'd have to actually leave the club to hear your new friend's name. Did we mention it's loud? *cash only; open every day; full bar; map:L5*

**UP & DOWN CLUB / 1151 Folsom St btwn 7th and 8th Sts; 415/626-2388** A trendy, professional crowd with steady incomes and designer duds unwinds with the help of top-shelf martinis at this small, popular SoMa jazz and supper club. The style of jazz veers toward newer styles of acid and fusion. It gets really crowded in here, so your best bet is to try to get in for dinner and stay for the show, which starts around 9:30pm. If you hang at the bar you'll be able to hear the music but may not be able to see the performers. When the booze kicks in and you're ready to groove, head upstairs for some dancing to deejay vinyl. Stiff cover, brother. *AE, V; no checks; open Mon, Wed–Sat; full bar; map:M5*

**WARFIELD THEATRE / 982 Market St at 6th St; 415/567-2060** This old-time theater was built in the 1920s, but big-name rock acts have played in the opulent space since the early '70s. Although it holds about 2,250 people, it somehow has the feel of an intimate club. The downstairs has a large dance floor in front of the elevated stage and an area for standing right behind the dance floor near the conveniently located bars. Toward the back are tables that can be reserved. Upstairs the balcony has theater seating. Depending on the show you can choose which area you want to be in. The Warfield brings in all types of major artists from the rock, rap, country, and alternative scenes. *AE, MC, V; no checks; call for show dates; full bar; map:M4*

# Bars, Pubs, and Taverns

San Francisco is teeming with bars in every neighborhood. The following is a sampling of some of the best. Keep in mind, though, that it's exploring the unknown that makes a trip an adventure. This is a good guide to start your journey, but go out and find some new places on your own.

**BALBOA CAFE / 3199 Fillmore St at Greenwich St; 415/921-3944** The city's beautiful, single, and overpaid pack themselves into this Marina pickup bar. Boys smoke cigars (yes, some jokers are still doing that), and girls look appropriately sexy. It's a classic old-school bar with the requisite brass and wood. Expect a stiff drink, a great burger, and a phone number by the end of the evening. *AE, DC, MC, V; no checks; open every day; full bar; map:K2*

**BAYSIDE SPORTS BAR AND GRILL / 1787 Union St at Octavia St; 415/673-1565** Bayside, one of the largest sports bars in the city, is popular with the clean-cut Marina yuppies outfitted in their ubiquitous ball caps, white T-shirts, and shorts. The place is loaded with cathode ray tubes, including a state-of-the-art super-large-screen television and 30 smaller ones, so there's no problem finding a place to watch the game. About 20 beers are on tap, and the pub-type menu offers good and big sandwiches, hamburgers, salads, and such. Happy hour is Monday to Friday from 4pm to 6pm. *MC, V; no checks; open every day; full bar; map:K2*

**BEAUTY BAR / 2299 Mission St at 19th St; 415/285-0323** Don't be thrown off by the chrome-domed hair dryers or the manicurist who's actually doing someone's nails—this is really a bar. The owners of this Mission District hot spot transported an entire vintage beauty salon from Long Island to create the magic that is the Beauty Bar. It's already worked in New York, and this place just keeps getting more popular here. It's a young, hip crowd that digs the novelty but stays for the laid-back atmosphere. *cash only; open every day; full bar; map:L7*

**BIX / 56 Gold St btwn Pacific and Jackson Sts; 415/433-6300** Named after jazz legend Bix Beiderbecke, this 1930s-style back-alley supper club attracts a professional cocktail-sipping crowd (the Bix cocktail is a San Francisco staple). It's a sophisticated scene with white-jacketed bartenders pouring strong drinks and live jazz in the background. Local politicians and high-powered business types rule this Financial District haunt. See also the review in the Restaurants chapter. *AE, CB, DC, DIS, MC, V; no checks; open every day; full bar; map:N2*

**BLONDIE'S BAR & NO GRILL / 540 Valencia St btwn 16th and 17th Sts; 415/864-2419** Sometimes there's just nothing better than sitting outside and drinking a giant neon-blue martini. Blondie's packs in the fresh-faced cool crowd nightly to its open, airy space. There's a long martini menu, with the Blue Funk mentioned above as the specialty. The friendly bartenders always give you the shaker to refill your glass, so it's rare to order more than one martini per person. There are a couple of pool tables and live music on Saturday nights. *cash only; open every day; full bar; map:L6*

**BUBBLE LOUNGE / 714 Montgomery St at Washington St; 415/434-4204** This super-chichi champagne bar is populated by the city's stylish and sophisticated, but is surprisingly comfortable and even fun. With over 300 types of champagne and sparkling wines, ordering can be a little intimidating, but the knowledgeable staff is helpful and friendly. If you prefer to forgo the bubbles, there's a full bar as well. The upstairs is more of a dig-me scene where people are checking each other out, but the downstairs Krug Room is intimate and laid back. There are also some equally extravagant treats to complement your bubbly, ranging from foie gras to caviar or something off the sushi cart. *AE, DC, MC, V; no checks; open Mon–Sat; full bar; www.bubblelounge.com; map:N2*

**BUENA VISTA CAFE / 2765 Hyde St at Beach St; 415/474-5044** Irish coffee: That's all that needs to be said about this San Francisco landmark. Located at the end of the Hyde Street cable car line, the Buena Vista was the first bar in the country to serve Irish coffee after the late journalist Stanton Delaplane returned from a trip to Dublin in 1952 and described  the concoction to his favorite bartender. The story is told and retold in articles and stories posted all over the bar. Watch the venerable bartenders line up the glasses and masterfully (or messily, depending on one's opinion) pour out the drinks, which make great pick-me-ups after a long day's sightseeing. There's a large tourist crowd here because of the proximity to the wharf and cable car line. *cash only; open every day; full bar; map:M1*

**BUS STOP / 1901 Union St at Laguna St; 415/567-6905** If you want to watch 49er fans at their rowdiest, this is the place to go. This Cow Hollow sports bar fills up fast when a big game is on, so get here early to snag a seat. The Gap-clad patrons watch their favorite teams over some beers in a loud but laid-back scene. The bar's not very big, but it's split into different areas to help break up the crowd and allow for more walls to put TVs on. In the back are a couple of pool tables you can lean on to watch the game. *cash only; open every day; full bar; map:K2*

**CAFE MARS / 798 Brannan St at 7th St; 415/621-6277** The Jetsons decor, cool patio, strong drinks, and great music draw 20- to 30-something urbanites to this popular SoMa hangout. It's a fun, festive atmosphere, and the friendly bartenders make a mean Martian martini. When Mars is really grooving, don't be surprised to see women dancing on the bar. There's also a bar menu of cosmic goodies. The heated patio is prime property, as is the pool room. The background music is jazzy and unobtrusive, but really starts pumping on weekend nights. This area is sketchy at night, so watch it on the way back to your car. *AE, MC, V; no checks; open every day; full bar; map:N5*

**COMET CLUB / 3111 Fillmore St at Filbert St; 415/567-5589** The Comet Club looks mighty weird from the outside—some sort of cosmic-themed funky metallic silver paint scheme—but it's a hopping singles scene inside with the Marina's prowling young ones checking each other out. It's a casual bar that can get crowded and loud as you try to talk over the pumping disco music. This is a good place to end your evening of debauchery along Union and Fillmore Streets. *MC, V; no checks; open Tues–Sat; full bar; map:K2*

**CROW BAR / 401 Broadway at Montgomery St; 415/788-2769** People love this huge dark bar in North Beach because it makes no promises: it's just a bar. All types congregate here peacefully, from the after-work Financial District suit set to your basic pierced and tattooed pool shark. It's a supercasual place to throw back one of the many beers or scotches available and unwind from a hard day's whatever. There's a great jukebox with a mix of classic and cutting-edge music, as well as pool tables and darts. *cash only; open every day; full bar; map:N2*

**DALVA / 3121 16th St at Valencia St; 415/252-7740** This ultracool bar in the gentrified Mission District is usually full of cute young professionals sipping on margaritas, fine scotch, or the house sangría. Dalva also has an extensive menu of beers, including some great Belgian ales. The bar is small but moody, with red walls and dim lighting. There's an even smaller back room that gets crowded on weekends. Later in the evening DJs come in to spin ambient and drum-and-bass music as a background to intimate conversations. Here's a little secret: The hostess from the crepe restaurant across the street, Ti Couz, will come over and get you at Dalva when your table is ready. *cash only; open every day; full bar; www.dalva.com; map:L6*

**THE EAGLE TAVERN / 398 12th St at Harrison St; 415/626-0880** This is the premier gay biker bar for the leather-loving set. All ages, colors, and sizes are represented here, decked out in various macho ensembles of leather, denim, and steel (or nothing but combat boots, as we discovered one night). Tattoos and body piercings are de rigueur. The focus here is to check out, be checked out, and hook up; even nongays are welcome as long as they don't make a scene. There's a pool table, some pinball machines, and a back patio that holds the Sunday Beer Bust (a dance and drink party in the late afternoon). Be sure to try the fantastic Queer Beer. *cash only; open every day; full bar; www.sfeagle.com; map:M5*

**ENRICO'S / 504 Broadway at Kearny St; 415/982-6223** Among the neon-lit strip clubs and porn stores on this part of Broadway sits Enrico's, a Parisian-style sidewalk cafe catering to a mixed group of bohemians, tourists, and wannabes. The heated patio is the place to be, as the inner restaurant area can get too noisy when the jazz band begins to play. Sit outside and people-watch while sipping a Mohito (a minty rum drink that goes down easy but packs a knockout punch) or an imported ale. Enrico's serves a full menu of California-infused Mediterranean food until 12:30am on weekends. See also the review in the Restaurants chapter. *AE, DC, DIS, MC, V; no checks; open every day; full bar; map:N2*

**15 ROMOLO / 15 Romolo Pl at Kearny St; 415/398-1359** You've got to know where you're going to find this little retro bar hidden on a secluded alley in North Beach (basically, bust a left at the porn store). The bar is part of the Basque Hotel, so you'll probably rub elbows with some international young tourists, but the main clientele is local youngish professionals relaxing after work. It's a laid-back type of place for mellowing out in one of the high-backed booths or comfy armchairs. This spot may be hidden away, but a lot of people have already found it and it can get crowded on weekends. *cash only; open every day; full bar; map:N2*

**GOLD DUST LOUNGE / 247 Powell St btwn Geary and O'Farrell Sts; 415/397-1695** You'd think the gold walls and red banquettes would be too garish and the Dixieland jazz music too cheesy, but for some reason this venerable Union Square joint still packs in the tourists and old-time locals. The Gold Dust Lounge has been around since the 1930s, and though its gilded glory has faded somewhat, it's still a fun spot to tilt a Manhattan after shopping or the theater. You can sit around the piano and sing along as the band plays and make a new friend or two from Vienna, Ohio. It's all very Old San Francisco. *cash only; open every day; full bar; map:N3*

**GREENS SPORTS BAR / 2239 Polk St at Green St; 415/775-4287** This popular Polk Street sports bar overflows onto the street when a big game is on, while passersby peer into the large open windows from the sidewalk to check the score on the large-screen television or 10 smaller ones. The crowd is loud and raucous, and there's always someone with a death wish who doesn't want the Niners to win. The walls are covered with old *Sports Illustrated* photos, autographed pictures, and the occasional girlie shot. When a game isn't on it's a pretty quiet locals' bar, where chances are a video of *Caddyshack* is playing on the TV and the pool table is open. A late-night happy hour runs Sunday to Wednesday from 10pm to 2am. *cash only; open every day; full bar; www.citysearch.com/sfo/greenssportsbar; map:L2*

**HARRINGTON'S BAR AND GRILL / 245 Front St at Sacramento St; 415/392-7595** An after-work Financial District crowd has been unwinding at this Irish pub for over 60 years. There's a mix of old-timers and whippersnappers sharing the day's war stories over a pint in one of the two large bars inside. The small heated patio space is snatched up quickly. A pub menu of basic American grub is available. *AE, MC, V; no checks; open Mon–Sat; full bar; map:N2*

**HAYES AND VINE WINE BAR / 377 Hayes St at Gough St; 415/626-5301**
 A great place to take a date, this stylish little wine bar in chic Hayes Valley caters to urbanites with a taste for the finer things. The attractive and knowledgeable staff is more than helpful when it comes to choosing

among the 750 wines (most of which you've probably never heard of), with about 50 offered by the glass. Try one of the flights, a four-glass sampling of certain wines. The vogue decor and tasty French-inspired snacks complete the picture in this cozy wine lover's haven. Cheese, olives, pâté, and other palate-cleansing noshables are also served. *MC, V; no checks; open every day; beer and wine; map:L4*

**JULIE'S SUPPER CLUB / 1123 Folsom St at 7th St; 415/861-0707** Seasoned and slightly pickled urban dwellers have been making this '50s-style cocktail joint a SoMa favorite since the early '90s. The bartenders serve stiff drinks (and great martinis) to a fun-loving crowd that congregates for the tasty happy-hour food and drink specials. More often than not that same crowd keeps partying well into the night, particularly when the large dinner parties in the back room are done eating and are ready to rock. It's got a swanky Old Hollywood feel, with black-and-white photographs on the wall and a swing soundtrack in the background. Trivia tip: This is one of the locations where the Symbionese Liberation Army held Patty Hearst hostage in the 1970s. *AE, MC, V; no checks; open every day; full bar; map:M4*

**LEXINGTON CLUB / 3464 19th St btwn Mission and Valencia Sts; 415/863-2052** Just around the corner from the many straight bars in the gentrified Valencia Corridor is this hip lesbian hangout, one of the few women-owned bars in the city. It offers a welcome respite from the busy Mission scene—the dark interior, moody lighting, and comfy booths make you settle right down. They have a great selection of beers and some good rock tunes on the jukebox. *cash only; open every day; full bar; map:L6*

**LI PO / 916 Grant Ave at Washington St; 415/982-0072** Chinatown is full of strange little divey bars like this one, but for some reason people of all types and ages are drawn to the Li Po. It's mysterious, dimly lit, and kind of creepy (no big surprise, since it once was an opium den). The whole place is scarlet red, and the large ancient lantern hanging from the ceiling looks as if it could disintegrate at any moment. This is definitely a late-night hot spot, with a friendly staff who will try to creep you out with ghost stories of opium junkies come back from the dead. *cash only; open every day; full bar; map:N2*

**LONDON WINE BAR / 415 Sansome St btwn Sacramento and Clay Sts; 415/788-4811** With its exposed brick walls and wood paneling, this après-work destination feels like a European tasting room. A 50-page list of wines features some really good deals. There's a menu of snacks to accompany your glass, but most of the regulars munch on the complimentary little cheese cubes. This is a great place to meet up with friends and chat before your next destination. *AE, CB, DC, DIS, MC, V; no checks; open Mon–Fri; beer and wine; map:N2*

**LONE PALM / 3394 22nd St at Guerrero St; 415/648-0109** Hidden among the crowded bars in the Mission District, this quiet (well, perhaps in the early afternoon) and romantic (well, maybe on weekday nights) bar is a convenient getaway. It's a great spot for couples to whisper sweet nothings in private at small candlelit tables. When there isn't someone playing the piano, the jukebox is belting out loungey background music. This is also a popular place for people who don't give a damn about San Francisco's no-smoking policy. *cash only; open every day; full bar; map:L6*

**MARINA LOUNGE / 2138 Chestnut St at Pierce St; 415/922-1475** This retro locals' hangout is an oasis of originality on a street full of retail shops and chain restaurants. Come in from the craziness outside to this dark mahogany bar with Sinatra crooning in the background, grab yourself a drink, and reaffirm your belief that all is right with the world. The clientele is mostly an upscale cocktail-drinking crowd looking to unwind. There's a pool table in the back and several vantage points for people-watching. When you see something you like, it's perfectly OK to strike up a conversation. *cash only; open every day; full bar; map:K2*

**MARTUNI'S / 4 Valencia St at Market St; 415/241-0205** It's kind of a strange place for an upscale gay piano bar, but for some reason this off-beat location on Market and Valencia Streets has become San Francisco's new hot spot for stiff martinis and classic sing-alongs à la Sinatra and Gershwin. As word gets around the various social circles (both straight and gay), more and more people are showing up at Martuni's for a boisterous evening of open-mic cabaret, show tunes, and cocktails. All types of people congregate here, yet so far it has avoided being dominated by a chummy clique. It's a great place for couples and groups to get together and chat in the dark alcoves as the piano man and aspiring lounge acts entertain. *MC, V; no checks; open every day; full bar; map:L5*

**O'REILLY'S IRISH BAR / 622 Green St at Columbus Ave; 415/989-6222** Literary types and serious drinkers (often one and the same) frequent this comfortable Irish pub in North Beach. On a nice night you'll want one of the outside tables, but more often than not it's like a wind tunnel and you'll need to take cover in the cozy interior. On the back wall there's a large mural of famous Irish authors (if you're having trouble naming them, look for the hints). At the bottom of the painting is a portrait of the owner's giant Irish wolfhound, who can sometimes be spotted blocking the door to the bathroom (don't worry, he's a real sweetie). They have a great Irish pub menu and pour a lovely Guinness. *MC, V; no*

## A VIEW WORTH DRINKING TO

One of the perks of being in a big city is being able to ride those super-fast elevators to the top of the hotel skyscrapers and hang out for a while in the bar. Sure, the drinks are overpriced, but for about $7 you get a million-dollar view of the city and the bay. Here's a list of our favorites; a few have a cover charge at night, but most are free during the day.

**The Carnelian Room** (555 California St btwn Kearny and Montgomery Sts; www.carnelianroom.com; 415/433-7500) Located on the 52nd floor of the Bank of America building, the Carnelian Room is a swanky reservations-only restaurant, but the adjoining cocktail lounge is open to everyone, and the view looking north toward the Golden Gate Bridge is phenomenal.

**Cityscape** (333 O'Farrell St at Mason St; 415/923-5002) OK, so it's a hokey Hilton hotel, but they can't corporatize the amazing views from high atop the 46th floor. Sit under the glass roof, knock down a few Long Islands, and ponder your existence among the stars.

**Crown Room** (950 Mason St at California St; 415/772-5131) Half the fun of getting here is riding in the glass elevator Willy Wonka style. The panoramic 360-degree view from the 24th floor of the Fairmont Hotel—the highest observation point in the city—is well worth that $9 Manhattan you're carrying around; in fact, it's widely considered *the* best view in the city.

**Equinox** (5 Embarcadero Center off Market St; 415/788-1234) The gimmick at this Hyatt Regency is the 17-story rooftop restaurant's revolving floor, which gives diners a 360-degree panoramic view of the city every 45 minutes. You'll never see a local there, but the tourists dig it.

**Harry Denton's Starlight Room** (450 Powell St at Sutter St; 415/395-8595) On the 21st floor of the Sir Francis Drake Hotel is a 1930s-style club complete with chandeliers, red-velvet banquettes, and glittering views of the city streets far below. Afternoon tea runs from 3pm to 5pm Monday through Friday, but it's the nightly dig-me and dance scene that everyone shows up for.

**Top of the Mark** (1 Nob Hill at California and Mason Sts; 415/616-6916) The "Meet Me at the Mark" is one of the most famous cocktail lounges in the world. During World War II, Pacific-bound servicemen toasted their good-byes to the States here, and you can kiss a $10 bill good-bye as you sip your cocktail and enjoy the magnificent 19th-floor view atop the Mark Hopkins Intercontinental.

**The View Lounge** (55 4th St btwn Market and Mission Sts; 415/442-6127) The name says it all: a cocktail lounge on the top floor of the San Francisco Marriott hotel that offers some of the best views in (and of) the city. Thick glass windows are the only thing separating you from one helluva first step. It's a very casual place where you can linger all day in your shorts and nobody will care.

*checks; open every day; full bar; www.oreillysirish.citysearch.com; map:N1*

**ROYAL OAK / 2201 Polk St at Vallejo St; 415/928-2303** This popular Russian Hill hangout has cozy antique couches and chairs arranged in a variety of little conversation areas lit by the soft glow of Tiffany lamps. In contrast to the sedate decor, this place gets packed with local urbanites on weekends and can be pretty raucous, with disco blaring in the background but nowhere to dance. The wait staff is attentive and quick and, for some reason, 100 percent female. If you can't get one of the prime seats in the main room, the turnover at the bar is high. *cash only; open every day; full bar; map:L2*

**SAN FRANCISCO BREWING COMPANY / 155 Columbus Ave at Pacific St; 415/434-3344** SF Brew Co. was one of the first microbreweries in the United States, built circa 1907. It's a classic old beer joint, with loads of polished wood and brass (notice the large kettle brewing away through the window). The bar is housed in one of the last standing Barbary Coast saloons and is full of local history. Locals vie for outdoor seating on the  sidewalk—great for people-watching—while quaffing $1 drafts at happy hour daily from 4pm to 6pm and midnight to 1am. There are usually about four to six different brews to choose from (you can have a cheap sample if you're not sure) and a good pub menu. A few nights a week a jazz band plays. *AE, MC, V; no checks; open every day; beer and wine; www.sfbrewing.com; map:N2*

**SKYLARK / 3089 16th St at Valencia St; 415/621-9294** Here is a dark, moody bar with no pretense in the midst of all the other bars in this area trying so hard to be hip. It is supremely hip for this very reason. Beautiful people huddle around the small candlelit tables in conversation while sipping cocktails, or crowd into the back and bar area where on weeknights and weekends you can enjoy downtempo and house music played by various local DJs (Tuesdays are particularly fun, with no cover). Relax and take in some of the beautiful paintings, especially Skylark herself up on the ceiling. *cash only; open every day; full bar; map:L6*

**SPECS' TWELVE ADLER MUSEUM CAFE / 12 Saroyan Pl off Columbus Ave; 415/421-4112** Specs' has been around forever and constantly goes in and out of fashion with the fickle hipsters of the city. Little do they know that the regulars like it more when Specs' is out and you can always  get a seat. Lately it's been in, especially on weekends, when this historically bohemian and decidedly irreverent hideaway gets jam-packed. If you can get a table, it's a great place to split some pitchers of Budweiser with friends and gab with people you've just met. Check out the giant wheel of cheese at the bar: for a nominal fee the bartender will cut you a chunk to have on saltine crackers. Other oddities to peruse are the collection of shrunken heads, the hanging whale penis bone, and the baskets of postcards sent from Specs' fans from around the world. If you're lucky Specs himself will come in and entertain you with stories of the old North Beach. *cash only; open every day; full bar; map:N2*

**TORONADO / 547 Haight St at Fillmore St; 415/863-2276** This edgy neighborhood bar offers a mind-numbing number of draft and bottled beers (over 100). It's fairly small, dark, and narrow, and seating (if any) is mainly at the long bar. Serious beer drinkers of the tattooed and pierced ilk make up most of this Lower Haight hangout's clientele. It's a more relaxed alternative to the dance clubs down the block, but it can get a little loud on weekend nights when a DJ comes in. FYI, the Toronado hats and shirts make great San Francisco souvenirs. *cash only; open every day; beer only; www.toronado.com; map:K5*

**TOSCA CAFE / 242 Columbus Ave btwn Broadway and Pacific Ave; 415/986-9651** Tosca is as pure classic North Beach as you can get nowadays. The leather booths and long, dark bar—as well as the crisply dressed bartenders—conjure images of another time. The clientele is a mix of young locals and visitors, and the bar can get crowded on weekends. If you can get a table in the back, settle in with a dry martini or a Tosca "cappuccino" (the house specialty, it contains no coffee—it's a frothy mix of brandy and hot chocolate) and soak up the atmosphere. The jukebox plays opera and big band–era tunes to accompany the hiss of the large brass espresso machines at either end of the bar. There is a secret back room reserved for friends of the owner (you may spot Nicolas Cage, Sean Penn, or Kevin Spacey heading back there on the occasional evening). *cash only; open every day; full bar; map:N2*

**TRAD'R SAM / 6150 Geary Blvd at 26th Ave; 415/221-0773** The last of the red-hot tiki bars is out of the way, but if you've got a group looking for a good time, this place is a ball. A menu of about 50 or so tropical drinks will get you in the party mood; one of them tastes just like a 50/50 bar—yum! OK, so it's pretty cheesy, but the Polynesian charm is intoxicating, and before you know it you and your buddies are all hovering over a bowl of scorpions and sticking paper umbrellas in your hair. The jukebox plays good tunes, and people will tend to sing along to the oldies. It's a mostly youngish crowd; expect a line on weekends. *cash only; open every day; full bar; map:F4*

**TWIN PEAKS TAVERN / 401 Castro St at 17th and Market Sts; 415/864-9470** This venerable San Francisco institution on the corner of Castro and Market Streets was the first openly gay bar in America. For almost 30 years the patrons of this comfortable, laid-back drinking establishment have looked out at the world through the large windows, and the wild world of the Castro has looked back. Now it's a mostly older crowd of gay men who live in the neighborhood. During the day it's very subdued, but in the evening it gets quite popular. As with most gay bars in the city, polite heteros are always welcome. *cash only; open every day; full bar; map:K6*

**VESUVIO CAFE / 255 Columbus Ave at Broadway; 415/362-3370** This Beat Generation hangout—situated along Jack Kerouac Alley across from the famed City Lights Bookstore—has remained pretty much the same since it opened in 1948. Vesuvio's, the preferred hangout for writer/beatnik Jack Kerouac, serves alcohol to a mix of brooding writers, career drinkers, bohemian artists, North Beach hipsters, and tourists on the hunt for beatnik lore. It's a great place to people-watch or feel the Beat by reading about the past, as the walls are papered with poems and articles about the bar and the Beat era. Upstairs there's a cool balcony with additional seating. The bar gets crowded in the evenings and on weekends. *cash only; open every day; full bar; www.vesuvio.com; map:N2*

# Coffee, Tea, and Dessert

**ALFRED SCHILLING RESTAURANT, CHOCOLATE, AND PASTRY / 1695 Market St at Valencia St; 415/431-8447** Step back into the Egyptian-inspired dining room of this candy shop/restaurant and you'll feel as if you're in some kind of surreal stage set, what with the desert (or is it dessert?) queen of the chocolate pyramids staring down at you from one of the exotic murals. If you're in an adventurous mood, gorge on the Willie Wonka Special, which is actually a full meal that includes chocolate in every course. You really can't go wrong with any of the outrageous sweet selections here—they are all amazingly decadent. Before you leave, pick up some of the pyramid-shaped truffles from the retail shop that made this candy maker famous. *AE, MC, V; no checks; open Mon–Sat; beer and wine; www.alfredschilling.com; map:L5*

**CAFE FLORE / 2298 Market St at Noe St; 415/621-8579** Cafe Flore is a place for the predominantly gay, beautiful, and well-coifed Castro Street crowd to see and be seen. It's always packed, and on a sunny day the open-air patio is prime real estate. It's a popular place for younger men to strut their stuff and hang out with a cappuccino while checking out the other patrons. There is a nice light menu of California cuisine, but eating is not what the customers are passionate about. *cash only; open every day; beer and wine; map:K6*

**CAFFE GRECO / 423 Columbus Ave btwn Vallejo and Green Sts; 415/397-6261** Try to grab a sidewalk table or at least one by the large sliding windows open to Columbus Avenue, then sit back and people-watch while enjoying one of the best Italian coffee drinks this side of Roma. Small, intimate tables, Italian dessert specialties in the refrigerated case, and the sound of many languages being spoken by the cosmopolitan customers enhance the cafe's European ambience. It's a great place to linger over an Italian pastry and take in the North Beach experience. You *must* try their Greco Grande cappuccino! *cash only; open every day; beer and wine; map:M2*

**CAFFE PUCCINI / 411 Columbus Ave btwn Vallejo and Green Sts; 415/989-7033** This North Beach cafe is decorated to honor the famed Italian composer Giacomo Puccini, with a framed photo of the artist and posters from his operas. Sit back and enjoy one of the homemade desserts (the tortes are phenomenal), a foamy cappuccino, and the opera music softly playing in the background. You can also order a meal or antipasto plate full of Italian treats as you soak up the action on Columbus Avenue. *No credit cards; checks OK; open every day; beer and wine; map:M2*

**CAFFE TRIESTE / 601 Vallejo St at Grant Ave; 415/392-6739** This Beat Generation hangout has been around since 1956, decades before "double decaf latte with nonfat milk and a twist" was ever uttered. You can sit here for hours enjoying the rich, locally roasted Italian coffee and taking in the bohemian aura. The staff is curt and detached, and that's how the locals like it, so know what you're going to order before you go to the counter. Trieste is a block off the main drag of Columbus, so the foot traffic isn't as heavy here except on Saturdays from 1:30 to 5 in the afternoon, when locals sing Italian operas and folk music for the cafe crowd. *cash only; open every day; beer and wine; www.caffetrieste. com; map:M2*

**JOE'S ICE CREAM / 5351 Geary Blvd at 18th Ave; 415/751-1950** A blast-from-the-past ice cream joint, Joe's has been around for over 50 years. Grab a seat at the old L-shaped counter for your trip back in time. Soda jerks serve amazing house-made ice cream treats to neighborhood families and the occasional lucky visitor. Try the Joe's It, much better than the store-bought It's It, or any of the sodas, shakes, malteds, sundaes, and such made with Joe's delicious ice cream. The really great thing about Joe's: It's open until 11pm on weekends, so you can satisfy that late-night craving. *cash only; open every day; no alcohol; map:G4*

**MUDDY WATERS COFFEE HOUSE / 521 Valencia St at 16th St; 415/863-8006** In the midst of the ultracool Valencia Corridor, this coffeehouse serves some majorly caffeinated beverages. You can sit here all night listening to the ambient tunes or get a quick fix that'll keep you going late into the night at the surrounding bars. The crowd is a mixed bag of locals, while outside the door you'll find the regular Mission District druggies.

It's a little rough around the edges on this block, so watch your back. *cash only; open every day; no alcohol; map:L5*

**THE NORTH END / 1402 Grant Ave at Green St; 415/956-3350** Away from busy Columbus Avenue and amid the cool boutiques and bars of Grant Avenue is the North End, the perfect place to relax and check out the stylish side of North Beach. Not only is the coffee great, they also carry sinfully good pastries from Victoria Pastry Co. (a North Beach institution). A fine selection of beers and some amazing sangría are available as well. While you're here, make a special trip to the bathroom and see the Elvis shrine—very cool. *cash only; open every day; beer and wine; map:N2*

**STEPS OF ROME / 348 Columbus Ave btwn Broadway and Vallejo Sts; 415/397-0435** Charming, flirty Italian waiters and an ultracool European crowd make this place the hot spot on Columbus Avenue. The restaurant spills out onto the sidewalk, with the young and the beautiful crowding around tables to chain-smoke cigarettes. It's a fun, lively scene, and, oh yeah, they serve food too. The gelato is fantastic, and the espresso drinks make an excellent accompaniment. But let's face it—it's the scene you come to Steps of Rome for, and you won't be disappointed. *AE, CB, DC, DIS, MC, V; no checks; open every day; beer and wine; map:N2*

**TOY BOAT DESSERT CAFE / 401 Clement St at 5th Ave; 415/751-7505** Kids rule at Toy Boat, and that includes the child within. The place is full of classic old toys that will bring back thoughts of your own childhood (all the old Saturday-morning stars are here, and for sale as well). When you're done perusing the toys, sit down for a slice of pie or the heavenly Fallen Angel Cake—chocolate cake with a mousse center covered in shaved chocolate. They've also got great ice cream desserts and, as a healthier alternative, terrific smoothies. *MC, V; checks OK; open every day; no alcohol; map:H3*

**ZERO DEGREES / 490 Pacific Ave btwn Montgomery and Sansome Sts; 415/788-9376** The stark urban-chic decor of Zero Degrees doesn't make you feel like settling down with your coffee and book, but it is a great late-night destination on your way home from the bars and nearby restaurants (its parent restaurant, MC2, is just down the block). You can get house-made ice creams in a variety of inventive flavors, as well as a selection of ports, champagnes, and scotches that make an elegant nightcap. *MC, V; no checks; open Mon–Sat; full bar; map:M2*

# ITINERARIES

# ITINERARIES

If we were going to spend three days vacationing in San Francisco, this is how we'd do it. Whether you're a first-time visitor or a San Francisco native, here's the insider advice on the best San Francisco has to offer. These are the must-see museums, attractions, restaurants, and nightclubs that make San Francisco one of the world's most exciting cities to explore, so keep this page dog-eared and get ready to have a ball.

Note: More information on the places in boldface below can be found in other chapters throughout this book and in the index.

## Three-Day Tour

### DAY ONE

Get your walking shoes on, because we're going to attempt to see the majority of San Francisco's most famous attractions in a single day.

**MORNING:** Start your day off in high style with a light breakfast of tea and scones at the **GARDEN COURT** within the Palace Hotel (2 New Montgomery St at Market St; 415/546-5010), one of the most elaborate and beautiful dining rooms ever built. Since you're in the neighborhood, it's time to do a little window-shopping at **UNION SQUARE**, with a mandatory stop at **NEIMAN MARCUS** (150 Stockton St at Geary St; 415/362-3900) to chuckle at the absurd price tags, and a stroll through the gilded lobby of the **WESTIN ST. FRANCIS** (335 Powell St btwn Geary and Post Sts; 415/397-7000). Next, hop on either the **POWELL-MASON** or **POWELL-HYDE CABLE CAR** to **FISHERMAN'S WHARF,** and head to Pier 41 to catch the fantastic **ALCATRAZ ISLAND TOUR** (415/705-5555); be sure to make a reservation far in advance, and ask for the headphone tour.

**AFTERNOON:** After the prison tour, walk west along the water near Fisherman's Wharf to the intersection of Jefferson and Taylor Streets and buy a fresh **DUNGENESS CRAB COCKTAIL** from the boisterous street vendors. Continue west along the wharf, making a few optional side trips to the **CANNERY** (2801 Leavenworth St at Beach St; 415/771-3112), **GHIRARDELLI SQUARE** (900 North Point St between Polk and Larkin Sts; 415/775-5500), and the **SAN FRANCISCO MARITIME NATIONAL HISTORICAL PARK** (foot of Polk St at Beach St; 415/561-7100). You're probably in need of a picker-upper by now, so head for the intersection of Beach and Hyde Streets to have a world-famous **IRISH COFFEE** at the **BUENA VISTA CAFE** (2765 Hyde St at Beach St; 415/474-5044). If you don't mind the long but beautiful walk (if you do, take the number 28 or 29 bus, or hail a taxi), continue west along the shoreline, past **AQUATIC PARK**, along the **GOLDEN GATE PROMENADE** to the **GOLDEN GATE**

## SAN FRANCISCO DAY BY DAY

There are some entertaining events going on in San Francisco that happen only on certain days of the week. Here are some local favorites:

**Farmers market** held every **Saturday morning** along the Embarcadero at the foot of Market Street.

A hand-clapping and foot-stomping praise to the Lord every **Sunday** at the **Glide Memorial Church** (330 Ellis St; 415/771-6300).

A sinfully sumptuous **Sunday brunch** at the **Ritz-Carlton hotel** (600 Stockton St; 415/296-7465).

**Operatic arias** from 2pm to 5pm every **Saturday** at **Caffe Trieste** (601 Vallejo St; 415/392-6739).

**Thursday night art and music** offerings at the **San Francisco Museum of Modern Art,** which stays open until 9pm and usually hosts live jazz and blues bands. It's quite popular with the locals.

**Rent roller skates,** in-line skates, or a tandem bicycle and cruise through **Golden Gate Park** on **Sunday,** when the main roads throughout the park are closed to auto traffic.

**Sunset tours** of **Alcatraz Island Thursday through Sunday** offer spectacular nighttime views of the city and an odd mix of romance and creepiness.

One of the best places to hear live rock in the city, **Bottom of the Hill,** also offers one of the best **all-you-can-eat barbecues** every **Sunday** from 4pm to 7pm.

**BRIDGE** for an at-least-once-in-your-lifetime stroll across the world's most famous bridge.

**EVENING:** OK, you've walked the bridge and now you're starving. Take a bus or taxi back to **NORTH BEACH** and head for **ENRICO'S** (504 Broadway at Kearny St; 415/982-6223). It's not the best restaurant in the city, but it has one of the best San Francisco vibes as well as live jazz nightly. Get a patio seat and order the burger and a rum-and-mint-infused *mojito* (very tasty). Afterward, cruise northwest up **COLUMBUS AVENUE,** soaking in the sights and smells and stopping in at classic San Francisco haunts such as **SPECS' TWELVE ADLER MUSEUM CAFE** (12 Saroyan Pl off Columbus Ave; 415/421-4112), **VESUVIO CAFE** (255 Columbus Ave at Broadway; 415/362-3370), and **CAFFE TRIESTE** (601 Vallejo St at Grant Ave; 415/392-6739). By now it's probably time for the second showing of **BEACH BLANKET BABYLON** at **CLUB FUGAZI** (678 Green St btwn Powell St and Columbus Ave; 415/421-4222), San Francisco's best and longest-running comedic musical (buy your tickets well in advance). If you're still up for more after the show, head back to

UNION SQUARE to the SIR FRANCIS DRAKE HOTEL and finish the night off in style with some drinking and dancing at the rooftop HARRY DENTON'S STARLIGHT ROOM (450 Powell St at Sutter St; 415/395-8595). Now go back to your hotel, take two aspirin, and recover.

## DAY TWO

More exploring of San Francisco's major attractions. Even if you have a car, you might want to pick up a bus map and purchase a day pass from a Muni driver, because you'll be adventuring all over the city today.

MORNING: There are still plenty more quintessential San Francisco sights to see. Start off with a Swedish pancake breakfast at SEARS FINE FOODS (439 Powell St btwn Post and Sutter Sts; 415/986-1160), a San Francisco classic. Next, spend a few hours wandering through San Francisco's world-famous CHINATOWN, exploring all the funky shops and back alleys, or take a guided WOK WIZ CHINATOWN WALKING TOUR (415/981-5588). This should work up enough of an appetite for lunch at HOUSE OF NANKING (919 Kearny St at Columbus Ave; 415/421-1429), another local landmark.

AFTERNOON: Now that you're refueled on pot stickers and Chinese greens, break out the map and head for COIT TOWER (415/362-0808) on the top of Telegraph Hill for a breathtaking view of the city (and some serious stair-climbing). Catch your breath, reload your camera, and head west to the famous winding block of LOMBARD STREET between Hyde and Leavenworth Streets (car or no car, it's worth a visit). Next, head to the fantastic SAN FRANCISCO CABLE CAR BARN MUSEUM (1201 Mason St at Washington St; 415/474-1887) to see how those amazing machines work in real time. Afterward, take the POWELL-MASON or POWELL-HYDE CABLE CAR back to Union Square.

EVENING: By now you're probably ready for some well-deserved R&R, so treat yourself to a blowout dinner at FARALLON (450 Post St btwn Mason and Powell Sts; 415/956-6969), POSTRIO (545 Post St btwn Mason and Taylor Sts; 415/776-7825), or the GRAND CAFÉ (501 Geary St at Taylor St; 415/292-0101), three of the best "big city" restaurants in San Francisco. Order a triple espresso for dessert and walk to BISCUITS & BLUES (401 Mason St at Geary St; 415/292-2583) for some toe-tappin' blues or, if you prefer a quieter evening, have a cocktail high above the city in the lounge of the CARNELIAN ROOM (555 California St btwn Kearny and Montgomery Sts; 415/433-7500). Back to the hotel; more aspirin.

## DAY THREE

You've seen a lot of the big-name attractions; now it's time to do what you really came to San Francisco for—eat, drink, shop, and repeat.

MORNING: Sleep in late and skip breakfast, then go for an early lunch where you'll be stuffing your face at YANK SING (101 Spear St at

Mission St; 415/957-9300), the most popular dim sum restaurant in the city (you can't go to San Francisco and not have a dim sum experience). Since you're already downtown, spend an hour shopping at **EMBARCADERO CENTER** (bordered by Drumm, Sacramento, Clay, and Battery Sts; 415/772-0500) or walking around the **FINANCIAL DISTRICT** marveling at the numerous skyscrapers.

**AFTERNOON:** Now take a bus, taxi, or long walk to San Francisco's SoMa district. Three must-stops here are the **SAN FRANCISCO MUSEUM OF MODERN ART** (151 3rd St between Mission and Howard Sts; 415/357-4000) and the adjoining **MUSEUMSTORE** for great souvenirs and gifts, the beautiful **YERBA BUENA GARDENS** (Mission St btwn 3rd and 4th Sts; 415/541-0312), and, especially if you have kids tagging along, the **METREON** megaplex entertainment center (4th and Mission Sts; 415/369-6000)—all right next to each other. This should take you well into the evening.

**EVENING:** Time for dinner. If you want small, intimate, and French, make a reservation right now for **FRINGALE** (570 4th St btwn Brannan and Bryant Sts; 415/543-0573). If you prefer a high-energy, big city–style dining experience, then either walk or taxi to the foot of Mission Street to **BOULEVARD** (1 Mission St at Steuart St; 415/543-6084), one of the city's most popular restaurants. When dinner is over, do something really romantic: Hail a taxi and ask the driver to take you to the top of **TWIN PEAKS** for a breathtaking view of the city lights. Or, if you're in the mood to party, walk south along the Embarcadero to **PIER 23** (Embarcadero at Greenwich St; 415/362-5125) for some stiff Long Island Iced Teas and dancing.

# San Francisco Family Style

**MORNING:** First it's a big pancake breakfast at **SEARS FINE FOODS** (439 Powell St btwn Post and Sutter Sts; 415/986-1160). Next, hop on either the **POWELL-MASON** or **POWELL-HYDE CABLE CAR** to **FISHERMAN'S WHARF** and head to Pier 41 to catch the **ALCATRAZ ISLAND TOUR** (415/705-5555), an adventure your kids will never forget (be sure to make a reservation far in advance, and ask for the headphone tour). After the tour, spend a few hours at Fisherman's Wharf, including **PIER 39** (pathetically touristy but a blast for kids), the **WAX MUSEUM** (415/202-0400), and the old sailing ships and submarine at the **HYDE STREET PIER**.

**AFTERNOON:** Grab sandwiches and fixins at Fisherman's Wharf (bring bread for the ducks), then either hail a cab or walk westward along the wharf to the **PALACE OF FINE ARTS**, where you'll enjoy a **PICNIC LUNCH**. The Palace also houses the **EXPLORATORIUM** (3601 Lyon St at

Marina Blvd; 415/563-7337), the most amazing science museum in the world, which will both astound and entertain your kids until closing time.

**EVENING:** For dinner we recommend two places that kids dig: **CAPP'S CORNER** in North Beach (1600 Powell St at Green St; 415/989-2589) or **MEL'S DINER** (2165 Lombard St at Fillmore St; 415/921-3039). Now for the coup de grâce: the **METREON** megaplex entertainment center (4th and Mission Sts; 415/369-6000), a small city of high-tech attractions and cinema screens (including an **IMAX THEATER**) in the SoMa district that will keep your kids entertained well past bedtime.

# A Day in the Park

You could spend a week touring **GOLDEN GATE PARK** and still not take advantage of everything it has to offer—the city's main playground is *that* big. But you can certainly see the highlights in a day, and here's the best way to do it.

**MORNING:** Start the day at **KATE'S KITCHEN** in the Haight-Ashbury district (471 Haight St at Fillmore St; 415/626-3984). Don your most comfortable shoes, then pick up some sandwiches at a nearby deli and head to **GOLDEN GATE PARK**. Start with the big attractions: the fantastic **STEINHART AQUARIUM, MORRISON PLANETARIUM**, and **NATURAL HISTORY MUSEUM** at the **CALIFORNIA ACADEMY OF SCIENCES** (off Middle Dr E, between John F. Kennedy and Martin Luther King Jr. Drs; 415/750-7145), as well as the serene **JAPANESE TEA GARDEN** (off Martin Luther King Jr. Dr; 415/752-4227).

**AFTERNOON:** Next, have a picnic lunch in the colorful **DAHLIA GARDEN** that fronts the resplendent **CONSERVATORY OF FLOWERS** (John F. Kennedy Dr near Conservatory Dr; 415/641-7978). If you're the romantic type, after lunch head to **STOW LAKE** (off John F. Kennedy Dr; 415/752-0347), rent a paddleboat, and spend a few hours paddling around the lake and feeding the swans. For a more adventurous option, go to **SKATES ON HAIGHT** (located half a block from Golden Gate Park at 1818 Haight St at Stanyan St; 415/752-8375), rent some conventional or in-line skates, and spend a few hours skating along the wide, tree-lined John F. Kennedy Drive. Don't worry if you suck at skating—the people having the most fun are the ones who forgot how to skate (besides, JFK Drive is closed to auto traffic on Sunday, so there's plenty of elbow room).

**EVENING:** OK, you've returned the skates, and it's probably getting toward the end of the day, so head to the west end of the park and watch the surfers and the sunset at **OCEAN BEACH** (dress warm). To cap off a perfect day, head back to Haight Street and have dinner at one of our all-time favorite restaurants, **CHA CHA CHA** (1801 Haight St at Schrader St; 415/386-5758), then waddle over to **KAN ZAMAN** (1793 Haight St at Schrader St; 415/751-9656) to smoke fragrant tobacco from an authentic hookah (trust us, it's a blast even if you don't smoke) and watch the belly dancers.

# The Locals-Only Tour

OK, you've seen all of San Francisco's major attractions, sampled the sourdough bread and Dungeness crab, and driven down Lombard Street, and now you're ready to see where the locals play and eat.

**MORNING:** The local's day starts with standing in line—with other locals, of course—at **ELLA'S** (500 Presidio Ave at California St; 415/441-5669) for breakfast (so worth the wait). If it's Sunday, be sure to attend either the 9am or 11am Sunday sermon sensation at the nondenominational **GLIDE MEMORIAL CHURCH** (330 Ellis St at Taylor St; 415/771-6300). Even if you're an ardent atheist, you can't help but whoop and holler along with the choir. Otherwise, take a bus to the **CASTRO** to check out one of the most renowned gay neighborhoods in the world. Besides just absorbing the positive energy flowing here, you can do some serious shopping along **CASTRO STREET** or, better yet, catch a classic flick at the incredible **CASTRO THEATRE** (429 Castro St at Market St; 415/621-6120).

**AFTERNOON:** Next, head east to the Mission District for a heavy dose of cross-cultures. Have a crepe for lunch at **TI COUZ** (3108 16th St at Valencia St; 415/252-7373), a burrito at **LA TAQUERIA** (2889 Mission St btwn 28th and 29th Sts; 415/285-7117), or the best Vietnamese food you'll ever eat at **THE SLANTED DOOR** (584 Valencia St at 17th St; 415/861-8032), then browse the dozens of shops along Valencia and Mission Streets. When you've had your fill of the high-energy Mission District scene, take a cross-town trip to Lincoln Park to spend a few

## THE 49-MILE SCENIC DRIVE

Introduce yourself to San Francisco's splendor by cruising in your automobile along the 49-Mile Scenic Drive-a four-hour, self-guided journey on the city's prettiest streets and past its most scenic sites, including Union Square, North Beach, Chinatown, Nob Hill, and Fisherman's Wharf. The route is well marked by blue-and-white signs featuring a picture of a seagull-but don't follow the birdie during rush hour unless you also enjoy staring at lots of license plates. A detailed map outlining the course is available at the San Francisco Visitor Information Center (900 Market St at Powell St, near the Union Square cable car turntable; 415/391-2000).

hours admiring one of the finest collections of **RODIN SCULPTURES** outside Paris at the gorgeous **CALIFORNIA PALACE OF THE LEGION OF HONOR** (34th Ave and Clement St in Lincoln Park; 415/750-3600), the most underrated (and nontouristy) museum in the city.

**EVENING:** By now it's time for dinner, so grab a cab to Cole Valley for some Euro-Asian fusion cuisine at **EOS RESTAURANT & WINE BAR** (901 Cole St at Carl St; 415/566-3063), a neighborhood favorite. If there's still gas in your tank, finish the day with some great live music and dancing at **CAFE DU NORD** (2170 Market St btwn Church and Sanchez Sts; 415/861-5016), one of the best live music venues in the city. Congratulations—you're now an honorary local.

# DAY TRIPS

# DAY TRIPS

## Berkeley

*10 miles northeast of San Francisco (approximately 15 to 20 minutes, traffic permitting). Cross the San Francisco–Oakland Bay Bridge, keep in the left lanes, take the Interstate 80 turnoff, then take the University Avenue exit; turn right onto University, which spills into the town of Berkeley. If you don't have a car, the Berkeley BART station is 2 blocks from the university, and the fare from any San Francisco BART station is under $3.*

You can still buy tie-dyed "Berserkley" T-shirts from vendors on Telegraph Avenue, but the wild days of this now middle-aged, upper-middle-class burg are gone. Although hot-button issues can still spark a march or two at the world-renowned University of California at Berkeley, these days most university students seem more interested in cramming for exams than in mounting a protest in People's Park. In some respects the action has moved from the campus to City Hall, where the town's residents—many of them former hippies, student intellectuals, and peace activists—rage on against everything from Columbus Day (Berkeley celebrates Indigenous People's Day instead) to the opening of a large video store downtown (too lowbrow and tacky). The *San Francisco Chronicle* once called Berkeley the "most contentious of cities," and it's a mantle most of its inhabitants wear with pride.

### EXPLORING

If you're a newcomer to Berkeley, start your tour of the town at the **UNIVERSITY OF CALIFORNIA AT BERKELEY** (also known as UC Berkeley, or Cal), the oldest and second largest of the nine campuses in the UC system. Driving through the campus is virtually impossible, so park on a side street or in a lot and set out on foot. The university isn't so huge that you'd get hopelessly lost if you wandered around on your own, but without guidance you might miss some of the highlights. Pick up a self-guided walking packet at the **UC BERKELEY VISITOR INFORMATION CENTER** (open Monday through Friday), or attend one of the free 90-minute tours offered Monday through Friday at 10am (meet at the visitor center), Saturday at 10am, and Sunday at 1pm (meet in front of the Campanile clock tower in the heart of the campus for the Saturday and Sunday tours). The visitor center is at 2200 University Avenue at Oxford Street, University Hall, Room 101; 510/642-5215 (recording) or 510/642-INFO; www.berkeley.edu (click on the Visitor's Services link).

A few paces north of the intersection of Telegraph Avenue and Bancroft Way is the university's legendary **SPROUL PLAZA**, where the Free

Speech Movement began in 1964. Walk up the famous steps of **SPROUL HALL**, where many demonstrators stood (and still stand) to speak their piece; pass through the double doors, and just beyond the entrance you'll see a display of photos commemorating those exciting times. Several hundred feet north of Sproul Plaza is the pretty bronzed-metal and white-granite **SATHER GATE**, the main campus entrance until the university was expanded in the '60s. If you head northeast toward the center of things you'll spot the **CAMPANILE** (officially named Sather Tower, though nobody calls it that), a 307-foot clock tower modeled after St. Mark's Campanile in Venice, Italy. Built in 1914, this is Cal's best-known landmark; for a small fee you can take the elevator to the top for a stunning view of the Bay Area. The only original building still standing on campus is just southwest of the Campanile: **SOUTH HALL**, built in 1873. Walk north past the tower and turn east on University Drive, and you'll eventually see, on your left, the Beaux Arts beauty known as the **HEARST MINING BUILDING**. Continue east on University Drive, and at the top of the hill, hidden in a eucalyptus grove, is the **GREEK THEATRE**, which architect Julia Morgan (of Hearst Castle fame) modeled after the amphitheater in Epidaurus, Greece. The popular theater was presented in 1903 as a gift by newspaper publisher William Randolph Hearst.

A visit to Berkeley wouldn't be complete without a stroll down bustling **TELEGRAPH AVENUE**, still the haunt of students, street people, runaways, hipsters, professors, and tarot readers. Start your trek down Telegraph at the intersection with Bancroft (at the southernmost edge of UC Berkeley), and make a loop around all the friendly street vendors hawking everything from top-quality tie-dyed shirts, dresses, and boxer shorts to handmade earrings and hand-painted ties. Along this street are some great bookstores, most notably **CODY'S BOOKS** (2454 Telegraph Ave at Haste St; 510/845-7852; www.codysbooks.com) and **MOE'S BOOKS** (2476 Telegraph Ave between Dwight Wy and Hayes St; 510/849-2087; www.moesbooks.com), and numerous cafes, including the popular **CAFE INTERMEZZO** (2442 Telegraph Ave at Haste St; 510/849-4592), where you can get a salad the size of your head and freshly made pastries. Across the street is **CAFFE MEDITERRANEUM** (2475 Telegraph Ave between Haste St and Dwight Wy; 510/549-1128), which made its film debut in *The Graduate*. "The Med" captures the bohemian flavor of Telegraph, and churns out good cappuccinos as well as burgers, pastas, and desserts.

Several museums grace this little city as well, including the highly regarded **UC BERKELEY ART MUSEUM** (2626 Bancroft Wy, between College Ave and Bowditch St; 510/642-0808), which has a small permanent collection of modern art and frequently hosts traveling exhibitions, as well as a sculpture garden and the **PACIFIC FILM ARCHIVE**. The **JUDAH L.**

## POWER TO THE PEOPLE'S PARK

On Dwight Way, between Telegraph Avenue and Bowditch Street, is People's Park, famous as a site of student riots that first flared when the university wanted to replace the park with a dormitory. On April 29, 1969, hundreds of activists gathered at the vacant lot with gardening tools and the intent to convert the dirt lot into a park. One month later Berkeley's mayor sent 250 police officers into the park to restore order, and a mass of 4,000 demonstrators assembled to challenge them. A riot ensued, police fired buckshot at the crowd, and one rioter was killed and another blinded. Then-governor Ronald Reagan called in the National Guard, and Berkeley became a war zone. For the next 17 days the guardsmen repeatedly gassed the activists, including university students and faculty. As a result, People's Park became the decade's most potent symbol of "people power." The dorm was never built, but in 1991 UC officials succeeded in placing a few sand volleyball courts and basketball courts in the park—and even that incited several protests.

**MAGNES MUSEUM** (2911 Russell St off Ashby and Pine Sts; 510/849-2710), the third-largest Jewish museum in the West, offers numerous exhibitions of Jewish art and culture, and a vast array of anthropological artifacts is showcased at the **PHOEBE HEARST MUSEUM OF ANTHROPOLOGY** (in UC Berkeley's Kroeber Hall, at the corner of College Ave and Bancroft Wy; 510/643-7648). Hands-on exhibits exploring the world of lasers, holograms, and cutting-edge computers are featured at the **LAWRENCE HALL OF SCIENCE** (One Centennial Dr near Grizzly Peak Blvd; 510/642-5133; www.lawrencehallofscience.org), and while you're there, duck outside to see (and hear) the giant, eerie wind chimes and take a peek at the Stonehenge-like solar observatory.

When you're ready for more pastoral (not to mention free) diversions, stroll through the **BERKELEY ROSE GARDEN**, a terraced park with 3,000 rosebushes (250 varieties) and a stellar view of San Francisco, particularly at sunset (on Euclid Ave between Bay View and Eunice Sts), or walk through the 30-acre **UNIVERSITY OF CALIFORNIA BOTANICAL GARDEN** (in Strawberry Canyon on 200 Centennial Dr; 510/642-3343), where you'll see more than 12,000 plants, including a spectacular collection of cacti from around the world, a Mendocino pygmy forest, and a Miocene-era redwood grove; free guided tours are offered on weekends.

The 2,065-acre **TILDEN REGIONAL PARK** (off Wildcat Canyon Rd; 510/562-PARK, press 7), set high in the hills above town, offers picnic sites, forests, open meadows, and miles of hiking trails, plus a steam train, a charming merry-go-round, pony rides, and a farm and nature area for kids. Tilden also boasts a beautiful **BOTANICAL GARDEN** (510/841-8732) specializing in California native plants, and tours of the garden are offered regularly. For kite flying, Frisbee throwing, and the very popular **ADVENTURE PLAYGROUND,** drive to the west end of town to the **BERKELEY MARINA** (at the foot of University Ave, just W of the Hwy 80 overpass, Berkeley; Adventure Playground is open weekends and holidays only; 510/644-8623), which extends 3,000 feet into the bay, providing a stunning view of the San Francisco skyline, the Bay Bridge, and the Golden Gate Bridge.

## SHOPPING

With its recent profusion of chichi stores and upscale outlets (Crate & Barrel, Dansk, Sur La Table, the Gardener, Sweet Potatoes, and so on), the **FOURTH STREET AREA** has become Berkeley's shopping mecca—a somewhat ironic development considering the city's traditional disdain for the bourgeoisie. Another favorite shopping area is in south Berkeley, near the Berkeley/Oakland border, in the small **ELMWOOD NEIGHBORHOOD,** which stretches along College Avenue and crosses Ashby Avenue. Poke your head into the tiny **TAIL OF THE YAK** boutique (2632 Ashby Ave, W of College Ave; 510/841-9891) for a look at the fabulous displays of Central American and other art treasures, then stroll along College, where you can pet the lop-eared baby bunnies and squawk back at the beautiful parrots at **YOUR BASIC BIRD** (2940 College Ave, N of Ashby Ave; 510/841-7617); dip into the huge candy jars at **SWEET DREAMS** (2901 College Ave at Russell St; 510/549-1211); munch on fantastic fresh-fruit cheese danish at **NABOLOM BAKERY** (2708 Russell St at College Ave; 510/845-BAKE); shop for clothes at numerous boutiques, and then drop by **ESPRESSO ROMA** (2960 College Ave at Ashby Ave; 510/644-3773), where you can sip strong coffee drinks, teas, fresh lemonade, beer on tap, or wine by the glass and eat some good calzones and sandwiches. On the other side of Berkeley, where the northwest border meets the little town of Albany, is **SOLANO AVENUE,** a popular mile-long street lined with shops and cafes frequented by locals.

Most folks around here agree that if you can't find what you want at **CODY'S BOOKS** (2454 Telegraph Ave at Haste St; 510/845-7852; www.codysbooks.com), Berkeley's best bookstore, it probably isn't worth reading. Almost every night, nationally known literary and political writers appear at Cody's and at **BLACK OAK BOOKS** (1491 Shattuck Ave between Rose and Vine Sts; 510/486-0698), a popular purveyor of new and used books. The four-story **MOE'S BOOKS** (2476 Telegraph Ave at Haste St; 510/849-2087) specializes in used tomes and remainders. And a **BARNES & NOBLE** megastore (2352 Shattuck Ave at Durant St; 510/644-0861), complete with a high-tech fountain and park benches for on-the-spot reading, offers discounts on the *New York Times* best-sellers and hardcover books and stocks hundreds of periodicals.

For some of the best bread in the Bay Area, go to Steve Sullivan's famous **ACME BREAD COMPANY** (1601 San Pablo Ave at Cedar St; 510/524-1327) or the **CHEESE BOARD** (1512 Shattuck Ave at Vine St; 510/549-3183), a collectively owned bakery and vast gourmet cheese shop. If you're a bagel lover, two Berkeley bagel shops rival Brooklyn's best: **NOAH'S BAGELS** (3170 College Ave at Alcatraz St, 510/654-0944; and 1883 Solano Ave at Alameda St, 510/525-4447) and **BOOGIE WOOGIE BAGEL BOY** (1281 Gilman St at Santa Fe Ave; 510/524-3104), formerly Brothers' Bagels.

## PERFORMING ARTS AND NIGHTLIFE

Music: The **BERKELEY SYMPHONY** blends new and experimental music with the classics at Zellerbach Hall (510/841-2800) on the UC Berkeley campus. Modern rock, funk, and acid jazz are blasted at **BLAKE'S** (2367 Telegraph Ave at Durant St; 510/848-0886). In the mood to dance? Drop in at **ASHKENAZ** (1317 San Pablo Ave at Gilman St; 510/525-5054). Live rock, jazz, folk, reggae, and other concerts are frequently held at UC Berkeley's intimate, open-air **GREEK THEATRE** (Gayley Rd off Hearst Ave; 510/642-9988), a particularly pleasant place for sitting beneath the stars and listening to music on warm summer nights. **CAL PERFOR-MANCES** (510/642-9988) presents up-and-coming and established artists of all kinds—from the Bulgarian Women's Choir to superstar mezzo-soprano Cecilia Bartoli; the concerts are held at various sites on the UC Berkeley campus.

Theater and Film: The **BERKELEY REPERTORY THEATRE** (2025 Addison St at Shattuck Ave; 510/845-4700) has a national reputation for experimental productions of the classics and innovative new works, and the **BLACK REPERTORY GROUP** (3201 Adeline St at Ashby St; 510/652-2120) offers a range of plays, dance performances, and art by African Americans. Every summer the **CALIFORNIA SHAKESPEARE FESTIVAL** (510/548-3422) performs in an outdoor theater in the Berkeley hills near Orinda (bundle up, 'cause it's usually freezing). Film buffs will appreciate the **PACIFIC FILM ARCHIVE** (2575 Bancroft Ave at Bowditch St; 510/642-1412), which shows underground avant-garde movies as well as the classics. For up-to-date listings of cultural events, pick up a free copy of **THE EXPRESS**, the East Bay's alternative weekly, available at cafes and newsstands throughout the area.

## RESTAURANTS

Just northwest of the university, on Shattuck Avenue, is the area well known as the "Gourmet Ghetto," thanks to the international reputation of Chez Panisse and other great neighborhood restaurants. **CHEZ PANISSE** (1517 Shattuck Ave between Cedar and Vine Sts; 510/548-5525) is one of the most famous restaurants in the nation. Owner and chef Alice Waters has been at the forefront of the California cuisine revolution since 1971, when she started cooking simple French-influenced meals for groups of friends, then opened her legendary restaurant. Other favored dining establishments in this neighborhood are **CAMBODIANA'S** (2156 University Ave between Shattuck Ave and Oxford St; 510/843-4630), a superb Cambodian restaurant open for lunch and dinner; **CHESTER'S CAFE** (1508-B Walnut Sq, off Vine St; 510/849-9995), which serves breakfast all day, lunch, and weekend brunch—search for a seat on the upstairs deck, where you can look out at the bay and the Golden Gate; **SAUL'S** (1475 Shattuck Ave at Vine St; 510/848-DELI), an old-fashioned deli offering breakfast from sunrise to sunset as well as classic "regular or full-figured" sandwiches; and **CHA AM** (1543 Shattuck Ave at Cedar St; 510/848-9664), for good, reasonably priced Thai food served on a glassed-in patio under towering palms.

Get a bite to eat at **BETTE'S-TO-GO** (also known as BTG) or, better yet, plan on indulging in a big breakfast here at the adjoining **BETTE'S OCEANVIEW DINER** (1807-A 4th St btwn Hearst Ave and Virginia St; 510/644-3230), a small, nouveau-'40s diner that doesn't have an ocean view (or any view, for that matter) but does have red booths, chrome stools, a checkerboard tile floor, a hip wait staff, the best jukebox around, and damn good breakfasts. On weekends bring the newspaper or a good book and expect a 45-minute stomach-growling wait, but consider the payoff: enormous, soufflé-style pancakes stuffed with pecans and ripe berries, farm-fresh eggs scrambled with prosciutto and Parmesan, outstanding omelets, corned beef hash, and the quintessential huevos rancheros. Nearby is the popular **CAFE ROUGE** (1782 4th St btwn Delaware and Hearst Sts; 510/525-1440), where you'll find everything from duck braised in white wine to grilled steaks for lunch and dinner. For less expensive fare or an inexpensive drink, belly up to the bar and hofbrau at **BRENNAN'S** (4th St and University Ave, under the overpass; 510/841-0960), a Berkeley landmark that's been serving hand-carved roasted-meat sandwiches with mashed potatoes and gravy since 1959. Brennan's handsome dark-wood bar serves great Irish coffee and beer.

A short drive away is another very popular breakfast and lunch spot, the diminutive **CAFE FANNY** (1603 San Pablo Ave, btwn Cedar and Virginia Sts; 510/524-5447), owned by Alice Waters (of Chez Panisse fame). This corner cafe, nestled next to the famous **ACME BREAD COMPANY** (be sure to swing by and pick up a few loaves to go), can handle fewer than a dozen stand-up customers at once, but that doesn't deter anyone. Named after Waters's daughter, the cafe recalls the neighborhood haunts so dear to the French. Breakfast on crunchy Cafe Fanny granola, jam-filled buckwheat crepes, or perfect soft-boiled eggs served on sourdough toast with a side of house-made jam, and sip a cafe au lait from a big, authentically French, handleless bowl. For lunch order a small pizza or one of the seductive sandwiches. You won't get trencherman portions, but you'll love every crumb.

When Berkeley carnivores hear the call of the wild and nothing but a big, rare burger will do, they head for **FATAPPLES** (1346 Martin Luther King Jr. Wy at Rose St; 510/526-2260), just a few blocks northwest of the famous Shattuck strip. A prime contender in the ongoing Berkeley burger wars, FatApples makes its burgers of exceptionally lean, high-quality ground beef and serves them on house-made wheat rolls. Don't miss the flaky olallieberry or pecan pie, the thick jumbo shakes, or the ethereal cheese puffs. For a hot dog and a good brewski, head south on Shattuck to the **TRIPLE ROCK BREWERY** (1920 Shattuck Ave at University Ave; 510/843-2739) and order the specialty beer of the day, then go way up the hill on Hearst to Top Dog (2503 Hearst Ave at Euclid St; 510/843-1241), a cheap, kinda grungy Berkeley institution that's been serving good hot dogs for years.

Where the northwest border of Berkeley meets the little town of Albany is **SOLANO AVENUE**, a popular mile-long street lined with shops and cafes. Solano is also home to one of the East Bay's best pizza joints, **ZACHARY'S CHICAGO PIZZA** (1853 Solano Ave at Alameda St; 510/525-5950). For years Bay Area transplants from the East Coast complained about the wretched local pizza. Then along came Zachary's with its tasty rendition of Chicago-style deep-dish: a deep-bottom crust packed with a choice of fillings, covered with a thin second crust, and topped with tomato sauce (the bottom crust turns crisp in the oven; the top one melts into the filling).

## LODGINGS

If you're looking for a place to stay in Berkeley, some of the favored spots are the grand, gleaming white, 279-room **CLAREMONT RESORT AND SPA** (41 Tunnel Rd, at Ashby and Domingo Aves; 510/843-3000 or 800/551-7266; www.claremontresort.com); the **ROSE GARDEN INN** (2740 Telegraph Ave btwn Ward and Stuart Sts; 510/549-2145; www.rosegardeninn.com), an attractive 40-room bed-and-breakfast surrounded by beautifully landscaped lawns; and the 18-room **FRENCH HOTEL** (1538 Shattuck Ave, btwn Cedar and Vine Sts; 510/548-9930), a simple, comfortable lodging in the heart of the Gourmet Ghetto. Note: Berkeley is a college town, so bear in mind that just about every accommodation will be booked three to four months in advance for May graduations; this guaranteed booking period also prompts most lodgings to jack up their rates for that month. The rest of the year you'll find that many of Berkeley's room rates are competitive with the ever-increasing rates of San Francisco's numerous hotels.

# The Marin Coast

When you consider that the San Francisco Bay Area has more people than the entire state of Oregon, and that Marin County has the highest per capita income in the nation, you would expect its coastline to be lined with fancy lodgings and resorts. Truth is, you won't find even a Motel 6 along the entire Marin coast, due partly to public pressure but mostly to the inaccessibly rugged, heavily forested terrain (it may look like a 15-minute drive from San Francisco on the map, but 90 minutes later you'll probably still be negotiating hairpin curves down the side of Mount Tamalpais). In fact, the Marin coast is just short of Eden, a veritable organic playground for city-weary 9-to-5ers in search of a patch of green or a square of sand to call their own for a day.

## MARIN HEADLANDS

*Head north across the Golden Gate Bridge, take the Alexander Avenue exit, and make your first left onto Conzelman Road, which leads into the Marin Headlands.*

On a sunny San Francisco day there's no better place to spend time outdoors than in the Marin Headlands. For more than a century following the Civil War, this vast expanse of grass-covered hills and rocky shore was off-limits to the public, appropriated by the U.S. Army as a strategic base for defending the bay against invaders. Remnants of obsolete and untested defenses—dozens of thick concrete bunkers and batteries recessed into the bluffs—now serve as playgrounds and picnic sites for the millions of tourists who visit each year.

There's a wealth of scheduled activities offered daily within the 15-square-mile **GOLDEN GATE NATIONAL RECREATION AREA**—birding clinics, bunker tours, wildflower hunts, geology hikes—but most visitors are satisfied with poking their heads into a bunker or two, snapping a photo of the San Francisco skyline, and driving home. For a more thorough approach buy the handy *Marin Headlands Map and Guide to Sites, Trails and Wildlife* at the Information Center at Fort Barry (415/331-1540; follow the signs in the headlands), and plan your day from there. Free hiking, mountain biking, and pet-friendly trail maps are available, too. The center is open daily from 9:30am to 4:30pm.

A popular Marin Headlands attraction is the **MARINE MAMMAL CENTER** (415/289-SEAL), a volunteer-run hospital for injured and abandoned mammals of the sea. It's virtually impossible not to melt at the sight of the cute sea lions and elephant and harbor seals as they lie in their pens (the center's staff, being no dummies, takes donations right on the spot). Signs list each animal's adopted name, species, stranding site, and injury—the latter of which is usually human-caused. Located at the east end of Fort Cronkhite near Rodeo Lagoon, the Marine Mammal Center is open daily from 10am to 4pm, and admission is free.

Closed to the public for several years due to storm damage, the precariously perched 1877 **POINT BONITA LIGHTHOUSE** (415/331-1540) is once again thrilling those tourists who are brave enough to traverse the long, dark tunnel and seven small footbridges leading to the beacon. (Because the cliffs along the passageway are so steep, one 19th-century lighthouse keeper rigged ropes around his children to prevent them from slipping into the raging sea below.) The reward for such bravery is, among other things, a rare and sensational view of the entrance to the bay. Call for tour times, and be sure to inquire about the full-moon tours, which take place twice a month by reservation only.

Also within the Marin Headlands is **HAWK HILL**, one of the most remarkable avian sites in the western United States and the biggest hawk lookout in western North America. Record count in 1992 was more than 20,000 birds, including 21 species of hawks. The best time to visit is during September and October, when thousands of birds of prey soar over the hill each day. The hill is located above Battery 129, where Conzelman Road becomes a one-way street. For a current schedule of the free ranger-led walks through the Marin Headlands—with topics ranging from bird-watching to wildflowers and war relics—call 415/331-1540.

## MUIR WOODS–MUIR BEACH

*Take the Stinson Beach/Highway 1 exit off Highway 101 just north of Sausalito and follow Highway 1 all the way to Muir Beach. A few miles before you reach the ocean there's a fork in the road to the Muir Woods turnoff (you'll see the sign). If you don't have a car you can book a bus trip with the Red & White Fleet (415/447-0597 or 877/855-5506), which takes you to Muir Woods and makes a short stop in Sausalito on the way back. The 3½-hour tours run several times daily and cost $33 for adults, $16 for children 5–11, and are free for kids under 5. Call for information and departure times.*

When you stand in the middle of Muir Woods, surrounded by a canopy of ancient redwoods towering hundreds of feet skyward, it's hard to fathom that San Francisco is less than 6 miles away. The park is a den of wooden giants; tourists speak in hushed tones as they crane their necks in disbelief, snapping photographs that don't begin to capture the immensity of these living titans, which once covered the entire coastal range.

Although the 560-acre park can get absurdly crowded on summer weekends (particularly on the flat trails along the canyon floor), you can usually circumvent the masses by hiking up the **OCEAN VIEW TRAIL** and returning via the **FERN CREEK TRAIL**. The park is open daily from 8am to sunset, and there's an admission price of $2 per person 17 or older. Picnicking is not allowed, although there is a snack bar (and gift shop) at the entrance. It's typically cool and damp here, so dress appropriately. For more information call 415/388-2595 or visit the Muir Woods website at www.nps.gov/muwo/.

Three miles west of Muir Woods, along Highway 1, is a small crescent-shaped cove called **MUIR BEACH**. Strewn with bits of driftwood and numerous tide pools, Muir Beach is a more sedate alternative to the beer-'n'-bikini crowds at the ever-popular Stinson Beach up north. If all you're looking for is a sandy, quiet place for some R&R, park your car right here and skip the trip to Stinson altogether (swimming, however, isn't allowed at Muir Beach because of the strong rip currents).

## STINSON BEACH

*Take the Stinson Beach/Highway 1 exit off Highway 101 just north of Sausalito, and follow Highway 1 all the way to Stinson Beach.*

On those treasured weekend days when the fog has lifted and the sun is scorching the Northern California coast, bleary-eyed Bay Area residents grab their morning paper and beach chairs, pile into their Mazda Miatas and Jeeps, and scramble to the sandy shores of Stinson Beach—the North Coast's nice-try answer to the fabled beaches of Southern California.

Stinson Beach is one of Northern California's most popular beaches, a 3.5-mile stretch of beige sand that offers enough elbow room for everyone to spread out beach blankets, picnic baskets, and toys. Swimming is allowed, and lifeguards are on hand from May to mid-September, though notices about riptides (plus the sea's toe-numbing temperatures and the threat of sharks) tend to discourage folks from venturing too far into the water. For recorded weather and surf conditions at Stinson call 415/868-1922. The beach is open daily from 9am to 10pm, and there's no charge for admission. Joined at the hip with *la playa* is the town of Stinson Beach, which does a brisk summer business serving lunch alfresco at its numerous cafes.

There are plenty of adventurous things to do around Stinson. For example, Scott Tye, a kayak instructor for **OFF THE BEACH BOATS** (15 Calle del Mar, Stinson Beach; 415/868-9445) in downtown Stinson Beach next to the post office, offers two-hour lessons on the basics of sea and surf kayaking. Rentals are surprisingly cheap (about $22 for two hours for surf kayaks), and they even rent a kayak that can hold an entire nuclear family.

A short drive north of Stinson Beach on Highway 1 leads to **BOLINAS LAGOON**, a placid saltwater expanse that serves as a refuge for numerous shorebirds and harbor seals sprawled out on the sandbars. Across from the lagoon is the **AUDUBON CANYON RANCH'S BOLINAS LAGOON PRESERVE** (4900 Hwy 1 just N of Stinson Beach; 415/868-9244; www.egret.org), a 1,014-acre wildlife sanctuary that supports a major heronry of great blue herons. This is the premier spot along the

Pacific Coast to watch immense, graceful seabirds as they court, mate, and rear their young, all accomplished on the tops of towering redwoods. Admission is free, though donations are requested; open mid-March to mid-July on Saturdays, Sundays, and holidays 10am to 4pm, and by appointment for groups.

And if you head back the other way, about a mile south of Stinson Beach off Highway 1 is **RED ROCK BEACH**, one of the few nude beaches on the Marin coast. It's easy to miss since you can't see it from the road; park at the first dirt pull-off on your right after leaving Stinson Beach and look for a steep trail leading down to the water.

## BOLINAS

*Take the Stinson Beach/Highway 1 exit off Highway 101 just north of Sausalito and follow Highway 1 past Stinson Beach to Bolinas.*

A sort of retirement community for aging rock stars, spent novelists, and former hippies, Bolinas is one of the most reclusive towns in Northern California. Residents regularly take down highway signs pointing the way to their rural enclave, an act that ironically has created more publicity for Bolinas than any road sign ever did. As a tourist you don't have to worry about being chased out of town by a band of machete-wielding Bolinistas, but don't expect anyone to roll out the welcome mat either. The trick is to look not like a tourist but more like a Bay Area resident who's only here to buy some peaches at the **PEOPLE'S STORE** (415/868-1433; open 8:30am–6:30pm every day).

What's the People's Store, you ask? It's a town landmark that's famous for its locally grown organic produce and exceptional service—the antithesis of the corporate supermarket. It's a little hard to find, hidden at the end of a gravel driveway next to the Bolinas Bakery (don't confuse it with the much larger general store down the street), but it's worth searching out just to see (and taste) the difference between Safeway and the Bolinas way.

Three side trips near Bolinas offer some adventurous exercise. Just before entering downtown Bolinas turn right (west) on Mesa Road, left on Overlook Road, and right on Elm Road and you'll dead-end at the **DUXBURY REEF NATURE RESERVE**, a rocky outcropping with numerous tide pools harboring a healthy population of starfish, sea anemones, snails, sea urchins, and other creatures that kids go gaga over. If you continue west on Mesa Road you'll reach the **POINT REYES BIRD OBSERVA-TORY**, where ornithologists keep an eye on more than 400 feathered species—it's one of the few full-time ornithological research stations in the United States. Admission to the visitor center and nature trail is free, and visitors are welcome to observe the tricky process of catching and banding the birds Tuesday through Sunday mornings, weather permitting, from May through October. It's open every day from 15 minutes after sunrise until sunset. Banding hours vary, so call 415/868-0655 for exact times and 415/868-1221, extension 40, for recorded general information. At the very end of Mesa Road is the **PALOMARIN TRAILHEAD**, a popular hiking trail that leads into the south entrance of Point Reyes National Seashore. The 6-mile round-trip trek—one of Point Reyes's prettiest hikes—passes several small lakes and meadows before it reaches Alamere Falls, a freshwater stream that cascades down a 40-foot bluff into Wildcat Beach.

---

# Point Reyes National Seashore

*The easiest route is via Sir Francis Drake Boulevard from Highway 101 at Larkspur. A much longer but more scenic route: Take the Stinson Beach/Highway 1 exit off Highway 101 just north of Sausalito and follow Highway 1 west to the ocean, then due north.*

Think of the Point Reyes National Seashore as Mother Nature's version of Disneyland, an outdoor-lover's playground with one doozy of a sandbox. Hiking, biking, swimming, sailing, wind surfing, sunbathing, camping, fishing, horseback riding, bird-watching, kayaking—all are fair game at this 71,000-acre sanctuary of forested hills, deep green pastures, and undisturbed beaches. Point Reyes is hardly a secret anymore—millions of visitors arrive each year—but the land is so vast and varied that finding your own space is never a problem. (As the old saying goes: If you want to be alone, walk up.)

As soon as you arrive at Point Reyes, stop at the **BEAR VALLEY VISITORS CENTER** (on Bear Valley Rd; 415/464-5100; www.nps.gov/pore)—look for the small sign posted just north of Olema on Highway 1—and pick up a free Point Reyes trail map; open weekdays 9am to 5pm and weekends 8am to 5pm. On the westernmost tip of Point Reyes, at the end of Sir Francis Drake Highway, is the **POINT REYES LIGHTHOUSE** (415/669-1534), the park's most popular attraction. Even if you loathe lighthouse tours, go anyway. The drive alone is worth the trip, a 45-minute scenic excursion through windswept meadows and working dairy ranches (watch out for cows on the road). When the fog burns off, the lighthouse and the headlands provide a fantastic lookout point for spying gray whales and thousands of common murres that inundate the rocks below. Visitors have free access to the lighthouse via a thigh-burning 308-step staircase; open 10am to 4:30pm Thursday through Monday, weather permitting.

That mighty pungent aroma you smell on the way to the Point Reyes Lighthouse is probably emanating from **JOHNSON'S OYSTER FARM**. It may not look like much—a cluster of trailer homes, shacks, and oyster tanks surrounded by huge piles of oyster shells—but that certainly doesn't detract from the taste of fresh-out-of-the-water oysters dipped in Johnson's special sauce. Eat 'em on the spot, or buy a bag for the road— either way you're not likely to find California oysters as fresh or as cheap anywhere else. The oyster farm resides within **DRAKES ESTERO** (415/669-1149), a large saltwater lagoon on the Point Reyes peninsula that produces nearly 20 percent of California's commercial oyster yield. It's located off Sir Francis Drake Highway, about 6 miles west of Inverness, and is open 8am to 4:30pm Tuesday through Sunday.

A popular Point Reyes pastime is **OCEAN KAYAKING**. Don't worry, the kayaks are very stable and there are no waves to contend with because you'll be paddling through placid Tomales Bay, a haven for migrating birds and marine mammals. Rental prices at **TOMALES BAY SEA KAYAKING** (415/663-1743; www.tamalsaka.com) start at about $35 for a half-day ($65 for a double-hulled kayak), and you can sign up for a guided day trip, a sunset cruise, or a romantic full-moon outing. Instruction, clinics, and boat delivery are available, and all ages and levels are welcome. The launching point is located on Highway 1 at the Marshall Boatworks in Marshall, 8 miles north of Point Reyes Station. It's usually open daily from 9am to 6pm.

---

# Marin County Communities

## SAUSALITO

Nestled on the east side of Marin County is the pretty little Mediterranean-style town of Sausalito, a former fishing village that's now home to about 7,500 residents, including several well-heeled owners of spectacular hillside mansions. Immediately after driving over the Golden Gate Bridge (heading north), turn right on Alexander Avenue, which after about a mile turns into Bridgeway, the main drag through the center of town. Pricey boutiques and waterfront restaurants line this street, and a paved promenade offers a truly breathtaking, unobstructed view of Angel Island, Alcatraz, and the San Francisco skyline.

If you have kids in tow, be sure to spend an afternoon or a day at the **BAY AREA DISCOVERY MUSEUM** (Fort Baker under the north end of the Golden Gate Bridge; 415/487-4398; www.badm.org), where children can sing and dance in the Discovery Theater, pretend to pump gas into a Model T in the Transportation Building, create a clay sculpture or paint a picture in the Art Sport Center, build a skyscraper in the Architecture & Design Building, dissect a squid in the Science Lab, and much more. This unique, hands-on interactive learning center is designed for ages 1 through 10, and it's a guaranteed child-pleaser.

To best appreciate the town of Sausalito, park your car near Bridgeway (you may have to hit a municipal lot or a side street to find a spot) and walk along the promenade and through the tiny village. For the perfect perch on the bay, walk through the touristy restaurant **HORIZONS** (558 Bridgeway; 415/331-3232) and grab a seat on the wind-sheltered deck in back, where you can sip the spirit of your choice and wave at the yachters sailing just a few feet under your nose. For a more upscale (literally—it's located above Horizons) experience, we highly recommend the unsurpassed views and innovative fusion menu at **ONDINE** (558 Bridgeway; 415/331-1133), a great place to spend a romantic evening (and a lot of money).

The **NO NAME BAR** (757 Bridgeway; 415/332-1392) is one of the few places on Bridgeway where you'll find a local resident. Don't try looking for the bar's name, because there's only a small, handsome wooden sign that says "Bar" in gold letters. The No Name's free jazz and R&B concerts (held Tuesday through Saturday night and Sunday afternoon) draw crowds. Stroll across the street and you'll see the pier, where you can catch a ferry to San Francisco. Nearby is the tiny **PLAZA VINA DEL MAR**, graced by a pair of elephant statues and a fountain from the Panama-Pacific International Exposition of 1915. One of the highlights of Sausalito is its gorgeous yachts—walk down the wooden planks and try to guess how many greenbacks it takes to own (and maintain) one of these glistening beauties.

The four-story **VILLAGE FAIR** (777 Bridgeway), on the west side of Bridgeway, is an attractive shopping mall honeycombed with shops and flowers and even a little waterfall. Don't expect to find any bargains here, but it's worth a quick look. You'll see many folks licking Lappert's ice cream in freshly made waffle cones, which is dished out in two shops on either side of Village Fair (689 Bridgeway, 415/331-3607; and 817 Bridgeway, 415/332-8175). One block west of Bridgeway is **CALEDONIA STREET**, where the locals hang out. Cafes, shops, and a movie theater line this street, as well as **SUSHI RAN** (107 Caledonia St, next to the Marin Theater; 415/332-3620), one of the Bay Area's best sushi restaurants; it's open for lunch and dinner.

At the north end of Sausalito is **FRED'S PLACE** (1917 Bridgeway; 415/332-4575), which has been making terrific French toast and other belly-packing breakfast fare since 1966. Eat a hearty breakfast, then head across the street and down the hill to the **BAY MODEL VISITORS CENTER** (2100 Bridgeway; 415/332-3871), a 1½-acre working hydraulic model of the San Francisco Bay and the Delta region used by the U.S. Army Corps of Engineers to study the tides and various bay problems. There's a 10-minute film and a tour, but the most interesting time to visit is when it's in use, so call ahead. The Bay Model also offers interactive exhibits and a World War II shipyard display; admission is free, and it's open Tuesday through Saturday (Sunday in summer). Just before Bridgeway merges with Highway 101 you'll find Sausalito's community of house-boat dwellers. Take a gander at the floating homes, which vary from funky little wooden abodes covered with pots of bright flowers to swanky residences with helipads (park at the Waldo Point Harbor Houseboat Marina at the north end of Bridgeway).

Before you say so long to Sausalito, take a spin through the lush, landscaped hills, zigzagging your way from one end to the other to get a taste of how the rich really live. It's hard to get really lost—all the streets eventually wind down to Bridgeway—just don't get too distracted by the magnificent mansions as you navigate the narrow, twisting roads.

## TIBURON

For a tour of Tiburon and Belvedere, the well-to-do waterfront towns that sit cheek by jowl directly across the bay, head north on Highway 101, turn right at the Tiburon/Highway 131 exit, then follow the signs to Tiburon Boulevard and downtown Tiburon (about a 15-minute drive from the city). Formerly a railroad town and until 1963 the terminus of the Northwestern Pacific Railroad, Tiburon (Spanish for "shark") now resembles a New England–style coastal village. Its short **MAIN STREET** is lined with expensive antique and specialty shops, as well as restaurants with incredible bay views. You can leave your car on the outskirts and walk to the village, or park in the large pay-lot off Main Street. (An even better way to get here is by bicycle or by taking the ferry from San Francisco; it drops off passengers at the edge of town.) At the tip of the Tiburon peninsula is a small grassy park with benches; on sunny days people flock here with picnics to admire the panoramic view of San Francisco and Angel Island.

For lunch or dinner, ask for a seat on the patio at **GUAYMAS** (5 Main St at the ferry landing; 415/435-6300)—you'll likely need reservations on sunny days—and indulge in the restaurant's classic Mexican fare and a frothy margarita or one of the fine tequilas. You can get lesser-quality fare but equally spectacular views at the ever-popular **SAM'S ANCHOR CAFE** (27 Main St; 415/435-4527), where Bay Area residents crowd the huge outdoor deck in back on sunny weekends for beers, margaritas, burgers, and big baskets of fries (it's quite the party scene on weekend afternoons). Be sure to bring sunscreen and a designated driver.

Stroll west on Main Street and you'll bump into the intimate **TIBURON DELI** (110 Main St; 415/435-4888), which offers Bud's ice cream, frozen yogurt, and healthy sandwiches. The deli is part of Tiburon's historic **ARK ROW**, an assembly of 100-year-old restored arks that now houses several shops. Another popular stop is the Victorian tasting room at **WINDSOR VINEYARDS**, (72 Main St; 415/435-3113 or 800/214-9463), which dates from 1888. About 35 wines are available for a free tasting with a wine purchase; gourmet sauces, wine accessories, and wine-related gifts are also available. Follow Main Street beyond the shops to Beach Road for another amazing view of the bay, one that includes the prized yachts docked in front of the members-only **SAN FRANCISCO YACHT CLUB**.

## BELVEDERE

At the southwest tip of the Tiburon peninsula is Belvedere (Italian for "beautiful view"), an ultra-exclusive community that makes Sausalito look like a poor cousin. The entire city consists of only half a square mile of land—but this is one seriously tony piece of real estate. To get a better view of Belvedere, reclaim your car and drive up the tiny town's steep, narrow roads for a glimpse of the highly protected, well-shielded multimillion-dollar homes where international celebs such as Elton John have been known to hide out. After your hillside cruise, drive along San Rafael Avenue, which hugs Richardson Bay on the north side of Tiburon, for another great view of the water. You can't see it very well from the street, but behind a stretch of houses on the east side of San Rafael Avenue is **BELVEDERE LAGOON**, where residents sail, canoe, kayak, and mingle with their neighbors on their sunny waterside decks (you can get a peek at the lagoon just steps from the intersection of San Rafael Avenue and Windward Road).

## MILL VALLEY

San Rafael Avenue winds its way north to Tiburon Boulevard, which leads back to Highway 101. If you stay on Tiburon Boulevard and follow it past the highway on-ramps, it turns into East Blithedale Avenue and leads directly into the heart of the idyllic town of Mill Valley. This is where many millionaires have forsaken bayside plots of land for the highly coveted real estate nestled in the redwoods. Introduce yourself to the town by walking along **THROCKMORTON AVENUE**, the main shopping strip off Blithedale. For more information on this city, contact the Mill Valley Chamber of Commerce (85 Throckmorton Ave next to the Depot Bookstore; 415/388-9700, www.millvalley.org). For additional not-to-be-missed Marin County attractions, see the Marin Coast section.

# Napa Valley

*55 miles north of San Francisco (approximately 1½ hours, traffic permitting). Take Highway 101 north across the Golden Gate Bridge, turn off at the Napa-Vallejo/Highway 37 exit, and follow the signs to Highway 121 and Napa.*

Despite the plethora of nouveau châteaus, fake French barns, and gimcrack stores selling wine bottles full of cabernet-flavored jelly beans, Napa Valley is still one of Northern California's most enchanting regions. In early spring the hills are a vibrant green, bright-yellow mustard blossoms poke up between the grapevines, and stands of fruit trees burst into showy flower. In summer tourists flood the valley and its hundreds of wineries, cranking up the energy level a few notches and conferring a patina of glamour and excitement that some locals delight in and others deplore. Later, after the grape harvest, the vineyards turn a bright autumnal scarlet, and the region's quaint, Old West–style towns assume a more relaxed, homey atmosphere.

At any time of year Napa Valley is blessed with an abundance of excellent restaurants, scores of welcoming bed-and-breakfasts, a couple of ultraluxurious resorts, enough interesting shops to keep Gold Cards flashing up and down the valley, and recreational opportunities galore: boating, biking, horseback riding, hot-air ballooning, gliding, hiking, soaking in mud baths or hot springs, and exploring historic sites. Diversity is the watchword here. You might grab a map of the region's numerous wineries and work on expanding the contents of your cellar (see Napa Valley Wineries and Sonoma Valley Wineries sidebars). Or engage in that ultimate food-to-go experience, the **NAPA VALLEY WINE TRAIN** (for information or reservations call 707/253-2111 or 800/427-4124), where passengers sip fine wines and sup on a meal while gazing out at the lush countryside on their cushy ride in a historically preserved vintage railcar. Winery maps and details about parks, hot-air balloon rides, and other recreational pastimes are readily available at many locations, including most hotels and the **NAPA VALLEY CONFERENCE AND VISITORS BUREAU** (1310 Town Center Mall off 1st St, Napa; 707/226-7459; www.napavalley.com; open daily).

The 35-mile-long Napa Valley is home to some of the most famous wineries in the world, and many of them are clustered along scenic Highway 29 and the verdant Silverado Trail, parallel roads running the length of the region through such quaint little towns as Yountville, Oakville, St. Helena, and Calistoga. The valley is a zoo on weekends—especially in summer and early fall, when traffic on narrow Highway 29 rivals rush hour in the Bay Area. Wise Wine Country visitors plan their trips here for weekdays, the misty months of winter, or early spring, when many room rates are lower and everything's less crowded, but the valley is no less spectacular.

## NAPA

At the southernmost end of Napa Valley is the sprawling town of Napa, where about half of the county's 123,340 residents live. Although its name is synonymous with wine, most of the wineries are actually several miles north of town. The city, founded in 1848, is well known for its imposing Victorian structures, many of them in the downtown area near the Napa River. Introduce yourself by taking a self-guided walking tour of downtown Napa's architectural gems. A detailed map highlighting everything from a Victorian Gothic church to an art deco brewery and a Beaux Arts bank is available for free at the Napa Valley Conference and Visitors Bureau (see the contact information above), or you may choose from a half-dozen walking-tour maps sold for a nominal fee by Napa County Landmarks (1030 1st St at Main St, in the Community Preservation Center, Napa, CA 94559; 707/255-1836; open Mon–Fri).

If you have time for only a quick tour, walk along **MAIN STREET**, which crosses the river. At the south end of Main, adjacent to Veteran's Park on the river's west bank, is a handsome century-old building that's now home to **DOWNTOWN JOE'S RESTAURANT AND BREWERY** (902 Main St at 2nd St; 707/258-2337). Grab a table on the covered outdoor patio and sample a microbrew or two; Downtown Joe's even makes its own root beer and ginger ale. A couple of blocks north on Main, the locals kick back at the **NAPA VALLEY COFFEE ROASTING COMPANY** (948 Main St at 1st St; 707/224-2233), a great little spot for a cup of freshly brewed java. Across the street at **COPPERFIELD'S** (1303 1st St at Randolph St; 707/252-8002), you'll find new and used books at reasonable prices.

For terrific deli sandwiches, fresh vegetable juices, and smoothies, walk west on First Street to the **FIRST SQUEEZE DELI & JUICE BAR & CAFE** (1126 1st St at Main St, in the Clock Tower Plaza; 707/224-6762). You'll have to drive to get to the best deli in town, **GENOVA DELICATESSEN** (1550 Trancas St, W of Jefferson St; 707/253-8686), which makes great sandwiches, roasted chickens, and a variety of salads and sweets. You can even sit at the espresso bar and order an Italian soda, a gelato, or a smooth cup of joe. Another Napa favorite for a casual breakfast, lunch, or early dinner is the **ALEXIS BAKING COMPANY AND CAFE** (1517 3rd St btwn Main and Jefferson Sts; 707/258-1827), which is also an ideal spot to pick up goodies-to-go such as chocolate-caramel cake and pumpkin-spice muffins. One of the town's best restaurants is the **BISTRO DON GIOVANNI** (4110 St. Helena Hwy/Hwy 29, just N of Salvador Ave; 707/224-3300), a friendly Italian trattoria.

## YOUNTVILLE

About 9 miles north of Napa, right off Highway 29 where the hills are covered with grapevines, is the tiny town of Yountville, home of Moet et Chandon's Napa Valley–based winery, Domaine Chandon. Yountville was founded in the mid-19th century by pioneer George Clavert Yount, reportedly the first American to settle in Napa Valley, and it's now the site of some of the best restaurants in the Wine Country, including chef Thomas Keller's **FRENCH LAUNDRY** (6640 Washington St at Creek St; 707/944-2380), which also happens to be one of the nation's best restaurants, so reservations (usually months in advance) are essential, though you might be able to sneak in during lunch. Other very popular restaurants are Philippe Jeanty's **BISTRO JEANTY** (6510 Washington St;

# NAPA VALLEY WINERIES

Napa's wineries are mainly clustered along Highway 29 and the Silverado Trail, parallel roads running the length of the valley. It's a busy place on weekends—expect backups in the summer and early fall, when Highway 29 traffic can be bumper-to-bumper. With the increasing numbers of visitors, most vintners now charge a small fee to taste their wines, and some require reservations for tours (don't let the latter deter you—the smaller establishments just need to control the number of visitors at any one time to make sure someone will be available to show you around).

As you whiz along the highway and see the signs announcing some of the most famous wineries in the world, you'll be tempted to pull over and stop at every one. But do yourself a favor and follow a tip from veteran wine tasters: Pick out the four or five wineries you're most interested in visiting over the weekend, and stick to your itinerary. Touring more than a couple of wineries a day will surely overwhelm and exhaust even the most intrepid wine connoisseur, although if you really want to see several wineries in a short period, skip the grand tours and just visit the tasting rooms.

If you're new to the wine-touring scene, you'll be relieved to know you won't ever be pressured to buy any of the wines you've sampled—the vintners are just delighted to expose you to their line of products (besides, you'll often find much better prices at some of the good wine stores in town). Here's a roster of some of Napa Valley's most popular wineries that offer tastings and/or tours of their facilities:

**S. Anderson** S. Anderson is the only family-owned champagne house in the United States. Lively candlelight tours of the caves educate the visitor on méthode champenoise—the method for making premium sparkling wines. 1473 Yountville Crossroad, Yountville; 707/944-8642; www.4bubbly.com.

**Beaulieu Vineyards** Nicknamed "BV," this winery is housed in a historic estate and is famous for its cabernet sauvignon. 1960 St. Helena Hwy, Rutherford; 707/967-5230; www.bvwine.com.

**Beringer Vineyards** Napa Valley's oldest continuously operating winery features a stately old Rhineland-style mansion and good $5 tours of the vineyards and caves every half hour between 10am and 4pm. It's well known for its chardonnay and cabernet. 2000 Main St, St. Helena; 707/963-4812; www.beringer.com.

**Château Montelena Winery** This gorgeous French château–style winery, built of stone, is celebrated for its chardonnay. The beautiful setting includes a lake with two islands. 1429 Tubbs Ln, Calistoga; 707/942-5105; www.montelena.com.

**Clos Pegase** Designed by architect Michael Graves, this stunning modern facility offers grand outdoor sculpture, a "Wine in Art" slide show every Saturday afternoon from

February through November, and guided tours of the winery, caves, and art collection. 1060 Dunaweal Ln, 2 miles S of Calistoga; 707/942-4981; www.clospegase.com.

**Domaine Chandon** Good sparkling wines come from this winery's handsome building. There's a four-star dining room and fantastic guided tours, too. 1 California Dr, Yountville; 707/944-2280; www.chandonusa.com.

**Hess Collection Winery** A stone winery in a remote, scenic location, the Hess Collection is well known for its cabernet sauvignon and chardonnay. Contemporary-American and European art is showcased in a dramatic building, part of the very well designed self-guided tour. 4411 Redwood Rd, Napa; 707/255-1144; www.hesscollection.com.

**Merryvale Vineyards** Within Merryvale's historic stone building are daily tastings and, by appointment only, informative, thorough tasting classes on Saturday and Sunday mornings. The winery is best known for its chardonnay. 1000 Main St, St. Helena; 707/963-7777; www.merryvale.com.

**Niebaum-Coppola Winery** Filmmaker Francis Ford Coppola now owns this former Inglenook grand château, built in the 1880s. There's a display on Coppola's film career and Inglenook's history, and a gift shop stocked with wine, pottery, books, T-shirts, and even Coppola's favorite cigars. Daily wine tastings are offered, and tours are by appointment. 1991 St. Helena Hwy, Rutherford; 707/968-1100; www.niebaum-coppola.com.

**Opus One** In a dramatic bermed neoclassical building, one daily tour with an expensive wine tasting ($25 per 4-ounce glass of wine) is offered by appointment at this extraordinary winery. 7900 St. Helena Hwy, Oakville; 707/944-9442; www.opus onewinery.com.

**Robert Mondavi Winery** This huge, world-famous winery, housed in a Mission-style building, offers excellent tours of the facilities. 7801 St. Helena Hwy, Oakville; 707/226-1395 or 800/R-MONDAVI; www.robertmondaviwinery.com.

**Schramsberg Vineyards** Schramsberg's first-rate sparkling wines are showcased in attractive, historic facilities and extensive caves. Interesting guided tours and tastings are available by appointment only. 1400 Schramsberg Rd just S of Calistoga; 707/942-2414; www.schramsberg.com.

**Sterling Vineyards** Sterling offers an excellent self-guided tour through its impressive white Mediterranean-style complex perched on a hill. Access is via an aerial sky tram offering splendid views, and there's a vast tasting room with panoramic vistas. 1111 Dunaweal Ln, 1 mile S of Calistoga; 707/942-3345 or 800/977-3242; www.sterling vineyards.com.

707/944-0103), Thomas Keller's **BOUCHON** (6534 Washington St; 707/944-8037), **DOMAINE CHANDON** (1 California Dr at Domaine Chandon Winery; 707/944-2892), and **MUSTARDS GRILL** (7399 St. Helena Hwy/Hwy 29; 707/944-2424).

In the heart of Yountville is the beautiful brick complex now known as **VINTAGE 1870** (6525 Washington St; 707/944-2451), a touristy mall with a few dozen shops and a handful of restaurants. The building was erected in 1870 as a winery, and now it's listed on the National Register of Historic Places.

## OAKVILLE

Just up the highway from Yountville is the tiny town of Oakville, which produces some of the best cabernet sauvignon in the world (as does its little nearby twin town, Rutherford). For a snack or quick lunch, stop at the popular **OAKVILLE GROCERY CO.** (7856 St. Helena Hwy/Hwy 29 at Oakville Cross Rd; 707/944-8802), a gourmet deli disguised as an old-fashioned country grocery store complete with a striking "Drink Coca-Cola" sign painted on the wall outside. Inside you'll find a fine variety of local wines (including a good selection of splits), a small espresso bar tucked in the corner, and pricey but delicious picnic supplies ranging from pâté and caviar to turkey sandwiches and freshly made sweets.

## ST. HELENA

If you continue north on this scenic stretch of Highway 29 you'll drive smack through the center of St. Helena, which has come a long way since its days as a rural Seventh Day Adventist village. For many years St. Helena has been entrenched in a never-ending battle to preserve its exclusive, small-town way of life—instead of becoming one more tourist haven for Wine Country visitors. Citizens have filed injunctions against everything from the Napa Valley Wine Train (forbidding it to stop in town) to Safeway (the grocery giant wanted to build a larger supermarket). Needless to say, Wal-Mart was out of the question.

As a result, Main Street has retained its Victorian Old West feel, and historic structures like **STEVE'S HARDWARE** (1370 Main St; 707/963-3423) coexist with the trendy **1351 LOUNGE** (1351 Main St; 707/963-1969), located in a former bank complete with vault. Just off the main drag you can find more down-home pleasures at the **NAPA VALLEY OLIVE OIL MANUFACTURING COMPANY** (835 Charter Oak Ave behind Tra Vigne restaurant; 707/963-4173), an authentic Italian deli and general store stuffed to the rafters with goodies like dried fava beans, biscotti, salami, and fresh mozzarella. For great gifts be sure to pick up a bottle or two of the top-notch extra-virgin olive oil or the olive oil soap. Just south of town, the notorious New York deli **DEAN & DELUCA** (607 S St. Helena Hwy, N of Zinfandel Ln; 707/967-9980) has opened a huge store selling a mind-boggling array of cheeses, wines, deli items, and cookware. For a picnic, take your treats to **LYMAN PARK** (on Main St between Adams and Pine) and sit on the grass or in the beautiful little white gazebo where bands sometimes perform summer concerts.

The town's most popular restaurant is the beautiful **RISTORANTE TRA VIGNE** (1050 Charter Oak Ave off Main St; 707/963-4444), where you'll need a reservation to get a table for lunch or dinner, although you don't need to plan in advance to get a good lunch at the adjoining **CANTINETTA TRA VIGNE** (1050 Charter Oak Ave; 707/963-8888), which offers a beautiful patio for enjoying focaccia pizzas, Italian sandwiches, interesting soups and salads, pastas topped with smoked salmon and other delights, and a surfeit of sweets. Two other hugely popular restaurants here are Hiro Sone's **TERRA** (1345 Railroad Ave; 707/963-8931) and Joachim Splichal's **PINOT BLANC** (641 Main St; 707/963-6191).

Leaving downtown St. Helena and heading north toward Calistoga, you'll pass under the **TUNNEL OF THE ELMS** (also called the "Tree Tunnel"), a fantastic row of dozens of elm trees arched across Main Street (Highway 29) in front of **BERINGER VINEYARDS**. They were planted by the Beringer brothers more than 100 years ago, and their interlaced branches form a gorgeous canopy about a quarter of a mile long. Beyond Beringer are two parks popular for hiking and picnics. **BALE GRIST MILL STATE HISTORIC PARK** (3369 Hwy 29 at Bale Grist Mill Rd, 3 miles N of St. Helena; 707/963-2236) holds a historic flour mill built in 1846 by a British surgeon named Bale. The 36-foot wooden waterwheel still grinds grain into meal and flour on weekends; it also appeared in the 1960 film *Pollyanna*. Next door is the 1,800-acre **BOTHE–NAPA VALLEY STATE PARK** (reservations: 707/942-4575 or 800/444-PARK; www.reserveamerica.com), offering about 100 picnic spots with barbecues and tables, a swimming pool open from mid-June through Labor Day, and 50 campsites. You can hike from one park to the other by following the moderately strenuous 1.2-mile History Trail.

## CALISTOGA

Mud baths, mineral pools, and massages are still the main attractions of this popular spa town, founded in the mid-19th century by California's first millionaire, Sam Brannan. Savvy Brannan made a bundle of cash supplying miners in the Gold Rush and quickly recognized the value of Calistoga's mineral-rich hot springs. In 1859 he purchased 2,000 acres of the Wappo Indians' hot springs land, built a first-class hotel and spa, and named the region Calistoga (a combination of the words *California* and *Saratoga*). He then watched his fortunes grow as affluent San Franciscans paraded into town for a relaxing respite from city life.

Generations later, city slickers are still making the pilgrimage to this sanctuary of spas. These days, however, more than a dozen enterprises touting the magical restorative powers of mineral baths line the town's

Old West–style streets. You'll see an odd combo of stressed-out CEOs and earthier types shelling out dough for a chance to soak away their worries and get the kinks rubbed out of their necks. While Calistoga's spas and resorts are less glamorous than the Sonoma Mission Inn & Spa (see the Sonoma section), many offer body treatments and mud baths you won't find anywhere else in this part of the state. Among the most popular spas are **DR. WILKINSON'S HOT SPRINGS** (1507 Lincoln Ave; 707/942-4102; www.napavalley.com/drwilkinson.html), where you'll get a great massage and numerous other body treatments for a fair price; **CALISTOGA SPA HOT SPRINGS** (1006 Washington St; 707/942-6269; www.napavalley. com/Calistoga), a favorite for families with young children that boasts four mineral pools in addition to several body-pampering services; **INDIAN SPRINGS** (1712 Lincoln Ave; 707/942-4913), for pricey spa treatments in a historic setting and the best (and largest) mineral pool in the area (you can even see—and hear—the steam from one of the geysers feeding hot mineral water into the pool); and **LAVENDER HILL SPA** (1015 Foothill Blvd/Hwy 29; 707/942-4495; www.lavenderhillspa.com), which provides aromatherapy facials, seaweed wraps, mud baths, and other sybaritic delights in one of the most attractive settings in town.

After you've steamed or soaked away all your tensions, head over to the pretty outdoor patio at the **CALISTOGA INN** (1250 Lincoln Ave; 707/942-4101) for a tall, cool drink. Try one of the house-brewed beers or ales, but save your appetite for one of the better restaurants in town. Once you're rejuvenated, stroll down the main street and browse through the many quaint shops marketing everything from French soaps and antique armoires to silk-screened T-shirts and saltwater taffy. For a trip back in time to Calistoga's pioneer past, stop by the **SHARPSTEEN MUSEUM AND BRANNAN COTTAGE** (1311 Washington St; 707/942-5911).

Along Calistoga's main drag are a number of restaurants and cafes. Walk south to north on Lincoln Avenue and you'll find California-style thin-crust pizza and calzone at **CHECKERS** (1414 Lincoln Ave; 707/942-9300), which also has an espresso bar and a children's menu. Or try the highly regarded **CATAHOULA RESTAURANT AND SALOON** (1457 Lincoln Ave; 707/942-2275) for gourmet pizza and chef-owner Jan Birnbaum's spirited brand of nouvelle Southern cuisine. Just off Lincoln Avenue is another very good restaurant serving a mix of cuisines for lunch and dinner: **WAPPO BAR & BISTRO** (1226-B Washington St off Lincoln Ave; 707/942-4712). And at the north end of the town's shopping district, across from Nance's Hot Springs, is the **CALISTOGA ROASTERY** (1631 Lincoln Ave; 707/942-5757), a casual, cozy spot where you can get great coffee and iced-coffee drinks, as well as a simple breakfast of poached eggs on toast or a lunchtime sandwich; open daily at 6:30am.

A short drive outside of town is the famous **OLD FAITHFUL GEYSER** (1299 Tubbs Ln, 2 miles N of Calistoga; 707/942-6463; open every day), which faithfully shoots a plume of 350°F mineral water 60 feet into the air at regular intervals. Other natural wonders abound at the **PETRIFIED FOREST** (4100 Petrified Forest Rd off Hwy 128, 6 miles N of Calistoga; 707/942-6667; www.petrifiedforest.org), where towering redwoods were turned to stone when Mount St. Helena erupted 3 million years ago; you can read about the fascinating event at the museum at the forest entrance. For a majestic view of the entire valley, hike through the beautiful redwood canyons and oak-madrone woodlands in **ROBERT LOUIS STEVENSON STATE PARK** to the top of Mount St. Helena (located off Hwy 29, 4 miles S of Calistoga; 707/942-4575).

## NAPA VALLEY LODGINGS

Napa Valley is rife with wonderful (albeit mostly pricey) lodgings. If money's no object, stay at either the gorgeous **AUBERGE DU SOLEIL** (180 Rutherford Hill Rd, Rutherford; 707/963-1211 or 800/348-5406), a 52-unit exclusive resort whose designers were inspired by the sunny architecture of southern France, or the impressive **MEADOWOOD RESORT** (900 Meadowood Ln off the Silverado Trail, St. Helena; 707/963-3646 or 800/458-8080), a 256-acre New England–style Eden that's a mecca to golfers. For those with thinner but still healthy wallets, a couple of other popular choices are **LA RESIDENCE** (4066 St. Helena Hwy/Hwy 29, Napa; 707/253-0337), one of the valley's most luxurious bed-and-breakfasts, and the **INN AT SOUTHBRIDGE** (1020 Main St, btwn Charter Oak Ave and Pope St, St. Helena; 707/967-9400 or 800/520-6800), the Meadowood Resort's sister inn.

# Sonoma Valley

*50 miles north of San Francisco (approximately 1½ hours, traffic permitting). Take Highway 101 north across the Golden Gate Bridge, turn off at the Napa-Vallejo/Highway 37 exit, and follow the signs to Highway 121 and Sonoma.*

Nestled between the Mayacama Mountains to the east and Sonoma Mountain to the west, the crescent-shaped Sonoma Valley is only 7 miles wide and 17 miles long. But what an impressive and historical stretch of land—after all, this is where California's world-renowned wine industry was born. Many California enophiles would argue that when it comes to comparing the Sonoma Valley's wine country with Napa's, less is definitely more: Sonoma is less congested, less developed, less commercial, and less glitzy than its rival. Smitten with the bucolic charm of the region, Sonomaphiles delight in wandering the area's back roads, leisurely hopping from winery to winery and exploring the quaint towns along the way. Before setting out for this verdant vineyard-laced region, stop at the **SONOMA VALLEY VISITORS BUREAU** (453 1st St E; 707/996-1090;

## SONOMA VALLEY WINERIES

California's world-renowned wine industry was born in the Sonoma Valley. Franciscan fathers planted the state's first vineyards at the Mission San Francisco Solano de Sonoma in 1823 and harvested the grapes to make their sacramental wines. Thirty-four years later, California's first major vineyard was planted with European grape varietals by Hungarian Count Agoston Haraszthy at Sonoma's revered Buena Vista Winery. Little did the count know that one day he would become widely hailed as the father of California wine—wine that is consistently rated as some of the best in the world. Today more than 100 wineries dot the Sonoma Valley, most offering pretty picnic areas and free tours of their winemaking facilities. Here's a roundup of some of Sonoma's best:

**Benziger Family Winery** Tram-ride tours take visitors through the vineyards here, and tastings are held in the wine shop. Home to good chardonnay and cabernet sauvignon. 1883 London Ranch Rd, Glen Ellen; 707/935-3000 or 800/989-8890; www.benziger.com.

**Buena Vista Winery** California's oldest premium winery (founded in 1857) is a large estate set in a forest with picnic grounds. It offers tours of the stone winery and the hillside tunnels, wine tasting, and a gallery featuring locals' artwork and a gift shop. 18000 Old Winery Rd, Sonoma; 707/938-1266 or 800/926-1266; www.buenavistawinery.com.

**Château St. Jean** Follow the self-guided tour through this beautiful 250-acre estate with tastings in the mansion and stunning views from a faux medieval tower. There is also a picnic area. 8555 Sonoma Hwy (Hwy 12), Kenwood; 707/833-4134 or 800/543-7572; www.chateaustjean.com.

**Gloria Ferrer Champagne Caves** See interesting subterranean cellars on the excellent guided tour. Tastings are also offered. 23555 Hwy 121, Sonoma; 707/996-7256; www.gloriaferrer.com.

www.sonomavalley.com) for lots of free, helpful information about the area's wineries, farmers markets, historic sites, walking tours, recreational facilities, and seasonal events.

## SONOMA

Sonoma, one of the most historic towns in Northern California, is a good place to experience the region's Mexican heritage. Designed by General Mariano Vallejo in 1835, Sonoma is set up like a Mexican town, with an 8-acre parklike plaza in the center—complete with a meandering flock of chickens and crowing roosters. In the mid-1800s the square was a dusty training ground for General Vallejo's troops. The plaza's **BEAR FLAG MONUMENT** marks the spot where the crude Bear Flag was raised in 1846, signaling the end of Mexican rule; the symbol was later adopted

**Gundlach-Bundschu Winery** This grand, historic building was established in 1858 and is set on impressive grounds. Gundlach-Bundschu is known primarily for its red wines. Picnic facilities and tastings are available at the winery. 2000 Denmark St, Sonoma; 707/938-5277; www.gunbun.com.

**Kenwood Vineyards** Founded in 1970, Kenwood is renowned for its red wines and quaint wooden barns. There's a tasting room, and the winery's Artist Series features a terrific collection of original art created especially for Kenwood wine labels. 9592 Sonoma Hwy (Hwy 12), Kenwood; 707/833-5891; www.kenwoodvineyards.com.

**Kunde Estate Winery & Vineyards** This century-old winery set on 2,000 gorgeous acres of rolling hills is one of Sonoma County's largest grape suppliers. It also boasts a good tasting room. 10155 Sonoma Hwy (Hwy 12), Kenwood; 707/833-5501; www.kunde.com.

**Matanzas Creek Winery** A beautiful drive northwest of the valley leads to this winery's attractive facilities. Matanzas offers outstanding chardonnay and merlot as well as guided tours, tastings, and picnic tables. 6097 Bennett Valley Rd, Santa Rosa; 707/528-6464 or 800/590-6464; www.matanzascreek.com.

**Sebastiani Vineyards** Sonoma's largest premium-variety winery, Sebastiani Vineyards provides tours of its aging cellar, which includes an interesting collection of carved-oak cask heads. There's also a tasting room and picnic tables. 389 4th St E, Sonoma; 707/938-5532 or 800/888-5532; www.sebastiani.com.

**Viansa Winery and Marketplace** These buildings and grounds modeled after a Tuscan village are owned by the Sebastiani family. Viansa produces good sauvignon blanc, chardonnay, and cabernet, plus gourmet Italian picnic fare and local delicacies perfect for the beautiful hillside picnic grounds. 25200 Hwy 121, Sonoma; 707/935-4700 or 800/995-4740; www.viansa.com.

by the state of California and placed on its flag. At the turn of the century a women's club transformed it into the lush park you see today, with more than 200 trees, rose gardens (look for the salmon-colored bloom called the Sonoma Rose), picnic tables and benches, a playground, and a duck-filled pond.

Sitting squarely in the center of the plaza is **SONOMA CITY HALL**, a stone Mission Revival structure built by San Francisco architect A. C. Lutgens in 1908. Note that all four sides of it are identical—Lutgens didn't want to offend any of the plaza merchants, so he gave them all the same view of his building. The city hall should look familiar to fans of the former hit TV show *Falcon Crest*, which featured it as the Tuscany County Courthouse. Several authentic adobe buildings hug the perimeter, most of them now housing an assortment of boutiques, restaurants, and also the vintage **SEBASTIANI THEATER** (476 1st St E; 707/996-2020). **MISSION SAN FRANCISCO SOLANO DE SONOMA** (on the corner of 1st St E and E Spain St; 707/938-1519), a.k.a. the Sonoma Mission, is the northernmost and last of the 21 missions built by the Spanish padres. For a nominal fee you can tour the interior of this early 19th-century adobe structure, as well as the nearby Sonoma Barracks (1st St E and E Spain St), a two-story adobe structure built between 1836 and 1840 to house Mexican Army troops, and General Vallejo's well-preserved yellow-and-white Victorian home.

A stroll around the plaza area offers interesting shopping, including two excellent bookstores, **READER'S BOOKS** (127 and 130 Napa St E; 707/939-1779) and **PLAZA BOOK SHOP** (40 W Spain St; 707/996-8474) for used and rare volumes. Or find everything for a Wine Country feast: cheeses and deli fare galore from the **SONOMA CHEESE FACTORY** (2 W Spain St; 707/996-1931) or pâtés, hams, bratwurst, and sausages from the **SONOMA SAUSAGE COMPANY** (414 1st St E; 707/938-1215). If you didn't have time to hit all the wineries you wanted, or if you want to ship wine home, stop by the **WINE EXCHANGE** (452 1st St E; 800/938-1794). Wine and beer tastings are available in the rear, and you can choose from an enormous selection of each to complete your picnic. **CUCINA VIANSA** (400 1st St E; 707/935-5656), which has the same take-out gourmet fare as Viansa Winery, also features wine tasting, an espresso bar, a lively cafe, and music on weekend nights. Listen to acoustic music at **MURPHY'S IRISH PUB** (464 1st St E; 707/935-0660), hidden in the courtyard behind the Sebastiani Theater.

Only four blocks from the Sonoma Plaza is the ever-popular **SEBASTIANI VINEYARDS** (389 4th St E; 707/938-5532 or 800/888-5532). After indulging in some wine tasting, walk or bicycle through the vineyards on the easy .75-mile paved path that leads to General Vallejo's home.

As you pound the pavement around the plaza, you'll pass many of the city's great restaurants. **DELLA SANTINA TRATTORIA** (133 Napa St E; 707/935-0576) offers excellent house-made pastas (the *gnocchi della nonna* with a tomato, basil, and garlic sauce would impress any Italian grandmother) and wonderful meats from the rosticceria. **RISTORANTE PIATTI** (405 1st St W in the El Dorado Hotel; 707/996-2351), part of a popular chain of chic nouvelle Italian restaurants, serves huge portions of wonderful Italian cuisine. The new **MAYA** restaurant (101 Napa St E; 707/935-3500), serving traditional Yucatan dishes, is also highly recommended.

When you're ready to venture beyond the city limits, drive north a few miles to the tiny town of **BOYES HOT SPRINGS**, home of the ever-popular **SONOMA MISSION INN & SPA** (18140 Sonoma Hwy/Hwy 12 at Boyes Blvd, Boyes Hot Springs; 707/938-9000 or 800/862-4945). This European-style spa offers everything from aerobics classes and Swedish massages to aromatherapy facials, seaweed wraps, and tarot card readings in perfectly groomed surroundings (the likes of Barbra Streisand, Tom Cruise, and Harrison Ford even come here to get pampered).

## GLEN ELLEN

A few more miles north is Jack London territory. There are more places and things named after Jack London in Sonoma County than there are women named María in Mexico, and this cult reaches its apex in Glen Ellen. This is where the author of *The Call of the Wild*, *The Sea Wolf*, and some 50 other books and numerous articles built his aptly named Beauty Ranch, an 800-acre spread now known as **JACK LONDON STATE HISTORIC PARK** (2400 London Ranch Rd off Hwy 12 and Arnold Dr, Glen Ellen; 707/938-5216). London's vineyards, piggery, horse stalls, and other ranch buildings are here, as well as the cottage where he wrote (and died) and a beautiful stone house-turned-museum called the House of Happy Walls. Lining those walls are pieces from London's interesting and worldly art collection as well as personal mementos, including some of the 600 rejection letters he received from publishers. The park is a pretty place for a picnic, with tables and barbecues set out under the oak and eucalyptus trees, a short walk from the parking lot. Carry your lunch to London's cottage to find the park's best table, next to a goldfish pond overlooking the grapevines.

Hard-core hikers should plan to spend the day trekking to **BATHHOUSE LAKE** and up **SONOMA MOUNTAIN**'s steep slopes (carry water), which are blanketed with grassy meadows and forests of madrone, manzanita, redwood, and Douglas fir. Or consider letting the friendly folks at the **SONOMA CATTLE COMPANY** (707/996-8566), based in the park, saddle up a horse for you. Call for the lowdown on their guided horseback trips; reservations are required.

A ticket to Jack London Park allows you free entrance (on the same day only) to the 2,700-acre **SUGARLOAF RIDGE STATE PARK** (2605 Adobe Canyon Rd, 3 miles E of Hwy 12, Kenwood; camping reservations: 800/444-PARK; www.reserveamerica.com), a 20-minute drive north. Sugarloaf has 25 miles of hiking and horseback-riding trails (with great views from the ridge), guided horseback rides, 50 tent campsites, and a horse corral.

## SONOMA VALLEY LODGINGS

For lodgings in Sonoma Valley, best bets are the **EL DORADO HOTEL** (405 1st St W, Sonoma; 707/996-3030 or 800/289-3031; www.sonoma mission.com), offering moderately priced rooms that overlook the Sonoma Plaza; the palatial **SONOMA MISSION INN & SPA** (see the contact information above); the **GAIGE HOUSE INN** (13540 Arnold Dr, Glen Ellen; 707/935-0237 or 800/935-0237; www.gaige.com), a gorgeous Victorian mansion that's possibly the finest B&B in California;

the **VICTORIAN GARDEN INN** (316 Napa St E, Sonoma; 707/996-5339; www.victoriangardeninn.com), an 1870s Greek Revival farmhouse converted into a charming B&B; or the posh 12-room **KENWOOD INN AND SPA** (10400 Sonoma Hwy/Hwy 12, 3 miles past Glen Ellen, Kenwood; 707/833-1293; www.kenwoodinn.com).

# Palo Alto

*30 miles south of San Francisco (approximately 45 to 50 minutes, traffic permitting). Take Highway 101 south to Palo Alto.*

The home of notable restaurants, fine-art galleries, foreign-movie houses, great bookstores, world-famous **STANFORD UNIVERSITY**, and some of the best shopping this side of heaven, Palo Alto is a beacon of cosmopolitan energy shining on the suburban sea. Much of the fuel for this cultural lighthouse comes, of course, from the university, which offers free tours of its attractive campus daily. Highlights include the **MAIN QUAD, HOOVER TOWER** (for a nominal fee you can get a great view from its observation platform), the huge **STANFORD BOOKSTORE**, and the gorgeous **MEMORIAL CHURCH**; call Visitor Information Services (650/723-2560) for more tour information. If you'd like to try to glimpse some atom smashing, visit the nearby **STANFORD LINEAR ACCELERATOR CENTER** (650/926-3300, press 9 to arrange a tour).

If you didn't find the tome you were looking for at the university's bookstore, Palo Alto and its neighbors contain many other outlets for bibliophiles. **KEPLER'S BOOKS AND MAGAZINES** (1010 El Camino Real, Menlo Park; 650/324-4321) is a wonderland for serious bookworms; you'll also find a healthy selection of mind food at **BORDERS BOOKS** (456 University Ave, Palo Alto; 650/326-3670) and **BOOKS INC.** (Stanford Shopping Center on El Camino Real near University Ave, Palo Alto; 650/321-0600). You'll probably need to follow up that literary excursion with a cup of joe. Some of the bookstores, such as Printer's Inc. and Borders, serve coffee and light snacks, but for authentic coffeehouse atmosphere and great espresso try **CAFFE VERONA** (236 Hamilton Ave at Emerson St, Palo Alto; 650/326-9942) or stop into **CAFE BORRONE** (1010 El Camino Real, Menlo Park; 650/327-0830), located next to Kepler's.

Moviegoers have a broad range of choices. The beautifully restored **STANFORD THEATER** (221 University Ave, Palo Alto; 650/324-3700), which showcases classic flicks, is especially worth a visit. If you prefer your performances live, check out the local **THEATREWORKS** troupe (650/463-1950), the **LIVELY ARTS** (650/725-2787) series at Stanford University, or the top-name talents currently appearing at the **SHORELINE AMPHITHEATER** (1 Amphitheater Pkwy, Mountain View; 650/967-3000). If you have nothing to wear for the show (or, indeed, if you have any other shopping need), Palo Alto won't let you down. **UNIVERSITY AVENUE** and its side streets contain a plethora of interesting stores. The **STANFORD SHOPPING CENTER** (on El Camino Real just N of downtown; 650/617-8585) is a sprawling, beautifully landscaped temple of consumerism, and includes such stores as Bloomingdale's, Macy's, Nordstrom, Ralph Lauren, the Gap, Crate & Barrel, the Disney Store, and many more. Recommended places to eat in this shopper's paradise include Bravo Fono and Max's Opera Cafe.

If you're looking for a good meal in town, Palo Alto offers many first-rate restaurants, including **BISTRO ELAN** (448 California Ave just off El Camino Real; 650/327-0284), which serves French fare with a California flair for lunch and dinner in a spare Parisian neighborhood bistro–style dining room; **EVVIA** (420 Emerson St btwn Lytton and University Aves; 650/326-0983), a warm and welcoming Greek restaurant with a sun-drenched, Mediterranean feel; **L'AMIE DONIA** (530 Bryant St btwn University and Hamilton Aves; 650/323-7614), an amiable, bustling French bistro and wine bar; and **MACARTHUR PARK** (27 University Ave just off El Camino Real near the train depot; 650/321-9990), in an attractive Julia Morgan–designed building, where crowds come for the lean, tender, oak-smoked ribs and first-rate mesquite-grilled steaks.

The favored lodging in Palo Alto is the modern, Mediterranean-style 62-room **GARDEN COURT HOTEL** (520 Cowper St btwn University and Hamilton Aves; 650/322-9000 or 800/824-9028), surrounded by Italianate architecture draped with arches and studded with colorful tile work and wrought-iron fixtures. And just outside of Palo Alto is another great choice: **STANFORD PARK HOTEL** (100 El Camino Real, N of University Ave, Menlo Park; 650/322-1234 or 800/368-2468; www. stanfordparkhotel.com), a 163-room lodging near Stanford University with handsome English-style furniture, fireplaces, balconies, vaulted ceilings, and courtyard views.

# Half Moon Bay

*The fastest way to Half Moon Bay is to take the Highway 92 exit off Interstate 280, which leads straight into town. Far more scenic, however, is the drive along Highway 1, which, aside from the section known as Devil's Slide, moves right along at a 50mph clip. The entrance to Main Street is located about 2 blocks up Highway 92 from the Highway 1 intersection. Head toward the Shell station, then turn south onto Main Street until you cross a small bridge.*

Most Bay Area families know Half Moon Bay as the pumpkin capital of the West, where thousands of pilgrims make their annual journey in search of the ultimate Halloween jack-o'-lantern. Since 1970 the **HALF**

**MOON BAY ART & PUMPKIN FESTIVAL** has featured all manner of squash cuisine and crafts, as well as the Giant Pumpkin weigh-in contest, won recently by a 974-pound monster. A Great Pumpkin Parade, pumpkin-carving competitions, pie-eating contests, and piles of great food pretty much assure a good time for all; for more information call the Pumpkin Hotline at 650/726-9652.

Pumpkins aside, Half Moon Bay is a jewel of a town, saved from mediocrity by diverting its historic Main Street well away from the fast-food chains and gas stations of Highway 1. The locals are disarmingly friendly, actually bestowing greetings as you walk along the rows of small shops and restaurants. Then, of course, there are the 4 miles of **GOLDEN CRESCENT-SHAPED BEACH**, one of the prettiest in all of California; bustling **PILLAR POINT HARBOR**, launching point for whale-watching and deep-sea-fishing trips; and myriad hiking and biking trails along the coast and into the **REDWOOD FORESTS**. Combine this with an array of commendable accommodations and restaurants, and you have the perfect ingredients for a peaceful weekend getaway.

The best way to explore the small, flat town of Half Moon Bay and its beaches is on a mountain bike. Lucky for you, they're available for rent at the **BICYCLERY** (101-B Main St at Hwy 1; 650/726-6000). Prices range from $8–$12 an hour to $25–$30 for all day. Be sure to ask one of the staffers about the best biking trails in the area, particularly the wonderful beach trail from Kelly Avenue to Pillar Point Harbor.

Once you have explored the town, take your mountain bike to **PURISIMA CREEK REDWOODS** (650/691-1200), a little-known sanctuary frequented mostly by locals. Located on the western slopes of the Santa Cruz Mountains, the preserve is filled with fern-lined creek banks, lush redwood forests, and fields of wildflowers and berries that are accessible to hikers, mountain bikers, and equestrians along miles of trails. From the Highway 1/Highway 92 intersection in Half Moon Bay, drive 1 mile south on Highway 1 to Higgins Purisima Creek Road and turn left, then continue 4.5 miles to a small gravel parking lot—that's the trailhead.

Another popular Half Moon Bay activity is **DEEP-SEA FISHING**. Even if you don't fish, it's worth a trip to **PILLAR POINT HARBOR** (4 miles N of Half Moon Bay off Hwy 1) to take in the pungent aroma of the sea; the rows of rusty trawlers and the salty men and women tending to endless chores evoke a sort of Hemingway-ish sense of romance. Visitors are encouraged to walk along the pier and even partake in a fishing trip. **CAPTAIN JOHN'S FISHING TRIPS** (650/726-2913 or 800/391-8787) and **HUCK FINN SPORTFISHING** (650/726-7133 or 800/572-2934) each charge around $55, including rod and reel, for a day's outing—a small price to pay for 30 pounds of fresh snapper or salmon. Between January and March, whale-watching trips also depart daily.

Near the harbor is one of the most infamous surf beaches in California: **MAVERICK BEACH**. If the name sounds familiar, that's because this local Half Moon Bay surf spot made national headlines as the site where famed Hawaiian surfer Mark Foo drowned in 1995 after being thrown from his board by a 20-foot wave. On calmer days, though, secluded Maverick Beach is still a good place to escape the weekend crowds because, although everyone's heard about the beach, few know where it is and you won't find it on any map. Here's the dope: From Capistrano Road at Pillar Point Harbor, turn left on Prospect Way, left on Broadway, right on Princeton, then right on Westpoint to the West Shoreline Access parking lot (on your left). Park here, then continue up Westpoint on foot toward the Pillar Point Satellite Tracking Station. Take about 77 steps, and on your right will be a trailhead leading to legendary Maverick Beach a short distance away.

If surfing isn't your thing, how about ocean kayaking? If you're one of those type A people who can't just lie on the beach and relax, **CALIFORNIA CANOE & KAYAK** (Pillar Point Harbor at the Half Moon Bay Yacht Club; 650/728-1803; www.calkayak.com) has the answer. For $89 they'll take you out on the bay for a 7-hour lesson in the fundamentals of the sea. Sure, it's expensive, but the rewards are priceless. Classes are usually held from 9am to 4pm Saturdays and Sundays, May through October (call to confirm); rentals are also available.

Back on land is the **ANDREOTTI FAMILY FARM** (227 Kelly Ave between Hwy 1 and the beach; 650/726-9461). If you like vegetables, you'll love this place. Every Friday, Saturday, and Sunday one of the family members slides open the old barn door at 10am sharp to reveal a cornucopia of just-picked artichokes, peas, brussels sprouts, beans, strawberries, and just about whatever else is growing in their adjacent fields. The Andreotti enterprise has been in operation since 1926, so it's a sure bet they know their veggies. (The farm's open till 6pm year-round.)

If you're a golfer, be sure to reserve a tee time at the oceanside 18-hole **HALF MOON BAY GOLF LINKS** (2000 Fairway Dr, next to the Half Moon Bay Lodge; 650/726-6384). Designed by Arnold Palmer, it's rated among the top 100 courses in the country, as well as number one in the Bay Area, according to the *San Francisco Business Times*. Greens fees are a bit steep, however, ranging from $85 to $115. Reserve as far in advance as possible.

On your way out of town, be sure to stop at **OBESTER WINERY'S WINE-TASTING AND SALES ROOM** (12341 San Mateo Rd; 650/726-9463), which is only a few miles from Half Moon Bay up Highway 92. It's a pleasant drive—passing numerous fields of flowers, Christmas tree farms, and pumpkin patches—to this wood shack filled with award-winning grape juice. Behind the tasting room is a small picnic area that's perfect for an afternoon lunch break. (The tasting room is open every day 10am–5pm.)

# Santa Cruz

*The most scenic route to Santa Cruz is along Highway 1 from San Francisco, which you can cruise at a steady 50mph along the coast. Faster but far less romantic is Route 17, which is accessed near San Jose from I-280, I-880, or Highway 101 and literally ends at the foot of the boardwalk. The exception to this rule is on weekend mornings, when Route 17 tends to logjam with Bay Area beachgoers while Highway 1 remains relatively uncrowded.*

For nearly a century Santa Cruz (Spanish for "holy cross") has been synonymous with "beach and boardwalk," as if this seaside city of 54,000 exists solely to sustain what is now the only major beachside amusement park left on the Pacific coast. Considering that the annual number of boardwalk visitors is 62 times greater than the city's population, it's no surprise that Santa Cruz's other highlights are all but ignored by the millions of thrill-seekers who head straight for the waterfront each year.

Not that the **SANTA CRUZ BEACH BOARDWALK** (400 Beach St, Santa Cruz; 831/423-5590)—now a cement walk—isn't worthy of the limelight. Ranked among the top amusement parks in the nation, with a higher attendance than either Marine World–Africa USA or Paramount's Great America, the privately owned amusement park has cleaned up its once-tarnished act by pouring a pile of money into improvements and security; the boardwalk is truly safe and clean these days. Then, of course, there's the legendary **GIANT DIPPER**, considered by those-who-would-know to be the greatest roller coaster ever built, and the hand-carved horses of the **LOOFF CAROUSEL**, the last bona fide brass-ring merry-go-round in North America. These two rides alone are worth a stroll down the boardwalk. Buy the reasonably priced day pass and stand in line for rides like **RIPTIDE** and the **BERMUDA TRIANGLE**, and you won't be disappointed. If you're among the crowds here on a Friday night in the summer, don't miss the boardwalk's **FREE CONCERTS**, featuring the likes of the Shirelles, Chubby Checker, and Sha Na Na.

Even without its celebrated amusement park, Santa Cruz would still be one of California's top coastal destinations. Where else can you find a vibrant, cross-cultural college town (remember, this used to be the LSD capital of the world) perched on the edge of an immense bay teeming with marine life, ringed by miles of golden beaches, and backed by dense redwood forests? Remove those boardwalk blinders for a day and you'll find out that there's a whole lot more to Santa Cruz than cotton candy and arcades.

Beaches are Santa Cruz's second most popular attraction. At the western edge of the city, on the north end of W Cliff Drive, is **NATURAL BRIDGES STATE BEACH**, named after archways carved into the rock formations here by the ocean waves (only one of the three original arches still stands). The beach is popular with surfers, wind surfers, tide-pool trekkers, and sunbathers, as well as fans of the migrating monarch butterflies that roost in the nearby eucalyptus grove from late October through February. On the south end of W Cliff Drive is **LIGHTHOUSE FIELD STATE BEACH**, the reputed birthplace of American surfing. This beach has several benches for sitting and gazing, a jogging and bicycling path, and a park with picnic tables, showers, and even plastic-bag dispensers for cleaning up after your dog (it's one of the few public places in town where canines are allowed). The nearby brick lighthouse is now home to the tiny **SANTA CRUZ SURFING MUSEUM** (W 753 41st Ave; 831/464-3233)—the first of its kind in the world—which is chock-full of hang-ten memorabilia (admission is free).

Between the lighthouse and the boardwalk is that famous strip of the sea known as **STEAMERS LANE**, the summa cum laude of California surfing spots (savvy surfers say *this*—not Southern California—is the place to catch the best breaks in the state). Watch the dudes ride the gnarly waves, then head over to the marvelous (but often crowded) white-sand Santa Cruz Beach fronting the boardwalk. The breakers are tamer here, and free volleyball courts and barbecue pits make this a favorite spot for sunbathing, swimming, picnicking, and playing volleyball on the sand courts. In the center of the action is the 85-year-old **MUNICIPAL WHARF**, where you can drive your car out to the shops, fish markets, and seafood restaurants.

So maybe you can't surf, but surely you can paddle a stable sea kayak around the Santa Cruz coast. **VISION QUEST KAYAKING** (831/425-8445), located on the northeast end of the Santa Cruz Wharf, rents single-, double-, and triple-seater kayaks for exploring the nearby cliffs and kelp beds where a multitude of sea otters, seals, sea lions, and other marine animals congregate. No experience is necessary, and all ages are welcome. Guided tours are also available. And if kayaking is out of your league, you might want to rent a bike and tour the town. The pedal-friendly downtown area is flat and wide (ditto the wharf and boardwalk), and the shoreline bike path along W Cliff Drive is sensational.

The **PACIFIC GARDEN MALL** (a.k.a. Pacific Avenue), Santa Cruz's main shopping district, was hit hard by the Loma Prieta earthquake in 1989 (the earthquake's epicenter was only 10 miles away), but the entire area has been rebuilt, and it's shinier and spiffier than before. Major retailers such as the Gap and Starbucks have settled in alongside book, antique, and vintage clothing stores; movie theaters; and sidewalk cafes. As you make your way down the mall, look for the **OCTAGON BUILDING**, an ornate, eight-sided Victorian brick edifice built in 1882 that has survived numerous quakes. The building once served as the city's Hall of Records and is now part of the **MCPHERSON CENTER FOR ART AND HISTORY** (705 Front St at Cooper St, Santa Cruz; 831/429-1964), where museums showcase 10,000 years of the area's past as well as contemporary art of the Pacific Rim.

One good thing about a college town—it knows how to party. The Cruz's coolest blues are at **MOE'S ALLEY** (1535 Commercial Wy at Commercial Crossing; 831/479-1854), featuring live music (and dancing) nightly. For traditional and modern jazz it's the **KUUMBWA JAZZ CENTER** (320 Cedar St at Maple St; 831/427-2227), a nonprofit (and nonsmoking) landmark that's been around for the past two decades. Local rock, reggae, blues, and world-beat bands mix it up at the **CATALYST** (1011 Pacific Ave between Elm and Cathcart Sts; 831/423-1336), which occasionally pulls in some big names, too. Bluegrass, Hawaiian, and folk music find a venue at cavernous **PALOOKAVILLE** (1133 Pacific Ave at Lincoln St; 831/454-0600), which also has its share of rock and reggae.

The nearby **BOOKSHOP SANTA CRUZ** (1540 Pacific Ave at Cooper St; 831/423-0900) has an inventory worthy of any university town, with a particularly good children's section, an adjacent coffeehouse, and plenty of places to sit, sip, and peruse a bit of your prospective purchase. For great organically grown produce and other picnic-basket goodies, shop at the farmers market held Wednesday from 2:30pm to 6:30pm on Lincoln Street between Pacific Avenue and Cedar Street. Another town highlight is the newly constructed **SEYMOUR MARINE DISCOVERY CENTER** (100 Shaffer Rd at the end of Delaware Ave; 831/459-3800; www.seymourcenter.ucsc.edu). The center's exhibit galleries, aquariums, and teaching laboratories provide an inside look at a marine research laboratory and the work of researchers at UC Santa Cruz's Institute of Marine Sciences. Can't-miss spectacles include the 87-foot blue whale skeleton and superb vistas of the bay.

For some serious hiking and mountain biking, drive about 23 miles north to the 18,000-acre **BIG BASIN REDWOODS STATE PARK,** California's first state park (established in 1902) and its second-largest redwood preserve. Big Basin is home to black-tailed deer and mountain lions, and 80 miles of trails wind past 300-foot-high redwoods and many waterfalls. Some trails even access the long golden strand of **WADDELL CREEK BEACH** (21600 Big Basin Wy off Hwy 236, 9 miles N of Boulder Creek; 831/338-8860); call for recorded directions.

Locomotive lovers, kids, and fans of Mother Nature should hop aboard one of the trains at **ROARING CAMP AND BIG TREES NARROW-GAUGE RAILROAD** (5355 Graham Hill Rd, Felton; 831/335-4400). The Roaring Camp Train is a narrow-gauge, steam-powered train that makes a 6-mile round-trip excursion through stately redwood groves to the summit of Bear Mountain; Big Trees Railroad offers an 18-mile round-trip ride through mountain tunnels and along ridges with spectacular views of the San Lorenzo River before stopping at the Santa Cruz Beach Boardwalk. Train schedules vary seasonally.

# RECREATION

# RECREATION

Surrounded by ocean, bays, mountain ranges, and rolling hills, the San Francisco Bay Area is the perfect natural arena for all manner of outdoor sports, from surfing and ocean kayaking to mountain biking, sailing, in-line skating, hiking, golfing, tennis, and much more. Even in drizzly winter months the weather is rarely severe enough to absolutely rule out a bit of fresh-air exercise—the sight of joggers splashing their way up and down the Embarcadero is not uncommon.

But for most of the year the sun beams down, the sky is blue, the weather mild, and the breezes refreshing even when brisk. And thanks to a slow-growth preservationist streak in its citizens, San Francisco and the surrounding Bay Area have plenty of wide-open space that's been kept in its natural condition and is open to the public.

The following is a list of many of the recreational activities available to both the local and the visitor, most of them either free or relatively inexpensive. Best of all, it'll get you off your fanny, get your blood flowing, and get you into some of the most beautiful scenery on the California coast.

## Indoor Activities

### GYMS

Only a few decades ago it was rare to find a gym where a member of the general public could feel comfortable; most workout facilities were havens for dedicated if not fanatical weight lifters and competition-minded bodybuilders. Thanks to the fitness explosion, however, almost every neighborhood now has a gym where you don't have to look like Schwarzenegger to fit in.

The **24 HOUR FITNESS TRAINING** (1200 Van Ness Ave at Post St; 415/776-2200; www.24hourfitness.com; map:L3) is one of seven franchise branches in San Francisco and Daly City. A day fee of $15 entitles you to use the wide range of machines (heavy on Nautilus) and free weights, step training, and cardiovascular cycles. Personalized training is available, and as the name states, they never close.

**GOLD'S GYM** (1001 Brannan St at 9th and Division Sts; 415/552-4653; www.goldsgym.com; map:M5) has a day fee of $15, or $10 if you are the guest of a member. Membership also includes classes in boxing, tai chi, and tai bo, among others; there are in-house as well as independent trainers. After using the wide selection of machines and free weights, enjoy the saunas and steam rooms. Hours are 5am to midnight

Monday through Thursday; 5am to 11pm Friday; 7am to 9pm Saturday; and 8am to 8pm Sunday.

Viewers of ESPN may know the **CRUNCH** chain from the TV show that originated in L.A. San Francisco's Crunch (1000 Van Ness Ave at O'Farrell St; 415/931-1100; www.crunchfitness.com; map:L3) offers, in addition to the usual free weights and cardiovascular equipment (Life Fitness, Star Track, Techno Gym), a dizzying array of classes, from step and aerobics to more esoteric offerings—everything from kick-boxing to yoga, with firefighter and GI-type training in between. There's a steam room and sauna; the day rate is $23. Hours are 5:30am to 11pm Monday through Thursday; 5:30am to 9:30pm Friday; 8am to 8pm Saturday; and 8am to 6pm Sunday.

A world away from the chains, with the feel of an unpretentious neighborhood gym (which is what it is), **VALENCIA STREET MUSCLE AND FITNESS** (333 Valencia St at 14th St; 415/626-8360; www.valencia streetmuscle.com; map:L5) promotes a low-key, work-at-your-own-pace philosophy that makes it one of the friendliest places in town. Operated by three-time Olympic coach Jim Schmitz, of the late and fondly remembered Sport Palace, it has a marvelously mixed clientele of all sizes, ages, weights, body types, and abilities. The staff is helpful but unintrusive: power lifter to stationary cyclist are all treated equally. A day pass is a bargain at $10; a no-time-limit 12-pack for $69 is an even better deal. Hours are 6am to 11pm Monday through Friday; weekends 8am to 8pm.

## ADVENTURE OUTFITTERS

OK, now you're a bit more toned up and ready to take on the world. But you'll have to get outfitted and pick up some pointers on your choice of new activities. Outdoors Unlimited and REI are good one-stop combination resources: not only can you buy or rent gear, but you'll find classes on the skills you'll need and groups of like-minded people to join up with for that kayaking expedition or bike tour. These organizations are much more than places to rent a tent or buy a new pair of shoes—they'll really help get you going.

**OUTDOORS UNLIMITED** (Box 0234-A, UCSF, San Francisco, CA 94143; 415/476-2078; www.outdoors.ucsf.edu/ou) is an expedition planning and outfitting group affiliated with the University of California at San Francisco, but it's also open to the public (which is invited to volunteer). It holds seminars in backwoods first aid, map and compass reading, and backpacking skills from basic to trip leader. OU also organizes excursions to locations that usually lie well outside the city limits (Yosemite, Mount Lassen, Death Valley); but the shorter bike trips sometimes originate in Golden Gate Park before heading out to Mount Tam or the Marin County town of Ross, and kayak training takes place on the bay. Autumn brings bonfires and volleyball at Ocean Beach and a sail through the Golden Gate on the square rigger the *Hawaiian Chieftain*. Visit the OU equipment rental facility at 550 Parnassus Avenue by 3rd Avenue (walk down the ramp leading under the campus library; map:H6) for a wide selection of tents, sleeping bags, lanterns and stoves, canoes, kayaks, wet suits, skis, and snowboards, to name just a few. OU members and volunteers receive a discount of up to 40 percent on seminars, excursions, and gear rental.

**REI** (1338 San Pablo Ave at Gilman St, Berkeley; 510/527-4140; www.rei.com; map:FF2) is an outfitter that, in addition to offering a full line of clothing, shoes, sleeping bags, and tents, also presents in-store seminars and slide lectures on a wide range of topics. Just one month, for instance, brought a talk on essentials in bike touring, lessons for beginning mountain climbers, and hints on how to travel safely through bear country. The store is of course open to the general public, but REI also offers a membership program that gives discounts on merchandise and first crack at some of the training sessions and lectures. It's worth checking out: The cost is only $15 for a lifetime membership. REI has stores across the country, and the website is a good place to find mountaineering, hiking, and backpacking clubs nationwide as well as in your own backyard.

## ROCK CLIMBING (INDOOR)

Northern California is home to dozens of outdoor rock-climbing locations, from Yosemite National Park to the formations at Ocean Beach from which the Cliff House got its name. But for indoor climbing, whether you're a beginner just getting a taste or an experienced mountaineer limbering up El Capitan, everyone agrees that the place to go is **MISSION CLIFFS ROCK-CLIMBING CENTER** (2295 Harrison St at 19th St; 415/550-0515; www.mission-cliffs.com; map:M6). They rent shoes and harnesses and offer basic, first climb, and kids' classes. But the main attraction is the center's massive simulated Matterhorn of a climbing wall, topping out at 55 feet; its 50 lead walls offer over 150 possible climbs (routes are changed regularly). Surface dimensions are 14,000 square feet, including 2,000 square feet of bouldering for the beginner. Designed by well-known climber Christian Griffiths, the surface is mostly vertical but features some overhangs as well as caves and crevasses. Prospective climbers are expected to pass a belay test (tying a figure-eight hitch and belaying another person) to obtain a card that allows them to start climbing; demonstrated mastery of belaying techniques waives the requirement so you don't have to take the test each time you want to climb. The center is also available for parties and corporate events.

# Outdoor Activities

## BICYCLING / MOUNTAIN BIKING

First, it should be said that anyone riding a bike in everyday San Francisco traffic should remain extra-alert: Even in this increasingly bike-friendly town, some drivers act as though they literally cannot see somebody on two wheels. In fact, raising the visibility of bicyclists is one of the goals of the monthly "bike-in" called Critical Mass (see below). Always wear a helmet and reflective gear, and remember that even if you have the right-of-way, the person who will come out on the short end of a car-bike collision will almost certainly be the one on the bike.

Close to Golden Gate Park are two dependable shops: **AMERICAN CYCLERY** (858 Stanyan St at Frederick St; 415/876-4545) and **VISION CYCLERY SAN FRANCISCO** (772 Stanyan St at Beulah St; 415/221-9766). Those of you interested in biking along Marina Boulevard and perhaps across the Golden Gate Bridge can visit **CITY CYCLE OF SAN FRANCISCO** (3001 Steiner St at Union St; 415/346-2242). **GOLDEN GATE PARK SKATE**

### BIKING MARIN

The hilly, scenic bike trails of Marin are a magnet for amateur and professional cyclists alike. A favorite not-too-strenuous route takes you north across the **Golden Gate Bridge,** then follows the bike trail under the bridge and down a very steep hill to downtown **Sausalito.** The paved trail hugs Sausalito's waterfront, leading past floating homes and marshes to Bayfront Park in **Mill Valley;** this gorgeous ride takes two to three hours (one-way) for the average recreational biker. To avoid riding (or pushing) your bike uphill to the bridge for the return trip, hop on a ferry in Sausalito or **Tiburon,** and take the leisurely route back to San Francisco's **Fisherman's Wharf** (call the Red & White Fleet for ferry info; 800/229-2784).

The **Marin Headlands** and **Mount Tamalpais** (also known as Mount Tam) are the bicycling hot spots for Bay Area mountain bikers. Maps of the numerous dirt trails are available at many Bay Area bike stores and bookstores, the Pan Toll Camp/Mount Tamalpais Ranger Station (on Pamoramic Hwy, 5.5 miles north of Hwy 1; 415/388-2070), and the Marin Headlands Visitor Center (at the corner of Bunker and Field Rds, Sausalito; 415/331-1540). Mount Tam offers fantastic scenic trails, but most are restricted to hikers only—and they're fiercely guarded. If you don't want to get slapped with a $200 fine for pedaling up the wrong path, be sure to look it up on a trail map first.

See "Bicycling / Mountain Biking" in the Outdoor Activities section for recommended bicycle rental shops.

**AND BIKE** (see the Roller Skating and In-line Skating section) also has a selection of bikes for hire.

Pleasure rides in the city suggest themselves from all sides. There are the perennial favorites, the Embarcadero and Golden Gate Park, or you might want to test yourself on one of the city's gut-busting hills. Many cyclists enjoy the northwestern edge of the city. Start out on the flat surface of the Marina Green, then explore the Presidio, with its many tree-lined roads. Or enter the Golden Gate National Recreational Area and follow the shore to reach ghostly Fort Point, a Civil War–era military outpost that protected California from the Confederates (who never bothered to show up). From here you can get on the Golden Gate Bridge for a 2-mile trip, then either continue into the Marin Headlands (see the "Biking Marin" sidebar) or turn back toward town.

Mountain biking in San Francisco is a more problematic matter. A mountain bike is useful for getting around the steeper parts of the Presidio or Golden Gate Park, but other than a few short single-track trails in the latter, the city offers little in the way of the rugged terrain that mountain bikers seek; for that you need to get out of town. The **PARNASSUS BIKE CLUB OF OUTDOORS UNLIMITED** (see the Adventure Outfitters section) frequently sponsors excursions to Marin. Also, several websites offer tips on good rides by region. Marin's Tennessee Valley is only one place discussed by Roger's Favorites at www.microweb.com/rogm/n-sf-bay-region.html. This is an amateur site put together by enthusiasts; surf around on the web and you should be able to find a lot more free information.

Finally, any discussion of biking in the city would be fatally flawed without a mention of **CRITICAL MASS**, a leaderless, often traffic-stopping grassroots pedalfest that takes place on the last Friday of each month. Bike riders gather by the thousands at Justin Herman Plaza (map:O2) by the Embarcadero to agree on a route, and then bike home via major thoroughfares in an awe-inspiring caravan that is part political demonstration on behalf of heightened "bike consciousness" and part just a plain ol' party. City officials have been cooperative for the most part, though they frown on the occasional breakaway; if you don't want to risk arrest, stay with the group. (For the record, some irate drivers tried a "Critical Gas car-in" once, but it fizzled.) Critical Mass has been a success not only by just continuing to exist but also by alerting the city to the needs of thousands of bike riders, resulting in more bike-only lanes on city streets.

## GOLF

Golf is a sport in the midst of reinvention. Not only is Tiger Woods the new face of the pro game, but the makeup of the amateurs is changing too. You'll find a different kind of player on the links these days, from blue-collars to Gen-Xers, rubbing elbows with the more traditional practitioners in plaid slacks. This is particularly true at the municipally owned and operated courses.

The City and County of San Francisco maintains an **AUTOMATED TEE TIME AND GOLF INFORMATION LINE** (415/750-4653), with a menu of detailed information on the city's five public courses. You can reserve a tee time, get directions to the courses, learn hours of operation, and get the rundown on greens fees, cart and club rentals, and lessons.

Dating from the turn of the century, the **PRESIDIO GOLF COURSE** (Arguello Blvd and W Pacific Ave; 415/561-4653; www.presidiogolf. com; map:H2) is the oldest continuously operating golf course in the West. Originally used by officers on the army post that used to occupy this site, it served as temporary housing following the earthquake and fire of 1906 and now hosts several pro tournaments each year. It's an 18-hole par 72 with a banked grass course, tree-lined fairway, and defined cut. Equipment is available for rent; call ahead for lessons. A rather plush driving range is here as well.

**LINCOLN PARK GOLF COURSE** (34th Ave and Clement St; 415/221-9911; map:E3), with 18 holes, is said to be one of the oldest municipal parks in the West. It features small greens, tricky traps, and plenty of Monterey cypress, as well as beautiful views of the Marin Headlands and the Golden Gate Bridge. There is no driving range. Pull carts are not available, but you can rent power carts. Clubs can be rented; call ahead to schedule lessons. Par is 68. Try to resist the temptation to drive a ball into the ocean from the hole that overlooks the Pacific. After all, it will cost you a stroke.

**HARDING PARK GOLF COURSE** and **JACK FLEMING GOLF COURSE** (corner of Harding Rd and Skyline Blvd, just south of the zoo; 415/664-4690), near Lake Merced, is a two-in-one course totaling 27 holes. Harding Park is thick with pine and Monterey cypress trees as well as traps. Beginners or those seeking an easier, perhaps less aggravating game will prefer 9-hole Jack Fleming, located inside the second 9 of Harding Park. This course's surface is softer and flatter. There is a small and rather crummy driving range as well. Par is 72 for Harding, 32 for Jack Fleming.

**GOLDEN GATE GOLF COURSE** (47th Ave off Fulton St; 415/751-8987; map:D5) follows the same pattern as Harding Park (see above), with well-trapped short greens requiring tight maneuvering. It's a fun, inexpensive course, and all of its 9 holes are par 3. Clubs are available to rent.

Those seeking a hitter's course should check out **SHARP PARK GOLF RANGE** (Fairway Dr west off Hwy 1; 650/355-0455; map:KK6), which the city operates in neighboring Pacifica. It's a long 18-hole course, flat and with the usual high number of traps; some players are put off by its occasionally marshy surface. There is no driving range; both power and pull carts as well as clubs are available for rental. Lessons are by appointment; call ahead.

If bad weather or the dark of night is keeping you from a game, you can always head down to **MISSION BAY GOLF CENTER** (1200 6th St at Channel St; 415/431-7888; map:O5). The 7-acre lighted facility consists of a weatherproofed double-decker steel and concrete arc containing 66 covered practice bays (all plastic mats) and a 300-yard range with nine target greens. You'll also find chipping and putting greens, target areas, and sand traps, as well as a fully stocked discount pro shop and a restaurant where you can contemplate your faults. The center is open Monday 11:30am to 11pm, Tuesday to Sunday 7am to 11pm. A bucket of balls costs $8, and the last bucket is sold at 10pm.

## HIKING

Although nobody disputes the thrill of a good climb up Mount Tam, there are plenty of trails in the city for those in need of the tranquility and renewal a quick day hike can provide. On some of these paths you can even forget you're in a major urban area. Whole books have been published on the subject of adventuring in San Francisco on foot: You could spend a lifetime in Golden Gate Park alone. You can head out in practically any direction and find something of interest. So these are just suggestions—it's easy to design your own walks.

Warm up with a jaunt down **AQUATIC PARK'S MUNICIPAL PIER** (map:L1); admire the boats in the bay and marvel at the bravery of the fishers who are seemingly going to eat what they're catching. Continue west through the **MARINA GREEN**, dodging joggers, skaters, and kite fliers. Following the **GOLDEN GATE PROMENADE**, a walking path just a few yards away from the water's edge, you can watch all manner of vessels, from sailboats to tankers. Keep going and you'll wind up at **FORT POINT**, where, as fans of Hitchcock's *Vertigo* will recall, Jimmy Stewart fished Kim Novak out of the drink. From here you can pick up the **COASTAL TRAIL** running under the toll plaza, near the abandoned artillery fortifications and then to the coast; you can follow the trail all the way to **BAKER BEACH**. Dress warmly.

In an opposite corner of the city, **BERNAL HEIGHTS PARK** (map:M8) offers a panoramic view from the top of what was once one of the early Spanish land grants on which San Francisco was founded. From Folsom and Ripley Streets, climb up the steep ascent of Bernal Heights Boulevard. People come from all over the city to walk dogs here, and there's a good deal of intercanine socializing. The dogs are generally friendly. Joggers enjoy the clear air and crisp breezes. There's also skateboard action—the downhill slopes are hard to resist if you want to see how fast you can get going. Keep an eye open, but don't be unduly worried: The kids usually post lookouts to make sure the coast is clear.

If you think hiking doesn't count unless it's done outside city limits, there are one or two organizations for you. One is **BAY TRAIL**, which can be reached at its website (www.abag.ca.gov/bayarea/baytrail/baytrail. html). Bay Trail is both the name of the group and its goal, "an endeavor to encircle the San Francisco Bay." Sometime in the future, proponents hope, there will be a "ring around the bay"—an unbroken corridor of park areas 400 miles long, so you can hopscotch from Marin to Mountain View and never leave a park. Until then, Bay Trail publicizes its program by organizing bike rides, hikes, and trail cleanups. Contact them if you want to be one of the 400 volunteers.

Since 1958, **GREENBELT ALLIANCE** (530 Bush St at Grant St; 415/398-3730 or 800/543-GREEN; www.greenbelt.org; map:N3) has spread its land planning and conservation message by way of free fun outings open to the public, although you must call 415/255-3233 to reserve. They tour parks, lakes, and the Bay Area's forgotten farms; watch hawks; and visit the Wine Country. The outings are thoughtfully ranked according to degree of difficulty, from easy to "hard-core," factoring in miles and elevation gain.

## HORSEBACK RIDING

Horses: Some people like to ride them, others like to bet on them. If you prefer the latter, then see "Horse Racing" in the Spectator Sports section. But if you want to hit the trail inside the city limits, the only place to go is **GOLDEN GATE PARK STABLES** (John F. Kennedy Dr at 36th Ave in Golden Gate Park; 415/668-7360; www.extendinc.com/ggps; map:E5), which offers rides and lessons. The guided rides take place every day, with the horses moving at a walk, and last about an hour, wending through the park to its western edge, by the tulip garden and the windmill, for a view of the Pacific (the horses do not go down to the beach, since the ocean has been known to overexcite them). Reservations are required, and the rides take place rain or shine; you may cancel if you don't want to ride in the rain, but be sure to do so far enough ahead that you don't get charged (no rain: Call by noon the previous day; rain: Call two hours before the ride). All riders must be under 230 pounds and over 8 years old; minors must have the permission of a parent or legal guardian. Riding boots and helmets are both required and provided. Lessons at the stables begin with six- and eight-week introductory courses ($168 and $208). Also offered are summer day camps (half-days for ages 5 to 8, full days for 8 and above) and pony-riding parties for the little ones. All prices are extremely reasonable.

## KAYAKING / CANOEING

Kayaking opportunities in San Francisco are divided into two areas, the bay and the Pacific Ocean. Those just starting out might want to confine themselves to practice jaunts in the bay before taking on the stronger currents and higher swells of the Pacific.

To find like-minded people seeking to improve their Eskimo rolls, check out **BAY AREA SEA KAYAKERS** (c/o Penny Wells, 229 Courtright Rd, San Rafael; 415/457-6094; www.bask.org) at its monthly general meeting (6:30 to 9:30pm on the last Wednesday of each month; check the website to confirm the meeting place). Dues of $25 admit you to workshops and clinics, get you a subscription to the *Bay Currents* newsletter, and provide access to the club's weekly excursions. Alcatraz is a favorite destination, although the club organizes trips to test the kayaking as far away as Chile. BASK also sponsors an Annual Kayak Rodeo. The club has more than 500 members and is rather loosely organized—it doesn't take much more than a suggestion to get things going. The **DOLPHIN CLUB** (see the Rowing section) also offers kayak training several times a year.

Canoes are larger than kayaks, and usually somewhat slower unless in the hands of experts. Some consider this roominess, safety, and stability an acceptable trade-off for the adrenaline rush of kayaking—still, always wear a life jacket, whatever kind of boat you're using. Canoes may be rented from **OUTDOORS UNLIMITED** (see the Adventure Outfitters section) for $40 for a weekend; the rate is $28 for OU members. OU's policy is that you "must have experience" before they rent to you.

## ROLLER SKATING / IN-LINE SKATING

Roller skating, once a weekend-only diversion, is now a day-to-day part of life. People are figuring out that they don't have to hang up their skates after childhood—and that skating can be a quick and clean way to get around in a crowded, traffic-jammed city. It's not uncommon to spot morning commuters taking the "in-line" to work.

For a recreational roll the action is at **GOLDEN GATE PARK**, particularly on Sundays, when much of the park is closed to cars. **JOHN F. KENNEDY DRIVE** in particular offers slow easy curves and modest bumps that accelerate without pushing you out of control. Skaters like rolling along the **EMBARCADERO**—it's long and level with pleasant breezes and an enjoyable view of the bay—and the **MARINA GREEN**. Gregarious types should check out the informal mass "skate-in" down **MARKET STREET** every Friday night. Assemble at the Ferry Building at the foot of Market Street in enough time to make the 8pm rollout.

**SKATES ON HAIGHT** (1818 Haight St at Stanyan St; 415/752-8375; www.skate.com; Mon–Fri 11am–7pm, Sat–Sun 10am–6pm; map:I5) is located half a block from Golden Gate Park. They rent both conventional and in-line skates for $6 per hour and $24 per day with a credit card. The store is known for its unannounced and unadvertised sales, so drop by and see if you can't pick up something on the sly.

GOLDEN GATE PARK SKATE AND BIKE (3038 Fulton St at 6th Ave; 415/668-1117; Mon–Fri 10am–6pm, Sat–Sun 10am–7pm; map:H4) rents conventional skates and Rollerblade-brand in-line, by the hour or by the day. Rates are $4 per hour for conventional skates, $12 for 24 hours; in-lines are $6 an hour, $24 for 24 hours. San Francisco residents must present an up-to-date driver's license; out-of-towners will have to use a credit card. They also sell both kinds of skates. The store is across the street from a primo skating area much favored by locals; roll on over, especially on a weekend, and you'll soon be surrounded by fellow skaters, some of them performing fairly intricate choreography to music flowing from boom boxes.

## ROWING

The SOUTH END ROWING CLUB (500 Jefferson St at Hyde St; 415/776-7372; www.south-end.org; map:M1), next to the Hyde Street Pier, has been hitting the water since its founding in 1873. There you will be able to hook up with other rowers, and you'll find a dazzling collection of vessels to choose from: The club's fleet of 30 different crafts ranges from kayaks and single-person sculls to a fearsome Viking-style rowboat. The club's signature craft is the *South Ender*, a 1915-vintage six-person scull that's controlled by a coxswain (the coxswain manipulates the rudder and coaches the rowers, usually by yelling). The club is open to the public Tuesdays, Thursdays, and Saturdays 10am to 6pm for a day-use fee of $6.50. In addition to rowing you can swim in the bay and return to the clubhouse for a sauna, a game of handball, or a workout in the gym. If you like what you see, $283 will cover your initiation fee ($100), key charge ($5), and first six months' dues ($178). The club participates in organized rowing competitions as well, including the Bridge to Bridge Regatta, in which teams race the 11.5 miles between the Bay and Golden Gate Bridges.

Literally next door to the South End, in a clubhouse built in 1896 and moved to its present location in 1938, you'll find the South End's friendly rivals, the DOLPHIN CLUB (foot of Hyde St at Jefferson St; 415/441-9329; www.dolphinclub.org; map:M1). Founded in 1877, the Dolphins began admitting women a mere 99 years later; women now make up about a third of the club's 900-person membership. Instructions in the art of kayaking are given several times a year; rowing training is offered once a month, with tips provided by former members of Olympic rowing teams and college champions. The club's fleet is less extensive than the South End's, composed of 16 rowboats, four of them double-rower shells, and one six-oared barge. The club also has a boathouse at Lake Merced for those who prefer flat water. Dolphin Club dues are $240 for the initiation fee and the first six months' membership, $31 per month subsequently. A day-use fee of $6.50 entitles a nonmember to use showers, sauna, lockers, and gym on Tuesdays, Thursdays, and Saturdays.

The **PACIFIC ROWING CLUB** (PO Box 27548, San Francisco, CA 94127; 415/242-0252; www.PacificRC.org) plies the flat water of Lake Merced. Much of this club's emphasis is on cultivating the next generation of rowers through its high school programs, in which older adult rowers pass along lore and enthusiasm.

Finally, mention should be made of what might be the first gay rowing club, named, of course, the **SAN FRANCISCO BAY BLADES**—get it? Any same-sexers who want to get out on the water should contact Dean at 510/482-1362; the group's e-mail address is goblades@aol.com.

## RUNNING

One of the advantages of running as a solitary sport is that it is uncomplicated—the runner really needs nothing more than a good pair of shoes and a fairly clear path. One of the advantages of running in San Francisco is the variety of terrain you can tackle. The **EMBARCADERO** is a long, even course of several miles from Berry Street to its terminus at Fisherman's Wharf, cooled by breezes all the way. It's a favorite jaunt for lunch-hour runners wanting to get back to the office for the afternoon but is never too crowded. A run on the **GOLDEN GATE BRIDGE** is 1 mile each way and provides a giddy sense of elevation. (There is no pedestrian traffic of any kind allowed on the Bay Bridge.) Running in **GOLDEN GATE PARK** allows you to alternate between the flat paved surfaces of the main roads and the dirt paths you find when you detour into the brush. These paths take you over steeper and trickier ground. The **GOLDEN GATE NATIONAL RECREATION AREA** also has that mix of well-established and off-the-beaten trails. Or take BART or the Muni streetcar to Glen Park and enjoy its forestlike atmosphere. And some swear by (and during) a run up **NOB HILL** along California Street from Market Street or up Taylor or Jones Street from either side. But be prepared to deal with traffic.

Let's say you don't want to run alone, that you like to test yourself in a crowd. Well, the biggest crowd in town is the one in the annual **BAY TO BREAKERS** foot race, held on the third Sunday of May with as many as 100,000 participants running the 7.5 miles from the Ferry Building to Ocean Beach. There are a number of serious runners who break away from the pack and actually compete for timed results and a new car, but the big draw here is the spectacle of silliness: people dressed as Elvis, as Brillo boxes, as animals, or sometimes in nothing at all. Call 415/777-7770 to register, or log on at www.baytobreakers.com. Finishers who paid the entry fee (not required, however) get a T-shirt and their names/results in the *San Francisco Chronicle*.

The **SAN FRANCISCO MARATHON**, sponsored by the *Chronicle*, is a more serious event, drawing 6,000 to 7,000 runners in comparison to Bay to Breakers' 80,000 to 100,000. The course is the standard 26.2 miles, and begins and ends in Golden Gate Park. It usually takes place in the middle of July. For more information contact West End Management at 415/284-9494.

If you seek a smaller group, a regularly scheduled Wednesday night run originates from the **FLEET FEET** running-apparel store in the Marina District (2086 Chestnut St at Steiner St; 415/921-7188; www.fleet-feet.com; map:K1). It is open to all abilities, draws on average 50 participants, and lasts 7 to 9 miles. There is also a Thursday night women's run of 3 miles.

An invaluable resource for hooking up with running groups and events is the **RUNNER'S SCHEDULE** (80 Mitchell Blvd, San Rafael, CA 94903; 415/472-7223; www.theschedule.com), an exhaustive listing of running-culture resources in California and Nevada, which you can pick up at shoe stores, gyms, and even some supermarkets. In the back pages are lists of group trainings, averaging 50 to 80 per issue, and a calendar boasting over 400 listings for races, clinics, and other events. The schedule is published monthly.

## STAIR CLIMBING

The biggest waste of money in San Francisco is a stair climbing machine. Although you can find a whole passel of stairs just about anywhere in the city, there are two places in the city where the locals prefer to power step:

The **LYON STREET STEPS**, between Green Street and Broadway. Built in 1916, this historic stairway street contains four steep sets of stairs totaling 288 unforgiving steps. This being Pacific Heights, it's quite the lovely setting, complete with flower gardens, manicured hedges, and a beeyootiful view of the bay. A block east, on Baker Street, another set of 369 steps descends to Green Street.

The **FILBERT STREET STEPS**, between Sansome Street and Telegraph Hill. This 377-step climb, which winds up the sheer eastern face of Telegraph Hill, sucks the life out of unaware tourists. She's a real charmer, though, wending through verdant flower gardens and charismatic 19th-century cottages. The trek starts at a narrow wooden plank walkway called Napier Lane, which leads to Montgomery Street. Turn right and follow the path to the end of the cul-de-sac, where another stairway continues up, up, and still more up to the top of Telegraph Hill. Your reward is a panoramic view of the city.

## SAILING

The San Francisco Bay has played a crucial role in making the city what it is: from Sir Francis Drake sailing past the Golden Gate (it seems he missed it in the fog), to entire ships' crews deserting their vessels to seek fortune in the Gold Rush, to the thriving waterfront that until recently served as the city's economic linchpin. Now, with most of the commercial shipping shifted across the bay to Oakland, the waterfront is primarily dedicated to amusement. On any sunny day the bay is festooned

## SEE LIFE AT THE FARALLON ISLANDS

Several miles due west of San Francisco is the small gaggle of islets called the Farallon Islands. On a very clear day you can see them just off the horizon, but what you can't see with the naked eye is the teeming sea and bird life—puffins, albatrosses, terns, whales, dolphins, seals, sea lions, great white sharks, and more—that congregates on or around these barren, windswept refuges. For a closer look you'll have to buy a ticket to board the 63-foot boat operated by the nonprofit **Oceanic Society Expedition** (415/474-3385; www.oceanic-society.org) and take an all-day guided nature cruise to the islands. The exceptional tour, which lasts eight or nine hours and costs about $67 per person, departs from the Fort Mason area in San Francisco's Marina District at 8:30am on Saturdays, Sundays, and occasional Fridays. Shorter, less expensive excursions to see gray whales are available, too. Note: If you're prone to seasickness, be sure to take some Dramamine before you depart—it can get real choppy out there.

with dozens of watercraft carrying passengers enjoying water, wind, and landscape.

Although it is extremely pleasant, sailing the bay is also good training for conditions the seagoer will meet in other parts of the world. There is, for example, the infamous "Potato Patch" beneath the Golden Gate Bridge, also known as Four Fathom Bank, where the depth of the bay changes from several hundred feet to a few dozen, causing the water to rush turbulently upward as if it were boiling, making for a bumpy and sometimes treacherous ride.

At that point you may wish you had attended **SPINNAKER SAILING SCHOOL** (Pier 40, South Beach Harbor; 415/543-7333; www.spinnaker-sailing.com), which has trained tens of thousands of new sailors since its founding in 1978. Courses can last from a weekend to two weeks, ranging from tips for beginners to preparation for a cruise to Hawaii. All courses are American Sailing Association certified.

After that you might feel confident enough to take on one of the rentals available from Spinnaker's **"BARE BOATS"** subsidiary. You can rent by the day, week, or month, skippering yourself if you complete the qualification procedure, or sailing with a captain provided by the school. For those more in the mood for sailing without the hassles of command, the Spinnaker location is also home to **RENDEZVOUS CHARTERS** (Pier 40, South Beach Harbor; 415/543-7333; www.rendezvouscharters.com), which provides skippered charters for day trips.

## SWIMMING

Almost any time during the day one can find swimmers bobbing in the water off **AQUATIC PARK** (map:L1), the best place in San Francisco for swimming in open water. This cove is less affected by the sometimes dangerous tides that prevail farther offshore, and the surrounding land serves as a windbreak to reduce the water's choppiness. Beginners should start out at slack tide; tide information can be found in the weather section of the daily newspapers. Open-water swimming at other locations, such as Ocean Beach and Baker Beach, is strongly not advised, no matter how tempting. The currents are much stronger, the waves more turbulent, and shark attacks are not unknown. If you must tackle the Pacific, use a surfboard. The same caution should be exercised when swimming in the bay: don't get too far out. Use the buoys as guidelines, and stay well inside them. For more San Francisco beach information call 415/391-2000.

Another problem faced by the outdoor swimmer is the question of temperature. The bay is basically cold, averaging between 50°–60°F. And remember, that's the average: winter can bring temperatures of 40°F or below, guaranteed to induce hypothermia in even the hardiest if they stay in the water too long (which is why Alcatraz was so hard to escape from). The warmth of a summer day can vanish the second you step into the water. Nobody should think less of you for using a wet suit to keep warm (it also allows you to stay in the water longer). If you decide to swim bareback—without a wet suit—start out by swimming a quarter hour at a time until you get the feel of it. And if you begin to feel unusually tired, get out of the water as fast as you can—it could be the onset of hypothermia.

You might want to build up your swimming skills at a practice pool before braving the bay. The **SHEEHAN HOTEL** (620 Sutter St at Mason St; 415/775-6500; map:M3) has an indoor pool that's open to the public. It's 21 yards long, ranges in depth from 4 to 10 feet, and is kept at a comfortable 82°F. Hours are Monday through Friday 6am to 10pm, Saturday 6am to 8pm, and Sunday 6am to 6pm. Admission is $10 for a single visit. Passes are also available for extended use: $85 for 15 visits; $150 for 30 visits with no time limit. Paid admission to the pool also entitles you to use of the adjacent gym.

Not only can you swim at the **ANGELO ROSSI PLAYGROUND AND POOL** (Arguello Blvd and Anza St; 415/666-7014; map:I4), you can sign up kids for swimming lessons Wednesdays, Thursdays, and Fridays in the summer months. Cost is $1.50 per lesson. Rates for regular swims are 50 cents for kids 17 and under, $3 for those 18 and over, and $5 for a family of two adults and two kids. The pool is indoors, runs from 4 to 10 feet deep, and is kept at 80° to 82°F.

After having built up your stamina and acclimated yourself to the conditions of the bay, it might be fun to join your fellow enthusiasts in a group swim. The **DOLPHIN CLUB** and the **SOUTH END ROWING CLUB** (see the Rowing section) sponsor regularly scheduled group swims. South End Rowing Club members swim together to Alcatraz twice a year—once in the summer and once on New Year's Day (brrr!). They also sponsor a group foray to the Golden Gate Bridge in the fall. All these swims embark from the club's headquarters at Aquatic Park. The Dolphin Club sponsors 20 group swims throughout the year, open to six-month members in good standing. Routes include the old favorites, the Golden Gate or Alcatraz, from Aquatic Park. The club's longest swim sets out from Fort Point and uses Aquatic Park as the finish line. For safety's sake, all group swims are accompanied by spotters in motorboats and on surfboards, ready to pluck out any swimmers whose enthusiasm turns out to be greater than their endurance.

For other opportunities to test your open-water swimming skills, you might contact the **SAN FRANCISCO BAY SWIMMING ASSOCIATION** (650/359-3773). This no-nonsense group declares itself "small on formality, organized coaching, and rules . . . no T-shirts, timed results, awards ceremonies, or post-race refreshments." It holds an organized swim once a month, with participants offered .5-, 1-, or 2-mile options. The club specializes in out-of-town jaunts: when these guys swim to Alcatraz, it's in the context of a combined 2.4-mile-swim/10-kilometer-run biathlon. This is not an event, or a group, for beginners. If you think you've got what it takes, give them a call.

## TENNIS

Unless it's simply pouring down rain, tennis enthusiasts can work on their backhands and net-rushing techniques at any of San Francisco's 153 municipal tennis courts, located at 69 sites throughout the city, including 21 courts at Golden Gate Park's Tennis Complex. If there are others waiting courtside, players at most municipal courts are expected to relinquish the court after a prescribed amount of play—five minutes of warm-up time and one set's worth for doubles or singles, or 30 minutes of rallying time for two players in lieu of a set. If there are no other players waiting you may, of course, go as long as you like (many of the courts, such as the ones at **DOLORES PARK**, are illuminated for night play; map:L6). There are no fees or reservations, but a set of rules is posted at each court; players count on good sportsmanship and common courtesy to see them observed. Call 415/753-7100 for a location near you.

The exception to all this is the **GOLDEN GATE PARK TENNIS COMPLEX** (map:I5), where procedures are more, well, complex. Courts are available in 90-minute increments starting at 9am; the last set must start by 4:30pm on weekends, 6pm on weekday evenings. There are two ways to claim a court: walk-up or reservation. Rates are lower for walk-up, which is first-come, first-served (or, since it's tennis, first serving), but a reservation secures your court—it all depends on how badly you need to play. Walk-up rates Monday through Friday are $4 for 90 minutes for San Francisco residents; $6 for nonresidents; $2 for seniors 65 and over; no charge for ages 18 or under. Evenings after 6pm and weekends will cost the walk-up San Franciscan $5, the out-of-towner $6. Seniors will pay $5; those under 18, $2.

To make weekend and evening reservations for the forthcoming week, call 415/753-7101 or 415/753-7102 on Wednesday from 4pm to 6pm; Thursday 9am to 5pm; or Friday 9am to noon. After 1pm on Friday, call the complex itself at 415/753-7001; you might be able to sneak in under the wire. Advance rates are $6 for city dwellers, $8 for nonresidents, $6 for seniors, and $2 for players 18 and under.

# Spectator Sports

Ticket availability fluctuates from team to team, from game to game, and according to a team's standing as the season progresses. Try the team's own box office first, although you may find slim pickings after the season ticket holders have staked their claims. Another useful source is **BASS** (510/762-2277) ticket service in the East Bay, with a spendy charge-by-phone service. For a particularly sought-after seat, you may have to avail yourself of the services of the ticket brokerages that have armies of buyers purchasing the individual limit. The brokerages then turn around and resell the seats at a hefty markup. Grit your teeth and check the news-paper. You generally find tickets being hawked in the classifieds and in display ads; the Yellow Pages also has a section for Ticket Sales. And, of course, there's always the scalpers on game day, but bring plenty of cash.

## PRO FOOTBALL

Five-time Super Bowl winners the **SAN FRANCISCO 49ERS** (415/468-2249; www.sf49ers.com) play their home games at 3Com Park at Candlestick Point on Sundays from August through December; kickoff is usually at 1pm. Unfortunately, tickets are usually snapped up in blocks far in advance, sometimes for the entire season. Consult the classifieds in the newspapers for offers from ticket brokers, or haggle with the scalpers at the gate. You can also try asking your hotel concierge, or call City Box Office at 415/392-4400 and cross your fingers. You get to the park by taking the 3Com exit off Highway 101 to Jamestown Avenue and Harney Way, but a highly recommended alternative is Muni's Ballpark Express—shuttle buses that get you to and from the game from a variety of locations at a price of $5 per round-trip. Call Muni at 415/673-6864 for stops and schedules. And for heaven's sake, bundle up: the wind from the bay whips into Candlestick Point something fierce—and then the fog sets in. FYI, the 49ers' archenemies, the **OAKLAND RAIDERS,** play at the Oakland Network Associates Coliseum, off the 880 freeway. Call 800/949-2626 for ticket information.

## PRO BASEBALL

The **SAN FRANCISCO GIANTS** (415/972-2000; www.sfgiants.com; map:O4), apparently having had enough of Candlestick Point's frigid winds, now play ball at the fabulous $319 million Pacific Bell Park at Third and King Streets in the China Basin section of SoMa. The season runs from April through October, and although tickets for most of the 40,800 seats are already sold, you can try to track them down through BASS Ticketmaster (510/762-2277) or stand in line the day of the game. Special express bus service is available from Market Street on game days; call Muni (415/673-6864) for pickup points and schedule information. For far more detailed info about PacBell Park and how to score tickets, see Top 25 Attractions in the Exploring chapter.

The American League's **OAKLAND ATHLETICS** play across the bay at the Network Associates Coliseum, at the Hegenberger Road exit off I-880, Oakland (510/430-8020). The ballpark holds close to 50,000 spectators and is accessible through BART's Coliseum Station. Tickets, which are far easier to score than Giants tickets, are available from the Coliseum Box Office or by phone through BASS Ticketmaster (510/762-2277).

## PRO BASKETBALL

Those craving hoops action have to go across the bay to catch the **GOLDEN STATE WARRIORS** (510/986-2200 or 888/479-4667; www.warriors.com) at the Oakland Coliseum Arena at the Hegenberger Road exit off of I-880. The easiest way to get out to see these three-time NBA Championship winners is to take BART to the Coliseum stop and follow the crowd. The fare is $2.75 one way from downtown San Francisco, $3 from the farther-flung Balboa Park Station. The arena holds 19,500 spectators, so seats are generally available. The season runs from November through April, and most games start at 7:30pm. Tickets are available at the arena and by phone through BASS Ticketmaster at 510/762-2277.

## HORSE RACING

**GOLDEN GATE FIELDS** (1100 Eastshore Hwy, Albany; 510/559-7300; www.ggfields.com; map:FF3) in the East Bay is the place to go if you want to watch horse racing, both on the track in front of you and via satellite from other racetracks around the country. Golden Gate Fields' own schedule is divided into two seasons: spring, from the end of March to the middle of June, and winter, from mid-November to mid-January. The track is open Wednesdays through Sundays, presenting 9 or 10 races per day. Satellite racing is offered year-round. Admission is $2 for the Club House and $10 for entry into the Turf Club, which offers a more elegant atmosphere with sit-down dining and a rigidly enforced dress code. The minimum bet is $1, with no upward limit for the races at the Fields and for televised races taking place in California; some restrictions may apply for bets placed on races in other states.

# Index

# We Stand By Our Reviews

Sasquatch Books is proud of *Best Places San Francisco*. Our editors and contributors go to great lengths and expense to see that all of the restaurant and lodging reviews are as accurate, up-to-date, and honest as possible. If we have disappointed you, please accept our apologies; however, if a recommendation in this 2nd edition of *Best Places San Francisco* has seriously misled you, Sasquatch Books would like to refund your purchase price. To receive your refund:

1. Tell us where and when you purchased your book and return the book and the book-purchase receipt to the address below.
2. Enclose the original restaurant or lodging receipt from the establishment in question, including date of visit.
3. Write a full explanation of your stay or meal and how *Best Places San Francisco* misled you.
4. Include your name, address, and phone number.

Refund is valid only while this 2nd edition of *Best Places San Francisco* is in print. If the ownership, management, or chef has changed since publication, Sasquatch Books cannot be held responsible. Tax and postage on the returned book is your responsibility. Please allow six to eight weeks for processing.

Please address to Satisfaction Guaranteed, *Best Places San Francisco*, and send to:

Sasquatch Books
615 Second Avenue, Suite 260
Seattle, WA 98104

# Best Places San Francisco Report Form

Based on my personal experience, I wish to nominate the following restaurant, place of lodging, shop, nightclub, sight, or other as a "Best Place"; or confirm/correct/disagree with the current review.

_____

_____

_____

_____

(Please include address and telephone number of establishment, if convenient.)

## REPORT

Please describe food, service, style, comfort, value, date of visit, and other aspects of your experience; continue on another piece of paper if necessary.

_____

_____

_____

_____

_____

_____

_____

I am not concerned, directly or indirectly, with the management or ownership of this establishment.

_____

**SIGNED**

_____

**ADDRESS**

_____

_____

**PHONE**                              **DATE**

Please address to Best Places San Francisco and send to:
**SASQUATCH BOOKS**
**615 SECOND AVENUE, SUITE 260**
**SEATTLE, WA 98104**
Feel free to email feedback as well: **BOOKS@SASQUATCHBOOKS.COM**